DISCARDED
Guatemala

El Petén
p225

The Highlands
p90

Central & Eastern Guatemala
p177

Antigua
p63

Guatemala City
p42

The Pacific Slope
p157

 D0486527

THIS EDITION WRITTEN AND RESEARCHED BY
Lucas Vidgen, Daniel C Schechter

Contents

CHURCH OF SAN ANDRÉS
XEQUL P144

SPACE IMAGES/GETTY IMAGES ©

BUS, PANAJACHEL P93

KELLY CHENG TRAVEL PHOTOGRAPHY/GETTY IMAGES ©

Contents

EASTER IN ANTIGUA P75

SPECIAL FEATURES

Welcome to Guatemala

Mysterious and often challenging, Central America's most diverse country offers landscapes and experiences that have been captivating travelers for centuries.

Colonial Grandeur

Say what you like about the Spanish in Latin America, you have to agree that they left behind some stunning architecture. From Antigua's crumbling ruins to the stately cathedral in Guatemala City's central plaza, there are plenty of opportunities to get snap-happy. In even the smallest towns you can find picturesque buildings – the small coastal town of Retalhuleu, for instance, has a charming central plaza – while larger coffee-boom towns such as Cobán and Quetzaltenango maintain vestiges of their glory days in their cathedrals, town halls and other public buildings.

The Timeless Maya

Many ask whatever happened to the Maya, but the simple answer is nothing – they're still here, and some traditions continue to thrive. If you're interested in archaeology, the must-see sites include Tikal, Copán (in Honduras), and Guatemala City's superb selection of museums. Living Maya culture can be witnessed in its 'pure' form in towns such as Rabinal and sacred sites such as Laguna Chicabal. And the Maya themselves? Well, they're everywhere. But the most traditional villages are in the highlands – the Ixil Triangle is a good place to start.

Adventure Awaits

Active souls tend to find their agenda very full once they get to Guatemala. Stunning trekking routes through the jungles and up volcanoes, world-class white-water rafting, miles of caves to explore, and what seems like a zip line strung between every two trees in the country are just the beginning. Like to take things up a notch? How about paragliding into a volcanic crater at Lago de Atitlán? Or scuba diving in the same place? You might even luck onto some good swell on the Pacific coast. Or you could just find a hammock and languidly consider your options. Your call.

Natural Highs

With not even 2% of its landmass urbanized, it's not surprising that Guatemala offers some superb natural scenery. National parks are few but impressive, particularly in the Petén region, and the lush canyons of the Río Dulce make for an unforgettable boat ride. The natural beauty of the volcano-ringed Lago de Atitlán has been captivating travelers for centuries, while the Verapaces are riddled with more caves than a spelunker could explore in a lifetime, and the swimming hole that launched a thousand postcards, Semuc Champey, just has to be seen to be believed.

Why I Love Guatemala

By Lucas Vidgen, Writer

Having lived here for over 10 years, I've found my love for Guatemala change and develop. At first it was purely visual – the dramatic, volcano-studded horizons, the lush forests and cobblestone streets. And then the little cultural jolts – traditionally dressed Maya toting iPhones, pistol-packing cowboys in boots, belt buckle and hat. But what I really came to appreciate was the Guatemalan spirit: that tragedies happen – wars, earthquakes, floods and hurricanes – but the simple things abide. A meal with family, a joke with friends – as crazy as everything else gets, these are the things to treasure.

For more about our writers, see page 324

Above: A woman in traditional dress, Quetzaltenango (p130)

Guatemala

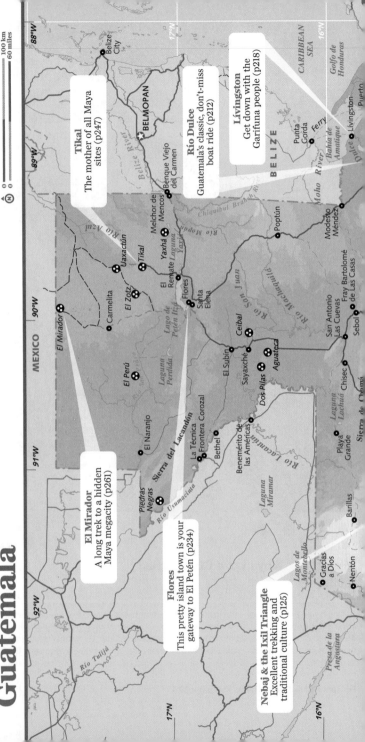

El Mirador
A long trek to a hidden Maya megacity (p261)

Flores
This pretty island town is your gateway to El Petén (p234)

Nebaj & the Ixil Triangle
Excellent trekking and traditional culture (p125)

Tikal
The mother of all Maya sites (p247)

Río Dulce
Guatemala's classic, don't-miss boat ride (p212)

Lívingston
Get down with the Garífuna people (p218)

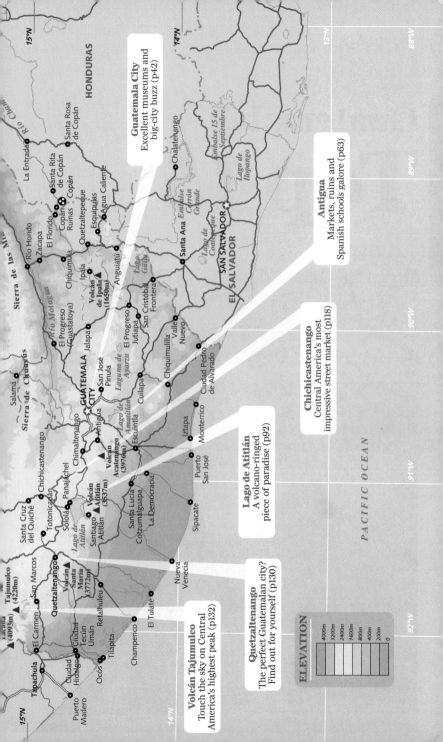

Guatemala City
Excellent museums and
big-city buzz (p42)

Antigua
Markets, ruins and
Spanish schools galore (p63)

Chichicastenango
Central America's most
impressive street market (p118)

Lago de Atitlán
A volcano-ringed
piece of paradise (p92)

Quetzaltenango
The perfect Guatemalan city?
Find out for yourself (p130)

Volcán Tajumulco
Touch the sky on Central
America's highest peak (p132)

ELEVATION

4000m
3200m
2400m
1600m
800m
400m
200m
0

Guatemala's
Top 15

Tikal

1 The remarkably restored temples (p247) that stand in this partially cleared corner of the jungle astonish for both their monumental size and architectural brilliance – as an early morning arrival at the Gran Plaza proves. Occupied for some 16 centuries, it's an amazing testament to the cultural and artistic heights scaled by this jungle civilization. A highlight is the helicopter-like vantage from towering Temple IV on the west edge of the precinct. Equally compelling is the abundance of wildlife, which can be appreciated as you stroll ancient causeways between ceremonial centers.

Below: Templo I, Gran Plaza (p250)

Antigua

2 With mammoth volcanic peaks and coffee-covered slopes as a backdrop for the scattered remnants of Spanish occupation, the former capital (p63) of Guatemala makes an appealing setting for learning Spanish, and a globally varied population come here to study at such quality institutes as Escuela de Español San José el Viejo. Nowhere else in the country packs in such a great culinary and nightlife scene, along with fabulous souvenir shopping in the markets, a sweet little central plaza replete with bubbling fountain, and picture-postcard vistas around every corner. Below: Street market

3

4

Lago de Atitlán

3 Atitlán (p92) elicits poetic outbursts from even the most seasoned traveler. Of volcanic origin, the alternately placid and turbulent lake is ringed by volcanoes and its shores are studded with villages such as Santiago Atitlán, with its thriving indigenous culture, and San Marcos, a haven for seekers who plug into the lake's cosmic energy. Plus there are enough activities – paragliding from Santa Catarina Palopó, kayaking around Santa Cruz La Laguna or hiking the glorious lakeshore trails – to make a longer stay viable.

Chichicastenango

4 More than just a place to shop, 'Chichi' (p118) is a vivid window on indigenous tradition, an ancient crossroads for the area's K'iche' Maya–speaking inhabitants, and a spiritually charged site. At Santo Tomás church in the center of town and the hill of Pascual Abaj on its southern edge, Maya rituals blend with Christian iconography. The twice-weekly market is a good place for souvenir hunting, though – particularly if you're after finely woven textiles or carved wooden masks. Above: Worshippers on the steps of Iglesia de Santo Tomás (p118)

Volcanoes

5 Sacred to the Maya and integral to the country's history, Guatemala's volcanoes dominate the skylines of the country's west, and are one of its emblematic features. You can gaze upon their domed beauty from the comfort of a cafe in Antigua or on Lago de Atitlán, or get up close and personal by climbing (at least) one. Favorites include the lava-spewing Pacaya (p72), Tajumulco (p132), which forms Central America's highest point, and San Pedro (p95), with its sweeping views over picturesque Lago de Atitlán. Top: Pacaya (p72)

Sweet River

6 The Río Dulce (literally, 'sweet river'; p212) connects Guatemala's largest lake with the Caribbean coast, and winding along it, through a steep-walled valley, surrounded by lush vegetation, bird calls and the (very occasional) manatee is Guatemala's classic, don't-miss-it boat ride. This is no tourist cruise – the river is a way of life and a means of transportation around here – but you get to stop at a couple of places to visit river-dwelling communities and natural hot springs, making for a magical, unforgettable experience.

Handicrafts & Textiles

7 Inextricably woven into the country's heritage, Guatemalan fabrics are much more than just tourist tat. The designs tell the stories of the wearer's community and beliefs. Likewise, handicraft production has always been a part of local life. Fine examples of craftwork and weaving can be seen on the streets all over the country, but if you're looking to take some home (or even to just get some priceless pics), you'll find the best selections in the markets in Guatemala City (p58), Antigua, Panajachel and Chichicastenango (p118). Below: Stall at Chichicastenango market (p118)

Guatemala City

8 Vibrant and raw, often confronting and occasionally surprising, the nation's capital (p42) is very much a love it or leave it proposition. Many choose the latter – and as fast as they can – but those who hang around and look behind the drab architecture and scruffy edges find a city teeming with life. For culture vultures, fine diners, mall rats, live-music lovers and city people in general, the capital has a buzz that's unmatched in the rest of the country. Below: Catedral Metropolitana (p45)

BERT DE RUITER / ALAMY STOCK PHOTO ©

AL ARGUETA / ALAMY STOCK PHOTO ©

Semuc Champey

9 Guatemala doesn't have all that many freshwater swimming holes that you'd really want to dive into, but the jungle-shrouded oasis of Semuc Champey (p189) is most definitely an exception. Turquoise-colored water cascades down a series of limestone pools, creating an idyllic setting that many call the most beautiful place in the country. You can make it out here on a rushed day tour, but you'd be mad to – Semuc and its surrounds are rural Guatemala at its finest.

Quetzaltenango

10 Quetzaltenango (p130) – 'Xela' to most everyone – is a kinder, gentler urban experience than the capital, and its blend of mountain scenery, highlands indigenous life, handsome architecture and urban sophistication attracts outsiders after an authentic slice of city life in Guatemala. Come here to study Spanish at the numerous language institutes, such as twhe well-regarded Celas Maya, or make it a base for excursions to such excellent high-altitude destinations as Laguna Chicabal, a crater lake/Maya pilgrimage site, or the Fuentes Georginas, a natural hot-springs resort ensconced in a verdant valley.

El Mirador

11 For true adventurers, the trek to El Mirador (p261) is a thrilling chance to explore the origins of Maya history; it is still being uncovered by archaeologists whom you're likely to meet at the site. Among the hundreds of vegetation-shrouded temples is the tallest pyramid in the Maya world, La Danta, which can be climbed for panoramic views of the jungle canopy. It's at least a six-day hike there and back through the mud and mosquitoes, unless you hop a chopper to the site. Above: View from atop La Danta (p261)

TRAVEL INK / GETTY IMAGES ©

Nebaj & the Ixil Triangle

12 A pocket of indigenous culture in a remote (though easily accessed) alpine setting, Nebaj (p125) is little visited, yet essential Guatemala. Homeland of the Ixil Maya people, whose language and culture survived harsh persecutions during the civil-war era, it's also a starting point for hikes through the Cuchumatanes mountain range, with dozens of traditional villages, such as Chajul, where community-run lodgings offer locals much-needed extra income and visitors a glimpse into this fascinating corner of the world. Above: Woman in traditional dress, Nebaj

Wildlife-Watching

13 While Guatemala's jungles, rivers, oceans and mountains don't exactly teem with life, there are several species that are worth keeping an eye out for. The Pacific coast is popular for whale-watching and turtle-spotting and there are manatees around the Río Dulce region. The Verapaces are a popular birding destination – you might even spot an endangered quetzal (p181) – as are the jungles of the Petén region, where you also stand a chance of spotting jaguars, howler monkeys, armadillos and agoutis, among others. Above right: Toucan (p289), Tikal

Flores

14 An isle of calm at the threshold of a vast jungle reserve, Flores (p234) is both a base for exploring El Petén and a stunning spot to recharge your rambling batteries. Unwinding at the numerous dining and drinking terraces that look across Lago de Petén Ixtá, or cruising in a weathered long boat to even smaller islets, you're likely to find companions for forays to Tikal or more remote places. But the picturesqueness of the town, with its captivating tableau of distant villages, is reason enough to head here.

Garifuna Culture, Lívingston

15 Descended from Carib, Arawak and West African people, the Garifuna are probably the most strikingly different of Guatemala's 23 indigenous language groups. They have their own religion, cuisine, dance and music styles, and a strong cultural identity that has survived despite direct and indirect attempts to quash it. Historically coastal dwellers, their heritage is strongly linked to the Caribbean; and the best place in Guatemala to immerse yourself in Garifuna culture is in the accessible-by-boat-only enclave of Lívingston (p218).

Need to Know

For more information, see Survival Guide (p293)

Currency
Quetzal (Q)

Language
Spanish (official), Maya languages (K'iche', Kaqchiquel and Mam most widespread), Garifuna

Visas
Many nationalities do not require tourist visas and will be given a 90-day stay upon entry, though citizens of some countries do need visas.

Money
Banks change cash and (sometimes) travelers checks, but *casas de cambio* (currency exchange offices) are usually quicker and may offer better rates.

Cell Phones
Cell phones are widely used. Roaming is available but expensive. Most travelers buy a local SIM card or a local prepaid phone on arrival.

Time
Central Standard Time (GMT/UTC minus six hours)

When to Go

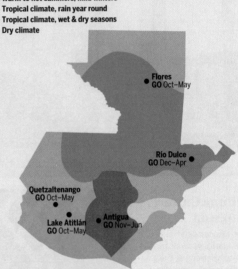

Warm to hot summers, mild winters
Tropical climate, rain year round
Tropical climate, wet & dry seasons
Dry climate

Flores
GO Oct–May

Río Dulce
GO Dec–Apr

Quetzaltenango
GO Oct–May

Lake Atitlán
GO Oct–May

Antigua
GO Nov–Jun

High Season
(Dec–Apr, Jun & Jul)

➡ Around key times (Christmas, New Year, Easter) hotel prices are at their highest.

➡ Accommodations should be booked well in advance for Easter in Antigua.

Shoulder
(Oct & Nov)

➡ Rains begin to ease up, but October is peak hurricane season.

➡ Mild temperatures and clear days make this a good time to be traveling and hiking in the highlands.

Low Season
(May, Aug–Sep)

➡ Prices drop, crowds thin out at archaeological sites, and booking accommodations is rarely necessary.

➡ Daily afternoon rains can make traveling chilly in the highlands and muddy in the jungle.

Useful Websites

Lanic Guatemala (www.lanic. utexas.edu/la/ca/guatemala) Excellent collection of Guatemala links.

Entre Mundos (www.entre mundos.org) Guatemalan social and political issues and NGO database.

Lonely Planet (www.lonely planet.com/guatemala) Destination information, hotel bookings, traveler forum and more.

Mostly Maya (www.mostly maya.com) Extensive information on remote Maya sites.

Xela Pages (www.xelapages. com) Information on the highlands and coast, plus forum.

Important Numbers

Guatemala has no regional, area or city codes; just dial the eight-digit number from anywhere in the country.

Guatemala country code	☎ 502
International access code	☎ 00
International collect calls	☎ 147120
Proatur (24hr tourist information & assistance)	☎ 1500

Exchange Rates

Australia	A$1	Q5.44
Canada	C$1	Q5.52
Euro zone	€1	Q8.62
Japan	¥100	Q6.66
New Zealand	NZ$1	Q5.10
UK	UK£1	Q11.09
US	US$1	Q7.60

For current exchange rates, see www.xe.com.

Daily Costs

Budget: Less than Q400

➡ Dorm bed: Q80–100

➡ Double room in a budget hotel: Q130–180

➡ Set meal in a *comedor* (basic, cheap eatery): Q30–45

➡ 'Chicken bus' ride (3hrs): Q20

Midrange: Q400–Q1000

➡ Double room in a hotel: Q320–500

➡ À la carte meal in a local restaurant: Q100–130

➡ Admission to archaeological site: Q50–150

➡ Shuttle bus ride (3hrs): Q150

Top End: More than Q1000

➡ Double room in a superior hotel: Q550 or more

➡ Meal in an elegant restaurant: Q130 or more

➡ Tour guide at archaeological site: up to Q450

➡ 4WD car hire, per day: Q650

Opening Hours

Hours provided are general guidelines, but there are many variations. Restaurant times, in particular, can vary by up to two hours either way.

The Ley Seca (dry law) stipulates that bars and *discotecas* must close by 1am, except on nights before public holidays; it is rigidly followed in large cities and universally mocked in smaller towns.

Banks 9am–5pm Monday to Friday, 9am–1pm Saturday

Bars 11am–midnight

Cafes & Restaurants 7am–9pm

Government offices 8am–4pm Monday to Friday

Shops 8am–noon and 2pm–6pm Monday to Saturday

Arriving in Guatemala

Aeropuerto Internacional La Aurora (p59; Guatemala City) Authorized taxis wait out the front of departures. Buy a coupon (Q80 for Zona 1) at the booth before the exit. Shuttle buses to Antigua (Q80) wait out the front, too – just listen for someone yelling 'Antigua, Antigua.'

Aeropuerto Internacional Mundo Maya (p240) Taxis wait outside, charging Q30 to Flores or Santa Elena. For Tikal or El Remate, go out to the main road and hail a passing minibus.

Getting Around

Pullman Bus Running only on major highways, these are the most comfortable choice. Seats are numbered and they run either semidirect or direct.

Shuttle Bus Booked through travel agents, hotels etc, these nonstop minibuses run between major tourist destinations, offering door-to-door service.

Chicken Bus Recycled US school buses, these are cheap, go everywhere, stop for everybody, and have no maximum capacity.

Pick-up truck In areas where there is no bus service this is a common way to get around. Flag one down wherever, climb into the back and hang on. Fares are equivalent to chicken buses.

Car If you're accustomed to crazy Latino traffic, driving is a great way to get off the beaten track.

Tuk-tuk These little three-wheelers are great for short hops around town at a fraction of a taxi fare.

For much more on **getting around**, see p304

First Time Guatemala

For more information, see Survival Guide (p293)

Checklist

➡ Make sure your passport is valid for at least six months past your arrival date

➡ Check visa requirements

➡ Arrange for appropriate travel insurance

➡ Organize necessary immunizations

➡ Read up on your government's Guatemala travel advisories

What to Pack

➡ International adapter (for non-US appliances)

➡ Spanish phrasebook

➡ Small medical kit

➡ Flashlight (torch)

➡ Money belt

➡ Good walking shoes

➡ Warm clothes if going to the highlands

➡ Padlock (if staying in dorms)

➡ Driver's license (if driving)

➡ Sunscreen and insect repellent

➡ Sunglasses

➡ Pocketknife

Top Tips for Your Trip

➡ Try to learn some Spanish before you arrive and some more when you get here – Guatemalans are extremely patient and will love you for just giving it a go.

➡ Pack as lightly as possible. Anything that locals use on a day-to-day basis can be bought cheaply. Anything remotely luxurious (electronics, imported goods etc) will be cheaper at home.

➡ Be aware of your surroundings (but not paranoid). If your gut tells you something is not right, it probably isn't.

What to Wear

Regardless of their economic status, Guatemalans do their best to look neat at all times, and you should do the same. This goes double when dealing with officialdom. The general look is neat-casual – pants and jeans are fine for both sexes, skirts should be (at least) below the knee. The only places you're really going to want to dress up for are fancy restaurants or Guatemala City *discotecas*.

Shorts and sleeveless tops are OK for the beach and coastal towns. In the highlands people tend to cover up more – a sensible move, considering the climate.

Dress conservatively when entering churches and visiting rural communities.

Sleeping

It's generally not necessary to book your accommodations in advance. If, however, you're planning on being in Antigua or down at the beach during Semana Santa, the sooner you book the better.

➡ **Hotels** From desperate dives out by the bus terminal to fancy-pants boutique numbers, there is no shortage of options.

➡ **Hostels** Starting to make a dent in the budget accommodations scene, especially in backpacker-favored destinations such as Antigua, Quetzaltenango and around Lago de Atitlán.

➡ **Homestays** Generally organized through Spanish schools, these are a great way to connect with local culture.

Money

Banks change cash and (sometimes) travelers checks, but *casas de cambio* (currency exchange offices) are usually quicker and may offer better rates.

Bargaining

Haggling is pretty much a national pastime in Guatemala and everything from a banana in the market to a speeding fine is negotiable to locals. Treat it as a game, and if you feel you're getting ripped off, just walk away (except, that is, if it's a speeding fine). Don't haggle in small stores and restaurants; always haggle in markets and with taxi drivers.

Tipping

A 10% tip is expected in restaurants (often automatically added to your bill in tourist towns such as Antigua). In small *comedores* (basic, cheap eateries) tipping is optional, but follow local practice and leave some spare change.

➡ **Homestays** Better to buy a gift than give cash

➡ **Hotels** Q10 per bag

➡ **Restaurants** 10% maximum (if not already included)

➡ **Taxis** Not customary

➡ **Trekking & tour guides** Q50 per person per day (extremely optional)

MICHAEL DEFREITAS / GETTY IMAGES ©

Cooking tortillas, Santiago Sacatepéquez (p89)

Etiquette

➡ **Dress** General standards of modesty in dress have relaxed somewhat. Coastal dwellers tend to show a lot more skin than highland types, but not all locals appreciate this type of attire.

➡ **Entering a Room** In public places such as a restaurant or waiting room, make a general greeting to everyone – *buenos días* or *buenas tardes* will do.

➡ **Greetings** When meeting someone personally, men shake hands with men, women air-kiss women, and men and women may air-kiss or shake – wait to see if she offers her hand, fellas.

➡ **Maya Women** Many Maya women avoid contact with foreign men, as virtuous Maya women don't talk with strange men. Male travelers in need of information should ask another man.

➡ **Photos** Understandably, the Maya can be very touchy about being photographed. Always ask for permission before taking pictures.

If You Like...

Colonial Architecture

Antigua Colonial show pony with a riot of gorgeous cobblestoned streetscapes, crumbling ruins and noble churches. (p63)

San Andrés Xecul Colonial/indigenous fusion at its wackiest, this small church's facade is laced with Maya imagery. (p144)

Guatemala City While most of the city is fabulously ugly, there are some definite gems here, particularly in the Centro Historico. (p44)

Cobán This cute hilltop town has a couple of real lookers, some of which have been converted into charming hotels. (p182)

Quetzaltenango The country's second city has some great old buildings, especially around the Parque Central. (p130)

Volcanoes

Tajumulco Central America's highest point is a relatively easy climb, particularly if you camp overnight. (p132)

Pacaya An easy day trip from Antigua, this peak is an all-time favorite for hikers. (p72)

Santa María Get an early start to catch the sunrise and views that stretch from Mexico to Antigua and out to the Pacific. (p132)

San Pedro A moderate half-day hike rewards you with gorgeous views of Lago de Atitlán and surrounds. (p95)

Ruins

Tikal This regional superstar is well on the tourist trail, but totally worth the visit for its soaring, jungle-shrouded temples. (p247)

El Mirador A little hard to get to (unless you pony up for the helicopter ride), you can watch archaeologists at work at this former megacity. (p261)

Copán Just over the border in Honduras, this site hosts some of the finest carvings and stonework in the region. (p201)

Quiriguá Snuggled among the banana plantations, this little-visited site has some impressively sized carved stelae. (p200)

Takalik Abaj The only really impressive ruins on the Pacific Coast show evidence of some of the earliest links between Olmec and Maya cultures. (p164)

Off-the-Beaten-Track Places

Chajul Step back in time and experience life as it has been lived for hundreds of years in this intensely traditional town. (p129)

Laguna Magdalena Take a two-day horseback ride with Unicornio Azul to this turquoise lagoon nestled in the Cuchamatanes mountain range. (p152)

San Mateo Ixtatán Up near the Mexican border, this cute village is surrounded by spectacular scenery. (p154)

Laguna Lachuá It's well worth the effort to visit this crystal-clear, circular lagoon that's surrounded by thick jungle. (p187)

Tilapita This classic one-hotel beach town is a great place to take a breather and watch the world go (slowly) by. (p160)

Wildlife

Monterrico Save a turtle, spot a whale or go birdwatching in the mangroves from this Pacific coast village. (p171)

Alta Verapaz The cloud forests around Cobán are home to a plethora of bird species, including the quetzal. (p180)

Río Dulce If you're very quiet and very lucky, you might just spot a manatee or a crocodile near the banks of this jungle-shrouded river. (p212)

Estación Biológica Las Guacamayas Biologists travel to this research station in a protected jungle reserve to study jaguars, crocodiles, turtles and exotic scarlet macaws. (p260)

Handicrafts & Textiles

Chichicastenango Central America's oldest and largest handicrafts market is a visual feast and souvenir heaven. (p118)

Antigua For a tourist-town market, prices are reasonable and shopping is reasonably hassle-free. (p83)

Santiago Atitlán Maya women weave textiles as they have for centuries in this Tz'utujil community on Lago de Atitlán's southern shore. See the work and the process at the excellent Cojolya Museum. (p106)

San Francisco El Alto Indigenous highlanders flock to this town north of Quetzaltenango for its vast and vivid market renowned for the quality and authenticity of its textiles. (p145)

Panajachel Sure, they're pushy, but the street vendors and roadside stalls in this lakeside town have some of the best collections of textiles, at very reasonable prices. (p102)

Doing Nothing

San Pedro La Laguna Taking it easy is pretty much a way of life in Guatemala's consummate chill zone. (p108)

Lanquín Sure there are caves to explore and rivers to tube... tomorrow... (p187)

Monterrico The ultimate in 'hammock swinging, no shoes, no shirt, no worries' Guatemalan beach towns. (p171)

Río Dulce Kick back riverside for a few days in a secluded jungle lodge. (p212)

Earth Lodge Chill out on an avocado farm in the hills above Antigua. (p86)

Top: Ruins at Gran Plaza (p203), Copán, Honduras
Bottom: Biotopo Monterrico-Hawaii (p172), Monterrico

PLAN YOUR TRIP IF YOU LIKE...

Month by Month

January

Generally cooler temperatures make this a good time to be traveling. In the first couple of weeks you're bound to meet plenty of Guatemalan families taking advantage of school holidays.

✯✯ El Cristo Negro de Esquipulas

Pilgrims in their thousands flock to the town of Esquipulas in the days leading up to January 15 to pay homage to the Black Christ.

✯✯ Rabinal Achí

In the highly traditional Baja Verapaz town of Rabinal, pre-Colombian dances are performed during the Fiesta de San Pedro from the 19th to the 25th.

March

The European spring break sees a mini high season – nothing books out, but things start to get a little more lively.

✯✯ Desfile de Bufos (The Parade of Fools)

On the Friday before Good Friday, this 100+ year old tradition sees thousands of hooded Guatemala City university students take to the streets in floats and costumes to mock the government.

April

On average the warmest month. All the foreigners want to be in Antigua and all the Guatemalans want to be at the beach – accommodations for both places should be booked well in advance.

✯✯ Semana Santa

While there are Easter processions all over the country, the most atmospheric are in Antigua and the most elaborate floats are in Guatemala City.

May

The semi-official start of the rainy season (although this is starting to vary wildly) sees afternoon showers across the country until the end of October (or thereabouts).

✯✯ Día del Trabajo (Labor Day)

On the first day of May there are celebrations, parades and protests throughout the country, the largest being in Guatemala City.

June

The end of the US college year sees a large influx of students arriving to study Spanish, volunteer and travel. The rainy season continues.

🏃 Turtle Nesting Season

Running until November, the main nesting season on the Pacific coast sees thousands of turtles come ashore to lay eggs. The best place to spot them is around Monterrico. (p172)

July

The college break continues, with many Spanish students finishing their studies and starting to travel. This is the depths of the rainy season, with the most rain and least sunshine.

 Fiesta de Cubulco

This small town is one of the few places left in the country to keep the Palo Volador (literally, 'flying pole') tradition alive. It happens on the last day of its five-day festival, on July 25.

Rabin Ajau

In the last week of July Cobán hosts this festival that showcases pre-Colombian traditions, including Maya ceremonies, traditional handicrafts, and plenty of music and dance.

August

Crowds start to thin out as college students return home. Often in this month there is a phenomenon called the *canicula* (dog days in English), which sees a warm, sunny break in the rains.

Fiesta de la Virgen de la Asunción

Peaking on August 15, this fiesta is celebrated with folk dances and parades in Sololá, Guatemala City and Jocotenango.

September

Temperatures start to cool and rains begin to ease up. This is the start of the real low season, and if you're into haggling on accommodations, now's a good time to start.

Independence Day

September 15 marks Guatemala's anniversary of independence. There are celebrations all over the country, but being that it coincides with Quetzaltenango's week-long festival, you'll find the most activity there, with loads of concerts and other cultural activities.

October

As the rains peter out, this month marks the start of volcano-trekking season, with spectacular cloud formations until mid-November.

Fiesta de San José Petén

On the night of the 31st a very curious ceremony takes place, as one of three skulls (thought to be of the village's founding fathers) is removed from the town church and paraded through this small town.

December

Seriously chilly temperatures hit the highlands – bring warm clothes or plan on buying some here. There's a little spike in vacationing Guatemalans, but most wait until after Christmas before they start traveling.

Orchid Festival

The misty hill country around Cobán makes for a perfect orchid habitat and this annual festival, held in the first week of December, showcases the variety of species that can be found in the area.

Quema del Diablo

All over the country (but particularly in the highlands) people haul their trash out into the street on December 7 and make huge bonfires while men dressed as devils run and dance amid the smoke.

Whale-Watching Season

From mid-December until the end of May, humpback and sperm whales can be seen migrating along the Pacific coast.

Plan Your Trip
Itineraries

Hit the Highlights

On a short break and want to see it all? Well, that's not going to happen, but with a week you can at least see Guatemala's Big Three.

Flying into **Guatemala City**, shuttle or taxi directly to **Antigua**. If you don't arrive too late, grab dinner at one of the city's fabulous restaurants and maybe a nightcap in a cozy bar. Next morning, take a walk around town – don't miss the Iglesia de la Merced or Las Capuchinas convent. You'll probably want an early night because the next day you'll be climbing a volcano – check with the locals to see which one is safe/recommended to climb at the moment. Back in town, catch dinner at the wonderfully atmospheric Mesón Panza Verde. The next day it's on to **Lago de Atitlán**. **Panajachel** is great for shopping and eating, but read up on the other villages around the lake – each is different and has its own appeal. Regardless of where you end up, spend a half a day exploring 'your' village and the next day exploring the rest of the lake. Next it's off to **Tikal**, so shuttle back to Guatemala City and then on to **Flores**. Head straight for the site, spend the day exploring and then return to Guatemala City for your flight home.

Above: Arco de Santa
Catalina (p84), Antigua

Right: Handicrafts,
Panajachel (p93)

Highland Fling

Guatemala's most spectacular scenery and strongest Maya traditions await along this well-traveled route. It could easily take a few months if you stop off to learn some Spanish or to take advantage of the great sightseeing and hiking possibilities along the way.

From the **capital** head first to picturesque **Antigua**, enjoying the country's finest colonial architecture, the great restaurants and the traveler and language-student scene. Several volcanoes wait to be climbed here including the fiery Volcán Fuego – but ask around for current conditions before planning anything.

From Antigua move on to **Panajachel** on volcano-ringed **Lago de Atitlán**. Hop in a boat to check out some of the quieter, more traditional Maya villages around the lake such as Santiago Atitlán, where the curious deity Maximón awaits, or San Pedro La Laguna, a party town with a certain fame countrywide. San Marcos La Laguna is much more laid-back and a magnet for yoga and natural-healing types. Santa Cruz La Laguna, meanwhile, is just plain tiny and gorgeous.

From the lake, hop a shuttle or 'chicken bus' north to **Chichicastenango** for its huge Thursday or Sunday market and, if you're lucky, a religious ceremony where it's hard to tell where the Maya-ism ends and the Catholicism starts.

From Chichicastenango you can follow the Interamericana Hwy west along the mountain ridges to **Quetzaltenango**, Guatemala's clean, orderly second city, with a host of intriguing villages, markets and natural wonders waiting within short bus rides away. From Quetzaltenango it's possible to go further into the hills to **Todos Santos Cuchumatán**, a fascinating Maya mountain town with great walking possibilities.

If you have extra time, consider pushing east to explore **Nebaj** and the Ixil Triangle, where you'll find great hiking opportunities and a strong Maya way of life amid stunning scenery. A rough but passable road leads further eastward from here, passing **Uspantan** and providing a back-door route to Alta Verapaz, where you can check out **Cobán**, **Semuc Champey** or head further north toward **Tikal**.

Top: Lago de Atitlán (p92)
Bottom: Young girl in Santiago Atitlán (p105)

3 WEEKS
The Big Loop

This 1900km round trip takes you to the best of Guatemala's Maya ruins, into its dense jungles and to some of its spectacular natural marvels, covering the center, east and north of the country. Really pushing, you might do it in two weeks, but if you have four, you'll enjoy it more.

Start out northeastward from **Guatemala City** and detour south into Honduras to see the great Maya site of **Copán**. Don't just make it a flying visit, though – Copán is a great town and there's plenty to do in the surrounding countryside.

Return to Guatemala and continue northeastward to another fine Maya site, **Quiriguá**, where you can marvel at the 10m-plus carved stelae and you may just have the place to yourself.

From there move on to the curious Garifuna enclave of **Lívingston** on the sweaty Caribbean coast. Soak up the atmosphere in this entirely different corner of Guatemala and get in some beach time on the country's finest beaches.

Take a boat up the jungle-lined **Río Dulce**, stopping for a dip in the hot springs along the way before reaching **Río Dulce town**.

Head north up Hwy 13 to chill out at **Finca Ixobel** before continuing to **Flores**, a quaint small town on an island in the Lago de Petén Itzá. From Flores, head for **Tikal**, the most majestic of all Maya sites. Spend a night at Tikal itself or nearby **El Remate**. While in the Flores/Tikal area, you should have time to take in further impressive Maya sites such as **Yaxhá** and **Uaxactún**.

From Flores head southwest to the relaxed riverside town of **Sayaxché**, which is at the center of another group of intriguing Mayan sites – **Ceibal**, **Aguateca** and **Dos Pilas**. The road south from Sayaxché is now paved all the way to **Chisec** and **Cobán**, jumping-off points for a whole series of pristine natural wonders, such as jungle-ringed **Laguna Lachuá**, the **Grutas de Lanquín** and the turquoise lagoons and waterfalls of **Semuc Champey**. Finally, make your way back to Guatemala City for your flight home.

Top: Fishers, Lívingston (p218)
Bottom: Ruins in Tikal (p247)

Guatemala: Off the Beaten Track

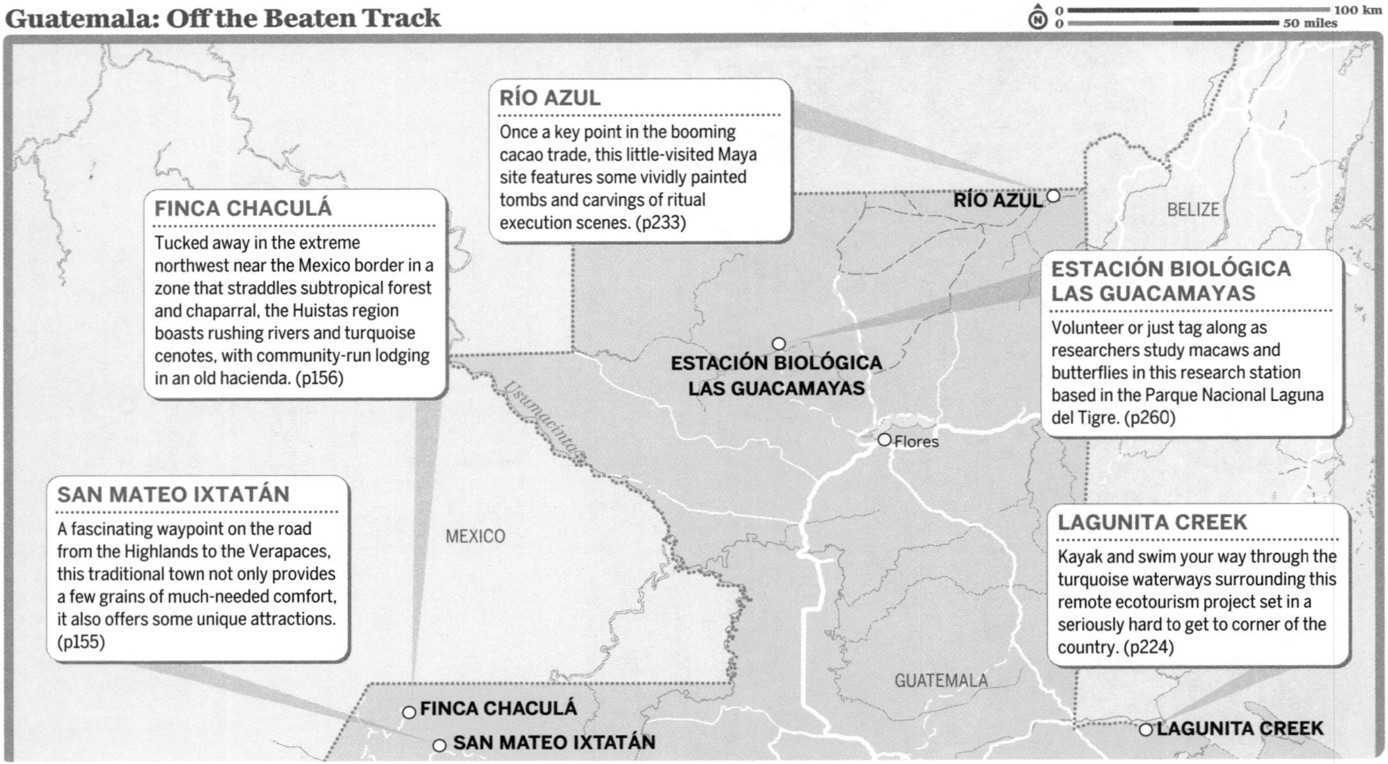

50 miles
100 km

ESTACIÓN BIOLÓGICA LAS GUACAMAYAS

Volunteer or just tag along as researchers study macaws and butterflies in this research station based in the Parque Nacional Laguna del Tigre. (p260)

LAGUNITA CREEK

Kayak and swim your way through the turquoise waterways surrounding this remote ecotourism project set in a seriously hard to get to corner of the country. (p224)

BELIZE

RÍO AZUL

RÍO AZUL

Once a key point in the booming cacao trade, this little-visited Maya site features some vividly painted tombs and carvings of ritual execution scenes. (p233)

Flores

GUATEMALA

ESTACIÓN BIOLÓGICA LAS GUACAMAYAS

LAGUNITA CREEK

FINCA CHACULÁ

Tucked away in the extreme northwest near the Mexico border in a zone that straddles subtropical forest and chaparral, the Huistas region boasts rushing rivers and turquoise cenotes, with community-run lodging in an old hacienda. (p156)

Usumacinta

MEXICO

FINCA CHACULÁ

SAN MATEO IXTATÁN

SAN MATEO IXTATÁN

A fascinating waypoint on the road from the Highlands to the Verapaces, this traditional town not only provides a few grains of much-needed comfort, it also offers some unique attractions. (p155)

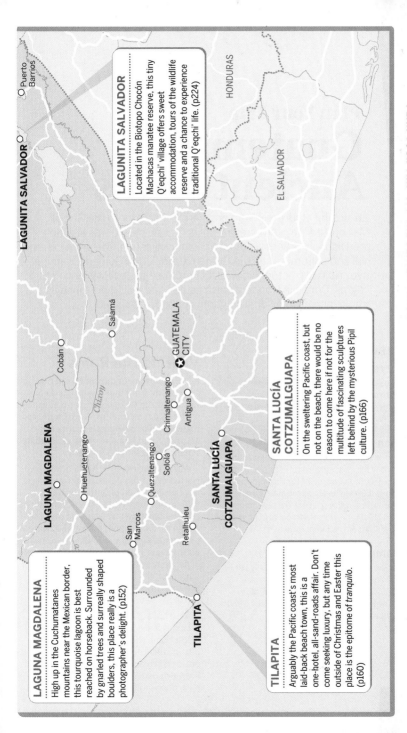

LAGUNITA SALVADOR

Located in the Biotopo Chocón Machacas manatee reserve, this tiny Q'eqchi' village offers sweet accommodation, tours of the wildlife reserve and a chance to experience traditional Q'eqchi' life. (p224)

SANTA LUCÍA COTZUMALGUAPA

On the sweltering Pacific coast, but not on the beach, there would be no reason to come here if not for the multitude of fascinating sculptures left behind by the mysterious Pipil culture. (p166)

LAGUNA MAGDALENA

High up in the Cuchumatanes mountains near the Mexican border, this turquoise lagoon is best reached on horseback. Surrounded by gnarled trees and surreally shaped boulders, this place really is a photographer's delight. (p152)

TILAPITA

Arguably the Pacific coast's most laid-back beach town, this is a one-hotel, all-sand-roads affair. Don't come here seeking luxury, but any time outside of Christmas and Easter this place is the epitome of *tranquilo*. (p160)

Plan Your Trip

Guatemala's Ancient Ruins

Stretching at its peak from northern El Salvador to the Gulf of Mexico, the Maya empire during its Classic period was arguably pre-Hispanic America's most brilliant civilization. The great ceremonial and cultural centers in Guatemala included Quiriguá, Kaminaljuyú, Tikal, Uaxactún, Río Azul, El Perú, Yaxhá, Dos Pilas and Piedras Negras. Copán in Honduras also gained and lost importance as the empire and its individual kingdoms ebbed and waned.

Need to Know

Where

The majority of Maya sites are in El Petén region, in the country's north. The other major grouping is in the southwest, roughly centered around Lago de Atitlán.

When

The ideal months to visit archaeological sites are outside of the rainy season. In El Petén you want to avoid the heat, while in the highlands seriously cold nighttime temperatures can make travel uncomfortable. Roughly speaking, the better times to visit El Petén are from November to April, while the highlands are best from February to May.

Opening Hours

Most sites are open from 8am to 4pm daily, but check times ahead of your visit. For the more popular sites, the best time to go is soon after opening time, thereby beating the tour bus crowds and the midday sun.

Visiting the Ruins

Maya achievement during this period rivaled anything that was going on in Europe at the time, boasting an advanced writing system, awe-inspiring engineering feats, advanced mathematics and astrology, and stone-working skills that remain impressive to this day.

Many legacies of the Maya have disappeared over time. Archaeological pieces have been carried off either by tomb raiders or foreign governments and much cultural heritage has been lost over the centuries due to government and church campaigns to assimilate the Maya into mainstream Hispanic culture. Outside of Guatemala City's fantastic selection of museums, the best way to get a feel for the amazing achievements of this unique culture is to visit archaeological sites.

Visiting a Maya ruin can be a powerful experience, a true step back in time. While some sites are little more than a pile of rubble or some grassy mounds, others (such as Tikal and Copán) have been extensively restored, and the temples, plazas and ballcourts give an excel-

Guatemala's Ancient Ruins

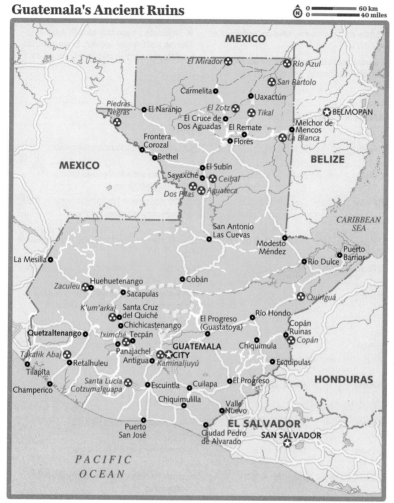

lent insight into what life must have been like in these places.

The most famous sites are generally thronged with visitors. Others are hidden away in thick jungle, reachable only by multiday treks or helicopter – for those with a sense of adventure, these can be the most exciting and rewarding to visit.

Site Practicalities

➡ Admission to sites costs between nothing (rare) and Q150 (also rare; generally reserved for top sites such as Tikal and Copán). Most sites charge around Q80.

➡ Protect yourself against the sun and, at jungle sites, mosquitoes.

➡ Sites such as Tikal and Copán have restaurants, bookstores, toilets and authorized guides.

➡ Little-visited sites may have no food or water available.

➡ Guided tours to many sites are usually available from nearby towns, although most of them (but not all) are accessible independently.

➡ Explanatory signs may be in Spanish only; Spanish and English; Spanish, English and the local Maya dialect; or completely nonexistent.

ANCIENT MAYA SITES

REGION	SITE	DESCRIPTION
El Petén	Tikal (p247)	Most famous of all Guatemalan Maya sites
El Petén	El Mirador (p261)	Late Preclassic site with the largest cluster of buildings in the Maya world
El Petén	San Bartolo (p233)	Over 100 structures in 1 sq km 'discovered' in 2003 after looters began sacking the site
El Petén	Piedras Negras (p233)	One of Guatemala's most extensive, least-accessible sites
El Petén	La Blanca (p233)	Late Classic period trading center with impressively preserved walls
El Petén	El Zotz (p233)	A sprawling, largely unexcavated site occupying its own *biotopo* abutting Tikal National Park
El Petén	Río Azul (p233)	Key trading post for cacao from the Caribbean in the early Classic period
El Petén	Ceibal (p230)	Ceremonial site featuring impressive stelae
El Petén	Aguateca (p230)	Easily accessible lakeside walled city
El Petén	Dos Pilas (p232)	Breakaway city from the Tikal group
Guatemala City	Kaminaljuyú (p47)	Important Preclassic site a few kilometers from downtown area
Highlands	Iximché (p106)	Naturally fortified ex-Kaqchiquel capital
Highlands	K'um'arkaj (p123)	Former K'iche' capital surrounded by ravines
Highlands	Zaculeu (p148)	Postclassic Mam religious center
Pacific Slope	Takalik Abaj (p164)	Important late Preclassic trading center
Pacific Slope	Santa Lucía Cotzumalguapa (p166)	Various small sites dotted around a modest town
Eastern Guatemala	Quiriguá (p201)	Important ceremonial center with strong links to nearby Copán
Honduras	Copán (p201)	Religious and political capital rivaling Tikal for importance

Resources

➡ Mesoweb (www.mesoweb.com) is a great, diverse resource on ancient Mesoamerican cultures, especially the Maya.

➡ *Archaeology of Ancient Mexico and Central America: An Encyclopedia*, a reference book by Susan Toby Evans and David L Webster, incorporates recent discoveries and scholarship.

➡ *Maya Art and Architecture*, by Mary Ellen Miller, is gorgeously illustrated and paints the

HIGHLIGHTS	LOCATION	TRANSPORTATION
Towering temples, including the 65m-high Templo IV	60km northeast of Flores	public transport or tour
La Danta, the largest Maya pyramid yet discovered	7km south of Mexican border	82km by bus plus two days' walking (or direct helicopter)
Features one of the best-preserved Maya murals with a depiction of the creation myth from the Popol Vuh	Approximately 40km north-east of Uaxactún	Tours from Uaxactún or Flores
Impressive carvings and a sizable acropolis complex	40km downstream from Yaxchilán	Tours from Flores or river cruises from Bethel
'Graffiti' dating back to the Early Postclassic era	On the Río Mopan near the Belize border	Tours from Flores or Melchor de Mencos
Views all the way to Tikal from the top of the Pirámide del Diablo	25km southwest of Uaxactún	Tours from Uaxactún or Flores; guide cooperative leads walks from Cruce de Dos Aguadas
Tombs featuring vibrant painted glyphs	Near the corner where the Belize, Guatemala and Mexico borders meet	Tours from Uaxactún
Intricate carvings, atmospheric riverboat ride to get there	17km from Sayaxché	Boat tour or bus from Sayaxché to 8km from site, then walk or hitch
Maya world's only bridge, intricate carvings	Southern tip of Laguna Petexbatún	Boat tour from Sayaxché
Heiroglyphic stairway, impressive carvings	16km from Sayaxché	Pick-up truck to Nacimiento followed by 20-minute hike
Ongoing excavations open to public	Guatemala City suburbs	Bus or taxi
Important ceremonial site for modern Maya	1km from Tecpán	Walk or bus
Sacred tunnel still used for Maya ceremonies	3km west of Santa Cruz del Quiché	Minibus
Spectacular setting, parklike grounds	4km west of Huehuetenango	Bus or taxi
Sculptures, ceremonial baths and broad stone causeway	19km north of Retalhuleu	Bus, taxi and pick-up
Stone sculptures, links with Mexican Olmec culture	29km west of Escuintla	Frequent buses
10m-plus stelae	45km south of Río Dulce	Frequent buses
Excellent sculpture museum, hieroglyphic staircase with longest-known Maya hieroglyphic carving	5km from the Guatemala–Honduras border, in Honduras	Bus; tours from Antigua

SIMON DANNHAUER / SHUTTERSTOCK ©

Top: Gran Plaza (p201), Quiriguá

Bottom: Ruins at Tikal (p247)

full picture, from gigantic temples to intricately painted ceramics.

➡ Mostly Maya (www.mostlymaya.com) is a hobby site devoted to exploring the Maya world, with practical info on how to get to some remote sites – it hasn't been updated in a while, but remains mostly excellent.

Don't Miss Sites

➡ Tikal – Guatemala's most famous Maya ruins.

➡ Copán – Across the border in Honduras, one of the most outstanding achievements of the Maya.

➡ El Mirador – Late-Preclassic metropolis buried in the deepest jungle.

➡ Ceibal – Memorable river journey to low, ruined temples.

➡ Santa Lucía Cotzumalguapa – Great stone heads carved with grotesque faces and fine relief scenes.

Top Museums

Some sites have their own museums – the ones at Tikal and Copán are well worth the extra admission fee – but there are also important city and regional museums that hold many of the most valuable and impressive pre-Hispanic artifacts.

Museo Nacional de Arqueología y Etnología, Guatemala City (p48) By far the most impressive collection of ancient Maya artifacts, with pieces from all the important ceremonial areas, including an impressive throne from the Piedras Negras site.

Museo Popol Vuh, Guatemala City (p48) A wealth of smaller pieces, including figurines, wooden masks, textiles and a faithful copy of the Dresden Codex.

Museo El Baúl, Santa Lucía Cotzumalguapa (p166) An open-air museum situated on the grounds of the sugar cane farm where dozens of human-sized stone sculptures have been found.

Colección Dr Juan Antonio Valdés, Uaxactún (p256) Housed in the Hotel El Chiclero, this private collection holds a remarkable wealth of Maya pottery from Uaxactún, Yaxhá, and as far away as Oaxaca, Mexico.

Regions at a Glance

The six regions outlined here could just as easily be six separate countries. Travel a hundred kilometers or so and everything changes: the food, the clothes, the way people talk and, of course, the scenery. The capital is all big-city buzz, while it's hard to imagine things getting any more laid-back than they do in the little beach towns down on the coast. Antigua is the epitome of stately colonial charm, whereas the temple-laden jungles and small towns of El Petén have a very rough-and-ready frontier atmosphere. The highlands of the center and west are probably the most similar, but where the volcano-studded west gets chilly and sometimes bleak, the cloud forest–covered center is much milder and more lush.

Guatemala City

Art & Archaeology
Nightlife
Urban Buzz

Museums & Galleries

You might be tempted to dodge the capital, but if you're at all interested in art and archaeology, you need to spend some time here. All the best pieces end up here, often in world-class, superbly curated spaces.

The Big Night Out

The capital's massive population of students, rock-steady live-music scene and burgeoning nightlife district just off the Central Park make it the best place to go out in the country, hands down.

That Feeling...

For all its craziness and stress, you're not going to get that big-city kick anywhere else in the country. Just walking down the street can be an adventure – keep your wits about you and you'll soon learn to love (or at least tolerate) it.

p42

Antigua

Colonial Architecture
Language Lessons
Food

Colonial Charms

Though much of the Spanish legacy in the former capital lies in ruins, even the remaining fragments add allure to the streetscapes, offering picture-postcard views at every corner and a chance to scramble through history.

Back to School

Despite some tough competition, Antigua remains the capital of Spanish-language study in Latin America. Dozens of small, affably run institutes offer personalized instruction in colonial/tropical surrounds at bargain prices.

Gourmet Traveling

Owing to its globally varied visitor profile, Antigua rivals much loftier destinations as a cuisine capital. Here you can enjoy everything from *escargots à la Bourguignonne* to Argentine *empanadas* at restaurants run by transplants from their culinary places of origin.

p63

The Highlands

Indigenous Attire
Volcanoes
Festivals

Fancy Dress

From the pom-pommed headdresses of women in Chajul to the flamboyant red-and-white striped trousers of men in Todos Santos Cuchumatán, traditional Maya clothing is a dazzling display of identity throughout the highlands.

Peaking Out

With a chain of 33 volcanoes, four of them active, climbers, geology buffs and landscape painters find plenty to inspire them here. An early morning hike up the Santa María volcano leads to a mesmerizing view of the periodically erupting Santiaguito.

Party Time

Every highlands town likes to let its hair down at an annual fest, and outsiders are always welcome. Good bets include Quetzaltenango's late September toast to its Virgen del Rosario and Todos Santos Cuchumatán's patron saint's day with madcap horse racing and drunken marimba dancing.

p90

The Pacific Slope

Beaches
Food
Wildlife

Sun, Sand & Surf

If you've been up in the hills or traveling hard, the whole Pacific coast is dotted with little beach towns where you can crank it back a notch or two and get in some quality do-nothing time.

This Fish is Delish!

With so much coastline it's no surprise that the seafood here is excellent – fried fish and shrimp are staples, but don't miss out on the *caldo de mariscos* (seafood stew) if you see it on a menu.

Animal Frenzy

With whales and turtles in the waters off the beaches and the mangroves buzzing with birdlife, this region is a wildlife-watcher's paradise. If you don't get your fill along the coast, stop by the drive-through Autosafari Chapín wildlife reserve.

p157

Central & Eastern Guatemala

Nature
Culture
Caves

Natural Paradise

From the lush cloud forests of the Verapaz to the verdant landscapes of Lago de Izabal and the Río Dulce, the rivers, lakes, canyons, waterfalls and jungles of this region showcase Guatemala at its natural best.

A Cultural Mosaic

Ethnically diverse and at times intensely traditional, the center and east of the country are home to Achi', Poqomchi', Ch'ortí and Q'eqchi' Maya, many of who maintain traditional customs. Over on the Caribbean, the culturally distinct Garifuna represent one more ingredient in Guatemala's ethnic stew.

Going Underground

The limestone crags, particularly north of Cobán, play host to a network of caves and caverns, making for great photo opportunities and fascinating forays for casual strollers and serious spelunkers alike.

p177

El Petén

Classic Maya Sites
Wildlife
Trekking

Site Seeing

With literally hundreds of sites sprinkled across the jungle lowlands, you may delve as deeply as you choose into the mysteries of Classic Maya civilization, from the oft-scaled temples of Tikal to the seldom-seen astronomical observatory of Uaxactún.

Animal Planet

Rare and endangered creatures still roam the protected expanses of the Maya Biosphere Reserve, and guides from *petenera* communities can help you track them down, whether it's nocturnal crocodile cruising at the Estación Biológica Las Guacamayas or awakening to howler monkeys at Biotopo Cerro Cahuí.

Going Bush

Seasoned guides at places such as Ni'tun Ecolodge on Lago de Petén Itzá or Aldana's Lodge in Uaxactún accompany you on multiday odysseys through the mud and mosquitoes to such remote Maya sites as El Zotz and El Mirador.

p225

On the Road

El Petén
p225

The Highlands
p90

Central & Eastern
Guatemala
p177

Antigua
p63

Guatemala City
p42

The Pacific Slope
p157

Guatemala City

POP 3.4 MILLION / ELEV 1500M

Best Places to Eat

➡ Ambia (p57)

➡ Arbol de la Vida (p56)

➡ La Cocina de Señora Pu (p55)

➡ Café de Imeri (p55)

➡ Kacao (p56)

Best Places to Sleep

➡ Dai Nonni (p54)

➡ Hotel Colonial (p53)

➡ Theatre International Hostel (p52)

➡ Eco Suites Uxlabil (p54)

➡ Posada Belen (p52)

Why Go?

Depending on who you talk to, Guatemala City (or Guate as it's known) is either big, dirty, dangerous and utterly forgettable or big, dirty, dangerous and fascinating. Either way, there's no doubt there's an energy here unlike anywhere else in Guatemala. It's a place where dilapidated buses belch fumes next to BMWs and Hummers, and where skyscrapers drop shadows on shantytowns.

Guate is busy reinventing itself as a people-friendly city. Downtown Zona 1, for years a no-go zone of abandoned buildings and crime hot spots, is leading the way with the pedestrianized 6a Calle attracting bars, cafes and restaurants.

Many travelers skip the city altogether, preferring to make Antigua their base. Still, you may want, or need, to get acquainted with the capital, because this is the hub of the country, home to the best museums and galleries, transport hubs and other traveler's services.

When to Go
Guatemala City

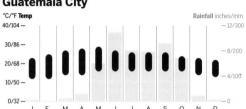

Mar & Apr The capital makes a good base for day trips to overcrowded Antigua during Easter.

Aug The Fiesta de la Virgen de la Asunción on the 15th features fireworks, parades and folk dancing.

Nov–Mar The drier, cooler months are a perfect time to visit the otherwise muggy city.

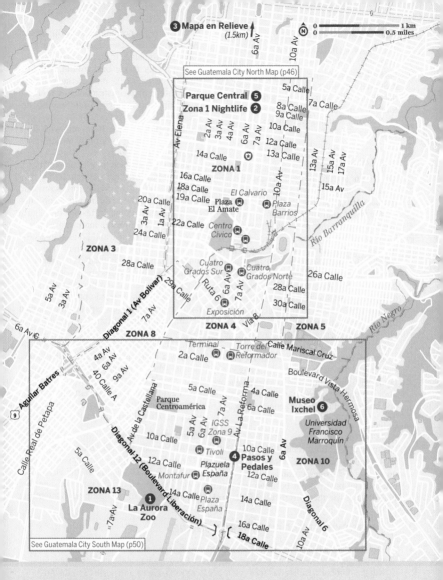

Guatemala City Highlights

1 Visiting the capital's surprisingly leafy and animal-friendly **La Aurora Zoo** (p49).

2 Heading straight for the rejuvenated **Zona 1** (p57) for the best night out on the town.

3 Being oddly mesmerized by the **Mapa en Relieve** (p45) 3D representation of the country – part engineering marvel, part tourist curio.

4 Joining pretty much everybody else in town for a stroll/bike ride/dog walk at **Pasos y Pedales** (p49).

5 Catching buskers, wandering preachers, free concerts and other random stuff in the always-bustling **Parque Central** (p44), or just stopping by to feed the pigeons.

6 Taking a journey through Guatemala's rich cultural heritage in **Museo Ixchel** (p48), devoted to indigenous textiles.

◉ Sights

The major sights are in Zona 1 (the historic center) and Zonas 10 and 13, where the museums are grouped. If you're in town on a Sunday, consider taking the TransMetro's SubiBaja (p49) hop-on, hop-off self-guided tour – it's an excellent way to see many of the city's sights without worrying about public transport or taxis.

◉ Zona 1

The main sights in Zona 1 are grouped around Parque Central (Plaza de la Constitución; Map p46; Zona 1). Back in the day, standard colonial urban planning required every town in the New World to have a large plaza for military exercises and ceremonies: on the north side of the plaza was usually the *palacio de gobierno* (colonial government headquarters); on another side, preferably the east, would be a church or cathedral; and the remaining sides of the square would boast additional civic buildings or the imposing mansions of wealthy citizens. Guatemala City's Parque Central is a classic example of the plan.

Parque Central and the adjoining Parque Centenario are never empty during daylight hours, with shoe-shine kids, ice-cream vendors and sometimes open-air political meetings and concerts adding to the general bustle.

Palacio Nacional de la Cultura   HISTORIC BUILDING
(Map p46; ☏ 2253-0748; cnr 6a Av & 6a Calle, Zona 1; Q40; ⊙ 9-11:45am & 2-4:45pm Mon-Sat) On the north side of Parque Central is this imposing presidential palace, built between 1936 and 1943 during the dictatorial rule of General Jorge Ubico at enormous cost to the lives of the prisoners who were forced to labor here. It's the third palace to stand on the site.

Despite its tragic background, architecturally the palace is one of the country's most interesting constructions, a mélange of multiple earlier styles from Spanish Renaissance to neoclassical. Today, most government offices have been removed from here and it's open as a museum and for a few ceremonial events.

Visits are by guided tour (available in English). You pass through a labyrinth of gleaming brass, polished wood, carved stone and frescoed arches. Features include an optimistic mural of Guatemalan history by Alberto Gálvez Suárez above the main stairway, and a two-ton gold, bronze and Bohemian-crystal chandelier in the reception hall. The banqueting hall sports stained-glass panels depicting – with delicious irony – the virtues of good government. From here your guide will probably take you out onto the presidential balcony, where you can imagine yourself a banana-republic dictator reviewing your troops.

In the western courtyard, the Patio de la Paz, a monument depicting two hands, stands where Guatemala's Peace Accords were signed in 1996; each day at 11am the rose held by the hands is changed by a military guard and the one from the previous day is tossed to a woman among the spectators.

Museo del Ferrocarril   MUSEUM
(Railway Museum; Map p46; www.museofegua.com; 9a Av 18-03, Zona 1; Q5; ⊙ 9am-4pm Tue-Fri, 10am-4pm Sat & Sun) This is one of the city's more intriguing museums. Documented here are the glory days of the troubled Guatemalan

---

ⓘ KNOWING EXACTLY WHERE YOU ARE

Guatemala City, like (almost) all Guatemalan towns, is laid out on a logical street grid. Avenidas run north–south; calles run east–west. Each avenida and calle has a number, with the numbers usually rising as you move from west to east and north to south. Addresses enable you to pinpoint exactly which block a building is in and which side of the street it's on. The address 9a Av 15-24, for instance, means building No 24 on 9a Av in the block after 15a Calle, while 4a Calle 7-3 is building No 3 on 4a Calle in the block after 7a Av. Odd-numbered buildings are on the left-hand side and even numbers are on the right as you move in the rising-numbers direction.

In addition, most cities and towns are divided into a number of zonas – 25 in Guatemala City, fewer in other places. You need to know the zona as well as the street address, for in some places the numbers of avenidas and calles are repeated in more than one zona. Beware, too, of a couple of other minor wrinkles in the system. Short streets may be suffixed 'A,' as in 14a Calle A, which will be found between 14a Calle and 15a Calle. In some smaller towns and villages no one uses street names, even when they're posted on signs.

rail system, along with some quirky artifacts, such as hand-drawn diagrams of derailments and a kitchen set up with items used in dining cars. You can climb around in the passenger carriages, but not the locomotives.

Casa MIMA　　　　　　　　　MUSEUM
(Map p46; ☑ 2253-4020; www.casamima.org; 8a Av 14-12, Zona 1; Q20; ⊙10am-5pm Mon-Sat) A wonderfully presented museum and cultural center set in a house dating from the late 1800s. The owners of the house were collectors with eclectic tastes ranging from French neo-rococo, Chinese and art deco to indigenous artifacts. The place is set up like a functioning house, filled with curios and furniture spanning the centuries.

Catedral Metropolitana　　　CATHEDRAL
(Map p46; 7a Av, Zona 1; ⊙6am-noon & 2-7pm) Facing Parque Central, this cathedral was constructed between 1782 and 1815 (the towers were finished in 1867). It has survived earthquake and fire well, though the earthquakes of 1917 and 1976 did substantial damage. Its heavy proportions and sparse ornamentation don't make for a particularly beautiful building, but it has a certain stateliness, and the altars are worth a look.

**Centro Cultural
Metropolitano**　　　　　　CULTURAL CENTER
(Map p46; 7a Av 11-67, Zona 1; ⊙9am-5pm Mon-Fri) To the rear of the ground floor of the *palacio de correos* (post office) you'll find a surprisingly avant-garde cultural center, hosting art exhibitions, book launches, handicraft workshops and film nights.

Banco de Guatemala　　NOTABLE BUILDING
(Map p46; 7a Av, Zona 1; ⊙9am-5pm Mon-Fri) More rewarding than you'd think is a visit to this bank building, which bears relief sculptures by Dagoberto Vásquez depicting his country's history.

Palacio de Justicia　　NOTABLE BUILDING
(High Court; Map p46; cnr 7a Av & 21a Calle, Zona 1) The imposing Palacio de Justicia lies nearby the Centro Cívico (p45).

Museo Nacional de Historia　　MUSEUM
(Map p46; ☑ 2253-6149; 9a Calle 9-70, Zona 1; Q10; ⊙9am-5pm Mon-Fri) This museum hosts a jumble of historical relics with an emphasis on photography and portraits. Check out the carefully coiffed hairstyles of the 19th-century generals and politicos.

**Municipalidad de
Guatemala**　　　　　　NOTABLE BUILDING
(City Hall; Map p46; 22a Calle, Zona 1) The city hall contains a huge mosaic by Carlos Mérida, completed in 1959.

⊙ Zona 2

Mapa en Relieve　　　　　MONUMENT
(Relief Map; www.mapaenrelieve.org; Av Simeón Cañas Final, Zona 2; Q30; ⊙9am-5pm) North of Zona 1, Zona 2 is mostly a middle-class residential district, but it's worth venturing along to Parque Minerva to see this huge open-air map of Guatemala showing the country at a scale of 1:10,000. The vertical scale is exaggerated to 1:2000 to make the volcanoes and mountains appear dramatically higher and steeper than they really are.

Constructed in 1905 under the direction of Francisco Vela, it was fully restored and repainted in 1999. Viewing towers afford a panoramic view. This is an odd but fun place, and it's curious to observe that Belize is still represented as part of Guatemala. It's an easy walk (or short cab ride) from Parque Central.

Parque Minerva　　　　　　　　PARK
(Av Simeón Cañas Final, Zona 2) Minerva, the Roman goddess of wisdom, technical skill and invention, was a favorite of President Manuel Estrada Cabrera. Her park is a placid place, good for walking among the eucalyptus trees and sipping a cool drink. Watch out, however, for pickpockets and purse-snatchers.

⊙ Zona 4

Centro Cívico　　　　　　ARCHITECTURE
(Map p46; Zona 4) Pride of Zona 4 (actually straddling its borders with Zonas 1 and 5) is the Centro Cívico, a set of large government and institutional buildings constructed during the 1950s and '60s. One is the headquarters of INGUAT (Guatemalan tourist institute), housing the city's main tourist office (p59).

⊙ Zona 5

Estadio Nacional Mateo Flores　STADIUM
(Map p46; 10a Av, Zona 5) Estadio Nacional Mateo Flores is the national stadium and plays host to football games, athletic conferences and big-name concerts.

Guatemala City North

N
0 — 400 m
0 — 0.2 miles

ZONA 3

6a Calle
7a Calle
8a Calle
9a Calle

Av Elena

1a Av

10a Calle

11a Calle
12a Calle

13a Calle

14a Calle

2a Av

15a Calle
15a Calle B
16a Calle
17a Calle
18a Calle
19a Calle
20a Calle
21a Calle

Av Centroamérica

2a Av

1a Av

22a Calle
23a Calle
24a Calle
25a Calle

Diagonal 1 (Av Bolívar)

ZONA 8

8a Av

27a Calle

Museo Miraflores (3.8km)

3a Av

4a Av

28 ⊗

21 🏛

20 🏛

41 ⊗

9a Calle A

6a Av

5a Av

38 🏛

46 🏛

34 ⊗

37 ⊗
43 ⊗ 35 ⊗

12a Calle A

36 22 32 ⊗
45 ⊗

ZONA 1

3a Av

4a Av

5a Av

6a Av A

31 ⊗

2 🏛
18 🏛
17 🏛
14 🏛

26 🏛

19 🏛
15 🏛

Fuente del Norte 🏛 ADN

Transportes Galgos
El Calvario 🏛

49 🔒

Diagonal 2

20a Calle

7a Av

Plaza Barrios

19a Calle

Transportes Galgos Inter

8a Av

9a Av

8 🏛

21a Calle

21a Calle
44 🏛

7 ⊙ 1 ⊙

10 ⊙

22a Calle

4 ⊙

CENTRO CÍVICO

6 ⊙

Proatur ℹ️ℹ️ Inguat

Ruta 3

Via 1

Cuatro Grados Sur 🏛

6a Av

7a Av

Via 3
Via 3

Ruta 2

Ruta 1

Departamento de Extranjería ℹ️

40 🏛

ZONA 4

Cuatro Grados Norte

Diagonal 6 (Av de la Barranquilla)

10a Av

12a Av

26a Calle

ZONA 5
27a Calle

28a Calle

29a Calle

30a Calle

13a Av
14a Av
15a Av

Via 2

Ruta 6

Ruta 5

Via 4
Via 4

Ruta 4

Plaza de la República

Exposición 🏛

Via 5

Ruta 7

Ruta 8

47 🏛

Via 7

6a Calle
7a Calle
8a Calle

5a Calle

16 🏛
11 🏛
12 ⊙ 13 ●
3 ✝

6a Calle
48 🏛

7a Calle
8a Calle

7a Av

8a Av

9a Av

9a Calle
42 ⊗
39 ⊗
29 ⊗

9 🏛 9a Calle

10a Av

11a Av

10a Calle

5 ⊠
23 🏛

24 🏛

13a Calle
13a Calle A
25 🏛
14a Calle

14a Calle A
Litegua 🏛 15a Calle

15a Calle A
Línea Dorada 🏛 16a Calle

17a Calle
18a Calle

Mapa en Relieve (2km)

12a Av

GUATEMALA CITY SIGHTS

Guatemala City North

GUATEMALA CITY SIGHTS

◔ Zona 7

Parque Arqueológico Kaminaljuyú ARCHAEOLOGICAL SITE

(cnr 11a Calle & 24a Av, Zona 7; Q50; ◷8am-4pm) With remnants of one of the first important cities in the Maya region, this park is just west of 23a Av and is some 4km west of the city center. At its peak, from about 400 BC to AD 100, ancient Kaminaljuyú had thousands of inhabitants and scores of temples, and probably dominated much of highland Guatemala.

Large-scale carvings found here were the forerunners of Classic Maya carving, and Kaminaljuyú had a literate elite before anywhere else in the Maya world. The city fell into ruin before being reoccupied around AD 400 by invaders from Teotihuacán in central Mexico, who rebuilt it in Teotihuacán's *talud-tablero* style, with buildings stepped in alternating vertical *(tablero)* and sloping *(talud)* sections. Unfortunately, most of Kaminaljuyú has been covered by urban sprawl: the archaeological park is but a small portion of the ancient city, and even here the remnants consist chiefly of grassy mounds. To the left from the entrance is La Acrópolis, where you can inspect excavations of a ball court and *talud-tablero* buildings from AD 450 to 550.

A couple of hundred meters south of the entrance and across the road are two burial statues from the late Preclassic era. They're badly deteriorated, but are the only examples of carving left at the site – the best examples have been moved to the new Museo Nacional de Arqueología y Etnología (p48).

You can get here on bus 35 from 4a Av, Zona 1, but check that the bus is going to the ruinas de Kaminaljuyú – not all do (and city buses are not really recommended). A taxi from Zona 1 costs around Q50.

◔ Zona 10

Two of the country's best museums are housed in large, modern buildings at the Universidad Francisco Marroquín, 1km east of Av La Reforma.

Museo Ixchel   MUSEUM
(Map p50; ☎ 2361-8081; www.museoixchel.org; 6a Calle Final, Zona 10; Q35; ☺ 9am-5pm Mon-Fri, to 1pm Sat) This museum is named for the Maya goddess of the moon, women, reproduction and, of course, textiles. Photographs and exhibits of indigenous costumes and other crafts show the incredible richness of traditional arts in Guatemala's highland towns. Guided tours are available in English (with prior reservation) or Spanish.

If you enjoy Guatemalan textiles at all, you must visit this museum. It has access for travelers with disabilities, a section for children, a cafe, a shop and a library.

Museo Popol Vuh   MUSEUM
(Map p50; ☎ 2338-7896; www.popolvuh.ufm.edu; 6a Calle Final, Zona 10; adult/child Q35/10; ☺ 9am-5pm Mon-Fri, to 1pm Sat) Behind Museo Ixchel you'll find well-displayed pre-Hispanic figurines, incense burners and burial urns, plus carved wooden masks and traditional textiles, filling several rooms of this museum. Other rooms hold colonial paintings and gilded wood and silver artifacts. A faithful copy of the *Dresden Codex,* one of the precious 'painted books' of the Maya, is among the most interesting pieces. There is also a colorful display of animals in Maya art.

Jardín Botánico   GARDENS
(Map p50; Calle Mariscal Cruz 1-56, Zona 10; Q15; ☺ 8am-3:30pm Mon-Fri, to noon Sat) The Universidad de San Carlos has a large, lush botanic garden on the northern edge of Zona 10. The admission includes the university's Museo de Historia Natural (p48) at the site.

Museo de Historia Natural   MUSEUM
(Natural History Museum; Map p50; Calle Mariscal Cruz 1-56, Zona 10; Q15; ☺ 8am-3:30pm Mon-Fri, to noon Sat) The university's Museo de Historia Natural is at the same site as the Universidad de San Carlos' botanical garden, which is also included in the admission price. The museum has a well-arranged collection of flora and fauna specimens from around the country – it's worth a quick visit if you're in the neighborhood.

◉ Zona 11

Museo Miraflores   MUSEUM
(☎ 2470-3415; www.museomiraflores.org.gt; 7a Calle 21-55, Zona 11; Q25; ☺ 9am-7pm Tue-Sun) This excellent modern museum is inauspiciously jammed between two shopping malls a few kilometers out of town. Downstairs focuses on objects found at Kaminaljuyú (p47), with fascinating trade route maps showing the site's importance. Upstairs there are displays on textiles and indigenous clothing, separated by region, from around the country.

Signs are in Spanish and (for the most part) English. Out back is a pleasant grassy area with paths and seating – a good place to take a breather.

To get here, catch any bus from the center going to Centro Comercial Tikal Futura. The museum is 250m down the road between it and the Miraflores shopping center.

◉ Zona 13

The attractions here in the city's southern reaches are all ranged along 5a Calle in the Finca Aurora area, northwest of the airport. While here you can also drop into the Mercado de Artesanías (p58).

Museo Nacional de Arqueología y Etnología   MUSEUM
(Map p50; ☎ 2475-4399; www.munae.gob.gt; 6a Calle, Sala 5, Finca La Aurora, Zona 13; Q60; ☺ 9am-4pm Tue-Fri, 9am-noon & 1:30-4pm Sat & Sun) This museum has the country's biggest collection of ancient Maya artifacts, but explanatory information is very sparse. There's a great wealth of monumental stone sculpture, including Classic-period stelae from Tikal, Uaxactún and Piedras Negras; a superb throne from Piedras Negras; and animal representations from Preclassic Kaminaljuyú.

Also here are rare wooden lintels from temples at Tikal and El Zotz, and a room with beautiful jade necklaces and masks. Don't miss the large-scale model of Tikal. The ethnology section has displays on the languages, costumes, dances, masks and homes of Guatemala's indigenous peoples.

Museo Nacional de Arte Moderno   GALLERY
(Map p50; ☎ 2472-0467; 6a Calle, Sala 6, Finca La Aurora, Zona 13; Q10; ☺ 9am-4pm Tue-Fri, 9am-12:30pm & 2-4pm Sat & Sun) Here you'll find a collection of 20th-century Guatemalan art including works by well-known Guatemalan artists such as Carlos Mérida, Carlos Valente and Humberto Gavarito.

Museo de los Niños   MUSEUM
(Children's Museum; Map p50; ☎ 2475-5076; www.museodelosninos.com.gt; 5a Calle 10-00, Zona 13; Q40; ☺ 8am-noon & 1-4:30pm Tue-Fri, 9:30am-1:30pm & 2:30-6pm Sat & Sun) Almost opposite the zoo entrance is this hands-on

affair that is a sure success if you have kids to keep happy. The fun ranges from a giant jigsaw-map of Guatemala to an earthquake simulator and, most popular of all, a room of original and entertaining ball games.

La Aurora Zoo ZOO
(Map p50; ☎2472-0507; www.aurorazoo.org.gt; 5a Calle, Zona 13; adult/child Q30/15; ⊘9am-5pm Tue-Sun) This is not badly kept as far as zoos in this part of the world go, and the lovely, parklike grounds alone are worth the admission fee.

Museo Nacional de Historia Natural Jorge Ibarra MUSEUM
(Map p50; ☎2472-0468; 6a Calle 7-30, Zona 13; Q10; ⊘9am-4pm Tue-Sun) This natural history museum, located behind the archaeology museum, boasts a large collection of dissected animals.

🏃 Activities

Pasos y Pedales FISHING
(Map p50; ⊘10am-2pm Sun) If you're here on a Sunday, check out a wonderful municipal initiative that sees the Av de las Americas in Zona 10, and its continuation, Av La Reforma in Zona 13, blocked off to traffic for 3km and taken over by jugglers, clowns, in-line skaters, dog walkers, food vendors, t'ai chi classes, skate parks and playgrounds for kids.

It's a great place to go for a walk (or you can hire bikes or in-line skates on the street) and check out a very relaxed, sociable side of the city that is rarely otherwise seen.

X-Park ADVENTURE SPORTS
(☎2380-2080; www.xpark.net; Av Hincapié, Km 11.5; Q15; ⊘10am-6pm) About 10 minutes' drive south of the airport is this very well-constructed 'adventure sports' park. Attractions (they prefer to call them 'challenges') cost from Q20 each and include bouldering and climbing walls, reverse bungees, mechanical bulls, a rope course, zip lines and a playground for kids. A fairly limited range of fast food is available at the cafeteria.

A taxi here from Zona 10 should cost you around Q35.

🚌 Tours

SubiBaja BUS TOUR
(Map p46; ⊘9am-2pm) **FREE** Modern, air-conditioned TransMetro buses run a hop-on, hop-off sightseeing circuit passing every 20 minutes, with 10 stops including Parque Central, Centro Cívico, the zoo (and museums), Zona Viva, Pasos y Pedales, Cuatro Grados Norte and Mapa en Relieve. Volunteer guides give an on-board commentary and each bus is staffed by a member of the Transit Police.

GUATEMALA CITY FOR CHILDREN

Guatemala City has enough child-friendly attractions to make it worth considering as an outing from Antigua if you have kids to please. The Museo de los Niños and La Aurora Zoo, conveniently over the road from each other in Zona 13, top the list. Kids might also relish the dead animals in various states of preservation at the nearby Museo Nacional de Historia Natural Jorge Ibarra .

The Mapa en Relieve (p45), north of the center, amuses most ages, and there are a few swings and climbing frames in the adjacent park.

On Sundays, kids and adults will enjoy the relaxed atmosphere and abundant free entertainment on offer at Pasos y Pedales.

It shouldn't be too hard to find some food that the little 'uns are willing to eat at the food courts in the Centro Comercial Los Próceres (p58) or Oakland Mall (p58), where everyone can also enjoy a little air-con and shopping (window or otherwise). At Oakland Mall you'll find the restaurant Nais (p56) – a winner with the kids for its huge aquarium filled with tropical fish (a scuba diver swims through periodically, cleaning the tank and feeding the inhabitants).

Facilities for families in Guatemala City are not easily found – change rooms are pretty much nonexistent and child car seats are pretty rare, although with some advance notice a rental car company could probably come up with one. For pram-pushers, sidewalks tend to be reasonably level and wide, but can get awfully crowded – consider bringing a baby carrier if you've got a really little one along.

Guatemala City South

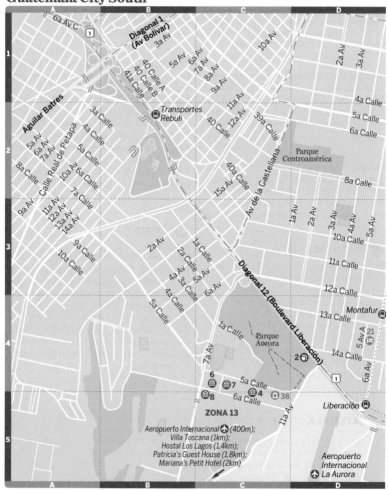

Guatemala City South

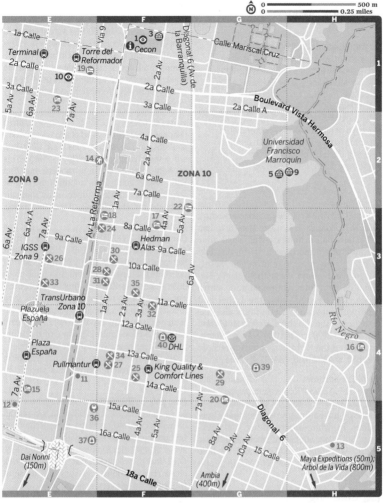

Clark Tours   BUS TOUR

(Map p50; ☑ 2412-4700; www.clarktours.com.gt; 7a Av 14-76, Zona 9; ☺ 9am-7pm Mon-Fri, to 1pm Sat) Guatemala's longest-established tour operator offers morning and full-day city tours. The morning tour (available Saturday to Wednesday) visits the Palacio Nacional de la Cultura, cathedral and Centro Cívico. The day tour adds the Ixchel and Popul Vuh museums. Clark Tours also has branches in the **Westin Camino Real** (Map p50; ☑ 2363-3920; cnr 14a Calle & Av La Reforma, Zona 10) and the **Hotel Barceló Guatemala** (Map p50; ☑ 2362-9716; 7a Av 15-45, Zona 9).

Maya Expeditions   ADVENTURE TOUR

(Map p50; ☑ 2363-4955; www.mayaexpeditions. com; 13a Av 14-70, Zona 10) Guatemala's most respected adventure-tourism company specializes in white-water rafting and trekking, but also offers archaeological trips, wildlife-watching expeditions and a whole lot more, mostly in the Alta Verapaz and Petén regions.

🛏 Sleeping

For budget and many midrange hotels, make a beeline for Zona 1. If you have just flown in or are about to fly out, there are a number of convenient guesthouses near the airport. Top-end hotels are mostly located around Zona 10.

🛏 Zona 1

Many of the city's cheaper lodgings are clustered in the area between 6a and 9a Avs and 14a and 17a Calles, 10 to 15 minutes' walk south from Parque Central. Keep street noise in mind as you look for a room.

★ Theatre International Hostel   HOSTEL $

(Map p46; ☑ 4202-5112; www.theatreihostel.com; 8a Av 14-17, Zona 1; dm Q60-80, r without bathroom from Q170; 🖥⏅) Zona 1's best hostel is a simple affair, but a welcome sight nonetheless. Rooms and dorms are spacious, the whole place is spotless and the small pool in the patio is a perfect refresher on those muggy city days.

Hotel Clariss   HOTEL $

(Map p46; ☑ 2232-1113; www.hotelclarissyasociados. amawebs.com; 8a Av 15-14, Zona 1; s/d Q190/240, s/d without bathroom Q145/190; 🅿@) This friendly place is set in a modern building with some good-sized rooms (and other, smaller ones). Those at the front get more air and light, but also the bulk of the street noise.

Hotel Spring   HOTEL $

(Map p46; ☑ 2230-2858; www.hotelspring.com; 8a Av 12-65, Zona 1; s/d from Q190/235, s/d without bathroom Q140/180; 🅿@🖥) With a beautiful courtyard setting, the Spring has a lot more style than other Zona 1 joints. It has central but quiet sunny patios. The 43 rooms vary greatly, but most are spacious and clean with high ceilings. Have a look around if you can. All rooms have cable TV; some of the more expensive ones are wheelchair accessible.

It's worth booking ahead. A cafeteria serves meals from 6:30am to 1:30pm.

Hotel Ajau   HOTEL $

(Map p46; ☑ 2232-0488; hotelajau@hotmail.com; 8a Av 15-62, Zona 1; s/d Q180/230, s/d without bathroom Q110/140; 🅿@🖥) One of the few budget hotels in Guate with any tangible sense of style, the Ajau is a pretty good deal, with lovely polished floor tiles and cool, clean rooms. Room sizes vary and those at the front can get very noisy.

★ Posada Belen   BOUTIQUE HOTEL $$

(Map p46; ☑ 2232-6178; www.posadabelen.com; 13a Calle A 10-20, Zona 1; s/d Q330/420; @🖥) One of Zona 1's most stylish options, this boutique hotel has just 10 rooms, arranged around a couple of lush patios. Rooms are well decorated with *típico* (traditional) furnishings and there's a good restaurant onsite.

Hotel Sevilla   HOTEL $$

(Map p46; ☑ 2230-0506; 9a Av 12-29, Zona 1; s/d Q180/220; 🖥) A step up from most hotels in this price range, the Sevilla doesn't quite live up to its self-awarded three-star status, but it still does a pretty good job. The location is supercentral and the somewhat aging rooms are spacious and light. Front rooms get some street noise.

Hotel Pan American
HOTEL $$

(Map p46; ☎2244-0850; www.hotelpanamerican.com.gt; 9a Calle 5-63, Zona 1; s/d Q360/520; P@☎) Guatemala City's only luxury hotel before WWII, the Pan American is one of the few hotels in the city with any air of history. There's a fine, art-deco lobby that's filled with plants and a not-too-shabby restaurant. Rooms are large and simple, often with three or more beds. The bathrooms are stylish and modern, with good-sized tubs.

Avoid rooms facing the noisy street.

Hotel Colonial
HOTEL $$

(Map p46; ☎2232-6722; www.hotelcolonial.net; 7a Av 14-19, Zona 1; s/d Q185/270, s/d without bathroom Q150/200; P@☎) This large converted house has spacious communal areas and heavy, dark, colonial decor. It's a very well-run establishment, with 42 clean, good-sized and adequately furnished rooms. Nearly all have a private bathroom and TV.

Hotel Quality Service
HOTEL $$

(Map p46; ☎2251-8005; www.qualityguate.com; 8a Calle 3-18, Zona 1; s/d incl breakfast Q230/300; P@☎) There's a pleasing, old-timey feel about this place, which is balanced perfectly by the modern-but-not-overly-so rooms. This is the best pick near the park.

Hotel Excel
HOTEL $$

(Map p46; ☎2253-2709; www.hotelexcel.amawebs.com; 9a Av 15-12, Zona 1; s/d Q205/255; P@☎) The Excel's bright, modern motel style may be a bit bland for some, but the rooms are spotless and the showers blast hot water.

Hotel Capri
HOTEL $$

(Map p46; ☎2232-8191; 9a Av 15-63, Zona 1; s/d Q175/250; P) This modern four-story number is in a decent location and rooms are set back from the street, so they're quiet. Big windows looking onto patios and light wells keep the place sunny and airy.

Hotel Centenario
HOTEL $$

(Map p46; ☎2338-0381; www.hotelcentenario.wordpress.com; 6a Calle 5-33, Zona 1; s/d Q200/250; P☎) Although it's looking a bit worn around the edges (and not that flash in the middle, either), the Centenario offers a pretty good deal, right on the park. Rooms are basic and unrenovated, with TV and hot showers.

Hotel Royal Palace
HOTEL $$$

(Map p46; ☎2416-4400; www.hotelroyalpalace.com; 6a Av 12-66, Zona 1; s/d Q530/645; P☀☎) A little island of glamor amid the rough and tumble of 6a Av, this place offers most comforts. The style is modern-reconstruction, with plenty of dark woods and fancy tiling around the place. Rooms are large, sparkling clean and wheelchair accessible. Those at the front have balconies overlooking the street – a fascinating, if noisy, spectacle.

Facilities include a restaurant, bar, gym, sauna and free airport transfers.

Zona 9

Hotel Villa Española
HOTEL $$

(Map p50; ☎2205-0200; www.hotelvillaespanola.com; 2a Calle 7-51, Zona 9; s/d Q465/535; P☀☎) One of the very few options with colonial stylings in this part of town, the Villa Española has some beautiful touches. It's on a busy road, but rooms are set well back, so there's little noise. There's a good restaurant on the premises.

Residencia del Sol
HOTEL $$$

(Map p50; ☎2360-4823; www.residenciadelsol.com; 3a Calle 6-42, Zona 9; s/d Q500/580; P☀☎) The spacious, good-looking rooms here make up for the slightly out-of-the-way location. Pay an extra Q80 for wooden floorboards and a balcony.

Mi Casa
HOTEL $$$

(Map p50; ☎2332-1364; www.hotelmicasa.com; 5a Av A 13-51, Zona 9; s/d incl breakfast Q420/640; P@☎) Set in a family house on a quiet street, Mi Casa offers big and sunny rooms with bathrooms, lino floors, standard acrylic paintings, fans and reading lamps. Breakfast is served in a leafy little patio out back. Call ahead for airport pickup.

Barceló Guatemala
BUSINESS HOTEL $$$

(Map p50; ☎4000-2378; www.barceloguatemalacity.com; 7a Av 15-45, Zona 9; r from Q625; P☀@☎☀) For that big, corporate, I'd-rather-not-be-here hotel experience, it's hard to go past the local outlet of the Spanish Barceló hotel chain.

Zona 10

Quetzalroo
HOSTEL $

(Map p50; ☎5746-0830; www.quetzalroo.com; 6a Av 7-84, Zona 10; dm/s/d without bathroom Q120/200/280; P@☎) Guatemala City's best downtown hostel has reasonable rooms and dorms, a cramped kitchen area and a great rooftop terrace. The location's handy for the Zona Viva eating and nightlife scene. Call for free pickup from the airport or bus terminal.

★ Eco Suites Uxlabil
APARTMENT **$$**

(Map p50; ☑2366-9555; www.uxlabil.com; 11a Calle 12-53, Zona 10; s/d incl breakfast Q395/495; ❄️🛜) If you're planning on being in town for a while (or even if you're not), you could do a lot worse than these sweet little apartments decked out in indigenous motifs and tucked away in a leafy corner of Zona 10. Weekly discounts apply.

Hotel Ciudad Vieja
HOTEL **$$$**

(Map p50; ☑2210-7900; www.hotelciudadvieja.com; 8a Calle 3-67, Zona 10; s/d incl breakfast Q685/760; ❄️🛜) A modern construction decked out superbly with old-world touches, the Ciudad Vieja is one of the few truly atmospheric hotels in this part of town. The rooms are good (although the singles can be a bit cramped), and the lovely, shady patio-atrium is perfect for taking a midday breather or enjoying a long and lazy breakfast.

La Inmaculada
HOTEL **$$$**

(Map p50; ☑2314-5100; www.inmaculadahotel.com; 14a Calle 7-88, Zona 10; r Q800-875, ste Q990; ❄️🛜) In a quiet corner of Zona 10, this newish hotel goes out of its way to please, with Egyptian cotton bedding, rainforest showers, balconies overlooking the lush gardens and a cool, understated design ethic.

Hotel San Carlos
HOTEL **$$$**

(Map p50; ☑2332-6055; www.hsancarlos.com; Av La Reforma 7-89, Zona 10; incl breakfast s/d Q740/835, apt from Q1390; 🅿️@🛜🏊) OK, so it goes a little heavy on the baroque furnishings, but this place is still a good deal. Set well back from the busy street, it's quiet and the well-appointed rooms and apartments are spacious and comfortable. Rates include airport pickup.

🛏️ Zona 13

The middle-class residential area around the airport in Zona 13 is filling up with guesthouses catering to arriving and departing travelers. All the room rates include breakfast and airport transfers (call from the airport on arrival). There are no restaurants out here, but hotel workers have the complete lowdown on fast-food home delivery options.

Hostal Los Lagos
HOSTEL **$**

(☑2261-2809; www.loslagoshostal.com; 8a Av 15-85 Aurora 1, Zona 13; dm/s/d Q120/170/320, s/d without bathroom Q140/180; 🅿️@🛜) This is the most hostel-like of the near-the-airport options. Rooms are mostly set aside for dorms, which are airy and spacious, but there are a couple of reasonable-value private rooms. The whole place is extremely comfortable, with big indoor and outdoor sitting areas.

Villa Toscana
HOTEL **$$**

(☑2261-2854; www.hostalvillatoscana.com; 16a Calle 8-20 Aurora 1, Zona 13; s/d incl breakfast Q260/380; 🅿️@🛜) One of the 'new breed' of airport hotels, this one features big, comfortable rooms, a tranquil atmosphere, a kitchen for guest use and a lovely backyard. Airport transfers are only available from 5:30am to 9:30pm – outside those hours, you pay the taxi.

Patricia's Guest House
GUESTHOUSE **$$**

(☑2261-4251; www.patriciashotel.com; 19 Calle 10-65, Aurora 2, Zona 13; s without bathroom incl breakfast Q260; 🅿️@🛜) This family house is a relaxed and comfortable airport-region option with a sweet little backyard where guests can hang out. It also offers private transport around the city and shuttles to bus stations.

Mariana's Petit Hotel
GUESTHOUSE **$$**

(☑2261-4105; www.marianaspetithotel.com; 20 Calle 10-17 Aurora 2, Zona 13; s/d incl breakfast Q280/345; 🛜) One of the better of the airport hotels, Mariana's features spacious rooms, a good breakfast and a range of hotel services and amenities.

★ Dai Nonni
HOTEL **$$$**

(☑2362-5458; www.dainonnihotel.com; 15 Av A 5-30, Zona 13; s/d Q695/790; 🛜) Just south of the Zona 10 action, this small hotel wins points for its eclectic decorations, backyard hangout areas and big rooms. Discounts are available for cash payments and longer stays.

🍴 Eating

For cheap eats head to Zona 1 – there are little *comedores* around the Mercado Central, and the cheapest of all are inside the market, on the lower floor. Zonas 10 and 14 have the lion's share of upscale restaurants, with a good selection of international cuisines.

American fast-food chains are sprinkled liberally throughout Zona 1 and across the city. Pollo Campero is Guatemala's KFC clone.

✕ Zona 1

Cheap eats are easy to find in Zona 1 – dozens of restaurants and fast-food shops are strung along, and just off, 6a Av between 8a and 15a Calles.

Coffee culture is just beginning to hit Zona 1, and there are a number of cool little cafes springing up where you can enjoy good coffee, sandwiches and snacks.

★Café de Imeri   CAFE $
(Map p46; 6a Calle 3-34, Zona 1; mains Q40-70; ⊙8am-6:30pm Mon-Sat; 🐾) Interesting breakfasts, soups and pastas. The list of sandwiches is impressive and there's a beautiful little courtyard area out the back.

Bar Céntrico   CAFE $
(Map p46; 7a Av 12-32, Zona 1; snacks Q25-45; ⊙9am-6pm Mon-Sat) A hip little bar-cafe with comfy sofas out on the passageway and local artworks on the walls.

Café-Restaurante Hamburgo   GUATEMALAN $
(Map p46; 15a Calle 5-34, Zona 1; set meal Q35-55; ⊙7am-9:30pm) This bustling spot facing the south side of Parque Concordia serves good Guatemalan food, with chefs at work along one side and orange-aproned waitstaff scurrying about. At weekends a marimba band adds atmosphere.

Restaurante Rey Sol   VEGETARIAN $
(Map p46; 11a Calle 5-51, Zona 1; mains Q20-30; ⊙7am-7pm Mon-Sat, to 4pm Sun; 🖋) Good, fresh ingredients and some innovative cooking keep this strictly vegetarian restaurant busy at lunchtime.

Fu Lu Sho   CHINESE $
(Map p46; 6a Av 12-05, Zona 1; mains Q40-70; ⊙8am-11pm) This classic Zona 1 Chinese joint has been going for years and is a reliable if somewhat unexciting choice. It's straight up Chinese with a few Guatemalan staples thrown in, but for late-night cheap eats, it's hard to beat.

★La Cocina de Señora Pu   GUATEMALAN $$
(Map p46; 6a Av A 10-16, Zona 1; mains around Q80; ⊙noon-8pm Mon-Sat) This tiny hole-in-the-wall eatery serves up excellent 'modernized' versions of classic Maya dishes. The menu is impressively wide – featuring beef, chicken, pork, duck, turkey, pigeon, rabbit, fish and shrimp – considering it's all done on a four-burner stove in front of your eyes and the flavors are delicious and sometimes surprising.

La Majo   GUATEMALAN $$
(Map p46; 12a Calle 3-08, Zona 1; mains Q50-80; ⊙10am-7pm; 🖋) Downtown Guatemala City's cultural renovation continues in this pleasing little boho cafe set in a crumbling colonial house. There's some OK food on offer and a couple of vegetarian and vegan dishes, but the big draw is the events calendar, featuring live music, theater and other local acts.

Café Leon at 12a Calle   CAFE $$
(Map p46; 12a Calle 6-23, Zona 1; breakfast Q50-70; ⊙7am-6pm Mon-Thu, to 7:30pm Fri, 8:30am-5pm Sat) A cozy branch of the popular coffee shop franchise, with a sweet little patio out back.

Café Leon   CAFE $$
(Map p46; 8a Av 9-15, Zona 1; breakfast Q50-70; ⊙7am-6pm Mon-Thu, to 7:30pm Fri, 8:30am-5pm Sat; 🐾) Hugely popular and atmospheric, with some great old photos of the city on the walls. Some good breakfasts and sandwiches are on offer, but the coffee is the drawcard.

Hotel Pan American   INTERNATIONAL $$
(Map p46; 📞2232-6807; 9a Calle 5-63, Zona 1; breakfast Q60-100, mains Q75-150; ⊙7am-9pm; 🐾) The restaurant at this venerable hotel is high on ambiance. It has notably experienced and polished wait staff sporting traditional Maya regalia. The food (Guatemalan, Italian and North American) is fine, although it is a little on the expensive side.

Picadilly   INTERNATIONAL $$
(Map p46; cnr 6a Av & 11a Calle, Zona 1; mains Q50-100; ⊙11am-9:30pm) Right in the thick of the 6a Av action, this bustling restaurant does OK pizzas and pastas and good steak dishes. The place is clean and street views out of the big front windows are mesmerizing.

Restaurante Altuna   SPANISH $$$
(Map p46; 📞2232-0669; 5a Av 12-31, Zona 1; mains Q130-180; ⊙noon-10pm Tue-Sat, to 4pm Sun) This large and classy restaurant has the atmosphere of a private club. It has tables in several rooms that open to a skylit patio. The specialties are seafood and Spanish dishes; service is both professional and welcoming.

Zona 9

Celeste Imperio　　　　CHINESE $$
(Map p50; cnr 7a Av & 10a Calle, Zona 9; mains Q80-150; ⊙11am-10:30pm Mon-Sat, to 9:30pm Sun) One of the city's many Chinese restaurants, this one gets the thumbs-up from locals. All your favorites are here, plus some unusual options, such as baked pigeon (Q85).

Puerto Barrios　　　　SEAFOOD $$
(Map p50; ☑ 2334-1302; 7a Av 10-65, Zona 9; mains Q100-200; ⊙noon-3:30pm & 6-11pm) Puerto Barrios specializes in tasty prawn and fish dishes and is awash in nautical themes: paintings of buccaneers, portholes for windows and a large compass by the door. If you're having trouble finding it, just look for the big pirate ship in which it is housed.

Zona 10

Zona 10's upmarket ambiance is matched by its range of restaurant choices – prices are higher here, but you're bound to find more variety on the menus and more comfortable surroundings.

★Arbol de la Vida　　　VEGETARIAN $
(17 Calle A 19-60, Zona 10; mains around Q50; ⊙7:30am-6pm Mon & Tue, to 8pm Wed-Fri, to 4pm Sat & Sun ; 🐾🖋) Zona 10's best vegetarian restaurant opens up for early breakfasts and offers a wide menu with tasty soups and mains featuring veg-friendly goodies such as tofu and quinoa.

ZONA 10 CHEAP EATS
· ·
A cheap lunch in GC's hoity-toity Zona 10? These places are nothing fancy, but they are popular with local office workers.

Paco's Café (Map p50; 1a Av 10-50, Zona 10; mains Q35-50; ⊙7am-4pm Mon-Sat) Down-home Guatemalan food served in an eatery at the side of a *kiosko* (small store).

Cafetería Solé (Map p50; 14a Calle, btwn 3a & 4a Avs, Zona 10; set lunch Q40; ⊙noon-4pm Mon-Sat) Good-value set meals.

Cafetería Patsy (Map p50; Av La Reforma 8-01, Zona 10; set lunch Q40-60; ⊙7:30am-8pm) A bright, cheerful place offering subs, sandwiches and good-value set lunches.

San Martín & Company　　CAFE, BAKERY $
(Map p50; 13a Calle 1-62, Zona 10; light meals Q40-60; ⊙6am-8pm; 🐾) Cool and clean, with ceiling fans inside and a small terrace outside, this Zona Viva cafe and bakery is great at any time of the day. For breakfast try a scrumptious omelet and croissant (the former arrives inside the latter); later there are tempting and original sandwiches, soups and salads.

La Chapinita　　　　GUATEMALAN $
(Map p50; 1a Av 10-24, Zona 10; set meals Q45; ⊙8am-7pm Mon-Sat) Down-home Guatemalan food served in more or less formal surrounds can be hard to come by in Zona 10, but this place does it well at good prices. Tables out front on the shady terrace are cool and breezy.

Los Alpes　　　　CAFE, BAKERY $
(Map p50; 10a Calle 1-09, Zona 10; breakfast Q40-60; ⊙7am-7pm Mon-Sat, 9am-7pm Sun) This relaxing garden restaurant-bakery is set well back from the road, behind a wall of vegetation, giving it a feeling of seclusion. Freshly made sandwiches and cakes really hit the spot.

★Kacao　　　　GUATEMALAN $$
(Map p50; ☑ 2337-4188; 2a Av 13-44, Zona 10; mains Q90-160; ⊙noon-4pm & 6-11pm Mon-Fri, 11am-10:30pm Sat & Sun) Set under a thatched *palapa* roof with a soft marimba soundtrack, this is Zona 10's best *comida típica* (regional food) restaurant. The atmosphere and food are both outstanding.

Nais　　　　INTERNATIONAL $$
(Map p50; Diagonal 6 13-01, Oakland Mall, Zona 10; mains Q60-100; ⊙6am-10pm) The food's OK here, but the kids will love the massive aquarium that forms the central wall of this restaurant, especially when the scuba diver comes swimming through, feeding the fish and manta rays.

La Maison de France　　FRENCH $$
(Map p50; ☑ 2337-4029; 13a Calle 7-98, Zona 10; mains Q90-200; ⊙noon-10:30pm Mon-Sat) French-Guatemalan probably isn't a combination you were expecting, but this little place does it well, with some good French dishes, such as garlic snails (Q60), imported wines and live music on Fridays.

Tamarindos　　　　FUSION $$$
(Map p50; ☑ 2360-2815; 11a Calle 2-19, Zona 10; mains Q130-210; ⊙noon-midnight; 🐾) A chic and delicious Asian-Italian restaurant with a Guatemalan twist. There's an inspiring range of salads on offer and some very good

Japanese and Thai-inspired dishes. The decor is stylish and the service prompt but friendly.

Pecorino ITALIAN $$$
(Map p50; ☎2360-3035; 11a Calle 3-36, Zona 10; mains Q120-250; ◉noon-1am Mon-Sat, to 6pm Sun; 🛜) With a beautiful courtyard setting, this is widely regarded as the city's best Italian restaurant. The menu features a huge selection of antipasto, pizza, pasta, meat and seafood dishes.

✖ Zona 14

★Ambia FUSION $$$
(www.fdg.com.gt; 10a Av 5-49, Zona 14; mains Q150-300; ◉noon-midnight Mon-Sat) As the prices may suggest, this is some of the city's finest dining, with a wide-ranging menu offering some good fusion dishes and leaning heavily on Asian influences. The presentation is fantastic and the ambiance superb. On balmy nights, the outdoor courtyard-lounge area is the place to be.

🍸 Drinking & Nightlife

Zona 1 boasts a clutch of good drinking places, including some Latin music and dance venues, all advantageously within half a block of each other just south of Parque Central.

Zona 10 has a few electronic dance clubs, but many of these have now moved further south to the outskirts of town. Check flyers around town for special nights.

Los Lirios CLUB
(Map p46; 7a Av 9-20, Zona 1; ◉5pm-1am Wed-Sat) With live Latin music and dancing most nights, this is a popular choice for the over-25 crowd.

El Gran Hotel PUB
(Map p46; 9a Calle 7-64, Zona 1; ◉6pm-1am Tue-Sun) You can't actually stay here, but the down-market renovated lobby of this classic hotel is one of Zona 1's better-looking bars. It also hosts one of the area's more reliable dance floors, alternating between Latin and electronic music.

Las Cien Puertas BAR
(Map p46; 9a Calle 6-45, Pasaje Aycinena 8-44, Zona 1; ◉noon-1am) This superhip little watering hole is set in a shabby colonial arcade that's said to have a hundred doors (hence the name) and is sometimes closed off for live bands.

LGBT VENUES

Don't get too excited: there are only a couple of places worthy of mention for men and nothing much for women.

Black & White Lounge (Map p46; www.blackandwhitebar.com; 11a Calle 2-54, Zona 1; ☾7pm-1am Wed-Sat) A well-established gay disco-bar in a former private house near the city center with drag shows and theme parties most weekends.

Genetic (Map p46; Ruta 3 3-08, Zona 4; from Q30; ☾9pm-1am Fri & Sat) This used to be called Pandora's Box, and it has been hosting Guatemala's gay crowd since the '70s, although these days it gets a mixed crowd and is one of the best places in town to go for trance/dance music. It has two dance floors, a rooftop patio and a relaxed atmosphere. Friday is 'all you can drink.'

Kahlua CLUB
(Map p50; cnr 15a Calle & 1a Av, Zona 10; from Q30; ☾7pm-1am Thu-Sat) For electronica and bright young things.

★ Entertainment

Guatemala City is home to nearly half the country's population, so it's no surprise that there are entertainment options to spare. The city's various cultural centers are the place to catch music and art shows, and there's live music most nights in the bars around Parque Central, and in the Parque itself most Sundays.

Cinema

Various multiscreen cinema complexes show Hollywood blockbuster movies, often in English with Spanish subtitles (unless it's a kids' movie, in which case it will most likely be dubbed into Spanish). Most convenient are **Cine Capitol Royal** (Centro Comercial Capitol; Map p46; ☎2251-8733; 6a Av 12-51, Zona 1) or **Cinépolis Oakland Mall** (Map p50; ☎2378-2300; www.cinepolis.com.gt; Diagonal 6 13-01, Zona 10). Tickets cost around Q35. Movie listings can be found in the *Prensa Libre* newspaper.

Live Music

★La Bodeguita del Centro LIVE MUSIC
(Map p46; ☎2230-2976; 12a Calle 3-55, Zona 1; ☾9pm-1am Tue-Sat) There's a hopping, creative local scene in Guatemala City, and this

large, bohemian hangout is one of the best places to connect with it. There's live music of some kind almost every night from Tuesday to Saturday, usually starting at 9pm, plus occasional poetry readings, films or forums.

Posters featuring the likes of Che, Marley, Lennon, Victor Jara, Van Gogh and Pablo Neruda cover the walls from floor to ceiling. Entry is usually free Tuesday to Thursday, with a charge of Q25 to Q60 on Friday and Saturday nights; food and drinks are served.

TrovaJazz   LIVE MUSIC
(Map p46; ☑ 2267-9388; www.trovajazz.com; Vía 6 3-55, Zona 4) Jazz, blues and folk fans should look into what's happening here.

Theater

The English-language magazine *Revue* (www.revuemag.com) has events details, although it focuses more on Antigua. Your hotel should have a copy or know where to get one. Free events mags in Spanish come and go. At the time of writing, *El Azar* (www.elazarcultural.blogspot.com) had the best info. Pick up a copy at the city's cultural centers.

Centro Cultural
Miguel Ángel Asturias   PERFORMING ARTS
(Map p46; ☑ 2332-4041; 24a Calle 3-81, Zona 1) Cultural events are held here.

Centro Cultural de España   PERFORMING ARTS
(Map p46; ☑ 2377-2200; www.cceguatemala.org; 6a Av 11-02, Zona 1; ⊙ 9am-7pm Tue-Fri, 10am-2pm Sat) The Spanish Cultural Center hosts an excellent range of events, including live music, film nights and art exhibitions, mostly with free admission.

🛍 Shopping

For fashion boutiques, electronics and other goods, head for large shopping malls such as Centro Comercial Los Próceres (Map p50; www.proceres.com; 16a Calle, Zona 10; ⊙ 8am-8pm) or Oakland Mall (Map p50; www.oaklandmall.com.gt; Diagonal 6 13-01, Zona 10; ⊙ 8am-8pm) in and around Zona 10. Zona 1's 6a Av is a fun window-shopping experience – half the city turns out to check out the shops, eat ice cream and just cruise the pedestrian mall.

Sophos   BOOKS
(Map p50; ☑ 2419-7070; www.sophosenlinea.com; 4a Av 12-59, Plaza Fontabella, Zona 10; ⊙ 10am-9pm Mon-Sat, to 7pm Sun) A relaxed place to read in the Zona Viva, with a good selection of books in English on Guatemala and the Maya, including Lonely Planet guides, and maps.

Mercado Central   MARKET
(Map p46; cnr 8a Av & 8a Calle, Zona 1; ⊙ 9am-6pm Mon-Sat, to noon Sun) Until the quake of 1976, Mercado Central, behind the cathedral, was where locals shopped for food and other necessities. Reconstructed after the earthquake, it now deals in colorful Guatemalan handicrafts such as textiles, carved wood, metalwork, pottery, leather goods and basketry. It's a pretty good place to shop for these kinds of things, with reasonable prices.

Mercado de Artesanías   MARKET
(Crafts Market; Map p50; ☑ 2475-5915; cnr 5a Calle & 11a Av, Zona 13; ⊙ 9:30am-6pm) This sleepy official market near the museums and zoo sells fabrics, clothes and other standard souvenirs without the crowds of the other markets.

Plaza El Amate   MARKET
(Map p46; cnr 18a Calle & 4a Av, Zona 1; ⊙ 8am-8pm) Less hectic than the central market, the Plaza El Amate features a satisfying jumble of everyday items, clothes, CDs and DVDs mixed in with souvenirs and food stalls.

🛈 Orientation

Guatemala City is quite spread out, with the airport to the south, the two major bus terminals to the southwest and northeast, the majority of interesting sights in the downtown Zona 1, and museums and higher-end accommodation clustered around Zona 10. None of these are really within walking distance from each other, but taxis are plentiful and cheap, and two relatively safe bus networks connect various parts of the city.

🛈 Information

DANGERS & ANNOYANCES

➤ Street crime, including armed robbery, has increased in recent years. Use normal urban caution (behaving as you would in, say, Manhattan or Rome).

➤ It's safe to walk downtown in the early evening, as long as you stick to streets with plenty of lighting and people. Stay alert, leave your valuables in your hotel and catch a taxi after dark.

➤ The more affluent sections of the city – Zonas 9, 10 and 14, for example – are safer, but crimes against tourists are not unknown.

➤ The Zona Viva, in Zona 10, has police patrols at night.

➤ Never try to resist if you are confronted by a robber.

EMERGENCY

Guatemala City (and, in fact, all of Guatemala) has no area codes – just dial the number as you see it.

INGUAT Tourist Information (☑ 2421-2854)
Tourist Police Liaison (24hr; ☑ 1500)

INTERNET ACCESS

Zona 1 throngs with inexpensive internet cafes. Elsewhere, rates tend to be higher, but there are still plenty of places to log on. Most hotels, and many restaurants and bars, offer wi-fi – if you're really stuck, the chain joints such as McDonalds, Burger King and Pollo Campero are a sure bet.

MEDICAL SERVICES

Guatemala City has many private hospitals and clinics. Public hospitals and clinics provide free consultations but can be busy; to reduce waiting time, get there before 7am.

Hospital Centro Médico (☑ 2279-4949; 6a Av 3-47, Zona 10; ☺ 24hr) Recommended. This private hospital has some English-speaking doctors.

Hospital General San Juan de Dios (☑ 2232-1187; 1a Av 10-50, Zona 1; ☺ 24hr) One of the city's best public hospitals.

MONEY

Card skimming is rife in Guatemala City – try to use ATMs that are under some sort of watch at all times, such as those inside stores or shopping malls.

American Express (☑ 2331-7422; 12a Calle 0-93, Centro Comercial Montufar, Zona 9; ☺ 8am-5pm Mon-Fri, to noon Sat) In an office of Clark Tours.

Banco Agromercantil (7a Av 9-11, Zona 1; ☺ 9am-7pm Mon-Fri, to 1pm Sat) Changes US dollars (cash, not traveler's checks).

Banrural (Aeropuerto Internacional La Aurora; ☺ 6am-8pm Mon-Fri, to 6pm Sat & Sun) Currency-exchange services. On the airport departures level.

Visa/MasterCard ATM, Zona 1 (18 Calle 6-85, Zona 1; ☺ 8am-10pm) Inside Paiz Supermarket.

Visa/MasterCard ATMs, Zona 10 (16a Calle, Zona 10; ☺ 10am-8pm Mon-Sat, to 7pm Sun) Inside Los Próceres mall.

POST

DHL (Map p50; ☑ 2379-1111; www.dhl.com; 12a Calle 5-12, Zona 10; ☺ 8am-7:30pm Mon-Fri, to noon Sat) Courier service.

Main Post Office (Map p46; 7a Av 11-67, Zona 1; ☺ 8:30am-5pm Mon-Fri, to 1pm Sat) In a huge yellow building at the Palacio de Correos. There's also a small post office at the airport.

TELEPHONE

Telgua/Claro (7a Av 12-39, Zona 1; ☺ 9am-6pm Mon-Fri, to 1pm Sat) Telephone office.

TOURIST INFORMATION

INGUAT (Map p46; ☑ 2421-2800; www.visit guatemala.com; 7a Av 1-17, Zona 4; ☺ 8am-4pm Mon-Fri) Main office of the Guatemalan tourism department. It has limited handout material, but staff are extremely helpful.

INGUAT (Aurora branch) (☑ 2322-5055; Aeropuerto Internacional La Aurora; ☺ 6am-9pm) Located in the arrivals hall; usually attended when flights arrive. Has reasonable info for onward travel and will call to confirm bus departures etc.

Instituto Geográfico Nacional (IGN; ☑ 2248-8100; www.ign.gob.gt; Av Las Américas 5-76, Zona 13; ☺ 9am-5pm Mon-Fri) The Instituto Geográfico Nacional sells maps, including 1:50,000 and 1:250,000 topographical sheets of all parts of Guatemala.

Proatur (Map p46; ☑ toll-free, in English 1500; 7a Av 1-17, Zona 4; ☺ 24hr) Tourist police liaison.

🛈 Getting There & Away

AIR

Guatemala City's **Aeropuerto Internacional La Aurora** (Map p50; ☑ 2260-6257) is the country's major airport. All international flights to Guatemala City land and take off here. The arrivals hall boasts a sometimes-working ATM, sometimes-attended tourist information booth and currency-exchange desks. Travelers have complained about the rates given at the exchange booth inside arrivals and instead recommend the Banrural bank in the departures hall. There is also a more reliable ATM in the departures hall, helpfully hidden behind the stairs leading up to the mezzanine.

At the time of writing, the country's only *scheduled* domestic flights were between Guatemala City and Flores with **Avianca** (☑ 2470-8222; www.avianca.com), leaving Guatemala City at 6am and 6:40pm, and **TAG** (☑ 2380-9494; www.tag.com.gt), which departs at 6:30am and 5:15pm. Domestic flights *may* leave from the domestic terminal, a 15-minute cab ride from the international terminal.

Tickets to Flores cost around Q910/1825 one-way/round-trip with Avianca and Q1065/1825 with TAG, but some travel agents, especially in Antigua, offer large discounts on these prices.

Fourteen international airlines also serve Guatemala, flying direct from North, Central and South America and Europe.

BUS

Buses from Guate run all over Guatemala and into Mexico, Belize, Honduras, El Salvador and beyond. Many bus companies have their own terminals, some of which are in Zona 1. The city council has been on a campaign to get long-distance bus companies out of the city center, so it may be wise to double-check with INGUAT or staff at your hotel about the office location before heading out.

Buses for the Pacific coast mostly leave from the CentraSur terminal in the southern outskirts of town. Departures for Central and Eastern Guatemala and El Petén mostly leave from CentraNorte in the city's northeast. Second-class buses (p62) for the Western Highlands leave from a series of roadside *paradas* (bus stops) on 41a Calle between 6a and 7a Avs in Zona 8.

International Bus Services

The following companies offer first-class bus services to international destinations.

Hedman Alas (Map p50; ☑ 2362-5072; www.hedmanalas.com; 2a Av 8-73, Zona 10) Serves multiple destinations in Honduras.

King Quality & Comfort Lines (Map p50; ☑ 2501-1000; www.king-qualityca.com; 4a Av 13-60, Zona 1) Serves most Central American capitals.

Línea Dorada (Map p46; ☑ 2415-8900; www.lineadorada.com.gt; cnr 10a Av & 16a Calle, Zona 1) Has a service to Tapachula, Mexico.

Pullmantur (Map p50; ☑ 2495-7000; www.pullmantur.com; 1a Av 13-22, Holiday Inn, Zona 10) Covers El Salvador and Honduras.

Tica Bus (☑ 2473-3737; www.ticabus.com; Calz Aguilar Batres 18-35, Zona 12) Covers all of Central America and Mexico.

Transportes Galgos Inter (Map p46; ☑ 2232-3661; www.transgalgosinter.com.gt; 7a Av 19-44, Zona 1) Can book connections to Tapachula, Mexico, and as far north as the US. Also goes to El Salvador.

National Pullman Bus Services

The following bus companies have Pullman services to Guatemalan destinations.

ADN (Map p46; ☑ 2251-0610; www.adnautobusesdelnorte.com; 8a Av 16-41, Zona 1) Flores and Quetzaltenango.

Fortaleza del Sur (☑ 2230-3390; CentraSur, Zona 12) Covers the Pacific coast.

Fuente del Norte (Map p46; ☑ 2251-3817; www.grupofuentedelnorte.com; 17a Calle 8-46, Zona 1) Covers the whole country.

Hedman Alas (p60) Daily departures between Guatemala City and Antigua.

Línea Dorada (p60) Luxury buses to El Petén, Quetzaltenango, Huehuetenango, Río Dulce etc.

Litegua (Map p46; ☑ 2220-8840; www.litegua.com; 15a Calle 10-40, Zona 1) Covers the east and Antigua.

Los Halcones (☑ 2433-9180; Calz Roosevelt 37-47, Zona 11) For Huehuetenango.

Monja Blanca (CentraNorte, Zona 18) For Cobán and points in between.

Rapidos del Sur (☑ 2232-7025; CentraSur, Zona 12) For the Pacific coast.

Rutas Orientales (☑ 2503-3100; CentraNorte, Zona 18) Covers the east.

Transportes Álamo (☑ 2471-8646; 12a Av A 0-65, Zona 7) For Quetzaltenango.

Transportes Galgos (Map p46; ☑ 2253-4868; 7a Av 19-44, Zona 1) For Quetzaltenango and Retalhuleu.

Transportes Rebuli (Map p50; ☑ 2230-2748; 41a Calle btwn 6a & 7a Av, Zona 8) For Panajachel.

CAR

Most major rental companies have offices both at La Aurora airport (in the arrivals area) and in Zona 9 or 10. Companies include the following:

Avis Airport (☑ 2324-9000; www.avis.com; Aeropuerto Internacional La Aurora; ☉ 6am-9pm)

INTERNATIONAL BUS DEPARTURES FROM GUATEMALA CITY

DESTINATION	COST (Q)	TIME (HOURS)	FREQUENCY (DAILY)	COMPANY
San José, Costa Rica	700-880	40-63	2	Tica Bus
San Salvador, El Salvador	175-390	5	6	King Quality & Comfort Lines, Pullmantur, Tica Bus
Copán, Honduras	410-650	5	2	Hedman Alas
La Ceiba, Honduras	450-690	12	2	Hedman Alas
San Pedro Sula, Honduras	410-655	8	2	Hedman Alas
Tegucigalpa, Honduras	305-705	10-35	6	Hedman Alas, King Quality & Comfort Lines, Pullmantur, Tica Bus
Tapachula, Mexico	175-230	5-7	4	Línea Dorada, Tica Bus, Transportes Galgos Inter
Managua, Nicaragua	465-625	16-35	2	King Quality & Comfort Lines, Tica Bus
Panama City, Panama	1040-1350	76	2	Tica Bus

Avis Downtown (☑ 2324-9000; www.avis.com; 6a Calle 7-64, Zona 9; ⊙ 8am-6pm Mon-Fri, to noon Sat)

Guatemala Rent a Car Airport (☑ 2208-9000; www.guatemalarentacar.com; Aeropuerto Internacional La Aurora; ⊙ 5:30am-9:30pm)

Guatemala Rent a Car Downtown (☑ 2329-9020; www.guatemalarentacar.com; 12a Calle 5-54, Oficina 15, Zona 9; ⊙ 8am-6pm Mon-Fri, to 1pm Sat)

Tabarini Airport (☑ 2331-4755; www.tabarini.com; Aeropuerto Internacional La Aurora; ⊙ 8am-9pm)

Tabarini Downtown (☑ 2444-4200; www.tabarini.com; 2a Calle A 7-30, Zona 10; ⊙ 8am-6pm Mon-Fri, 9am-1pm Sat)

Tally Renta Autos Airport (☑ 2261-2526; www.tallyrentaautos.com; Aeropuerto Internacional La Aurora; ⊙ 8:30am-10pm)

Tally Renta Autos Downtown (☑ 2230-3783; www.tallyrentaautos.com; 7a Av 14-60, Zona 1; ⊙ 8:30am-6:30pm Mon-Fri, 9am-2pm Sat)

SHUTTLE MINIBUS

Shuttle services from Guatemala City to popular destinations such as Panajachel and Chichicastenango (via Antigua; both around Q260) are offered by travel agencies in Antigua. Quetzaltenango-based travel agents also have shuttles to and from Guatemala City.

❶ Getting Around

TO/FROM THE AIRPORT

Aeropuerto Internacional La Aurora Guatemala City's international airport is in Zona 13, a Q80 taxi ride to Zona 1 and Q70 to Zona 10. If you're arriving late at night, a popular option is to spend the night in one of the guesthouses close to the airport and get a fresh start the next day.

Bus Arriving from other parts of the country, you'll most likely be coming in on a bus. Guatemala City's bus stations are scattered all over town. Wherever you're going, if it's more than a few blocks away it's a good idea to grab a taxi. Taxis are plentiful (especially around bus stations) and a whole lot cheaper than getting mugged while lugging your backpack around.

BUS & MINIBUS

Due to an alarming increase in (often violent) crime on Guatemala City's red city buses, it is pretty much universally accepted that tourists should only use them in case of dire emergency. The major exceptions are the TransMetro and TransUrbano buses, which are most useful for getting to the CentraSur and CentraNorte bus terminals, respectively.

For the thrillseekers out there, we've listed the most useful red bus routes. Buses will stop anywhere they see a passenger, but street corners and traffic lights are your best bet for hailing them – just hold out your hand. Buses should cost Q1 per ride in the daytime (but this can as

NATIONAL PULLMAN BUS DEPARTURES FROM GUATEMALA CITY

DESTINATION	COST (Q)	TIME (HOURS)	FREQUENCY	COMPANY
Antigua	75	1	4 daily	Hedman Alas, Litegua
Chiquimula	60	3	half hourly, 4:30am-6pm	Rutas Orientales
Cobán	60-75	5	hourly, 4am-5pm	Monja Blanca
El Carmen	90	7	hourly, 4am-5pm	Fortaleza del Sur
Esquipulas	60	5	half hourly, 4:30am-6pm	Rutas Orientales
Flores & Santa Elena	140-160	8-10	6 daily	ADN, Fuente del Norte, Línea Dorada
Huehuetenango	90-100	5	4 daily	Línea Dorada, Los Halcones
Poptún	120-150	8	3 daily	Línea Dorada
Puerto Barrios	80	5	half hourly, 3:45am-7pm	Litegua
Quetzaltenango	80	4	10 daily	Álamo, Línea Dorada, Transportes Galgos
Retalhuleu	85	3	5 daily	Fuente del Norte
Río Dulce	70	5	half hourly, 6am-4:30pm	Litegua
Tecún Umán	75	6	4 daily	Fortaleza del Sur

much as quadruple on public holidays or the driver's whim). You pay the driver or the driver's helper as you get on. Don't catch them at night.

Airport to Zona 1 (Bus No 82) Travels via Zonas 9 and 4.

Zona 1 to Airport (Bus No 82) Travels via 10a Av in Zona 1 then down 6a Av in Zonas 4 and 9.

Zona 1 to Zona 10 (Bus No 82 or 101) Travels via 10a Av, Zona 1, then 6a Av and Ruta 6 in Zona 4 and Av La Reforma.

Zona 10 to Zona 1 (Bus No 82 or 101) Travels via Av La Reforma then 7a Av, Zona 4 and 9a Av, Zona 1.

TransMetro

In early 2007, in answer to growing concerns about traffic congestion and insecurity on urban buses, Guatemala City inaugurated the TransMetro system (http://transmetro.munig uate.com). TransMetro buses differ from regular old, red urban buses because they are prepaid (the driver carries no money, thus reducing the risk of robberies), travel in their own lanes (not getting caught in traffic jams), only stop at designated stops and are new, comfortable and bright green.

There are currently two routes in operation – one connects Zona 1's Plaza Barrios with the CentraSur bus terminal, from where the majority of buses for the Pacific coast depart. The other runs south from Plaza Barrios through Zonas 9 and 10.

Crime has increased so much on Guate's regular red buses that travelers are advised not to use them, but TransMetro buses are safe, fast and comfortable. All rides cost Q1, payable with a Q1 coin at the bus stop before boarding.

TransUrbano

A more recent improvement to the city's bus scene is **TransUrbano** (Map p50; www.trans urbano.com.gt; cnr Av Reforma & 12a Calle, Zona 10), a much wider network of buses that aren't quite as slick as TransMetro but are still safe, reliable and comfortable. They're slower because they don't have a dedicated lane, but safer than the old red buses because to board you need a magnetic rechargeable card (card and first ride free), which can only be obtained by showing your passport or Guatemalan ID card. The rechargeable cards are available from special booths, the most useful for travelers being in Zona 1's Plaza Barrios, the CentraNorte bus terminal and the Zona 10 TransUrbano office on Av La Reforma.

TAXI

Plenty of taxis cruise most parts of the city. Fares are negotiable; always establish your destination and fare before getting in. Zona 1 to Zona 10, or vice-versa, costs around Q50 to Q70. If you want to phone for a taxi, **Taxi Amarillo Express** (🖉1766) has metered cabs (figure on Q5 per kilometer) that often work out cheaper than others, although true *capitaleños* (capital city residents) will tell you that taxi meters are all rigged and you get a better deal bargaining.

SECOND-CLASS BUS ('CHICKEN BUS') SERVICES

DESTINATION	COST (Q)	TIME (HOURS)	FREQUENCY	DEPARTS
Amatitlán	8	30min	every 5min, 7am-8:45pm	CentraSur, Zona 12
Antigua	13	1	every 5min, 7am-8pm	Calz Roosevelt btwn 4a Av & 5a Av, Zona 7
Chichicastenango	30	3	hourly, 5am-6pm	Parada, Zona 8
Ciudad Pedro de Alvarado	55	2½	half hourly, 5am-4pm	CentraSur, Zona 12
Esquintla	25	1	half hourly, 6am-4:30pm	CentraSur, Zona 12
Huehuetenango	65	5	half hourly, 7am-5pm	Parada, Zona 8
La Democracia	30	2	half hourly, 6am-4:30pm	CentraSur, Zona 12
La Mesilla	100	8	hourly, 8am-4pm	Parada, Zona 8
Monterrico	45	3	3 daily	CentraSur, Zona 12
Panajachel	40	3	half hourly, 7am-5pm	Parada, Zona 8
Puerto San José	25	1	every 15min, 4:30am-4:45pm	CentraSur, Zona 12
Salamá	50	3	half hourly, 5am-5pm	17a Calle 11-32, Zona 1
San Pedro La Laguna	45	4	hourly, 2am-2pm	Parada, Zona 8
Santa Cruz del Quiché	45	4	hourly, 5am-5pm	Parada, Zona 8
Santiago Atitlán	45	4	half hourly, 4am-5pm	Parada, Zona 8
Tecpán	20	2	every 15min, 5:30am-7pm	Parada, Zona 8

Antigua

POP 34,685 / ELEV 1539M

Best Places to Eat

➡ Cactus Grill (p80)

➡ Bistrot Cinq (p81)

➡ Zoola Antigua (p79)

➡ Mesón Panza Verde (p81)

Best Places to Sleep

➡ El Hostal (p76)

➡ Earth Lodge (El Hato; p86)

➡ Posada del Ángel (p78)

➡ Hotel Quinta de las Flores (p78)

➡ Casa Santo Domingo Hotel (p78)

Why Go?

A place of rare beauty, major historical significance and vibrant culture, Antigua remains Guatemala's must-visit destination.

A former capital, the city boasts an impressive catalog of colonial relics in a magnificent setting. Streetscapes of pastel facades unfold beneath three volcanoes. Many old ecclesiastical and civic structures are beautifully renovated, while others retain tumbledown charm, with fragments strewn about parklike grounds.

Thanks to the dozens of Spanish-language schools that operate here, Antigua is a global hot spot. Yet it remains a vibrant Guatemalan town; its churches, plazas and markets are throbbing with activity. Outside the city, indigenous communities, coffee plantations and volcanoes offer ample opportunities for exploration.

Perhaps the real miracle of Antigua is its resilience. Despite earthquakes, volcanic eruptions and floods, followed by virtual abandonment, it has re-emerged with a vengeance, buoyed by the pride of its inhabitants.

When to Go

Blessed with a springlike climate year round, Antigua is a great destination at any time. Ample sunshine prevails most days with slightly cooler temperatures from mid-May to October when afternoon downpours are the norm.

Antigua's biggest deal is Semana Santa (Holy Week), which precedes Easter, when religious processions enliven the streets, passion plays are performed and hotels are fully booked.

Other particularly lively times include Corpus Christi (May/June) and All Saints' Day (November 1) with obligatory feasts of *fiambre* (chilled mixed salad) and festive visits to the graveyard.

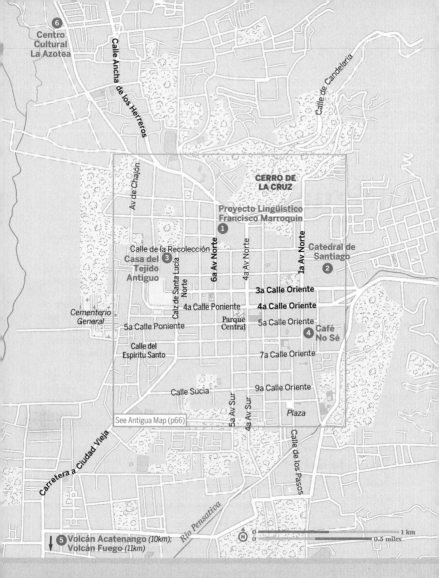

Antigua Highlights

1 Resurrecting your high-school Spanish at highly regarded **language schools** (p72).

2 Witnessing scattered slabs of masonry, such as at the **Catedral** (p65), that display mute evidence of Antigua's quake-ridden history.

3 Admiring and acquiring traditional Maya wear at **Casa del Tejido Antiguo** (p69), with its seminal collection of *huipiles* (embroidered tunics) and *cortes* (wraparound skirts).

4 Sampling a clandestine mescal at **Café No Sé** (p82), the low-lit lair of choice for Antigua's expats.

5 Scaling **Acatenango** (p72) for jaw-dropping views of its sister volcanoes, including fire-spewing Fuego.

6 Savoring volcanic coffee beans at the **Centro Cultural La Azotea** (p86).

⊙ Sights

Echoes of the city's former grandeur are everywhere, rewarding a stroll in any direction. At the heart of it all, verdant Parque Central, surrounded by superb colonial administrative buildings, makes an excellent place to begin explorations. Dotted around town are dozens of ecclesiastical complexes established by the myriad Catholic orders in the city's heyday, now in various states of decay. Once glorious in their gilded baroque finery, Antigua's churches and monasteries have suffered indignities from both nature and humankind. Rebuilding after earthquakes gave the churches thicker walls, lower towers and belfries, and unembellished interiors. Furthermore, moving the capital to Guatemala City deprived Antigua of the population needed to maintain the churches in their traditional richness, though they remain impressive. Aside from their architectural interest, most of the complexes feature tranquil cloisters and gardens, and a few contain museums, notably the Convento de Santo Domingo.

◉ Parque Central & Around

Palacio de los Capitanes Generales   HISTORIC BUILDING
(Palace of the Captains General; Map p71; ☑ 7832-2868; www.centroculturalrealpalacio.org.gt; 5a Calle Poniente; ⊙ 9am-4:30pm Wed-Sun) `FREE` Dating from 1549, the palace was colonial headquarters for all of Central America, from Chiapas to Costa Rica, until the capital was relocated in 1776. The stately double-arcaded facade that anchors the south side of the plaza is all that remains of the original complex. Following extensive renovations, the palace now serves as a cultural center with art exhibits and performances.

Catedral de Santiago   CATHEDRAL
(Map p71; cnr 4a Av Norte & 5a Calle Oriente; ruins Q8; ⊙ ruins 9am-5pm, parish 6:30am-noon & 3-6:30pm Mon, Tue, Thu & Fri, 8am-noon & 3-7pm Sat, 5:30am-1pm & 3-7:30pm Sun) Antigua's cathedral was begun in 1545, wrecked by the quake of 1773, and only partially rebuilt over the next century. The present sliver of a church – the parish of San José – occupies only the entrance hall of the original edifice. Behind it are the roofless ruins of the main part of the cathedral, which is entered from 5a Calle Oriente.

The ruin is a haunting place, with massive chunks of pillars strewn beneath sweeping brick archways and vegetation sprouting from cracks in the walls. Reproductions of the intricate plasterwork figures and moldings between the arches seem all that more impressive against the ruined backdrop. Behind the main altar, steps lead down to a former crypt, now serving as a chapel, with a smoke-blackened Christ.

Antiguo Colegio de la Compañía de Jesús   HISTORIC BUILDING
(Map p71; ☑ 7932-3838; www.aecid-cf.org.gt; 6a Av Norte; ⊙ 9am-6pm) `FREE` Established in 1626, the Jesuit monastery and college was a vital component of Antigua life until the order was expelled in 1767; just six years later, the great earthquake left it in ruins. Rescued from the rubble by the Spanish government, the complex has been reborn as a cultural center, the **Centro de Formación de la Cooperación Española**.

The former offices, classrooms and refectories now contain lecture halls, exhibit spaces, a fashionable cafe and an excellent library. The three cloisters have been made over with fine wood columns and balconies, a brilliant setting for photo exhibits, concerts, films and festivals. One component remains respectfully unrestored, though: the Compañía de Jesús church, the grand facade of which stands to the left of the main entrance of the complex.

Palacio del Ayuntamiento   HISTORIC BUILDING
(City Hall Palace; Map p71; 4a Calle Poniente) This double-decker structure on the north side of the park dates from the 18th century. Besides town offices, the palace houses the **Museo del Libro Antiguo** (Old Book Museum; Map p71; ☑ 7832-5511; Q30; ⊙ 9am-4pm Tue-Fri, 9am-noon & 2-4pm Sat & Sun), showcasing the early days of Guatemalan printing. The stone benches beneath the lower arcade make a fine people-watching perch.

◉ West of Parque Central

Iglesia y Convento de Nuestra Señora de la Merced   CHURCH, MONASTERY
(Map p66; monastery ruins Q15; ⊙ church 6am-noon & 3-8pm, ruins 8:30am-5:30pm) At the northern end of 5a Av is La Merced – a striking yellow building trimmed with plaster filigree. The squat, thick-walled structure was built to withstand earthquakes, and three centuries after its construction it remains in

ANTIGUA SIGHTS

ANTIGUA

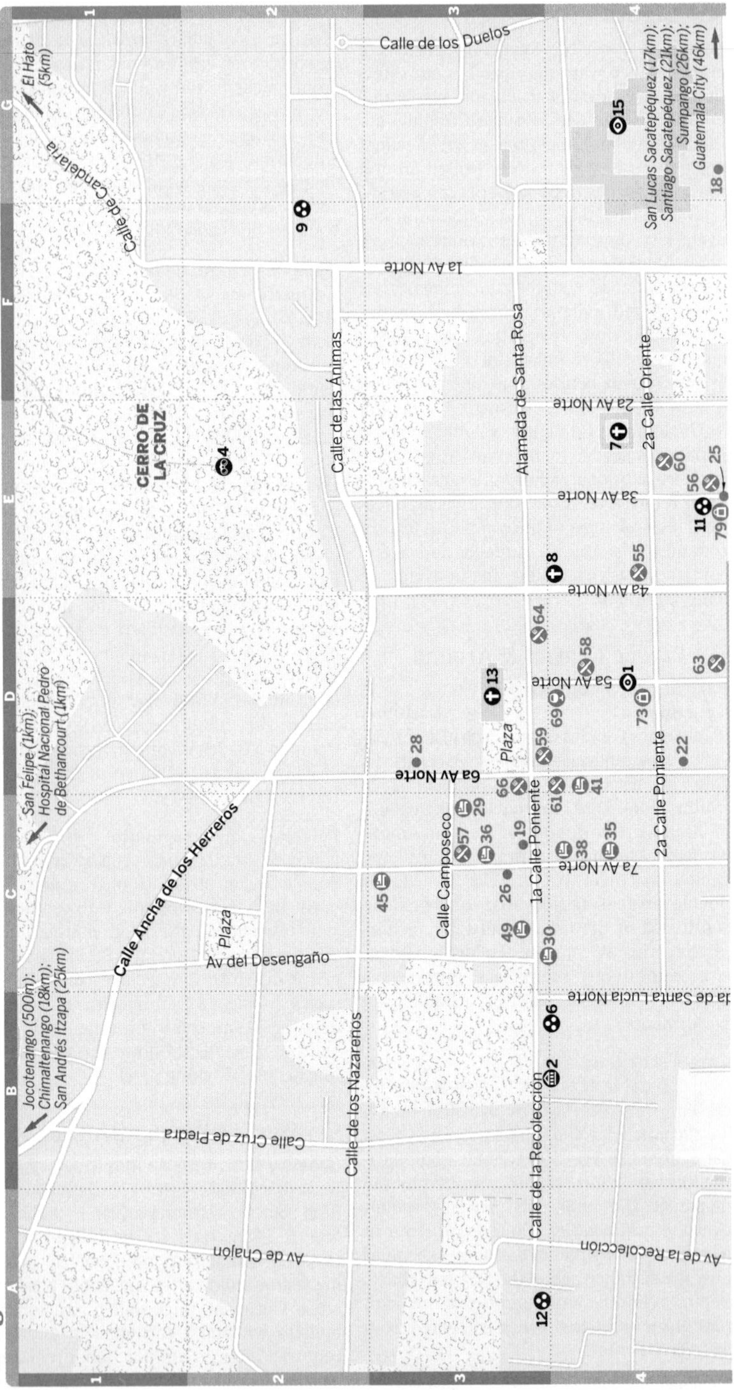

Antigua

0 — 200 m
0 — 0.1 miles

El Hato
(5km)

Calle de Candelaría

CERRO DE
LA CRUZ

San Felipe (1km);
Hospital Nacional Pedro
de Bethancourt (1km)

Jocotenango (500m);
Chimaltenango (18km);
San Andrés Itzapa (25km)

Calle Ancha de los Herreros

Calle de los Duelos

Calle de las Ánimas

Alameda de Santa Rosa

1a Av Norte

2a Av Norte

3a Av Norte

4a Av Norte

5a Av Norte

6a Av Norte

7a Av Norte

Calle Camposeco

1a Calle Poniente

2a Calle Poniente

2a Calle Oriente

Av del Desengaño

Plaza

Plaza

Calle de los Nazarenos

Calle Cruz de Piedra

Calle de la Recolección

Av de Chajón

Av de la Recolección

Calle de Santa Lucía Norte

San Lucas Sacatepéquez (17km);
Santiago Sacatepéquez (21km);
Sumpango (26km);
Guatemala City (46km)

15
18
9
4
8
7
11
60
56
25
79
55
64
58
1
63
13
69
59
73
22
28
66
29
36
57
19
61
41
35
38
26
45
49
30
6
2
12

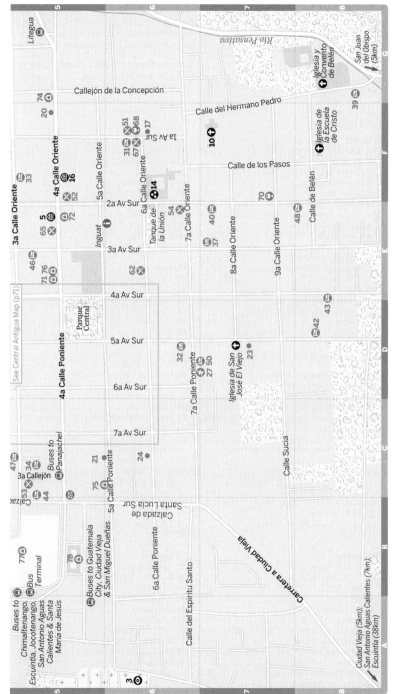

good shape. Only the church is still in use; a candlelit procession, accompanied by bell ringing and firecrackers, starts and ends there on the last Thursday evening of each month.

Inside the monastery ruins is a fountain 27m in diameter, said to be the largest in Hispanic America. It's in the shape of a water lily (traditionally a symbol of power for Maya lords), and lily motifs also appear on the church's entrance arch. Go upstairs for a bird's-eye view of the fountain and the town.

Iglesia y Convento de la Recolección RUIN
(Map p66; Av de la Recolección; Q40; ⊘ 9am-5pm)
A serene air pervades the remains of the

Antigua

monastery of La Recolección, which stands well west of the center. Erected in the early 1700s by the Récollets (a French branch of the Franciscan order), its church was one of the largest in Antigua at the time. The earthquake of 1773 toppled the structure, of which only the great arched doorway remains intact.

Beyond the monaastery are strewn the massive chunks of masonry that formed the original walls. The adjoining cloisters, laid out on an equally grand scale, have been cleared of debris and have variously served as fairgrounds and swimming pool following the complex's short life as a monastery.

Casa del Tejido Antiguo   MUSEUM
(Map p66; ☑7832-3169; Calle de la Recolección 51; Q15; ⊙9am-5pm Mon-Fri, 9am-4pm Sat) This space is like a museum, market and workshop all rolled into one, with exhibits on regional outfits and daily demonstrations of backstrap weaving techniques. Founder Alicia Pérez, an indigenous Kaqchiquel woman, is an expert on the significance of designs that appear on the *tocoyales* (head coverings), *tzutes* (shawls) and *huipiles* displayed here. Weaving classes are offered.

Colegio de San Jerónimo   RUIN
(Real Aduana; Map p66; cnr Calz de Santa Lucía Norte & Calle de la Recolección; Q40; ⊙9am-5pm) Completed in 1757, the Colegio de San Jerónimo was used as a school by friars of the Merced order, but because it did not have royal authorization, it was taken over by Spain's Carlos III and, in 1765, designated for use as the Royal Customs House. Today it's a tranquil, mostly open-air site in an excellent state of preservation.

The handsome cloister centers upon an octagonal fountain, an evocative setting for occasional dance and other cultural performances. Upstairs you'll find excellent photo angles of Volcán Agua through stone archways.

Cementerio General   CEMETERY
(Map p66; Calle San Bartolome Becerra; ⊙7am-noon & 2-6pm) Antigua's municipal cemetery, southwest of the market and bus terminal, is a conglomeration of tombs and mausoleums decked with wreaths, exotic flowers and other signs of mourning. Proatur (p84) offers an escort to this out-of-the-way site on request.

◉ East of Parque Central

Iglesia y Convento de Santo Domingo   MONASTERY
(Map p66; ☑7820-1220; 3a Calle Oriente 28; Q42; ⊙9am-6pm Mon-Sat, 11:45am-6pm Sun) Founded by Dominican friars in 1542, Santo Domingo became the biggest and richest monastery in Antigua. Following three 18th-century earthquakes, the buildings were pillaged for construction material. The site was acquired as a private residence in 1970 by a North American archaeologist, who performed extensive excavations before it was taken over by the Casa Santo Domingo Hotel (p78).

The archaeological zone has been innovatively restored as a 'cultural route.' It includes the picturesque ruined monastery church, the adjacent cloister with a replica of the original fountain, workshops for candle and pottery makers, and two underground crypts that were discovered during the church excavations. One of these, the **Calvary Crypt**, contains a well-preserved mural of the Crucifixion dating from 1683.

Also part of the archaeological zone are six museums, which can all be visited with one admission ticket. This museum route may be entered either through the hotel or the Universidad de San Carlos extension on 1a Av Norte. Starting from the hotel side, the route includes the following museums: the **Museo de la Platería**, with silver-work masterpieces including incense burners, candelabras and crowns; the **Museo Colonial**, with canvases and wood sculpture on religious themes from the 16th to 18th centuries; the **Museo Arqueológico**, with ceramic and stone objects from the Maya Classic period; the **Museo de Arte Precolombino y Vidrio Moderno**, with glass works by modern artists and the pre-Hispanic ceramic pieces that inspired them; the **Museo de Artes y Artesanías Populares de Sacatepéquez**, with exhibits on traditional handicrafts from the Antigua region; and the **Museo de la Farmacia**, a restored version of a 19th-century apothecary's shop from Guatemala City.

A recently added component to the complex is a cultural park upon Cerro Santa Inés, a hill located 1km to the southeast of the monastery complex. Aside from stunning views of Antigua and Volcán Agua, **Santo Domingo del Cerro** offers a museum devoted to artist Efraín Recinos, whose murals and sculptures (including one featuring his VW bug) grace the gardens. Another small **museum** covers Pope John Paul II's 2002 visit to Guatemala. A free shuttle service runs from the hotel to Santo Domingo del Cerro every 15 minutes.

La Antigua Galería de Arte   GALLERY

(Map p66; ☑ 7832-2124; www.laantiguagaleria. com; 4a Calle Oriente 15; ⊙ 10am-7pm Mon-Sat, noon-6pm Sun) FREE Displaying works by more than 70 artists, most Guatemalan, in the halls and patio of a colonial mansion, Antigua's premier art gallery merits an extended visit.

Iglesia de San Francisco   CHURCH, MONASTERY

(Map p66; ☑ 7882-4438; cnr 7a Calle Oriente & Calle de los Pasos; museum & monastery adult/ child Q6/3; ⊙ 9am-5:30pm) This church is imbued with the spirit of Hermano Pedro de San José de Bethancourt, a Franciscan monk who founded a hospital for the poor in Antigua and earned the gratitude of generations. On the south side are the ruins of the adjoining monastery, with some vivid frescoes still visible amid the rubble.

Hermano Pedro's intercession is still sought by the ill, who pray fervently by his tomb, housed in an elaborate pavilion since his canonization in 2002. Devotees may enter via a garden north of the church. A museum is haphazardly strewn with relics from the church and Santo Hermano's well-preserved personal belongings, while the corridor is plastered with thank-you notes for miracles attributed to the saint.

Convento de Capuchinas   CONVENT

(Iglesia y Convento de Nuestra Señora del Pilar de Zaragoza; Map p66; cnr 2a Av Norte & 2a Calle Oriente; adult/student Q40/20; ⊙ 9am-5pm) Inaugurated in 1736 by nuns from Madrid, the convent of Las Capuchinas was seriously damaged by the 1773 earthquake and thereafter abandoned. Thanks to meticulous renovations in recent decades, it's possible to get a sense of the life experienced by those cloistered nuns, who ran an orphanage and women's hospital.

Wander round to admire the fine cloister with its stout columns and high arched passageways, remarkably restored washbasins and well-tended gardens. At the rear you'll find the convent's most unique feature, a towerlike structure of 18 nuns' cells built around a circular patio.

Iglesia y Convento de Santa Clara   RUIN

(Map p66; 2a Av Sur, btwn 6a & 7a Calles Oriente; Q40; ⊙ 9am-5pm) Established by sisters from Puebla, Mexico, Santa Clara was inaugurated in 1734, destroyed four decades later by the great quake and abandoned. Fortunately some elements of the original structure remain intact, such as the church's stonework facade, the arched niches along the nave that served as confessionals, and an underground chamber where provisions were stored. Most captivating of all is the cloister, centering on a fountain bordered by gardens, though only one side of the upper-level arcade is still in place.

Choco Museo   MUSEUM

(Map p66; ☑ 7832-4520; www.chocomuseo.com; 4a Calle Oriente 14; ⊙ 10am-6:30pm Sun-Thu, 10am-7:30pm Fri & Sat; 🖈) FREE It was the Maya who discovered the culinary uses of the cacao bean, which later became a form of currency for the Aztec empire. These are a few of the things you'll learn at this kid-friendly expo, the Antigua branch of a hemisphere-wide project. The museum also offers chocolate-making workshops and cacao plantation tours.

A branch of the museum, on 5a Av Norte, a block north of Parque Central, features an attractive courtyard where you can whip up and enjoy your own Maya chocolate.

🏃 Activities

Antigua has a number of professional, established outfits offering a range of activities. Drop into the local offices to chat about possibilities.

For those wanting to move to a different beat, you can learn to dance at several places around town. **New Sensation Salsa Studio** (Map p66; ☑ 5033-0921; 7a Av Norte 78; per hour Q85) offers one-on-one instruction in salsa, merengue, bachata and cha-cha.

Old Town Outfitters   ADVENTURE SPORTS

(Map p71; ☑ 5399-0440; www.adventureguat emala.com; 5a Av Sur 12C) 🌿 Mountain-biking, rock-climbing, kayaking and trekking are among the high-energy activities offered by this highly responsible operator, which works with guides from local communities. It also rents quality mountain bikes (Q125/200 per half/whole day).

Old Town Outfitters can take you on a three-day trek through the Western Highlands, following the Maya trade routes that linked Lago de Atitlán to Quetzaltenango.

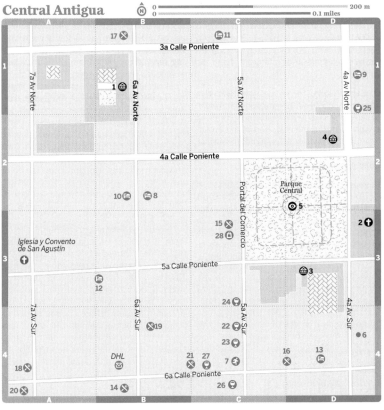

Central Antigua

ANTIGUA ACTIVITIES

Central Antigua

◉ Sights

1 Antiguo Colegio de la Compañía de Jesús B1
2 Catedral de Santiago D3
   Museo del Libro Antiguo ....(see 4)
3 Palacio de los Capitanes Generales D3
4 Palacio del Ayuntamiento D2
5 Parque Central D2

⊕ Activities, Courses & Tours

6 El Frijol Feliz D4
7 Old Town Outfitters C4

⬤ Sleeping

8 Bigfoot Hostel B2
9 Hotel Casa del Parque D1
10 Hotel Casa Rústica B2
11 Hotel El Mesón de María C1
12 Posada de San Carlos B3
13 Tropicana Hostel D4

◈ Eating

14 Cactus Grill B4
15 Café Condesa C3
16 Caffé Mediterráneo D4
17 El Viejo Café B1
18 Rainbow Café A4
19 Sabe Rico B4
20 Samsara A4
21 Travel Menu B4

⊜ Drinking & Nightlife

22 La Sin Ventura C4
23 Lucky Rabbit C4
24 Monoloco C3
25 Ocelot Bar D1
26 Reilly's en la Esquina C4
27 Snug C4

⬢ Shopping

28 Librería La Casa del Conde C3

It also has a popular range of guided half-day mountain-bike rides (Q400) in the hills around Antigua, at varying levels of difficulty. Its two-day Pedal & Paddle Tour (Q2075 per person with three or more people) includes kayaking and hiking at Lago de Atitlán.

Ox Expeditions ADVENTURE SPORTS
(Map p66; ☑ 5801-4301; www.oxexpeditions.com; 7a Calle Poniente 17) Offers rigorous climbing opportunities in the area, plus such adrenaline-fueled activities as paragliding, surfing and zip-lining. Part of their profits go to local environmental projects.

Ravenscroft Riding Stables HORSEBACK RIDING
(☑7830-6669; 2a Av Sur 3, San Juan del Obispo; per hour beginners/experienced riders Q190/230) This outfit, 3km south of Antigua on the road to Santa María de Jesús, offers English-style riding, with scenic rides of two to three hours around the foothills of Volcán Agua.

Volcano Ascents

All three volcanoes overlooking Antigua – **Agua**, **Acatenango** and **Fuego** – are tempting challenges. How close you can get to Fuego depends on recent levels of activity. In many ways the twin-peaked Acatenango (3975m), overlooking Fuego, is the most exhilarating summit. For an active-volcano experience many people take tours to **Pacaya** (2552m), 25km southeast of Antigua (a 1½-hour drive).

Old Town Outfitters (p70) leads strenuous hikes up Volcán Acatenango, traversing four ecosystems to reach the summit (Q1070, including lunch and transport to the trailhead in the village of La Soledad). The expedition departs at 5am. Overnight hikes are another option, camping just below the treeline, then ascending to the summit the following morning (Q1300 per person with two people).

Most agencies run seven-hour Pacaya trips daily for Q90 (leaving Antigua at 6am and 2pm); food and drinks are not included, nor is the Q50 admission to the Pacaya protected area. It takes about 1½ hours to make the steep ascent to the simmering black cone. (If you're out of breath, kids will rent you horses on the way up.) From the summit there are stupendous views northwest to Agua and northeast to Lago de Atitlán. The descent is quicker as you slide down the powdery slope.

Ascents of Volcán Agua (3766m) take off from the village of Santa María de Jesús (Q3.50 from Antigua bus terminal) on the volcano's northeast slopes. You can hire INGUAT-authorized guides (one day/overnight Q200/250 per person, plus park entry fee of Q40) from the tourist office just off Santa María's Parque Central. Note that a high number of assaults on the slopes have been reported; guides recommend that those attempting the climb hire a police escort (Q300) as an additional precaution.

🏃 Courses

Antigua's Spanish-language schools attract students from around the world. There are dozens of schools to choose

---

SAINT HERMANO PEDRO

The spirit of Hermano Pedro, Antigua's most venerated Christian, looms large more than three centuries after his death. The saint's tomb, inside the Iglesia de San Francisco (p70), overflows with devotional plaques, amulets and tokens from the faithful offering gratitude for his miraculous healing powers. Antigua's only public hospital, southeast of Parque Central, was dubbed in his honor and carries on his mission of providing health services to those unable to afford them.

Born on Tenerife in the Canary Islands in 1627, Pedro de Bethancourt labored as a shepherd until he hung up his staff at the age of 24 and made for Guatemala to help the poor, though the arduous journey left Pedro himself impoverished. Further hardship awaited when he flunked his studies at the Franciscan seminary in Antigua. Undaunted, he took to picking up dying Maya off the streets and treating them during the plagues of the 1600s. He had found his true calling, and a few years later he built a hospital devoted to healing the indigent, then built homeless shelters and schools for poor students. His efforts gave rise to a new religious order, the Bethlehemites, which took on his mantle after his death in 1667. To this day, flocks of devotees visit his tomb, a phenomenon the Vatican recognized when Pope John Paul II canonized the good brother in 2002, making him Guatemala's only officially authorized saint.

from. Price, teaching quality and student satisfaction vary greatly. Often the quality of instruction depends upon the particular teacher and, thus, may vary even within a single school.

Visit a few schools before you choose and, if possible, talk to people who have studied recently at schools you like the look of – you're bound to run into a few. The INGUAT tourist office (p85) has a list of authorized schools.

Classes start every Monday at most schools, though you can usually be placed with a teacher any day of the week. Most schools cater for all levels and allow you to stay as long as you like. Three or four weeks is typical, though it's perfectly OK to do just one week. The busiest seasons are during January and from April to August, and some schools request advance reservations for these times.

Instruction is nearly always one-on-one and costs Q1000 to Q1800 per week for four hours of classes daily, five days a week. Most schools offer to arrange room and board with local families, usually with your own room and three meals daily (except Sunday), for around Q800 per week (a bit more with private bathroom). Some schools may offer accommodations in guesthouses or their own hostels.

Homestays are meant to promote the total immersion concept of language learning, but this becomes less viable where there are several foreigners staying with one family or where there are separate mealtimes for students and the family. Indeed, there are so many foreigners about Antigua, it takes some real discipline to converse in Spanish rather than your native tongue. Many enjoy this social scene, but if you think it may deter you, consider studying in Quetzaltenango, El Petén or elsewhere, where there are fewer foreign students.

★ **Proyecto Lingüístico Francisco Marroquín**   LANGUAGE COURSE
(Map p66; 7832-1422; www.spanishschool plfm.com; 6a Av Norte 43) Antigua's oldest Spanish school, founded in 1969, is run by a nonprofit foundation to preserve indigenous languages and culture, with capacity to teach K'iche' and Kaqchiquel, among other Maya tongues.

Academia de Español Sevilla   LANGUAGE COURSE
(Map p66; 7832-5101; www.sevillantigua.com; 1a Av Sur 17C) This well-managed institute offers plenty of free activities, and they can arrange volunteer work in local community projects. One-on-one classes are conducted amid the remnants of a colonial monastery. Shared student housing is offered as an accommodations option.

Escuela de Español San José el Viejo   LANGUAGE COURSE
(Map p66; 7832-3028; www.sanjoseelviejo.com; 5a Av Sur 34) Long-standing school with parklike study environment, complete with tennis court and pool and its own tasteful accommodations. Students may switch teachers each week. Accredited by the Guatemalan Ministry of Education.

Christian Spanish Academy LANGUAGE COURSE
(Map p66; 7832-3922; www.learncsa.com; 6a Av Norte 15) Originally established to train missionaries, this modern outfit is favored by mature language learners with specific professional needs.

Escuela de Español Tecún Umán   LANGUAGE COURSE
(Map p66; 5513-4349; www.tecunumanschool.com; 6a Calle Poniente 34A) Long-standing Guatemalan-run outfit with university-trained staff. Classes are held on the pleasant rooftop terrace of a nearby cafe.

Antigüeña Spanish Academy   LANGUAGE COURSE
(Map p66; 5735-4638; www.spanishacademy antiguena.com; 1a Calle Poniente 10) Oft-recommended school, authorized by the Ministry of Education. It can arrange volunteer work for social workers at Hermano Pedro hospital on request.

Centro Lingüístico Maya   LANGUAGE COURSE
(Map p66; 7832-0656; www.clmaya.com; 5a Calle Poniente 20) Large, professionally managed, pricier institute with 30 years of experience in training diplomatic personnel and journalists.

El Frijol Feliz   COOKING COURSE
(Map p71; 7832-5274; www.frijolfeliz.com; 4a Av Sur 1; 3hr class Q350) Hands-on instruction preparing Guatemalan meals; students may choose their own menu.

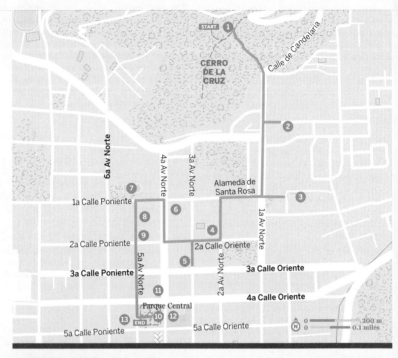

🏃 City Walk
Splendor in the Ruins

START CERRO DE LA CRUZ
END CAFÉ CONDESA
LENGTH 2.3KM; 2½ HOURS

For the big picture, take a taxi up **1 Cerro de La Cruz** (p76), north of town. Beyond the stone cross that gives the hill its name, spreads Antigua, with the majestic Volcán Agua as a backdrop. Descend the wooded slopes via the path to the left. At the bottom, turn right down a cobblestone street. You'll come to a basketball court backed by the ruins of **2 Iglesia de la Candelaria**. Examine it closely – there's a lot going on between the swirly columns.

Go one block south to a small plaza, then head left alongside a high yellow wall to glimpse the **3 Templo de Santa Rosa de Lima**, a small church with an elaborate facade. Turn around and head west along jacaranda-lined Alameda de Santa Rosa. Take the first left, onto 2a Av Norte, past an ironworks shop. At the next corner on the right are the ruins of the **4 Convento de Capuchinas** (p70), with its unique tower. Go right on 2a Calle Oriente. Passing 3a Av Norte, look down to your left to see the multicolumned facade of **5 Iglesia El Carmen** and the adjacent handicrafts market.

Continue another block west and turn right on 4a Av Norte. Near the next corner on the right is the old **6 Convento de Santa Teresa**, which until recently served as the men's prison. Go left on 1a Calle Poniente. You'll see the yellow bell tower of the **7 Iglesia de Nuestra Señora de la Merced** (p65). Turn left down 5a Av Norte, jam-packed with tourist-friendly locales, including the handicrafts center **8 Nim Po't** (p83). Proceed beneath the **9 Arco de Santa Catalina** (p84). A remnant of the 17th-century convent that stood here (now occupied by a luxury hotel and B&B), the arch enabled nuns to cross the street unseen.

Continue down 5a Av Norte to **10 Parque Central** (p75). Ascend to the balcony of the **11 Palacio del Ayuntamiento** (p65) for photo ops of the square and **12 Catedral de Santiago** (p65). Finally, stop into the square's **13 Café Condesa** (p80), for a well-deserved cappuccino and wedge of pie.

🚩 Tours

INGUAT-authorized guides around Parque Central offer city walking tours, with visits to convents, ruins and museums, for around Q80 per person. Similar guided walks are offered daily by Antigua travel agencies such as Atitrans (p85). Also on offer are trips to the surrounding villages and coffee plantations.

Elizabeth Bell, a local scholar of Antigua history, or her knowledgeable associates lead three-hour cultural walking tours of the town (in English and/or Spanish) on Tuesday, Wednesday, Friday and Saturday mornings. The cost is Q190. Reservations can be made through **Antigua Tours** (Map p66; ☑ 7832-5821; www.antiguatours.net; 3a Calle Oriente 22; tour incl museum fees Q190), inside the Café Condesa off Parque Central; groups congregate at the park's fountain at the appointed hour. Bell's book, *Antigua Guatemala: The City and its Heritage,* is well worth picking up: it has extensive descriptions of all the monuments and neatly encapsulates the city's history and fiestas. Bell and company also offer tours to the nearby villages of San Antonio Aguas Calientes and San Andrés Itzapa to investigate weaving workshops and Maya shrines, respectively.

La Antigua City Tour (Map p66; ☑ 7832-6151; www.antiguacitytour.com; Q200; ☺ 9am-5pm) runs a little bus around town, hitting all the key sites from Cerro de la Cruz to Parque Central.

De la Gente (☑ 5585-4450; www.dlgcoffee.org; tour per person (min 2 people) Q200) 🍃 offers tours of coffee plantations around San Miguel Escobar, a suburb of Ciudad Vieja, with local growers demonstrating cultivation, harvesting and processing techniques. At the end, participants are guided through traditional roasting methods and share a cup with the family. Tours (three to five hours) depart at 9am or 1pm and should be booked at least a day in advance.

Agencies also offer tours to more distant places, including Tikal, the Cobán area, Monterrico, Chichicastenango and Lago de Atitlán (although these options often depart from Guatemala City). Two-day trips to Tikal, flying from the capital to Flores and back, start at Q3000 per person. Two-day land tours to Copán (some including Quiriguá and Río Dulce) run around Q1140 per person.

CATours (☑ 7832-9638; www.catours.co.uk; 6a Calle Oriente 14; ☺ 9am-5pm Tue-Sun) offers two-day motorbike tours to Lago de Atitlán or Monterrico from Q1435.

🎊 Festivals & Events

The most exciting time to be in Antigua is **Semana Santa** (Easter), when hundreds of devotees garbed in deep purple robes bear revered icons from their churches in daily street processions in remembrance of Christ's crucifixion and the events surrounding it. Dense clouds of incense envelop the parades and the streets are covered in elaborate *alfombras* (carpets) of colored sawdust and flower petals. These fragile works of art are destroyed as the processions shuffle over them, but are re-created each morning for another day of parades.

The fervor and the crowds peak on Good Friday, when an early-morning procession departs from La Merced (p65), and a late afternoon one leaves from the **Escuela de Cristo** (Map p66; cnr Calle de los Pasos & Calle de Belén; ☺ 9am-1pm & 3-7pm Thu-Tue). There may also be an enactment of the crucifixion in **Parque Central** (Map p71; btwn 4a Calle & 5a Calle). Have ironclad Antigua room reservations well in advance of Semana Santa, or plan to stay in Guatemala City or elsewhere and commute to the festivities.

Processions, *velaciones* (vigils) and other events actually go on every weekend through Lent, the 40-day period prior to Semana Santa. Antigua's tourist office and the booklet *Lent and Holy Week in Antigua* by Elizabeth Bell gives explanations.

🛏 Sleeping

With an estimated 140 hotels, *posadas* (guesthouses) and hostels, Antigua has a wide range of accommodations to suit any traveler's style or budget. Some of Antigua's midrange hotels allow you to wallow in colonial charm for a moderate outlay of cash. Rates listed are for Friday and Saturday nights, and customarily drop around 20% during the week. Finding a room is generally a simple task, with the major exception of Semana Santa, for which you should book as far ahead as possible and be prepared to pay double normal rates.

⭐ **Yellow House** HOSTEL **$**
(Map p66; ☑ 7832-6646; yellowhouseantigua@hotmail.com; 1a Calle Poniente 24; dm incl breakfast Q70, s/d without bathroom incl breakfast Q110/200; @) 🍃 Thoughtfully designed, ecologically conscious and damn friendly, this makes a fine budget choice. Rooms vary in style and size, but comfy beds, recessed lighting

and screened windows are the norm. It can get crowded with just three bathrooms downstairs, but they're kept clean and use solar-heated water. The plant-filled terrace is perfect for enjoying the huge, healthy breakfast served each morning.

★El Hostal
HOSTEL $

(Map p66; ☑7832-0442; www.elhostal-antigua .com; 1a Av Sur 8; dm incl breakfast Q90, s/d/tr without bathroom Q200/270/360; �﹅) Within stumbling distance of the popular Café No Sé (p82), El Hostal is a cordially run budget option with a bit of colonial style. Set around a cheery little patio-cafe are half a dozen neatly kept private rooms and dorms with sturdy single beds or well-spaced bunks, a few sticks of furniture and creatively painted walls.

There's a sparkling guest kitchen and good gas-heated showers.

Tropicana Hostel
HOSTEL $

(Map p71; ☑7832-0462; www.tropicanahostel. com; 6a Calle Poniente 2; dm Q70, r with/without bathroom Q300/200; �﹅☒) The new standard for party hostels, the Tropicana is a smash hit. Check in any time you like and join the flock of global youth sunning by the poolside bar or soaking in the hot tub against a backdrop of ruins. Mixed-gender dorms feature as many as 15 beds (on three tiers), each with built-in lockers, privacy curtains and smartphone docks.

Zoola Antigua
HOSTEL $

(Map p66; ☑7832-0364; www.zoolaantigua.wix. com/zoola; 7a Calle Poniente 15; dm/r incl breakfast Q70/180; �﹅) The Antigua branch of the Israeli-run hostel on Lago de Atitlán translates successfully to a colonial setting: sparsely furnished dorms surround an open courtyard where global travelers chill and nosh on healthy Middle Eastern snacks beneath a rainbow canopy. New chillage options include a spectacular roof-terrace bar with hot tub.

Hostal Antigua
HOSTEL $

(Map p66; ☑7832-8090; http://es.hostalantigua .com; 5a Av Sur 22; dm/d/q Q70/295/340; �﹅☒) Just a block and a half from Parque Central, this low-key hostel favors cleanliness and comfort over frenetic socializing. Twelve- and four-bed dorms and private rooms, featuring sturdy wood beds and ceiling fans, line up along a pretty leafy corridor. Up above is a roof terrace with guest kitchen and tiled tables.

Bigfoot Hostel
HOSTEL $

(Map p71; ☑7832-0489; www.bigfoothostel antigua.com; 6a Av Norte; dm/d/tr/q Q75/225/ 275/325; ☒�﹅) Newly renovated by a Nicaragua-based outfit, this place is always hopping, both as a hostel and bar. Though the tall, narrow structure remains cramped, dorms feature comfy carved-wood beds with curtains for privacy and roomy lockers, and air-con is available. Perks for global youth include a pool table, TV lounge, snack bar and the ever-popular Monday pub crawl.

Villa Esthela
HOSTEL $

(Map p66; ☑7832-5162; www.hostelantigua.com; 2a Av Sur 48, Casa A-3; dm/r Q45/150; �﹅) Run by a Dutch expat, this humble but popular hostel is in a quiet part of town five blocks south of Parque Central. Approached down an alley, the old house contains a six-bed dorm with metal bunk beds and several private rooms sharing basic bathrooms. Budget travelers get together in the TV lounge or relax up on the terrace.

ANTIGUA FOR CHILDREN

With gaudily painted buses roving around town, rainbow candles burning in the churches and gigantic volcanoes in the background, Antigua holds an innate magic that appeals to children. Within most of the monastic complexes are parklike expanses where kids can run around amid the ruined walls and fountains. The craft shop Nim Po't (p83) overflows with colorful kites and tiny replicas of those buses to look at, while the market (p83) holds many novel sights, sounds and smells. At the Choco Museo (p70), you can make your own chocolate confections. Lunchtime at Posada de Don Rodrigo (p81) is a festive affair with marimbas making music, and there are matinee movies at the Centro de Formación de la Cooperación Española (p65) every Saturday. Otherwise, take the kids up to **Cerro de la Cruz** (Hill of the Cross; Map p66) for mesmerizing views of the town and surrounding volcanoes, sign up with Ravenscroft Riding Stables (p72) for a bit of horseback riding, or consider a trip to Earth Lodge (p86), a kid-friendly retreat with a playground, fanciful cabins and plenty of hiking trails.

Terrace Hostel HOSTEL $
(Map p66; ☎7832-3463; www.terracehostel.com; 3a Calle Poniente 24; dm incl breakfast Q70, r incl breakfast without bathroom Q200; 📶) The key feature at this fun-filled establishment is the rooftop terrace, a fabulous perch for both volcano views and Q10 Brahvas (happy hour starts at noon). Below deck, rooms are fairly bare, but kept tidy. Don't miss the Monday pub crawl, taking off from here at 3pm.

Hotel Burkhard HOTEL $
(Map p66; ☎7832-4316; hotelburkhard@hotmail.com; 3a Calle Oriente 19A; r Q150; 📶) This tiny establishment has a dozen compact, colorfully decorated rooms over two levels.

Casa Jacaranda HOSTEL $
(Map p66; ☎7832-7589; www.casajacaranda.hotel.com; 1a Calle Poniente 37; dm incl breakfast Q95, s/d incl breakfast without bathroom Q115/230; @📶) At this original hostel (not a party center), the rooms (all sharing bathrooms) are simple but display a bit of flair. So does the airy front lounge, with plasma TV and a mural after Klimt (except the female figure is garbed in a *huipil*). If possible, stay out back behind the jacaranda, a tranquil retreat from the traffic.

An abundant breakfast is served.

Posada Los Búcaros BOUTIQUE HOTEL $$
(Map p66; ☎7832-2346; www.hotelbucaros.com; 7a Av Norte 94; s/d Q300/400; P📶) West of La Merced in a quiet zone of pretty cobbled streets, this converted 150-year-old residence strikes a nice balance between colonial splendor and contemporary comfort. Rooms with pastel walls and high wood-beam ceilings open onto three lushly planted courtyards graced with *los búcaros* – semicircular fountains that are set into the walls.

Posada de San Carlos HOSTEL, HOTEL $$
(Map p71; ☎7832-4698; www.posadadesancarlos.com; 5a Calle Poniente 11; dm/r incl breakfast Q60/300; 📶🐾) A hip global inn with an emphasis on comfort, the San Carlos features spacious rooms along a corridor that opens onto a neat patio with fountain. Both private rooms and the seven-bed dorm have colonial flair, with carved wood beds and chests, plus LED TVs. The front cafe whips up tasty natural fare and there are fat-tire bikes on loan.

Posada Juma Ocag HOTEL $$
(Map p66; ☎7832-3109; www.posadajumaocag.com; Calz Santa Lucia Norte 13; s/d Q150/200; 📶) Juma Ocag's seven spotless, comfortable rooms have quality mattresses and traditional appointments including wrought-iron bedsteads, armoires and mirrors crafted in-house, and there's a spiffy little kitchen for guests. Despite the hectic location opposite the market, it remains peaceful – especially the upstairs rooms – with a rooftop patio and well-tended little garden. Reservations are accepted in person only.

Casa Cristina BOUTIQUE HOTEL $$
(Map p66; ☎7832-0623; www.casa-cristina.com; Callejón Camposeco 3A; s/d downstairs Q190/230, s/d upstairs Q270/340; 📶) There are just a dozen rooms at this hotel on a pretty backstreet near La Merced. Though compact, all are quaintly appointed with *típico* (traditional) bedspreads, brushed-on pastels and wood-stained furniture, and the plant-laden roof terrace makes a nice retreat. *Muy tranquilo.*

Posada San Sebastián GUESTHOUSE $$
(Map p66; ☎7832-2621; www.posadasansebastian.com; 3a Av Norte 4; s/d/tr Q420/490/570; 📶) As carpenter, antique restorer and occasional xylophone player, Luis Méndez Rodríguez is the auteur of this converted mansion. Each of the nine uniquely appointed rooms display his knack for finding and refurbishing art and furniture. Big bathrooms with tub are a bonus, as are the roof terrace, pretty little courtyard garden and use of a kitchen.

Hotel Palacio Chico BOUTIQUE HOTEL $$
(Casa 1940; Map p66; ☎7832-3895; http://1940.palaciochico.com; 7a Av Norte 15; s/d/tr incl breakfast Q330/435/510; 📶) Though on the small side, rooms at this stylish establishment are nicely decked out, with classic tile work, crafted iron bed frames and sponged-on paint. Get a pedicure at the ground-level spa or catch some rays on the top-deck terrace.

Hotel Posada San Pedro II HOTEL $$
(Map p66; ☎7832-4122; www.posadasanpedro.net; 7a Av Norte 29; s/d/tr Q270/345/380; P) Somebody has restored this place with a whole lot of love and attention to detail. Rooms are spacious and well-furnished and look out onto two lush patios surrounded by hanging plants.

Hotel Posada San Pedro HOTEL $$
(Map p66; ☎7832-3594; www.posadasanpedro.net; 3a Av Sur 15; s/d/tr Q230/300/345) The 10 rooms at the San Pedro are neat and inviting, with swabbed-on mustard or chocolate

tones, *azulejo*-tiled bathrooms and cable TV. A guest kitchen, several spacious sitting rooms and two terraces with great views add to the comfortable, friendly atmosphere.

Hotel la Casa de Don Ismael   HOTEL $$
(Map p66; ☎7832-1932; www.casadonismael.com; 3a Calle Poniente 6, Lotificación Cofiño 2a Callejón; s/d Q165/250, incl breakfast Q215/335; ☎) Expect to share the premises with the family at this homey, humble guesthouse, hidden down a side street and overseen by its kind, cordial namesake. Seven rustic rooms share three hot-water bathrooms, and there's a pleasant roof terrace.

Las Golondrinas   APARTMENT $$
(Map p66; ☎7832-3343; aptslasgolondrinas@gmail.com; 6a Av Norte 34; s/d Q150/250; ☎) The humble apartments here are an excellent option for self-caterers. Units are set around a tranquil, tree-studded garden, and all feature front terraces suitable for alfresco dining. The place is run by an inveterate traveler who's climbed hundreds of volcanoes. Good weekly and monthly discounts are available.

Hotel Santa Clara   HOTEL $$
(Map p66; ☎7832-0342; www.hotelsantaclara antigua.com; 2a Av Sur 20; s/d/tr Q290/400/480; ℗) In a quiet area south of the center, the Santa Clara boasts brilliantly restored antique chambers alongside a small courtyard, with carved-wood bedsteads and skylights set into the roof beams. Toward the rear are two levels of newer, mostly brighter rooms, with glimpses of the Iglesia de San Francisco from the upper level.

Hotel Posada La Merced   HOTEL $$
(Map p66; ☎7832-3197; www.posadalamerced antigua.com; 7a Av Norte 43; s/d from Q275/350; ℗☺☎) Behind the big wooden doors, La Merced sports a modern interior. Rooms in the rear section have a bit more pizzazz (and are pricier), with *típico* weavings and colonial furniture. Bonuses include a rooftop terrace, well-appointed guest kitchen, morning coffee and gracious staff.

Hotel Casa Rústica   HOTEL $$
(Map p71; ☎7832-3709; www.casarusticagt.com; 6a Av Norte 8; s/d Q350/425, without bathroom Q280/340; @☎) Everything about the 'rustic house' feels right, from the lily-shaped fountain in the patio to the tiled tables on the top deck. It's also one of the few hotels in this price range to offer guests full kitchen access, not to mention a pool table and

entertainment lounge. Attractively done up with regional textiles, the 14 rooms occupy two buildings.

★Posada del Ángel   BOUTIQUE HOTEL $$$
(Map p66; ☎7832-0260; www.posadadelangel.com; 4a Av Sur 24A; r/ste from Q1480/2270; ℗☎☀) The Posada became Antigua's most celebrated inn when Bill Clinton bedded down here in 1999. Behind an unassuming garage door, the luxury just keeps unfolding. The five rooms and two suites all have fireplaces, fresh lilies, four-poster beds and highly polished tile floors. If you didn't think it was possible to fit a lap pool into an Antigua patio, stop by.

★Mesón Panza Verde   BOUTIQUE HOTEL $$$
(Map p66; ☎7955-8282; www.panzaverde.com; 5a Av Sur 19; r/ste from Q765/1410; ℗@☎☀) Possibly the ultimate in Antigua luxury, the Panza Verde is cloistered in a serene compound south of the center. The three doubles and nine lavishly appointed suites open onto private terraces amid gardens overflowing with orchids, ferns and bamboo. Along with its renowned restaurant (p81), the hotel also features its own art gallery.

★Casa Santo Domingo Hotel   HOTEL $$$
(Map p66; ☎7820-1220; www.casasantodomingo.com.gt; 3a Calle Oriente 28A; r from Q1425; ℗@☎☀) 🌀 Innovatively created from the remains of the sprawling Santo Domingo monastery, this is Antigua's premier lodging. The 128 rooms and suites are of an international five-star standard, while the grounds retain their colonial splendor, dotted with archaeological relics and featuring a large swimming pool, several fine restaurants, shops and five museums. The Dominican friars never had it so good.

Free shuttles from the hotel take you to Santo Domingo del Cerro, a recently developed component of the complex atop a hill to the south, with a fine restaurant, an art and sculpture garden and stunning views.

★Hotel Quinta de las Flores   HOTEL $$$
(Map p66; ☎7832-3721; www.quintadelas flores.com; Calle del Hermano Pedro 6; s/d from Q495/595, bungalow Q1145; ℗@☀) More a village than a hotel, this property on the southeastern edge of town is bursting with charms. Pebbly paths weave by stands of bird-of-paradise, cobblestoned plazas with weathered fountains, a good-sized pool and an open-air restaurant. There are eight luxu-

rious rooms in the main building, most with fireplaces, and five more 'garden rooms' with private terraces.

There are also two-story *casitas* (cottages), each with two bedrooms, a kitchen and living room. Considerable discounts are offered for stays by the week.

Hotel El Mesón de María   HISTORIC HOTEL $$$
(Map p71; 7832-6068; www.hotelmesonde maria.com; 3a Calle Poniente 8; s/d incl breakfast from Q790/975;) Bask in antique splendor at this impressively restored colonial mansion in the center of town, replete with lushly vegetated courtyards and various luxurious salons. Plush chambers vary in layout, but all feature giant beds with sumptuous spreads and carved headboards, rustic furniture and beautifully tiled bathrooms. Take breakfast or cocktails on the fabulous roof terrace.

Hotel Casa del Parque   BOUTIQUE HOTEL $$$
(Map p71; 7832-0961; www.hotelcasadelpar que.com; 4a Av Norte 5; s/d Q745/900;) One of Antigua's original boutique hotels, this little place near the park combines a designer's eye with colonial charms. Each room has a unique layout, but all are picture perfect. The upstairs units are spectacular, with sweeping views, luxurious baths and minibars. Cheaper downstairs rooms lack views but give easier access to the pool, spa and sauna.

✗ Eating

For global gourmands, Antigua is a banquet. Within 10 minutes' walk of Parque Central you can dine well and inexpensively on Italian, Belgian, French, Thai, Indian, Irish, Israeli, German, Chinese, Mexican and Salvadoran cuisines.

On Saturday and Sunday, tables are set up in front of Convento La Merced (p65), serving, among other snacks, chicken salad sandwiches, *rellenitos*, *enchiladas*, tamales and *chuchitos* laced with hot sauce and pickled cabbage, along with bowls of *atol blanco* (corn-based hot beverage). Talk about comfort food!

Note that most formal restaurants in Antigua whack on a 10% tip before presenting the bill. It should be itemized, but if in doubt, ask.

★Zoola Antigua   ISRAELI $
(Map p66; www.zoolaantigua.wix.com/zoola; Calle de Santa Lucia 15; salads Q45, sandwiches Q35-50; 8am-10pm;) The restaurant component

of Zoola hostel (p76) whips up highly authentic Israeli fare. Nosh on falafel, kebabs or *sabich* – a wrap stuffed with hummus, eggplant and salad. Seating is at low coffee tables surrounded by pillows. On Friday evenings Zoola offers a buffet-style spread of salads.

★Restaurante Doña Luisa Xicotencatl   CAFE $
(Map p66; 7832-2578; 4a Calle Oriente 12; sandwiches & breakfast mains Q20-45; 7am-9:30pm) Refreshingly local in character, this cafe is a place to enjoy the colonial patio ambiance over breakfast or a light meal. The selection of pastries are from the attached bakery; banana bread comes hot from the oven around 2pm daily.

Samsara   VEGETARIAN $
(Map p71; 7832-2200; 6a Calle Poniente 33; salads Q40-50; 7am-9pm;) At this small veggie cafe, fresh organic ingredients are excitingly combined in soups, salads and drinks – how about a kale, peanut butter and avocado smoothie? For breakfast there's quinoa porridge or banana and amaranth-seed pancakes, along with French-press coffee and numerous tea blends. If you don't mind the new-age soundtrack, Samsara can be a culinary thrill.

Y Tu Piña También   SANDWICHES $
(Map p66; www.ytupinatambien.com; 1a Av Sur 10B; sandwiches & salads Q40-50; 7am-7pm;) An international crossroads, this natural-foods cafe does healthy, sophisticated fare for foreign students on the go. There's a tempting array of sandwiches (served on whole wheat, pita or bagel) and salads. It opens early and makes a good breakfast stop, with omelets, abundant fruit salads and banana pancakes, plus excellent coffee.

Tienda La Canche   GUATEMALAN $
(Map p66; 6a Av Norte 42; set lunch Q25; 7am-10pm) A hole in the wall if there ever was

🛈 VOLUNTEERING

Many of Antigua's language schools, such as Academia de Español Sevilla (p73), Antigüeña Spanish Academy (p73) and **Cambio Spanish School** (Map p66; 7832-8033; www. cambiospanishschool.com; 4a Calle Oriente 28), can help you find volunteer work.

one, this eatery behind a 'mom and pop' store consists of just two tables. A couple of traditional options are prepared daily, such as *pepián de pollo* (a hearty chicken stew containing chunks of *huizquil,* a yucca-like tuber), accompanied by thick tortillas. *Frescos,* home-squeezed fruit beverages, are served alongside.

Café Condesa
CAFE $

(Map p71; ☑7832-0038; www.cafecondesa.com.gt; Portal del Comercio 4; cakes & pies Q20-26; ☺7am-8pm Sun-Thu, to 9pm Fri & Sat) Baked goods – pies, cakes, quiches, scones and house-baked whole-wheat sandwich bread – are the strong suit at this grand old cafe set around the patio of a 16th-century mansion off the main square. The lavish Sunday buffet (Q78; 9am to 1pm) is an Antigua institution.

Fernando's Kaffee
CAFE $

(Map p66; ☑7832-6953; www.fernandoskaffee. com; cnr 7a Av Norte & Callejón Camposeco; cinnamon rolls Q10, empanadas Q40; ☺7am-7pm Mon-Sat, noon-7pm Sun; ☏) Long a draw for coffee and chocolate mavens, this friendly corner cafe also bakes an array of fine pastries, including some delightfully gooey cinnamon rolls. Beyond the counter is an inviting patio ideal for a low-key breakfast and linger.

Luna de Miel
CREPERIE $

(Map p66; ☑7882-4559; www.lunademielantigua .com; 6a Av Norte 40; crepes Q34-55; ☺10am-9:30pm Mon & Tue, 9am-9:30pm Wed-Sun; ☏) Loungey Luna de Miel offers dozens of variations on the classic crepe – try the *chapín* version stuffed with avocado, cheese and fried tomatoes – plus tropical smoothies. As if that weren't enough, the graffitied roof deck makes a remarkably relaxing place to enjoy them.

Casa de las Mixtas
GUATEMALAN $

(Map p66; 3a Callejón; mains Q20-30; ☺8am-9pm Mon-Sat) For down-home Guatemalan fare, try this family-run operation on a quiet backstreet across from the market. Aside from its namesake snack (*mixtas* are Guatemalan-style hot dogs, wrapped in tortillas), it also serves a range of set breakfasts. Regulars make for the little terrace upstairs.

Travel Menu
INTERNATIONAL $

(Map p71; ☑7832-2937; 6a Calle Poniente 14; mains Q40-50; ☺noon-11pm; ☑) This recently renovated and expanded restaurant-bar is indeed aimed at travelers (on a budget), serving up a global greatest hits selection (veggie curries, fish burgers, salads) in a relaxed, roomy space.

★Cactus Grill
MEXICAN $$

(Map p71; ☑7832-2163; 6a Calle Poniente 21; tacos Q45; ☺noon-10pm) Created by a Mexico City native, this colorful little place does a brisk trade in authentic Mexican fare, both traditional and new wave, with superb salsas served in clay bowls. The fish tacos are heartily recommended. It's along the nightlife corridor; start the evening with a chili-fringed margarita or quality mescal from Oaxaca.

El Viejo Café
CAFE $$

(Map p71; ☑7832-1576; www.elviejocafe.com; 3a Calle Poniente 12; mains Q50-95; ☺7am-9pm; ☏☺) Popular with tourists and *chapínes* (Guatemalans) alike, this atmospheric cafe strewn with antique curios makes an ideal breakfast stop. Choose from an array of fresh-baked croissants and well-roasted Guatemalan coffees and settle into a window nook.

Hector's Bistro
FRENCH $$

(Map p66; ☑7832-9867; 1a Calle Poniente 9A; mains Q70-175; ☺noon-10pm) This tiny, intimate salon across the way from La Merced has just a few tables, with the kitchen behind the bar. Guatemala City native Hector has garnered acclaim for his versions of *bœuf bourguignon,* grilled duck breast and so on. There's no proper sign: check the chalkboard for daily specials and the quiche of the week.

Caffé Mediterráneo
ITALIAN $$

(Map p71; ☑7882-7180; 6a Calle Poniente 6A; mains Q90-130; ☺noon-3pm & 6-10pm Wed-Mon) Here you'll find the finest, most authentic Italian food in Antigua, plus superb service, in a lovely candlelit setting. Hailing from Calabria, chef Francesco does a tantalizing array of salads and pasta, using seasonally available ingredients.

Como Como
BELGIAN $$

(Map p66; ☑5514-5014; 2a Av Sur 12; mains Q100-150; ☺noon-3pm & 6-10pm Tue-Sun) Guatemalan ingredients fuse with Euro recipes at this Belgian bistro, popular with the expat crowd. Flemish specialties include *waterzooi,* a creamy fish stew, and *filet americain* (steak tartar). Dining is alfresco in the candlelit courtyard.

Origami
JAPANESE $$

(Map p66; ☑7882-4250; 6a Calle Oriente 6; mains Q50-65; ☺noon-3pm & 6-9pm Mon-Wed

& Fri, 6-9pm Sat, noon-4pm Sun; 🖉) Rather than striving for authenticity, the Japanese couple who run Origami just serve the sort of things they'd make at home: pulled pork *donburi,* red curry and wasabi-dressed salad (100% organic) are among the more popular items. It's a cozy place with several salons and some tables in the courtyard. Be sure to try the homemade ginger ale.

Angie Angie
ARGENTINE **$$**

(Map p66; 🖉 7832-3352; 1a Av Sur 11A; mains Q65-95; ⊙noon-11pm Wed-Mon) Equal parts South American eatery, art gallery and social club, Angie's place is always worth stopping into, if only to lounge around the tropically abundant back garden. Besides the *empanadas,* mixed grills and homemade pastas, there's a good-value set lunch. Bonfires nightly, plus live blues and jazz on weekends.

Epicure
DELI **$$**

(Map p66; 🖉 7832-5545; 3a Av Norte 11B; sandwiches Q75-90, mains Q90-145; ⊙10am-9pm Mon-Sat, 10am-7pm Sun) A good place to stock up on sandwiches for the volcano climb is this Euro-standard deli, with all kinds of gourmet items. Offers elegant open-air dining under the rear arbor.

Quesos y Vino
ITALIAN **$$**

(Map p66; 🖉 7832-7785; 5a Av Norte 32A; pizzas Q60-150; ⊙noon-4pm & 6-10pm Wed-Mon) This Italian-owned establishment is comprised of three rustic buildings, with a lovely outdoor patio and adjoining deli. Like the restaurant's name, the food is basic and satisfying: hearty soups, well-stuffed sandwiches on homemade bread, salads and wood-fired pizzas. Enter from 1a Calle Poniente.

Posada de Don Rodrigo
GUATEMALAN **$$**

(Map p66; 🖉 7832-0387; www.posadadonrodrigo. com; 5a Av Norte 17; mains Q125-150; ⊙6am-10pm) The seafood crepes, steaks and sausages have a subtle Guatemalan accent here. The real draw, though, is the setting, a gorgeous courtyard with plenty of wrought iron, blossoming flowers and tinkling fountains, with marimbas and painters adding local color.

La Cuevita de Los Urquizú
GUATEMALAN **$$**

(Map p66; 🖉 7882-4532; 2a Calle Oriente 9D; lunch combo Q80; ⊙8am-4pm Mon & Tue, to 8pm Wed-Sun) Sumptuous *típico* food is the draw here, all kept warm in earthenware pots out front. Choose from *pepián* (chicken and vegetables in a piquant sesame and pump-

kin seed sauce), *kaq'ik* (spicy turkey stew), *jocón* (green stew of chicken or pork with green vegetables and herbs) or other such Guatemalan favorites, and you'll get two accompaniments.

Sabe Rico
DELI **$$**

(Map p71; 🖉 7832-0648; www.saberico.com.gt; 6a Av Sur 7; sandwiches & salads Q65-80; ⊙8am-7pm Mon & Wed, to 4pm Tue, to 9pm Thu-Sat, 9am-4pm Sun) This little deli whips up tasty salads and sandwiches, using ingredients from its herb garden. It also offers fresh-baked breads and brownies, fine wines and imported foods. Eat in one of the various salons or stock up for a picnic.

El Papaturro
SALVADORAN **$$**

(Map p66; 🖉 7832-0445; 2a Calle Oriente 4; pupusas Q30, mains Q70-85; ⊙noon-10pm Tue-Sun) This homey spot run by natives of El Salvador serves authentic *pupusas* – thick tortillas stuffed with cheese or *chicharrónes* (fried pork fat) and garnished with *curtido* (marinated cabbage) – and other snacks from Guatemala's southern neighbor in a relaxed courtyard setting. The obvious accompaniment is *horchata,* a beverage blend of cacao, ice, cinnamon, cashews and more.

Fridas
MEXICAN **$$**

(Map p66; 🖉 7832-1296; 5a Av Norte 29; mains Q75-140; ⊙noon-midnight) Dedicated to Ms Kahlo, this ever-busy bar-restaurant does Jalisco-style posole, shrimp tacos and other tasty Mexican fare. Live music on Thursday and Friday evenings.

★ Mesón Panza Verde
FUSION **$$$**

(Map p66; 🖉 7832-2925; www.panzaverde.com; 5a Av Sur 19; mains Q150-200; ⊙6-10pm Mon, noon-3pm & 6-10pm Tue-Sun) The restaurant of the exclusive B&B Mesón Panza Verde (p78) dishes up divine continental cuisine in an appealing Antiguan atmosphere. The menu features an eclectic global lineup, with the French-trained chef putting an emphasis on fresh seafood and organic ingredients. Live music (jazz, Cuban) enhances the ambiance Wednesday to Saturday nights.

★ Bistrot Cinq
FRENCH **$$$**

(Map p66; 🖉 7832-5510; www.bistrotcinq.com; 4a Calle Oriente 7; mains Q135-175; ⊙noon-10:30pm) Popular among the mature expat crowd, the Cinq is a faithful replica of its Parisian counterparts, offering zesty salads and classic entrees such as mahi-mahi *amandine* and filet mignon. Check the blackboard for exciting nightly specials. Be sure to make it down for Sunday brunch (served from noon to 5pm). Now serving absinthe.

🍷 Drinking & Nightlife

The bar scene jumps, especially on Friday and Saturday evenings when the hordes roll in from Guatemala City for some Antigua-style revelry. Besides the watering holes, the restaurants Fridas (p81) and Bistrot Cinq (p81) are at least as popular for the cocktails as the cuisine. Start drinking early and save: *cuba libres* and mojitos are half price between 5pm and 8pm at many bars.

To get an overview of Antigua's nightspots, join the pub crawl that embarks every Monday at 3pm from the Terrace Hostel (p77).

★Por Qué No? PUB
(Map p66; ☑4324-5407; www.porquenocafe. com; cnr 2a Av Sur & 9a Calle Oriente; ⊙6-10pm Mon-Sat) This alternative cafe is a vertically oriented space that takes up an absurdly narrow corner of an old building (grab the rope to reach the upper level) with vintage bric-a-brac hanging from the rafters and every surface scrawled with guest-generated graffiti. The vibe is relaxed and conversational and a crowd spills out the door each evening.

Host Carlos is an ace in the kitchen, whipping up scrumptious shrimp and eggplant dishes nightly, and the musical mix is similarly splendid.

Ocelot Bar PUB
(Map p71; ☑5658-9028; 4a Av Norte 3; ⊙4:30pm-1am) Just off Parque Central, this Welsh tavern feels like a large living room, with wall-length sofas, murals of literary and sports heroes, and board games, not to mention the best-stocked bar in town. It's highly popular with the mature expat crowd; the Monday evening pub quiz really packs them in.

Ocelot is part of a nightlife center that consists of at least three other bars, including the Tiki-themed Vudu and game-center Bullseye.

Café No Sé BAR
(Map p66; www.cafenose.com; 1a Av Sur 11C; ⊙3pm-1am) This downbeat little bar is a point of reference for Antigua's budding young Burroughses and Kerouacs. It's also the core of a lively music scene, with players wailing from a corner of the room most evenings. A semiclandestine attached salon serves its own brand of mescal, 'smuggled' over from Oaxaca (two-shot minimum). After hours, just bang on the door.

Reilly's en la Esquina IRISH PUB
(Map p71; ☑7832-6251; 6a Calle Poniente 7; ⊙noon-12:30am) Holding the key corner of Antigua's nightlife corridor, the new and improved Reilly's packs in both Guatemalans and gringos on weekends. The sprawling pub counts no fewer than four bars, with most of the action focusing on the central patio. Midweek it's mellower, with the billiard table, pub grub and Guinness on tap pulling in a faithful following.

Snug PUB
(Map p71; ☑5838-5390; 6a Calle Poniente 14; ⊙noon-11pm) It's a tight squeeze, but spirits are high at the aptly dubbed Snug, a new anchor on the expat drinking scene. Live music on Sundays.

Monoloco PUB
(Map p71; ☑7832-4235; 5a Av Sur 6, Pasaje El Corregidor; ⊙11am-12:45am) As much Guatemala weekender as tourist hangout, the 'wacky monkey' serves up a good blend of comfort foods and local dishes, as well as ice-cold beers, in a relaxed environment with sports TV on dozens of sets.

La Sin Ventura CLUB
(Map p71; 5a Av Sur 8; ⊙4pm-1am Tue-Fri, noon-1am Sat, noon-8pm Sun) The liveliest dance floor in town is packed with Guatemalan youth toward the weekend. DJs pump out *cumbias* (Colombian dance tunes) and reggaetón most nights, while musicians play live salsa on Tuesdays.

Las Vibras de la Casbah CLUB
(Map p66; ☑3141-5311; www.lasvibrasantigua.com; 5a Av Norte 30; ⊙5pm-1am Wed-Sat) It's quite a party most nights at this split-level disco near the Santa Catalina arch: plenty of selfies, vapor shots and EDM form the scene. To take a breather, make your way to the open-air terrace out front.

Lucky Rabbit BAR
(Map p71; ☑7832-5099; 5a Av Sur 8; ⊙7pm-1am Mon-Sat) A former cinema, this upstairs space favored by Guatemalan youth has morphed into a game room/dance hall, though the movies are still continuously projected throughout the evening.

☆ Entertainment

The Centro de Formación de la Cooperación Española (p65) runs thematic series of documentaries or foreign art-house films on Wednesday nights.

Café No Sé, Angie Angie (p81), the **Rainbow Café** (Map p71; ☑ 7832-1919; www.rainbow cafeantigua.com; 7a Av Sur 8; ⊙ 8am-11pm) and Mesón Panza Verde (p81) host folk, rock and jazz performances.

🔒 Shopping

Woven and leather goods, ironwork, paintings and jade jewelry are some of the items to look for in Antigua's various shops and markets. For beautiful *típico* fabrics, first get educated at the Casa del Tejido Antiguo (p69), then have a look around Nim Po't or the big handicrafts markets near the bus terminal and next to Iglesia El Carmen.

Market　　　　　　　　　　MARKET
(Map p66; Calz de Santa Lucía Sur; ⊙ 6am-6pm Mon, Thu & Sat, 7am-6pm Tue, Wed & Fri, 7am-5pm Sun) Antigua's market – chaotic, colorful and always busy – sprawls north of 4a Calle Poniente. The best days are the official market days – Monday, Thursday and especially Saturday – when villagers from the vicinity roll in and spread their wares north and west of the main market building.

La Casa del Jade　　　　　　　JEWELRY
(Map p66; www.lacasadeljade.com; 4a Calle Oriente 10; ⊙ 9am-6pm) More than just a jewelry shop, the Casa has a museum that displays dozens of pre-Hispanic jade pieces and an open workshop where you can admire the work of contemporary craftspeople. It's inside the Casa Antigua El Jaulón shopping arcade.

Nim Po't　　　　　　　　　HANDICRAFTS
(Map p66; ☑ 7832-2681; www.nimpotexport.com; 5a Av Norte 29; ⊙ 9am-9pm Sun-Thu, 9am-10pm Fri & Sat) This sprawling hall boasts a huge collection of Maya clothing, as well as hundreds of masks, wood carvings, kites, paintings, refrigerator magnets and assorted Maximón figurines. The *huipiles, cortes, fajas* and other garments are arranged by region, so it makes for a fascinating visit whether you're buying or not.

Mercado del Carmen　　　　　HANDICRAFTS
(Map p66; cnr 3a Calle Oriente & 3a Av Norte; ⊙ 9am-6pm) Next to the ruins of the Iglesia El Carmen, this market is a good place to browse for textiles, pottery and jade, particularly on weekends, when activity spills out onto 3a Av Norte.

Doña María Gordillo Dulces Típicos　FOOD
(Map p66; 4a Calle Oriente 11; ⊙ 10am-6pm Mon-Sat) This shop is filled with traditional Guatemalan sweets, such as coconut macaroons, *dulces de leche* and marzipan, and there's often a crowd of *antigüeños* lined up to buy them.

El Reino del Jade　　　　　　JEWELRY
(Map p66; ☑ 7832-1593; 5a Av Norte 28; ⊙ 9am-6:30pm) This shop near the Santa Catalina arch specializes in designer jewelry featuring jade and other gems.

Librería La Casa del Conde　　　BOOKS
(Map p71; ☑ 7832-3322; Portal del Comercio 4; ⊙ 9am-6pm) Excellent selection of Central American history and politics, plus nature guides in English, literature in Spanish and Lonely Planet titles.

Mercado de Artesanías　　　HANDICRAFTS
(Map p66; 4a Calle Poniente; ⊙ 9am-6pm) Masses of Guatemalan handicrafts fill the stalls of this building at the west end of town just below the main market. While not at the top end of the quality range, it has a variety of colorful masks, blankets, jewelry, purses and so on. Don't be afraid to bargain.

Jade Maya　　　　　　　　JEWELRY
(Map p66; www.jademaya.com; 4a Calle Oriente 34; ⊙ 9am-6pm) Started by a North American couple who discovered a jade quarry in the Motagua Valley, this shop features a jade workshop and a small museum (free

LGBT VENUES

A continuous influx of foreign visitors has granted Antigua a veneer of cosmopolitanism and tolerance beyond that of other similar-size Guatemalan cities. So despite the strong religious undercurrent, gays and lesbians find a sort of haven here, and the nightlife scene embraces every persuasion. In particular, the restaurant Fridas (p81) hosts a queer gathering with DJs on the final Saturday of each month (upstairs), and the dance club Las Vibras de la Casbah (p82) stages alternative events weekly.

admission) with an assortment of pre-Hispanic pieces.

Centro de Arte Popular ARTS
(Map p66; 4a Calle Oriente 10; ⏲9:30am-6:30pm) Inside the Casa Antigua El Jaulón, a courtyard shopping arcade, this shop/museum displays Tz'utujil oil paintings, cedar figurines, masks and other crafts. The art is thematically arranged to illustrate the various aspects of indigenous life.

La Bodegona ELECTRONICS
(Map p66; 5a Calle Poniente 32; ⏲7am-8pm) The front section of this supermarket has a good-value cell-phone shop.

ℹ Orientation

Antigua's focal point is the broad Parque Central (p75); few places in town are more than 15 minutes' walk from here. Compass points are added to the numbered Calles and Avs, indicating whether an address is *norte* (north), *sur* (south), *poniente* (west) or *oriente* (east) of Parque Central.

Three volcanoes provide easy reference points: Volcán Agua is south of the city and visible from most points within it; Volcán Fuego and Volcán Acatenango rise to the southwest (Acatenango is the more northerly of the two).

Another useful Antigua landmark is the **Arco de Santa Catalina** (Map p66; 5a Av Norte), an arch spanning 5a Av Norte, two and a half blocks north of Parque Central, on the way to La Merced church.

ℹ Information

DANGERS & ANNOYANCES

- Antigua generally feels safe to walk around, but muggings do occur, so don't let your guard down completely. This holds doubly true after the bars close at 1am; after 10pm, consider taking a taxi back to your accommodations.
- Pickpockets work the busy market, doing overtime on paydays at the middle and end of the month. December (bonus time) brings a renewed wave of robberies.
- Some of the more remote hiking trails have been the scene of muggings, though stepped-up police patrols have reduced the likelihood of such incidents. If you're planning on hiking independently, check with Proatur about the current situation.

EMERGENCY

Proatur (☎5578-9835; operacionesproatur@inguat.gob.gt; 6a Calle Poniente Final; ⏲24hr) The helpful tourism assistance agency has its headquarters on the west side of town, three blocks south of the market. If you're the victim of a crime, staff will accompany you to the national police and assist with the formalities, including any translating that's needed. Given advance notice, it can provide an escort for drivers heading out on potentially risky roads.

Ambulance	☎128
Fire	☎123
Police	☎120
Tourist police	☎1500 or ☎2421-2810

INTERNET ACCESS

Aside from an abundance of affordable cybercafes, wi-fi is available in restaurants, cafes and elsewhere.

Funky Monkey (5a Av Sur 6, Pasaje El Corregidor; per hour Q12; ⏲8am-12:30am) Inside Monoloco.

MEDIA

The Antigua-based *Revue Magazine* (www.revuemag.com) runs about 90% ads, but has reasonable information about cultural events; it's available everywhere. *La Cuadra* (www.lacuadraonline.com), published by Café No Sé (p82), presents the gringo-bohemian perspective, mixing politics with irreverent commentary; pick up a copy at the cafe.

MEDICAL SERVICES

Farmacia Cruz Verde Ivori (☎7832-8318; 7a Av Norte; ⏲24hr)

Hospital Nacional Pedro de Bethancourt (☎7831-1319; ⏲24hr) A public hospital in San Felipe, 2km north of the center, with emergency service.

Hospital Privado Hermano Pedro (☎7832-1190; www.hospitalhermanopedro.net; Av de la Recolección 4; ⏲24hr) Private hospital that offers 24-hour emergency service and accepts foreign insurance.

MONEY

Banco Agromercantil (4a Calle Poniente 8; ⏲9am-7pm Mon-Fri, to 5pm Sat & Sun) Changes US dollars and euros (cash or traveler's checks). Also houses a branch of Western Union.

Banco Industrial (5a Av Sur 4; ⏲9am-7pm Mon-Fri, to 1pm Sat) Has a reliable ATM and changes US dollars. Another useful BI ATM is inside Café Barista, on the northwest corner of Parque Central.

Citibank (cnr 4a Calle Oriente & 4a Av Norte; ⏲9am-4:30pm Mon-Fri, 9:30am-1pm Sat) Changes US dollars and euros.

Visa & MasterCard ATM (Portal del Comercio) Facing Parque Central.

OPENING HOURS

With travelers visiting Antigua year-round, opening hours remain pretty consistent throughout the year.

Banks 9am-6pm Monday to Friday, 9am-1pm Saturday

Bars and clubs Afternoon or late afternoon to 1am, though some open earlier; dance clubs generally shut on Sundays and some on Mondays

Cafes 7am-7pm, some to as late as 10pm

Restaurants Noon-10pm or 11pm, some close 3pm-6pm

Shops 9am-6pm Monday to Friday, 9am-5pm Saturday; many shops also stay open Sunday

POST

DHL (Map p71; ☑ 2339-8400; 6a Calle Poniente 16; ☺ 8am-6pm Mon-Fri, 8am-noon Sat) Offers door-to-door service.

Post Office (Map p66; cnr 4a Calle Poniente & Calz de Santa Lucía; ☺ 8:30am-5:30pm Mon-Fri, 9am-1pm Sat) Opposite the market.

TELEPHONE

Most internet cafes offer cut-rate international calls, though Skype calls may be even cheaper. If you plan to be around a while, consider purchasing a local cell phone; you can pick one up at La Bodegona.

TOURIST INFORMATION

INGUAT (Map p66; ☑ 7832-0787; info-antigua@inguat.gob.gt; 5a Calle Oriente 11; ☺ 8am-4pm Mon-Fri, 9am-5pm Sat & Sun) The tourist office has free city maps, bus information and helpful, bilingual staff.

TRAVEL AGENCIES

Atitrans (☑ 7832-3371; www.atitrans.net; 6a Av Sur 8; ☺ 8am-9pm) Multipurpose agency with recommended shuttle service.

LAX Travel (☑ 7832-2674; laxantigua@hotmail.com; 6a Av Sur 12; ☺ 9am-6pm Mon-Fri, 9am-5pm Sat) International flight specialist.

Onvisa Travel Agency (☑ 5226-3441; onvisatravel@hotmail.com; 6a Calle Poniente 40) Operates shuttles to Copán, Lake Atitlán and elsewhere.

Rainbow Travel Center (☑ 7931-7878; www.rainbowtravelcenter.com; 7a Av Sur 8; ☺ 9am-6pm Mon-Fri, 9am-5pm Sat) Specializes in student and teacher airfares.

ⓘ Getting There & Around

CAR & MOTORCYCLE

To park in Antigua, you're supposed to have a *marbete* (label) hanging from your rearview mirror, or risk a fine. Purchase these from traffic cops for Q10.

If you're planning to drive out of town on a reportedly hijack-prone road (such as to Panajachel via Patzún), you may request an escort from Proatur by emailing them at least 72 hours in advance. There's no fee other than the escort's expenses.

CATours (p75) Rents scooters and offers one- to seven-day motorcycle tours from Q800.

Guatemala Renta Autos (☑ 2329-9030; www.guatemalarentacar.com; 4a Av Norte 6; rental per day from Q260; ☺ 8am-6pm Mon-Fri, to 3pm Sat)

Tabarini (☑ 7832-8107; www.tabarini.com; 6a Av Sur 22; rental per day from Q300; ☺ 8am-6pm)

ANTIGUA BUSES

DESTINATION	FARE	DURATION	FREQUENCY	SERVICE
Chimaltenango	Q5	30min	every 10min	
Ciudad Vieja	Q3	15min	every 15min	Take a San Miguel Dueñas bus.
Escuintla	Q8	1hr	every 20min	
Guatemala City	Q10	1hr	every 15min from 7am to 8pm	A Pullman service (Q45; 9:30am and 4pm) by **Litegua** (Map p85; ☑ 7832-9850; www.litegua.com; 4a Calle Oriente 48) also runs from its office at the east end of town.
Panajachel	Q36	2½hr	one bus daily at 7am	Transportes Rebulli service, departing from Panadería Colombia on 4a Calle Poniente, half a block east of the market.
San Antonio Aguas Calientes	Q4	20min	every 10min	

BUS

Buses (Map p66; cnr 5a Calle Poniente & Av de la Recolección) from Guatemala City, Ciudad Vieja and San Miguel Dueñas arrive and depart from a street just south of the market, across from the Mercado de Artesanías.

Buses (Map p66; Av de la Recolección) to Chimaltenango, Escuintla, San Antonio Aguas Calientes and Santa María de Jesús go from a lot behind the main market building. If you're heading out to local villages, go early in the morning and return by midafternoon, as bus services decrease dramatically as evening approaches.

To reach highland towns such as Chichicastenango, Quetzaltenango, Huehuetenango or Panajachel, take one of the frequent buses to Chimaltenango, on the Interamericana Hwy, then catch an onward bus. Making connections is easy, as many folks will jump to your aid as you alight from one bus looking for another, but stay alert.

SHUTTLE MINIBUS

Numerous travel agencies and tourist minibus operators offer frequent shuttle services to places tourists go, including Guatemala City and its airport, Panajachel and Chichicastenango. They cost more than buses, but they're comfortable and convenient, with door-to-door service at both ends. Some typical one-way prices include Chichicastenango (Q115), Cobán (Q250), Copán (Honduras; Q270), Guatemala City (Q80), Monterrico (Q115), Panajachel (Q115) and Quetzaltenango (Q195).

EXPLORE MORE OF ANTIGUA

While Antigua itself is pretty much well-trodden territory from end to end, there are plenty of little villages just outside of town that are begging to be explored:

Santa María de Jesús At the foot of Volcán Agua, holds a major market on Sundays.

San Juan del Obispo Has a wonderful colonial church and panoramic views of Antigua.

San Felipe An artisans' village with some of the finest jade, silver and ceramic work in the area.

Pastores Ground zero for leatherwork. This is the place to come for handmade cowboy boots and stock whips.

Confirm departure times with shuttle operators and whether they require a minimum number of passengers.

TAXI & TUK-TUK

Taxis wait where the Guatemala City buses stop and on the east side of Parque Central. An in-town taxi ride costs Q25 to Q30. *Tuk-tuks* are Q5 to Q10. Note that *tuk-tuks* are not allowed in the center of town, so you'll have to hike a few blocks out to find one; they do not operate after 8pm.

AROUND ANTIGUA

Jocotenango

This village just northwest of Antigua opens a window on a less self-conscious, less Unesco-authorized version of Guatemalan life compared with central Antigua. Aloof from the traffic of the main thoroughfare stands the church, as it has for centuries, its peach facade graced by baroque columns and elaborate stuccowork, behind elaborate gardens and a majestic ceiba tree. The town is known for its processions during Lent – or perhaps more so as the birthplace of Latin American pop star Ricardo Arjona.

Though accommodations are sparse in Jocotenango, it is practically a suburb of Antigua, where there are numerous hotels and hostels.

Outstanding coffee can be enjoyed at the Centro Cultural La Azotea ([☎]7831-1120; www.azoteaestate.com; Calle del Cementerio Final; adult/child Q50/30; ⊗8:30am-5pm Mon-Fri, 8.30am-3pm Sat) plantation, which is Jocotenango's main draw; for nightlife, nearby Antigua is a better bet.

Any bus from Antigua bound for Chimaltenango can drop you off in front of the church (Q3, 5 minutes); or catch a *tuk-tuk* (Q5).

El Hato

★ **Earth Lodge**   LODGE **$**
([☎]5664-0713; www.earthlodgeguatemala.com; dm Q55, s/d cabin from Q230/310, without bathroom Q130/200; [⊗][☎]) [⊘] High in the hills above Jocotenango, this 40-acre spread is set on a working avocado farm, and the views of the Panchoy valley and volcanoes are truly mesmerizing. Developed and overseen by an affable North American couple, the eco-friendly retreat offers plenty to do: hiking

trails, birdwatching, Spanish lessons, yoga sessions, a *chuj* (Maya sauna) or just hanging in a hammock.

Accommodations are in comfortable A-frame cabins, an eight-bed dorm and a couple of fabulous tree houses. Lip-smacking, nutritious vegetarian food is served with a slew of avocado-based fare at harvest time (January and July).

A portion of the profits buys supplies for the village school, where guests can do volunteer work.

To get there, your best bet is to call at least a day in advance to see if the lodge can pick you up from Antigua (Q30 per person with two passengers). Otherwise, an 'El Hato' bus leaves from behind the market in Antigua at least six times Monday, Thursday and Saturday, less often the rest of the week. From there it's a 25-minute walk downhill – any villager can give you directions – just ask for 'los gringos.'

Ciudad Vieja & Around

Seven kilometers southwest of Antigua along the Escuintla road is Ciudad Vieja (Old City), near the site of the first capital of the Captaincy General of Guatemala. Founded in 1527, it met its demise 14 years later when Volcán Agua let loose a flood of water that had been penned up in its crater. The water deluged the town with tons of rock and mud, leaving only the ruins of La Concepción church.

The actual site of the former capital is a bit to the east at San Miguel Escobar; Ciudad Vieja was populated by survivors of the flood. The pretty church on the main square has an impressive stuccowork facade, though it's about two centuries newer than the plaque by the door boasts it to be.

A good way to tour this area is by bicycle. Head out of Antigua along the Ciudad Vieja road east of the market. It's a 4km ride along a moderately busy road to Ciudad Vieja. Take 4a Calle west through the restored colonial part of town. Back at the main road, turn left. When you reach the cemetery, go right, following signs for San Miguel Dueñas. From there, it's about a 10-minute ride downhill to the Valhalla Experimental Station, on the left side. The road goes on to San Miguel Dueñas.

Coming into that town, you'll go over a small bridge. Bear right, then turn right at the sign for San Antonio Aguas Calientes.

This road, unpaved for much of the way, winds for the next 5km through coffee *fincas* (plantations), hamlets and vegetable fields. Arriving in San Antonio, turn right at the communal washbasins to reach the main plaza. Leaving town, go around the left side of the church, then head left up 2a Calle. From there, it's a steep climb but you're rewarded with breathtaking views of the village. Beyond the Finca Los Nietos coffee plantation, you'll reach the RN-14 Hwy. Turn left there and go 2km, taking the second right onto a dirt road. This will take you back to the Ciudad Vieja–Antigua road, where a left turn leads you back into town.

🤾 Activities

Niños de Guatemala   CULTURAL TOUR
(☑ 7832-8033; www.ninosdeguatemala.org; tours Q200-250; ⊙ Tue & Thu) The NGO Niños de Guatemala, which runs three schools for low-income kids in and around the town, leads alternative tours of Ciudad Vieja that really get beneath the surface of the community. A half-day tour, every Thursday morning, takes you through the poorer section of town, then focuses on two of its principal industries: 'chicken bus' rebuilding and coffin-making.

On another tour, given Tuesday mornings, participants visit a woodworking workshop in the outlying district of San Lorenzo el Cubo and learn how to make *quitapeñas* (worry dolls). Tour fees include transport, guide and a snack.

Valhalla Experimental Station   TOUR
(☑ 7831-5799; www.exvalhalla.net; ⊙ 8am-4:30pm) 🖉 Between San Antonio Aguas Calientes and Ciudad Vieja, near the village of San Miguel Dueñas, is this macadamia farm raising 300 species of the remarkable nut. You can tour this organic, sustainable agriculture project and sample nuts, oils and cosmetics made from the harvest. Be sure to sample the macadamia pancakes, served in an open-air cafe surrounded by lush tropical foliage.

🛏 Sleeping

Hotel Santa Valentina   HOTEL $$
(☑ 7831-5044; 2a Av 0-01, Zona 3; s/d Q200/250; 🅿) Your best bet for accommodations in Ciudad Vieja offers rooms with bathroom and TV. An abundant breakfast is served in the hotel's café.

WORTH A TRIP

SAN ANTONIO AGUAS CALIENTES

This tranquil village surrounded by farmed volcanic slopes is noted for its textiles, and the **Mercado de Artesanías** (handicrafts market) stands prominently beside the town hall. Inside, women work on hip-strap looms and on the upper level there's an exhibit of traditional outfits, with examples from all over Guatemala. Ceremonial *huipiles*, embroidered on both sides, can go for as much as Q2800 here.

San Cristóbal El Alto

Just 3km south of Antigua along the road to Santa María de Jesús, San Cristóbal El Alto sits about 300m higher than its sister village down by the turnoff, a perch that affords superb views of the Panchoy valley. The forested slopes here are laced with trails, and members of the tight-knit community can guide you around. It's also a center for woodwork, pottery and textiles, which are displayed on the plaza every Sunday.

◎ Sights & Activities

Cerro San Cristóbal   GARDENS
(☑ 5941-8415; www.restcerrosancristobal.com; ⊙ tours Mon-Fri by request) **FREE** Perched on a hillside overlooking the Panchoy valley, this is a well-managed organic farm that's packed with small pleasures. Tours are given of a medicinal plant garden, neatly arrayed plots of organic veggies and a greenhouse full of orchids. There are also demonstrations by weavers on a bicycle-powered loom, a consecrated shrine to Maximón and a traditional sauna (Q300).

Cooperativa COSENDER   HIKING
(☑ 5560-5081; per person Q140) This community guide association leads half-day hikes from San Cristóbal El Alto up into the hills, then down to a gorge that's a sacred site for the community.

🛏 Sleeping & Eating

Casa Xicayá   GUESTHOUSE $
(☑ 5560-5081; veronicaxicayortega@yahoo.es; Calle Principal 41 Oriente; r per person incl breakfast Q160) San Cristóbal El Alto's single lodging option, two blocks east of the main square, enjoys a tranquil setting on grounds dotted with avocado and loquat trees. There are two options, both with bathroom: three upstairs rooms with volcano views, and a nine-bed cabin in the woods. The rate includes a huge breakfast with plenty of beans, plantains and tortillas.

Restaurant Cerro San Cristóbal   VEGETARIAN $
(☑ 5941-8145; www.restsancristobal.com; Calle Principal 5; mains Q35-50; ⊙ 8am-5:30pm Mon-Thu, 8am-8pm Fri-Sun) Contender for the slow food star of the Antigua area, this restaurant puts its own organically grown produce on the table. Giant salads are loaded with avocados, nasturtiums, greens and herbs from the surrounding gardens. They also serve tilapia from their own fish pond. Dine on a terrace with stupendous views of the Panchoy valley.

❶ Getting There & Away

Shuttles to Cerro San Cristóbal, about 1km below the center of the village, depart from Nim Po't (p83) crafts shop in Antigua between 8am and 6pm daily (Q10, 15 minutes).

San Juan Comalapa

Set on the side of a deep ravine, this village 16km north of Chimaltenango is best known for its tradition of primitive folk painting. Its setting is alluded to in its original Kaqchiquel name, Chixot, 'on the edge of a frying pan.' Though poor and a bit rundown, Comalapa is worth visiting for glimpses of both the realities and artistic reflections of contemporary Kaqchiquel life, particularly on market days (Tuesday, Friday and Sunday).

Comalapa gained its reputation during the 1950s when native son Andrés Curruchich (1891–1969) rose to fame for his primitive paintings of village life, ceremonies and legends, and his works ended up on display as far away as San Francisco, Dallas and Detroit. Considered the father of Guatemalan 'primitivist' painting, he was awarded the prestigious Order of the Quetzal.

Comalapa is also known as the birthplace of Rafael Álvarez Ovalle, composer of Guatemala's national anthem.

In 1976 a major earthquake caused widespread devastation in Comalapa and took the lives of 3500 inhabitants. The **Templo de San Juan Bautista**, the town's oldest church and a survivor of four previous quakes, was mostly toppled but later rebuilt. Scenes from the earthquake and other events appear on a major set of murals – at 184m reputedly the country's longest – that cover the walls along the southern approach. Painted by students in 2002, the panels allude to the origins of Maya culture and envision a possible future.

You can visit the house Curruchich was born in, on the main street. His daughter and granddaughter will show you around and there is some information about the artist. His legacy lives on as other villagers took up the brush and started working in a similar primitive style. Their works can be viewed at the **Galería de Arte Gabriel** (☑ 7849-8168; 0 Av 2-88; ☺ 9am-5pm) FREE and **Museo de Arte Maya** (☑ 5068-4047; 3a Calle 0-74, Zona 1; ☺ 8am-4pm Mon-Sat, 10:30am-4pm Sun), the latter also featuring archaeological finds and vintage photos.

🛏 Sleeping & Eating

Hotel Pixcayá   HOTEL **$**
(☑ 7849-8260; 0 Av 1-82; s/d with bathroom Q70/140, without bathroom Q40/80; 🅿) If you want to stay the night in Comalapa, your best bet is the Pixcayá, a block south of the church. It has three levels of neat and simple rooms around a plant-laden courtyard.

El Rinkoncito Chapin   GUATEMALAN **$**
(0 Av 251; mains Q25-50; ☺ 7am-9pm) The best choice for food is this friendly establishment on the main street with polished log tables and a brilliant panorama of the surrounding hills from the rear window. Grilled steaks and seafood are its specialty, and it serves Spanish wines.

❶ Getting There & Away

Buses (Q8, 45 minutes, every half hour) run from Chimaltenango; minibuses and pick-ups leave when full.

Santiago Sacatepéquez & Sumpango

All Saints' Day (November 1) is best known in Guatemala as the time when families visit cemeteries to spruce up the tombstones of loved ones with poignant floral designs, but locals add another quirk to this seasonal ritual. It's also the time of the **Feria del Barrilete Gigante** (Festival of the Giant Kite).

The biggest parties happen in Santiago Sacatepéquez and Sumpango, about 20km and 25km north of Antigua respectively. Fabricated weeks ahead of the event, these kites really are giants. Made from tissue paper with wood or bamboo braces, and with guide ropes as thick as a human arm, most are more than 13m wide, with intricate, colorful designs that combine Maya cosmology and popular iconography. In Santiago they're flown over the cemetery, some say to communicate with the souls of the dead. Kids fly their own small kites right in the cemetery, running around the gravestones. Food and knickknack vendors sell their wares next to the graveyard. In Sumpango it's a somewhat more formal affair (and the crowds are more manageable), with the kites lined up at one end of a football field and bleachers set up at the other. Judges rank the big flyers according to size, design, color, originality and elevation. Part of the fun is watching the crowd flee when a giant kite takes a nose dive!

Various travel agencies run day trips from Antigua to Santiago Sacatepéquez on November 1 (charging around Q200 per person including lunch and an English-speaking guide), though you can easily get there on your own by taking any Guatemala City–bound bus and getting off with the throngs at the junction for Santiago (Q4, 20 minutes). From here, take one of the scores of buses covering the last few kilometers (Q2.50, 15 minutes). The fastest way to Sumpango is to take a bus to Chimaltenango (Q5, 30 minutes) and backtrack to Sumpango (Q3, 15 minutes); this will bypass all of the Santiago-bound traffic, which is bumper to bumper on fair day.

ANTIGUA SANTIAGO SACATEPÉQUEZ & SUMPANGO

The Highlands

Best Places to Eat

➜ Restaurante Hana (p101)

➜ Café El Artesano (p113)

➜ Café Sabor Cruceño (p117)

➜ Allala (p115)

➜ Mayan Inn (p120)

Best Places to Sleep

➜ La Fortuna (p117)

➜ Mayan Inn (p120)

➜ Hacienda Mil Amores (p130)

➜ La Casa del Mundo (p116)

➜ Posada Rural Finca Chaculá (p156)

Why Go?

Guatemala's most dramatic region – El Altiplano – stretches from Antigua to the Mexican border. Traditional values and customs are strongest here. Maya dialects are spoken far more widely than Spanish, and over a dozen distinct groups dwell within the region, each with its own language and clothing. Such extraordinary diversity is perhaps most evident in the weekly markets of Chichicastenango and San Francisco El Alto. This is where indigenous tradition blends most tantalizingly with Spanish, and it is common to see Maya rituals taking place in front of and inside colonial churches.

Most travelers spend a spell at volcano-ringed Lago de Atitlán. West of the lake stands Guatemala's second city, Quetzaltenango. Northward spread the Cuchumatanes mountains, where indigenous life follows its own rhythms amidst fantastic mountain landscapes. For hikers, this is the promised land.

When to Go

If you're up for trekking the Ixil Triangle or scaling Volcán Santa María, trails tend to be less muddy and volcano visibility is best from November to April.

Key events to plan a trip around include Quetzaltenango's annual party (late September or early October); devil-burning ceremonies in Chichicastenango (early December); and folk saint Maximón's spring move in Santiago Atitlán (Holy Week).

Try to be in Todos Santos Cuchumatán on November 1, when the normally sedate town hosts a no-holds-barred celebration with rowdy horse races and all-male marimba dancing.

The Highlands Highlights

1 Soaring over, diving under or relaxing by sublime **Lago de Atitlán** (p92).

2 Hunting for *huipiles* (embroidered tunics) and other Maya weavings at vibrant indigenous markets in **Chichicastenango** (p118) and **San Francisco El Alto** (p145).

3 Upgrading your Spanish and ascending volcanoes in and around **Quetzaltenango** (p130).

4 Taking in the stunning scenery and village life of the Ixil Triangle around **Nebaj** (p125).

5 Mingling with the Maya in **Todos Santos Cuchumatán** (p152), **San Mateo Ixtatán** (p154) and other remote villages.

ℹ️ Getting Around

Public transportation connections between towns and villages in the highlands are easy and cheap, accommodations are plentiful, and people are generally welcoming and helpful, making it a cinch to get around.

The meandering Interamericana (Hwy 1), running 345km along the mountain ridges between Guatemala City and the Mexican border at La Mesilla, passes close to all of the region's most important places, and countless buses roar up and down it all day, every day. Two key intersections act as major bus interchanges: Los Encuentros for Panajachel and Chichicastenango, and Cuatro Caminos for Quetzaltenango and Huehuetenango. If you can't find a bus going to your destination, simply get one to either of those points. Transfers are usually seamless, with not-too-frustrating waiting times and locals who are ready to help travelers find the right bus.

Travel is easiest in the morning and, for smaller places, on market days. By mid- or late afternoon, buses may be scarcer. Further off the beaten track you may be relying more on pick-ups than buses for transportation.

Microbuses – large vans that depart as soon as they fill with passengers – are becoming the dominant mode of transport along highland routes such as Santa Cruz del Quiché–Nebaj and Chichicastenango–Los Encuentros. They're preferred by many locals for their convenience and are only slightly more expensive than buses.

Otherwise, vans run by tour operators shuttle tourists between the major destinations of the region and beyond. They are faster, more comfortable and more expensive than buses.

LAGO DE ATITLÁN

Nineteenth-century traveler/chronicler John L Stephens, writing in *Incidents of Travel in Central America,* called Lago de Atitlán 'the most magnificent spectacle we ever saw,' and he had been around a bit. Today even seasoned travelers marvel at this incredible environment. Fishermen in rustic crafts ply the lake's aquamarine surface, while indigenous women in multicolored outfits do their washing by the banks where trees burst into bloom. Fertile hills dot the landscape, and over everything loom the volcanoes, permeating the entire area with a mysterious beauty. No wonder many outsiders have fallen in love with the place and made their homes here.

Though volcanic explosions have been going on here for millions of years, today's landscape has its origins in the massive eruption of 85,000 years ago, termed Los Chocoyos, which blew volcanic ash as far away as Florida and Panama. The quantity of magma expelled from below the earth's crust caused the surface terrain to collapse, forming a huge, roughly circular hollow that soon filled with water – the Lago de Atitlán. Smaller volcanoes rose out of the lake's southern waters thousands of years later: Volcán San Pedro (today 3020m above sea level) about 60,000 years ago, followed by Volcán Atitlán (3537m) and Volcán Tolimán (3158m). The lake today is 8km across from north to south, 18km from east to west, and averages around 300m deep, though the water level has been on the rise since 2009.

Around AD 900, when the Maya highland civilization was in decline, the region was settled by two groups that had migrated from the Toltec capital of Tula in Mexico, the Kaqchiquel and Tz'utujil. The latter group settled at Chuitinamit, across the way from the present-day village of Santiago Atitlán, while the former occupied the lake's northern shores; this demographic composition persists to this day. By the time the Spanish showed up in 1524, the Tz'utujil had expanded their domain to occupy most of the lake shore. Pedro de Alvarado exploited the situation by allying with the Kaqchiquels against their Tz'utujil rivals, whom they defeated in a bloody battle at Tzanajuyú. The Kaqchiquels subsequently rebelled against the Spanish and were themselves subjugated by 1531.

Today, the main lakeside town is Panajachel, or 'Gringotenango' as it is sometimes unkindly called, and most people initially head here to launch their Atitlán explorations. Santiago Atitlán, along the lake's southern spur, has the strongest indigenous identity of any of the major lake towns. Up the western shore, the town of San Pedro La Laguna has a reputation as a countercultural party center. On the north side, San Marcos La Laguna is a haven for new-agers, while Santa Cruz La Laguna and Jaibalito, nearer to Panajachel, are among the lake's most idyllic, picturesque locales.

The lake is a three-hour bus ride west from Guatemala City or Antigua. There is an ersatz town at the highway junction of Los Encuentros, based on throngs of people changing buses here. From La Cuchilla junction, 2km further west along the Interamericana, a road descends 12km southward to Sololá, and then there's a sinuous 8km descent to Panajachel. Sit on the right-hand side of the bus for views of the lake and its surrounding volcanoes.

Sololá

POP 30,155 / ELEV 1978M

Long before the Spanish showed up, the Kaqchiquel town of Sololá held importance due to its location on trade routes between the *tierra caliente* (hot lands of the Pacific Slope) and *tierra fría* (the chilly highlands). Traders still meet here, and Sololá's **market** (⊙Tue & Fri) is one of the most vivid in the highlands.

An enormous new market building is under construction in front of the cathedral. Until it's finished, the sprawling Mercado Mayoreo (wholesale market), 10 blocks north (uphill) from the central plaza, is the stage for the twice-weekly market, held Tuesday and Friday, when the building and vicinity are ablaze with the colorful costumes of people from surrounding villages and towns. Displays of meat, vegetables, fruit, homewares and clothing are neatly arranged in every available space, with tides of buyers ebbing and flowing around the vendors. Elaborate stands are stocked with brightly colored yarn used to make the traditional costumes you see around you.

Sunday mornings the officers of the traditional *cofradías* (religious brotherhoods) parade ceremoniously to the cathedral.

◎ Sights

Museo de Sololá   MUSEUM
(Q10; ⊙9am-6pm Mon-Fri, 8am-5pm Sun) Housed atop the elaborate Swiss-built clock tower that fronts the city hall, the museum is devoted to photograph exhibits and the clock mechanism itself, though the biggest thrill is the view it affords down the slope to Lake Atitlán.

⌷ Sleeping & Eating

Hotel Cacique Ralón   HOTEL $$
(☑7762-4657; www.hotelcaciqueralon.webnode.es; 4a Calle 6-43; s/d/tr Q150/250/375; ℗) The best choice for lodging in Sololá is this tranquil retreat halfway between the bustling market and the central plaza. Simply adorned rooms and several terraces surround a garden studded with birds of paradise and an avocado tree, with a small cafe.

Comedor Eben Ezer   GUATEMALAN $
(6 Av; set lunch Q20; ⊙7am-6:30pm) This simple lunch hall at the base of the town hall is a gathering place for the Kaqchiquel community. Expect hearty helpings of such down-home fare as *caldo de res* (broth with meat and veggies) and *carne guisado* (stewed beef) with abundant side portions of rice and veggies.

⌂ Shopping

Mercado de Artesanías   HANDICRAFTS
(Handicrafts market; 6 Av) On the upper level of the town hall is this small but excellent market, displaying beautiful *huipiles,* beadwork, bags and other crafts produced by a cooperative of 30 indigenous groups from around Sololá department.

Panajachel

POP 10,238 / ELEV 1584M

The busiest and most built-up lakeside settlement, Panajachel ('Pana' to pretty much the entire country) has developed haphazardly and, some say, in a less-than-beautiful way. Strolling the main street, Calle Santander, crammed with cybercafes, travel agencies, handicraft hawkers and rowdy bars, dodging noisome *tuk-tuks* all the way, you may be forgiven for supposing this paradise lost.

A hike down to the lakeshore, though, will give you a better idea of why Pana attracts so many visitors. Aside from the astounding volcano panorama, the town's excellent transportation connections, copious accommodations, varied restaurants and thumping nightlife make it a favorite destination for weekending Guatemalans.

Several different cultures mingle on Panajachel's dusty streets. *Ladinos* (people of mixed indigenous and European heritage) and gringos control the tourist industry. The Kaqchiquel and Tz'utujil Maya from surrounding villages come to sell their handicrafts to tourists. Tour groups arrive by bus for a few hours or overnight. This mix makes Pana a curiously cosmopolitan crossroads in an otherwise remote, rural vicinity. All of this makes for a convenient transition into the Atitlán universe – but to truly experience the beauty of the lake, most travelers venture onward soon after arrival.

◎ Sights

Reserva Natural Atitlán   PARK
(☑7762-2565; www.atitlanreserva.com; adult/child Q50/25; ⊙8am-5pm) A former coffee plantation being retaken by natural vegetation, this reserve is 200m past the Hotel Atitlán on the northern outskirts of town. It makes a good outing on foot or bicycle. You can leisurely walk the main trail in an hour: it

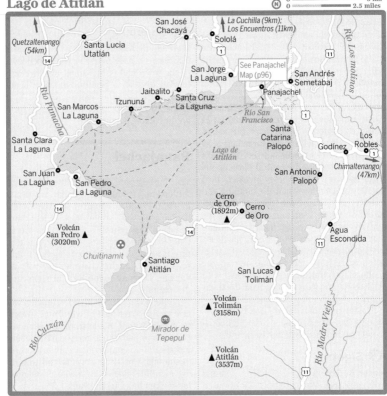

leads up over swing bridges to a waterfall, then down to a platform for viewing local spider monkeys.

You should also see pisotes (coatis), relatives of the raccoon with long snouts and long, upright, furry tails. The reserve includes a butterfly enclosure and herb garden, an interpretive center, a small coffee plantation and an aviary. For more extreme thrills, there are various zip lines spanning canyons and forest, the longest of which extends nearly a kilometer. For longer stays, there are some excellent rooms with private decks, and camping.

Casa Cakchiquel   ARTS CENTER
(☏ 7762-0969; Calle 14 de Febrero; ☺ 7am-8pm) Pana's cultural center started life as one of the first hotels on the lake, built by a Swedish countess in 1948. Now it holds a radio station, Japanese restaurant and a gallery of photos and postcards of Atitlán in simpler times, when steamboats plied the lake.

During its 1950s heyday such illustrious guests as Ingrid Bergman, Aldous Huxley and Ernesto 'Che' Guevara chatted around the fireplace.

La Galería   GALLERY
(☏ 7762-2432; panagaleria@hotmail.com; Calle Rancho Grande; ☺ 9am-noon & 2-6pm Wed-Mon) FREE Overflowing with art by Guatemalan painters and sculptors, this gallery functions as both an exhibit space and cultural center, hosting lectures, films and occasional concerts. Started in 1971 by Nan Cuz, an indigenous Guatemalan painter who resided in Germany during WWII, the gallery holds a number of the hallucinatory landscapes that garnered Cuz recognition in the European art world.

Museo Lacustre Atitlán   MUSEUM
(Calle Santander; Q35; ☺ 8am-6pm) Inside the Hotel Posada de Don Rodrigo, this museum has displays on the history of the Atitlán re-

gion and the volcanic eruptions that created its landscape, plus a collection of ancient artifacts recovered from the lake. A hall below the main gallery covers Samabaj, an ancient ceremonial center discovered at the bottom of the lake near Cerro de Oro.

🏃 Activities

Cycling, Hiking & Kayaking

Lago de Atitlán is a cycling and hiking wonderland, spreading across hill and dale. But before setting out for any hike or ride, make enquiries about safety with Proatur (p103), and keep asking as you go. Volcán San Pedro climbs via numerous operators in town cost around Q700 per person, including boat transportation, taxi to the trailhead, entry fees and guide. Kayaks are available for rent from **Diversiones Acuáticas Balam** (☑ 5514-8512; Playa Pública; per hour Q25), operating from a shed between the Santiago boat dock and the public beach.

Roger's Tours   CYCLING

(☑ 7762-6060; www.rogerstours.com; Calle Santander; bike rental per hour/day Q35/170) This outfit rents quality mountain bikes and leads a variety of cycling tours (Q460 per person including helmet, guide and lunch). One tour travels by boat from Panajachel to Tzununá, then by bike west via dirt trail to San Marcos La Laguna and road to San Pedro La Laguna, finally returning to Pana by boat.

Another tour hits the villages on the lake's east side.

Paragliding

'Too much of a good thing' is how Aldous Huxley described Lago de Atitlán in his 1934 travel work *Beyond the Mexique Bay*. That applies well to the experience of soaring over Lago de Atitlán with parachute-like wings, enjoying a falcon's view of the lake's rippling expanse and the villages that tumble down from green hills to its shores. The lake has become a center for paragliding enthusiasts and several operators provide tandem flights, with passengers seated in a canvas chair attached to the flyer's harness so they're free to take photos or simply gaze in amazement at the panorama below.

RealWorld Paragliding   GLIDING

(☑ 5634-5699; www.realworldparagliding.jimdo. com; Calle Santander, Centro Comercial San Rafael; tandem flights Q700) Certified by the US Hang Gliding & Paragliding Association,

Christian Behrenz is a patient, personable English-speaking guide who's made more than 2500 tandem flights. If wind conditions are right, you'll take off from above Santa Catarina Palopó and land at Panajachel. Flights last for 20 minutes to an hour, depending on the wind and passenger preferences.

In optimal conditions, you can fly as high as 700m above the lake (2300m above sea level). You might also do a few acrobatics, approaching the cliffs to pick up dynamic winds that lift you up like a wave.

🚣 Courses

Panajachel has a niche in the language-school scene. Two well-set-up schools are **Jardín de América** (☑ 7762-2637; www.jardindeam erica.com; Calle del Chalí) and **Jabel Tinamit** (☑ 7762-6056; www.jabeltinamit.com; cnr Avenida de Los Árboles & Callejón Las Armonías; 4/5 hours daily instruction per week Q880/1075, homestay per week additional Q650). The former is set amidst ample gardens while the latter is in the center of town. Four hours of one-on-one study five days per week, including a homestay with a local family, will cost around Q1500 per week.

🧭 Tours

If you're pressed for time, a boat tour of the lake, stopping at a few villages, is a fine idea. Boats leave the Playa Pública quay daily at 8:30am and 9:30am for tours to San Pedro, San Juan and Santiago Atitlán, stopping for an hour or two at each village; both return at 3:30pm and cost Q100 per person. The earlier tour also takes in San Marcos La Laguna. Travel agencies offer more extensive tours, which may include weaving demonstrations, visits to the shrine of Maximón in Santiago, and so on.

The women's empowerment organization Oxlajuj B'atz' (p102) offers day tours of Panajachel and other lakeside villages (Q340 per person, including lunch) with visits to its member weaving cooperatives.

Posada Los Encuentros   TOUR

(☑ 7762-2093; www.losencuentros.com; Callejón Chotzar 0-41) Offers half and full-day educational tours to lakeside villages, focusing on such topics as Maya medicine, Tz'utujil oil painting and organic coffee cultivation. Guide Richard Morgan is a scholar of Maya history and culture and longtime lake resident. Hiking tours and volcano climbs are also offered.

THE HIGHLANDS PANAJACHEL

Panajachel

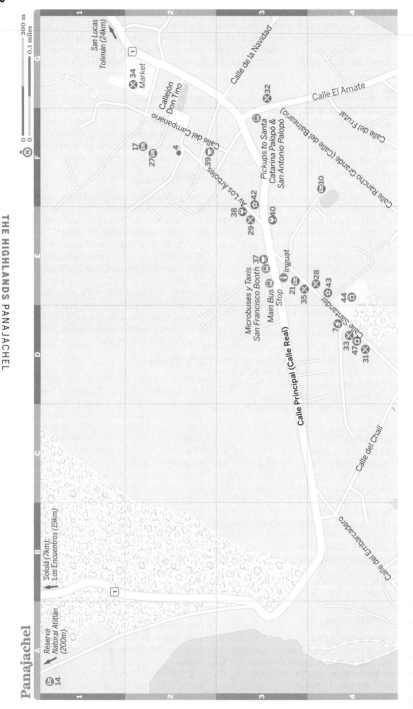

200 m
0.1 miles

Reserva
Natural Atitlán
(200m)
14

Sololá (7km);
Los Encuentros (19km)
1

San Lucas
Tolimán (24km)
1

34 Market
Callejón
Don Tino
Calle del Campanario

Calle de la Navidad
32
Calle El Amate

17
27
4
39
Pickups to Santa
Catarina Palopó &
San Antonio Palopó

Calle Rancho Grande (Calle del Balneario)
Calle del Frutal

Av Los Árboles
38
29 42
40
10

Microbuses y Taxis
San Francisco Booth
37
Main Bus
Stop
21
35
Inguat
28
43
44
Calle Principal (Calle Real)

Calle Santander
33
47
31

Calle del Chalí

Calle del Embarcadero

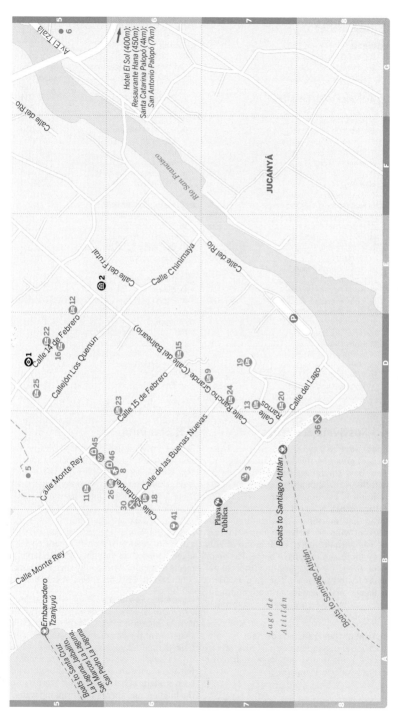

Panajachel

⚝ Festivals & Events

Independence Day   SPORTS
On September 14, the day before Independence Day, torch-bearing athletes run in marathons throughout the country, but the tradition is celebrated with special fervor in Panajachel, where it all started in 1957. Early that morning schoolchildren from different villages arrive in buses to visit the lake; around noon, each group of kids gets a torch and runs back home. The main event, though, is the marathon from Guatemala City to Panajachel. The runners arrive in Pana's main square around midnight, heralded by cheering crowds, marimbas and fireworks displays.

Festival of San Francisco de Asís   FERIA
The festival of San Francisco de Asís, on October 4, is celebrated with massive drinking and fireworks in Panajachel.

🛏 Sleeping

Budget travelers will rejoice at the profusion of family-run *hospedajes* (guesthouses). They're simple – perhaps two rough beds, a small table and a light bulb in a bare room – but cheap. The pricier ones offer generous discounts for longer stays.

Midrange lodgings are busiest on weekends. From Sunday to Thursday you may get a discount; likewise if you're planning on staying for longer than four days. Many establishments raise rates during July, August, Semana Santa and the Christmas–New Year holidays.

Hospedaje El Viajero   HOTEL $
(☑ 7762-0128; www.hospedajeelviajero.com; Final de la Av Santander; s/d/tr Q100/180/240; ☎) El Viajero is at the end of a short lane off lower Calle Santander, making it quiet and peaceful yet near everything. Nothing fancy here but the rooms are spacious and bright and there's plenty of balcony seating. You can use the kitchen, and there's free drinking water.

Villa Lupita
HOTEL **$**

(☎ 5054-2447; Callejón Don Tino; s/d Q75/150, s/d without bathroom Q50/100) Family-run Lupita is great value for the town center. Facing a plaza below the church, it's removed from the tourist drag. Accommodations are basic but nicely maintained, with art from San Juan wrapping around a flower-filled patio with broken-tile mosaic.

Mario's Rooms
HOTEL **$**

(☎ 7762-2370; www.mariosroomsatitlan.com; Calle Santander; s/d incl breakfast Q150/230; @) Among the best in the budget category, Mario's scrupulously maintained rooms are arranged on two floors facing a plant-filled courtyard. It's in the middle of everything but somehow remains low-key, with helpful staff.

Hospedaje Sueño Real
HOTEL **$**

(☎ 7762-0608; hotelsuenorealpana@hotmail.com; Calle Ramos; s/d from Q150/180; P @ 🛜) Better than most of the budget options along this lane, the Sueño Real has cheerfully decorated, if smallish, rooms with TV and fan. The best are the upstairs triples, opening on a plant-festooned lake-view terrace.

Hospedaje Casa Linda
GUESTHOUSE **$**

(☎ 7762-0386; Callejón El Capulin; r Q180, s/d/tr without bathroom Q80/160/180) Spotless little rooms surround a lush garden at this tranquil family-run establishment. Upstairs units get a nice breeze and the balconies are good for afternoon siestas. Ask Basilio, the kindly proprietor, for details of his next marimba performance.

Hotel Larry's Place
HOTEL **$**

(☎ 7762-0767; www.hotellarrysplace.com; Calle 14 de Febrero; r Q150; P) Set back from the road behind a wall of vegetation, Larry's Place offers good-sized, cool rooms in a sylvan setting. Furnishings are tasteful, ceilings high and the balconies welcome. No TV or internet, but who needs 'em anyway?

Hotel Jere
HOTEL **$**

(☎ 7762-2781; www.jerehotel.com; Calle Rancho Grande; s/d/tr Q100/125/180; P @) Jere's brick-walled rooms are enlivened with traditional textiles, and some open on to sun-splashed balconies. You can book shuttle buses and lake tours on the spot and rent bicycles.

Hotel Posada Viñas del Lago
HOTEL **$**

(☎ 7762-0389; braulio.pana@hotmail.com; Playa Pública; s/d/tr Q85/150/200; P @ 🛜) Steps from the lakefront, this garishly painted lodging is managed by a Kaqchiquel extend-ed family whose activities are on full view. Mattresses sag and water outages are common but the lake views make up for it, particularly from units 21 to 23.

Hospedaje García
HOTEL **$**

(☎ 7762-2187; Calle 14 de Febrero; s/d Q130/160, s/d without bathroom Q70/130; P 🛜) Located on a side street off Santander, this is a sprawling, airy place with an affable manager and numerous rooms of varying shape and size. If you don't mind the frayed furniture, some of the upper-level units are very good with huge bathrooms and balconies looking out onto the patio.

Jenna's River B&B
B&B **$$**

(☎ 5458-1984; www.jennasriverbedandbreakfast.com; Calle Rancho; s/d incl breakfast Q350/500; ☻ @ 🛜) Jenna's place, near the lake shore, has seven uniquely decked-out rooms, a studio apartment and a traditional Mongolian yurt that's starlit by night. Jenna and pooches welcome travelers to their tropically abundant garden, gazebo and breakfast room, where the table is set with fresh-baked bread and homemade jams.

Art, antiques and textiles adorn the rooms and can be bought in the adjacent shop.

Posada Los Encuentros
LODGE **$$**

(☎ 7762-1603; www.losencuentros.com; Callejón Chotzar 0-41; s/d incl breakfast Q300/335, s/d with kitchen Q380/420; @ 🛜) Just across the river is this 'ecocultural B&B,' featuring seven cozy rooms in a relaxed home, plus a volcanically heated tub, medicinal plant garden, sunning terrace and fitness center. Owner Richard Morgan is happy to share his encyclopedic knowledge of the lake and offers cultural tours (p95) of the area.

Hotel Utz-Jay
HOTEL **$$**

(☎ 7762-0217; www.hotelutzjay.com; Calle 15 de Febrero 2-50; s/d/tr from Q225/360/495; P @ 🛜) These eight adobe cottages stand amidst lovely gardens bursting with heliconia, orange trumpet and ferns where no fewer than 46 types of birds have been spotted. Rooms are decorated with traditional fabrics and have cozy porches out front. Good breakfasts are available and there's a *chuj* (traditional Maya sauna).

The attentive staff can also arrange shuttles, make you a box lunch or do your laundry.

Posada de los Volcanes
HOTEL **$$**

(☎ 7762-0244; www.posadadelosvolcanes.com; Calle Santander 5-51; s/d incl breakfast from

Q380/460) Sharing the property with its own travel agency, this chalet-style lodging has lovely pine-paneled rooms. On the 4th floor, you'll be rewarded with your own private terrace, suitable for kicking back with cocktails and surveying the lake.

Hotel Montana   HOTEL $$
(☑ 7762-0326; atitlanhotelmontana@hotmail.com; Callejón Don Tino; s/d Q175/275; P) Down a narrow street near the church, the Montana is an old-fashioned establishment with wonderful plant-laden balconies fronted by pot-bellied railing. Choose a room on the upper level for brilliant views of the mountainside.

Hotel Posada K'amol B'ey   HOTEL $$
(☑ 7762-0215; hotelkamolbey@yahoo.com; Final Calle Ramos; r/bungalows for 5 people Q150/550; P 🛜) At the end of the row of hotels leading up from the Playa Pública, the 'king of the road' is about the tidiest and quietest option, and everything works. Two levels of spacious units with quality beds face a clipped suburban lawn where hummingbirds flit around. At the rear are three bungalows, each with two rooms and kitchen.

Hotel El Sol   HOTEL $$
(☑ 7762-6090; www.hotelelsolpanajachel.com; Carretera a Santa Catarina Palopó; dm/s/d/tr Q60/160/210/260; P 🛜) Along the road to Santa Catarina, about a 15-minute walk or lightning *tuk-tuk* ride outside Pana, this modern hostel is a slice of Japan. Hailing from Hiroshima, owner Kazuomi and family offer free bicycles, use of a kitchen and a tub fed by natural hot springs. Accommodations include an eight-bed dorm and five private rooms.

Hotel Utz Rajil   HOTEL $$
(☑ 7762-0303; www.hotelutzrajil.webs.com; Calle 14 de Febrero; s/d/tr Q125/200/275; 🛜) A modern, three-story hotel with 13 large, well-maintained rooms and quality furniture, the Utz Rajil (Kaqchiquel for 'good deal') features cool balconies for photo ops of the street activity below. (Don't expect to get any sleep past 6am, though.)

Hotel Primavera   HOTEL $$
(☑ 7762-2052; www.primaveraatitlan.com; Calle Santander; r Q300; 🛜) This stylish Norwegian-owned hotel near Pana's main intersection just feels right. Ten large rooms with plant-filled window boxes, soft lighting and handsome fabrics face a sleek wood-decked patio, making for a relaxing atmosphere. Chez Alex, the restaurant downstairs, serves foie gras, escargot *und wienerschnitzel* in a Euro-toned setting.

Hotel Atitlán   HERITAGE HOTEL $$$
(☑ 7762-1441; www.hotelatitlan.com; Finca San Buenaventura; r incl breakfast from Q1450; P @ 🛜 ⛅) A coffee plantation for much of the 20th century, this estate was remade as Pana's loveliest hotel in the 1970s. Located on the lake shore 1.5km northwest of the town center, it's a rambling, semicolonial affair surrounded by manicured tropical gardens.

The 60 rooms all have lake-facing balconies; decorations go heavy on religious imagery, wood carvings and wrought iron. A restaurant, bar and lakefront pool with killer volcano views ensure you'll never want to leave the premises.

Casa Texel   HOTEL $$$
(☑ 7762-2076; www.casatexel.com; Calle Rancho Grande; s/d/tr incl breakfast Q445/843/1134; P 🛜) This pristine new hotel a block from the lakefront is a semiluxurious spread with a proper dose of indigenous style (*texel* is the Kaqchiquel term for the wife of a religious leader). Rooms on three levels line up along brick balconies with terraces at the end. Decor is modern with colorful bedspreads, pretty tiles, cast-iron fixtures and vintage photos.

Hotel Posada de Don Rodrigo   HOTEL $$$
(☑ 7832-9858; www.posadadedonrodrigo.com; Calle Santander; d/ste from Q1225/1400; P ⛅) Down by the lakeside, this hotel has landscaped grounds that hold many delights – squash courts, a swimming pool with waterslide, a couple of saunas and a fine museum. Large rooms are decorated in colonial style and open onto the lawn. Breakfast is served on the fabulous lake-view terrace.

✖️ Eating
Near the south end of Calle del Lago, an agglomeration of thatched-roof restaurants crowds the lakefront. All serve lake *mojarra* (bream, Q95) and black bass (Q140), with skinny, bow-tied youths taking your order. Restaurante El Atitlán, the last one on the left, offers the best quality and variety.

Another obvious choice for cheap meals are the myriad taco and fried chicken stalls that proliferate along Calle Santander every afternoon and evening. You might try the appropriately named **Humo en Tus Ojos**, last spotted near the intersection of Calles Principal and Santander; this is where the cops eat.

For food shopping, there's the Despensa Familiar (p102), at the north end of Calle El Amate.

Chero's Bar
SALVADORAN $

(Av Los Árboles; pupusas Q10; ⏰12:30pm-1am Tue-Sat) Located in the nightlife zone, Chero's can get pretty lively, with beer-drinking patrons gathering around simple wood tables as *tuk-tuks* zip by. Salvadoran staff slap out *pupusas,* either straight up or filled with such items as *güicoy* (a kind of squash) or the spinach-like herb *chipilín*, and served with the customary pickled cabbage and salsa.

Fuentes de Vida
GUATEMALAN $

(market; lunch Q20; ⏰7:30am-4pm) This is the largest of a group of rather rustic cook stalls at the rear of the market building, near the pork vendors. It offers half a dozen menu options daily, all of which come with beans, tortillas and a fiery salsa made from dried red chilies.

Deli Jasmín
ORGANIC $

(☑7762-2585; Calle Santander; items Q25-45; ⏰7am-6pm Wed-Mon; ✏️) This tranquil garden restaurant serves a range of healthy foods and drinks to the strains of soft classical music. Breakfast is served all day, and you can buy whole-wheat or pita bread, hummus or mango chutney to take away.

Café Loco
CAFE $

(Calle Santander; ⏰9am-8pm Tue-Sun, 3-8pm Mon) The latest wrinkle in Pana's crazy quilt of storefronts is this Korean-run cafe, which has caught the fancy of the travelers who crowd the long counter. The youthful staff set up a formidable range of espresso variations, from 'Brown Cloud' (a small espresso with a bit of milk and foam) to 'Habana Blues,' with brown sugar sprinkled over espresso grounds.

★Restaurante Hana
JAPANESE $$

(☑4298-1415; www.restaurantehana.com; Calle 14 de Febrero; mains Q65-85; ⏰noon-9pm Tue-Sun) Serving absolutely authentic Japanese cuisine, Hana is ensconced in the serene courtyard of the Casa Cakchiquel (p94) graced by hanging plants and a gallery of photos of old Pana. Besides preparing such classics as nigiri sushi, sashimi and tempura, Chef Mihoko does *uramaki* ('inside-out' sushi), *donburi* and cold udon noodles just as they're done in her native Japan.

Mister Jon's
AMERICAN $$

(☑4710-8697; www.mister-jon.com; Calle Santander; breakfast Q35-50; ⏰7am-10pm Tue-Sun;

☎) All the perks of a US diner are here in abundance, including buttermilk pancakes, great omelets with hash browns or country biscuits on the side, and free coffee refills (of Guatemala's finest). But it's no gringo ghetto – *chapínes* (Guatemalans) who've been up north like it, too.

Guajimbo's
STEAK $$

(☑7762-0063; Calle Santander; mains Q60-95; ⏰7:30am-9:30pm Fri-Wed) This Uruguayan grill serves up generous helpings of steak, sausage and chicken dishes with vegetables, salad, garlic bread and rice or boiled potatoes. Vegetarians can enjoy tofu kebabs. You won't leave hungry.

El Patio
GUATEMALAN $$

(☑7762-2041; Plaza Los Patios, Calle Santander; mains Q38-60; ⏰7am-9:30pm) This is a locally popular joint for lunch; the front terrace makes an obvious meeting place. Try to make it for Monday lunch when everyone chows down on *caldo de res* (chunky broth), served with all the trimmings.

Deli Llama de Fuego
ORGANIC $$

(☑7762-2586; Calle Santander; items Q40-55; ⏰7am-9pm Thu-Tue) Offering a variety of healthy food and drink, this natural-foods haven revolves around a *llama de fuego* tree (African tulip).

Restaurante El Atitlán
SEAFOOD $$

(Calle del Lago; black bass Q140; ⏰7am-9pm) The last of a string of thatched-roof restaurants along the lakefront, El Atitlán offers the best quality and variety. The main draw, aside from the stunning setting, is the lake fish, highlighted by *mojarra* (bream) and black bass.

Las Chinitas
ASIAN $$

(Calle Santander, Plaza Los Patios; mains Q45-60; ⏰8am-10pm; ✏️) Indonesian-run Las Chinitas has a pan-Asian menu – miso, Singapore salad, stir-frys and pot stickers, as well as changing *menú del día* features with tofu and shiitake mushrooms. Dining is under the open-air dome of the Centro Comercial El Patio.

Chez Alex
EUROPEAN $$$

(☑7762-0172; www.primaveraatitlan.com; Calle Santander, Hotel Primavera; mains Q135-160; ⏰noon-10pm) The restaurant component of the Hotel Primavera serves some of Pana's finest cuisine, with a hefty dash of European influence. After a meal of mussels in white-wine sauce or Camembert-stuffed schnitzel, kick back with a Habana cigar.

Despensa Familiar SUPERMARKET
(Calle El Amate) Self-caterers will find all they need at this large, well-stocked supermarket.

🍷 Drinking & Nightlife

Panajachel's miniature Zona Viva (party zone) focuses on Av Los Árboles.

★ Crossroads Café CAFE
(☑ 5292-8439; www.crossroadscafepana.com; Calle del Campanario 0-27; ⊙ 9am-1pm & 2:30-6pm Tue-Sat) Bay Area native Mike Roberts has made Panajachel a major crossroads for coffee aficionados. When he's not roasting beans or working the Cimbali at his narrow cafe near the center of town, Mike spends his time combing the highlands for small estate coffees to add to his roster, now starring the tangy Acatenango Eighth Wonder and smooth Huehue Organic.

La Palapa PUB
(Calle Principal; ⊙ 9am-1am) As the name suggests, this party center unfolds beneath a thatched-roof shelter (actually two), with a beachy ambiance. It's favored by Peace Corps volunteers and other gringos, but all sorts crowd in for the Saturday afternoon BBQ. There's a convenient hostel round back for those who've neglected to secure a bed (Q61 per person). Diversions include live music Friday and Saturday nights, trivia quiz Thursdays and sports TV.

Café La Parada CAFE
(Centro Comercial El Dorado; ⊙ 6am-7pm; 🛜) Right by the main bus stop (hence the name), this friendly cafe is popular with local travelers for its excellent iced coffee and free wi-fi.

Chapiteau CLUB
(☑ 7762-2056; Av Los Árboles; ⊙ 7pm-1am Wed-Sat) This strobe-lit disco-bar is the anchor of Pana's little Zona Viva. Check out the phantasmagoric marquee before you cross the threshold.

Sunset Café BAR
(cnr Calles Santander & del Lago; ⊙ 11am-11pm) This open-air lounge at the end of Calle Santander is the place to enjoy those dreamlike volcano sundowns. In high season, there's live music Friday to Sunday evenings.

☆ Entertainment

Circus Bar LIVE MUSIC
(☑ 7762-2056; Av Los Árboles; ⊙ noon-midnight) Behind the swinging doors, Circus Bar has a cabaret atmosphere, with live music nightly from 7:30 to 10:30pm. Flamenco, folk or marimbas nicely complement the cozy atmosphere, as do the substantial list of imported liquors, Q10 cocktails and good pizza.

Pana Rock Café LIVE MUSIC
(☑ 7762-2194; Calle Santander 1-74) Like a Hard Rock by the lake, this lively little pub hosts plugged-in bands nightly from 9pm. It's big with Guatemala City youth, who settle in with a *cubetazo* (bucket of beer) or two.

🔒 Shopping

Some travelers prefer the Pana shopping scene to the well-known market at Chichicastenango (p118) because the atmosphere is lower key. Calle Santander is lined with booths, stores and complexes that sell (among other things) traditional Maya clothing, jade, Rasta berets with built-in dreadlocks, colorful blankets, leather goods and wood carvings. Otherwise, head for the traditional market building in the town center, busiest on Sundays when every square meter of ground alongside is occupied by vendors in indigenous garb.

La Señora de Cancuén CLOTHING
(☑ 7762-2602; Calle Santander; ⊙ 9:30am-7pm) Displays the innovative clothing and jewelry of Guatemalan designer Ana Kayax, produced by indigenous weavers and craftspeople from around Guatemala. There's a story behind every item sold here.

Libros del Lago BOOKS
(Calle Santander; ⊙ 10am-6:30pm) Excellent books in English and other tongues on Guatemala, the Maya and Mesoamerica, plus maps and Latin American literature in English.

The Book Store BOOKS
(Calle Santander, Centro Comercial El Patio; ⊙ 9am-6pm) Eclectic selection of fiction and nonfiction run by a well-read gringo; also features a lending library.

Oxlajuj B'atz' HANDICRAFTS
(Thirteen Threads; ☑ 7762-2921; www.oxlajujbatz.org.gt; Plaza Hotel Real Santander; ⊙ 10am-6pm) Supporting an NGO for the empowerment of indigenous women, this fair-trade shop features naturally dyed rugs, handbags, hand-woven goods and beaded jewelry.

Comerciales de Artesanías Típicas Tinamit Maya HANDICRAFTS
(⊙ 7am-7pm) Be sure to browse the many stalls of this extensive handicrafts market, which has an impressive variety of bags,

clothing, blankets, belts and hammocks. More booths line up along the beach end of Calle Santander.

ℹ️ Orientation

Most buses stop at the intersection of Calle Principal and Calle Santander, the main road to the lake with a plethora of lodgings and other tourist-oriented businesses. Calle Principal continues 400m to 500m northeast to the town center, where you'll find the daily market (busiest on Sunday and Thursday), church, town hall and a further smattering of places to sleep and eat.

ℹ️ Information

EMERGENCY

Proatur (Programa de Asistencia al Turista; 📞 5874-9450; proatur.solola@gmail.com; Calle Rancho Grande; 🕐 9am-5pm)

INTERNET ACCESS

MayaNet (Calle Santander, Centro Comercial El Patio)

MEDICAL SERVICES

Pana Medic (📞 4892-3499; drzulmashalom@hotmail.com; Calle Principal 0-72) Clinic run by an English-speaking doctor.

MONEY

Banco de América Central (Calle Santander, Centro Comercial San Rafael; 🕐 9am-5pm Mon-Fri, 9am-1pm Sat) Reliable ATM; Visa, American Express and MasterCard cash advances.

Banco Industrial (Calle Santander, Comercial Los Pinos; 🕐 9am-4pm Mon-Fri, 9am-1pm Sat) Visa/MasterCard ATM.

POST

DHL (Calle Santander, Edificio Rincón Sai) Courier service.

Post Office (cnr Calles Santander & 15 de Febrero)

RealWorld Export (📞 7762-0543; Calle Santander, Centro Comercial San Rafael) For bulk shipments (over 100kg), this reliable outfit offers competitive rates.

TOURIST INFORMATION

INGUAT (📞 2421-2953; info-pana@inguat. gob.gt; Calle Principal 1-47; 🕐 9am-5pm) This tourist office is opposite the main bus stop on Calle Principal 50m west of Calle Santander. The English-speaking director provides a wealth of information.

TRAVEL AGENCIES

Atitrans (📞 7762-0146; www.atitranspana-jachel.com; Calle Santander; 🕐 8am-8pm) Trips, tours and shuttle services.

Eternal Spring (📞 7762-6043; eternalspring_conexiones@hotmail.com; Calle Santander) Shuttles to San Cristóbal de Las Casas, Mexico.

Magic Travel (📞 7762-0755; www.magictravel. com.gt; Calle Santander, Edificio Rincón Sai) Interesting tours with English-speaking guides. Reliable shuttle services to San Cristóbal de Las Casas daily at 6:30am.

ℹ️ Getting There & Away

BOAT

Passenger boats for Santiago Atitlán (35 minutes) depart from the Playa Pública (public beach) at the foot of Calle Rancho Grande. All other departures leave from the Embarcadero Tzanjuyú, at the foot of Calle del Embarcadero. Frequent canopied *lanchas* (small motorboats) go counterclockwise around the lake, with direct and local service to San Pedro La Laguna. The local services stop in Santa Cruz La Laguna (15 minutes), Jaibalito, Tzununá, San Marcos La Laguna (30 minutes), San Juan La Laguna and San Pedro La Laguna (45 minutes). The first boat to San Pedro departs at 7am, the last around 7:30pm.

One-way passage to San Pedro, Santiago or San Lucas costs Q25 (though local inhabitants are charged less). *Lanchas* are also available for private hire from the Playa Pública or Embarcadero Tzanjuyú: expect to pay around Q400 to San Pedro La Laguna.

SHUTTLE MINIBUS

Tourist shuttle buses take half the time of buses, for several times the price. You can book at a number of travel agencies on Calle Santander. The **Microbuses y Taxis San Francisco booth** (📞 7762-0556; mitafsa_56@hotmail.com; Calle Principal) near the main bus stop also sells shuttle-bus seats.

Typical one-way fares include Antigua (Q95), Chichicastenango (round trip Thu & Sun; Q95), Guatemala City (Q175), San Cristóbal de Las Casas, Mexico (Q280) and Quetzaltenango (Q150).

Around Panajachel

Southeast of Pana, 5km and 10km respectively along a winding road, lie the lakeside hamlets of Santa Catarina Palopó and San Antonio Palopó. (The name 'Palopó' is a Spanish-Kaqchiquel amalgam referring to a type of fig tree that grows here.) Compared with nearby Pana, the Palopós feel sublimely remote, with narrow streets paved in stone blocks and adobe houses with roofs of thatch or tin. Many villagers, both men and women, go about their daily activities clad in traditional outfits, and these are good places

BUSES FROM PANAJACHEL

Panajachel's main bus stop is at the junction of Calles Santander and Principal, immediately west of the Centro Comercial El Dorado. Departures – approximately and subject to change – are as follows:

DESTINATION	FARE	TIME	FREQUENCY	ALTERNATIVE
Antigua	Q45	2½hr	A direct bus by Transportes Rebuli departs at 11am Monday to Saturday.	Or take a Guatemala City bus and change at Chimaltenango.
Chichicastenango	Q20	1½hr	Five buses depart between 6:45am and 6pm daily.	Or take any bus heading to Los Encuentros (via Sololá) and change buses there.
Ciudad Tecún Umán (Mexican border)				By the Pacific route (via Mazatenango) take a bus to Cocales and change there; by the highland route, transfer at Quetzaltenango.
Guatemala City	Q35	3½hr	Five departures daily from 4:30am to 3pm by Transportes Rebuli.	Or take a bus to Los Encuentros (via Sololá) and change there.
Huehuetenango		3½hr		Take a bus to Los Encuentros (via Sololá), then wait for a Huehue- or La Mesilla–bound bus. Or catch one heading to Quetzaltenango, alight at Cuatro Caminos and change buses there. There are buses at least hourly from these junctions.
Los Encuentros	Q5.50	40min		Take one of the frequent buses to Sololá, from where there are buses to Los Encuentros every 10 minutes until 6 pm.
Quetzaltenango	Q25	2½hr	Four buses daily starting at 5am, the last leaving at 1pm.	Or take a bus to Los Encuentros (via Sololá) and change there.
Sololá	Q3	15min	Every 10 minutes from 7am to 7pm.	

to look for the luminescent indigo weavings you see all around Lago de Atitlán. Also out here is a surprising little clutch of midrange and top-end places to stay.

Santa Catarina Palopó

POP 4976 / ELEV 1585M

On weekends and holidays textile vendors line the path to the lakeside at Santa Catarina Palopó, and you can step into wooden storefronts hung thick with bright cloth.

🛏 Sleeping

Villa Santa Catarina HOTEL $$$
(☎ 7762-1291; www.villasdeguatemala.com; s/d/ste Q790/935/1400; P@✆) In stark contrast to its humble surroundings stands this luxury spread with elegant restaurant and pool fringed by palm trees and sumptuous gardens. The 38 spacious and simply furnished rooms sport tasteful weavings and cool adobe walls. Rooms 23 to 27 (partly) and the two suites face across the lake to Volcán San Pedro.

ℹ Getting There & Away

Pick-ups to Santa Catarina leave about every half hour from Calle El Amate in Panajachel, near its intersection with Calle Principal (Q3, 20 minutes). The last pick-up back to Pana leaves about 6pm.

San Antonio Palopó

POP 4035 / ELEV 1773M

San Antonio Palopó is a remote and captivating hillside village where entire families tend their terraced fields in traditional garb – women in indigo-striped *huipiles* (long embroidered tunics), dark blue *cortes* (long skirts) and sparkly headbands, and men in traditional wool skirts. At the top, a gleaming white church forms the center of activity. About 150m down the path to the right, the **Tienda Candelaria** houses a weaving cooperative where women produce shawls, *huipiles* and *tocoyales* (headdresses) on backstrap looms and get a fair price for them.

🛏 Sleeping

⭐**Hotel Terrazas del Lago**　　HOTEL **$$**
(☑7762-0157; www.hotelterrazasdellago.com; s/d/tr Q180/240/310; [P][🤙]) At this magical and affordable retreat, 15 attractive stone-walled rooms climb the hillside, with small terraces and hammocks. Good inexpensive meals (Q50 to Q80) are served on the lakefront deck with views straight across to Volcán Tolimán.

❶ Getting There & Away

Pick-ups to San Antonio leave about every half-hour from Calle El Amate in Panajachel, near its intersection with Calle Principal (Q5, 30 minutes). The last pick-up back to Pana leaves San Antonio about 6pm.

San Lucas Tolimán

POP 12,675 / ELEV 1591M

Further around the lake from San Antonio Palopó, but reached by a different, higher-level road, San Lucas Tolimán is busier and more commercial than most lakeside villages. Set at the foot of the dramatic Volcán Tolimán, it's a coffee-growing town and a transportation point on a route between the Interamericana and the Carretera al Pacífico. Market days are Sunday, Tuesday and Friday. Atypically not standing on the town's plaza but along the street to the lakefront is the 16th-century **Parroquia de San Lucas** parish church. The parish, aided by Catholic missionaries from Minnesota and volunteers from North America and Europe, has been active in redistributing coffee-plantation land, setting up a fair-trade coffee cooperative and founding a women's center, a clinic and a reforestation program. For visits to the cooperative and information on volunteering, contact the **parish office** (☑7722-0112; www.sanlucasmission.org).

🛏 Sleeping

Hotel Don Pedro　　HOTEL **$**
(☑7722-0028; Final de Calle Principal; s/d/tr Q60/130/190; [P][🤙]) Down by the waterfront, this hotel is made entirely of stone and rough-hewn timber beams. The unfinished construction feels like a medieval inn, and the relaxed restaurant/bar (meals Q45 to Q80) sports the same motif.

Hotel Tolimán　　HOTEL **$$$**
(☑7722-0033; www.hoteltoliman.com; Calle Principal Final; s/d incl breakfast from Q520/640; [P][🤙][🏊]) This is a low-key resort on the site of a former coffee-processing plant, with 20 colonial-style rooms and suites in cottages around a spreading *amate* tree. A terrace restaurant overlooks a fountain-fed pool on landscaped grounds leading down to the lakeshore.

❶ Getting There & Away

From Panajachel, take any bus heading for Cocales, get off at Santa Alicia and walk or take a *tuk-tuk* 1km into town.

Santiago Atitlán

POP 28,665 / ELEV 1606M

Across the lake from Panajachel, on an inlet between the volcanoes of Tolimán and San Pedro, lies Santiago Atitlán, the largest of the lake communities, with a strong indigenous identity. Many *atitecos* (as its people are known) proudly adhere to a traditional Tz'utujil Maya lifestyle. Women wear purple-striped skirts and *huipiles* embroidered with colored birds and flowers, while older men still wear lavender or maroon striped embroidered pants. The town's *cofradías* maintain the syncretic traditions and rituals of Maya Catholicism. There's a large arts and crafts scene here, too. Boatbuilding is a local industry, and rows of rough-hewn *cayucos* (dugout canoes) are lined up along the shore. The best days to visit are Friday and Sunday, the main market days, but any day will do.

It's the most workaday of the lake villages, home to Maximón (mah-shee-*mohn*), who is ceremonially moved to a new home on May 8 (after Semana Santa). The rest of the year, Maximón resides with a caretaker, receiving offerings. He changes house every year, but he's easy enough to find by asking around.

The Tz'utujil had been in this area for generations when the Spanish arrived, with

WORTH A TRIP

IXIMCHÉ

The remnants of the Kaqchiquels' 15th-century capital stand some 15km due east of Lago de Atitlán. The 'palaces' and temples uncovered here are modest in scale but ensconced in a serene, park-like setting. Iximché remains an important ceremonial site for indigenous pilgrims, who visit the area to perform magic rituals, burning liquor, paraffin or sticks of wood in front of the pyramids to ward off illness or bring down enemies.

K'icab the Great, leader of the Kaqchiquels, relocated his capital here in 1463 from its previous location near the K'iche' Maya stronghold of K'umarcaaj. At that time, the Kaqchiquel were at war with the K'iche', and the natural defences of the new location, a flat promontory surrounded by ravines, served them well. The Spanish, who arrived in 1524, set up their first Guatemalan headquarters here, forming an alliance with the resident Kaqchiquels against their K'iche' enemies. However, the Europeans' demands for gold and other loot soon put an end to their alliance with the Kaqchiquel, who were defeated in an ensuing guerrilla war.

Entering the archaeological site (Q50; ⊗ 8am-4:00pm), visit the small museum (closed Monday) on the right, then continue to the four ceremonial plazas, which are surrounded by temple structures up to 10m high, and ball courts. Some structures have been uncovered; on a few the original plaster coating is still in place.

The ruins are reached from the town of Tecpán, off the Interamericana. Buses traveling east from La Cuchilla junction can drop you at the turnoff; from there it's about a 1km walk (or, if you're lucky, a short ride on an urban bus) to the center of town. 'Ruinas' microbuses to the site (Q5, 10 minutes) leave from near Tecpán's main plaza every 15 minutes till 4pm. The last bus back leaves the site no later than 4:30pm.

their ceremonial capital at Chuitinamit, across the inlet. Santiago was established by Franciscan friars in 1547, as part of the colonial strategy to consolidate the indigenous population. In the 1980s left-wing guerrillas had a strong presence in the area, prompting the Guatemalan army to kill or disappear hundreds of villagers.

◉ Sights

**Cojolya Association of
Maya Women Weavers** MUSEUM
(☑ 7721-7268; www.cojolya.org; Calle Real, Comercial Las Máscaras, 2nd fl; donation requested; ⊗ 9am-5pm Mon-Fri, 9am-2pm Sat) This small museum is devoted to the art of backstrap loom weaving. The well-designed exhibit shows the history of the craft and the process from spinning the cotton fibers to the finished textile. There are also daily demonstrations of backstrap loom techniques, and a small shop.

**Iglesia Parroquial
Santiago Apóstol** CHURCH
The formidable parish church was built by the Franciscans in the mid-16th century. A memorial plaque just inside the entrance on your right commemorates Father Stanley Francis Rother, a missionary priest from Oklahoma. Beloved by the local people, Rother was murdered by ultrarightists in the par-

ish rectory next door in 1981; the bedroom where he slept remains open to visitors.

Along the walls of the church are wooden statues of the saints, each of whom has new clothes made by local women every year. At the front stand three colonial altarpieces that were renovated between 1976 and 1981 by brothers Diego Chávez Petzey and Nicolás Chávez Sojuel. These symbolize the three volcanoes around Santiago, which are believed to protect the town. The central one was subtly changed from a traditional European vision of heaven to a more Maya representation of a sacred mountain with two *cofradía* members climbing towards a sacred cave.

Parque de Paz MEMORIAL
(Peace Park) During the civil war Santiago became the first village in the country to succeed in expelling the army, following a notorious massacre of 13 villagers on December 2, 1990. The site of this massacre, where troops were encamped, is now the Parque de Paz, about 1km south of the Parque Central along the road toward San Pedro La Laguna.

Parque Central PLAZA
Here you'll find a stone monument that commemorates Concepción Ramírez, the woman on the back of the 25-centavo coin, and a basin that contains a relief version of the lake.

☂ Activities

There are several rewarding day hikes around Santiago. Most enticing of all are the three volcanoes in the vicinity: Tolimán, Atitlán and San Pedro. Before attempting a climb, enquire about the current security situation. It's best to go with a guide; the Posada de Santiago can set up a reliable one. Guided volcano climbs run about Q425 for two to five people.

Less daunting a challenge than the massive volcanoes in the vicinity, Cerro de Oro (1892m) still yields great views and features several Maya ceremonial sites. It's some 8km northeast, about halfway between Santiago and San Lucas Tolimán.

Milpas Tours leads a variety of fascinating tours in and around Santiago Atitlán. They can take you to the Tz'utujil community of Chuk Muk on the slopes of Volcán Tolimán, with an unexcavated archaeological site; show you the temporary shrine devoted to locally worshiped saint Maximón (Q170); or visit the workshops of local weavers, painters and sculptors and chefs.

Another worthy destination is the Mirador de Tepepul, about 4km south of Santiago, near where the inlet ends (four to five hours round trip, Q225 per person). The hike goes through cloud forest populated with many birds, including parakeets, curassows, swifts, boat-tailed grackles and tucanets, and on to a lookout point with views all the way to the coast.

The pre-Hispanic Tz'utujil capital of Chuitinamit is across the inlet from Santiago. The hilltop archaeological site features some carved petroglyphs as well as some fanciful painted carvings of more recent vintage. From the dock, it's a 20-minute hike to the top, where there are good views of Santiago. Milpas Tours can take you across the inlet by *cayuco* and accompany you up the tenuous trail to the site.

☞ Tours

Dolores Ratzan Pablo CULTURAL TOUR

(☎ 5730-4570; dolores_ratzan@yahoo.com) This English-speaking Tz'utujil woman can introduce you to the wonders of Maya birthing and healing, point out examples of Maya-Catholic syncretism at the church and *cofradías,* and describe the incidents that led to the massacre at the Parque de Paz in 1990. Tours typically last two hours and cost Q300 per person.

Milpas Tours CULTURAL TOUR

(☎ 5450-2381; milpastours@yahoo.es) INGUAT-authorized local guide Miguel Pablo Sicay is a personable *atiteco* who leads various fascinating tours in and around Santiago Atitlán. He'll lead you up to the observation point of Rey Tepepul (Q225), near where the inlet ends; show you the temporary shrine devoted to locally worshiped saint Maximón (Q170); or convey you by *cayuco* (wooden rowboat) to the ancient Tz'utujil capital of Chutinamit.

⌨ Sleeping

Hotel Ratzán HOTEL **$**

(☎ 7721-7840; www.hotelyposadaratzan.blogspot.nl; Calle Principal; s/d Q100/200; ☞) This budget option, near the center of town, is a family-run establishment with nice wood-beam ceilings and large, modern bathrooms. Only three of the five rooms have exterior windows but considering it's just down the street from the massive Evangelical church, with raucous nightly services, maybe that's a good thing.

Posada de Santiago LODGE **$$**

(☎ 7721-7366; www.posadadesantiago.com; s/d Q235/400, cottages s/d/tr Q500/615/690, ste from Q765; ▣@☞☒) Striking a balance between rustic charm and luxury, the North American–owned *posada* makes a great retreat. Seven cottages and five suites, all with stone walls, fireplaces, porches, hammocks and folk art, are set amid rambling gardens. Across the road stretches a lakeside resort with pool and bar. The restaurant serves delicious, natural fare, as well as homegrown roasted coffee.

The *posada* is 1.5km from the town dock. Catch a *tuk-tuk* (Q10) or hire a *lancha* over to the hotel's own dock.

Hotel La Estrella HOTEL **$$**

(☎ 7721-7814; www.hotel-laestrella.blogspot.com; Calle Campo; s/d/tr Q175/300/425; ▣☞) A short hike north of the ferry dock along the road to San Lucas is this excellent value option, featuring modern, comfortable units with handsome wood ceilings and locally woven bedspreads. Room 13, adjacent to the top terrace, takes best advantage of the hotel's lakeside position looking straight across the inlet at Volcán San Pedro.

Hotel Bambú LODGE **$$$**

(☎ 7721-7332; www.ecobambu.com; Carretera San Lucas Tolimán Km 16; s/d/tr incl breakfast

Q535/690/765; P 🛜 🏊) 🅿 Run by an amiable Spaniard, the Bambú is an ecologically harmonious hotel. Scattered around wild yet manicured grounds, the 10 spacious rooms are in grass- or bamboo-roofed buildings, with cypress fittings and earthy tile floors. A pebbly path leads to a swimming pool in a serene, jungly setting.

It's 600m from the dock; if you're arriving by boat, ask to be dropped off at the hotel's own dock.

✗ Eating & Drinking

Comedor Santa Rita GUATEMALAN $
(Calle de Santa Rita 88; lunch Q25-30; ⊙7am-9pm Mon-Fri) The latest incarnation of a generations-old dining hall is a good place to try Maya specialties like *pulique* (veggie-rich stew) and *patín,* served with a stack of tortillas. It was overseen by doña Hélida Esther Cabrera, Santiago's resident ethnographer; her granddaughter's now the chef. Half a block east of the Parque Central.

Restaurant El Gran Sol GUATEMALAN $$
(📋4271-4642; Cantón Tzanjuyú; mains Q55; ⊙8am-7pm Mon-Sat) One block up from the dock on the left, this family-run establishment is a good bet for breakfast, lunch or snacks, with a spiffy kitchen and breezy deck over a cacophonous junction. Thelma and clan love to cook; try their soups, pancakes or *quesadillas* (with homemade cheese).

Café Quila's PUB
(⊙5-10pm Wed-Sun) Quila's is a casual gathering place where expats and lake dwellers can bond over sports TV or ping-pong. Some of the best burgers (Q20 to Q30) on the lake are served in the cozy front lounge or rear patio with a mural of Santiago. Coming up from the dock, take the first right.

🛍 Shopping

Colorful textiles, wooden animals, beadwork jewelry, leather belts and paintings are produced and sold at workshops along the street leading up from the dock.

For contemporary bags, clothing and accessories with Tz'utujil elements, check out the Cojolya Association of Maya Women Weavers (p106), whose shop displays woven items designed by the association's North American founder, Candis E Krummel.

ℹ Information

G&T Continental (⊙8:30am-5pm Mon-Fri, 9am-1pm Sat) There's a Cajero 5B ATM at G&T Continental, on the south side of the Parque Central.

Nuevo Hospitalito Atitlán (📋7721-7683; www.hospitalitoatitlan.org; Canton Ch'utch'aj) The Nuevo Hospitalito Atitlán, on the way out of town toward San Lucas Tolimán, is a modern hospital staffed by English-speaking doctors and American volunteers. Primarily providing health care to the Maya community, it has a 24-hour emergency clinic.

San Pedro La Laguna

POP 10,150 / ELEV 1592M

Spreading onto a peninsula at the base of the volcano of the same name, San Pedro remains among the most visited of the lakeside villages – due as much to its reasonably priced accommodations and global social scene as to its spectacular setting. Travelers tend to dig in here for a spell, in pursuit of (in no particular order) drinking, firetwirling, African drumming, Spanish classes, painting classes, volcano hiking, hot-tub soaking and hammock swinging.

While this scene unfolds at the lakefront, up the hill San Pedro follows more traditional rhythms. Clad in indigenous outfits, the predominantly indigenous *pedranos* (as the locals are called) congregate around the market zone. You'll see coffee being picked on the volcano's slopes and spread out to dry on wide platforms at the beginning of the dry season.

◉ Sights

Galería de Arte Tz'utujil GALLERY
(⊙3-6pm) FREE This little gallery, up in the center of town opposite the main church, displays the work of local contemporary artists, with a new exhibition each month.

Museo Tz'unun 'Ya MUSEUM
(7a Av; Q35; ⊙8am-noon & 2-5pm Mon-Fri) This museum focuses on the history of the Tz'utujil people and geology of the region, with a film on the formation of the lake and a gallery of colorized photos of San Pedro in former days. As a bonus, they'll identify and interpret your *nahual* (animal counterpart), based on your birth date.

🏃 Activities

Looming above the village, Volcán San Pedro almost asks to be climbed by anyone with an adventurous spirit. It is the most accessible of the three volcanoes in the zone and, classified as a municipal ecological park, it's regularly patrolled by tourism police.

Another popular hike goes up the hill referred to as **Indian Nose** – its skyline resembles the profile of an ancient Maya dignitary. **Asoantur** (☑4379-4545; asoantur@gmail.com; 4a Av A 3-60; ☺7am-7pm), an association made up of 16 INGUAT-authorized guides from the local community, leads expeditions to the peak for Q100 per person. It also offers cultural tours of San Pedro and nearby coffee plantations, horseback-riding tours, and kayak, bicycle and motorbike rentals. It operates from a hut on the lane up from the Pana dock.

Kayaks are available for hire (Q10 per hour), turning right from the Pana dock. Ask at Natalí hairdressers.

Geo Travel   HIKING
(☑3168-8625; GeoTravelGuatemala@gmail.com) These tours, led by a geology expert, focus on the natural environment. One popular tour ascends before dawn to the Rostro Maya (Indian Nose; Q200 per person), from which you may observe eight volcanoes, and locally based geologist Matt Purvis explains how they came to stand in a line and how Lake Atitlán was formed.

Matt also leads overnight trips to Santiaguito, Fuego and Pacaya (all active volcanoes) for Q700 per person.

Café Chuasinayi   SWIMMING
(☑7721-8381; adult/child Q10/5; ☺7am-5pm Sun-Fri) The pool on the grounds of campground/cafe Chuasinayi is a global gathering place, particularly on Sundays when a character known as Smokin' Joe barbecues baby back ribs. Coming from the Santiago dock take the first right and go along 100m or so.

Solar Pools   SPA
(7a Av 2-22) After a day's hiking or cycling, it's time for a good soak in one of these spring-fed pools (Q40 per person), near the bend in the trail between the two docks. Book ahead so that your pool is already hot when you arrive.

🍃 Courses

San Pedro is making a name for itself in the language game with ultra-economical rates at its various Spanish institutes. The standard price for four hours of one-on-one classes, five days a week, is Q850. Accommodations with a local family, with three meals daily (except Sunday) typically costs Q650. Volcano hikes, Maya culture seminars and dance classes are among the extracurricular activities offered.

**Community
Spanish School**   LANGUAGE COURSE
(☑5466-7177; www.communityspanishschool.com) This is a professionally managed school staffed by accredited local instructors, who lead one-on-one classes in thatched huts along a strip of garden running down to the lakefront. Arriving at the Pana dock, go 300m left.

San Pedro Spanish School   LANGUAGE COURSE
(☑5715-4604;   www.sanpedrospanishschool.org; 7a Av 2-20) Well-organized school on the street between the two docks, with consistently good reviews. Classes are held under thatched-roof huts amidst an attractive garden setting. The school supports Niños del Lago, an organization that provides education, health care and nutrition for local Tz'utujil children.

Celas Maya   LANGUAGE COURSE
(☑5933-1450; www.spanishschool.com.gt) The lake branch of the prestigious Quetzaltenango institute takes documentaries, news reports and storytelling as the basis for one-on-one classes aimed at building speaking and listening skills. Classes in Tz'utujil are also offered. It's at the end of the lakefront trail from the Pana dock.

Casa Rosario   LANGUAGE COURSE
(☑(in US) 415-282-7684; www.casarosario.com) Classes are held in little huts amid gardens near the lake. Weaving classes and *huipil* appreciation (from the owner's voluminous collection) are among the extracurricular activities. In addition to homestays, language learners may stay in one of the primitive elevated shelters on the premises. Look for the sign along the path between the docks.

🛏 Sleeping

In many places in San Pedro it is possible to negotiate deals for longer stays and during the low season. It's also possible to rent a room or an entire house in town – ask around.

Near the Pana Dock

Hotel Mansión del Lago HOTEL $
(☑ 7721-8124; www.hotelmansiondellago.com; 3a Vía & 4a Av, Zona 2; s/d Q75/150) If you'd just like to drop your bags, this massive L-shaped property is just above the Pana dock. Sparkling clean rooms are done up in cloud or dove motifs, with rockers on wide balconies looking right at Indian Nose.

Hotel Gran Sueño HOTEL $
(☑ 7721-8110; 8a Calle 4-40, Zona 2; s/d Q75/150; ☎) Though certainly not in the prettiest part of town, beyond its plant-draped entryway and up a spiral staircase are bright rooms with colorful abstract designs, comfortable beds and uniquely designed bathrooms. Rooms 9 and 11 are fantastic lake-view perches. From the Pana dock, it's a few doors left of the first crossing.

Mr Mullet's Hostel HOSTEL $
(☑ 4419-0566; www.mrmullets.com; dm Q60, r with/without bathroom Q140/95; ☎) Word of mouth has ensured the success of the newest party point in lakeside San Pedro, often overflowing with fun seekers who pile into the four-bed dorms (each bed featuring a large locker and essential charging outlet) and cell-like private rooms on two levels or crowd the patio/bar at rear, which shuts at 11pm for those who actually want to sleep.

From the Pana dock, it's a five-minute walk to the left; look for the man with the mullet.

Hostel Fe HOSTEL $
(☑ 3486-7027; www.hostelfe.com; dm/r Q70/200) A runaway smash, this new hostel takes up a massive concrete block 100m south of the Pana dock. It's the destination of choice for global youth, as much for its rockin' waterfront cafe and adjacent sundeck bar (with waterslide) as for the sparsely furnished steel-doored rooms and dorms. Local *pedranos* keep the bathrooms and hangout terraces neat and clean.

Between the Docks

Zoola HOSTEL $
(☑ 5847-4857; dm Q50, r with/without bathroom Q160/130; ☎) 'Laid-back' best describes this Israeli-run establishment, a place to crash after a Mideast feast at the adjoining restaurant (p111). It's reached down a long, jungly boardwalk opposite the Museo Tz'unun 'Ya. Behind the cafe/chill-out lounge, low adobe blocks of dorms extend to the lake, where

---

TZ'UTUJIL OIL PAINTINGS

Emanating primarily from the Lago de Atitlán towns of Santiago Atitlán, San Pedro La Laguna and San Juan La Laguna, Tz'utujil oil painting has a distinctive primitivist style, with depictions of rural life, local traditions and landscapes in vibrant colors.

This distinctly Maya mode is generally handed down through generations of the same family, and the leading artists share surnames. In San Pedro La Laguna the name of note is González. Legend has it that Tz'utujil art began when Rafael González y González noticed some dye that had dripped and mixed with the sap of a tree; he made a paintbrush from his hair and began creating the type of canvases still popular today. His grandson Pedro Rafael González Chavajay and Pedro's cousin Mariano González Chavajay are leading contemporary exponents of the Tz'utujil style. The artist Emilio González Morales pioneered the motif of depicting rural scenes from above – the *vista del pájaro*, or bird's-eye view – as well as from below, an ant's-eye view.

The granddaddy of Santiago painting was Juan Sisay; success at an international art exhibition in 1969 sparked an explosion of painters working in his style. You can even learn to paint in this style at several studios around town.

Among the leading figures in San Juan are husband and wife Antonio Vásquez Yojcom and Juana Mendoza Cholotío, whose paintings are exhibited at the **Galería Xocomeel** on the way up from the main dock.

Artists in all three communities are experimenting with new forms while continuing to explore Maya cultural themes.

If you've got more than a passing interest, consider taking the 'Maya Artists & Artisans' tour offered by Posada Los Encuentros (p99) in Panajachel or visit the website Arte Maya Tz'utuhil (www.artemaya.com).

a canopied swimming pool is the focus of nightly parties. Two-night minimum stay.

Hotel Sak'cari El Amanecer
HOTEL **$$**

(☑7721-8096; www.hotel-sakcari.com; 7a Av 2-12, Zona 2; s/d/tr Q275/305/385; P🖥🐾) About midway along the trail between the two docks, the ecofriendly Sak'cari (Tz'utujil for 'sunrise') has 20 clean wood-paneled rooms with lots of shelves. Rooms at the rear are best (and priciest), with big balconies overlooking the lake past a landscaped lawn that's a splendid place for hammock swinging. More active guests can grab a kayak and navigate the lake.

Hotel Mikaso
HOTEL **$$**

(☑7721-8232; www.mikasohotel.com; 4a Callejon A-88; dm/s/d/tr Q80/150/250/300; 🖥) Despite encroaching lake waters, the Mikaso still stands proudly at Atitlán's shores. Big rooms with carved wood furniture and ceiling fans ring a garden bursting with birds of paradise; a few have private patios. The rooftop bar/restaurant boasts fantastic lake views and a deck/lounge features a Jacuzzi and pool table.

✖ Eating

Café La Puerta
CAFE **$**

(☑4050-0500; 7a Av 2-20; breakfast Q30-40; ⊙7am-5pm; 🖋) The resident cafe for the San Pedro Spanish School (p109), La Puerta is an appealing spot for natural fare. Breakfast on homemade granola, grainy bread, delicious raspberry jam and avocado milkshakes, all served on beautiful mosaic tile tables by the sweetest waitstaff ever to wear a *huipil*. Traditional Guatemalan dishes fused with Asian influences are the highlights of the lunch menu.

Shanti Shanti
ISRAELI **$**

(8a Calle 3-93; mains Q20-30; ⊙7am-11pm; 🖋) With terraced seating cascading down to the lakeside, this makes a pleasant perch for Mideast staples such as falafel, baba ghanouj and hummus, as well as hearty soups.

Idea Connection
CAFE **$$**

(panini & pastas Q30-50; ⊙7am-5pm; 🖥) Yes, you can get connected on one of the computers at this cybercafe along gringo lane, but it's even more appealing as a bakery/garden cafe. Run by Massimo from Milan, it's a real oasis in the shade, with fantastically fresh croissants, cinnamon rolls and muffins, not to mention super smoothies.

🍷 Drinking & Nightlife

While many *pedranos* spend their evenings shouting the lord's praises at evangelical congregations, visitors tend to prowl San Pedro's hard-partying bar scene.

D'Juice Girls
JUICE BAR

(⊙7am-11pm) D'Juice Girls are young Hebrew-speaking Tz'utujil women who squeeze the tropical fruits of Guatemala into supernutritious combos, such as carrot-ginger-beet. Their popular stand is a five-minute walk east of the Pana dock.

Café Las Cristalinas
CAFE

(⊙7am-9pm; 🖥) To savor a shot of the coffee grown on the surrounding slopes (and roasted here), head for this thatched-roof structure on the way up from the Pana dock to the center of town. Be sure as well to try their excellent banana bread, which you may enjoy on various inviting terraces. It also functions as a cybercafe.

Zoola
LOUNGE

(⊙11am-midnight; 🖥) Zoola remains San Pedro's premier global chillage venue. Travelers kick back on cushions around low tables, munching scrumptious Mideast fare, grooving on Manu, playing board games and generally unwinding. For serious DJ sessions, follow the cobblestone path to the sensational lakefront lounge with swimming pool.

Alegre Pub
PUB

(8a Calle 4-10; ⊙9am-1am) Some nights are more *alegres* than others at this long-running upstairs pub at the corner up from the Pana dock, but it remains a watering hole for San Pedro's cast of characters. Shoot pool with the locals (Tz'utujil rules) in the way-laid-back rooftop garden.

🛍 Shopping

Grupo Ecológico Teixchel
CLOTHING

(☑5932-0000; berta_nc@yahoo.com; ⊙8:30am-noon & 2-6pm) This is a Tz'utujil women's collective that sells fair-trade woven goods and offers weaving classes for Q30 per hour (not including materials). It's about 150m uphill from the Pana dock toward the center of town.

Tony's Bookstore
BOOKS

Secondhand bookstore run by a Dutchman, with a decent selection of fiction in English and other languages. It's at the start of the path to Hotel Mikaso, about

100m north up the path from the Santiago dock street.

ⓘ Orientation

San Pedro has two docks, about 1km apart. The one on the southeast side of town serves boats going to and from Santiago Atitlán; the other, on the northwest side, serves Panajachel. From each dock, streets run ahead to meet outside the market in the town center, a few hundred meters uphill.

Most of the tourism activity is in the lower part of town, between and on either side of the two docks. To work your way across this lower area from the Panajachel dock, turn left at the first intersection. Follow this path about 200m until you reach a store called La Estrellita, then take the trail on the right. Soon afterward, the path angles left and passes the Museo Tz'unun 'Ya, then takes a sharp left into a busy bar and restaurant zone. From the Santiago dock, turn right immediately before the Hotel Villasol.

ⓘ Information

Banrural (⊙ 8:30am-5pm Mon-Fri, 9am-1pm Sat) You can change US dollars and euros at Banrural, two blocks east of the market in the town center, which has a Visa ATM.

Clínica Los Volcanes (☑ 7823-7656; www.clinicalosvolcanes.com) A private clinic providing medical and dental services, with English-speaking staff; foreign medical insurance accepted. It's near the Pana dock.

ⓘ Getting There & Away

Passenger boats arrive and depart here for Panajachel and Santiago Atitlán. Boats from San Pedro to Santiago (Q25, 25 minutes) run hourly from 6am to 4pm. Boats from San Pedro to Panajachel (Q25) run every half hour or so from 6am to 5pm. Some go direct; others make stops at San Juan, San Marcos (Q10) and Jaibalito/Santa Cruz (Q20) en route.

San Pedro is connected by paved roads to Santiago Atitlán (although this stretch is plagued by bandits) and to the Interamericana at Km 148 (about 20km west of Los Encuentros), the latter a hair-raising journey with spectacular lake vistas on the way up. A paved branch of the San Pedro–Interamericana road runs along the northwest side of the lake from Santa Clara to San Marcos La Laguna.

Seven buses leave for Quetzaltenango (Q35, three hours) from San Pedro's Catholic church, up in the town center, between 4:45am and 1:30pm Monday to Saturday; three buses leave on Sunday, including Pullman buses at 8:30am and 1:30pm.

San Juan La Laguna

POP 5868 / ELEV 1605M

Just 2km east of San Pedro, on a rise above a spectacular bay, this mellow village has escaped many of the excesses of its neighbors, and some travelers find it a more tranquil setting in which to study Spanish or experience indigenous life. San Juan is special: the Tz'utujil inhabitants take pride in their craft traditions – particularly painting and weaving – and have developed their own tourism infrastructure to highlight these traditions to outsiders.

Perhaps part of what makes it all run so well is the communal spirit: coffee growers, fishers, organic farmers, natural dyers and widows are among the like-minded groups who've formed cooperatives here.

As you wander around the village, you'll notice various murals depicting aspects of San Juan life and legend.

ⓕ Tours

Asociación de Guías de Ecoturismo Rupalaj K'istalin   TOUR
(☑ 5623-7351; www.sanjuanlalaguna.org; ⊙ 8am-5pm) The association offers a worthwhile tour of San Juan La Laguna's points of interest, led by indigenous guides (Q110 per person), in Spanish. You'll visit two weaving cooperatives, both of which use dyes from native plants, and an art studio/gallery featuring the Tz'utujil primitivist painting style. The office is 300m up the hill from the dock.

Other tours offered include trips with local fishermen in rustic *cayucos* to learn about traditional lake fishing techniques and a demonstration of the harvesting of the lakeshore reeds, which are used as material for *petates*, the woven mats the town is known for.

The association can also set up guides for one-way walks to San Marcos La Laguna (Q200 per person), returning by *lancha,* and hikes up Rupalaj K'istalin (Q175 per person), the mountain that towers above San Juan and is the site of Maya religious rituals.

ⓔ Courses

Eco Spanish School   LANGUAGE COURSE
(☑ 4727-6481; www.ecolanguages.net) Located on a coffee plantation with views of the lake, this school offers one-on-one classes based on an immersion methodology with opportunities to experience Tz'utujil culture. They can arrange homestays with local

ATITLÁN RISING

At San Juan La Laguna an art gallery is half submerged, its upper floor abandoned. At Tzununá, only the roof is visible of what used to be a shelter for waiting boat passengers. And in Panajachel the public beach has been washed off the map. New docks have been built in all the lakeside villages, and in Santa Cruz, a plank walk has replaced the lakeside trail, now underwater. It may appear that a tsunami or some similar disaster has struck. But what's actually happening is that the lake level is rising, inexorably – around 5m since 2009. In the process, it keeps swallowing dwellings and businesses, most of them owned by outsiders. Foreign residents are learning the hard way why it is that almost all local towns are built well above the lake shore. The lake's capricious behavior is well-lodged in the community's collective memory. The elders of Atitlán know of its cyclical rise and fall, a phenomenon noted as far back as the 16th century by the Spanish conquistadors. The water level has been considerably higher in the past and it will no doubt drop again. In the meantime, the rising trend is the talk of the lake, with various theories proposed. Some attribute it to the deforestation of the lakeside slopes, which causes soil erosion. When Tropical Storm Agatha hit in 2010, it might have washed a great deal of this sediment into the lake, clogging the crevices in its basin that provide natural drainage. A more authoritative theory attributes the phenomenon to the lake's volcanic origins. According to this view, seismic activity heats the ground beneath the lake bed and forms a sort of subterranean 'bladder' that keeps expanding until exit vents appear. This periodic expansion causes the lake level to rise.

families. A path to the school is signed near the Catholic church.

🛏 Sleeping & Eating

Mayachik' LODGE $
(☑ 4218-4675; www.mayachik.com; dm/bungalows Q50/150; 🅿 🛜) 🏊 Immediately southwest of town, this European-managed ecoresort blends harmoniously with its surroundings. Various traditionally built accommodations with compost toilets and solar-powered showers include a circular bungalow, 8-bed dorm, and at the top of the hill a large adobe house with three bedrooms. A kitchen prepares vegetarian meals and serves home-grown coffee.

Guests may use the *temascal,* a formidable stone structure, infused with aromatic herbs. Spanish classes and volunteering are options.

Hotel Pa Muelle HOTEL $
(☑ 4141-0820; hotelpamuelle@turbonett.com; Camino al Muelle; s/d Q100/175) The small hotel has a delightful setting, with blue rooms along a patch of lawn high above the lake. A plant-laden lounge has been added on top, providing even more fantastic views. It's near the top of the hill coming up from the dock.

★ Uxlabil Eco Hotel HOTEL $$
(☑ 5990-6016; www.uxlabil.com; N-14 Km 175; s/d incl breakfast Q351/444) The Uxlabil stands on a small coffee plantation on the southern edge of San Juan's bay. Made by local artisans from natural materials, the four-level structure blends seamlessly into the hillside gardens, populated by more than 80 kinds of birds. Featuring hand-carved stone trimmings, all the rooms face the lake and have excellent terraces looking straight at the Rostro Maya.

The restaurant serves organic food and coffee. You can ask to be dropped off at the dock; if arriving from the town, hike down to the lake and follow the path along the bank.

Alma de Colores VEGETARIAN $
(☑ 4261-2646; www.almadecolores.org; set lunch Q25; ⊘ 8am-5pm Mon-Fri) Bread, pizza and focaccia are baked at this pleasant open-air bakery/cafe on the way out to San Pablo, and there are two lunch options daily prepared with vegetables from a local organic farm. It's run by an Italian NGO as part of a program to integrate young adults with disabilities into the workplace.

Café El Artesano EUROPEAN $$
(☑ 4555-4773; Salida a Guatemala; cheese platter Q80; ⊘ noon-4pm Mon-Fri) Bring a group of friends and make an afternoon of it at this unique restaurant. Fine cheeses (25 varieties, all produced in Guatemala and aged in-house), smoked meats and artisan breads are served under a delightful arbor, with wines personally selected by the manager, a young man of Swiss heritage. Reservations are essential.

THE HIGHLANDS SAN JUAN LA LAGUNA

ℹ Getting There & Away

To get to San Juan, ask any boat coming from Pana or San Pedro to drop you off at the dock. Otherwise it's a 15-minute pick-up or *tuk-tuk* ride (Q10) to/from San Pedro.

San Marcos La Laguna

POP 2585 / ELEV 1580M

Without doubt the prettiest of the lakeside villages, San Marcos La Laguna lives a double life. The mostly Maya community occupies the higher ground, while expats and visitors cover a flat jungly patch toward the shoreline with paths snaking through banana, coffee and avocado trees. The two converge under the spreading *matapalo* (strangler fig) tree of the delightful central plaza.

San Marcos has become a magnet for global seekers, who believe the place has a spiritual energy that's conducive to learning and practicing meditation, holistic therapies, massage, reiki and other spiritually oriented activities. Whatever you're into, it's a great spot to kick back and distance the everyday world for a spell. Lago de Atitlán is beautiful and clean here, and you can swim off the rocks. Boats put in at a central dock below Posada Schumann. The path leading from there to the village center, and a parallel one about 100m west, are the main axes for most visitors.

It's an outlandish melange of cultures – evangelical Christians, self-styled shamans, Kaqchiquel farmers and visionary artists – against a backdrop of incredible natural beauty. Someone ought to make a movie about it.

◉ Sights & Activities

Cerro Tzankujil   PARK
(Q15; ⊙ 8am-6pm) This nature reserve is on a sacred hill west of San Marcos village. Well-maintained pebbly trails lead to swimming areas with shelters by the bank and a diving platform. The water is crystal clear here. A branch off the main trail ascends to a Maya altar on the summit, while a lower spur reaches a volcano lookout.

Rent kayaks by the entrance (Q20 per hour, available until 11am).

Yoga Forest   YOGA
(☑ 3301-1835; www.theyogaforest.org) Up in the hills north of town amid lush forest, this is a blissfully secluded perch to learn and practice shamanic healing and other esoteric arts, with a magnificent yoga platform built into the hillside. A cafe prepares vegetarian

food and accommodations are available in shared adobe *cabañas* with thatched roofs and magnificent lake views.

Yoga-teacher training and permaculture courses are offered, as well as workshops on such techniques as Thai massage; check the website for the upcoming program. If you'd just like to check it out you may join a forest tour every Thursday at 10am (Q50).

East-West Center   MEDITATION
(☑ 3102-4666) Deep tissue massage (Q250 per hour), reflexology, acupuncture and Bach flowers are among the holistic therapies offered here, along with workshops in I-Ching readings, herbal remedies and so on. It's near the top of the main trail from the dock.

Las Pirámides
Meditation Center   MEDITATION
(☑ 5205-7302; www.laspiramidesdelka.com) San Marcos La Laguna's claim to fame, this retreat by the lake has been providing spiritual guidance for more than two decades. Most structures on the property are pyramidal and oriented to the four cardinal points, including the two temples where sessions are held. A one-month personal development course begins every full moon, with three sessions daily (US$700).

There's also a three-month solar course running from each equinox to the following solstice (the moon course is a prerequisite). Nonguests can come for the meditation or Hatha yoga (7am to 8am, Q50) sessions. Accommodations are available to course participants, including use of the sauna and access to the esoteric library. The center also has a vegetarian restaurant and room to wander about in the medicinal herb garden.

🛏 Sleeping

There aren't any street signs but most lodgings have posted their own fancifully painted versions to point you in the right direction.

Circles   HOSTEL $
(☑ 3327-8961; www.circles-cafe.com; dm/r without bathroom Q75/150) Near the top of the path from the dock is this casual cafe/hostel providing the essentials: good espresso and a comfy place to sleep. Upstairs are two private rooms and a thoughtfully designed dorm with curtains on each bunk. A chill-out terrace looks over a garden with cushioned nooks.

Hotel La Paz   HOSTEL $
(☑ 5061-5316; www.lakeatitlanlapaz.com; dm/r/bungalows Q60/150/250) 🖉 Along the upper trail

that links the two main paths, the holistically minded La Paz has rambling gardens holding bungalows of traditional *bajareque* (a stone, bamboo and mud material) with thatched roofs. A vegetarian restaurant, traditional Maya sauna, Spanish lessons and morning yoga sessions are additional attractions.

★ **Hotel Jinava Bay** RESORT **$$**
(☑ 5299-3311; www.hoteljinava.com; r with/without bathroom Q350/250; P ☀) Cobbled paths weave through gardens bursting with flowers, coffee, palms and a profusion of hummingbirds at this tropical lakeside spread 300m west of the village. Bungalows are terraced down the hillside, with jaw-dropping views over the bay – though the lower ones are nicer, with stone walls and beds of tropical hardwoods. Children may not stay here.

Reception is below, by the lakefront restaurant, so it's best approached by boat.

Dragon Hotel BOUTIQUE HOTEL **$$**
(www.eldragonhotel.com; s/d Q340/565, s/d without bathroom Q215/380; ☀) Definitely a work in progress, this lakefront spread created by a North American artist could be the wackiest of San Marcos lodgings. Signs of artistic exuberance pop up everywhere, from the dining area with its hanging spheres to the waterfront deck/bar with its trademark serpent. But not at the expense of luxury: uniquely designed rooms feature plasma TVs, loft beds and private terraces.

The kitchen is equally inspired; the key lime pie here is legendary. To find El Dragon, head east off the main trail past Restaurante Fé and follow this lane to a football field; look for the horned monster at the far right corner.

Lush HOTEL **$$$**
(www.lushatitlan.com; r per week/month from Q1720/4200, ste from Q4580/9920; ☀) ✦ Eco-chic Lush seems to sprout organically from the living rock of the hillside, with recycled glass, plastic and other flotsam ingeniously incorporated as construction materials. Each of its seven suites and three rooms is unique, with handcrafted furnishings and beautiful stained-glass windows, and most feature private balconies with lake or garden views. Primarily for long-term stays, the accommodations also include kitchens.

There are also a few budget rooms available on a drop-in basis. From the dock, it's a six-minute walk to the left (west) along the lakeside path.

 Eating

Allala JAPANESE **$**
(☑ 5166-8638; mains Q35-45; ☺ 3-9pm Thu-Tue; ✦) This groovy little shack can be found by the creek east of the village. Japanese owner Seiko makes a mean miso soup, plus vegetarian sushi and tempura platters, and the plum wine is divine. All this, and complimentary cheesecake for dessert. Service can be slow, but the funky decor gives you something to look at.

Moonfish HEALTH FOOD **$**
(sandwiches & burritos Q30; ☺ 7:30am-8pm Wed-Mon; ☀ ✦) Along the main thoroughfare west of the square, Moonfish whips up hippie-friendly fare including tempeh sandwiches, tofu scrambles and mighty fine falafel with ingredients fresh from the garden. Check the bulletin board for upcoming yoga retreats and events.

Restaurante Fé INTERNATIONAL **$$**
(mains Q55-80; ☺ 7:30am-10pm; ☀) Fé, about midway down the main trail, offers informal candlelit dining in a pleasant, open-air hall with a tree in the middle. The pastas, curries and pan-fried fish are all well worth savoring here, and the mulligatawny stew is excellent. A good place to while away the evening.

Blind Lemon's BURGERS **$$**
(www.blindlemons.com; mains Q55-70; ☺ noon-10pm; ☀) This hangout brings the Mississippi Delta to Atitlán, with weekly blues jams by owner Carlos and special guests in a colonial-style mansion. The menu features chicken platters, Cajun-blackened fish, pizza, burgers and other gringo comfort food. It's at the top of the western path.

ⓘ Getting There & Away

The last dependable boat to Santa Cruz La Laguna and Panajachel departs about 5pm.

A gravel road runs east from San Marcos to Tzununá and a paved one west to San Pablo and Santa Clara, where it meets the road running from the Interamericana to San Pedro. You can travel between San Marcos and San Pedro by pick-up, with a transfer at San Pablo.

Jaibalito

POP 750 / ELEV 1562M

This Kaqchiquel hamlet is only accessible by boat (a 20-minute *lancha* ride from Panajachel or San Pedro, Q20) or on foot via a ridgeline trail from Santa Cruz La Laguna,

4km to the east (45 minutes). The hike west to San Marcos (6km) is equally picturesque. There are several marvelous places to stay.

🛏 Sleeping & Eating

Posada Jaibalito HOSTEL **$**

(📞5192-4334; dm/s/d Q35/70/95; 🛜) Jaibalito's budget choice is just up from the dock on the left. The German-owned operation is a remarkable value, with dorm and a few private rooms occupying a garden flanked by coffee plants. Some little houses are available for longer-term renters. Authentic bratwurst and goulash (Q24) are served at the cafe, along with shots of aged Zacapa rum (Q15).

★La Casa del Mundo Hotel & Café HOTEL **$$$**

(📞5218-5332; www.lacasadelmundo.com; r with/without bathroom Q585/315) On a secluded cliff facing the volcanoes is one of Guatemala's most spectacular hotels. It features sumptuous gardens, lake swimming from Mediterranean-style terraces, and a wood-fired hot tub overhanging the lake. The best rooms seem to float above the water, with no land visible beneath. Every room is outfitted with comfortable beds, Guatemalan fabrics and fresh flowers. Reservations are advisable.

The restaurant prepares a toothsome four-course dinner (Q85 to Q95), served family style. You can rent kayaks (Q50 per hour) for exploring the lake.

Club Ven Acá FUSION **$$**

(📞5122-6047; www.clubvenaca.com; menú del día Q150) Right at the dock is this trendy restaurant with a seasonally varying menu and a popular happy hour highlighted by purple-basil mojitos. Sunday brunch is a big deal with to-die-for eggs Benedict. Guests tend to unwind in the hot tub or infinity pool.

Santa Cruz La Laguna

POP 6000 / ELEV 1833M

With the typically dual nature of the Atitlán villages, Santa Cruz comprises both a waterfront resort – home of the lake's scuba-diving outfit – and an indigenous Kaqchiquel village, about 600m uphill from the dock. The cobblestoned road up is frequented by villagers lugging sacks of avocados or firewood. The inaccessibility of the spot – it can only be reached by boat or on foot – may impede its development but it also enhances its rugged beauty.

🏃 Activities

ATI Divers DIVING

(📞5706-4117; www.atidivers.com) Lago de Atitlán is one of the rare places in the world where you can dive at altitude without using a dry suit. This group leads dive trips from Santa Cruz. It offers a four-day PADI open-water diving certification course (Q1915), as well as a PADI high-altitude course and fun dives. It's based at La Iguana Perdida hotel.

The lake fills a collapsed volcanic cone with bizarre geological formations and aquatic life such as cichlids, which spawn near an active fault line where hot water vents into the lake. Diving at altitude brings its own challenges – you need better control over your buoyancy, and visibility is reduced. During the rainy season the water clouds up, so the best time to dive is between October and May.

Los Elementos Adventure Center KAYAKING

(📞5359-8328; www.kayakguatemala.com; 2-day tour Q1250) Offers kayak rentals and multiday excursions around the lake. Two-day paddle-and-hike tours include a visit to Santa Catarina Palopó, with kayaking along the lake's northern shore and hiking along the old Maya trail through Tzununá and Jaibalito. The price includes meals and a night's lodging.

Its base is a 10-minute walk west of La Iguana Perdida along the lakeside trail.

🛏 Sleeping & Eating

Hotel Isla Verde BUNGALOW **$$**

(📞5760-2648; www.islaverdeatitlan.com; s/d Q375/420, s/d without bathroom Q285/330; 🛜) 🍃 This stylish, environmentally friendly lodging makes the most of its spectacular setting. A mosaic stone path winds through exuberant vegetation to the nine hillside cabins (six with private bathroom); the higher you go, the more jaw-dropping the picture-window views. Simple rooms are tastefully decorated with art and recycled elements. Bathrooms are jungle-chic affairs, and water and electricity are solar powered.

A terrace restaurant serves slow-food cuisine, and there's a pavilion for meditation and dance. It's a 10-minute walk west of the dock along the lakefront trail.

La Iguana Perdida LODGE **$$**

(📞5706-4117; www.laiguanaperdida.com; dm Q45, r from Q270, s/d without bathroom Q95/125; @🛜) The first place you see as you step off the dock, La Iguana Perdida makes a great hangout to enjoy the lake views and meet other travelers, go scuba diving or kayaking, learn Spanish or sweat it out in the sauna. Don't miss the Saturday night cross-dressing, fire and music BBQs!

Managed mainly by alternative-minded gringos (volunteers often needed), it features a range of rooms, from primitive (electricity-free dorm in an A-frame cabin) to luxurious (an adobe structure with stylish furnishings and private balconies). Meals are served family-style; a three-course dinner is Q60.

★ **La Fortuna** BUNGALOW $$$
(☑ 5203-1033; www.lafortunaatitlan.com; bungalows from Q600) 🦋 As luxurious as it is wild and remote, this ecologically outfitted retreat is at Patzisotz, a secluded bay just east of Santa Cruz around a rocky cliff. Four thatched-roof cabins are elegantly constructed of locally forested guanacaste with Asian influences. Each features a porch and upper deck overlooking the lake, mosquito-netted beds and open-air bathrooms with rain showers.

The old coffee plantation is the creation of North American owners Kat and Steve; the latter a former guide and chef who prepares delectable meals from his own garden. Meals are brought to your cabin or served in the stunning dining room/clubhouse, in front of which stands a wood-fired hot tub. *Lanchas* will drop you at the dock (Q10 from Santa Cruz).

Café Sabor Cruceño GUATEMALAN $
(mains Q35-40; ⊙ 8am-3pm Mon-Sat) Up in the village, this innovative *comedor* is run by local students who are learning to make traditional Guatemalan dishes to global tourism standards. Such Kaqchiquel fare as *subanik* (a tomato sauce of ground seeds and chilies accompanied by *tamalitos*) is prepared with locally grown herbs and veggies and served in the bay-view dining hall.

It's inside the CECAP training center, at the lower end of the Santa Cruz' central plaza.

❶ Getting There & Away

Santa Cruz is a 15-minute *lancha* ride from Panajachel (Q15) or 25 minutes from San Pedro (Q20). The last boat back to Pana passes at around 5:15pm.

Tzununá
POP 2000 / ELEV 1571M

If there's such a thing as an up-and-coming spot on Lago de Atitlán, Tzununá, located 2km east of San Marcos by a paved road, may be it.

Despite recent gringo incursions, the 99 per cent Kaqchiquel village ('Hummingbird of the Water') retains a strong indigenous character and a lush natural beauty with year-round rivers springing from forested mountain slopes. Women in scarlet *huipiles* tread the paths between traditionally managed groves of coffee, avocados, bananas and *jocote*. Whereas foreign travelers head for San Pedro to party or San Marcos to meditate, the few who come here are into sustainable agriculture, which they can study at a project called Atitlán Organics (☑ 4681-4697; www.atitlanorganics.com).

Both of the shoreline lodgings in Tzununá prepare meals for guests.

🛏 Sleeping

Maya Moon Lodge LODGE $$
(☑ 5533-2433; www.mayamoonlodgeatitlan.com; dm Q75, r from Q300; 🐕) Definitely off the beaten track, this retreat a bit west of the main dock consists of large, simply furnished cabins at various levels of a florally abundant hillside, all with hammock-slung balconies facing the lake. The lodge is stamped with the patient, generous character of its English owners. A cafe at the lakefront serves meals with organic veggies from the garden.

Lomas de Tzununá RESORT $$$
(☑ 5201-8272; www.lomasdetzununa.com; s/d/tr incl breakfast Q670/750/845; @ 🛜 🏊) 🦋 Perched high on a cliff at the east end of the bay with astounding views, this semi-luxurious property features cypress cabins and a restaurant with a terrific balcony. From the main dock it may be reached by *tuk-tuk* up a tortuous track through the forest; otherwise arrive by boat if you can handle the precipitous ascent.

Massage, Bach flower remedies and reiki are available at the hotel spa.

❶ Getting There & Away

Regular *lanchas* running between Panajachel (Q20) and San Pedro (Q15) stop at Tzununá. The last boat back to Pana passes at around 5:15pm. Alternatively, you could hike here from San Marcos La Laguna via a gravel road.

QUICHÉ

The road into Quiché department leaves the Interamericana at Los Encuentros, winding northward through pine forests and cornfields. Quiché is the homeland of the K'iche' people, though other groups form the fabric of this culturally diverse region, most notably the Ixil of the eastern Cuchumatanes mountains. Most visitors who come to this largely forgotten pocket of the country are on a jaunt to the famous market at Chichicastenango. Similarly captivating commerce is conducted in Santa Cruz del Quiché, the departmental capital to the north, and it is less trammeled territory. On its outskirts lie the mysterious ruins of K'umarcaaj, the last capital city of the K'iche'. Adventurous souls push further north for Nebaj, heart of the culturally vibrant Ixil Triangle, with myriad hiking opportunities.

Chichicastenango

POP 148,855 / ELEV 2172M

Surrounded by valleys with mountains serrating the horizons, Chichicastenango can seem isolated in time and space from the rest of Guatemala. When its narrow cobbled streets and red-tiled roofs are enveloped in mist, it's downright magical. The crowds of crafts vendors and tour groups who flock in for the huge Thursday and Sunday markets lend it a much worldlier, more commercial atmosphere, but Chichi retains its mystery. Masheños (citizens of Chichicastenango) are famous for their adherence to pre-Christian beliefs and ceremonies, and the town's various *cofradías* (religious brotherhoods) hold processions in observance of their saints around the church of Santo Tomás.

Once called Chaviar, Chichi was an important Kaqchiquel trading town long before the Spanish conquest. In the 15th century the group clashed with the K'iche' (based at K'umarcaaj, 20km north) and were forced to move their headquarters to the more defensible Iximché. When the Spanish conquered K'umarcaaj in 1524, many of its residents fled to Chaviar, which they renamed Chugüilá (Above the Nettles) and Tziguan Tinamit (Surrounded by Canyons). These are the names still used by the K'iche' Maya, although everyone else calls the place Chichicastenango, a name given by the Spaniards' Mexican allies.

Today, Chichi has two religious and governmental establishments. On the one hand, the Catholic Church and the Republic of Guatemala appoint priests and town officials; on the other, the indigenous people elect their own religious and civil officers to manage local matters, with a separate council and mayor, and a court that decides cases involving only local indigenous people.

◉ Sights

Take a close look at the mural running alongside the wall of the town hall on the east side of the plaza. It's dedicated to the victims of the civil war and tells the story using symbology from the Popol Vuh.

INGUAT-authorized guides in beige vests offer cultural walks of Chichi and up to Pascual Abaj.

Market   MARKET

(Plaza Principal; ⊙ Thu & Sun) Some villagers still walk for hours carrying their wares to reach Chichi's market, one of Guatemala's largest. At dawn on Thursday and Sunday they spread out their vegetables, chunks of chalk (ground to a powder, mixed with water and used to soften dried maize), handmade harnesses and other merchandise, and wait for customers.

In the past vendors erected their stands of tree limbs and covered them with cotton sheeting each market day, but these days a sea of tin roofs remains a permanent fixture atop the plaza.

Tourist-oriented handicraft stalls selling masks, textiles, pottery and so on now occupy much of the plaza and the streets to the north. Things villagers need – food, soap, clothing, sewing notions, toys – cluster at the north end of the square and in the Centro Comercial Santo Tomás off the north side, whose upper deck offers irresistible photo opportunities of the business conducted below.

Iglesia de Santo Tomás   CHURCH

(5a Av) This church on the plaza's east side dates from 1540 and is often the scene of rituals that are more distinctly Maya than Catholic. Inside, the floor of the church may be dotted with offerings of maize, flowers and bottles of liquor wrapped in corn husks; candles are arranged in specific patterns along low stone platforms.

The front steps serve much the same purpose as did the great flights of stairs leading up to Maya pyramids. For much of the day (especially Sunday), they smolder with incense of *copal* resin, while indigenous prayer leaders called *chuchkajaues* (mother-fathers) swing censers (usually tin cans poked with holes) and chant magic words marking the days of the ancient Maya calendar and in honor of ancestors. The candles and offerings inside recall those ancestors, many of whom are buried beneath the floor just as Maya kings were buried beneath pyramids. Note that photography is not permitted.

Galería Pop-Wuj
GALLERY

(☑ 4629-9327; www.galeriapopwuj.wix.com/galeriapopwuj; Casa 2-27, Calle Pascual Habaj) [FREE] On the way down the hill to the shrine at Pascual Abaj, you might stop into this interesting gallery. Developed as an art institute for local children with the backing of Project Guggenheim, it holds a small but unique collection of oil paintings by the artist brothers Juan and Miguel Cortéz and their pupils. K'iche' classes are offered.

Pascual Abaj
SHRINE

On a hilltop south of town, Pascual Abaj (Sacrifice Stone) is a shrine to the Maya earth god Huyup Tak'ah (Mountain Plain). A stone-faced idol stands amid a circle of squat stone crosses in a clearing. Said to be hundreds – perhaps thousands – of years old, it has suffered numerous indignities at the hands of outsiders, but local people still revere it.

Chuchkajaues come regularly to offer incense, food, cigarettes, flowers, liquor and perhaps even a sacrificial chicken, in thanks and hope for the earth's continuing fertility. The area is littered with past offerings. The worshippers won't mind if you watch the goings on, but be sure to request permission before taking any photos. You may be asked if you want to make an offering yourself.

Even if there are no ceremonies going on, you can still see the idol and enjoy the walk up the pine-clad hill. To get there from the plaza, walk down 5a Av, turn right into 9a Calle and proceed downhill. At the bottom, bear left along a path and head up through either of the *morerías* (ceremonial mask workshops) that are signposted here; the one on the right houses a museum of local culture. Exiting at the rear, follow the path uphill through the trees to the top of the hill.

Capilla del Calvario
CHURCH

(4a Av) On the west side of the plaza, this whitewashed church is similar in form and function to Santo Tomás, but smaller. Ceremonies go on continually in front of the church, as worshippers ring a bonfire of fragrant *copal*, while within candles are placed upon blackened stone slabs.

Museo Arqueológico Regional
MUSEUM

(5a Av 4-47; Q5; ☉ 8am-12:30pm & 2-4:30pm Tue, Wed, Fri & Sat, 8am-4pm Thu, 8am-2pm Sun) Chichi's archaeology museum holds the collection of Hugo Rossbach, a German who served as the town's Catholic priest until his death in 1944. It includes some beautiful jade necklaces and figurines, along with ceremonial masks, obsidian spearheads, incense burners, figurines and *metates* (grindstones for maize). A second hall features a portrait gallery of *cofradía* leaders.

🎭 Festivals & Events

Feast of Santo Tomás
CULTURAL

(☉ Dec) This celebration of the patron saint's day goes on for most of December, starting on the 5th with an inaugural parade and culminating on the 21st when pairs of brave (some would say mad) men fly about at high speeds suspended from a tall, vertical pole. Traditional dances, concerts and fireworks also feature.

Quema del Diablo
CULTURAL

(Burning of the Devil; ☉ Dec 7) In this ceremony, residents burn their garbage in the streets and usher a statue of the Virgin Mary to the steps of the Iglesia de Santo Tomás. There are lots of incense and candles, a marimba band and a fireworks display that has observers running for cover.

Feast of the Immaculate Conception
CULTURAL

(☉ Dec 8) Don't miss the early-morning dance of the giant cartoon characters in the plaza.

🛏 Sleeping

If you want to secure a room the night before the Thursday or Sunday market, it's a good idea to call or arrive early the day before.

Hotel Girón
HOTEL $

(☑ 5601-0692; hotelgiron@gmail.com; 6a Calle 4-52; s/d/tr Q85/145/180; P @) It won't win any prizes for decor but this motel-style place a block north of the plaza is functional and feels secure. It's reached through a shopping alley, so it's slightly removed from the hubbub of the center.

Hotel Mashito
HOTEL $

(☑ 5168-7178; 8a Calle 1-72; s/d Q70/140, s/d without bathroom Q40/80) On the road to the cemetery, the family-run Mashito is built around a plant-filled patio. Though a bit frayed, at least it's colorful, with green paint framing the brick, and patchwork blankets on the beds. The wood-paneled rooms up top (with shared bath) are in better shape.

Chalet House
GUESTHOUSE $$

(☑ 5842-2100; www.chalethotelchichicastenango.com; 3a Calle C 7-44; r incl breakfast Q240) In a quieter residential zone north of the center, this feels like an apartment building, though the rooftop terrace is an exotic extra. Simply furnished rooms have thick blankets, real solar-powered showers, and there's a guest kitchen. Gregarious owner Manuel has plenty to tell you about his town.

Also provided is reliable shuttle service to Los Encuentros with connections to Antigua and Cobán.

Posada El Arco   GUESTHOUSE **$$**
(☑ 3469-1590; 4a Calle 4-36; s/d/tr Q225/244/305) 🌿 Near the Arco Gucumatz, this homey, solar-powered spread is one of Chichi's more original accommodations. All nine rooms are idiosyncratically appointed, with Maya weavings, colonial bedsteads and fireplaces. Rooms 3,4, 6 and 7 have views over the tranquil rear garden and northward to the mountains. Well-read owner Pedro likes to converse in English. Reservations are a good idea.

Mayan Inn   HOTEL **$$$**
(☑ 2412-4753; www.mayaninn.com.gt; 8a Calle A 1-91; ⊙ s/d/tr Q878/1122/1239) Founded in 1932, the inn today encompasses several restored colonial houses on either side of 8a Calle. The courtyards are planted with tropical flora and the walls draped in indigenous textiles. Each of the 16 rooms is uniquely appointed, with carved armoires and fireplaces. Those on the south side have the best views. The **restaurant** (☑ 2412-4753; 8a Calle A 1-91; mains Q70-125; ⊙ 7am-10pm) here does some of Chichi's finest cuisine.

✖ Eating

As may be expected, most restaurants here remain empty when not occupied by tour groups, with meek underage waiters hovering in the background. The real action is in the central plaza, where attentive *abuelitas* (grandmas) ladle chicken soup, beef stew, tamales and *chiles rellenos* from huge pots as their daughters and granddaughters minister to the throngs of country folk sitting at long tables covered with oilcloth. At least four vendors line up by the central fountain, where a *chuchito* – small tamal wrapped in a corn husk – and chocolate will get you change from Q10. What are called tamales here are made of rice and laced with sauce. Sliced watermelon and papaya can be had at other stalls. On nonmarket evenings you'll find enchiladas and *pupusas* in front of the cathedral, served with *atole de plátano,* a warm plantain beverage spiked with cinnamon.

Comedor Típico   GUATEMALAN **$**
(4a Av 4-23; dishes Q20) One of the few nontouristy eateries in town, this locally popular lunch hall does cow's foot soup and other hearty fare for the traveler's soul.

Casa San Juan   GUATEMALAN **$$**
(☑ 7756-2086; 6a Av 7-30; mains Q60; ⊙ 10am-9:30pm Tue-Sun) One of the more stylish eateries, the San Juan occupies a beautiful colonial structure beside Santo Tomás with candlelit dining in various salons. Offerings range from burgers and sandwiches to more traditional fare, including good *chiles rellenos* laced with zesty salsa.

COFRADÍAS

Chichicastenango's religious life is centered on traditional brotherhoods known as *cofradías*. Membership is an honorable civic duty, and election as leader is the greatest honor. Leaders must provide banquets and pay for festivities for the *cofradía* throughout their term. Though it is expensive, a *cofrade* (brotherhood member) happily accepts the burden, even going into debt if necessary.

Each of Chichi's 14 *cofradías* has a patron saint. Most notable is the *cofradía* of Santo Tomás, the town's patron saint. *Cofradías* march in procession to church on the Sundays that follow their saints' days, with the officers dressed in costumes showing their rank. Before them is carried a ceremonial staff topped by a silver crucifix or sun-badge that signifies the patron saint of the *cofradía*. A drum, flute and perhaps a trumpet may accompany the procession, as do fireworks.

During major church festivals, effigies of the saints are carried in grand processions, and richly costumed dancers wearing wooden masks act out legends of the ancient Maya and of the Spanish conquest. For the rest of the year, these items are kept in storehouses-cum-workshops called *morerías;* two prominent ones are at the start of the trail leading up to the Maya shrine of Pascual Abaj (p119).

Chichicastenango

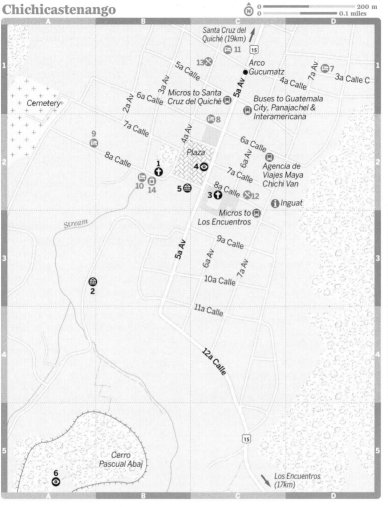

Chichicastenango

🛍 Shopping

Ut'z Bat'z
HANDICRAFTS

(8a Calle 3-14; ⊘1-5pm Wed, 10am-5pm Thu, Sat & Sun) This fair-trade shop by the plaza's southwest corner displays the work of a local women's cooperative comprising 30 weavers, including scarves, shawls, table runners, bags and pillows.

ℹ Information

DANGERS & ANNOYANCES

Hola, amigo! is the refrain you'll hear from the myriad vendors and touts who depend on tourism for their livelihood; it can wear you down, but try to be polite. Ignore touts offering assistance in finding a hotel; you'll have no difficulty finding lodgings on your own.

Chichi is plagued by traffic and exhaust fumes. Keep an eye out for buses tearing around corners.

MEDICAL SERVICES

Hospital El Buen Samaritano (☑7756-1163; 6a Calle 3-60) Has a 24-hour emergency clinic.

MONEY

Chichi's many banks all stay open on Sunday.

Banco Industrial (6a Calle 6-05) Visa/MasterCard ATM.

Visa/MasterCard ATM (cnr 5a Av & 6a Calle)

TOURIST INFORMATION

INGUAT (☑5966-1162; info-quiche@inguat. gob.gt; 7a Av 7-14; ⊘8am-4pm Sun-Thu) Authorized guides can be hired here for cultural tours of the town and up to Pascual Abaj.

Getting There & Away

Buses heading south to Panajachel, Quetzaltenango and all other points reached from the Interamericana arrive and depart from 5a Calle near the corner of 5a Av, one block uphill from the Arco Gucumatz. Buses approaching from the south go up 7a Av, dropping off passengers two blocks east of the central plaza.

Agencia de Viajes Maya Chichi Van (☑5007-2051; mayachichivan@yahoo.es; 6a Calle 6-45) offers shuttles to Guatemala City (Q125), Antigua (Q90) and Panajachel (Q55) on Thursday and Sunday at 2pm, plus service to San Cristóbal de las Casas, Mexico, at 7am daily. In most cases it needs at least five passengers. It also runs tours to K'umarcaaj near Santa Cruz del Quiché, Nebaj and elsewhere.

The hotel Chalet House (p119) provides reliable shuttle service to Los Encuentros with connections to Antigua, Lago de Atitlán and Quetzaltenango.

PHONE FEUD

Due to a long-running land dispute between the indigenous community and Telgua, Chichicastenango has been without landlines for the past two years. Telgua owner Mexican mogul Carlos Slim contends that he purchased the plot behind the cathedral where the telephone antennas stand while one of Chichi's *cofradías* insists it belongs to them, and the case has been tied up in court for at least three years. The result has been a spike in business for cell phone providers, one of which, Claro, is also Slim's.

Santa Cruz del Quiché

POP 102,782 / ELEV 1979M

Without Chichicastenango's big market and attendant tourism, Santa Cruz – or just El Quiché – presents a less self-conscious slice of regional life and is refreshingly free of competition for tourist lucre. Just 19km north of Chichi, Santa Cruz is the capital of Quiché department, drawing a diverse populace on business and administrative affairs. The main market days are Thursday and Sunday, boosting the bustle considerably. Travelers who come here usually do so to visit K'umarcaaj, the ruins of the old K'iche' Maya capital, or to change buses en route further north.

The most exciting time to be here is mid-August during the **Fiestas Elenas** (www.fiestaselenas.com; ⊘mid-August), a week of festivities and a proud display of indigenous traditions, culminating in *Convite Femenino,* when El Quiché's women don masks and dance up a storm to marimba accompaniment.

⊙ Sights

Most points of interest are within a few short blocks of the tripartite plaza, usually a hive of activity. The top square is flanked on the east by Gobernación (the departmental government palace), the middle one by the cathedral and town hall, and the bottom one by the big domed events hall, in front of which stands a statue of K'iche' warrior Tecún Umán in a fierce posture, though these days sadly engulfed by the stalls of the informal economy. The main market occupies a series of buildings east of the plaza.

BUSES FROM CHICHICASTENANGO

DESTINATION	FARE	TIME	FREQUENCY	ALTERNATIVE
Antigua	Q25	3½hr		Take any bus heading for Guatemala City and change at Chimaltenango.
Guatemala City	Q30	2½hr	Every 30 minutes from 3am to 5pm.	
Los Encuentros	Q6	30min	Frequent.	Microbuses leave from in front of the Telgua building on 7a Av.
Panajachel	Q20	2hr		Take a microbus to Los Encuentros and change there.
Quetzaltenango	Q20	2hr	Every half hour until 3pm.	Take a microbus to Los Encuentros and change there.
Santa Cruz del Quiché	Q6	40min	Frequent microbuses depart from 5a Calle on the west side of 5a Av between 7am and 8pm.	

K'umarcaaj ARCHAEOLOGICAL SITE
(Q'um'arkaj, Utatlán; Q30; ⊙8am-4pm) The ruins of the ancient K'iche' Maya capital of K'umarcaaj remain a sacred site for the Maya, and contemporary rituals are customarily enacted here. Archaeologists have identified more than 80 large structures in 12 groups, but only limited restoration has been done. The ruins have a fine setting, shaded by tall evergreens and surrounded by ravines. Bring a flashlight.

The kingdom of K'iche' was established in late Postclassic times (about the 14th century) by a mixture of indigenous people and invaders from the Tabasco-Campeche border area in Mexico. King Ku'ucumatz founded K'umarcaaj, which owing to its naturally fortified position commanded an extensive valley, and conquered many neighboring settlements. During the long reign of his successor Q'uik'ab (1425–75), the K'iche' kingdom extended its borders to Huehuetenango, Nebaj, Rabinal and the Pacific Slope. At the same time the Kaqchiquel, a vassal people who once fought alongside the K'iche', rebelled, establishing an independent capital at Iximché.

When Pedro de Alvarado and his Spanish conquistadors hit Guatemala in 1524, it was the K'iche', under their king Tecún Umán, who led the resistance against them. In the decisive battle fought near Quetzaltenango on February 12, 1524, Alvarado and Tecún engaged in mortal combat. Alvarado prevailed. The defeated K'iche' invited him to visit K'umarcaaj. Smelling a rat, Alvarado enlisted the aid of his Mexican auxiliaries and the anti-K'iche' Kaqchiquel, and together they captured the K'iche' leaders, burnt them alive in K'umarcaaj's main plaza and then destroyed the city.

The museum at the entrance will help orientate you. The tallest of the structures round the central plaza, the **Templo de Tohil** (a sky god), is blackened by smoke and has a niche where contemporary prayermen regularly make offerings to Maya gods. The L-shaped ball court alongside it has been extensively restored.

Down the hillside to the right of the plaza is the entrance to a long tunnel known as the *cueva*. Legend has it that the K'iche' dug the tunnel as a refuge for their women and children in preparation for Alvarado's coming, and that a K'iche' princess was later buried in a deep shaft off this tunnel. Revered as the place where the K'iche' kingdom died, the *cueva* is sacred to highland Maya and is an important location for prayers, candle burning, offerings and chicken sacrifices.

If there's anyone around the entrance, ask permission before entering. Inside, the long tunnel (perhaps 100m long) is blackened with smoke and incense and littered with candles and flower petals. Use your flashlight and watch your footing: there are several side tunnels and at least one of them, on the right near the end, contains a deep, black shaft.

The ruins of K'umarcaaj are 3km west of El Quiché. Gray 'Ruinas' microbuses depart from in front of the cathedral in Santa Cruz every 20 minutes (Q1). The last one back is at 6:50pm.

🛏 Sleeping

The main hotel district is along 1a Av (Zona 5) north of the bus terminal, with at least five hotels within two blocks, while other hotels are located along 9a Calle.

For budget grub, there's plenty of grilling going on around and within the market.

Hotel Rey K'iche HOTEL $

(☑ 7755-0827; 8a Calle 0-39, Zona 5; s/d Q100/180; @🛜) Between the bus station and plaza, the Rey K'iche is excellent value with well-maintained, brick-walled rooms around a quiet interior and affable staff. There's free drinking water and a decent cafe upstairs serving breakfast and dinner. All things considered, it's the best place to stay.

Posada Santa Cecilia HOTEL $

(☑ 5180-1194; cnr 1a Av & 6a Calle; s/d Q125/190) Just south of the chaotic main plaza, this modern establishment takes up the top level of a small shopping center. Although the handful of comfortable units have large firm beds with pretty quilts, the property is sketchily maintained and unfortunately open to the constant rumble of traffic and car exhaust from the plaza during working hours.

El Sitio Hotel HOTEL $$

(☑ 7755-3656; elsitiohotel@gmail.com; 9a Calle 0-41, Zona 5; s/d/tr Q175/300/400; 🅿🛜) From the outside, this business-class hotel two blocks north of the bus terminal resembles a modern evangelical church. Though rather sterile with a cavernous lobby, rooms are modern and well-maintained and have a bit of local-style decor.

Café San Miguel BAKERY $

(☑ 7755-1488; 2 Av 4-42; sandwiches Q12; ☺8am-8pm; 🛜) Opposite the cathedral, this little bakery-cafe is a popular gathering place, with good coffee and fresh-baked goods on offer. Muffins are called *cubos* here; *tostadas* and *champurradas* are kinds of cookies; *pan dormido* is bread that's been allowed to lie around for a few days.

Restaurant El Chalet STEAK $$

(☑ 7755-0618; 1a Calle 2-39, Zona 5; mains Q60-70; ☺7am-9pm) The specialty here is grilled meats, served with homemade salsas. You could make a light meal of the tortilla-sized portions. Dining is beneath an arbor flanked by a strip of garden. It's part of a posh hotel/conference center a few blocks east of the big clock tower.

Uspantán

POP 41,892

Most travelers who pass through Uspantán are on their way to Cobán. Though the sky-high journey through the Cuchumatanes is reason enough to travel there, Uspantán, a benevolent town halfway between Huehuetenango and Cobán along the 7W road, offers a few attractions of its own.

The setting is stunning, in a fertile valley at the base of green forested mountains over which a bank of clouds roll in each afternoon. Women wear lacy, loose-fitting *huipiles* in bright orange or pink.

Founded by the Uspanteko Maya around the 6th century AD, it was originally dubbed Tz'unun Kaab' – place of hummingbirds. The

---

BUSES FROM QUICHÉ

El Quiché is the jumping-off point for the remote reaches of northern Quiché department, which extend all the way to the Mexican border. The main bus terminal, a dusty lot in Zona 5, is located four blocks south and two blocks east of the plaza.

DESTINATION	FARE	TIME	FREQUENCY
Chichicastenango	Q6	40min	Frequent microbuses depart from the corner of 5a Calle and 2 Av, opposite Café San Miguel.
Guatemala City	Q35	3hr	Every 10 minutes from 3am to 5pm.
Huehuetenango	Q25	2hr	Microbuses from the south side of the lot depart every half hour from 5am to 6pm.
Nebaj	Q20	2hr	Every half hour from 6am to 7pm.
Sacapulas	Q12	1hr	Microbuses depart from 1a Av off the northeast corner of main plaza every half hour until 7:30pm.
Uspantán	Q30	2-2½hr	Frequent microbuses depart from the west side of the lot from 5:30am to 7pm.

LOOK, UP IN THE SKY

Surely one of the most spectacular pre-Hispanic rituals alive today is that of the *palo volador* (flying pole). Dating from the Postclassic era, the ritual involves the installation of a tree trunk measuring up to 30m in the town square. One man sits atop the pole, playing the flute and directing the ceremony. Four flyers, or angels (the number four symbolizing the cardinal points of the compass), then leap off the top of the trunk, attached by ropes, and spin back to earth.

If all goes according to plan, the four flyers will circle the pole 13 times – thus making the number 52, which corresponds to the number of years in a Maya calendar round. In some places there are only two flyers, symbolizing Hun Hunahpu and Ixbalanque, the wizard twins from the Popul Vuh, who descended to the underworld to battle the lords of darkness.

The tradition has changed somewhat since the time of its origins – the tree trunk is no longer carried by hand to town for one, and the flyers' costumes have become increasingly gaudy over the years, incorporating such nontraditional items as mirrors sewn into the fabric. The *palo volador* is widely practiced in Mexico, most notably in Puebla and Veracruz, but is becoming less common in Guatemala. Your best chance of seeing it is during the fiestas of Chichicastenango (December 21), Cubulco (July 25) and nearby Joyabaj (August 15) in the department of Quiché.

severe repression it experienced during the armed conflict of the 1980s forged indigenous leader Rigoberta Menchú, who grew up a five-hour walk through the mountains in the village of Laj Chimel – though some locals gripe over why she hasn't returned to her hometown. Cardamom is grown, pigs and sheep are raised on the surrounding slopes and gravel mining is a key industry.

To get the big picture, hike up to Cerro Xoqoneb', a Maya ceremonial center 1.5km east of town. Signage is sparse; the tourism association **ACAT** (ACAT; ☏ 7951-8027; amalia.urizar@yahoo.com) can set you up with a guide.

🛏 Sleeping & Eating

Hotel Don Gabriel　　　　　HOTEL $
(☏ 7951-8540; hoteldongabriel@yahoo.es; 7a Av 6-22; s/d/tr Q75/150/210; 🅿 🛜) Rooms at this excellent value lodging, just around the corner from the Parque Central, have plenty of thick blankets for the evening chill. If possible, choose a room on the top level opening on a Gaudí-esque terrace with various plant-laden gazebos and fabulous views of the mountains. Downstairs is a neat and clean little restaurant serving breakfast from 7am.

Hotel Posada Doña Leonor　　　HOTEL $
(☏ 7951-8041; calutis54@hotmail.com; 6a Calle 4-25, Zona 1; s/d/tr Q80/160/240; 🅿 🛜) This well-maintained option a block east of the plaza features 21 rooms around a courtyard with a jacaranda tree in the middle and a cook shack for breakfast and supper. You'll find firm beds, fresh paint, and spotless bathrooms with electric showerheads.

Comedor Yeimy　　　　GUATEMALAN $
(7a Calle; meals Q20; ⊙ 7:30am-8pm) This unusually clean establishment has silver tablecloths and several pink-walled salons. Home-cooked platters of chicken, steak or eggs are nicely presented and served with a bowl of pickled carrots and onions. It's one block south, 1½ blocks east of the plaza.

ℹ Getting There & Away

Microbuses for Quiché (Q30, 2½ hours), via Sacapulas, leave whenever full from Uspantán's bus terminal on 6a Calle, three blocks west of the Parque Central, until 7pm. For Cobán (Q30, three hours), microbuses go hourly from 4am to 3:30pm; a 35km stretch of that journey is over a perilously unpaved surface. For Nebaj, there are a couple of direct microbuses (coming from Cobán), or get a microbus to Sacapulas where you'll find frequent connections up to the Ixil Triangle.

Nebaj

POP 18,484 / ELEV 2000M

Hidden in a remote fold of the Cuchumatanes mountains north of Sacapulas is the Triángulo Ixil (Ixil Triangle), a 2300-sq-km zone comprising the towns of Santa María Nebaj, San Juan Cotzal and San Gaspar Chajul, as well as dozens of outlying villages and hamlets. The local Ixil Maya people, though they suffered perhaps more than anybody in Guatemala's civil war, cling proudly to their traditions and speak the Ixil language. Nebaj women are celebrated for their beautiful purple, green and yellow pom-pommed hair braids, scarlet *cortes,* and their *huipiles* and *rebozos* (shawls) featuring bird and animal motifs.

Living in this beautiful mountain vastness has long been both a blessing and a curse. The invading Spaniards found it difficult to conquer, and they laid waste to the inhabitants when they did. During the civil war years, massacres and disappearances were rife, with more than two dozen villages destroyed. According to estimates by church groups and human-rights organizations, some 25,000 Ixil inhabitants (of a population of 85,000) were either killed or displaced by the army between 1978 and 1983 as part of

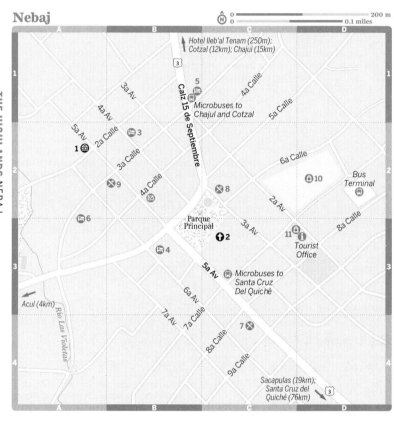

Nebaj

◉ Sights
1 Centro Cultural Kumool A2
2 Iglesia de Nebaj C3

✪ Activities, Courses & Tours
Guías Ixiles ....(see 9)
Nebaj Language School ....(see 9)

🛏 Sleeping
3 Hotel Santa María B2
4 Hotel Turansa B3

5 Hotel Villa Nebaj B1
6 Media Luna Medio Sol A3

✗ Eating
7 Asados El Pasabien C4
8 Comedor El Si'm C2
9 El Descanso B2

🛍 Shopping
10 Market D2
11 Mercado de Artesanías C3

LAJ CHIMEL

Renowned as the place that spawned Nobel Peace Prize winner Rigoberta Menchú, **Laj Chimel** (🖉 5729-7610; tour per person Q190, min 2 people) offers homegrown tours of the community and surroundings, as well as basic accommodations. Local K'iche' guides lead relaxed walks along a well-conditioned trail through the cloud forest, pointing out birds and wildlife and stopping at a lookout point for impressive views over the Cuchumatanes range.

Along the way, you'll learn about medicinal plants, *milpa* (cornfield) cultivation and the civil war atrocities that occurred here. The tour includes lunch at a local home.

Pick-up trucks from Uspantán's bus terminal can take you as far as Laguna Danta (Q20), a secluded lake one hour's walk from Laj Chimel. It's best to travel up in the morning and spend the night at a community-run hostel (Q50 per person). Simple meals are offered. The village is off the grid but solar panels provide some power.

the campaign to expunge guerrilla activity. You may hear some appalling personal experiences from locals while you're here.

The people of the Ixil Triangle are making a heroic effort to build a new future with the help of development organizations and NGOs, whose workers you're likely to encounter during your visit.

◉ Sights

A block east of Parque Principal is the market (busiest on Thursday and Sunday). Calz 15 de Septiembre runs northeast from the Parque to become the road to Cotzal and Chajul.

Centro Cultural Kumool MUSEUM
(5a Av 1-32; Q20; ⊙9am-noon & 1-6pm Mon-Fri, 8am-1pm Sat) Housed in the Radio Ixil building, this small museum displays a collection of mostly ceramic objects excavated in the Ixil region, all arranged by historical period. Among the more interesting pieces are a ceremonial ax with a skull handle and a giant funerary urn with a jaguar face, plus some well-preserved polychrome vases.

Iglesia de Nebaj CHURCH
This formidable church dominates the south side of Parque Principal. Inside, to the left of the entrance is a memorial to Juan José Gerardi, the socially progressive priest who as bishop of Quiché witnessed widespread human rights abuses here. Soon after he released a report about these atrocities, Gerardi himself was assassinated. Several hundred crosses around the monument memorialize the Nebaj inhabitants who were murdered during a massacre in the early 1980s.

🔗 Tours

Guías Ixiles HIKING
(🖉 5847-4747; www.nebaj.com; 3a Calle, El Descanso Bldg, Zona 1; ⊙8am-12:30pm & 2-5pm) Guías Ixiles offers half-day walks to Las Cataratas (Q55 for one person plus Q25 for each extra person), a series of waterfalls north of town, or around town with visits to the sacred sites of the *costumbristas* (people who still practice non-Christian Maya rites). Guías Ixiles also leads three-day treks over the Cuchumatanes to Todos Santos Cuchumatán.

🍴 Courses

Nebaj Language School LANGUAGE COURSE
(🖉 5847-4747; www.nebaj.com/nls.html; 3a Calle, El Descanso Bldg, Zona 1; 1 week Q615) Offers instruction in Spanish. A package (Q1110) is available, including accommodations with a local family, two meals a day, two guided hikes to nearby villages and internet use. Instruction in the indigenous Ixil language is another option.

You can also learn how to make regional dishes like *boxboles* (corn dough wrapped in squash leaves, served with a spicy peanut sauce).

✨ Festivals & Events

Nebaj's annual **festival**, coinciding with the Assumption of the Virgin Mary, runs for 10 days in mid-August.

🛏️ Sleeping & Eating

Hotel Turansa HOTEL **$**
(🖉 4144-7609; cnr 5a Calle & 6a Av; s/d from Q85/150; 🅿🤶) This friendly, central establishment – just a block from the Parque Principal – has decent-sized rooms with big comfy beds and flat-screen TVs along

plant-draped balconies. Top-floor triples open on a sunny terrace. The only downside is the pervasive engine noise from outside.

Media Luna Medio Sol
HOSTEL $

(☑5749-7450; www.nebaj.com/medialuna.html; 3a Calle 6-25; dm Q35, r per person Q45; ☜) Nebaj's hostel is around the corner from its parent organization, El Descanso (p128), where you can check in. Two six-bed dorms and a few private rooms with thin mattresses share clean toilets and showers. You're welcome to use the kitchen, though facilities are minimal.

★ Hotel Santa María
HOTEL $$

(☑4212-7927; www.hotelsantamarianebaj.com; cnr 4a Av & 2a Calle; s/d Q150/200; P☜) Scarlet woven bedspreads, carved-wood headboards and other Ixil handicrafts decorate the bright, spotless rooms at this well-maintained property three blocks northwest of the main plaza.

Hotel Villa Nebaj
HOTEL $$

(☑7756-0005; www.hotelvillanebaj.com; Calz 15 de Septiembre 2-37; s/d Q150/225; P☜) Behind the elaborate facade is a neat, modern hotel with fountains in the courtyard and elaborate paintings of *nebajenses* in fiesta wear. Rooms on three levels have a dash of style, withcolorful bedspreads, carved headboards and piping hot showers.

Comedor El Si'm
GUATEMALAN $

(3a Av; breakfast Q30; ☉7am-9pm) This below-street-level place off the main plaza is great for a gut-stuffing *desayuno* (breakfast), served with a bonus bowl of *mosh* (warm cereal) and freshly baked cookie, and they refill your coffee cup. It's usually crammed with local characters by 8am.

El Descanso
CAFE $

(☑5847-4747; www.nebaj.com; 3a Calle, Zona 1; mains Q28-35; ☉6:30am-9:30pm) This cozy restaurant features a bar and lounge areas in Nebaj's most alternative ambiance. A range of snacks, salads and soups is served.

Asados El Pasabien
STEAK $

(cnr 5a Av & 9a Calle; mains Q35-45; ☉noon-3pm & 6-10:30pm) Steaks, chicken and shrimp are skillfully grilled and served up with heaping portions of halved potatoes, salad and home-made salsas at this locally popular dining hall.

🔒 Shopping

Mercado de Artesanías
HANDICRAFTS

(Handicrafts Market; cnr 7a Calle & 2a Av, Zona 1; ☉8am-6pm) The numerous vendor stalls

---

TRADITIONAL MAYA CLOTHING

Anyone visiting the highlands can delight in the beautiful *traje indígena* (traditional Maya clothing). The styles, patterns and colors used by each village – originally devised by the Spanish colonists to distinguish one village from another – are unique, and each garment is the creation of its weaver, with subtle individual differences.

The basic elements of the traditional wardrobe are the *tocoyal* (head covering), *huipil* (blouse), *corte* or *refago* (skirt), *calzones* (trousers), tzut or *kaperraj* (cloth), *paz* (belt) or *faja* (sash) and *caítes* or *xajáp* (sandals).

Women's head coverings are beautiful and elaborate bands of cloth up to several meters long, wound about the head and often decorated with tassels, pom-poms and silver ornaments.

Women proudly wear *huipiles* every day. Though some machine-made fabrics are now being used, many *huipiles* are still made completely by hand. The white blouse is woven on a backstrap loom, then decorated with appliqué and embroidery designs and motifs common to the weaver's village. Many of the motifs are traditional symbols. No doubt all motifs originally had religious or historical significance, but today that meaning has often been lost.

Cortes (refagos) are pieces of cloth 7m to 10m long that are wrapped around the body. Traditionally, girls wear theirs above the knee, married women at the knee and old women below the knee, though the style can differ markedly from region to region.

Both men and women wear *fajas*, long strips of backstrap-loom-woven cloth wrapped around the midriff as belts. When they're wrapped with folds upward like a cummerbund, the folds serve as pockets.

Tzutes (for men) or *kaperraj* (for women) are the all-purpose cloths carried by local people and used as head coverings, baby slings, produce sacks, basket covers and shawls. There are also shawls for women called *perraj*.

here offer well-made *rebozos, cintas* (the pom-pommed braid woven into Ixil women's hair) and *huipiles,* which can cost anywhere from Q300 to Q5000, depending on quality.

ℹ Information

Banrural (⊙8am-4:30pm Mon-Fri, 7-11am Sat) Changes traveler's checks.

Post Office (5a Av 4-37) One block northwest of the park.

Tourist Office (☑3072-4224; cnr 7a Calle & 2a Av, Zona 1; ⊙8am-6pm Mon-Sat, 8am-noon Sun) The tourist office, inside the Mercado de Artesanías, can answer questions in Spanish.

ℹ Getting There & Away

The bus terminal is just below the market. Microbuses bound for Santa Cruz del Quiché, via Sacapulas, go every half hour from 4am until 5pm (Q20, two hours), departing from behind the church at the corner of 5a Av and 7a Calle. To head west to Huehuetenango or east to Uspantán and Cobán, change at Sacapulas.

Microbuses to Chajul (Q7, 45 minutes) depart every 20 minutes or so until 6pm from in front of the Hotel Villa Nebaj, on Calz 15 de Septiembre.

The main bus terminal, behind the market, mainly serves outlying villages such as Tzalbal, Vicalama and Palop; one bus travels all the way to Guatemala City (Q50, 5½ hours) via Chichicastenango, departing at 2am.

Chajul

POP 53,089

A good paved road winds northeast through piney slopes to Chajul, an impoverished but intensely traditional village, where centuries-old customs are still practiced. Women stroll arm-in-arm wearing maroon *cortes* (wraparound skirts), earrings made from silver coins, and bright blue or purple *huipiles* woven with geometric patterns. Along the dirt streets, adobe structures with tile roofs propped up by carved wooden pillars are interspersed with patches of maize and squash. Tuesday and Friday are market days.

◉ Sights

Museo Maya Ixil   MUSEUM
(☑4586-8238; centroculturalmayaixil08@gmail.com; Q20; ⊙8am-6pm) The musical instruments, stone implements, weapons, indigenous outfits and archaeological finds crammed into this humble adobe home have been painstakingly selected by a local historian, along with evidence of Chajul's resistance during the armed conflict of the

1980s. From the Parque Central, turn left at the bank, then right uphill. If there's no one around, inquire at the Banrural.

⌨ Tours

Limitless Horizons Ixil   CULTURAL TOUR
(☑5332-6264; www.limitlesshorizonsixil.org) This California-based NGO works to expand educational opportunities for local children. It offers 'community engagement trips' (Q11,140), 10-day excursions that involve visiting homes of local families, learning backstrap weaving, speaking the Ixil language, exploring the highlands and collaborating on community service projects.

🛏 Sleeping & Eating

Posada Vetz K'aol   LODGE $
(☑5784-8802; www.asociacionchajulense.org; dm/r per person Q65/75) Standing in a patch of forest, the *posada* is a former stable, built in the local style with carved wood columns along an arcade. Most of the pine-paneled rooms have four or five bunk beds and there's one double with its own bathroom. A cozy sitting room has a large fireplace and coffee maker.

Just a 10-minute stroll from the center of Chajul, down a path off the road from Nebaj, it's owned by a local coffee growers' cooperative that offers half-day tours with visits to beekeepers and a sacred hill where devotees perform ceremonies (Q50 per person). Host Eduardo can meet you in the village and accompany you to the lodge.

Comedor Sarai   GUATEMALAN $
(set lunch Q15; ⊙7am-9pm) Join the *chajulenses* for lunch at this humble hall next to the pharmacy. The one or two items on the menu usually consist of chicken or beef and are served at rude wooden tables covered with oilcloth.

ℹ Getting There & Away

From Nebaj, microbuses to Chajul (Q7, 45 minutes) depart every 20 minutes or so until 6pm from in front of the Hotel Villa Nebaj, on Calz 15 de Septiembre. The last micro back to Nebaj departs around 5pm.

Acul

Acul, 4km west of Nebaj, was founded as the first *polo de desarrollo* (pole of development) in 1983. Considered 'strategic hamlets', these settlements were constructed to enable the army to keep inhabitants from having contact with the guerrillas. After the civil war, some people returned to their original homes but others stayed on. Set astride the bucolic Río Azul valley, it retains a functional appearance, with stores and evangelical prayer halls along either side of a broad dirt street. These days the main activities are weaving, cattle ranching and loom building.

Just north of Acul is a pair of farms devoted to the making of cheese. They were started by two immigrant brothers, the Azzaris, cheese makers in their native Italian Alps who moved to Guatemala in the 1930s, perhaps choosing the Acul valley because of its alpine appearance. Older brother José gained renown as a prize wrestler before being killed in the ring.

Both farms offer excellent accommodations. The first you come to, the **Hacienda Mil Amores** (☎5704-4817; itaazzari.33@hotmail.com; r per person Q185), has four country cabins on a hillside and it serves a superb lunch (Q55, by reservation). Just across the way, the humbler **Hacienda San Antonio** (☎5702-1907; www.quesochancol.com; r per person Q155) has half a dozen neat, wood-floored rooms, some with hot-water bathroom, and does meals (Q55).

Microbuses ply the paved road between Nebaj and Acul every half hour, or consider hiking over with Nebaj-based Guías Ixiles (p127) and taking the bus back.

WESTERN HIGHLANDS

The mountainous departments of Quetzaltenango, Totonicapán and Huehuetenango are generally less frequented by tourists, but with extraordinarily dramatic scenery and vibrant indigenous culture, this part of the country presents an invariably fascinating panorama. Highlights of any visit include Quetzaltenango, Guatemala's second-largest city, with an ever-growing language-school and volunteer-work scene; the pretty nearby town of Zunil, with its volcanically heated springs; ascents of the volcanoes around Quetzaltenango; and the remote mountain enclave of Todos Santos Cuchumatán, north of Huehuetenango, with a strong traditional culture and excellent walking possibilities.

Quetzaltenango

POP 152,743 / ELEV 2367M

Quetzaltenango may well be the perfect Guatemalan town – not too big, not too small, enough foreigners to support a good range of hotels and restaurants, but not so many that it loses its national flavor. The Guatemalan 'layering' effect is at work in the city center – once the Spanish moved out, the Germans moved in and their architecture gives the zone a somber, even Gothic, feel.

Quetzaltenango is big, like its name – which the locals kindly shorten to Xela (*shell*-ah), itself an abbreviation of the original K'iche' Maya name, Xelajú – but by Guatemalan standards, it is an orderly, clean and safe city. It tends to attract a more serious type of traveler – people who really want to learn Spanish and then stay around and get involved in the myriad volunteer projects on offer.

Xela also functions as a base for a range of spectacular hikes through the surrounding countryside – the ascent to the summit of Volcán Tajumulco (Central America's highest point) and the three-day trek to Lago de Atitlán, to name a few.

Quetzaltenango came under the sway of the K'iche' Maya of K'umarcaaj when they began their great expansion in the 14th century. Before that it had been a Mam Maya town. It was near here that the K'iche' leader Tecún Umán was defeated and killed by the Spanish conquistador Pedro de Alvarado in 1524.

The town prospered in the late-19th-century coffee boom, with brokers opening warehouses and *finca* (plantation) owners coming to town to buy supplies. (Fans of urban decay will appreciate the abundance of unrestored structures still standing from that period.) This boom busted when a combined earthquake and eruption of Santa María in 1902 wreaked mass destruction. Still, the city's position at the intersection of roads to the Pacific Slope, Mexico and Guatemala City guaranteed it some degree of prosperity. Today it's again busy with commerce, of the indigenous, foreign and *ladino* varieties.

◎ Sights

Centro Intercultural de Quetzaltenango CULTURAL CENTER
(Map p134; 4a Calle & 19 Av, Zona 3) FREE Quetzaltenango's railroad station, 1km east of the Templo de Minerva along 4a Calle, lay dormant for years until the city converted it into this center, which now houses schools of art and dance, plus three interesting museums.

The Museo Ixkik' is devoted to Maya weaving and traditional outfits, while some 400 paintings by Guatemala's leading modernists are exhibited in the Museo de Arte, including works by Efraín Recinos, Juan Antonio Franco and the landscape artist José Luis Álvarez. The Museo del Ferrocarril de los Altos covers the ambitious rail project that connected Quetzaltenango to the Pacific coast but operated for just three years from 1930 to 1933.

Museo de Arte MUSEUM
(Map p134; 4a Calle & 19 Av, Zona 3; donation requested; ☺9am-1pm & 3-7pm) An interesting if chaotic collection of some 400 paintings by Guatemala's leading modernists is exhibited here, including works by Efraín Recinos, Jorge Mazariegos and the landscape artist José Luis Álvarez. Most prominently displayed are the fantastic canvases of Rodrigo Díaz, who also happens to be the curator.

Museo Ixkik' MUSEUM
(Map p134; ☑5653-5585; 4a Calle & 19 Av, Zona 3; donation requested Q35; ☺9am-5pm Mon-Fri) Devoted to Maya weaving, with traditional outfits arranged by region. Director Raquel García is an expert on the symbols of indigenous clothing and provides interesting commentary.

Parque Centro América PLAZA
(Map p138) Most of Xela's sights crowd in and around the broad central plaza. The original version, designed by Italian architect Alberto Porta in the 1800s, comprised two separate parks; these were combined in a 1930s update into its current oblong shape. The most notable of the monuments scattered along its expanse is a rotunda of Ionic columns dedicated to the composer Rafael Álvarez Ovalle.

In the center of the plaza is a pillar dedicated to Justo Rufino Barrios, the 19th-century president whose 'reforms' transferred land ownership from Maya peasants to coffee-plantation owners.

Templo de Minerva MONUMENT
(Map p134) FREE Rising incongruously from an island in the middle of traffic-choked 4a Calle, the temple was erected by dictator Estrada Cabrera to honor the Roman goddess of education and to inspire Guatemalan education. Bizarre contrast notwithstanding, it makes a handy shelter during a rainstorm.

Cathedral CATHEDRAL
(Map p138) The ornately carved facade of the Iglesia del Espíritu Santo marks the site of the original 1532 construction, which was pulverized by the quakes of 1853 and 1902. The modern Metropolitan Cathedral behind it was finished in the 1990s.

Parque Zoológico Minerva ZOO
(Map p134; ☑7763-5637; Av Las Américas 0-50, Zona 3; adult/child under 1.2m Q2/free; ☺9am-4pm Tue-Sun) About 2km northwest of Parque Centro América is this zoo/city park with spider monkeys, coyotes, turtles, gray foxes and numerous tropical birds, plus a few rides for children. The entrance is around the corner from the Templo de Minerva.

Museo del Ferrocarril de los Altos MUSEUM
(Map p134; 4a Calle & 19 Av, Zona 3; Q6; ☺9:30am-1pm & 3-6pm) This museum covers the ambitious rail project that connected Quetzaltenango to the Pacific coast but operated for just three years, from 1930 to 1933. Though the exhibit is woefully neglected, there's still plenty to see.

CHAJUL'S HIDDEN MURALS

While renovating the kitchen of his ancient dwelling in Chajul, resident Lucas Ariscona made a momentous discovery. Removing several layers of plaster revealed a series of murals that had probably not seen light for centuries. The paintings, which cover several walls of Ariscona's home, depict some kind of procession made up of both Spaniards and Mayas. Though they're seriously faded by sudden exposure to the elements after being concealed for so long, it is still possible to make out a figure in European attire playing a drum for another character in Maya ceremonial costume as well as a caped reveler bearing a human heart in his hand. Though Ariscona has made efforts to preserve the murals, his resources are limited and in the smoke-filled environment of a typical Chajul home, the rare testament to a Euro-Maya encounter faces inevitable deterioration.

As many as four other old houses in the community harbor ancient paintings beneath the plaster, some of them rich in Maya symbolism. Inquire at the Museo Maya Ixil (p129) to locate and visit these long-dormant works of art. A small donation is requested.

Museo de Historia Natural MUSEUM
(Map p138; ☑ 7761-6427; 7a Calle; Q6; ☺ 8am-noon & 2-6pm Mon-Fri, 9am-5pm Sat & Sun) The natural history museum holds a hodgepodge of Maya artifacts, vintage photos, old coins, knick-knacks and stuffed animals. Most interesting, perhaps, is the section devoted to the liberal revolution in Central American politics and the Estado de Los Altos, of which Quetzaltenango was once the capital.

🏃 Activities

There are many exciting walks and climbs to be done from Xela. **Volcán Tajumulco** (4220m), 50km northwest, is the highest point in Central America, and it's a challenging trek of one long day from the city or two days with a night camping on the mountain. This includes about five hours of walking up from the starting point, Tuhichan (2½ hours by bus from Xela).

With early starts, **Volcán Santa María** (3772m), towering to the south of the city, and the highly active **Santiaguito** (2488m), on Santa María's southwest flank, can both be done in long mornings from Xela, though the tough, slippery trail is recommended only for seasoned hikers. You start walking at the village of Llanos del Pinal, 5km south of Xela (Q5 by bus), from where it's four to five hours up to the summit of Santa María. Getting too close to Santiaguito is dangerous, so people usually just look at it from a point about 1½ hours' walk from Llanos del Pinal.

Highland Partners VOLUNTEERING
(Map p134; ☑ 7761-6408; www.highlandpartners. org; 5a Av & 6a Calle 6-17, Zona 1) This group seeks to empower Maya women in five rural communities near Quetzaltenango by helping them to become economically sustainable. You can join one of its Maya Viva tours to experience life in these villages, or go further and get involved in special projects such as building fuel-efficient stoves, transplanting trees or teaching art to schoolchildren.

In Xela, Highland Partners runs Pixan (p141), an outlet for weavings made by Maya women.

Los Vahos SWIMMING
(The Vapors; Q10; ☺ 8am-6pm) Just a short hike south of Xela are the rough-and-ready sauna/steam baths at Los Vahos (the Vapors). These natural saunas are just two dark stone rooms behind plastic curtains – occasionally the vents are carpeted with eucalyptus leaves, giving the steam a herbal quality. The baths are a 2km (1.2mi) uphill walk away, with good views of the city.

🎓 Courses

Language Courses

Quetzaltenango's many language schools attract students from around the world. Unlike Antigua, it isn't overrun with foreigners, though there is a growing social scene revolving around language students and volunteer workers.

Most schools provide opportunities to get involved in social action programs working with the local K'iche' Maya. The standard weekly price is Q920/1000 for four/five hours of instruction per day, Monday to Friday. Add around Q325 for room and board with a local family. Some places charge up to 20% more for tuition from June to August, and many require nonrefundable registration fees. Extras range from movies and free internet to dancing, cooking classes and lectures on Guatemalan politics and culture.

Proyecto Lingüístico
Quetzalteco de Español LANGUAGE COURSE
(Map p134; ☑ 7763-1061; www.plqe.org; 5a Calle 2-40, Zona 1) This collectively managed and politically minded institute also runs the **Escuela de la Montaña**, a limited-enrolment language-learning program in a rural zone near the town of Colomba. Courses in K'iche' are also offered.

El Quetzal Spanish School LANGUAGE COURSE
(Map p134; ☑ 7761-2784; www.elquetzalspanish.com; 7a Calle 4-24, Zona 1) One of the few indigenous-run businesses in town, offering plenty of activities.

El Portal Spanish School LANGUAGE COURSE
(Map p134; ☑ 7761-5275; www.spanishschoolelportal.com; 9a Callejón A 11-49, Zona 1) Small outfit with enthusiastic and supportive atmosphere. Earnings provide scholarships for children of single mothers.

Inepas LANGUAGE COURSE
(Instituto de Español y Participación en Ayuda Social; Map p138; ☑ 7765-1308; www.inepas.org; 15a Av 4-59) Guatemalan social issues are woven into the Spanish lessons at this Unesco-recognized NGO that promotes educational development in rural communities, and students can participate in a variety of worthy projects. The institute offers a selection of inexpensive accommodations as well as homestays.

**Centro de Estudios
de Español Pop Wuj** LANGUAGE COURSE
(Map p134; ☑ 7761-8286; www.pop-wuj.org; 1a
Calle 17-72, Zona 1) Pop Wuj's profits go to development projects in nearby villages, in
which students can participate.

Celas Maya LANGUAGE COURSE
(Map p138; ☑ 7765-8205; www.celasmaya.edu.gt;
6a Calle 14-55, Zona 1) Busy, professional outfit
with a good library and internet cafe. Official training and testing center for DELE
(test of Spanish as a foreign language).

Other Courses

Bakanos Dance Studio DANCING
(Map p138; ☑ 5651-4474; 15 Av 3-51; group/individual session Q35/125) Learn or improve
your salsa, merengue, bachata and *cumbia*
moves at this locally recommended studio.

Trama Textiles WEAVING
(Map p138; www.tramatextiles.org; 3a Calle 10-56, Zona 1) A fair-trade shop representing 17
weaving cooperatives from five different
regions of Guatemala, Trama Textiles also
offers backstrap-loom weaving classes. Options range from a simple demonstration
of techniques (Q35) to a 20-hour course in
which students produce an embroidered table runner (Q650).

🖐 Tours

★ **Guate Guides** ADVENTURE TOUR
(☑ 5195-7734; www.guateguides.com) This
small, locally run outfit offers tours to area
volcanoes, villages and nature reserves with
an emphasis on quality equipment and
knowledgeable guides. Experts in hiking and cycling respectively, guides Marvín
and Martín are certified in first-aid and survival situations.

Among the more interesting excursions
it offers are half-day cycling trips to San
Andrés Xequl via the Samalá river valley
(Q260), climbs up Santa María and Tacaná
volcanoes, and photography tours to the
quetzal reserve near San Marcos (one-day/
overnight Q390/700).

Altiplano's Tour Operator CULTURAL TOUR
(Map p138; ☑ 7766-9614; www.altiplanos.com.
gt; 6a Calle 7-55, Zona 1; half-day tours per person
Q250-350) This outfit offers some interesting
half-day tours to indigenous villages and
markets, colonial churches and coffee plantations around Xela, plus reliable shuttle
services.

Maya Viva CULTURAL TOUR
(Map p134; ☑ 7761-6408; www.highlandpartners.
org; cnr 5a Av & 6a Calle 6-17, Zona 1) This community tourism program is organized by
Highland Partners, a group that seeks to
empower Maya women in the countryside.
Visitors get to experience life in one of five
rural communities near Quetzaltenango and
learn about their customs, traditions and
daily activities.

Quetzaltrekkers ADVENTURE TOUR
(Map p134; ☑ 7765-5895; www.quetzaltrekkers.
com; Diagonal 12 8-37, Zona 1) Most of the guides
at this unique outfit are foreign volunteers
(and experienced trekkers can join their
ranks). Based at the Casa Argentina hotel, it
provides both monetary and logistical support for various social projects.

One-day hikes to Fuentes Georginas and
Santa María volcano, three-day trips to Lago
de Atitlán (Q750 per person) and six-day
treks from Nebaj to Todos Santos Cuchumatán (Q1300) run on a weekly basis; check
the calendar to see when they go. Also offered are rock-climbing expeditions to La
Muela, a pilgrimage site in the Almolonga
Valley where rock pillars rise out of an extinct lava field.

Adrenalina Tours TOUR
(Map p138; ☑ 7761-4509; www.adrenalinatours.
com; 13 Av & 4a Calle, Pasaje Enríquez) Provides a
range of trips in the Xela area, including to
Laguna de Chicabal (Q270), Fuentes Georginas (Q115) and El Aprisco nature reserve
plus weeklong itineraries focused on Maya
cosmogeny and Guatemala's natural attractions (per person from Q7250). INGUAT-certified guides.

Tranvía de los Altos TOUR
(Map p138; ☑ 5752-8369; www.tranviadelosaltos.
com) This pseudostreetcar does various circuits of the city, complete with knowledgeable commentary (in Spanish) and cheesy
sound effects. Two-hour tours start at 11am
and 3pm (Q50 per person), departing from
the Casa No'j (p141) on the south side of the
Parque Central.

✪ Festivals & Events

Xela Music Festival MUSIC
Organized by the French Cultural Institute,
this performance event usually takes place
in November, with local musicians playing
on five or six stages around the city center.

Quetzaltenango

0 0.25 miles
0 500 m

Salcajá (5km);
Cuatro Caminos &
Interamericana (9km);
San Andrés Xecul (11km);
San Francisco El Alto (13km);
Totonicapán (20km);
Momostenango (24km)

Zunil (via
Cantel, 14km)

Río Seco

San Martín
Sacatepéquez (20km)

Río Seco

6a Av

13a Calle

3a Av

4a Av

7a Calle

Long-Distance
Bus Stop

7a Av (Calzada Independencia)

Calle Cirilo Flores

Av El Cenizal

Diagonal 2

2a Av
3a Av
4a Av
5a Av
6a Av

5a Calle

Diagonal 3

Av Jesus Castillo

12a Av

Línea
Dorada

Estadio
Mario
Camposeco

1a Calle

14a Av

14a Av
13a Av

Buses to San Martín
Sacatepéquez (Chile Verde)

Transportes
Álamo

8a Calle
7a Calle
6a Calle
5a Calle

4a Calle

Parque
Benito
Juárez

18a Av
17a Av
16a Av
15a Av

3a Av
1a Calle

Transportes
Galgos

ZONA 3

8a Av
9a Av

Parque
Centro
América

8a Calle
9a Calle
10a Calle
11a Calle

13a Av

ZONA 1

1a Calle
2a Calle
3a Calle
4a Calle

12a Av

See Central Quetzaltenango Map (p138)

21a Av
22a Av
23a Av
24a Av

6a Calle
4a Calle
3a Calle

20a Av
19a Av
18a Av

1a Calle

Parque El
Calvario

Cemetery

Calle Rodolfo Robles

Diagonal 14

Diagonal 11

Diagonal 8

Diagonal 13

Diagonal 12

Microbuses
to City Center

Terminal
Minerva

Complejo
Deportivo

Feria de la Virgen del Rosario CULTURAL
(Feria Centroamericana de Independencia) Held in late September or early October, this is Xela's big annual party. Students create colorful carpets of sawdust upon the streets of the city, taxi drivers shoot fireworks and the sirens of the firetrucks wail. Residents kick up their heels at a fairground on the city's perimeter and there's plenty of entertainment at selected venues around town, including a battle of the brass bands in the Parque Centro América.

An international Spanish-language literary competition, hosted by the city, goes simultaneously.

🛏 Sleeping

With a continual influx of foreign volunteers and language students, Xela counts numerous long-term-stay options. Some guesthouses offer furnished apartments and most language institutes can set up homestays with local families. Look for leads in the classified section of the publication *XelaWho*.

Casa Seibel HOSTEL $
(Map p138; ☑ 7765-2130; www.casaseibel.com; 9 Av 8-10; dm/r Q50/110; 🛜) Brilliantly incorporated into a vintage Xela house, the recently opened Casa Seibel is cozy and comfortable. Set around two plant-fillled courtyards, its dorms and private rooms (sharing two bathrooms, one with tub) have attractive wood floors and painted ceilings and retain some original furniture with plenty of shelves and closet space. Guests can mingle in the shared kitchen and TV lounge.

Hotel Kiktem-Ja HOTEL $
(Map p138; ☑ 7761-4304; www.hotelkiktem-ja. com; 13a Av 7-18, Zona 1; s/d/tr Q135/180/230; Ⓟ) Set in a great hundred-year-old house downtown, the Kiktem-Ja is all floorboards at weird angles, stone arches and squiggly wood columns along plant-draped corridors. Rooms are spacious with sturdy bedsteads, fireplaces and pretty tiled bathrooms.

★ Casa Renaissance HOTEL $
(Map p138; ☑ 3121-6315; www.casarenaissance. com; 9a Calle 11-26, Zona 1; r with/without bathroom Q160/125; 🛜) This colonial mansion has been reborn as a casual guesthouse with five huge, beautifully restored rooms (two with private bathroom) along a delightful patio. The Dutch-managed place has a relaxed atmosphere: take drinks from the cooler, prepare your own meals in the kitchen or watch

videos from a voluminous collection. Rates drop significantly by the week.

Casa Nativos HOSTEL $
(Map p138; ☑ 7765-4723; www.casanativos.com; Pasaje Enríquez, 13a Calle, Zona 1; dm Q40, d without bathroom Q125; 🛜) One component of a cultural center occupying the rear of the Pasaje Enríquez, this Euro/Guate-run hostel contains basic but stylishly renovated rooms that accent the vintage beauty of the building; some feature balconies. There's a two-room apartment for long-term stays, including use of a shared kitchen.

Hostel Nim Sut HOSTEL $
(Map p138; ☑ 7761-3083; www.hostelnimsutquet-zaltenango.weebly.com; 4a Calle 9-42, Zona 1; dm Q45, s/d Q100/170, s/d without bathroom Q85/130; 🛜) Conveniently placed a block east of the Parque Centro América, this restored colonial relic has plenty of large rooms with basic bedding and clean parquet floors, some considerably brighter than others (room 5 is best). The terrace, from which you can occasionally glimpse the plumes of Santiaguito,

is a good place to enjoy an espresso from the cafe downstairs.

Guest House El Puente   HOSTEL $

(Map p138; ☑7761-4342; celasmaya@gmail.com; 15a Av 6-75, Zona 1; s/d/tr Q75/150/225) The three thoroughly restored rooms here, all with bathroom, surround a large, well-tended garden. Connected to Celas Maya (p133) Spanish school, it's often occupied by language learners who congregate in the large, well-equipped kitchen.

Black Cat Hostel   HOSTEL $

(Map p138; ☑7761-2091; 13a Av 3-33; dm incl breakfast Q70, r Q175; ☎) A great place to stay if you're looking to meet up with other travelers, this full-service hostel features a sunny courtyard, a bar-restaurant and lounge/TV area. Though sparsely furnished, the rooms are done up in soothing colors with nice wood floors.

Casa Argentina   HOSTEL $

(Map p134; ☑7763-2320; casargentina.xela@ gmail.com; Diagonal 12 8-37, Zona 1; dm Q30, s/d Q60/100; ☎) This sprawling guesthouse west of the center is a port of call for itinerant quetzal-pinchers. Steer clear of the outrageously overcrowded dorm and opt for the marginally pricier private rooms with cinderblock decor and bathroom. Overseen by an extended family that is eager to please.

Hostal Casa
Doña Mercedes   BOUTIQUE HOTEL $$

(Map p138; ☑7765-4687; www.hostalcasadonamercedes.com.gt; 6a Calle 13-42; s/d Q184/290, s/d without bathroom Q90/184; ☎) Two blocks west of Parque Centro América is this tranquil, excellent-value establishment. Neat rooms have a bit of colonial flair with burnished wood floors and wicker bedsteads, and there's plenty of space to lounge around. Well-equipped guest kitchen.

VOLUNTEERING IN XELA

The Quetzaltenango area has many nonprofit organizations working on social projects with the local K'iche' Maya people that need volunteers. Volunteer jobs can range from designing websites for indigenous organizations to working in animal shelters. You can volunteer part-time for a week or two while also studying Spanish, or you can live and work in a close-knit indigenous village for a year. Indeed, some schools exist primarily to generate funds for social projects and can help students to participate in their free time. Skills in fields such as medicine, nursing, teaching, youth work and computers are prized, but there are possibilities for anyone with the will to help. Volunteers must normally meet all their own costs and be willing to commit to a project for a specified minimum time. Three months is fairly typical for full-time posts, though the minimum can be as little as a week or as long as a year.

EntreMundos (Map p138; ☑7761-2179; www.entremundos.org; 6a Calle 7-31, Zona 1; ◷2-4pm Mon-Thu) is a nonprofit that works with NGOs and community groups, offering skill-building workshops and computer classes to local NGO workers. Its website has details of 100 projects all over Guatemala looking for volunteers, and its free bilingual bimonthly magazine features articles about social development and human rights issues, as well as local volunteer opportunities. EntreMundos asks a donation of Q25 for drop-in visitors wanting to be placed.

A few of the short-term volunteer opportunities provided by EntreMundos:

Amigo Fiel An animal-rights project with a shelter and focus on street-dog rehabilitation.

Chico Méndes Project Reforestation project in rural village just outside of Xela.

FUNDABIEM A foundation providing social and medical support to individuals with physical and mental disabilities; two-week minimum.

La Red Kuchub'al Fair-trade organization working with over 20 community organizations; two-week minimum.

The Quetzaltenango-based **Do Guatemala** (Map p138; ☑4899-3614; www.do-guatemala.com; 14 Av 3-06) sets up personalized trips that combine travel, volunteering and Spanish lessons in any combination possible. It offers volunteer placements throughout the country and provides orientation upon arrival.

Hostal 7 Orejas HOSTEL **$$**

(Map p134; ☑ 7768-3218; www.7orejas.com; 2a Calle 16-92, Zona 1; dm/s/d/tr Q75/170/305/365; [P] [@]) The 'Seven Ears' (named after a nearby mountain range) is a cordially managed and scrupulously maintained hostel on a quiet street northwest of the center. The pseudocolonial structure features spacious, fresh-smelling rooms alongside a strip of garden. Each has three queen-size beds with carved-wood chests for storage. Breakfast (Q30) is served on the excellent rooftop terrace.

Casa San Bartolomé B&B **$$**

(Map p134; ☑ 7761-9511; www.casasanbartolome. com; 2a Av 7-17, Zona 1; s/d/tr Q215/300/375; [P] [�]) In the family for generations, this atmospheric old residence has been converted into a cozy B&B. All six rooms have beautiful furniture and modern art. Guests may prepare meals in a shared kitchen and take tea on the lovely upper terrace. Located in a quiet, lovely neighborhood a 15-minute walk east of the park.

Hotel Casa Mañen HOTEL **$$**

(Map p138; ☑ 7765-0786; www.comeseeit.com; 9a Av 4-11, Zona 1; s/d from Q375/470) The town residence of coffee barons through the 19th century, this atmospheric guesthouse was thoughtfully renovated by a North American couple in the 1980s, with traditionally outfitted rooms, tranquil gardens and a fine roof terrace/bar. The furniture could use an upgrade and the staff some training, but these are quibbles.

Hotel Modelo HOTEL **$$**

(Map p138; ☑ 7761-2529; www.hotelmodelo1892. com; 14a Av A 2-31, Zona 1; r from Q500; [P] [@] [host] [🌀]) A few blocks below the Teatro Municipal, the colonial-style Modelo offers atmospheric rooms with wooden floorboards, firm beds and spacious bathrooms, lined up alongside pretty patios with seasonal flower arrangements and volcano paintings. A solid midrange option.

Hotel Pensión Bonifaz HOTEL **$$$**

(Map p138; ☑ 7723-1100; www.pensionbonifaz.com. gt; 4a Calle 10-50, Zona 1; s/d/tr Q625/740/850; [P] [@] [🌀]) The oldest and grandest hotel in Xela looms above the Parque Centro América. Rooms are on the top three floors; the 2nd-floor chambers surround a leafy colonial patio where breakfast is served. Though interior decor is not as fabulous as you might expect, the opulent front bar makes up for it.

 Eating

Quetzaltenango has a good selection of places to eat in all price ranges. Cheapest are the food stalls on the lower level of the central market, where snacks and main-course plates are sold for Q10 or less. One popular breakfast spot is **Doña Cristy** (Map p138; ⊙ 7am-7pm), serving *atol de elote* (a hot maize beverage), *empanadas* and *chuchitos* (small tamales garnished with chopped beets and grated cheese).

★**Café Canela** GUATEMALAN **$**

(Map p138; ☑ 7761-6654; 6a Calle 15-16; set lunch Q20; ⊙ 7am-3pm Mon-Fri; [🌀] [✈]) For breakfast and lunch on weekdays, Martha, aka *la nicaragüense*, has a simple setup with a sunny patio and alternative vibe. You'll find creative variations on the essential *menú del día* (Q20), nicely dressed salads and tasty soups. There are three set lunch choices daily including a vegan option.

Café Nativos CAFE **$**

(Map p138; ☑ 7765-4723; 13a Calle; breakfast Q25-30; ⊙ 10am-10pm) Part of a hostel/arts center in the Pasaje Enríquez, Café Nativos is an inviting place with good natural fare, espresso, French toast for breakfast, falafel and tofu in *mole*. A terrific balcony terrace, with counter along the edge, looks right at the ex-Gutierrez bank building, a deco wonder, and the burned-out shell of the Café Baviera.

La Chatia Artesano BAKERY **$**

(Map p138; ☑ 7765-0031; 7a Calle 15-20; sandwiches Q30-40; ⊙ 6:30am-9pm) A good place to stock up for that volcano climb, this craft bakery makes whole-wheat sandwiches (tofu, tempeh, eggplant, cheese), excellent cookies and granola.

Aj de Lunas GUATEMALAN **$**

(Map p138; ☑ 7761-0097; 9a Calle 11-16; lunch combos Q25; ⊙ 8am-9pm Mon-Sat; [🌀] [✈]) This recently upgraded dining hall is a good place to savor Quetzalteco home cooking, with daily specials like *jocóm* and *caldo de patas* (cow foot soup) served with a pile of tortillas and little dishes of lemons and tiny chilies. Vegetarian options are available.

★**Sabor de la India** INDIAN **$$**

(Map p138; ☑ 7765-2555; 15a Av 3-64; mains Q50-70; ⊙ noon-10pm Tue-Sun; [🌀] [✈]) Authentic south Indian fare is whipped up here by a fellow from Kerala. Servings are huge; the *thalis* – platters of curried veggies, chicken or beef – are highly recommended. Often

THE HIGHLANDS QUETZALTENANGO

Central Quetzaltenango

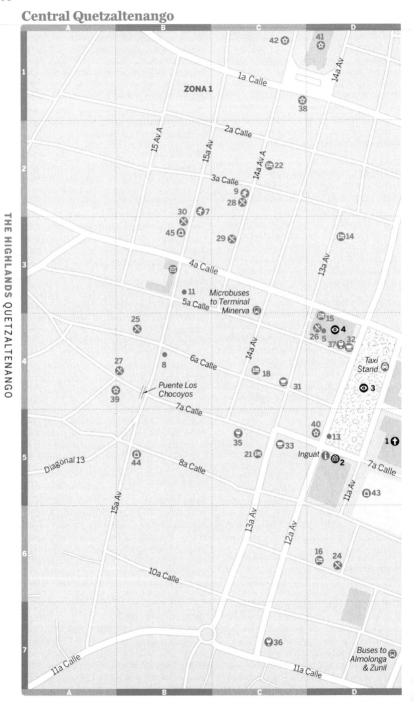

Central Quetzaltenango

◎ Sights
1 Cathedral D5
2 Museo de Historia Natural...................D5
3 Parque Centro América D4
4 Pasaje Enríquez....................................D4

✚ Activities, Courses & Tours
5 Adrenalina Tours D4
6 Altiplano's Tour Operator F5
7 Bakanos Dance Studio.......................B2
8 Celas Maya B4
9 Do Guatemala......................................C2
10 EntreMundos.......................................F5
11 Inepas..B3
12 Trama Textiles E2
13 Tranvía de los Altos...........................D5

🛏 Sleeping
14 Black Cat Hostel D3
15 Casa Nativos D4
16 Casa Renaissance..............................D6
17 Casa Seibel...E6
    Guest House El Puente ....(see 8)
18 Hostal Casa Doña Mercedes...........C4
19 Hostel Nim Sut E4
20 Hotel Casa Mañen F4
21 Hotel Kiktem-Ja C5
22 Hotel Modelo......................................C2
23 Hotel Pensión Bonifaz E4

🍴 Eating
24 Aj de Lunas D6
25 Café Canela..B4
26 Café Nativos D4
    Doña Cristy ....(see 43)
27 La Chatia Artesano B4
28 Royal Paris..C2
29 Sabe Delis C3
30 Sabor de la India B3

🍷 Drinking & Nightlife
31 Café Armonía C4
32 Café El Balcón del Enríquez...............D4
33 Café El Cuartito..................................C5
34 Café La Luna.......................................F4
35 King & Queen......................................C5
36 Pool & Beer...C7
37 Salón Tecún..D4

✪ Entertainment
38 Bari..C1
39 Blue Angel Video Café........................A4
40 Casa No'j...D5
41 Teatro Municipal.................................D1
42 Teatro Roma.......................................C1

🛍 Shopping
43 Central Market D5
44 North & South Bookstore B5
45 Vrisa Books...B3

populated by groups of gringos, the old stone-walled house makes an atmospheric setting for an extended meal.

Sabe Delis CREPERIE **$$**
(Map p138; ☑ 7761-2635; 14 Av A 3-38; crepes Q35-50; ☎) Crepes and wood-fired pizzas are the main attractions at this upscale dining hall, which also prepares exceptionally zesty salads. Popular with both foreigners and *chapines* (Guatemalans).

Panorama EUROPEAN **$$**
(Map p134; ☑ 7765-8580; www.restaurante panorama.com; 13a Av A, D16-44; fondue Q80; ⊙ noon-midnight) A 10-minute hike up the hill at the south end of town with views worthy of its name, Panorama makes a romantic spot for that special night out. Fondues and melted raclette cheese are the stars of the table at the Swiss-owned establishment.

Royal Paris FRENCH **$$**
(Map p138; ☑ 7761-1942; www.royalparis-quet zaltenango.blogspot.nl; 14 Av A 3-06; salads Q60; ⊙ noon-10pm Tue-Sun; ☎) Overseen by the French consul himself, this bistro ought to be authentic, and the escargots, baked Camembert and filet mignon approach Parisian standards. Check the blackboard for nightly specials. The cozy ambiance is augmented by a sweet terrace and live folk and jazz Wednesday, Friday and Saturday nights.

🍷 Drinking & Nightlife

Coffee plays an important part in Xela's economy, and there are plenty of places to grab a cup.

Xela's Zona Viva revolves around the Teatro Municipal, with discos and clubs popping up along 1a and 2a Calles and up 14 Av.

★**Café La Luna** CAFE
(Map p138; ☑ 7761-4354; 8a Av 4-11; ⊙ 11am-9pm Mon-Fri, 4-9pm Sat; ☎) For chocolate aficionados, this is a shrine. Made from scratch on the premises, the chocolate is velvety smooth and served in a variety of beverages: the chocolate cappuccino is mind-blowing. Groups of friends gather in the various salons, which are littered with vintage bric-a-brac.

★**Salón Tecún** PUB
(Map p138; Pasaje Enríquez; ⊙ 9:30am-12:30am) On the plaza end of the elegant Pasaje Enríquez, alive day and night with a healthy mix of Guatemalans and foreigners quaffing Cabro, the Tecún claims to be the country's longest-

running bar (since 1935). It also serves good pizza and pub food. Don't miss it.

Café El Cuartito CAFE
(Map p138; 13a Av 7-09; ⊙ 8am-11pm; ☎) This offbeat cafe with quirky decor is a point of reference for travelers and language students. It serves a good range of vegetarian snacks, herbal teas and organic coffee just about any way you want it, plus some creative cocktails – how about a raspberry mojito? There's live music most nights.

Café Armonía CAFE
(Map p138; ☑ 7765-3509; www.cafearmonia.com; 13 Av 5-48; ⊙ 7:30am-8:15pm Mon-Sat) This simple place is Xela's main outlet for the small growers of Guate's chief coffee-growing regions, including Acatenango, Huehuetenango, Atitlán and San Marcos beans, which are grown at a higher altitude and are thus more acidic than beans from Quetzaltenango. Herbert, one of the smart baristas here, grew up on a coffee *finca* and is an expert roaster.

King & Queen PUB
(Map p138; 7a Calle 13-27; ⊙ 6pm-1am) This tiny pub packs in a mixed crowd. Whether there's a band in the corner (Wednesday and Friday) or a heated trivia quiz (Tuesday), the face cards on the wall take it all in.

Café El Balcón del Enríquez CAFE
(Map p138; 12 Av 4-40, Pasaje Enríquez; ⊙ 8am-10pm) With specially designed viewing counters overlooking the Parque Centro América, this lively cafe on the upper level of the Pasaje Enríquez makes a nice perch for morning espresso or evening cocktails.

Pool & Beer PUB
(Map p138; 12a Av 10-21; ⊙ 7:30pm-1am Thu-Sat) The pool tables are worn and the cues crooked, but this ramshackle clubhouse remains a friendly and refreshingly nontrendy spot. Later in the evening day-glo imagery fires up a throbbing dance floor.

☆ Entertainment

It gets chilly when the sun goes down, so you won't want to sit out in the Parque Centro América enjoying the balmy breezes – there aren't any. Nevertheless, it's a pleasant place for an evening stroll.

The music scene is particularly strong in Xela. Many of the town's restaurants, cafes and bars double as performance venues, including the Royal Paris and El Cuartito. To see what's on, pick up a copy of *XelaWho* or check www.xelawho.com.

Teatro Municipal — THEATER

(Map p138; ✆7761-2218; 14a Av & 1a Calle) Quetzaltenango's grand neoclassical theater north of the center is the main venue for plays, concerts and dance performances. An elaborate two-tiered curved balcony has private boxes for prominent families.

Casa No'j — PERFORMING ARTS

(Map p138; ✆7761-4400; www.centroculturalcasanoj.blogspot.com; 7a Calle 12-12, Zona 1; ⊙8am-6pm Mon-Fri) Just off the park's southwest corner, the 19th-century former Convent of Bethlehem now houses Xela's premier cultural center. Besides photo and art exhibits, it stages anything from poetry festivals to marimba recitals to archaeology conferences, and it occasionally hosts internationally acclaimed artists and literary figures. Regional food festivals take place here on Sundays. Check the blog for upcoming events.

Bari — LIVE MUSIC

(Map p138; 1a Calle 14-31; ⊙8pm-1am Wed-Sat) One of several nightspots opposite the Teatro Municipal, Bari regularly hosts live *trova* (protest folk), rock and pop.

Teatro Roma — THEATER

(Map p138; ✆3010-0100; 14a Av A-34) This palace of culture is a showcase primarily for political comedy revues, with the occasional dance program.

Blue Angel Video Café — CINEMA

(Map p138; 7a Calle 15-79, Zona 1) Maintains an extensive library of both commercial and art films that may be viewed upon request, besides serving a range of vegetarian meals, herbal teas and hot chocolate.

🛍 Shopping

Pixan — HANDICRAFTS

(Map p134; ✆7761-6408; www.amaguate.org; 5a Av 6-17; ⊙9am-5pm Mon-Fri) The fashion outlet for the women's empowerment association AMA (highland women's association), Pixan sells quality textiles and clothing produced by Maya weavers in collaboration with designers from London, New York and elsewhere.

Pasaje Enríquez — SHOPPING CENTER

(Map p138; btwn Calles 4a & 5a) On the west side of the park, Pasaje Enríquez is an imposing arcade patterned after a structure in Florence, Italy, housing an assortment of travel agencies, language institutes, cafes and one major bar.

Central Market — MARKET

(Map p138) Xela's central market is three floors of reasonably priced handicrafts and souvenirs. Bargain hard.

Mercado La Democracia — MARKET

(1a Calle, Zona 3) For a more intense, everyday marketing experience, hit the Mercado La Democracia, about 10 blocks north of Parque Centro América in Zona 3, with food, clothing, CDs and other necessities for city dweller and villager alike.

Vrisa Books — BOOKS

(Map p138; 15a Av 3-64) This secondhand bookstore stocks over 4000 titles in English and will trade used books.

North & South Bookstore — BOOKS

(Map p138; ✆7761-7900; 12 Av 3-43, Zona 1; ⊙8am-8pm Mon-Sat) Broad selection of titles on Latin America, politics, poetry and history. Also plenty of new and used travel guidebooks and Spanish student resources. All this, plus bagels and coffee.

ℹ Orientation

The heart of Xela is the oblong Parque Centro América, graced with neoclassical monuments and surrounded by the city's important buildings. Most accommodations are within a few blocks of this plaza.

The main bus station is Terminal Minerva, on the western outskirts and next to one of the principal markets.

ℹ Information

EMERGENCY

Bomberos (Fire) ✆7761-2002
Cruz Roja (Red Cross) ✆7761-2746
Policía Nacional ✆7761-0042
Proatur ✆1500 or 2421-2810

INTERNET ACCESS

Wi-fi is widespread in cafes and accommodations. The language institute Celas Maya (p133) runs one of the few remaining cybercafes.

MEDIA

English-language publications are available free in bars, restaurants and cafes around town. EntreMundos (p136) publishes a bimonthly magazine, which has plenty of information on political developments and volunteer projects in the region.

XelaWho (www.xelawho.com) Billing itself as 'Quetzaltenango's leading Culture & Nightlife Magazine,' this little monthly lists cultural events in the city, with some irreverent takes on life in Guatemala in general.

MEDICAL SERVICES

Hospital Privado Quetzaltenango (☏7774-4700; www.hospitalprivadoquetzaltenango. com; Calle Rodolfo Robles 23-51; ☺24hr) Usually has an English-speaking doctor on staff.

Hospital San Rafael (☏7761-4381; 9a Calle 10-41, Zona 1; ☺24hr) Foreign insurance policies accepted.

MONEY

Banco Industrial (4 Calle 11-38, Zona 1; ☺9am-6pm Mon-Fri, 9am-1pm Sat), on the north side of Parque Centro América, changes US dollars and euros and gives advances on Visa cards. There's a Cajero 5B ATM in the Edificio Rivera just north of the *municipalidad* building.

POST

Main Post Office (Map p138; 4a Calle 15-07, Zona 1)

TOURIST INFORMATION

INGUAT (Map p138; ☏7761-4931; www.vive xela.visitguatemala.com; 7a Calle 11-35, Zona 1; ☺9am-5pm Mon-Fri, 9am-1pm Sat), usually staffed by an English speaker, is at the southern end of Parque Centro América.

There's a plethora of tourist maps circulating; look for them at internet cafes, language schools and hotels. Though they're essentially advertising flyers, the better ones like *Xelamap* include plenty of useful information.

TRAVEL AGENCIES

Besides hikes and tours, Altiplano's Tour Operator (p133) offers luggage storage, bike rentals and hotel bookings.

USEFUL WEBSITES

Xela Pages (www.xelapages.com) Packed with information about Xela and nearby attractions, with a useful discussion forum.

🛈 Getting There & Away

BUS

All 2nd-class buses depart from **Terminal Minerva** (Map p134; 7a Calle, Zona 3), a dusty, crowded yard in the west of town, unless otherwise noted. First-class companies operating between Quetzaltenango and Guatemala City have their own terminals.

Leaving or entering town, buses bound for Salcajá, Cuatro Caminos, San Francisco El Alto and Totonicapán make a **stop** (Map p134) east of the center at the Rotonda, a traffic circle on Calz Independencia, marked by the **Monumen-**

to a la Marimba (Map p134). Getting off here when you're coming into Xela saves the 10 to 15 minutes it will take your bus to cross town to Terminal Minerva.

Note that service is generally less frequent on Sunday.

First-Class Bus Terminals

Linea Dorada (Map p134; ☏7767-5198; www. lineadorada.com.gt; 5a Calle 12-44, Zona 3)

Transportes Galgos (Map p134; ☏7761-2248; Calle Rodolfo Robles 17-43, Zona 1)

Transportes Álamo (Map p134; ☏7767-4582; 14a Av 5-15, Zona 3)

CAR & MOTORCYCLE

Tabarini (☏7763-0418; www.tabarini.com; 9a Calle 9-21, Zona 1) rents cars for about Q300 per day.

SHUTTLE MINIBUS

Most Xela travel agencies, including Altiplano's (p133), run shuttle minibuses to such destinations as Antigua (Q195), Chichicastenango (Q195), Panajachel (Q160) and San Cristóbal de Las Casas, Mexico (Q240).

Around Quetzaltenango

The beautiful volcanic country around Xela offers up numerous exciting day trips. For many, the volcanoes themselves pose irresistible challenges. You can feast your eyes and soul on the wild church at San Andrés Xequl, hike to the ceremonial shores of Laguna Chicabal or soak in the idyllic hot springs at Fuentes Georginas. Or simply hop on a bus and explore the myriad small traditional villages that pepper this part of the highlands. Market days are great opportunities to observe locals in action, so Sunday and Wednesday in Momostenango, Monday in Zunil, Tuesday and Saturday in Totonicapán and Friday in San Francisco El Alto are good days to visit.

Zunil

POP 12,356 / ELEV 2262M

As you speed downhill toward Zunil from Quetzaltenango, you'll see this pretty market town spreading across a lush valley framed by steep hills and dominated by a towering volcano, its white colonial church gleaming above the red-tiled roofs of the low houses. A road on the left bridges a river and, 1km further, reaches Zunil's plaza.

Founded in 1529, Zunil is a typical Guatemalan highland town, where traditional indigenous agriculture is practiced. The cul-

BUSES FROM QUETZALTENANGO

DESTINATION	FARE	TIME	FREQUENCY	ALTERNATIVE
Almolonga	Q3	10min	Every 15min, 6am-10pm.	Buses depart from the **Shell station** (Map p143) at the corner of 9a Av and 10a Calle.
Antigua				Take any bus bound for Guatemala City via the Interamericana and change at Chimaltenango.
Chichicastenango	Q25	2½hr	Every 30min, 8am-5pm.	Or take a bus heading to Guatemala City and change at Los Encuentros.
Ciudad Tecún Umán (Mexican border)	Q40	3hr	Direct buses hourly.	Or take a bus to Coatepeque (every 15min, 4am-5:45pm) and change for Ciudad Tecún Umán.
El Carmen/ Talismán (Mexican border)				Take a bus to San Marcos (Q10, 2hr, every 15min), then catch another to Malacatán (Q15, 1hr) where you can find a collective taxi (Q5) to El Carmen.
Guatemala City	Q35	3½hr	Every 15min, 2am-5pm.	1st-class companies operating between Quetzaltenango and Guatemala City have their own terminals.
Huehuetenango	Q20	2hr	Every 15min, 4am-6:30pm.	Or take a bus to Cuatro Caminos, where you can catch Pullmans by Los Halcones and Velasquez.
La Mesilla (Mexican border)	Q40	4hr	4 buses, 7am-2:15pm.	Or take a bus to Huehuetenango and change there.
Momostenango	Q7	1½hr	Every 15min, 6am-7pm.	
Panajachel	Q30	2hr	5 buses, 10am-5pm.	
Retalhuleu	Q13	1hr	Every 10min, 5am-7:30pm.	
San Andrés Xequl	Q8	30min	Every half hour, 6am-3pm.	
San Pedro La Laguna	Q25	3hr	6 buses, 11:30am-5:30pm.	
Zunil	Q5	25min	Every 15min, 6am-10pm.	Buses depart from the Shell station at the corner of 9a Av and 10a Calle.

tivated plots, divided by stone fences, are irrigated by canals; you'll see the farmers scooping up water with a shovel-like instrument and tossing it over their plants. Locals wash their clothes near the river bridge in pools of hot water that come out of the rocks.

◉ Sights

Zunil boasts a particularly striking church. Its ornate facade, with eight pairs of serpentine columns, is echoed inside by a richly carved gilt altar, with saints garbed in silver-embroidered robes. On Tuesday, Thursday and Saturday, the plaza in front is bright with the purple-striped *huipiles* and richly patterned *cortes* of the local K'iche' Maya women buying and selling.

Half a block downhill from the church plaza, the Cooperativa Santa Ana (☺8am-6pm Mon-Fri, 8am-1pm Sat) is a handicrafts cooperative made up of more than 600 local women. Finely woven vests, jackets and traditional *huipiles* (from Q400) are displayed and sold here. You can try them on and discuss their making with the weavers, who may sometimes be creating new items at the loom.

While you're in Zunil, visit the image of San Simón, the name given here to the much-venerated non-Christian deity known elsewhere as Maximón. His effigy, propped up in a chair, is moved each year to a different house during the festival of San

Simón, held on October 28. Ask any local where to find him.

🛏 Sleeping

Hotel Las Cumbres   HOTEL $$

(☑ 5399-0029; www.lascumbres.com.gt; Carretera al Pacífico, Km 210.5; s/d incl breakfast Q345/400, s/d with sauna Q485/555; P) Located 500m south of Zunil, Las Cumbres seems like a colonial village amid a volcanic landscape where great plumes of steam emanate from the earth. The hotel is built on top of natural steam vents, and some of the 20 cozy rooms come equipped with their own sauna and/or hot-spring-fed Jacuzzi.

There's a good restaurant (mains Q50 to Q80) serving organic vegetables from the hotel garden, along with a squash court, gymnasium and handicrafts store. Nonguests can use the public sauna (Q30 per hour, open 7am to 7pm), a modern pine-paneled installation, or spa, offering massages and facials. Any bus bound for Retalhuleu or Mazatenango can drop you at the entrance (Q5).

ℹ Getting There & Away

Buses (Q5) depart from the Shell station at the corner of 9a Av and 10a Calle in Quetzaltenango every 15 minutes from 6am to 10pm. Returning, buses depart from the main road beside the bridge.

Fuentes Georginas

A superb natural spa in a spectacular setting, **Fuentes Georginas** (☑ 4766-7066; info@fuentesgeorginas.com; Q50; ⊙ 9am-6pm) is an 8km drive uphill from Zunil. It's named after the wife of 'benevolent dictator' Jorge Ubico, who customarily comandeered the installations on weekends for his personal use. Four pools of varying temperatures are fed by hot sulfur springs and framed by a steep, high wall of tropical vines, ferns and flowers. Though the setting is intensely tropical, the mountain air currents keep it deliciously cool through the day. There is a little 500m walk starting from beside the pool, worth doing to check out the birds and orchids. Bring a bathing suit; towels are available (Q10 plus deposit). Lockers cost Q5. Hurricane Agatha ripped through the spa in 2010, all but destroying the installations. Fortunately, it's been completely rebuilt and restored, though patches of the road there remain perilously damaged.

Trails lead to two nearby volcanoes: **Volcán Zunil** (15km, about three hours one way) and **Volcán Santo Tomás** (25km, about five hours one way). Guides (essential) are available for either trip. Ask at the restaurant.

Down the valley a bit from the pools are nine rustic but cozy **cottages** (per person Q160), each with a hot tub and cold shower, BBQ and a fireplace to ward off the mountain chill at night (wood and matches provided). Included in the price of the cottages is access to the pools all day and all night, when rules are relaxed.

Besides the **restaurant/bar** (meals Q70-85; ⊙ 8am-7pm), which serves great grilled steaks, sausage and *papas,* there are three sheltered picnic tables with cooking grills.

Daily shuttles to Fuentes Georginas (Q120 return, including entrance fee) are offered by most Xela agencies, including Altiplano's (p133), leaving at 9am and 2:30pm. Shuttles return to Xela at noon and 6:30pm respectively.

San Andrés Xequl

A few kilometers past Salcajá, the road from Quetzaltenango passes the Morería crossroads, where a branch heads west to San Andrés Xequl. After about 3km on this uphill spur, you'll start seeing rainbow cascades of hand-dyed thread drying on the roofs and you'll know you have arrived in San Andrés Xequl. Boxed in by fertile hills, this small town boasts the most bizarre, stunning **church** imaginable. Technicolored saints, angels, flowers and climbing vines fight for space with angels frolicking on the ledges and a pair of jaguars scratching the top column on a shocking yellow facade. The cones on the bell towers are straight from the circus big top.

Inside, a carpet of candles illuminate bleeding effigies of Christ. Above the altar, 'Fisher of Men' is written in blue neon, a reference to the town's patron saint.

The community **tourist office** (☑ 4778-4851; ⊙ 9am-5pm), to the left of the church, echoes its playful facade. Here you can set up a guided walk of the town with visits to *huipil* embroiderers, and dyers and candle makers, continuing up to **El Calvario**, the little yellow church at the top of the hill. Maya ceremonies, with plenty of burnt offerings, are still held at the triple-cross altar alongside, and the panoramic view across the valley is phenomenal. The tourist office also offers tours of surrounding villages.

Friday is the big market day. The annual festival, on November 30, features tightrope walkers.

There are no restaurants as such in town, but you'll find cheap, filling meals in the *comedores* around the market.

To get here take any northbound bus from Xela, alighting at the Esso station at the Morería crossroads, and hail a pick-up or walk the 3km uphill. Buses returning to Xela line up at the edge of the plaza and make the trip until about 5pm.

Totonicapán

POP 134,373 / ELEV 2476M

San Miguel Totonicapán is known for its artisans. Shoemakers, weavers, tinsmiths, potters, leather workers and carpenters all make and sell their goods here. Market days are Tuesday and Saturday; it's a locals market, not a tourist affair, and it winds down by late morning.

The ride from Cuatro Caminos is along a pine-studded valley. From Totonicapán's bus station it's a 600m hike up 3a Calle to the twin main plazas, or you can take a *tuk-tuk*. The lower plaza has a **statue of Atanasio Tzul**, leader of an indigenous rebellion that started here in 1820, while the upper one, known as Parque San Miguel, is home to the large **colonial church** and neoclassical **municipal theater**.

🏃 Activities

Sendero Ecológico El Aprisco   HIKING
(☑ 5355-0280; Q25; ☺ 8am-5pm) Encompassing some 13 hectares of old-growth forest northeast of Totonicapán, this eco-reserve makes for some delightful hiking. Well-marked trails traverse the community-run site, domain of the endangered *pinabete* tree and 29 endemic bird species, such as the amethyst-throated hummingbird and plumed quetzalillo. For overnight stays, there are adobe cabins with fireplaces, bunk beds and straw bedding, and meals are prepared.

El Aprisco is 5km up the Santa Cruz del Quiché road from Toto; microbuses bound for El Quiché can drop you at the entrance in about 20 minutes. Alternatively, Altiplano's (p133) in Xela can organize early-morning birdwatching expeditions to the reserve.

🧭 Tours

Aventura Maya K'iche'   CULTURAL TOUR
(☑ 5696-2207; www.aventuramayakiche.org; tour Q615) This program introduces visitors to the town's traditional crafts as well as other aspects of life in Toto. A day-long cultural tour, with an English-speaking guide, includes visits to weaving and pottery workshops, a bit of sightseeing and a traditional lunch with a marimba concert and dance performance. (Book at least five days in advance.)

🎉 Festivals & Events

Feria Titular de San Miguel Arcángel   RELIGIOUS
(Name-Day Festival of Archangel St Michael; ☺ Sep 24-30) Runs from September 24 to 30, peaking on September 29.

Apparition of the Archangel Michael   RELIGIOUS
(☺ May 8) Features fireworks and traditional dances.

🛏 Sleeping

Aventura Maya K'iche' can arrange stays with local families, including breakfast and dinner (groups of two/three/four Q385/345/310 per person).

Aventura Maya K'iche' offers the option to have a traditional lunch in a private home with a marimba concert (48 hours' notice required).

Hospedaje Paco Centro   HOTEL $
(☑ 7766-2810; 3a Calle 8-18, Zona 2; s/d Q65/120, s/d without bathroom Q40/70) Practically hidden inside a shopping center a couple of blocks from the lower plaza, this sternly managed place has bare, minimally maintained rooms of three to five beds each. Avoid those facing the street.

Restaurante Bonanza   GUATEMALAN $$
(☑ 7766-1064; 7a Calle 7-17, Zona 4; mains Q45-60; ☺ 7am-9pm; 🖥) Totonicapán's most conventional restaurant is a meat-and-tortillas sort of place, where bow-tied waitstaff deliver heaping helpings of steak, chicken and seafood.

ℹ Getting There & Away

Toto buses from Quetzaltenango depart every 10 minutes or so (one hour) throughout the day from the Rotonda on Calz Independencia (passing through Cuatro Caminos). The last direct bus to Quetzaltenango leaves Toto at 6:30pm.

San Francisco El Alto

POP 33,240 / ELEV 2582M

High on a hilltop overlooking Quetzaltenango some 17km away stands the town of San Francisco El Alto, whose Friday **market** is regarded as the biggest and most authentic in the country. The large plaza in front of the 18th-century church is covered in goods. Stalls are crowded into neighboring streets, and the press of traffic is so great that a special system of one-way roads is put in place to avoid colossal traffic jams.

The whole town is Guatemala's garment district: every inch is jammed with vendors selling sweaters, socks, blankets, jeans, scarves and more. Bolts of cloth spill from storefronts packed to the ceiling with miles of material.

Around mid-morning when the clouds roll away, panoramic views can be had from the roof of the church. The caretaker will let you go up for a small tip. On the way through, have a look at the six elaborate gilded altarpieces and remains of what must once have been very colorful frescoes.

San Francisco's big party is the Fiesta de San Francisco de Asís, celebrated around October 4 with traditional dances.

Good *chuchitos* (small tamales), *chiles rellenos* and other prepared foods are sold from stacks in the marketplace.

Banco Reformador (2a Calle 3-23; ⊙ 9am-4pm Mon-Fri, 9am-1pm Sat) has a Visa ATM.

🛏 Sleeping

Hotel Real Plaza HOTEL $
(☑ 7738-4110; 3a Av 2-22, Zona 1; s/d Q75/150, s/d without bathroom Q35/70) This hotel does indeed have beautiful views out over the valley to the Santa María volcano. Rooms are spacious, with balconies and (thankfully) hot showers. Thursday nights it's likely to fill up.

ℹ Getting There & Away

Buses to San Francisco leave Quetzaltenango from the Rotonda on Calz Independencia (passing through Cuatro Caminos) frequently throughout the day (Q5, 40 minutes). Arriving on market day, get off on 4a Av at the top of the hill and walk towards the church.

Momostenango

POP 128,728 / ELEV 2259M

Beyond San Francisco El Alto, 26km from Quetzaltenango, this town, set in a pretty mountain valley along a road through pine woods, is famous for the making of *chamarras* (thick woollen blankets), as well as ponchos and other woolen garments. The best days to look for these are Wednesday and Sunday, the main market days.

Momostenango is noted for its adherence to the ancient Maya calendar and observance of traditional rites. The town's five main altars are the scene of ceremonies enacted on important celestial dates such as the summer solstice, the spring equinox, the start of the Maya solar year (known as El Mam, observed in late February), and Wajshakib' B'atz, the start of the 260-day *tzolkin* year. Should you be allowed access to these ceremonies, be sure to treat altars and participants with the utmost respect.

A few basic *comedores* provide cheap, filling meals while the restaurant of the Hotel Otoño is a classier option.

☞ Tours

Takiliben May Wajshakib Batz CULTURAL TOUR
(☑ 7736-5537; wajshakibbaztz13@yahoo.es; 3a Av A 6-85, Zona 3) This is a Maya mission, dedicated to studying and teaching Maya culture and sacred traditions. Its director, Rigoberto Itzep Chanchavac, is a *chuchkajau* (Maya priest) responsible for advising the community on when special days of the Maya calendars fall. His full- or half-day workshops focus on customs that usually remain hidden from outsiders.

The mission also leads a tour of Momostenango, with visits to the sacred hill of Paclom and the ritual hot springs of Payashú (Q100, including a homestay with a local family).

✪ Festivals & Events

Wajshakib' B'atz (eight thread), marking the start of the ritual *tzolkin* calendar, is considered the holiest day in the cycle, when Maya 'daykeepers' are ordained. During the ceremony, usually enacted atop sacred Paclom hill (accessed from the end of 5a Calle), the candidates for priesthood are presented with a 'sacred bundle' of red seeds and crystals – used for divination readings based on the ritual calendar – and then they dance around the ceremonial fire holding their bundle. As the festival falls at the end of a 260-day cycle, the date varies from year to year. Contact Takiliben May to find out when it falls in the current year.

🛏 Sleeping

Hotel Otoño HOTEL $
(☑ 7736-5313; gruvial.m@gmail.com; 3a Av A 1-48, Zona 2; r per person Q100; 🅿 🗟) Momostenango's poshest lodging has 14 modern rooms with glossy tile floors and huge bathrooms. Some feature balconies or picture windows taking in the surrounding hills. The hotel restaurant serves all meals.

EXPLORE MORE OF QUETZALTENANGO

The wide-open spaces and mountainous countryside around Xela offer an almost endless array of opportunities for getting out there and doing a bit of solo exploration. Small villages dotted around the valley mean that you shouldn't ever have much trouble getting directions, and the relative safety of the area means that the biggest danger you're likely to face is that of a yapping dog (carry a stick). A few destinations to head towards:

Santiaguito lookout Get a close-up view of volcanic eruptions, going off like clockwork every 20 minutes.

Lava fields Over near Mt Candelaria, these extensive fields are a great place for a picnic and a spot of sunbathing.

San Cristóbal waterfall Halfway between Xela and San Francisco, the falls are most impressive in the wet season.

Las Mojadas The walk to this pretty flower-growing village takes you from Llanos del Pinal and past the Santiaguito volcano. You can catch a bus back.

ℹ️ Information

BAC Reformador (1a Av 1-13, Zona 1; ⊙9am-5pm Mon-Fri, 8am-noon Sat & Sun) Changes traveler's checks and has a Cajero 5B ATM.

ℹ️ Getting There & Away

You can get buses to Momostenango from Quetzaltenango's Terminal Minerva (Q7, 1½ hours) or from San Francisco El Alto (45 minutes). Buses run about every 15 minutes, with the last one back to Quetzaltenango normally leaving Momostenango at 4:30pm.

Laguna Chicabal

This magical lake is nestled in the crater of Volcán Chicabal (2712m) on the edge of a cloud forest. Considered a cosmic convergence point by the Mam and K'iche' Maya, it is a sacred place and a hotbed of ceremonial activity. There are Maya altars at each of the four cardinal points along its sandy shores, and Maya and worshippers come from far and wide to perform ceremonies and make offerings here. Forty days after Easter Sunday is the observance of 13 Q'anil, when faithful farmers flock here to pray for rain. By observing the level of the lagoon and seeing if the roots of surrounding trees are submerged, they can judge whether to plant. Because the lake and grounds have great ceremonial significance, campers and hikers are asked to treat them with the utmost respect.

Adding to the atmosphere of mystery, a veil of fog dances over the water, alternately revealing and hiding the lake's placid contours. Birdwatchers might spot quetzals, horned guan and pink-headed warblers.

From the visitor center (☎4957-5983; Q25; ⊙7am-3pm), a trail leads another 3km uphill to the site. About two-thirds of the way up you'll reach a fork, where you can bear right to go directly to the lagoon, or left up to a *mirador* (observation post) and then a whopping 615 steep steps down to the edge of the lake. Start early for best visibility.

🛏️ Sleeping & Eating

There are good accommodations at the visitor center, which is managed by the local Mam community, including a pair of six-sided bungalows with four bunks each (per person Q50) sharing a cold-water bath house, and a two-level log cabin with private bathrooms (double per person Q75).

Bring food if you plan to stay: there's no restaurant and the store has just the basics.

ℹ️ Getting There & Away

Access to Laguna Chicabal is via the community of Toj Mech, southwest of San Martín Sacatepéquez (also known as Chile Verde) along the road to Colomba. Microbuses from Xela (Q5) depart every 20 minutes, Monday to Saturday, from 15a Av and 6a Calle in Zona 3. These vehicles drop you at a parking lot in Toj Mech. From here, a cheerful fellow named Juan can take you up the steep, deeply rutted road to the park's visitor center in his bullish pick-up truck (Q75, 15 minutes).

Huehuetenango

POP 111,108 / ELEV 1909M

Often used as a stop off on the journey to or from Mexico, or as a staging area for forays deeper into the Cuchumatanes mountain range, Huehuetenango offers few charms

SALCAJÁ

Entering Salcajá, 7km from Xela, you pass a **monument** to a heroic figure, the undocumented emigrant to the USA. But aside from this distinction, Salcajá harbors some other special qualities to which it alone can lay claim.

Dating from 1524, the **Iglesia de San Jacinto**, two blocks west on 3a Calle from the main road, was the first Christian temple in Central America. It is also known as the Concepción la Conquistadora, a reference to Pedro de Alvarado, the devout Catholic who conquered the territory. The small squat structure appears quite austere from outside, but within are original paintings and a beautiful painted-wood altar.

Salcajá is famed for its traditional *ikat*-style textiles, remarkable for the hand-tied and dyed threads that are laid out in the preferred pattern on a loom. Shops selling bolts of this fabric are ubiquitous here, and you can usually visit the workshops before purchasing.

Perhaps the town is best known, though, for its production of two alcoholic beverages that locals consider akin to magic elixirs. *Caldo de frutas* (literally, fruit soup) is like a high-octane sangria, made by combining *nances* (cherry-like fruits), apples, peaches and pears and fermenting them for six months or so. You can purchase fifths of it for around Q30 after viewing the production process. *Rompopo* is an entirely different type of potent potable, made from rum, egg yolks, sugar and spices. Little liquor shops all over Salcajá peddle the stuff, but you may like to try the friendly shop of José Daniel Sandoval Santizo, a block east of the main road along 4a Calle.

of its own, though some may appreciate its welcoming if scruffy character. Fortunately, 'Huehue' *(way-way)* packs in plenty of eating and sleeping options along with some striking mountain scenery.

Huehuetenango was a Mam Maya region until the 15th century, when the K'iche', expanding from their capital K'umarcaaj (near present-day Santa Cruz del Quiché), pushed them out. But the weakness of K'iche' rule soon brought about civil war, which engulfed the highlands and provided a chance for Mam independence. The turmoil was still unresolved in 1525 when Gonzalo de Alvarado, the brother of Pedro, arrived to conquer Zaculeu, the Mam capital, for Spain.

⊙ Sights

The lively indigenous market is filled daily with traders who come down from surrounding villages. Actually, it's about the only place you'll see traditional costumes in this town, as most citizens are *ladinos* in modern garb.

Zaculeu   ARCHAEOLOGICAL SITE
(Q50; ⊙8am-4pm) A remnant of the Mam capital, the Zaculeu ('White Earth' in the Mam language) archaeological zone was restored by the United Fruit Company in the 1940s, leaving its pyramids, ball courts and ceremonial platforms covered by a thick coat of graying plaster. Though hardly authentic, the work goes further than others in simulating the appearance of an active religious center.

With ravines on three sides, the Postclassic religious center occupies a strategic location that served its Mam Maya inhabitants well. It finally failed, however, in 1525, when Gonzalo de Alvarado, aided by Tlaxcalan and K'iche' forces, laid siege to the site for two months. Starvation ultimately defeated the Mam.

A small museum at the site holds, among other things, skulls and grave goods found in a tomb beneath Estructura 1, the tallest structure at the site.

Zaculeu is located 4km west of Huehuetenango's main plaza. Buses to the site (Q2.50, 15 minutes) leave about every 30 minutes between 7:30am and 6pm from in front of the **school** at the corner of 2a Calle and 7a Av. A taxi from the town center costs Q30 one way. One hour is plenty of time to look around the site and museum.

Parque Central   PLAZA
Huehuetenango's main square is shaded by cylindrical ficus trees and surrounded by the town's imposing buildings: the **municipalidad** (Town Hall) (with a band shell on the upper floor) and the imposing neoclassical **church**. For a bird's-eye view of the situation, check out the little relief map of Huehuetenango department, which lists altitudes, language groups and populations of the various municipal divisions.

Huehuetenango

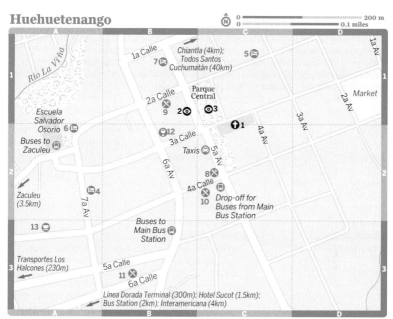

0   200 m
0   0.1 miles

🛏 Sleeping

Hotel San Luis de la Sierra   HOTEL **$**

(✆ 7764-9217; hsanluis@gmail.com; 2a Calle 7-00; s/d Q135/190; 🅿🛜) The simple, smallish rooms here have pine furniture and homey touches, and the hotel remains pleasantly aloof from the racket outside. The real attraction, though, is the rambling coffee plantation out back, with paths for strolling.

Hotel Sucot   HOTEL **$**

(✆ 7764-2511; Terminal de buses; s/d Q80/140, s/d without bathroom Q50/80; 🅿🛜) For travelers just needing a sleepover between bus journeys, this is the least scary of the bunch beside the terminal. The beds are decent, showers functional, staff jovial and there's a cafe (and events hall!). It's the next to last one on the right.

Hotel Mary   HOTEL **$**

(✆ 7764-1618; 2a Calle 3-52; s/d Q80/130; 🅿) This echoey older hotel has a cafe on the ground floor and a useful map of the province in the lobby. Though drably furnished, rooms do have comfy beds and large tiled bathrooms. At least one – No 310 – features a balcony.

Hotel Zaculeu   HOTEL **$$**

(✆ 7764-1086; www.hotelzaculeu.com; 5a Av 1-14; s/d/tr Q125/250/330; 🅿@🛜) The

Huehuetenango

long-standing Zaculeu has loads of character, and despite its advanced age it remains quite spiffy. Rooms in the 'new section' (just 20 years old) are a bit pricier but larger and more stylish. The sprawling patio area, overflowing with plants and chirping birds, is conducive to lounging, as is the excellent bar.

BUSES FROM HUEHUETENANGO

The bus terminal is in Zona 4, 2km southwest of the plaza along 6a Calle. A number of companies ply the same routes, though information is not posted in any coherent fashion. Microbuses leave from the south end of the station. Another stop, for microbuses to Cobán and Barrillas, via Soloma and San Mateo Ixtatán, is by a gas station at El Calvario, at the corner of 1a Av and 1a Calle, four blocks northeast of the Parque Central.

DESTINATION	FARE	TIME (HR)	FREQUENCY	ALTERNATIVE
Antigua				Take a Guatemala City–bound bus and change at Chimaltenango.
Barillas	Q50	6	Microbuses every 30min, 2am-4:30pm.	
Cobán	Q40	7	Microbus at 1pm Mon-Sat from El Calvario gas station.	
Gracias a Dios (Mexican border)	Q50	5	Hourly, 3am-1pm by Chiantlequita.	
Guatemala City	Q60	5	5 Pullman buses by Velázquez Plus 5:30am-2:30pm.	Two lines run Pullman buses from their own private terminals: **Transportes Los Halcones** (☎7765-7985; 10a Av 9-12, Zona 1) leaves 7 times a day 1am-3:30pm (Q65), with deluxe service (Q75) at 7am, 10:30am and 2pm; **Linea Dorada** (☎7768-1566; www.lineadorada.com.gt; 8a Calle 8-70, Zona 1) departs at 11pm (Q110).
La Mesilla	Q20	2	Every 15min, 3am-7pm by Transportes Los Verdes.	
Nebaj				Take a microbus to Sacapulas from where there are frequent connections to Nebaj.
Panajachel				Take a Guatemala City–bound bus and change at Los Encuentros.
Quetzaltenango	Q20	2	Every 15min, 3:30am-7pm.	
Sacapulas	Q20	2	Frequent microbuses 5:30am-5:30pm.	Via Aguacatán.
Santa Cruz del Quiché	Q25	2	Frequent microbuses 5am-5pm.	
Soloma	Q25	3	Hourly microbuses 4:30am-2:30pm from El Calvario gas station.	
Todos Santos Cuchumatán	Q20	2	Every 30min, 3am-3pm from El Calvario gas station.	

Hotel Casa Blanca HOTEL **$$**
(☎7769-0777; 7a Av 3-41; s/d Q220/280; P☎) Hanging ferns and sculpted shrubs grace the attractive courtyard here, ringed by spacious, modern rooms with arched pine ceilings and good hot showers. The patio restaurant out back serves up good-value set lunches (Q22), and its Sunday breakfast buffet (Q40) is a major deal.

✖ Eating & Drinking

★ La Tinaja   GUATEMALAN $
(☎7764-1513; 4a Calle 6-51; set menu Q25; ⊙noon-10pm) As much a cultural center as a cafe, the home of historian/gourmand Rolando Gutiérrez has an interesting library and a collection of old clocks, radios and namesake *tinajas* (urns), all displayed in a series of inviting salons. Aside from quesadillas and tamales (served with salt from San Mateo Ixtatán), you'll find such local snacks as *sangüichitos* (Huehue-style sandwiches) and *rellenitos*.

Cafetería Las Palmeras   GUATEMALAN $
(4a Calle 5-10; mains Q27-50; ⊙7am-8:30pm; 🛜) Popular Las Palmeras features a breezy upper level with views over the Parque Central. The *caldo de pollo criollo* (Q27) is a must, brimming with chicken, *güisquil* and corn. On Saturdays there are tasty tamales.

La Fonda de Don Juan   PIZZA $$
(2a Calle 5-35; pizzas Q45-75; ⊙24hr) The place for Huehue's night owls and early risers, La Fonda serves varied Guatemalan and international fare including good-value pizzas.

Restaurante Lekaf   INTERNATIONAL $$
(☎7764-3202; 6a Calle 6-40; mains Q50-100; ⊙10am-11pm) This modern, airy dining hall has a varied menu, including sandwiches, pizza and seafood. Live music (marimbas, folk) attracts a lively crowd nightly from 7pm to 10pm.

Café Museo   CAFE
(☎7764-1101; 4a Calle 7-40; ⊙7am-9:30pm Mon-Sat, 2-9:30pm Sun; 🛜) This 'museum' serves some of Huehue's best coffee, and that's saying something. More than just a place to get a well-prepared cup, it also provides some background on this bewitching bean that has so influenced Guatemala's history. The various salons and delightful patio buzz with java hounds from early morning till late evening.

Besides examining antique coffee-processing paraphernalia and some diagrams demonstrating coffee production techniques, you can roast your own beans for purchase. Owner Manrique López, son of a small-scale producer from Barillas, also organizes coffee plantation tours during harvest season (January to April).

Café D'Carlo   BAR
(☎7764-2204; 6 Av 2-59) Opposite the Royal Park Hotel, this upper-level, open-air lounge has a friendly, relaxed vibe and a terrace/counter facing the street, a good spot for snacks and a bucket of chilled Gallos. Friday and Saturday nights from around 9pm there are performances by singer-songwriters.

ℹ Information

The town center is 4km northeast of the Interamericana, and the bus station is off the road linking the two, about 2km from each.

Banco Industrial (6a Av 1-26), a block west of the main plaza, has a reliable ATM.

ℹ Getting Around

City buses circulate between the bus station and the town center from 5am to around 7:30pm. Arriving in Huehue, leave the east side of the station through the gap between the Transportes Fortaleza and El Condor offices; walk through a small covered market, then the main market building to the next street, where 'Centro' buses depart every few minutes (Q2). To return to the bus station from the center, catch buses outside the Hotel La Sexta.

Around Huehuetenango

Except for Todos Santos Cuchumatán, the mountainous far northwest of Guatemala is little visited by travelers. The adventurous few will often be a novelty to the local Maya folks they meet. Spanish skills, patience and tact will pave the way in these parts. Beyond the coffee lands of the Huistas (Santa Ana and San Antonio) the lower northwestern corner of the department is cut through by rivers and dotted with cenotes (circular pools in limestone craters).

Chiantla

POP 7737 / ELEV 1463M

Just before the climb into the Cuchumatanes, you'll come across the village of Chiantla, the former seat of the municipality, now practically a suburb of Huehuetenango. Its church holds the **Virgen del Rosario**, a silver statue donated by the owner of a local mine. The virgin is believed to have mystical healing powers and people come from all over the country to seek her assistance. The main date for the pilgrimage is February 2, when the town packs out with supplicants and the infirm.

Also in the church are some interesting **murals** painted in the 1950s, showing local Maya having miraculous experiences while working in the silver mines.

Another 4km on from Chiantla, **El Mirador Juan Diéguez Olaverri** overlooks

Huehuetenango from a point up in the Cuchumatanes. On a clear day it offers a great view of the entire region and many volcanoes. Mounted on plaques here is the poem, *A Los Cuchumatanes,* penned by the lookout point's namesake. Local kids will recite it to you for a tip.

Any bus from Huehue heading for Todos Santos, Soloma or Barillas goes through Chiantla and past the turnoff for the Mirador.

Chancol

The Guatemalan/French-run **Unicornio Azul** (☑ 5205-9328; www.unicornioazul.com; s/d/tr incl breakfast Q300/480/600) ranch is at Chancol, about 25km by road northeast of Huehuetenango. It offers horseback riding through the Cuchumatanes along trails used only by local inhabitants, camping out or staying in rural accommodations. Unicornio Azul also functions as a *posada rural,* with 10 simple but comfortable rooms in the estate home or a separate building.

Rides can range from one hour (included in the room rate) to two/three days (per person Q2400/3700, with a minimum four riders). Among the options is a two-day journey to **Laguna Magdalena**, a turquoise lagoon nestled in the mountains, with massive boulders and ancient, gnarled trees scattered around. There are also day trips (Q690) for those who'd rather sleep at the *posada*.These rides are done only during the dry season (November to April), preferably by experienced riders. All tours are guided by Pauline Décamps, a member of the French Equestrian Federation, who zealously looks after the 14 robust horses stabled here.

❶ Getting There & Away

To get to Chancol, take any bus heading for Todos Santos or Barillas and get off in La Capellanía; the owners will come pick you up (Q45).

Chiabal

High in the Sierra de los Cuchumatanes (3400m) amid a rocky plateau dotted with maguey plants and sheep, Chiabal, 17km east of Todos Santos, welcomes visitors looking to experience rural life in a tiny **Mam community** (☑ 5381-0540; esteban. matias@hotmail.com). The villagers provide simple accommodations and prepare hearty local fare. A community-built 2.5km interpretive trail leads to the Piedra Cuache, an oddly shaped boulder at a 3666m lookout point. Guides can take you to various sites in the 18,000-hectare Parque Regional Municipal de Todos Santos Cuchumatán, including the summit of La Torre. There is also the chance to participate in community activities such as herding llamas, weaving *huipiles* and planting potatoes while getting to know the local inhabitants.

The villagers provide simple accommodations in four local houses for those visiting the Mam community (Q130 for three meals and a night's stay).

Microbuses go directly to Chiabal (Q10) from the El Calvario gas station at the corner of 1a Av and 1a Calle in Huehuetenango. Otherwise, hop a Todos Santos bus and get off at Chiabal, 4km west of the turn off the Huehue–Barillas road.

Todos Santos Cuchumatán

POP 2980 / ELEV 2470M

Way up in the highlands, the community of Todos Santos is nestled at the bottom of a deep valley and bordered by forested slopes. After a 1½-hour climb up from Huehuetenango, the bus leaves the Huehue–Soloma highway to follow a narrow paved road alongside precipitous cliffs, pulling into town about an hour later.

Traditional clothing is very much in use here and, unusually, it's the male costume that is the more eye-catching. Men wear red-and-white-striped trousers, little straw hats with blue ribbons, jackets with multicolored stripes and thick woven collars. Saturday is the main market day; there's a smaller market on Wednesday.

Reasons to visit Todos Santos include good walking in the hills and getting to know a traditional and close-knit but friendly community. Todos Santos suffered terribly during Guatemala's civil war when, by some accounts, 2000 area inhabitants were murdered. It is still very poor. To supplement their subsistence from agriculture, families travel in the early part of the year to work for meager wages on coffee, sugar and cotton plantations on the Pacific Slope. Working in the US is, however, proving a more lucrative alternative for some *todosanteros* today, as the amount of new construction in the valley demonstrates, not to mention the incorporation of urban elements into the traditional outfit.

If you're coming to Todos Santos in the wet season (mid-May to November), bring warm clothes, as it's cold up here, especially at night.

◎ Sights

Museo Balam   MUSEUM
(Q5; ⊙8am-6pm) Todos Santos' museum is in a two-story house along a side street one block east of the plaza. The collection of outfits and masks, traditional kitchen implements, archaeological finds and musical instruments comes to life when Fortunato, its creator and a community leader, is there to provide commentary.

Tuj K'man Txun   MONUMENT
This ceremonial site, 500m up the street beside the central plaza, consists of two wooden crosses upon a stone altar for contemporary Maya offerings. The crosses commemorate the incidents of August 1982, when the army executed hundreds of alleged guerrilla collaborators, then torched many homes.

🏃 Activities

Parque Regional Todos Santos Cuchumatán   HIKING
The section of the Cuchumatanes range to the north and east of Todos Santos presents superb hiking opportunities through subtropical montane wet forest, much of it above 3700m. Among the unique species of vegetation found at these heights is the coniferous shrub known as *huitó.* One of the most spectacular destinations is La Torre (3837m), the highest nonvolcanic point in Central America.

Las Cuevas   HIKING
The walk to Las Cuevas, a sacred cave still used for Maya rituals, starts from La Maceta, a tree growing out of rock beside a football field, 15 minutes by bus up the Huehue road from Todos Santos (Q5).

☞ Tours

Red de Turismo Natural y Cultural de Huehuetenango   HIKING
(☑4051-5597; robjerbautista@yahoo.es; hikes from Q250) This network of ecologically oriented guides throughout the department is locally represented by Roberto Jerónimo Bautista. He leads hikes to the isolated mountain community of San Juan Atitán, where the women wear dazzling *huipiles,* in about six hours, returning by bus to Todos Santos. The trail climbs through old-growth forest to summits that afford views all the way to the Mexican border.

Roberto also leads three-day treks to Nebaj (per person from Q700, with minimum of two), including food and lodging in community dwellings.

Mam Trekking   HIKING
(☑5206-0916; rigoguiadeturismo@yahoo.com; hikes from Q100) Knowledgeable, English-speaking *todosantero* Rigoberto Pablo Cruz leads walks around the Parque Regional Todos Santos Cuchumatán, including a climb to the peak of La Torre followed by a descent to La Maceta. In addition, Rigoberto leads walks to Tzunul, a community where men weave women's *cortes* on a loom and women weave men's shirt collars by hand.

Mam also offers the chance to relax in a traditional Maya *chuj,* a welcome option in Todos Santos' chilly climate. A *chuj* is a small adobe building with wooden boards covering the entrance. A wood fire burns in a stone hearth within, and water is sprinkled on the stones to provide steam.

Rigo also leads three- and four-day hikes to Nebaj (per person from Q700, with a minimum of two).

🛏 Sleeping & Eating

For such a small place, Todos Santos has a assortment of good, cheap accommodations, three of which are nearby the main plaza.

There are a couple of basic *comedores* in the center of town for good home-cooked fare. For a little more variety, try the dining hall at the Hotel Casa Familiar.

Tourist Hotel   HOTEL $
(☑4491-0220; r with/without bathroom Q75/50) In a quieter part of town, the Tourist is quite clean and well maintained, with functional hot showers, quality mattresses and plenty of (synthetic) blankets for the evening chill. Around 200m east from the main square, turn left downhill by a shop called La Todosanterita to find the solitary pink concrete structure.

Hotel Casa Familiar   HOTEL $
(☑5737-0112; hotelyrestaurante_casafamiliar@yahoo.com; s/d Q100/150, s/d without bathroom Q60/90) This cheerfully run lodging just down from the main plaza has four cozy rooms with hardwood floors, traditional textile bedspreads, good hot showers and private terraces. More recently built units on the upper level have less character with tile floors and cheap furniture. Have a breakfast

TODOS SANTOS' BIG DAY

Todos Santos Cuchumatán is renowned for its wildly colorful horse races, the highlight of El Día de Todos los Santosa, a no-holds-barred annual celebration held on November 1. It's the culmination of a week of festivities and an all-night spree of male dancing to marimbas and *aguardiente* (cane liquor) drinking on the eve of the races – which rather than a competitive event is a chance for *todosanteros* to ride up and down as fast as they can while getting progressively drunker the whole day long (with a break for lunch). The authentically indigenous event attracts throngs of inhabitants from surrounding communities who gather on a grassy hillside alongside the sand track or upon the rooftops opposite to observe the riders decked out in their finest traditional garb. Todos Santos, incidentally, is the only place in Guatemala where the Day of the Dead is not observed on November 1, since that day is reserved for a celebration of autonomy within Huehuetenango province. Instead, the traditional visit to the cemetery is postponed to the following day, when graves are decorated and marimbas serenade groups of mourners as they arrive to pay their respects.

bowl of *mosh* (porridge) or fresh-baked banana bread at the cafe downstairs.

Guests may use a *chuj* (Maya sauna) for Q30 per person.

Hotelito Todos Santos   HOTEL $
(② 3030-6950; s/d Q75/150, s/d without bathroom Q45/90) South of the plaza, up a side street that branches left, this backpackers' fave has small and bare but well-scrubbed rooms with tile floors and firm beds. Room 15, one of the four private bath units in the tower, has excellent views over the valley. The casual cafe here is noted for its pancakes.

Comedor Katy   GUATEMALAN $
(meals Q20; ⊘ 7:30am-8pm) Women in traditional garb attend to great vats bubbling over glowing embers at this rustic cook shack just above the central plaza. There are tables on a terrace overlooking the market activity.

Comedor Evelín   GUATEMALAN $
(meals Q15; ⊘ 7am-9pm) Inside this often busy eatery you'll find the menu scrawled on a styrofoam board. At lunch time it serves such traditional fare as *pepián de pollo* (chicken in pumpkin-seed sauce) and *caldo de res*. It's 100m east of the plaza, turning uphill at the bookstore.

ⓘ Information

Todos Santos' main street is about 500m long. Towards its west end are the church and market, with the central plaza raised above street level on the south side.

The Grupo de Mujeres weaving shop at the base of the Hotel Casa Familiar (p153) functions as a de facto information center.

Banrural (Central Plaza) changes US dollars and has a Cajero 5B ATM.

ⓘ Getting There & Away

Buses depart from the main street between the plaza and the church. About 10 buses leave for Huehuetenango (Q20, two hours) between 4:30am and 2pm. Microbuses going as far as Tres Caminos (the junction with the Huehue-Barillas highway) leave throughout the day, whenever they fill up. There are two buses daily heading northwest to Jacaltenango. A Huisteca bus heads for La Mesilla at 5am.

Soloma & Around

North of the Todos Santos turnoff, the paved road winds up between often mist-shrouded cliffs and a precipitous gorge. Out of the mists emerge a pair of massive fingers of granite, known as the **Piedras de Captzín**. Soon after, you arrive in **San Juan Ixcoy**, where the women wear traditional white *huipiles* embroidered at the collar and hanging almost to their ankles.

Some 70km north of Huehuetenango, Soloma fills a valley and spreads up into the hills. This agricultural town is one of the biggest in the Cuchumatanes. The Maya here speak Q'anjob'al, but some of the *ladino* cowboys may greet you in English. Soloma's prosperity and its residents' language skills can be attributed to the migratory laborers who annually make the arduous trip to the US to work. On Sunday, market day, the town floods with people from surrounding villages. The pink-and-pastel **Hotel Don Chico** (② 7780-6087; 4a Av 3-65, Soloma; s/d/tr Q90/180/270; ℗ @ ⑮), opposite the massive gold-domed Catholic church, is the most comfortable lodging in town.

From Soloma the road cuts through a lushly wooded canyon, then climbs to the town of **Santa Eulalia**, which feels much more remote and traditional. It can get quite chilly here. This is sheep-farming territory, and you'll see shepherds wearing *capixays* (short woollen ponchos) in the fields. The town has a reputation for producing some of the finest marimbas in the country, as a little monument in front of the town hall proclaims, with locally grown hormigo trees providing the wood for the keys. A new Gothic version of Santa Eulalia's church is springing up with intricate floral motifs on its cement facade and a Maya inscription dedicated to the mother of the patron saint. There's reasonable lodging here at **Hotel Del Coronado** (☎5734-5850; Santa Eulalia; s/d Q60/120, s/d without bath Q45/90), a weird modernistic structure with bright spotless rooms and wonderful views of the surrounding slopes.

From Santa Eulalia the narrow road keeps climbing through pasture and occasional pine forest – sit on the left and you can see all the way to Mexico – and after 30km reaches **San Mateo Ixtatán**, the logical place to break the journey if you're heading for Laguna Lachuá from Huehue. Perched on an aerie with the jagged peaks of the Cuchumatanes trailing off into the clouds, the town unfolds organically over the green slopes. (The mist can descend early here, wiping out visibility by early afternoon.) Quaint buildings with pillared verandas and painted designs on the doors line largely traffic-free paths. The women of this small Chuj town wear captivating *huipiles,* lacy white affairs with concentric floral patterns embroidered on the neckline. San Mateo's church has a primitive charm. Beyond a rather dumpy facade is an austere interior with crude fruit motifs painted on the pillars. The real action seems to be out front in the atrium, where a smoking altar attests to the enduring Maya influence.

San Mateo holds an interesting archaeological site, **Wajxaklajunh**. It consists mostly of unexcavated mounds, with their stone foundations visible, and a large polygonal structure, whose top platform makes an ideal observation point for the surrounding hills. At the base stand a group of surprisingly intact stelae. To get there from the main plaza, go down the main street, then turn right downhill at a blue shop.

The **Hotel Magdalena** (☎5336-2823; dfpa85@icloud.com; San Mateo Ixtatán; s/d Q65/130; 📶) is easily the best option in town and the showers are scalding hot (but ask if the heater is on beforehand). From the park, go uphill and take the first street on the right; the yellow box is adjacent to the Banco Agromercantil. Right above the turnoff is spiffy **Los Picones al Chaz Chaz** (San Mateo Ixtatán; meals Q25; ⏰6am-8pm), where you can have fresh tamales with delicious salsas in the morning, as well as tacos and burritos.

Barillas-bound buses from Huehuetenango stop in Soloma, Santa Eulalia and San Mateo.

Barillas

POP 75,000 / ELEV 1450M

Leaving San Mateo, the road drops and weather becomes slightly kinder. After 28km, you'll reach Barillas, a prosperous coffee-growing town with a lowland feel.

Sleeping & Eating

Hotel Villa Virginia HOTEL $

(☎7780-2236; cnr 3a Calle & 3 Av; r per person Q80; P 📶) Barillas' most straightforward option is right on the plaza, with decent beds on clean tile floors – but get a room away from the street. Across the way are a couple of popular cafes.

Restaurant El Café CAFE $

(3a Calle 2-40; mains Q30-40; ⏰6:30am-9:30pm; 📶) This bright, clean and lively spot just up from Barillas' main square won't win any awards for originality, but makes a mean *huevos a la ranchera*, served with plenty of beans and tortillas.

Getting There & Away

Tuk-tuk drivers can convey you from the bus terminal to the town center (Q10, seven minutes).

If you're moving on for Cobán or El Petén, get an early start. Microbuses head for Playa Grande (Q50, 3½ hours) hourly from 3am to 3pm, departing from the traffic light by Mercado No 1 in the center of town. The road goes through the remote villages and forests of the Ixcán region, much of the way traveling above the landscape with vistas of vast distances. It starts out alternating between packed gravel and a tortuous exposed-boulder surface, then at Mayalán meets up with a recently completed section of the Transversal del Norte, after which the drive accelerates tenfold.

Yalambojoch & Laguna Brava

In a lower lying, more lushly vegetated zone between the Cuchumatanes and the Mexican border, the northwest corner of Huehuetenango department has a distinctive culture where the Awakateko language is spoken. About 20km east of the border post at Gracias a Dios is the hamlet of Yalambojoch. Most of the inhabitants fled during the conflict of the 1980s and have only recently returned to pick up the pieces of their lives.

A European NGO has contributed toward the redevelopment of the community of Yalambojoch, constructing wells, houses and a school/cultural center, **Niwan Nha** (☑5068-4163; per@cnl.nu), where indigenous girls learn *huipil* weaving skills.

One of the chief attractions for visitors is the Laguna Brava (also known as Laguna Yolnajab), 6.5km to the north, an extension of Mexico's Lagunas de Montebello. There's good swimming in the crystalline waters of the lagoon, reached by a two-hour descent on foot or horseback from Yalambojoch (best attempted from March to June). There's a Q25 entry fee to the lagoon, and guides charge Q75 to take you down, plus Q75 per day for horses.

East of Yalambojoch, a series of surprisingly intact **Maya pyramids** dating from the 10th century stand near the site of what used to be the village of San Francisco, the site of one of the civil war's most atrocious massacres, part of Rios Montt's scorched earth campaign.

West of Yalambojoch toward the border post at Gracias a Dios is the Finca La Trinidad junction, where a paved road leads south to the Interamericana. Approximately 5km south of the Finca La Trinidad junction is the turnoff for **Posada Rural Finca Chaculá** (☑5780-4855; www.turismochacula.com; s/d/tr incl breakfast Q270/420/525), a community-tourism project started by returnees from five different ethnic groups who took refuge in Mexico during the civil war. Their 37-sq-km farm features a small lagoon, some Maya archaeological sites, a waterfall and abundant forest. The old estate house has been outfitted with three comfortable rooms with hot showers, and meals are served. INGUAT-trained guides lead excursions to the Laguna Brava (Laguna Yolnajab) and **Hoyo Cimarrón**, a gigantic, almost perfectly cylindrical crater near the Mexican border.

🍴 Sleeping & Eating

Good home-cooked meals are served at Finca Chaculá (p156), a community-run ecotourism project.

Hospedaje Niwan Nha   BUNGALOW **$**
(per@cnl.nu; dm Q50, bungalows per person Q100) Accommodations at Yalambojoch include a few comfortable cabins and a large, well-maintained dorm. Guests have access to a well-equipped kitchen or can get meals at a pair of *comedores* for about Q20.

La Mesilla

With an early start from Huehuetenango you should have no trouble getting through this border point and onward to San Cristóbal de las Casas, Mexico. From the bus terminal, it's a hike of about 1km to the Guatemalan immigration post. Mexican immigration is at Ciudad Cuauhtémoc, 4km west of the border; taxis charge 10 Mexican pesos for the ride. About 30m past Mexican immigration, you'll find TAOSA buses to Comitán (50 pesos, every half hour), from which there are onward connections to San Cristóbal (55 pesos, 2¾ hours) over a road that is currently under repair.

The strip in La Mesilla leading to the border post has a variety of services, including a police station, a post office and a bank. There are also money changers who will do the deal – at a mediocre rate, but as no banks on either side of the border will perform this exchange it's your only option. For changing dollars, you're better off going to a bank in Huehue or Xela.

If you're stuck at the border there are a couple of straightforward places to spend the night.

ℹ Getting There & Away

Entering Guatemala via La Mesilla, you'll find chicken buses leaving for Huehuetenango (Q20, two hours) every 20 minutes till 6pm, as well as transport to Quetzaltenango (Q40). Otherwise, Línea Dorada runs a Pullman to Guatemala City (Q180, eight hours) at 8pm.

The Pacific Slope

Best Places to Eat

➜ Taberna El Pelicano (p174)

➜ Cafetería La Luna (p163)

➜ Max Café (p161)

➜ Robert's (p169)

Best Places to Sleep

➜ Takalik Maya Lodge (p164)

➜ Driftwood Surfer (p170)

➜ Hotel Pez de Oro (p174)

➜ Hotel Casa y Campo (p162)

➜ Finca Santa Elena (p168)

Why Go?

Separated from the highlands by a chain of volcanoes, the flatlands that run down to the Pacific are universally known as La Costa. It's a sultry region – hot and wet or hot and dry, depending on the time of year – with rich volcanic soil good for growing coffee, palm-oil seeds and sugarcane.

Archaeologically, the big draws here are Takalik Abaj and the sculptures left by pre-Olmec civilizations around Santa Lucía Cotzumalguapa.

The culture is overwhelmingly *ladino* (mixed indigenous and European heritage), and even the biggest towns are humble affairs, with low-rise houses and the occasional palm-thatched roof.

Guatemalan beach tourism is seriously underdeveloped. Monterrico is the only real contender, helped along by a nature reserve protecting mangroves and their inhabitants. Sipacate is slowly developing as a surf resort, although serious surfers find more joy in Mexico or El Salvador.

When to Go

You can't escape the heat on the coast, although temperatures do get a little more moderate from November to March. Beaches pack out on weekends and places like Monterrico will often double their room rates. Guatemalans love the beach for the main vacation periods – Easter and Christmas – and booking accommodations around this time is a very good idea.

The Pacific surf is rough at any time of year, but surfers find the best waves towards the end of hurricane season, late October through to November.

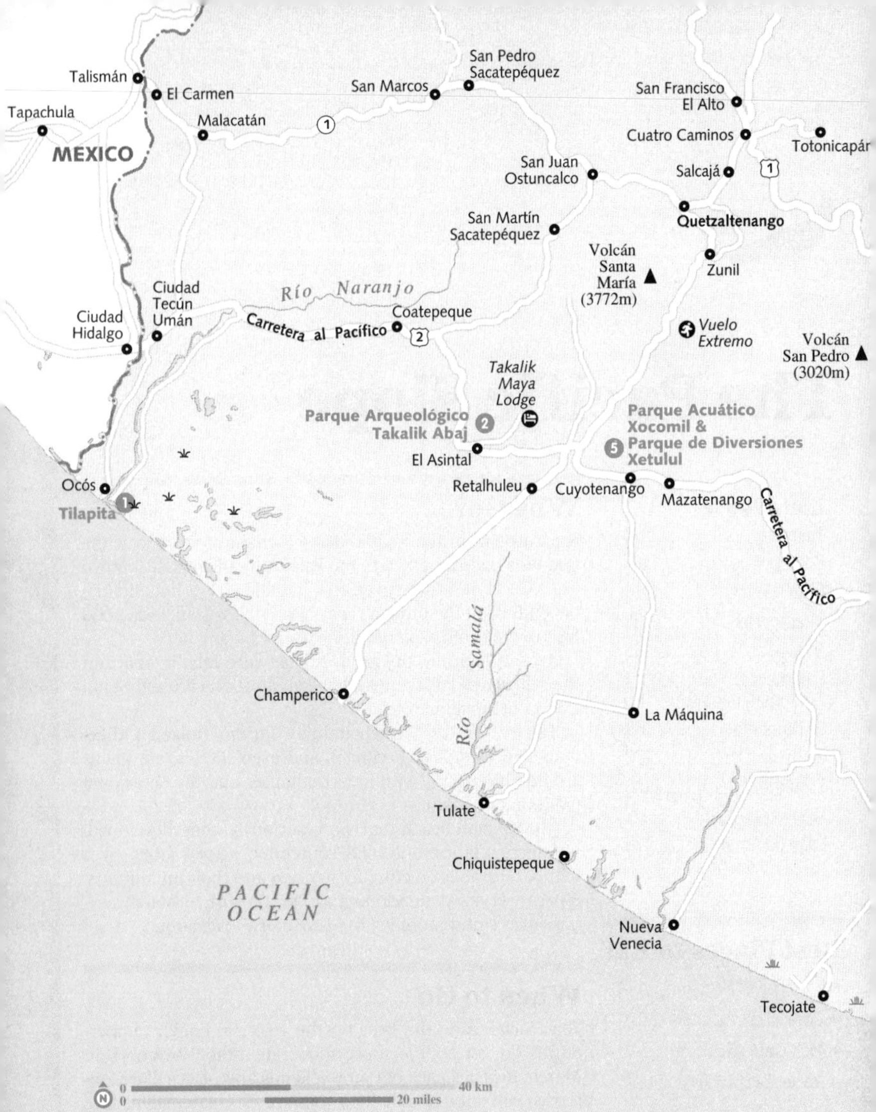

Talismán
El Carmen
Tapachula
San Marcos
San Pedro
Sacatepéquez
San Francisco
El Alto
Malacatán
MEXICO
Cuatro Caminos
Totonicapár
Salcajá
San Juan
Ostuncalco
Quetzaltenango
San Martín
Sacatepéquez
Volcán
Santa
María
(3772m)
Zunil
Ciudad
Tecún
Umán
Río Naranjo
Coatepeque
Ciudad
Hidalgo
Carretera al Pacífico
Vuelo
Extremo
Volcán
San Pedro
(3020m)
Takalik
Maya
Lodge
Parque Acuático
Xocomil &
Parque de Diversiones
Xetulul
Parque Arqueológico
Takalik Abaj
El Asintal
Ocós
Tilapita
Retalhuleu
Cuyotenango
Mazatenango
Carretera al Pacífico
Río Samala
Champerico
La Máquina
Río
Tulate
Chiquistepeque
PACIFIC
OCEAN
Nueva
Venecia
Tecojate

N
0   40 km
0   20 miles

The Pacific Slope Highlights

❶ **Tilapita** (p160) Getting away from absolutely everything in this one-hotel town.

❷ **Parque Arqueológico Takalik Abaj** (p164) Investigating the bridge in history between the Olmec and the Maya while strolling this grassy archaeological site.

❸ **Biotopo Monterrico-Hawaii** (p172) Spotting wildlife among the mangrove-lined canal and lagoons.

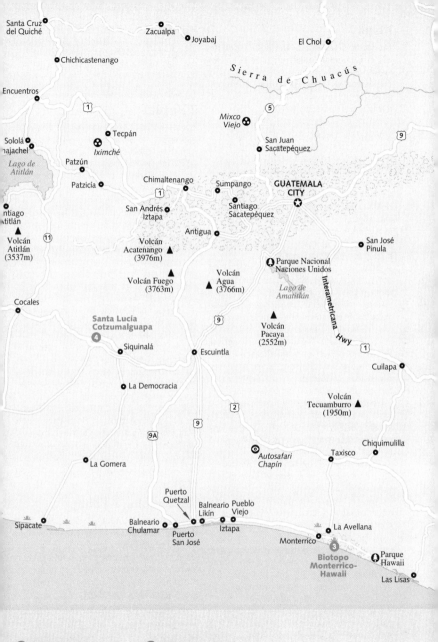

Santa Cruz
del Quiché

Zacualpa

Joyabaj

El Chol

Chichicastenango

Sierra de Chuacús

Encuentros

1

5

9

Sololá
Panajachel

Tecpán

Iximché

Patzún

Lago de
Atitlán

Patzicía

Chimaltenango

1

San Andrés
Iztapa

Mixco
Viejo

San Juan
Sacatepéquez

Sumpango

GUATEMALA
CITY

Santiago
Sacatepéquez

Santiago
Atitlán

Volcán
Atitlán
(3537m)

11

Antigua

San José
Pinula

Volcán
Acatenango
(3976m)

Parque Nacional
Naciones Unidos

Cocales

Volcán Fuego
(3763m)

Volcán
Agua
(3766m)

Lago de
Amatitlán

Interamericana Hwy

Santa Lucía
Cotzumalguapa

4

9

Volcán
Pacaya
(2552m)

1

Siquinalá

Escuintla

Cuilapa

La Democracia

2

Volcán
Tecuamburro
(1950m)

9

9A

Chiquimulilla

La Gomera

Autosafari
Chapín

Taxisco

Puerto
Quetzal

Sipacate

Balneario
Chulamar

Puerto
San José

Balneario
Likín

Iztapa

Pueblo
Viejo

La Avellana

Monterrico

Biotopo
Monterrico-
Hawaii

3

Parque
Hawaii

Las Lisas

4 **Santa Lucía**
Cotzumalguapa (p166)
Checking out the big
mysterious heads carved by
members of the non-Maya
Pipil culture.

5 **Amusement parks**
(p163) Getting wet at Parque
Acuático Xocomil and dizzy at
Parque de Diversiones Xetulul,
two fun parks near Retalhuleu.

History

Despite it being one of the first settled areas in Guatemala, relatively little is known about the Pacific region's early history. Many archaeological sites are presumed overgrown by jungle; others have been destroyed to make way for agriculture.

What *is* known is that the Olmecs were among the first to arrive, followed by the Ocós and Iztapa, whose cultures appear to have flourished around 1500 BC.

Although these cultures were much more humble than those of their northerly counterparts, they developed a level of sophistication in stone carving and ceramics. It's also thought that the coastal region acted as a conduit, passing cultural advances (like the formation of writing and the Maya calendar) from north to south.

Between AD 400 and 900, the Pipil moved in, most likely displaced by the turmoil in the Mexican highlands, and began farming cacao, which they used to make a (rather bitter) chocolate drink. They also used cacao beans as currency.

Towards the end of the Postclassic period, the K'iche', Kaqchiquel and Tz'utujil indigenous groups began moving in as population expansion in Guatemala's highlands made food scarce and land squabbles common.

Pedro de Alvarado, the first Spaniard to land in Guatemala, arrived here in 1524, pausing briefly to fight the K'iche' as a sort of forerunner to a much larger battle around present-day Quetzaltenango.

Further agricultural projects (mostly indigo and cacao) were started around this time, but it wasn't until independence that the region became one of the country's main agricultural suppliers, with plantations of coffee, bananas, rubber and sugarcane.

In the languid tropical climate, not much changes, particularly the social structure. The distribution of land – a few large landholders and many poorly paid, landless farm workers – can be traced back to these early post-independence days. You'll see the outcome as you travel around the region – large mansions and opulent gated communities alongside squalid, makeshift workers' huts.

🛈 Getting There & Around

The Pacific Slope has good road connections to Mexico to the north, El Salvador to the south, Antigua, Guatemala City and the Western Highlands. The major bus hubs are at Escuintla and Retalhuleu – coming from elsewhere in the country, it's more than likely that you will be passing through (and possibly changing buses in) one of these towns.

Tilapita

Just south of the Mexican border, this little fishing village is the place to come for some seriously laid-back beach time. There's exactly one hotel here (and it's a good one) and it's a world away from the often hectic, scruffy feel of other towns along the coast.

The village, which sits on a sandbar cut off from the mainland by the Ocós estuary, is only reachable by boat from the town of Tilapa. There's some excellent swimming to be had here, although as with all the beaches along this coast, the undertow can be quite serious and there are no lifeguards. If you're not a strong swimmer, don't go too far out.

There's not a whole lot to do (which is kind of the point), but local fisherfolk offer fascinating **boat tours** of the estuary, mangroves and adjoining **Reserva Natural El Manchón** for Q150 to Q300 per boat. There are no guarantees to sightings, but local wildlife includes iguanas, crocodiles, white herons, egrets and kingfishers.

Back in Tilapita, the **Tortugario Tilapita**, across the path from Hotel Pacifico del Mar, is fighting an uphill battle to preserve the local sea turtle population and would be quite happy for whatever help they can get if you're looking for some volunteer work.

🛏 Sleeping & Eating

The only place to eat on the island is at the Hotel Pacifico del Mar, where delicious meals (around Q60) are served in an oversized *palapa* (thatched palm-leaf shelter) and generally consist of the catch of the day. Shrimp, fish and *caldo de mariscos* (seafood stew) are always a good bet.

Hotel Pacifico del Mar   HOTEL $
(📱 5914-1524; www.playatilapa.com; s/d Q75/100; 🆒) Pacifico del Mar is nothing fancy, but it has decent-sized, clean concrete rooms. The good-sized swimming pool is a welcome addition, as things can get slightly warm here.

❶ Getting There & Away

Coming from Tecún Umán, you might luck onto a direct minibus (Q15, 45 minutes) to Tilapa – if not, take any bus heading out of town, get off at the Tilapa turnoff and wait for an onward bus there. A much more scenic option is to take a bus to Ocós (Q15, 30 minutes) and a *lancha* (small motorboat; around Q40, 45 minutes) to Tilapita from there. Coming in the other direction, direct buses run from Coatepeque to Tilapa (Q15, 1½ hours). Once you get to Tilapa, turn left down the side street and follow it to the dock, where you will find *lanchas* waiting. The 10-minute ride to Tilapita costs Q10 per person in a shared *lancha*, or you can hire a private one to make the trip for Q50. Tell the *lanchero* you are going to *el hotel* (although he will probably know that already).

Pullman drivers doing the Guatemala City–Tecún Umán run often stop in at Tilapa. If you're headed straight for the capital (Q70, four hours) or anywhere in between, ask around to find out when the next departure is.

Coatepeque

POP 58,300

Set on a hill and surrounded by lush coffee plantations, Coatepeque is a brash and chaotic commercial center, noisy and humid at all times. If you read the papers, the name Coatepeque should be familiar. A major stopover on the Colombia–Mexico drugs 'n' guns route, this town probably has more gang-related activity than any other outside of Guatemala City. Tourists are never the target and rarely get caught in the crossfire, but keep your wits about you. This *is* another facet of Guatemala, and probably not one you want to get too acquainted with.

If you're here to see the ruins at Takalik Abaj, Retalhuleu is a much better bet. If you really want to stay here or (more likely) get stuck, there are a couple of places in the relatively quiet town center that will put you up admirably.

Maya Expeditions (p52) runs rafting expeditions on the nearby Río Naranjo.

🛏 Sleeping & Eating

Hotel Baechli   HOTEL **$**
(☑ 7775-1483; 6a Calle 5-45, Zona 1; s/d Q85/105; 🅿) Cool, simple rooms with fan in a central location.

Hotel Europa   HOTEL **$**
(☑ 7775-1396; 6a Calle 4-01, Zona 1; r per person Q120) A cool and tranquil older-style hotel.

Front rooms have balconies overlooking the plaza, but can be noisy during the day.

Max Café   CAFE **$$**
(4a Calle 3-52, Zona 1; mains Q40-80; 🕒7am-9pm Mon-Sat, to 1pm Sun) Vaguely hip and completely out of place in otherwise workaday Coatepeque, Max Café serves up a good range of salads and sandwiches, some OK mains and the best coffee in town.

❶ Getting There & Away

Coatepeque is a major transport hub for the Pacific Slope, and bus connections here are good. The bus terminal is 2km to the north of town, but most buses stop in the center. There are departures to El Carmen (Q30, two hours), Tecún Umán (Q30, two hours), Quetzaltenango (Q35, 2½ hours), Tilapa (Q15, 1½ hours) and Retalhuleu (Q15, one hour), among others. Several Pullman bus companies stop here on the Guatemala City–Tecún Umán run, providing much more comfort and possibly a welcome spot of air-conditioning in the tropical heat. They stop on the street one block east of the bus terminal and charge Q70 for the four-hour run to Guatemala City.

Retalhuleu

POP 34,300

Arriving at the bus station in Retalhuleu, or Reu (*ray*-oo) as it's known to most Guatemalans, you're pretty much guaranteed to be underwhelmed. The neighborhood is a tawdry affair, packed out with dilapidated wooden *cantinas* (canteens) and street vendors.

The town center, just five blocks away from the bus station, is like another world – a majestic, palm-filled plaza, surrounded by some fine old buildings. Even the city police get in on the act, hanging plants outside their headquarters.

The real reason most people visit is for access to Takalik Abaj, but if you're up for some serious downtime, a couple of world-class fun parks are just down the road.

◎ Sights

Museo de Arqueología y Etnología   MUSEUM
(6a Av 5-68; Q15; 🕒8:30am-5pm Mon-Fri) This is a small museum of archaeological relics. Upstairs are historical photos and a mural showing locations of 33 archaeological sites in Retalhuleu department.

Retalhuleu

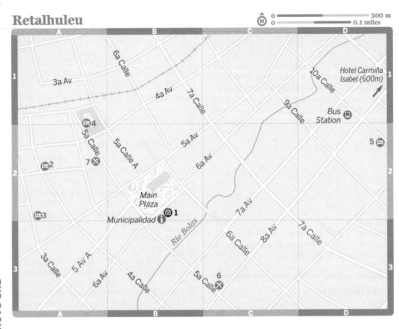

Retalhuleu

◎ **Sights**

1 Museo de Arqueología y
Etnología B2

🛏 **Sleeping**

2 Hostal Casa Santa María A2
3 Hotel Casa y Campo A2
4 Hotel Posada Don José A1
5 La Estancia D2

🍴 **Eating**

6 Cafetería La Luna C3
7 Hotel Astor A2

🛏 Sleeping

Out on the Carretera al Pacífico are several hotels. These tend to be 'tropical motels' by design, with bungalows, pools and restaurants. They are convenient if you have a car or can get a bus to drop you on the spot. Downtown has some good options, too.

Hotel Casa y Campo HOTEL **$$**

(☑ 7771-3289; 3a Calle 4-73, Zona 1; s/d Q160/300; **P ❋ 🛜**) Comfortable, good-value rooms a couple of blocks from the plaza. This one books up fast, so it's worth calling ahead.

Hotel Carmiña Isabel HOTEL **$$**

(☑ 7771-7832; Calz Las Palmas 2-71, Zona 2; s/d Q180/300; **P ❋ 🛱**) Calz Las Palmas used to be *the* place to live in Reu, and is still lined with stately mansions. This hotel is a fine example – rooms aren't huge, but the grounds and pool area are lovely.

Hostal Casa Santa María HOTEL **$$**

(☑ 7771-6136; 4a Calle 4-23, Zona 1; s/d from Q180/280; **❋ 🛜 🛱**) One of the more atmospheric options in town, this small hotel offers eight cool and spacious rooms with minimal but tasteful decorations. The small swimming pool in the courtyard is a good place for a dip.

La Estancia HOTEL **$$**

(☑ 7771-3053; 10a Calle 8-50, Zona 1; s/d Q120/240; **P ❋ 🛜**) A good, reasonably priced option is this family-run hotel offering simple, clean rooms a couple of blocks from the bus stop.

Hotel Posada de Don José HOTEL **$$**

(☑ 7771-0180; www.posadadedonjose.com; 5a Calle 3-67, Zona 1; r from Q440; **P ❋ 🛜 🛱**) A beautiful colonial-style hotel built around a huge swimming pool. Swan dives from the top balcony are tempting, but probably unwise. Rooms are spacious and comfortable – they're slowly remodeling here, so it's worth having a look at a few before deciding.

Eating

Reu seems to be slightly obsessed with pizza – 5a Av north of the plaza is almost wall-to-wall pizzerias. The dining rooms of the Posada de Don José (p162) and the **Hotel Astor** (📞7771-2559; 5a Calle 4-60, Zona 1; mains Q60-120; ☉7:30am-11pm) both offer more refined dining options.

Cafetería La Luna　　　　　GUATEMALAN $
(cnr 8a Av & 5a Calle, Zona 1; mains Q35-75; ☉8am-10pm) In a new location a block off the plaza, this remains a town favorite for simple but filling meals in a low-key environment.

ℹ Orientation

The town center is 4km southwest of the Carretera al Pacífico, along Calz Las Palmas, a grand boulevard lined with towering palms. The **main bus stop** (10a Calle, Zona 1) is northeast of the plaza. To find the plaza, look for the twin church towers and walk toward them.

ℹ Information

There is no official tourist office, but people in the **municipalidad** (Town Hall; 6a Av, Zona 1), facing the east side of the church, will do their best to help.

Banco Agromercantil (5a Av, Zona 1) Changes US dollars and traveler's checks and has a MasterCard ATM.

Banco Industrial (cnr 6a Calle & 5a Av, Zona 1) Changes US dollars and traveler's checks and has a Visa ATM.

ℹ Getting There & Away

Most buses traveling along the Carretera al Pacífico detour into Reu. Shared taxis (Q9) are the best way to get to El Asintal (for Takalik Abaj). Look for station wagons with 'Asintal' painted on the windshield around the bus stop and plaza.

Most buses make two stops in town, at the **main terminal** (5a Av, Zona 5) and a smaller bus station.

Around Retalhuleu

Parque Acuático Xocomil & Parque de Diversiones Xetulul

If you have children along, or your own inner child is fighting to get out, head to one of these two gigantic theme parks next door to one another on the Quetzaltenango road, about 12km north of Retalhuleu.

Both Xocomil and Xetulul are run by Irtra (Instituto de Recreación de los Trabajadores de la Empresa Privada de Guatemala; Guatemalan Private Enterprise Workers' Recreation Institute), which administers several fun sites around the country for workers and their families. Between them, the two sites comprise the most popular tourist attraction in Guatemala, with over a million visitors a year.

◉ Sights

Parque de Diversiones Xetulul　　　AMUSEMENT PARK
(📞7722-9450; www.irtra.org.gt; Carretera CITO, Km 180.5; adult/child Q100/50; ☉10am-5pm Fri-Sun) Xetulul is a surprisingly well organised amusement park, with first-class rides for all ages. Themed areas include representations of a Tikal pyramid, historical Guatemalan buildings and famous buildings from many European cities. An all-you-can-ride bracelet costs Q50 on top of admission.

Parque Acuático Xocomil　　　AMUSEMENT PARK
(📞7772-9400; www.irtra.org.gt; Carretera CITO, Km 180.5; adult/child Q100/50; ☉9am-5pm Thu-Sun) With a distinct Guatemalan theme, this world-class water park offers aquatic diversions for all ages (under-fives must have a flotation device; BYO, or hire one for Q20).

THE PACIFIC SLOPE AROUND RETALHULEU

RETALHULEU BUSES

DESTINATION	COST (Q)	TIME (HR)	FREQUENCY
Champerico	15	1	every few minutes, 6am-7pm
Guatemala City	50-95	3	every 15min, 2am-8:30pm
Quetzaltenango	20	1	every 30min, 4am-6pm
Santa Lucía Cotzumalguapa	30	2	every 15min, 2am-8:30pm
Tecún Umán (Mexican border)	20	1½	every 20min, 5am-10pm

Among the 14 waterslides, two swimming pools and two wave pools are re-creations of Maya monuments from Tikal, Copán and Quiriguá. Visitors can bob along a river through canyons flanked with ancient temples and Maya masks. Three real volcanoes – Santiaguito, Zunil and Santa María – can be seen from the grounds.

🛏 Sleeping

IRTRA Hostales HOTEL $$
(☑ 7722-9100; www.irtra.org.gt; Carretera CITO, Km 180; r with fan/air-con from Q400/440; 🅿 ❄ ☄) Set on lush, tropical grounds that feature swimming pools, a spa bath, various sports fields and probably the most impressive minigolf course in the country, this is the best accommodations for miles around. There are seven main buildings within the complex, each decorated in a different style – Colonial, Mediterranean, Polynesian, Indonesian, Thai, African, Maya – but rooms are spacious, modern and comfortable throughout.

Note that the Hostales is quieter from Sunday to Wednesday; Thursday to Saturday nights (when the parks are open) the place packs out and prices rise considerably.

ℹ Getting There & Away

Any bus heading from Retalhuleu toward Quetzaltenango will drop you at Xocomil, Xetulul or the IRTRA Hostales (Q8, 30 minutes).

Vuelo Extremo

If you're into the whole zip-line thing, **Vuelo Extremo** (☑ 5908-8193; www.vueloextremo.com; Carretera a Retalhuleu, Km 198; 3/4/11 cables Q75/100/150; ⊙ 6am-6pm) is one of the better-value ones in the country. Located almost exactly halfway between Retalhuleu and Quetzaltenango, it starts and ends with a terrifying 300m-long, 29m-high zip across the valley over the highway and then follows a circuit zigzagging down the hill on the other side.

For the fainter of heart there are some nice walking trails (Q25), crossing swinging bridges and passing by small waterfalls.

Parque Arqueológico Takalik Abaj

About 25km northwest of Retalhuleu, the Parque Arqueológico Takalik Abaj is a fascinating archaeological site set on land now occupied by coffee, rubber and sugarcane plantations. Takalik Abaj was an important trading center in the late Preclassic period,

before AD 250, and forms a historical link between Mesoamerica's first civilization, the Olmecs, and the Maya. The Olmecs flourished from about 1200 to 600 BC on Mexico's southern Gulf coast, but their influence extended far and wide, and numerous Olmec-style sculptures have been found at Takalik Abaj.

The city, which had strong connections with the town of Kaminaljuyú (in present-day Guatemala City), was sacked in about AD 300 and its great monuments, especially those in Maya style, were decapitated. Some monuments were rebuilt after AD 600 and the site retained a ceremonial and religious importance for the Maya, which it maintains to this day. Maya from the Guatemalan highlands regularly come here to perform ceremonies.

⊙ Sights

**Parque Arqueológico
Takalik Abaj** ARCHAEOLOGICAL SITE
(www.takalikabajpark.com; Q50; ⊙ 7am-5pm) This 6.5-sq-km archaeological site spreads over nine natural terraces, which were adapted by its ancient inhabitants. The parklike grounds boast temple mounds, ball courts and flights of steps paved with rounded river stones, along with an impressive number of stone sculptures. These works include numerous representations of animals and aquatic creatures (some in a curious pot-bellied style known as *barrigón*), miniature versions of the characteristic Olmec colossal heads and early Maya-style monuments depicting finely adorned personages carrying out religious ceremonies.

Archaeological work is continuing outside the kernel of the site, which is the Grupo Central on terrace No 2, where the most important ceremonial and civic buildings were located. Classic-era baths and multicolored floors were discovered here in late 2005.

The largest and tallest building is Estructura 5, a pyramid 16m high and 115m square on terrace No 3, above No 2. This may have formed one side of a ball court. Estructura 7, east of Estructura 5, is thought to have been an observatory.

🛏 Sleeping

★ **Takalik Maya Lodge** HOTEL $$
(☑ 2334-7693; www.takalik.com; farmhouse/bungalows Sun-Wed Q330/490, Thu-Sat Q400/590) Set on the grounds of a working farm 2km past the entrance to Takalik Abaj (and on top of a large, unexcavated section of it), this is by far

the most comfortable place to stay in the area. Accommodations options include the old farmhouse or newly constructed 'Maya-style' houses set in the middle of the forest.

Check the website for package deals including accommodations, meals and tours of the coffee, macadamia and rubber plantation as well as guided horseback tours of the waterfalls on the property and the archaeological site. Any pick-up from El Asintal passing Takalik Abaj will drop you at the entrance.

ℹ️ Getting There & Away

To reach Takalik Abaj by public transportation, catch a shared taxi from Retalhuleu to El Asintal (Q9, 30 minutes), which is 12km northwest of Reu and 5km north of the Carretera al Pacífico. Less frequent buses leave from a bus station on 5a Av A, 800m southwest of Reu plaza, about every half-hour from 6am to 6pm. Pick ups at El Asintal provide transportation on to Takalik Abaj (Q5), 4km further by paved road. You'll be shown around by a volunteer guide, whom you will probably want to tip (Q20 per person is a good baseline). You can also visit Takalik Abaj on tours from Quetzaltenango.

Champerico

POP 8700

Built as a shipping point for coffee during the boom of the late 19th century, Champerico, 38km southwest of Retalhuleu, is a tawdry, sweltering, dilapidated place that sees few tourists. Nevertheless, it's one of the easiest ocean beaches to reach on a day trip from Quetzaltenango, and heat-starved students still try their luck here. Beware of strong waves and an undertow if you go in the ocean, and stay in the main, central part of the beach: if you stray too far in either direction you put yourself at risk from impoverished, potentially desperate shack dwellers who live towards the ends of the beach. Tourists have been victims of violent armed robberies here.

🛏️ Sleeping & Eating

Most beachgoers come only to spend the day, but there are several cheap hotels. Most accommodations options are scattered along the beachfront or a block or two inland. Be aware that hotels here are all very basic.

Hotel Maza HOTEL $$
(☑7773-7180; s/d Q180/270; ❄️) With large clean rooms just across the road from the beach, the Hotel Maza is a good bet.

7 Mares SEAFOOD $
(mains from Q40; ⏰8am-7pm) Offers a shaded swimming pool, leafy dining area and upstairs deck that catches good breezes and views. And the seafood is delicious.

ℹ️ Getting There & Away

Regular buses connect Champerico with other Pacific Slope towns, Quetzaltenango and Guatemala City. The bus stop is two blocks back from the beach on the road out of town. The last buses back to Quetzaltenango leave at about 6pm, and a bit later for Retalhuleu.

Tulate

Tulate is a beach town that has yet to make it onto the radar of most travelers. The great thing about this beach is that, unlike others along the coast, the water gets deep very gradually, making it a great place to swim and just hang around and have some fun. The waves rarely get big enough to surf, but bodysurfers should be able to get a ride any time of the year. To get to the beach you have to catch a boat (Q5) across the estuary. Once on the other side, the water is 500m in front of you, straight down the only paved street.

🛏️ Sleeping & Eating

Of the three hotels in Tulate worth mentioning, the Villa Victoria, on the main drag, is the easiest to find. If you're heading toward either the Paraíso or Iguana, avoid the long hot walk along the beachfront by taking the riverfront path to the left as soon as you get off the *lancha* (small motorboat). If you don't feel like walking, a *lancha* to the Paraíso/Iguana costs Q60/130.

All the hotels have restaurants, but the best, most atmospheric dining is at the little shacks right on the beachfront, where good, fresh seafood meals start at around Q40.

Playa Paraíso BUNGALOW $$
(☑7872-1191; bungalows Q420; ❄️) This comfortable, if slightly worn, option is about 1km down the beach to the left from the main street. The bungalows here have two double beds, a sitting room and laid-back little balconies out front. There are hammocks strung around the property, and a good, if somewhat pricey, restaurant serves meals any time. Things can get a little hectic on weekends, but midweek you may just have the place to yourself.

Villa Victoria   HOTEL **$$**

(☏ 7763-1139; www.turicentrosvillavictoria.com; r with fan/air-con Q150/290; ❄ ▣) On the main street, halfway between the boat landing and the beach, this is a reasonable deal. Rooms are fresh and simple, with two double beds. It also doubles as a *turicentro,* meaning that local kids come and use the pool (which has an awesome waterslide, by the way) and may crank up the music ridiculously early on weekends.

Hotel La Iguana   BUNGALOW **$$**

(☏ 2478-3135; iguanabungalows@yahoo.com; bunga-lows midweek/weekend Q350/400; ▣) La Iguana has pleasant, somewhat basic rooms with a double bed and a bunk in each. It's a fair walk from the center, but simple meals (Q40) are available in the restaurant, and bungalows come equipped with kitchen.

❶ Getting There & Away

Buses run direct to Tulate from Mazatenango (Q40, two hours). Coming from the west, it's tempting to get off at Cuyotenango and wait for a bus there to avoid backtracking. The only problem with this is that buses tend to leave Mazatenango when full, so you might miss out on a seat.

Santa Lucía Cotzumalguapa

POP 49,480

Santa Lucía Cotzumalguapa, though benign enough, is unexciting. The region, though, is an important stop for anyone interested in archaeology. In the fields and *fincas* (plan-tations or farms) near the town stand great stone heads carved with grotesque faces and fine relief scenes, the product of the enig-matic Pipil culture that flourished here from about AD 500 to 700.

In your explorations of the area, you may also get to see a Guatemalan sugarcane *fin-ca* in full operation.

The local people of this region are de-scended from the Pipil, an ancient culture that had linguistic and cultural links with the Nahuatl-speaking peoples of central Mexico. In early Classic times, the Pipil who lived here grew cacao, the money of the age. They were obsessed with *juego de pelota* (a ball game) and with the rites and mysteries of death. Pipil art, unlike the flowery, almost romantic style of the Maya, is cold, gro-tesque and severe, but still very finely done. Exactly when these 'Mexicans' settled in this pocket of Guatemala, and where they came from, is not known, though connections with the Gulf Coast of Mexico, whose culture was also obsessed with the ball game, have been suggested.

◉ Sights

There are three main sites to visit, all out-side town: El Baúl hilltop site, about 4.5km north; the museum at Finca El Baúl, 2.75km further north; and the Museo Cultura Cotzu-malguapa, off the highway about 2km north-east of town.

Taxi drivers in Santa Lucía's main square will take you around all three sites for about Q300 without too much haggling. In this hot and muggy climate, riding at least part of the way is the least you can do to help yourself.

Museo El Baúl   MUSEUM

(◷ 8am-4pm Mon-Fri, to noon Sat) **FREE** This museum, about 2.75km on foot or 5km by vehicle from El Baúl hilltop site, comprises a very fine open-air assemblage of Pipil stone sculpture collected from around Finca El Baúl's sugarcane fields. A large stone jaguar faces you at the entrance.

Other figures include four humans or monkeys with arms folded across their chests; a grinning, blank-eyed head reminis-cent of the one at the hilltop site; carvings of skulls; and, at the back, a stela showing a personage wearing an animal headdress, standing over a similarly attired figure on the ground: seemingly winner and loser of a ball game.

To get there, if driving, leave town north-ward on the road passing **El Calvario** church. From the intersection just past the church, go 2.7km to a fork in the road just beyond a bridge; take the left fork and fol-low the paved road 3km to the headquarters of the Finca El Baúl sugarcane plantation. Buses trundle along this road every few hours. (If you're on foot, you can walk from the hilltop site back to the crossroads with the paved road. Cross the road and contin-ue along the dirt track. This will eventually bring you to the asphalt road that leads to the *finca* headquarters. When you reach the road, turn right.)

Approaching the *finca* headquarters (6km from Santa Lucía's main square), you cross a bridge at a curve. Continue uphill and you will see the entrance on the left, marked by a guard post and a sign 'Ingenio El Baúl Bienvenidos.' Tell the guards that you would

Santa Lucía Cotzumalguapa

like to visit the *museo,* and you should be admitted. Pass the sugar refinery buildings to arrive at the museum on the right.

Museo Cultura Cotzumalguapa MUSEUM
(Q30; ⊙ 8am-1pm & 2:30-4:30pm Mon-Fri, 8am-1pm Sat) At the headquarters of the Finca Las Ilusiones sugarcane plantation, you'll find this museum, which holds a collection of sculptures found around Las Ilusiones' lands. There is some explanatory material and you'll probably be shown around by the caretaker.

The museum includes a reconstruction of a sacrificial altar with the original stones, and photos of some fine stelae that were removed to the Dahlem Museum in Berlin in 1880. The most impressive exhibit, Monumento 21, is actually a fiberglass copy of a stone that still stands in the fields of Finca Bilbao (part of Las Ilusiones' plantations), depicting what may be a shaman holding a sort of puppet on the left, a ball-game player in the middle with a knife in one hand, and a king or priest on the right holding what may be a heart. Another copy of this stone, along with one of Monumento 19, lies on the ground across the street from the museum. Along the road just before the bridge to the *finca* house are copies of some of the sculptures from El Baúl museum.

To find the museum, head about 1.5km east of the town center on Carretera al Pacífico (Hwy 2). Take a left shortly before the **Tecún farm supplies** depot and travel about 400m north.

El Baúl Hilltop Site ARCHAEOLOGICAL SITE
With two great carved stones, this archaeological site has the additional fascination of being an active place of pagan worship for local people. Maya people visit regularly, especially on weekends, and make offerings, light fires and candles, and sacrifice chickens. They will not mind if you visit as well, and may be happy to pose with the idols for photographs in exchange for a small contribution.

Of the two stones, the large, grotesque, half-buried head is the most striking, with its elaborate headdress, beak–like nose and 'blind' eyes with big bags underneath. The head is stained with wax from candles, splashes of liquor and other drinks, and with the smoke and ashes of incense fires, all part of worship. People have been coming here to pay homage for more than 1400 years.

The other stone is a relief carving of a figure with an elaborate headdress, possibly a fire god, surrounded by circular motifs that may be date glyphs.

To get here, leave town northward on the road passing El Calvario church. From the intersection just past the church, go 2.7km to a fork in the road just beyond a bridge; the fork is marked by the entrance to the Ciudad España housing development (signposted from the center). Buses heading out to Finca El Baúl, the plantation headquarters, pass this sign. Take the right-hand fork, passing a settlement called Colonia Maya on your right. After you have gone 1.5km from the Los Tarros sign, a dirt track crosses the road: turn right here, between two concrete posts. Ahead now is a low mound topped by three large trees: this is the hilltop site. After about 250m, fork right between two more identical concrete posts, and follow this track around in front of the mound to its end after some 150m. Then take the path up on to the mound, which is actually a great ruined temple platform that has not been restored.

PACIFIC SLOPE FARMSTAYS

With so many beautiful *fincas* (farms) in gorgeous rural settings, it was only a matter of time before agritourism started to take hold in Guatemala. This is seriously low-impact tourism – often you can stay in the original farmhouse, and tours basically consist of walking around the property. Most *fincas* offering tours and accommodations still make most of their money from agriculture – they're not just sitting around waiting for you to show up. If you're planning on staying on a *finca,* get in touch a few days in advance to let them know you're coming.

Aldea Loma Linda (☑5724-6035; r per person without bathroom volunteers/visitors Q30/60) A beautiful little village set right on the southern foothills of the Santa María volcano. There are some great walks (Q60 to Q80 for around three hours) in the surrounding countryside, which is populated by an estimated 280 bird species (including the quetzal) throughout the year. Accommodations are basic but comfortable, and meals (Q25) are eaten with local families. Volunteers can work in the community's organic vegetable garden, the worm farm or in forest conservation. Buses for Loma Linda (Q10, two hours) leave from Retalhuleu at midday, 12:30pm, 1:30pm and 3pm.

Finca Santa Elena (☑7772-5294; www.fincasantaelena.com; Carretera a Quetzaltenango, Km 187; r per person without bathroom Q150-180; ☎) Set just off the main highway, this is one of the most easily accessible *fincas* in the region. Accommodations are in the original farmhouse, a lovely wooden building, and most rooms have great views. Home-cooked meals cost around Q70. Tours (Q60 to Q85 per person) are wonderfully informative. One tour demonstrates the coffee production process, while the other plunges into the local forest, passing rivers, waterfalls, bamboo forest and a spot that thousands of butterflies naturally inhabit. To get here, take any bus between Quetzaltenango and Retalhuleu and ask to be let off at the Entrada a Palmarcito (Km 187). The *finca* entrance is up the concrete road, 400m on the right.

Reserva El Patrocinio (☑7771-4393; www.reservapatrocinio.com; campsites/s/d Q150/ 510/830) This working coffee, macadamia and rambutan (among other crops) farm has been converted into a private nature reserve. Accommodations are in a stylish, modern house set on the hillside overlooking the valley. If you're staying here, all meals and activities are included in the price. Sitting on 140 hectares, there are walks galore, canopy zip lines (Q120), informative tours through the plantations (Q25 to Q50, more for birdwatching) and a decent restaurant (meals Q60 to Q120) with panoramic views. The reserve is 14km off the main road, about 18km north of Retalhuleu – ask for transportation options when making reservations.

🛏 Sleeping

The best hotel options are out on the entrance to town. You're not missing much by being out here.

Hotel Internacional   HOTEL $
(☑ 7882-5504; Calle los Mormones; s/d Q130/180; P❄) Down a short lane (signposted) off Carretera al Pacífico is the best budget hotel in town. It has clean, good-sized rooms with fan, cold shower and TV. Air-con is Q70 extra.

Hospedaje Reforma   HOTEL $
(☑ 7882-1731; 4a Av 4-71; s/d Q80/160) This hotel has exactly three things going for it: it's cheap, it's central and the patio is decorated with stuffed boars' heads. And if you like sleeping in small, dark and airless concrete cells, make that four.

Hotel Santiaguito   HOTEL $$
(☑ 7882-5435; www.hotelsantiaguito.com; Carretera al Pacífico, Km 90.4; s/d Q330/435; P❄≋) On the highway on the west edge of town, the Santiaguito is fairly lavish for Guatemala's Pacific Slope, with spacious tree-shaded grounds and a nice swimming pool (nonguests Q20). The large rooms have huge, firm beds and are set around a jungly patio/parking area. The big restaurant is shaded by ceiling fans and serves up good cheeseburgers and slightly overpriced meals (Q30 to Q80).

Hotel El Camino   HOTEL $$
(☑ 7882-5316; Carretera al Pacífico, Km 90.5; s/d Q180/300; P❄🛜) Hotel El Camino's rooms are almost ridiculously large, with a few sticks of furniture, such as clothes racks and writing tables. You could organize a game of soccer with the rest of the floor space, but don't tell management it was our idea.

🍴 Eating

The Hotel Internacional and El Camino both have restaurants attached (mains Q30 to Q50 and Q50 to Q100, respectively).

Robert's   STEAK $$
(Carretera al Pacífico, Km 89; mains Q60-180; ⊙11am-10pm) Probably the nicest place to eat in town is this steak house with leafy outdoor seating.

Beer House   BURGERS $$
(Carretera al Pacífico, Km 89; mains Q50-100; ⊙1-11pm) Does good burgers and OK meals.

ℹ Getting There & Away

As Hwy 2 now bypasses Santa Lucía, a lot of buses do not come into town. Coming to Santa Lucía from the east, you will almost certainly need to change buses at Escuintla (Q12, 30 minutes). From the west you will probably have to change at Mazatenango (Q20, 1¼ hours). At Cocales, 23km west of Santa Lucía, a road down from Lago de Atitlán meets Hwy 2, providing a route to or from the highlands. Eight buses daily run from Cocales to Panajachel (Q30, 2½ hours, 70km; between about 6am and 2pm). Ask about the current situation, as there have been reports of robberies along this stretch of road in the past.

La Democracia

POP 17,500

La Democracia, a nondescript Pacific Slope town located 10km south of Siquinalá, is hot day and night, rainy season and dry season. During the late Preclassic period (300 BC to AD 250), this area, like Takalik Abaj to the northwest, was home to a culture showing influence from southern Mexico. As you come into town from the highway, follow signs to the regional *museo,* which is on the plaza. You'll find a 5B ATM there, too.

⦿ Sights

At the archaeological site of Monte Alto, on the outskirts of La Democracia, huge basalt heads and pot-bellied sculptures have been discovered. These heads resemble crude versions of the colossal heads that were carved by the Olmecs on Mexico's southern Gulf Coast some centuries previously.

Today, these great Olmecoid heads are arranged around La Democracia's newly renovated main plaza, set in their own little roofed stands and illuminated at night.

Museo Regional de Arqueología   MUSEUM
(☑ 7880-3650; Q30; ⊙8:30am-1pm & 2-4:30pm Tue-Sat) Facing the plaza, along with the church and the modest Palacio Municipal, is this small, modern museum that houses some fascinating archaeological finds. The star of the show is an exquisite jade mask. Smaller figures, yokes used in *juego de pelota* (a ball game), relief carvings and other objects make up the rest of this small but important collection.

🛏 Sleeping & Eating

Guest House Paxil de Cayala   GUESTHOUSE **$**
(☑ 7880-3129; s/d without bathroom Q60/120)
Half a block from the plaza, La Democracia's
only place to stay is OK for the night, with
big, mosquito-proofed rooms.

Burger Chops   FAST FOOD **$**
(mains Q25-45; ⊙ 8am-9pm) Just off the
square, this is as close as the town gets to
a restaurant.

❶ Getting There & Away

The Chatía Gomerana company runs buses
every half hour from 6am to 4:30pm, from the
CentraSur terminal in Guatemala City to La
Democracia (Q25, two hours) via Escuintla. From
Santa Lucía Cotzumalguapa, catch a bus 8km
east to Siquinalá and change there.

Sipacate

An hour and a half down the road from Santa Lucía Cotzumalguapa is Guatemala's surf
capital. Waves here average 1.8m, with the
best breaks between December and April.
The town is separated from the beach by the
Canal de Chiquimulilla.

🛏 Sleeping & Eating

Oddly unexploited, the beach here has only
a few hotels. The best places to eat are in
those hotels, where the superfresh seafood is
your best bet.

★ Driftwood Surfer   HOSTEL **$**
(☑ 3036-6891; www.driftwoodsurfer.com; dm/d
Q65/295; ❉ ❉) The new kid on Sipacate's
block is this excellent little surf hostel right
on the beachfront. The air-conditioned
dorms are a big draw, as is the swim-up bar
in the pool overlooking the beach. Surf classes and board hire are available.

El Paredon   BUNGALOW **$**
(☑ 4994-1842; www.paredonsurf.com; dm Q85, s/d
from Q270/360) This budget choice is a rustic little surf camp to the east of the village.
It's run by a couple of Guatemalan surfers.
Board and kayak hire, surf lessons and good,
simple meals (Q50 to Q80) are available.
Book in advance.

To get here you can catch the daily bus
from Puerto San José (departs 1pm Monday
to Friday, Q20) or a *tuk-tuk*/pick-up to the
El Escondite pier from Sipacate, then a boat
(Q20 one-way) to El Paredon.

Rancho Carillo   BUNGALOW **$$$**
(☑ 5517-1069; www.marmaya.com; r/6-person
bungalows Q550/1200; ❉ ❉ ❉) Located
straight across the canal from Sipacate,
this property is a short boat ride (Q10 re-
turn) from town. The only trouble you'll
have sleeping is from the noise of crashing
waves. Call ahead and you'll probably be
able to get a better price – there's a 25%
discount on weekdays. Surfboards are
available for rent.

❶ Getting There & Away

Buses from Guatemala City's CentraSur termi-
nal (Q40, 3½ hours) pass through La Democ-
racia en route to Sipacate every two hours. If
you're coming from Antigua, the easiest way is
on the shuttle (tickets sold in every travel agen-
cy in town), which costs around Q100.

Escuintla

POP 116,000

Surrounded by rich green foliage, Escuint-
la should be a tropical idyll where people
swing languidly in hammocks and con-
coct pungent meals of readily available
exotic fruits and vegetables. In fact, it's a
hot, shabby commercial and industrial city
that's integral to the Pacific Slope's econo-
my, but not at all important to travelers, ex-
cept for making bus connections. Banks are
located around the plaza. There's an ATM
in the **Farmacia Herdez** (cnr 13a Calle & 4a
Av; ⊙ 7am-10pm), one block uphill from the
bus terminal.

🛏 Sleeping & Eating

There are simple eateries all along the main
street and around the bus terminal. For
something a little upscale, head to **Jaco-
bo's** (4a Av 14-62; mains Q30-50; ⊙ 11am-10pm),
which offers reasonable Chinese food in
clean and tranquil surrounds.

Hotel Costa Sur   HOTEL **$**
(☑ 7888-1819; 12a Calle 4-13; s/d with fan Q90/120,
s/d with air-con Q130/150 ; ❉) Just off the main
street, offering decent, cool rooms with TV
and fan.

Hotel Sarita   HOTEL **$$**
(☑ 7888-1959; Av Centro América 15-32; s/d
Q340/380; ❉ ❉ ❉) One of the better hotels
in town, with a large swimming pool and a
good onsite restaurant.

ℹ️ Getting There & Away

All buses from the terminal pass along 1a Av, but if you really want to get a seat, head to the main bus station in the southern part of town, just off 4a Av. The station entrance is marked by a Scott 77 fuel station. If you're heading to Monterrico and can't find a direct bus, catch one to Puerto San José or Iztapa and make a connection there.

Buses coming along the Carretera al Pacífico may drop you in the north of town, necessitating a sweaty walk through the hectic town center if you want to get to the main station.

Autosafari Chapín

Located about 25km southeast of Escuintla, **Autosafari Chapín** (☑ 2222-5858; www. autosafarichapin.com; Carretera a Taxisco, Km 87.5; adult/child Q60/50; ⊙ 9:30am-5pm Tue-Sun) is a drive-through safari park and animal conservation project earning high marks for its sensitivity and success in breeding animals in captivity. Species native to Guatemala include white-tailed deer, tapir and macaws. Around the grounds also roam non-native species such as lions, rhinos and leopards. There is a restaurant and pool, and it makes a good day out if you're traveling with kids.

It's more fun if you have your own vehicle, but if not, a 20-minute cruise through the park in a minibus is included in the admission price. Various companies run buses here (Q20, 1½ hours) from the Centra Sur terminal in Guatemala City. They leave every 10 minutes, from 4:30am to 5:30pm.

Iztapa

POP 6100

About 12km east of Puerto San José is Iztapa, Guatemala's first Pacific port, used by none other than Pedro de Alvarado in the 16th century. When Puerto San José was built in 1853, Iztapa's reign as the port of the capital city came to an end, and it relaxed into a tropical torpor from which it has yet to emerge.

There's not much to do in town. If you're not heading out fishing, the best option is to get a boat across the river to the sandbar fronting the ocean, where the waves pound and a line of palm-thatched restaurants offers food and beer.

🏃 Activities

Iztapa has gained renown as one of the world's premier deep-sea fishing spots. World records have been set here, and enthusiasts can fish for marlin, sharks and yellowfin tuna, among others. November through June is typically the best time to angle for sailfish. **Buena Vista Fishing** (☑ 7880-4203; www.buenavistasportfishing.com) and **Fishing International** (☑ toll-free in USA & Canada 800-950-4242; www.fishinginternational.com) run all-inclusive deep-sea fishing tours to Iztapa from the USA. It is also possible to contract local boat owners for fishing trips, though equipment and comfort may be nonexistent and catch-and-release could prove a foreign concept. The boat owners hang out at the edge of the Río María Linda – bargain hard. Yellowfin tuna will likely be out of reach for the local boats, as these fish inhabit the waters some 17km from Iztapa.

🛏️ Sleeping & Eating

There are a couple of hotels in town, but if you're looking for a beach holiday, this isn't the place. Small *comedores* (cheap eateries) can be found along the main street and in the area around the market.

Sol y Playa Tropical　　　　　HOTEL $$
(☑ 7881-4365; a Calle 5-48; s/d Q230/300; ❋ ⚏) This place has tolerable rooms with fan and bathroom on two floors around a swimming pool that monopolizes the central patio. Aircon costs an extra Q50.

ℹ️ Getting There & Away

The bonus about Iztapa is that you can catch a bus from Guatemala City all the way here (Q30, 1½ hours). They leave about every half hour, from 5am to 6pm, traveling via Escuintla and Puerto San José. The last bus heading back from Iztapa goes around 5pm.

Most people will be just passing through here en route to Monterrico. If you're driving, follow the signs on the road east until you get to the new bridge (Q15 one-way) across to Pueblo Viejo.

Monterrico

The coastal area around Monterrico is a totally different Guatemala. Life here is steeped with a sultry, tropical flavor, with rustic wooden-slat and thatched-roof architecture and awesome volcanoes that shimmer in the hinterland. It's fast becoming popular with foreigners as a beach break from Antigua or Guatemala City. On weekdays it's relatively quiet, but on weekends and holidays it teems with Guatemalan families.

Monterrico itself is a coastal village with a few small, inexpensive hotels right on the beach, a large wildlife reserve and two centers for the hatching and release of sea turtles and caimans. The beach here is dramatic, with powerful surf crashing onto black volcanic sand at odd angles. This wave-print signals that there are rip tides; deaths have occurred at this beach, so swim with care. Behind the town is a large network of mangrove swamps and canals, part of the 190km Canal de Chiquimulilla.

◉ Sights

Biotopo Monterrico-Hawaii WILDLIFE RESERVE
(Reserva Natural Monterrico) This reserve, administered by Cecon (Centro de Estudios Conservacionistas de la Universidad de San Carlos), is Monterrico's biggest attraction. The 20km-long nature reserve of coast and coastal mangrove swamps is bursting with avian and aquatic life. The reserve's most famous denizens are the endangered leatherback and ridley turtles, who lay their eggs on the beach in many places along the coast. The mangrove swamps are a network of 25 lagoons, all connected by mangrove canals.

Boat tours of the reserve, passing through the mangrove swamps and visiting several lagoons, take around 1½ to two hours and cost Q75 for one person, Q50 for each additional person. It's best to go just on sunrise, when you're likely to see the most wildlife. If you have binoculars, bring them along for birdwatching; January and February are the best months. Locals will approach you on the street (some with very impressive-looking ID cards), offering tours, but if you want to support the *tortugario* (which, incidentally, has the most environmentally knowledgeable guides), arrange a tour directly through Tortugario Monterrico.

Some travelers have griped about the use of motorboats (as opposed to the paddled varieties), because the sound of the motor scares off the wildlife. If you're under no time pressure, ask about arranging a paddled tour of the canal.

Parque Hawaii WILDLIFE RESERVE
(☑ 4743-4655; www.arcasguatemala.com; ☺ 8am-5pm) This nature reserve operated by Arcas (Asociación de Rescate y Conservación de Vida Silvestre) comprises a sea-turtle hatchery and some caimans, 8km east along the beach from Monterrico. The reserve is separate from the neighboring Biotopo Monterrico-Hawaii, but engages in the same line of conservation. Volunteers are welcome year round, but the sea-turtle nesting season is from June to November, with August and September being the peak months.

Volunteers are charged Q1330 a week for food and board onsite at the project. Homestays are available with local families for around the same cost. Jobs for volunteers include hatchery checks and maintenance, mangrove reforestation, basic construction and data collection. See the website for the complete lowdown on volunteering here. Most of the egg collection happens at night. It's a way out of town, but there are usually other volunteers to keep you company, and while you're here you can kayak, go on village trips and fish in the sea and mangroves.

A bus (Q5, 30 minutes) leaves the Monterrico jetty every couple of hours during the week and every hour on weekends for the bumpy ride to the reserve. Pick-ups also operate on this route, charging Q35 per person.

Tortugario Monterrico WILDLIFE RESERVE
(Q50; ☺ 7am-5pm) The Cecon-run Tortugario Monterrico is just a short walk east down the beach from the end of Calle Principal and then a block inland. Several endangered species of animals are raised here, including leatherback, olive ridley and green sea turtles, caimans and iguanas.

There's an interesting interpretative trail and a little museum with pickled displays in bottles. The staff offer lagoon trips, and night walks (Q50) from August to December to look for turtle eggs, and will accept volunteers. Around sunset nightly from September to January on the beach in front of the *tortugario,* workers release baby turtles. For a Q10 donation you can 'buy' a turtle and release it. Despite what everybody else is doing, please refrain from using flash cameras and flashlights.

◈ Courses

Proyecto Lingüístico Monterrico LANGUAGE COURSE
(☑ 5475-1265; www.proyectolinguisticomonterrico.com; Calle Principal) About 250m from the beach, this place is quite professional. Classes are generally held outdoors in a shady garden area. You can study in the morning or afternoon, depending on your schedule. Twenty hours of study per week costs Q760, or Q1300 with homestay.

Even if you're not studying here, the school is the best source of tourist information in town.

Tours

Productos Mundiales   BOAT TOUR

(📞 2366-1026; www.productos-mundiales.com) This outfit offers marine wildlife-watching tours (six hours, from Q1775 per person), leaving from Marina Pez Vela in nearby Puerto Quetzal. Throughout the year you stand a pretty good chance of seeing pilot whales, bottlenose dolphins, spinner dolphins, olive ridley turtles, leatherback turtles, giant manta rays and whale sharks. From December to May, humpback and sperm whales can also be seen.

Reservations (five days in advance via bank account deposit) are essential – see the website for details. To get to the marina, catch any Guatemala City–bound bus (Q12, one hour) to Puerto Quetzal, then a taxi or *tuk-tuk* from there.

🛏 Sleeping

To save a difficult, hot walk along the beach, take the last road to the left or right off Calle Principal before you hit the beach. Many places offer discounts for stays of three nights or more. Reservations on weekends are a good idea. Midweek, you'll have plenty more bargaining power.

📋 Left of Calle Principal

Johnny's Place   HOTEL **$**

(📞 5812-0409; www.johnnysplacehotel.com; dm Q45, r without bathroom Q145, r with air-con from Q320, bungalows Q550-1200; P❄☎) While Johnny's may not be everyone's cup of tea, it's easy enough to find – it's the first place you come to turning left on the beach – and one of the biggest operations here. It's got a decent atmosphere, though, and attracts a good mix of backpackers and family groups.

Every pair of bungalows shares a barbecue and small swimming pool. There's also a larger general swimming pool. The cheaper rooms are not glamorous, but have fans and screened windows. Pay extra and things start to get very swish. The bar-restaurant overlooks the sea and is a popular hangout: the food is not gourmet, but there are plenty of choices and imaginative *licuados* (fresh fruit drinks) and other long cool drinks.

Brisas del Mar   HOTEL **$**

(📞 5517-1142; r per person with fan/air-con Q120/180; P❄☎) One block back from the beach, this popular option offers good-sized rooms, a 2nd-floor dining hall with excellent sea views and a large swimming pool.

THE PACIFIC SLOPE MONTERRICO

FISHING ALONG THE PACIFIC COAST

Somewhere between five and 40 miles off the coast of Iztapa, chances are that right now a sportfisher is hauling in a billfish. This area is recognized as one of the world's top sportfishing locations – the coastline here forms an enormous, natural eddy and scientists who have studied the area have concluded this might be the largest breeding ground for Pacific sailfish in the world.

Catches of 15 to 20 billfish per day are average throughout the year. During high season (October to May) this number regularly goes over 40. Guatemala preserves its billfish population by enforcing a catch-and-release code on all billfish caught. Other species, such as dorado and tuna, are open game, and if you snag one, its next stop could well be your frying pan. If you'd like lessons, or you're looking for an all-inclusive accommodations-and-fishing package, check www.greatsailfishing.com.

Fish here run in seasons. There's fishing all year round, but the best months are: dorado (May to October); roosterfish (June to September); marlin (September to December); yellowfin tuna (September to January); sea bass (October); and sailfish (October to May).

As in any part of the world, overfishing is a concern in Guatemala. The prime culprits here, though, are the commercial fishers, who use drag netting. Another concern, particularly for inland species and shrimp, is the practice of chemical-intensive agriculture. Runoff leeches into the river system, decimating fish populations and damaging fragile mangrove ecosystems.

It's estimated that Guatemala's Pacific coast has lost more than 90% of its original mangrove forests. The mangroves serve as nurseries for fish and shellfish and the trees maintain water quality and prevent erosion. They also provide food and income for local populations, but all along the Pacific coast, commercial shrimp farming is moving in. Over the past decade, commercial shrimp farms have consumed about 5% of all the remaining mangroves in the world.

★ **Hotel Pez de Oro** BUNGALOW **$$**
(☑2368-3684; www.pezdeoro.com; s/d Q400/
500; [P][❄]) This is the funkiest-looking place
in town, with comfortable little huts and
bungalows scattered around a shady prop-
erty. The color scheme is a cheery blue and
yellow, and the rooms have some tasteful
decorations and large overhead fans. The
excellent restaurant, with big sea views,
serves up great Italian cuisine and seafood
dishes.

Dos Mundos Pacific Resort RESORT **$$$**
(☑7823-0820; www.dosmundospacific.com; bun-
galows from Q930; [P][❄][🛜][❄]) The biggest
complex around is pushing resort status –
manicured grounds, two swimming pools
and a gorgeous beachfront restaurant. The
bungalows are spacious and simple, but
beautifully presented, with wide shady balconies out front.

🛏 Right of Calle Principal

Hotel El Delfin HOTEL **$**
(☑4661-9255; www.hotel-el-delfin.com; dm
Q40, s/d from Q125/200, s/d without bathroom
Q50/100; [🛜][❄]) A humble but sprawling
beachside setup that's been slowly improving over the years. Rooms are big and
well-appointed, but the place can get noisy
on weekends.

Café del Sol HOTEL **$$**
(☑5810-0821; www.cafe-del-sol.com; s/d with
fan from Q205/305, r with air-con from Q560;
[P][❄][🛜][❄]) Set all under one big thatched
roof, the 'economy' rooms here are a bit dis-
appointing compared to the rest of the place.
Across the road, the new annex offers 'stand-
ard' rooms that are a better deal – larger and
with an onsite swimming pool. The restau-
rant's menu has some original dishes and you
can eat on the terrace or in the big *palapa*
(thatched) dining area.

Hotel Atelie del Mar HOTEL **$$$**
(☑5752-5528; www.hotelateliedelmar.com; s/d with
fan incl breakfast Q500/660; [P][❄][🛜][❄]) This is
one of the most formal hotels in town, with
lovely landscaped grounds and spacious,
simple and beautiful rooms. It's got the
best swimming pool around, along with the
widest menu and an onsite art gallery.

✗ Eating

There are many simple seafood restaurants
on Calle Principal. For the best cheap eats,
hit either of the two nameless *comedores*

(basic, cheap eateries) on the last road to the
right before the beach, where you can pick
up an excellent plate of garlic shrimp, rice
tortillas, fries and salad for Q50.

Most hotels have restaurants serving
whatever is fresh from the sea that day.

★ **Taberna El Pelicano** ITALIAN, SEAFOOD **$$**
(mains Q60-150; ⊙noon-2pm & 6-10pm Wed-Sun)
By far the best place to eat in town, with the
widest menu and most interesting food, such
as seafood risotto (Q80), beef carpaccio (Q75)
and a range of jumbo shrimp dishes (Q140).

🍷 Drinking & Nightlife

Playa Club CLUB
(⊙8am-1am) This venue, located at Johnny's
Place (p173), heats up on weekends, with
plenty of reggaetón, house music and drinks
specials keeping the crowd moving.

Las Mañanitas BAR
(⊙noon-late) On the beachfront at the end of
the main street, this little bar is what Mon-
terrico really needed – plenty of hammock
chairs looking out over the beach, a good
range of drinks and low-key music playing
in the background.

ℹ Orientation & Information

From where you alight from the La Avellana boat,
it's about 1km to the beach and the hotels; you
will pass through the village en route. From the
embarcadero (wharf), walk straight ahead and
then turn left. Pick-ups (Q5) meet scheduled
boats or *lanchas* (small motorboats).

If you come by bus from Pueblo Viejo, from the
stop walk about 300m toward the beach on Calle
Principal.

Banrural, just off the main street on the road
to Parque Hawaii, changes cash and may change
traveler's checks. There's an ATM in the Super-
mercado Monterrico.

ℹ Getting There & Away

There are two ways to get to Monterrico. Coming
from Guatemala City or Antigua, it's most logi-
cal to catch a bus that, with the new bridge at
Pueblo Viejo, goes right through to Monterrico.
The other option is to head to La Avellana, where
lanchas and car ferries depart for Monterrico.
The Cubanita company runs a handful of direct
buses to and from Guatemala City (Q45, four
hours, 124km). Alternatively, you reach La Avellana
by changing buses at Taxisco on Hwy 2. Buses
operate half-hourly from 5am to 4pm between
Guatemala City and Taxisco (Q40, 3½ hours)
and roughly hourly from 7am to 4:30pm between
Taxisco and La Avellana (Q10, 40 minutes),

although taxi drivers will tell you that you've missed the last bus, regardless of what time you arrive. A taxi between Taxisco and La Avellana costs around Q80.

From La Avellana catch a *lancha* or car ferry to Monterrico. The collective *lanchas* charge Q5 per passenger for the half-hour trip along the Canal de Chiquimulilla, a long mangrove canal. They start at 4:30am and run more or less every half hour or hour until late afternoon. You can always pay more and charter your own boat. The car ferry costs Q100 per vehicle.

Shuttle buses also serve Monterrico. The most reliable leaves from outside the Proyecto Lingüístico Monterrico (p172) at 1pm and 4pm (Q80/160 to Antigua/Guatemala City); book tickets and inquire about other destinations at the language school. Contact any travel agent in Antigua to arrange a shuttle to Monterrico from Guatemala City or Antigua.

Around Monterrico

Isleta de Gaia

East down the coast from Monterrico, near Las Lisas, is the Guatemalan Pacific coast's best-kept secret – a bungalow-hotel built on a long island of sand and named for the Greek earth goddess. Overlooking the Pacific on one side and mangroves on the other, this small, friendly, ecological, French-owned **resort** (☑7885-0044; www.isleta-de-gaia.com; 2-/4-person bungalow Q600/1050; @☎☒) ✆ is constructed from natural materials.

There are 12 bungalows, on one and two levels, with sea, lagoon or pool views. Each has good beds, fan, bathroom, balcony and hammock; decorations are Mexican and Costa Rican. The seafront restaurant (mains Q70 to Q150) offers Italian, Spanish and French cuisine, with fresh fish naturally the star. There are boogie boards and kayaks for rent and a boat for fishing trips. Reserve your stay in this little paradise by email four days in advance.

The staff run a shuttle service to and from Guatemala City and Antigua. From Monterrico there is no road east along the coast beyond Parque Hawaii, so you have to backtrack to Taxisco and take Carretera al Pacífico for about 35km to reach the turnoff for Las Lisas. From the turnoff it's 20km to Las Lisas, where you take a boat (Q100) to Isleta de Gaia.

Chiquimulilla & El Salvador Border

Surfers found in this part of Guatemala will likely be heading to or returning from La Libertad in El Salvador. Most people shoot straight through Escuintla and Taxisco to Chiquimulilla and on to the Salvadoran border at Ciudad Pedro de Alvarado–La Hachadura, from where it is about 110km along the coast of El Salvador to La Libertad.

Should you need to stop for the night before crossing the border, you could do worse than the friendly cowboy town of Chiquimulilla (population 15,100), some 12km east of Taxisco. There isn't much going on here, but it's a decent enough place to take care of errands and regroup. The new bus terminal is on the outskirts of town, but *tuk-tuks* will take you anywhere you want to go for Q4.

🛏 Sleeping & Eating

All but the cheapest hotels in this region tend to have swimming pools. Mosquitoes can be a concern; check for well-sealed or (preferably) screened windows.

There are two serviceable *hospedajes* (guesthouses) in La Hachadura on the El Salvador side of the border, but the *hostales* (budget hotels) in Ciudad Pedro de Alvarado on the Guatemalan side are not recommended.

Beef is very much a part of the diet in this region, although there is usually some seafood on offer. With the exception of hotel restaurants, places to eat tend to be more informal than restaurant-quality.

Hotel San Carlos HOTEL $
(☑7885-0817; 2a Calle, Zona 2; s/d Q120/180; ☑☎) A few blocks from the bus terminal, this family-run option offers reasonable rooms and an onsite restaurant.

❶ Getting There & Away

Chiquimulilla and the El Salvador Border are served by buses from Guatemala City and those running along the Pacific Hwy.

Buses leave Taxisco for the border every 15 minutes until 5pm.

The other option for getting to El Salvador is to turn north from Chiquimulilla and take local buses through Cuilapa to the border at Valle Nuevo–Las Chinamas, traveling inland before veering south to La Libertad.

Cuilapa

POP 25,400

Surrounded by citrus and coffee plantations, the capital of Santa Rosa department isn't much of a tourist attraction in its own right, although the area's fame for wood carvings, pottery and leather goods may turn up a couple of decent souvenirs.

People coming this way are usually headed for the border with El Salvador, but there are a couple of volcanoes just out of town that are easily climbed and afford some excellent views.

Hotels in Cuilapa are very basic. Your best bet is in nearby Chiquimulilla or day-tripping from further afield. Basic *comedores* (cheap eateries) can be found around the bus terminal/market area.

Sights

Tecuamburro VOLCANO
The Tecuamburro volcanic complex comprises various peaks, including Cerro de Miraflores (1950m), Cerro la Soledad (1850m) and Cerro Peña Blanca (1850m). This last, which has several small vents releasing steam and sulfur, provides the most interesting climb, although its forested slopes mean no views until you're almost at the top.

Buses and minibuses (Q15, 1½ hours) leave regularly for the village of Tecuamburro from Cuilapa. From there it's a two- to three-hour hike (14km) to the summit of Peña Blanca.

Volcán Cruz Quemada VOLCANO
This dormant volcano towers 1700m over the tiny village of Santa María Ixhuatán at its base. Coffee plantations reach about one third of the way up its slopes. The summit, littered with radio towers, offers excellent views of the land running down to the coast, the Cerro La Consulta mountain range and the nearby Tecuamburro volcanic complex. From Santa María it's an easy-to-moderate climb to the top that should take about three hours.

The 12km hike is possible to do on your own, asking for plenty of directions along the way. Alternatively, guides can be hired in Santa María – ask at the taxi stand on the main square. To get to Santa María, catch a minibus (Q8, 25 minutes) from Cuilapa.

Getting There & Away

Cuilapa is connected by a good road with Guatemala City. Buses (Q30, 2½ hours) leave from the CentraSur bus terminal in Guatemala City.

Minibuses leave from Cuilapa's bus terminal for the El Salvador border crossing at Valle Nuevo.

Lago de Amatitlán

Lago de Amatitlán is a placid lake backed by a looming volcano and situated a mere 25km south of Guatemala City, making it a good day trip. After suffering years of serious neglect, the lake is slowly being rejuvenated, thanks mainly to local community groups who hope to see it once again function as a tourist attraction. On weekends, people from Guatemala City come to row boats on the lake (its waters are too polluted for swimming) or to rent a hot tub for a dip. Many people from the capital own second homes here.

Sights & Activities

Shared/private boat tours cost Q10/80. If you're feeling energetic, rowboats rent from Q30 per hour.

Teleférico CABLE CAR
(adult/child return Q20/10; ⊙9am-5pm Fri-Sun) When it's operating, this cable car heads out over the lakeshore then pretty much straight up the hillside. It's a half-hour ride with some stunning views of the surrounding countryside from the top.

Sleeping & Eating

There are a few decent hotels scattered around the lake's edge, and some more in the town, but most travelers come here on a day trip (if at all).

A string of *comedores* along the lakefront offer fried fish, tacos and simple meals. For something a bit more refined, follow the signs up the hill to the right to **La Rocarena** (mains Q50-120; ⊙8am-9pm), which has a decent menu, lovely grounds, good views and a couple of warm-water swimming pools.

Getting There & Away

The lake is situated just off the main Escuintla–Guatemala City highway (Hwy 9). Coming from Guatemala City (Q10, one hour), just ask to be dropped at the *teleférico*. The waterfront is about half a kilometer from the signposted turnoff. Coming from Escuintla, or heading back to Guatemala City, buses stop on the main road, about 1km away. It's an easy 10- to 15-minute walk; taxis are rare.

Central & Eastern Guatemala

Best Places to Eat

➡ Xkape Koba'n (p183)

➡ La Abadia (p184)

➡ Restaurante Buga Mama (p222)

➡ Sundog Café (p213)

➡ Restaurante Safari (p217)

Best Places to Sleep

➡ Hotel Restaurant Ram Tzul (p181)

➡ Hotel La Posada (p183)

➡ Utopia (p189)

➡ Finca Tatin (p223)

Why Go?

Stretching from the steamy lowland forests of El Petén to the dry tropics of the Río Motagua valley, and from the edge of the Western Highlands to the Caribbean Sea, this is Guatemala's most diverse region.

The Carretera al Atlántico (Hwy 9) shoots eastward to the sea from Guatemala City, passing the turnoffs for the wonderfully preserved ruins of Copán (Honduras), Quiriguá with its impressive stelae and Río Dulce, a favored resting spot for Caribbean sailors and gateway to the Refugio de Vida Silvestre Bocas del Polochic (Bocas del Polochic Wildlife Reserve). While you're here don't miss the gorgeous boat ride down the Río Dulce to Lívingston, the enclave of the Garifuna people.

The north of the region is lush and mountainous coffee-growing country. The limestone crags around Cobán attract cavers the world over, and the beautiful pools and cascades of Semuc Champey rate high on Guatemala's list of natural wonders.

When to Go

This region encompasses a huge area, measuring about one quarter of Guatemala's land mass, and the climate is predictably diverse. Cobán and the Alta Verapaz are best avoided in the cooler months from November to February, as many of the attractions involve swimming. Garifuna National Day in Lívingston at the end of November is worth putting on your calendar, as is Cobán's Rabin Ajau festival in July.

Birdwatchers hoping to see Guatemala's national bird, the quetzal, will have better luck during their laying period from March to June. Accommodations prices remain relatively stable throughout the year, with the usual exceptions of steep hikes during Christmas and Easter.

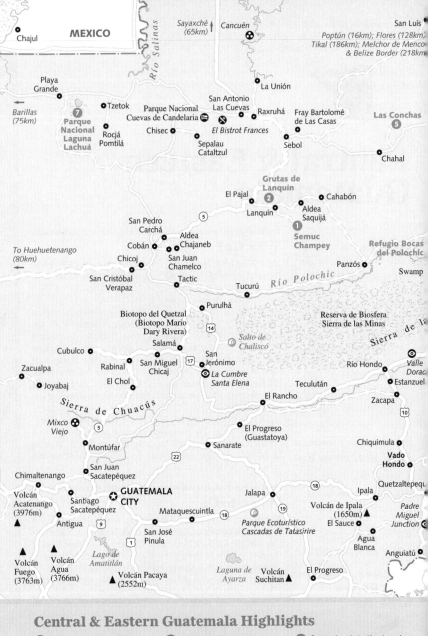

Central & Eastern Guatemala Highlights

1 Splashing around the turquoise waters of **Semuc Champey** (p189).

2 Getting deep in the caves at **Grutas de Lanquín** (p187).

3 Admiring the impressive carvings at **Copán** and **Quiriguá** (p201).

4 Relaxing in the Antigua-rivaling beauty of **Copán Ruinas** (p206).

5 Going bush in the jungle hideaway of **Las Conchas** (p193), where waterfalls, jungle treks and village tours await.

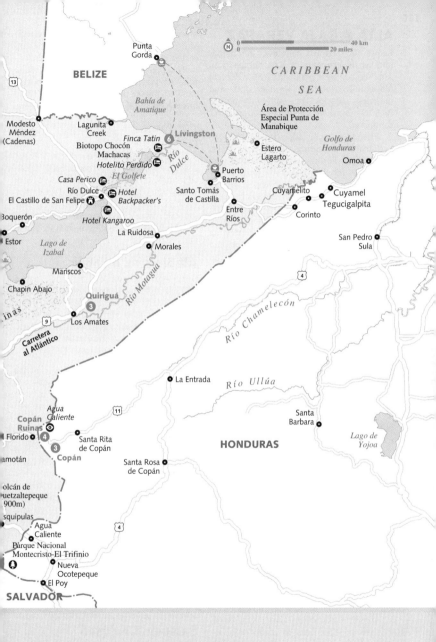

ALTA & BAJA VERAPAZ

Before the Spanish conquest, the mountainous departments of Baja Verapaz and Alta Verapaz were populated by the Rabinal Maya, noted for their warlike habits and merciless victories. They battled the powerful K'iche' Maya for a century but were never conquered.

When the conquistadors arrived, they too had trouble defeating the Rabinal Maya. It was Fray Bartolomé de Las Casas who convinced the Spanish authorities to try peace where war had failed. Armed with an edict that forbade Spanish soldiers from entering the region for five years, the friar and his brethren pursued their religious mission and succeeded in pacifying and converting the Rabinal Maya, renaming their homeland Verapaz (True Peace). It is now divided into Baja Verapaz, with its capital at Salamá, and Alta Verapaz, which is centered on Cobán. The Rabinal Maya have remained among the most dedicated and true to ancient Maya customs, and there are many intriguing villages to visit in this part of Guatemala, including Rabinal itself.

Salamá & Around

A wonderful introduction to Baja Verapaz' not-too-hot, not-too-cold climate, the area around Salamá hosts a wealth of attractions, both post-colonial and indigenous.

Salamá itself is known for its ornate church (complete with grisly depiction of Jesus) and bustling Sunday market. A photogenic ex-sugar-mill-turned-museum and impressive stone aqueduct can be found in the neighboring town of San Jerónimo.

Salamá also marks the starting point for a back-roads route to Guatemala City, passing Rabinal, whose annual fiesta of San Pedro (January 19 to 25), is a beguiling mix of pre-Columbian and Catholic traditions, and Cubulco, where the *palo volador* (flying pole) tradition is still observed. There are basic, adequate *pensiones* (family-run guesthouses) in both Rabinal and Cubulco.

From there it's 100km south to Guatemala City, passing the turnoff to Mixco Viejo, one of the least-visited and most spectacularly sited Maya sites in the country. The former Poqomam capital, it lies wedged between deep ravines with just one way in and one way out; the Poqomam further fortified the site by constructing impressive rock walls

around the city. It took Pedro de Alvarado and his troops more than a month of concerted attacks to conquer it. When they finally succeeded, they furiously laid waste to this city, which scholars believe supported close to 10,000 people at its height. There are several temples and two ball courts here.

🖝 Tours

EcoVerapaz   TOUR
(☑5722-9095; ecoverapaz@hotmail.com; 8a Av 7-12, Zona 1, Salamá; 1-day tour per person Q400) Located in the shop Imprenta Mi Terruño – a block west of the plaza on the road to La Cumbre. Its local, trained naturalists offer interesting tours throughout Baja Verapaz including caving, birdwatching, hiking, horseback riding and orchid trips.

🍴 Sleeping & Eating

Hotel Real Legendario   HOTEL $
(☑7940-0501; www.hotelreallegendario.com; 8a Av 3-57, Salamá; s/d Q160/180; ℗ 🖥) You'll recognize this place, three blocks east of the plaza, by the stands of bamboo in the parking lot. The clean, secure rooms have fan, hot-water bathroom and cable TV.

Posada de Don Maco   HOTEL $
(☑7940-0083; 3a Calle 8-26, Salamá; s/d Q120/160; ℗) This clean, family-run place has simple but spacious rooms with fan and good bathrooms. The courtyard boasts a collection of caged squirrels.

Antojitos Zacapanecos   FAST FOOD $
(cnr 6a Calle & 8a Av, Salamá; mains Q25; ⊙10am-9pm) For something a little different in the fast-food vein, check out the huge flour tortillas filled with pork, chicken or beef from this place. Better yet, grab one to go and have a picnic in the plaza.

❶ Getting There & Away

Buses leave Salamá's downtown bus terminal frequently for Cobán (Q30, 1½ to two hours), Guatemala City (Q40 to Q55, three hours) and neighboring villages.

Salto de Chaliscó

What's claimed to be Central America's highest waterfall (Q20) lies 12km down a dirt road from a turnoff at Km 145 on Hwy 14 to Cobán. At 130m and surrounded by cloud forest, it's an impressive sight, especially if it's been raining and the fall is running at full force. Another waterfall, the **Lomo de Macho**, lies 8km away – an enjoyable walk, or you can hire a horse from the visitors center in town (about 5km from the falls).

Buses to Chaliscó leave every half hour from Salamá (Q17, 1½ hours), passing La Cumbre Santa Elena (Q10, 45min) on Hwy 14.

Biotopo del Quetzal

Along Hwy 14, 34km beyond the La Cumbre turnoff for Salamá, is the Biotopo Mario Dary Rivera nature reserve, commonly called **Biotopo del Quetzal** (Hwy 14, Km 161; Q40; ⊘ 7am-4pm), just east of Purulhá village.

You need a fair bit of luck to see a quetzal, as they're rare and shy, though you have the best chance of seeing them from March to June. Even so, it's well worth stopping to explore and enjoy this lush high-altitude cloud-forest ecosystem that is the quetzal's natural habitat – and you may happen to see one. Early morning or early evening are the best times to watch out for them – they're actually more prevalent around the grounds of the nearby hotels.

The reserve has a visitors center, a little shop for drinks and snacks, and a camping and BBQ area. The ruling on camping changes from time to time. Check by contacting **Cecon** (Centro de Estudios Conservacionistas de la Universidad de San Carlos; Map p50; www.cecon.usac.edu.gt; Av La Reforma 0-63, Zona 10, Guatemala City), which administers this and other biotopes.

Two excellent, well-maintained **nature trails** wind through the reserve: the 1800m **Sendero los Helechos** (Fern Trail) and the 3600m **Sendero los Musgos** (Moss Trail). As you wander through the dense growth, treading on the rich, spongy humus and leaf mold, you'll see many varieties of epiphytes (air plants), which thrive in the reserve's humid atmosphere. Deep in the forest is Xiu Gua Li Che (Grandfather Tree), some 450 years old, which germinated around the time the Spanish fought the Rabinal in these mountains.

🛏 Sleeping & Eating

Ranchitos del Quetzal   HOTEL $
(☑ 4130-9456; www.ranchitosdelquetzal.com; Hwy 14, Km 160.5; r per person from Q100; ℗) Carved out of the jungle on a hillside 200m away from the Biotopo del Quetzal entrance, this place has good-sized simple rooms with warm (ie tepid) showers in the older wooden building and hot showers in the newer concrete one. Reasonably priced, simple meals (mains from Q30) are served, and there are vegetarian options.

★ **Hotel Restaurant Ram Tzul**   HOTEL $$
(☑ 5908-4066; www.ramtzul.com; Hwy 14, Km 158; s/d Q290/425; ℗ 🛜) Quite likely the most beautiful hotel in either of the Verapaces, this place features a restaurant/sitting area in a tall, thatched-roofed structure with fire pits and plenty of atmosphere. The rustic, upmarket theme extends to the rooms and bungalows, which are spacious and elegantly decorated. The hotel property includes waterfalls and swimming spots.

❶ Getting There & Away

Any bus to or from Guatemala City will set you down at the park entrance. Heading in the other direction, it's best to flag down a bus or microbus to El Rancho and change there for your next destination.

COURTING THE QUETZAL

The resplendent quetzal, which gave its name to Guatemala's currency, was sacred to the Maya. Its feathers grace the plumed serpent Quetzalcóatl and killing one was a capital offense. In modern times it has enjoyed no such protection, and hunting (mostly for the male's long emerald-green tail feathers) and habitat loss have made the bird a rarity in Guatemala. You may well have a much better chance of seeing one in Costa Rica or Panama.

However, the best place to look for a quetzal in Guatemala is in the cloud forests of the Alta Verapaz, especially in the vicinity of the Biotopo del Quetzal. Look out for avocado and fruit trees as they are the preferred food of the quetzal (along with insects, snails, frogs and lizards). But you'll have to look closely – the quetzal's green plumage is dull unless it's in direct sunlight, providing perfect camouflage, and it often remains motionless for hours.

The females lay two eggs per year, from March to June, and this is the best time to go looking, as the males' tail feathers grow up to 75cm long during this period. Keep an ear out for their distinctive call – sharp cackles and a low, burbling whistle: *keeeoo-keeeoo*.

Cobán

POP 68,900 / ELEV 1320M

Not so much an attraction in itself, but an excellent jumping-off point for the natural wonders of Alta Verapaz, Cobán is a prosperous city with an upbeat air. Return visitors will marvel at how much (and how tastefully) the town has developed since their last visit.

The town was once the center of Tezulutlán (Tierra de Guerra, or 'Land of War'), a stronghold of the Rabinal Maya.

In the 19th century, when German immigrants moved in and founded vast coffee and cardamom *fincas* (plantations), Cobán took on the aspect of a German mountain town, as the *finca* owners built town residences. The era of German cultural and economic domination ended during WWII, when the USA prevailed upon the Guatemalan government to deport the powerful *finca* owners, many of whom actively supported the Nazis.

◉ Sights

Orquigonia
GARDENS

(☑ 4740-2224; www.orquigonia.com; Hwy 14, Km 206; Q40; ☺ 7am-4pm) Orchid lovers and even the orchid-curious should not miss the wonderfully informative guided tour of this orchid sanctuary just off the highway to Cobán. The 1½ to two hour tour takes you through the history of orchid collecting, starting with the Maya, as you wend your way along a path in the forest. There are sweet little cabins on the grounds where you can stay for Q350 per night.

To get here catch any bus from Cobán headed for Tontem and get off when you see the sign, about 200m up the dirt road off Hwy 14.

Parque Nacional Las Victorias
PARK

(3a Calle, Zona 1; Q15; ☺ 8am-4:30pm, walking trails 9am-3pm) This forested 82-hectare national park, right in town, has ponds, BBQ and picnic areas, children's play areas, a lookout point and kilometers of trails. The entrance is near the corner of 9a Av and 3a Calle. Most trails are very isolated – consider hiking in a group. You can camp here.

Templo El Calvario
CHURCH

(3a Calle, Zona 1) You can get a fine view over the town from this church atop a long flight of stairs at the north end of 7a Av. Indigenous people leave offerings at outdoor shrines and crosses in front of the church. Don't linger here after 4pm, as muggings are not unknown in this area.

The **Ermita de Santo Domingo de Guzmán**, a chapel dedicated to Cobán's patron saint, is 150m west of the bottom of the stairs leading to El Calvario.

Mercado Terminal
MARKET

The local market is always good for a wander, even if you're not looking to buy.

☞ Tours

Chicoj Cooperative
COFFEE TOUR

(☑ 5524-1831; www.coffeetourchicoj.com; tours Q60) Just 15 minutes out of town by bus, this is a community tourism initiative offering 2km, 45-minute tours of its coffee farm. Halfway through there's the standard stop for a canopy zip-line tour. The tour winds up with a cup of coffee made from beans grown and roasted at the farm.

Cobán tour operators offer this tour for Q160, but you can easily catch a bus from the stop near the police station on 1a Calle, which goes straight to the village of Chicoj.

Misterio Verde
TOUR

(☑ 7952-1047; 2a Calle 14-36, Zona 1; ☺ 8:30am-5:30pm) Acts as a booking agent for various community tourism projects in the area, including the Chicacnab cloud forests (near Cobán) and the subtropical rainforests of Rocjá Pomtilá (near Laguna Lachuá) in which participants stay in villages with a Q'eqchi' Maya family. For Q350 to Q450 you get a guide, lodging for two nights and four meals.

Your guide will take you hiking to local places of interest. The men of the family are the guides, providing them a sustainable way to make a living. Reservations are required at least one day in advance. It also rents boots, sleeping bags and binoculars at reasonable prices, so you need not worry if you haven't come prepared for such a rugged experience. Participants should speak at least a little Spanish. With a month's notice, this outfit also offers quetzal-viewing platforms.

Finca Santa Margarita
COFFEE TOUR

(☑ 7952-1586; 3a Calle 4-12, Zona 2; tours Q40; ☺ guided tours 8:30-11am & 2-4pm Mon-Fri, 8:30-11am Sat) This working coffee farm in the middle of downtown Cobán offers stellar guided tours. From propagation and planting to roasting and exporting, the 45-minute tour will tell you all you ever wanted to know about these powerful beans. At tour's end, you're treated to a cup of coffee and you can purchase beans straight from the roaster.

The talented guide speaks English and Spanish.

Aventuras Turísticas TOUR
(✆ 7951-2008; www.aventurasturisticas.com; 1a Calle 4-25, Zona 1) Leads tours to Laguna Lachuá, the Grutas de Lanquín, Rey Marcos and Parque Nacional Cuevas de Candelaria, as well as to Semuc Champey, Tikal, Ceibal and anywhere else you may want to go; it will customize itineraries. French, English and Spanish speaking guides are available.

★☆ Festivals & Events

Guatemala's most impressive festival of indigenous traditions, the national folklore festival of **Rabin Ajau** with its traditional dance of the Paabanc, takes place here in the latter part of July or in the first week of August. The **national orchid show** is hosted here every December.

⌂ Sleeping

When choosing a room in Cobán, you may want to ensure that the showers have hot water; it can be cold in these parts.

Casa Luna HOSTEL $
(✆ 7951-3528; www.cobantravels.com/casaluna; 5a Av 2-28, Zona 1; dm/s/d without bathroom Q50/60/120; @🛜) Modern rooms set around a pretty, grassy courtyard. Dorms have lockers and private rooms are well decorated. The shared bathrooms are spotless and the atmosphere is laid-back.

Campground CAMPGROUND $
(Parque Nacional Las Victorias; campsite per person Q50) Camping is available at Parque Nacional Las Victorias, right in town. Facilities include water and toilets but no showers.

Hotel La Paz HOTEL $
(✆ 7952-1358; 6a Av 2-19, Zona 1; s/d Q55/80; P) This cheerful, clean budget hotel, 1.5 blocks north and two blocks west of the plaza, is an excellent deal. It has many flowers and a good cafeteria next door.

★ Hotel La Posada HOTEL $$
(✆ 7952-1495; www.laposadacoban.com; 1a Calle 4-12, Zona 2; s/d Q450/490) Just off the plaza, this colonial-style hotel is Cobán's best, though rooms streetside suffer from traffic noise. Its colonnaded porches are dripping with tropical flowers and furnished with easy chairs and hammocks. The rooms are

a bit austere, with plenty of religious relics around the place, but they have nice old furniture, fireplaces and wall hangings of local weaving.

Hotel Central HOTEL $$
(✆ 7952-1442; 1a Calle 1-79, Zona 1; s/d Q140/200; P🛜) Reasonably sized rooms and lovely outdoor sitting areas make this a decent choice. Try for a room at the back for better ventilation and views out over the town.

Pensión Monja Blanca HOTEL $$
(✆ 7952-1712; 2a Calle 6-30, Zona 2; s/d Q185/250, s/d without bathroom Q135/175; P) This place is peaceful despite being on busy 2a Calle. After walking through two courtyards, you come to a lush garden packed with fruit and hibiscus trees around which the spotless rooms are arranged. Each room has an old-time feel to it and is furnished with two good-quality single beds with folksy covers. Also has cable TV.

The hotel's central location and tranquil atmosphere make it a good place for solo women travelers.

Posada de Don Antonio HOTEL $$
(✆ 7951-1792; 5a Av 1-51, Zona 4; s/d Q270/490; P✳🛜) This atmospheric two-story place provides some of the best value accommodations in town. Rooms are spacious with two (or even three!) double beds, high ceilings and loving attention to detail. Breakfast (Q30 to Q50) in the lush patio area is a great way to start the day.

Casa Duranta HOTEL $$
(✆ 7951-4716; www.casaduranta.com; 3a Calle 4-46, Zona 3; s/d Q310/420; P🛜) Some rooms at this carefully restored, eclectically decorated place are excellent value, while others are a bit cramped for the price. Have a look around if you can.

✖ Eating

Most of the hotels in Cobán come with their own restaurants. In the evening, food trucks (kitchens on wheels) park around the plaza and offer some of the cheapest dining in town. As always, the one to go for has the largest crowd of locals hanging around and chomping down.

★ Xkape Koba'n GUATEMALAN $
(2a Calle 5-13, Zona 2; snacks/mains Q25/50; ⊙10am-7pm) 🌿 The perfect place to take a breather or while away a whole afternoon, this beautiful, artsy little cafe has

Cobán

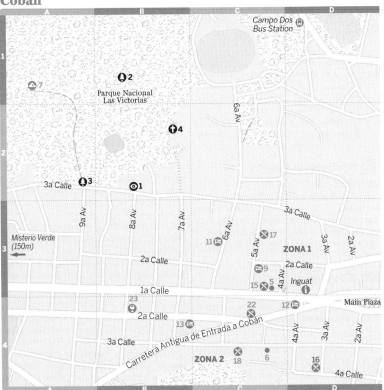

a lush garden out back. Some interesting indigenous-inspired dishes are on the small menu. The cakes are homemade, the coffee is delectable and there are some interesting handicrafts for sale.

★ La Abadia
FUSION $$

(cnr 1a Calle & 4a Av, Zona 3; mains Q90-160; ⊘6-10pm Mon-Sat) Cobán's dining scene has improved dramatically over the years and this is another welcome addition. The surrounds are refined yet relaxed, the menu offers a great selection of local, international and fusion dishes and there's a pretty good wine list, too.

La Casa del Monje
STEAK $$

(4a Av 2-16, Zona 3; mains Q60-150; ⊘6:30am-11pm; ⊚) Cobán's best steak house is set in a lovely colonial-era monastery a few blocks from the park. If you're not in the mood for big chunks of meat, local dishes like *cack'ik* (turkey stew) come highly recommended.

Casa Chavez
INTERNATIONAL $$

(1a Calle 4-25, Zona 1; mains Q50-100; ⊘8am-8:30pm; ⊚) Set in a lovely old house, Casa Chavez offers an ample, if a little uninspired, menu. Still, the location's great, and breakfast out back overlooking the garden and hills beyond is hard to beat.

Kardamomuss
FUSION $$

(3a Calle 5-34, Zona 2; mains Q60-130; ⊘8am-9pm; ⊚) The widest menu in town is at this chic new place a few blocks from the plaza. Billing itself as 'fusion' food, it takes a pretty good stab at Indian, Chinese and Italian dishes, with locally grown cardamom as the featured ingredient.

El Bistro
INTERNATIONAL $$

(4a Calle 3-11, Zona 2; mains Q80-150; ⊘6:30am-10pm) This restaurant, at Casa D'Acuña hotel, offers authentic Italian and other European-style dishes served in an attractive oasis of tranquillity to a sound track

Cobán

Sights
1 Ermita de Santo Domingo de
   Guzmán...B2
2 Parque Nacional Las Victorias B1
3 Parque Nacional Las Victorias
   Entrance...A2
4 Templo El Calvario.............................B2

Activities, Courses & Tours
5 Aventuras Turísticas C3
6 Finca Santa Margarita........................ C4

Sleeping
7 Campground A1
8 Casa Duranta.....................................F4
9 Casa Luna C3
10 Hotel Central E3
11 Hotel La Paz.....................................C3
12 Hotel La Posada D4
13 Pensión Monja Blanca.......................B4
14 Posada de Don Antonio F3

Eating
15 Casa Chavez.....................................C3
16 El Bistro.. D4
17 El Peñascal.......................................C3
18 Kardamomuss.................................... C4
19 La Abadia F4
20 La Casa del Monje F4
21 Supermarket E3
22 Xkape Koba'n C4

Drinking & Nightlife
23 Bohemios...B4

Shopping
24 Mercado Terminal E3

of classical music. In addition to protein-oriented mains, there is a range of pastas (Q40 to Q65), salads, homemade breads, cakes and outstanding desserts.

El Peñascal   GUATEMALAN $$
(5a Av 2-61; mains Q70-150; ⊘11:30am-9pm) Probably Cobán's finest stand-alone restaurant, El Peñascal has plenty of regional specialties, Guatemalan classics, mixed meat platters, seafood and snacks in a relaxed, up-market setting.

Supermarket   SUPERMARKET
(⊘9am-9pm Mon-Sat, to 7pm Sun) Everyday supermarket items, just off the plaza.

🍷 Drinking & Nightlife

Bohemios   CLUB
(cnr 8a Av & 2a Calle, Zona 2; Q15-30; ⊘Thu-Sat) About as close as this town gets to a mega-disco, with balcony seating and bow-tied waitstaff.

ℹ Orientation

Most buses will drop you at the terminal known as **Campo Dos** (Campo Norte), just north of town. It's a 15-minute walk (2km) or Q15 taxi ride to the plaza from there.

ℹ Information

Banco G&T (1a Calle) Has a MasterCard ATM.
Banco Industrial (cnr 1a Calle & 7a Av, Zona 1) Has a Visa ATM.
INGUAT (☑4210-9992; 1a Calle 3-13, Zona 1; ⊘8am-4pm Mon-Sat, 9am-1pm Sun) More useful than other INGUAT offices tend to be.
Lavandería Econo Express (7a Av 2-32, Zona 1; ⊘7am-7pm Mon-Sat) Laundry places are in short supply in Cobán – these folks wash and dry a load for Q50.
Police Station (☑7952-1225) Police station.
Post Office (cnr 2a Av & 3a Calle, Zona 3) A block southeast from the plaza.

ℹ️ Getting There & Away

The highway connecting Cobán with Guatemala City and Hwy 9 is the most traveled route between Cobán and the outside world. The road north through Chisec to Sayaxché and Flores is now paved all the way, providing much easier access than before to El Petén. The off-the-beaten-track routes west to Huehuetenango and northeast to Fray Bartolomé de Las Casas and Poptún are mostly unpaved and still provide a bit of an adventure (although this second one was being paved at the time of research). Always double-check bus departure times, especially for less frequently served destinations.

Buses leave from a variety of points around town, including the Campo Dos (p185) bus terminal. Minibuses, known as microbuses, are replacing or are additional to 'chicken' buses (former US school buses) on many routes. Please be aware that the road to Uspantán and Nebaj is prone to landslides – get the latest before setting out.

Destinations not served by Campo Dos terminal include the following:

Cahabón (Q30; 4½ hours) Same buses as to Lanquín.

Guatemala City (Q60 to Q70; four to five hours) **Transportes Monja Blanca** (☑ 7951-3571; 2a Calle 3-77, Zona 4) has buses leaving for Guatemala City every 30 minutes from 2am to 6am, then hourly until 4pm.

Lanquín (Q30; 2½ to three hours) **Transportes Martínez Cobán** (6a Calle 2-4 , Zona 4) has multiple departures throughout the day.

Minibuses to Lanquín (cnr 5a Calle & 3a Av, Zona 4) also depart from 7am to 4pm, some continuing to Semuc Champey. Do check these times, though, as they seem to be fluid.

San Pedro Carchá (Q5; 20 minutes; every 10 minutes) Buses depart from 6am to 7pm from the lot in front of the Monja Blanca terminal.

BUSES FROM CAMPO DOS BUS TERMINAL

DESTINATION	COST (Q)	TIME
Biotopo del Quetzal	15	1¼hr
Chisec	25	2hr
Fray Bartolomé de Las Casas	50	4hr
Nebaj	75	5½–7hr
Playa Grande, for Laguna Lachuá	60	3hr
Raxruhá	35	2½–3hr
Salamá	30	1½hr
Sayaxché	75	4hr
Tactic	10	40
Uspantán	40	4½hr

CAR

Cobán has a couple of places that rent cars. Reserve your choice in advance. If you want to go to Grutas de Lanquín or Semuc Champey, you'll need a 4WD vehicle.The most reliable company in town is **Inque Renta Autos** (☑ 7952-1994; inque83@hotmail.com; 3a Av 1-18, Zona 4).

San Cristóbal Verapaz

Throughout the region around Cobán, there are scores of villages where you can experience traditional Maya culture in some of its purest extant forms. One such place is San Cristóbal Verapaz a Poqomchi' Maya village set beside Lake Chicoj, 19km west of Cobán. During Semana Santa (Easter Week), local artists design elaborate *alfombras* (carpets) of colored sawdust and flower petals rivaled only by those in Antigua.

San Cristóbal is also home to the Centro Communitario Educativo Pokomchi (Cecep), an organization dedicated to preserving traditional and modern ways of Poqomchi' life. Cecep inaugurated the Museo Katinamit (Calle del Calvario 0-33, Zona 3; Q10; ⊗ 8am-5pm Mon-Sat, 9am-12pm Sat), which re-creates a typical Poqomchi' house. It also offers volunteer and ethno-tourism opportunities and houses the Aj Chi Cho Language Center (courses incl homestay per week Q1300) for teaching Spanish. El Portón Real (☑ 7950-4604; oscar_capriel@hotmail.com; 4a Av 1-44, Zona 1; s/d Q80/130) is a Poqomchi'-owned and -operated hotel, a few blocks away from the museum and school.

San Pedro Carchá

At the town of San Pedro Carchá, 6km east of Cobán on the way to Lanquín, is the Balneario Las Islas (Q15; ⊗ 7am-4pm), a tributary of the river Cahabon coming down past rocks and into a natural pool that's great for swimming. It's a five- to 10-minute walk from the bus stop in Carchá; anyone can point the way.

Buses operate frequently between Cobán and Carchá (Q8; 20 minutes).

Grutas Rey Marcos

Near Aldea Chajaneb, 12km east of Cobán, is the cave system Grutas Rey Marcos (☑ 7951-2756; Q30; ⊗ 8am-5pm). It's set in the Balneario Cecilinda (Q10; ⊗ 8am-5pm), which is, incidentally, a great place to go for a swim or a hike on scenic mountain trails. The caves themselves go for more

PARQUE NACIONAL LAGUNA LACHUÁ

This national park (☏ 4084-1706; entry fee adult/child Q50/25, campsite per adult/child Q30/15, bunk with mosquito net Q80/40, tent hire Q20) is renowned for the perfectly round, pristine turquoise lake (220m deep) for which it was named. Until recently, this Guatemalan gem was rarely visited by travelers because it was an active, violent area during the civil war and the road was in pathetic disrepair. Now it fills up quickly on weekends and public holidays, and if you're thinking about coming at these times, it's a good idea to call and reserve a space.

You can no longer rent canoes for exploring the lake, but there are about 4km of interpretative trails to explore. Overnight visitors can use the cooking facilities, so come prepared with food and drink (there is no food available to buy in the park). There is only one shower.

A wonderfully rustic bunkhouse has been constructed on the lake's edge, but if you don't want to stay in the park, there are hotels and restaurants in nearby Playa Grande. There's also a community tourism initiative in Rocjá Pomtilá (☏ 5381-1970; rocapon@ yahoo.com; r for 2 nights, incl guide & 4 meals Q350-450) on the eastern edge of the park. Contact the community directly or Misterio Verde (p182) in Cobán to make arrangements.

A new road means you can get to the park entrance from Cobán in a bit over two hours by bus (Q70). Take a Playa Grande (Cantabal) bus from Cobán via Chisec and ask the driver to leave you at the park entrance, from which it's about a 2km walk to the lake. From Playa Grande there are buses and pick-ups leaving for Barillas (Q70, five hours), the first stop on the back route to Huehuetenango in the Western Highlands. The Cobán tour outfits offer two-day and one-night trips out here.

than 1km into the earth, although chances are you won't get taken that far. A river runs through the cave (you have to wade through it at one point) and there are some impressive stalactites and stalagmites. Headlamps, helmets and rubber boots are included in the admission price to the cave. According to local legend, any wishes made in the cave are guaranteed to come true.

To reach the caves, take a bus or pick-up (Q5, 15 minutes) from San Juan Chamelco towards Chamil and ask the driver to let you off at the turnoff. From there it's about a 1km walk to the entrance. Alternatively, hire a taxi from Cobán (Q120).

Lanquín

One of the best excursions to make from Cobán is to the pretty village of Lanquín, 61km to the east. People come for two reasons: to explore the wonderful cave system just out of town and as a jumping-off point for visiting the natural rock pools at Semuc Champey.

◉ Sights

Grutas de Lanquín   CAVE
(Q35; ⊘ 8am-6pm) These caves are about 1km northwest of the town, and extend for sev-

eral kilometers into the earth. There is now a ticket office here. The first cave has lights, but do take a powerful flashlight (torch) anyway. You'll also need shoes with good traction as inside it's slippery with moisture and bat droppings.

Though the first few hundred meters of the cavern have been equipped with a walkway and lit by diesel-powered electric lights, most of this subterranean system is untouched. If you are not an experienced spelunker, you shouldn't wander too far into the caves; the entire extent has yet to be explored, let alone mapped.

As well as featuring funky stalactites, mostly named for animals, these caves are crammed with bats. Try to time your visit to coincide with sunset, when hundreds of them fly out of the mouth of the cave in formations so dense they obscure the sky. For a dazzling display of navigation skills, sit at the entrance while they exit. Please be aware that bats are extremely light-sensitive and, tempting as it may be, flash photography can disorient and, in some cases, blind them.

The river here gushes from the cave in clean, cool and delicious torrents. You can swim in the river, which has some comfortably hot pockets close to shore.

🏃 Activities

Guatemala City–based Maya Expeditions (p52) offers exciting one- to five-day rafting expeditions on the Río Cahabón.

ADETES   RAFTING
(☑5069-3518;   www.guaterafting.com)   This excellent community tourism initiative is based in Aldea Saquijá, 12km out of Lanquín. It offers rafting trips led by well-trained community members on the Río Cahabón. Prices range from Q266 to Q1216 per person for a two- to five-hour trip. To get to the headquarters, catch any bus leaving Lanquín headed towards Cahabón.

🛏 Sleeping

There are a few OK hotels in the actual town, but to get the full experience you really want to be out on the riverbanks somewhere. Accommodations tends toward the backpackers hostel end of the spectrum, but some more refined options are springing up.

Zephyr Lodge   HOSTEL $
(☑5168-2441; www.zephyrlodgelanquin.com; dm Q50, r Q150-250; ☎) Lanquín's party hostel is all class – great rooms with spectacular views, OK dorms and some good hangout areas, including the big thatched-roof bar/restaurant. The river's a five-minute walk downhill.

Rabin Itzam   HOTEL $
(☑7983-0076; s/d Q170/220, s/d without bathroom Q70/120) A no-frills budget hotel in the center. The beds sag a bit, but rooms upstairs at the front (without bathroom) have good valley views.

El Retiro Lodge   BUNGALOW $
(☑4638-3008; www.elretirolanquin.com; dm Q50, r with/without bathroom from Q200/150; ℗@☎) This sublimely located hotel is about 500m along the road beyond Rabin Itzam. Dorm rooms have only four beds. Individual decor includes some clever use of tiles, shells, strings of beads and local fabrics. Thatched-roof huts look down over the greenest of green fields to a beautiful wide river. It's safe to swim and to use an inner tube if you're a confident swimmer.

Viñas Hotel   HOTEL $$
(☑4800-0061; r with/without bathroom Q310/275; ❄☎❖) On the outskirts of town, heading towards Semuc Champey, this is the best full-service hotel around. Rooms are by no means fancy, but they do come with air-con

and there's a big pool here, with lush, looming mountains in the background. It makes great use of its hillside location, with fantastic views from the multiple balconies on offer.

El Muro   HOSTEL $$
(☑4904-0671; www.elmurolanquin.net; dm Q50, r Q150-250; ☎) By far the best option in the town itself, El Muro is a happy little hostel/bar featuring good-sized dorms and rooms. Most have attached bathroom and all have breezy balconies overlooking the hills or garden.

🍴 Eating

The food is pretty good in Lanquín – there are some good-priced *comedores* (cheap eateries) in the town and most of the hotels offer gringo-friendly menus.

Restaurante Champey   GUATEMALAN $
(mains Q30-60; ⊙8am-11pm) This large outdoor eatery halfway between town and El Retiro serves up good-sized plates of steak, eggs and rice and gets rowdy and beer-fueled at night.

ℹ Information

The Banrural on Lanquín's main square changes US dollars and traveler's checks, but at the time of writing did not have an ATM.

ℹ Getting There & Away

Overnight tours to Grutas de Lanquín (p187) and Semuc Champey, offered in Cobán for Q400 per person, are the easiest way to visit these places, but it's really not that complicated to organize yourself. Tours take about two hours to reach Lanquín from Cobán; the price includes a packed lunch.

Buses operate several times daily between Cobán and Lanquín, continuing to Cahabón. There are eight buses to Cobán (Q35, three hours) between 6am and 5:30pm. Shuttles for Semuc Champey (Q25 one way) leave at 9:30am (book at your hotel) and pick-ups (Q20) leave whenever they are full, half a block from the main square.

If it's been raining heavily and you're driving, you'll need a 4WD vehicle. The road from San Pedro Carchá to El Pajal, where you turn off for Lanquín, is paved. The 11km from El Pajal to Lanquín is not. You can head on from Lanquín to Flores in 14 to 15 hours via El Pajal, Sebol, Raxrujá and Sayaxché. The road from El Pajal to Sebol was being paved at time of research. Or you can head from Lanquín to Sebol and Fray Bartolomé de Las Casas and on to Poptún.

If you're heading towards Río Dulce, a back road exists, although it's unpaved for most of the way and gets washed out in heavy rains. Transportation schedules along here are flexible at best. Ask around to see what the current situation is. A daily shuttle (Q180, six hours) runs on this road and is the most reliable, easy option. Book at any of the hotels.

Semuc Champey & Around

Eleven kilometers south of Lanquín, along a rough, bumpy, slow road, is Semuc Champey (Q50; ☺8am-6pm), famed for its great 300m-long natural limestone bridge, on top of which is a stepped series of pools with cool, flowing river water good for swimming. The water is from the Río Cahabón, and much more of it passes underground, beneath the bridge. Though this bit of paradise is difficult to reach, the beauty of its setting and the perfection of the pools, ranging from turquoise to emerald-green, make it worth it. Many people consider this the most beautiful spot in all Guatemala.

If you're visiting on a tour, some guides will take you down a rope ladder from the lowest pool to the river, which gushes out from the rocks below. Plenty of people do this and love it, though it is a bit risky.

◉ Sights

K'anba Caves   CAVE

(Q75; ☺9am-3pm, tours 9am, 10am, 1pm, 2:30pm & 3pm) About a kilometer before Semuc Champey, just before the large bridge crossing the river, you'll see a turnoff to the right for these caves, which many find to be much more interesting than Grutas de Lanquín (p187). Bring a flashlight for the two-hour tour or you'll be stumbling around by candlelight.

A half hour of river tubing costs an extra Q10. There have been reports of serious overcrowding on these cave tours. If you can, arrive for the 9am tour, before the tour groups start showing up. And, as always, evaluate the conditions before setting out.

⬛ Sleeping & Eating

A simple restaurant at the parking area serves OK meals (including *cack'ik* – turkey stew; Q50) but is a long way from the pools. It's a better idea to bring a picnic.

Campground   CAMPGROUND $

(campsite per tent Q50) It's possible to camp at Semuc Champey, but be sure to pitch a tent only in the upper areas, as flash floods are common down below. It's also risky to leave anything unattended, as it might get stolen. The place now has 24-hour security, which may reassure potential campers, but you should keep your valuables with you.

★Utopia   HOSTEL $$

(☑3135-8329; www.utopiaecohotel.com; campsites per person Q30, hammock/dm Q35/65, r with/without bathroom Q425/165; ☀) Set on a hillside overlooking the small village of Semil, 3km from Semuc Champey, this is the most impressive setup in the area. Every range of accommodations imaginable is available, from luxurious riverside cabins to campsites. The restaurant/bar (serving vegetarian family-style meals) has fantastic valley views and the stretch of river that it sits on is truly idyllic.

The turnoff to Semil is 2km before Semuc Champey. From there it's about 1km to the hotel. Call from Lanquín (or drop into the office at the crossroads where the bus arrives) for free transport out here.

El Portal   HOSTEL $$

(☑4091-7878; www.elportaldechampey.com; dm Q60, r with/without bathroom Q300/185; ℗☀) About 100m short of the entrance to Semuc Champey, this is the obvious choice for convenient access to Semuc. There's only daytime electricity (thanks to a generator), but the well-spaced wooden huts built on the bank sloping down to the river are by far the best accommodations deal in the area. Meals and tours are available.

❶ Getting There & Away

If you're into walking, the 2½-hour trip from Lanquín is a fairly pleasant one, passing through lush countryside and simple rural scenes. If not, there are plenty of transportation options. Pick-ups run from the plaza in Lanquín to Semuc Champey – your chances of catching one are better in the early morning and on market days: Sunday, Monday and Thursday. Expect to pay somewhere between Q15 and Q30. All the Lanquín hotels and hostels run shuttle services out here, too.

Chisec & Around

POP 35,000

The town of Chisec, 66km north of Cobán, is becoming a center for reaching several exciting destinations. This is thanks to the paving of the road from Cobán to Sayaxché and Flores, which runs through here, and some admirable community tourism programs aiming to help develop this long-ignored region, the population of which is almost entirely Q'eqchi' Maya. The best source of information on these programs is the office of **Puerta al Mundo Maya** (5978-1465; www.puertamundomaya.com.gt; Lote 135, Barrio El Centro), which administers quite a few of them.

◉ Sights

Cuevas de B'ombi'l Pek   CAVE
(Q140; ⊘8am-4pm) A mere 3km north of Chisec, these painted caves remained undiscovered until 2001. They haven't been fully mapped yet, but some claim that they connect to the caves of Parque Nacional Cuevas de Candelaria. The community-run guide office is by the roadside. Pay the entrance fee and the guide will take you on the 3km walk through cornfields to the entrance.

The entire tour takes about four hours. The first, main cavern is the most impressive for its size (reaching 50m in height; you have the choice of rappelling or descending via a slippery 'jungle ladder' to enter), but a secondary cave – just 1m wide – features paintings of monkeys and jaguars. River tubing (Q70) is also possible, starting at the guide office.

Any bus running north from Chisec can drop you at the guide office.

Lagunas de Sepalau   OUTDOORS
(Q200; ⊘8am-5pm) Surrounded by pristine forest, these turquoise lagoons are 8km west of Chisec. Recently developed as a community ecotourism project by local villagers, tours of the area include a fair bit of walking and some rowboat paddling. The obligatory zip-line is also present. The area is rich in wildlife: jaguars, tapir, iguanas, toucans and howler monkeys are all in residence.

There are three lagoons, the most spectacular of which is the third on the tour, Q'ekija, which is ringed by steep walls of thick jungle. From February to June the first two lagoons dry up.

Pick-ups leave Chisec's plaza for the village of Sepalau Cataltzul throughout the day and there's usually a bus (Q10, 45 minutes) at 10:30am. On arrival at the village, you pay the entrance fee and a guide will take you on the 3km walk to the first lagoon.

⊨ Sleeping

Chisec's not very touristy, but there is one basic hotel on the plaza and one more out on the highway.

Hotel Nopales   HOTEL $
(5514-0624; Parque Central; s/d Q80/140; 🖭) This has surprisingly large rooms (with that classic musty budget-hotel smell) set around a courtyard dominated by a permanently empty (unless it's been raining) swimming pool.

Hotel La Estancia de la Virgen   HOTEL $$
(5514-7444; www.hotelestanciadelavirgen.com; Calle Principal; s/d with fan Q100/160, s/d with aircon Q150/200; P ❋ @ 🖭 🖭) Chisec's best hotel, on the main road at the northern exit from town, has neat and sensible rooms, a restaurant and a pool with some excellent waterslides in the shape of fallen tree trunks.

✕ Eating

Apart from the ubiquitous *comedores* (cheap eateries) out on the highway and the restaurant in the Hotel La Estancia de la Virgen, Chisec actually has one pretty good restaurant – the **Restaurante Bonapek** (Parque Central; mains Q40-60; ⊘8am-9pm).

ℹ Getting There & Away

Buses leave Chisec for Cobán (Q25, two hours) eight times daily, from 3am to 2pm. Buses or minibuses to San Antonio and Raxrujá (one hour) go hourly, from 6am to 4pm. Some of these continue to Fray Bartolomé de Las Casas. There are also regular minibuses to Playa Grande (two hours), for the Parque Nacional Laguna Lachuá. Some Cobán–Sayaxché minibuses and buses pass through Chisec.

Raxruhá

POP 35,000

A sleepy little crossroads town, Raxruhá provides a good base for exploring the nearby attractions of Cancuén and Cuevas de Candelaria.

⊨ Sleeping

There are exactly two hotels in town, both within about 500m of each other, on the road into town. Don't expect anything fancy.

Hotel Cancuén   HOTEL $
(5764-0478; www.cuevaslosnacimientos.com; s/d Q100/140, without bathroom Q35/70; P ❋) The best hotel in town is a family-run affair just on the outskirts of town (a two-minute walk from the center). Rooms are clean and well decorated (air-con is an additional Q50), and there's a good little *comedor* (cheap eatery) onsite. It has good information about visiting Cancuén.

You can arrange walking/tubing tours (Q150 per person, four to six hours) of the nearby Cueva los Nacimientos, the northernmost point in the Candelaria complex.

Hotel El Amigo HOTEL $
(☑5872-4136; r per person Q70; P☀☀) Large, vaguely clean rooms around an oversized parking lot. The place has great potential but is terribly rundown – it may have been fixed up by the time you get there.

Eating

Both of the hotels in town serve basic meals and there are good-value *comedores* (cheap eateries) around the market/bus terminal area. The best eating for miles around is oddly located a few kilometers west of town on the road to the Candelaria caves. The small French-inspired menu at **El Bistrot Frances** (☑5352-9276; www.candelarialodge.com; Km 318; mains Q70-120, s/d from Q220/350; ☉7am-8pm) offers decent variety and the daily special is always worth investigating. They also have extremely comfortable rooms and bungalows. Any bus heading to Chisec can drop you here.

Information

Banrural at the main intersection changes cash but not traveler's checks. The nearest ATMs are in Chisec and Fray Bartolomé.

Getting There & Away

Pick-ups and the occasional bus for La Unión (to access Cancuén; Q15, one hour) leave from the stop one block uphill. There are at least five scheduled departures daily to both Sayaxché (Q35, 2½ hours) and Cobán (Q35, two hours) from Raxruhá.

Around Raxruhá

Parque Nacional Cuevas de Candelaria

Just west of Raxruhá, this 22km-long cave system, dug out by the subterranean Río Candelaria, boasts some monstrous proportions – the main chamber is 30m high, 200m wide and has stalagmites measuring up to 30m in length. Natural apertures in the roof allow sunlight in, creating magical, eerie reflections.

The caves were used by the Q'eqchi' Maya and you'll see some platforms and ladders carved into the stone. The **El Mico** (www.cuevasdecandelaria.com; Km 316.5; tubing/walking tour Q60/80; ☉9am-5pm) complex is probably the most easily accessible and spectacular of the various cave tours. Look for the sign from the highway.

A couple of kilometers west on the same highway is the turnoff to **Comunidad Mucbilha'** (Km 315; tubing or walking tour Q80; ☉8am-4pm). It's 2km along a dirt road to the parking lot, then another 1km to the visitors center, where you can walk or tube through the **Venado Seco cave.**

Another couple of caves can be visited nearby at the **Cuevas de Candelaria Camposanto** (Km 309.5; tubing or walking tours Q80; ☉8am-4pm).

Community-run operations offer tours into the various entrances to the cave complex. You can walk, tube and spelunk the entire underground passage in about two days, but you must do so with a guide. Prices depend on group size but will probably average around Q3200 per person, not including food. Contact Maya Expeditions (p52) for details.

Guides can be organized at the roadside *tienda* (store) for the short walk to the Cuevas de Candelaria Camposanto. With a couple of days notice, they will put on a Maya ceremony (Q35 per person) for visitors. For more information about Mucbilha' and Candelaria Camposanto, contact Puerta al Mundo Maya in Chisec.

Sleeping & Eating

Complejo Cultural de Candelaria HOTEL $$
(☑4035-0566; www.cuevasdecandelaria.com; Km 316.5; s/d from Q350/500) The best place to eat for miles around, the Complejo Cultural de Candelaria offers supremely comfortable, stylishly decorated cabins, with excellent French-influenced meals included in the rates. Some slightly cheaper cabins without bathrooms may be available.

Getting There & Away

Any bus running between Chisec and Raxruhá can drop you at El Mico, Comunidad Mucbilha or Cuevas de Candelaria Camposante.

Cancuén

This large **Maya site** (Q80; ☉8am-4pm) hit the papers when it was 'discovered' in 2000, even though it had already been 'discovered' back in 1907. Excavations are still under way, but estimates say that Cancuén may rival Tikal (p247) for size.

Cancuén's importance seems to stem from its geographical/tactical position. Hieroglyphics attest to alliances with Calakmul (Mexico) and Tikal, and its relative proximity to the southern Highlands would have given it access to pyrite and obsidian, prized minerals of the Maya. Artisans certainly worked here – their bodies have been discovered dressed, unusually, in royal finery. Several workshops have also been uncovered, one containing a 17kg piece of jade.

It's thought that Cancuén was a trading center rather than a religious center, and the usual temples and pyramids are absent. In their place is a grand palace boasting more than 150 rooms set around 11 courtyards. Carvings here are impressive, particularly the grand palace, but also along the ball courts and the two altars that have been excavated to date. Casual visitors will need about an hour to see the main, partially excavated, sections of the site and another hour or two to see the rest.

You can camp here and eat in the *comedor* (dining room), but if you're planning on doing so, contact the community tourism office Puerta al Mundo Maya (p190) in Chisec a few days beforehand to let them know your plans.

Cobán tour companies make day trips to Cancuén. To get here independently, catch a pick-up (leaving hourly) from Raxruhá to La Unión (Q15, 40 minutes), from where you can hire a boat (Q200 to Q350 for one to 16 people, round trip) to the site. You can also hire a guide (Q100 to Q200, depending on group size) to take you on the 4km walk to the site from La Unión, but in the rainy season this will be a very muddy affair. If walking or going by *lancha* (small motorboat), pay at the small store where the bus stops – the boat dock is an easy 1km walk from there. Pay your entrance fee at the site when you arrive. The last pick-up leaves La Unión for Raxruhá at 3pm.

Fray Bartolomé de Las Casas

POP 9200

This town, often referred to simply as Fray, is a way station on the back route between the Cobán/Lanquín area and Poptún on the Río Dulce–Flores highway (Hwy 13). This route is dotted with traditional Maya villages where only the patriarchs speak Spanish, and then only a little. This is a great opportunity for getting off the 'gringo trail' and into the heart of Guatemala.

Fray is substantial considering it's in the middle of nowhere, but don't let its size fool you. This is a place where the weekly soccer game is the biggest deal in town, chickens languish in the streets and siesta is taken seriously.

The town itself is fairly spread out, with the plaza – where you'll find the *municipalidad* (town hall) – and most tourist facilities at one end and the market and bus terminus at the other. Walking between the two takes about 10 minutes. Coming from Cobán, you'll want to hop off at the central plaza.

🍴 Sleeping & Eating

Eating options are limited here – try Comedor Jireh and Restaurante Doris on the main street. Otherwise, grab a steak (with tortillas and beans, Q20) at the informal BBQ shacks that open up along the main street at night.

Hotel La Cabaña HOTEL $
(☑ 7952-0352; 2a Calle 1-92, Zona 3; r per person with/without bathroom Q80/60) This friendly place has the best accommodation in town. It's two blocks from the main street, near the triangular traffic circle. Ask around – everybody knows it.

ℹ Information

Banrural, near the plaza, changes US dollars and traveler's checks and has an ATM.

ℹ Getting There & Away

At least two daily buses depart from the plaza for Poptún (Q40, five hours). Buses for Cobán leave hourly between 4am and 4pm. Some go via Chisec (Q50, 3½ hours). Others take the slower route via San Pedro Carchá.

EL ORIENTE

Heading east from Guatemala City brings you into the long, flat valleys of the region Guatemalans call El Oriente (the East). It's a dry and unforgiving landscape of stunted hillsides covered in scraggly brush. They breed 'em tough out here and the cowboy hats, boots, buckles and sidearms sported by a lot of men in the region fit well against this rugged backdrop.

Most travelers pass through on their way to Copán in Honduras or to visit the pilgrimage town of Esquipulas. Further east, the landscape becomes a lot more tropical and you'll see plenty of fruit for sale at roadside

WORTH A TRIP

LAS CONCHAS

From Fray you can visit **Las Conchas** (Q50), a series of limestone pools and waterfalls on the Río Chiyú, which some say are better than those at Semuc Champey (p189). The pools are up to 8m deep and 20m wide and connected by a series of spectacular waterfalls, but they're not a turquoise color like those at Semuc.

You can stay right by the pools at the rustic but charming **Oasis Chiyú** (☎4826-5247; www.naturetoursguatemala.com; campsite per person Q75, s/d without bathroom Q160/240) – make reservations well in advance – or in nearby Chahal at the clean and comfortable family-run **Villa Santa Elena** (☎5000-9246; Ruta 5, Km 365 ; campsite per person Q25, s/d Q170/230; P❄@☏).

Both the Oasis Chiyú and Villa Santa Elena have restaurants. If you're just cruising through without booking a room, the latter is much more likely to be open – you'll need to book in advance if you're planning on eating at the Oasis.

Regular minibuses (Q15, one hour) leave Fray for Chahal when full. From there you must change buses for Las Conchas (Q10, one hour). If you're in your own vehicle, look for the marked sign to Las Conchas, 15km east of Chahal. If you're coming south from El Petén, get off in Modesto Mendez (known locally as Cadenas), catch a Chahal-bound minibus to Sejux (say-whoosh) and walk or wait for another minibus to take you the remaining 3km to Las Conchas. Whichever direction you're coming from, travel connections are easiest in the morning and drop off severely in the late afternoon.

stalls. If you've got some time in this area, a quick side trip to the ruins at Quiriguá is well worth your while.

Río Hondo

POP 10,500

Río Hondo (Deep River), 50km east of El Rancho junction and 130km from Guatemala City, is where Hwy 10 to Chiquimula heads south off the Carretera al Atlántico (Hwy 9). Beyond Chiquimula are turnoffs to Copán, just across the Honduras border; to Esquipulas and on to Nueva Ocotepeque (Honduras); and the remote border crossing between Guatemala and El Salvador at Anguiatú, 12km north of Metapán (El Salvador).

The actual town of Río Hondo is northeast of the junction. Places to stay hereabouts may list their address as Río Hondo, Santa Cruz Río Hondo or Santa Cruz Teculután. Nine kilometers west of the junction are several attractive motels right on Hwy 9. By car, it's an hour from here to Quiriguá, half an hour to Chiquimula and 1½ hours to Esquipulas.

Activities

Valle Dorado WATER PARK

(☎7943-6666; www.hotelvalledorado.com; Hwy 9, Km 149; adult/child Q100/60; ⊙9am-5pm Wed-Sun) An attraction near Río Hondo is Valle Dorado, an aquatic park and tourist center. This large complex 14km past the Hwy 10 junction includes an aquatic park with giant pools, waterslides, toboggans and other entertainment. Check the website for promotional deals and make reservations on weekends.

If you really like the place, you can stay here, in large, comfortable rooms (Q550).

Parque Acuatico Longarone WATER PARK

(Hwy 9, Km 126.5; adult/child Q70/50; ⊙9am-5pm Fri-Sun) Río Hondo is home to the Parque Acuatico Longarone with giant waterslides, an artificial river and other water-based fun.

Sleeping & Eating

For some reason Río Hondo is a favorite location for vacationing residents of Guatemala City. The upside of this is that there are some good (if tending toward overpriced) hotels around. Most have pools that nonguests can use for around Q25 per person.

All the hotels have restaurants. There are a couple of little BBQ joints set up on the main street, too, along with an impressive array of fruit vendors.

Hotel El Atlántico HOTEL $$

(☎7933-0598; Hwy 9, Km 126.5; s/d Q280/400; P❄@☏≋) The best-looking place in town has plenty of dark-wood fittings and well-spaced bungalows. The pool area is tranquil, with some shady sitting areas.

DEM BONES

Most of the people you hear about who are digging stuff up in Guatemala these days are archaeologists. Or mining companies. But there's another group out there, sifting patiently through the soil in search of treasure – paleontologists.

While it's unclear whether dinosaurs ever inhabited what is now Guatemala, evidence shows that large prehistoric mammals – such as giant armadillos, 3m-tall sloths, mammoths and saber-toothed tigers certainly did. As they migrated southwards from North America they found they could not go much further than present-day Guatemala – back then the landmass stopped at northern Nicaragua, and 10 million years would pass before South and Central America joined, creating the American continents more or less as they are today.

Various theories seek to explain the disappearance of the dinosaurs and other large prehistoric mammals – the most widely accepted one being that a massive meteorite slammed into the Yucatán Peninsula, 66 million years ago, causing global climate change.

The great bulk of the fossil and bone evidence uncovered in Guatemala has been in the country's southeast corner, but giant sloth and mastodon remains have been found in what is now Guatemala City. Paleontologist Roberto Woolfolk Saravia, founder of the **Museo de Paleontología, Arqueología y Geología** (Roberto Woolfolk Saravia Archeology & Paleontology Museum; Hwy 10, Estanzuela; ☉8am-5pm Mon-Fri) FREE, claims to have collected more than 5000 fragments and skeletons, and he says there are a lot more out there, just that (you guessed it) the funding isn't available to dig it up.

If you have even a passing interest in prehistoric life, the museum makes for a worthy detour – it's been remodeled recently, and on display are remains of mastodons, giant sloths and armadillos, a prehistoric horse measuring 50cm, and two molar teeth from a mammoth.

Hotel Nuevo Pasabién HOTEL $$
(☏7933-0606; www.hotelpasabien.com; Hwy 9, Km 126.5; s/d with fan Q120/250, s/d with air-con Q250/400; P❋@☀) On the north side of the highway, this hotel is a good choice for families – kids will enjoy the three pools with all manner of fancy slides.

Hotel Longarone HOTEL $$$
(☏7933-0488; www.hotel-longarone.com; Hwy 9, Km 126.5; s/d from Q430/620; P❋@☂☀) Attached to Parque Acuatico Longarone (p193), with good-looking grounds, playgrounds for kids and a surprisingly fine Italian restaurant. Rooms are comfortable if somewhat dated.

❶ Getting There & Away

Frequent buses traveling east–west on the Atlantic Hwy pass through Río Hondo. If you're coming from Honduras and heading east, be aware that the turnoff for Guatemala City is just west of the town – ask your driver to drop you in town as it is a much better place to wait for your onward connection.

Chiquimula

POP 55,400

Thirty-two kilometers south of Río Hondo on Hwy 10, Chiquimula is a major market town for all of eastern Guatemala. For travelers it's not a destination but a transit point. Your goal is probably the fabulous Maya ruins at Copán in Honduras, just across the border from El Florido. There are also some interesting journeys between Chiquimula and Jalapa, 78km to the west. Among other things, Chiquimula is famous for its sweltering climate and its decent budget hotels (a couple have swimming pools).

⌷ Sleeping

There is a range of good hotels within easy walking distance of the central plaza.

Hotel Posada Don Adan HOTEL $
(☏7942-3924; 8a Av 4-30, Zona 1; s/d Q120/180; P❋) The Don offers the best deal in this price range – neat, complete rooms with TV, fan, air-con, a couple of sticks of furniture and good, firm beds. They lock the doors at 10pm.

Hotel Hernández
HOTEL $

(☎7942-0708; 3a Calle 7-41, Zona 1; s/d with fan Q90/140, s/d with air-con Q150/220, s/d without bathroom Q60/100; P ❄ 🛜 🏊) It's hard to beat the Hernández – it's been a favorite for years and keeps going strong, with its central position, spacious, simple rooms and good-sized swimming pool.

Hostal Casa Vieja
HOTEL $$

(☎7942-7971; www.hostalcasaviejachiquimula.com; 8a Av 1-60, Zona 2; s/d/ste Q200/400/500; ❄🛜) A short walk from the center, this is probably the best hotel in town. Rooms are smallish but delicately decorated and the garden areas are lovely. The whole place radiates a tranquillity sorely missing in the rest of town.

Hostal Maria Teresa
HOTEL $$

(☎7942-0177; 6a Calle 6-21, Zona 1; s/d Q200/380; P ❄🛜) Set around a gorgeous colonial courtyard with wide shady passageways, the single rooms are a bit poky, but the doubles are generous and all the comforts are here: cable TV, hot showers and air-con.

Posada Perla de Oriente
HOTEL $$

(☎7942-0014; 2a Calle 11-50, Zona 1; s/d with fan Q140/250, s/d with air-con Q170/300; P ❄ 🛜 🏊) Surprisingly tranquil for its location just around the corner from the bus terminal, with some of the best-value rooms in town. The rooms are large and unadorned, but the grounds are quiet and leafy and the big swimming pool is a bonus.

🍴 Eating

There's a string of *comedores* (cheap eateries) on 8a Av behind the market. At night, snack vendors and taco carts set up along 7a Av opposite the plaza.

Corner Coffee
CAFE $

(6a Calle 6-70, Zona 1; bagels Q30, breakfast Q30-40; ⊙7am-10pm Mon-Sat, 3-10pm Sun) You could argue with the syntax of the name, but this air-con haven right on the lovely Parque Calvario serves up the best range of sandwiches, burgers and bagels in town.

Charli's
INTERNATIONAL $$

(7a Av 5-55, Zona 1; mains Q60-120; ⊙8am-9pm) Chiquimula's 'fine dining' option (tablecloths!) has a wide menu featuring pasta, pizza, seafood and steaks, all served up amid chilly air-con, with relaxed and friendly service.

Parillada de Calero
STEAK $$

(7a Av 4-83, Zona 1; breakfast from Q40, mains Q60-110; ⊙8am-10pm) An open-air steakhouse, serving the juiciest flame-grilled cuts in town. This is also the breakfast hot spot – the Tropical Breakfast (pancakes with a mound of fresh fruit) goes down well in this climate.

ℹ️ Orientation

Though it's very hot, Chiquimula is easy to get around on foot.

ℹ️ Information

Banco G&T (7a Av 4-75, Zona 1; ⊙9am-8pm Mon-Fri, 10am-2pm Sat) Half a block south of the plaza. Changes US dollars and traveler's checks, and gives cash advances on Visa and MasterCard.

Post Office (10a Av; ⊙9am-4pm Mon-Fri, to 1pm Sat) Between 1a and 2a Calles.

Telgua (3a Calle) Plenty of card phones; a few doors downhill from Parque Ismael Cerna.

ℹ️ Getting There & Away

Several companies operate buses and microbuses, arriving and departing from the bus

BUSES FROM CHIQUIMULA

DESTINATION	COST (Q)	TIME	FREQUENCY
Anguiatú, El Salvador border	20	1hr	leaves when full 5am to 5:30pm
El Florido, Honduras border	28	1½hr	leaves when full 5:30am to 4:30pm
Esquipulas	25	45min	every 20min, 5am to 9pm
Flores	120	7–8hr	2 daily
Guatemala City	60	3hr	every 30min, 3am to 3:30pm
Ipala	10	1½hr	hourly, 5am to 7pm
Puerto Barrios	50	4½hr	every 30min, 3:30am to 4pm
Quiriguá	35	2hr	every 30min, 3:30am to 4pm
Río Hondo	18	35min	every 15min, 5am to 6pm

station area on 11a Av, between 1a and 2a Calles. **Litegua** (☑ 7942-2064; www.litegua.com; 1a Calle, btwn 10a & 11a Avs), which operates buses to El Florido (the border crossing on the way to Copán), has its own bus station a half block north. For the Honduran border-crossing at Agua Caliente, take a minibus to Esquipulas and change there. If you're headed to Jalapa, you'll need to go to Ipala to make the connection. For Río Dulce, take a Flores bus or a Puerto Barrios bus to La Ruidosa junction and change there. If you're going to Esquipulas, sit on the left for the best views of the basilica housing the shrine of El Cristo Negro.

Ipala

Typical of many towns in El Oriente, Ipala is hot and dusty and holds little of interest for the average traveler. If you're not here to see the Volcán de Ipala, there's a good chance you are lost.

Volcán de Ipala (Q10) is notable for its especially beautiful, clear crater lake measuring nearly 1km around and nestled below the summit at 1493m. The dramatic hike to the top takes you from 800m to 1650m in about two hours, though you can drive halfway up in a car. There are trails, a visitors center and a campsite on the shores of the lake.

Of the very limited accommodations in downtown Ipala, the **Hotel Peña** (☑ 7942-8064; 2a Calle 2-26; s/d Q70/100; **P**) is about the best, although it may be worth the 10-minute walk to the **Hotel Dorado** (☑ 7942-8334; Barrio El Rostro; s/d with fan Q120/140, r with air-con Q180; **P**❋❀), which offers new, vaguely modern rooms out on the highway to Agua Blanca.

There are fast-food joints and *churrasco* (barbecued meat) stands around the plaza.

ⓘ GETTING TO EL SALVADOR

Between Chiquimula and Esquipulas (35km from Chiquimula and 14km from Esquipulas), Padre Miguel junction is the turnoff for Anguiatú, at the border with El Salvador, which is 19km (30 minutes) away. Minibuses pass by frequently, coming from Chiquimula, Quetzaltepeque and Esquipulas.

The border at Anguiatú is open 24 hours, but you're best crossing during daylight. Plenty of trucks cross here. Across the border there are hourly buses to the capital, San Salvador, passing through Metapán and Santa Ana.

Slightly more upscale is the **Restaurante El Original** (2 Av; mains Q50-80; ◷ 11:30am-9pm Mon-Sat).

There are banks with ATMs around the plaza.

To get here, take a bus from Chiquimula (Q10, 1½ hours) or Jalapa (two hours) to Ipala and transfer to a microbus to Agua Blanca (Q8, every 15 minutes). The trailhead is at El Sauce just before Agua Blanca; look for the blue INGUAT sign. You might luck on to a pick-up to Aldea Chigüiton, where the road ends, 2km from the highway running south from Ipala. You may also be able to hire a horse in Chigüiton. Buses pull up a block away from Ipala's plaza. Besides the connections to Chiquimula and Jalapa, there are also connections to Guatemala City (Q60, 3 hours).

Quetzaltepeque

A bustling little town between Chiquimula and Esquipulas, Quetzaltepeque holds very little of interest for the visitor with the exception of the nearby volcano of the same name.

⊙ Sights

Volcán de Quetzaltepeque VOLCANO
About 10km east of the village of Quetzaltepeque, this volcano tops out at 1900m. The walk to the top is tough going, through thick subtropical pine forest, and the trail disappears in sections, but if you have a car you can drive almost all the way to the top. From the summit there are excellent views of the nearby Ipala and Suchítan volcanoes and the surrounding countryside.

Due to the condition of the trail and some security concerns, you really need a guide to undertake this trek. Ask in the **Quetzaltepeque municipalidad** (Town Hall; ☑ 7944-0258; ◷ 8am-4pm Mon-Sat) on the main plaza to be put in touch with a local guide.

⊨ Sleeping & Eating

There are *comedores* (cheap eateries) and small restaurants around the plaza.

Hotel El Gringo HOTEL **$**
(☑ 7944-0186; 3a Av 2-25, Zona 2; r per person Q60) This very friendly, very basic hotel has bright, spacious rooms and very suspect beds. All things considered, you're probably better off staying in either Chiquimula or Esquipulas.

JALAPA

Jalapa is a small, friendly town 78km west of Chiquimula, and the route between the two is a stunning one: verdant gorges choked with banana trees alternate with fog-enveloped valleys.

While you're here, consider making a day trip to **Parque Ecoturístico Cascadas de Tatasirire** (☑5202-4150; www.cascadasdetatasirire.com; Q100; ☉8am-5pm), a lovely private nature reserve with waterfalls and walking trails just out of town. You can camp out here or stay in an extremely rustic 'ecolodge.'

Sleeping

Jalapa has probably the best-value accommodations in the country – it's a pity there isn't more to do around here.

Hotel Recinos (☑7922-2580; 2a Calle 0-80, Zona 2; s/d Q70/150) If you're just passing through, this very pink cheapie on the west side of the terminal/market area is a decent bet. The clean rooms with fan are a good deal, although it can get cramped when they squeeze two beds in.

Posada de Don José Antonio (☑7922-5751; Av Chipilapa A 0-64, Zona 2; s/d Q180/250; P@☎) Beautifully decorated with colonial flourishes, the rooms here are huge and the bathrooms massive. There are some lovely sitting areas, a shady patio and an onsite restaurant.

Eating

Eating options are limited – a short stroll along the main street will get you up to speed. Also look around the market area, where you will find the oddly out of place yet completely welcome **Florencia** (Av Chipilapa 1-72, Zona 1; mains Q40-80; ☉7am-9pm).

Getting There & Away

Despite the construction of a shiny new terminal at the south end of town, most buses continue to use the chaotic market/bus terminal area a block back from the main street. Buses leave regularly for Chiquimula (Q28, 1½ hours) and Guatemala City (pullman/2nd class, Q35/28). For Esquipulas, change in Chiquimula.

❶ Getting There & Away

Buses running between Chiquimula (Q12, 30 minutes) and Esquipulas (Q10, 20 minutes) pass through Quetzaltepeque.

Esquipulas

POP 27,400

From Chiquimula, Hwy 10 goes south into the mountains, where it's a bit cooler. After an hour's ride through pretty country, the highway descends into a valley ringed by mountains, where Esquipulas stands. Halfway down the slope, about 1km from the center of town, there is a *mirador* (lookout) from which to get a good view. The reason for a trip to Esquipulas is evident as soon as you catch sight of the place, dominated by the great Basílica de Esquipulas towering above the town, its whiteness shimmering in the sun. The view has changed little in over 150 years since explorer John L Stephens saw it and described it in his book *Incidents of Travel in Central America, Chiapas and Yucatan* (1841).

History

This town may have been a place of pilgrimage before the Spanish conquest. Legend has it that the town takes its name from a noble Maya lord who ruled this region when the Spanish arrived and who received them in peace.

With the arrival of the friars a church was built here, and in 1595 an image that came to be known as El Cristo Negro (Black Christ) was installed behind the altar. In response to the steady increase in pilgrims to Esquipulas, a huge new church was inaugurated in 1758, and the pilgrimage trade has been the town's livelihood ever since.

◉ Sights & Activities

Basílica de Esquipulas   BASILICA

(11a Calle) A massive pile of stone that has resisted the power of earthquakes for almost 250 years, the basilica is approached through a pretty park and up a wide flight of steps. The impressive facade and towers are floodlit at night.

Inside, the devout approach the surprisingly small El Cristo Negro (Black Christ) with extreme reverence, many on their knees. Incense, murmured prayers and the scuffle of feet fill the air. When there are throngs of pilgrims, you must enter the church from the side to get a close view of the famous shrine. Shuffling along quickly, you may get a good glimpse or two before being shoved onward by the crowd behind you. On Sundays, religious holidays and (especially) during the **Cristo de Esquipulas festival** (January 15), the press of devotees is intense. On weekdays, you may have the place to yourself, which can be very powerful and rewarding.

Cruising the religious kitsch sold by the throngs of vendors around the basilica is an entertaining diversion. When you leave the church and descend the steps through the park and exit right to the market, notice the vendors selling straw hats that are decorated with artificial flowers and stitched with the name 'Esquipulas' – perfect for pilgrims who want everyone to know they've made the trip. These are very popular rearview mirror novelties for chicken-bus drivers countrywide.

Centro Turístico Cueva de las Minas CAVE
(Q25; ⊗8am-4pm) This has a 50m-deep cave (bring your own light), grassy picnic areas and the Río El Milagro, where people come for a dip and say it's miraculous. The cave and river are half a kilometer from the entrance, which is behind the basilica's cemetery, 300m south of the turnoff into town on the road to Honduras. Refreshments are available.

Parque Chatún AMUSEMENT PARK
(☑7873-0909; www.parquechatun.com; adult/child incl lunch Q80/70; ⊗9am-6pm Tue-Sat) If you've got kids along (or even if you don't), this fun park 3km out of town should provide some light relief from all the religious business. There are swimming pools, a climbing wall, campgrounds, a petting zoo, a canopy tour and a mini bungee jump. Entry includes the use of all these except the canopy tour

If you don't have a vehicle, look for the minibus doing rounds of the town or get your hotel to call it – it will take you out there for Q5.

🛏 Sleeping

Esquipulas has an abundance of places to stay. On holidays and during the annual Cristo de Esquipulas festival (January 15), every hotel in town is filled, whatever the price;

EL CRISTO NEGRO

Attracting more than a million pilgrims from Mexico, Central America, the US and further afield every year, the Black Christ of Esquipulas is one of Guatemala's top tourist draws.

Myths surround the sculpture's color. It was long believed that the Spaniards who commissioned it in 1594 requested a Christ with a skin tone resembling Esquipulas' Ch'ortí' natives, so that they would be easier to convert. Studies have shown, though, that it is made from a light wood, possibly cedar. Some believers say it turned black mysteriously overnight – others say that it happened as a result of human contact and the amount of incense burnt in the church over the centuries.

The Black Christ first gained widespread attention when the Archbishop of Guatemala recovered miraculously from a chronic illness after visiting Esquipulas in 1737, and the town got a healthy publicity kick when Pope John Paul II visited in 1996.

But the statue's popularity has also been explained by the syncretism of pre-Christian and Christian beliefs. All throughout the Americas, when the Spanish arrived, indigenous peoples soon discovered it was less painful to appear to accept the new religion, basically retaining their traditional beliefs and renaming the old gods accordingly. In Maya culture, black was the color of warriors and associated with magic, death, violence and sacrifice. Accordingly, El Cristo Negro can be seen as a warrior Christ, defeater of death.

There are two authorized copies of Esquipulas' El Cristo Negro in the US. One in New York has come to represent the sufferings and hardships experienced by the Latino community there, while the one in Los Angeles (which was smuggled into the country, allegedly aided by bribed officials) has taken on a special significance for undocumented immigrants.

weekends are superbusy as well, with prices substantially higher. These rates reflect weekend prices. On weekdays (excluding the festival period), there are *descuentos* (discounts). For cheap rooms, look in the streets immediately north of the towering basilica.

Hotel Portal de la Fe   HOTEL $$
(☑ 7943-4261; 11 Calle 1-70, Zona 1; s/d Q280/500; P ✻ @ ⚂ ☒) One of the few hotels with any real style in town. Subterranean rooms are predictably gloomy, but upstairs the situation improves considerably.

Hotel Mahanaim   HOTEL $$
(☑ 7943-1131; 10a Calle 1-85, Zona 1; r Q380; P ✻ @ ⚂ ☒) This establishment is on three levels around a covered courtyard. Rooms are comfortable but plain. It wouldn't be such a good deal if it weren't for the big covered swimming pool out back.

Hotel Monte Cristo   HOTEL $$
(☑ 7943-1453; 3a Av 9-12, Zona 1; s/d Q200/280, s/d without bathroom Q90/120; P) Good-sized rooms with a bit of furniture and superhot showers. A policy of not letting the upstairs rooms until the downstairs ones are full might see you staying at ground level.

Hotel Vistana al Señor   HOTEL $$
(☑ 7943-4294; hotelvistana@gmail.com; 1a Av 'B' 1-42; s/d Q280/360; ⚂) By far the best deal in this price range are these sweet little rooms just south of the market. There's a pretty common balcony area with good views upstairs.

Hotel La Favorita   HOTEL $$
(☑ 7943-1175; 2a Av 10-15, Zona 1; r Q220, s/d without bathroom Q70/120; P) A real budget choice, the rooms without bathroom are a bit grim, but those with bathrooms are good enough.

Hotel Legendario   HOTEL $$$
(☑ 7943-1824; www.hotellegendario.com; cnr 3a Av & 9a Calle, Zona 1; r Q950; P ✻ @ ⚂ ☒) The fanciest hotel downtown goes all out on the services, right down to a separate kids' swimming pool. Rooms are reasonable – big enough, with new beds, large windows opening onto a grassy courtyard, and all the comforts you'd expect for the price.

✗ Eating

Restaurants are slightly more expensive here than in other parts of Guatemala. Budget restaurants are clustered at the north end of the park, where hungry pilgrims can find them readily.

Restaurante Calle Real   GUATEMALAN $
(3a Av; mains Q40-80; ⊘ 8am-10pm) Typical of many restaurants here, this big eating-barn turns out cheap meals for the pilgrims. It has a wide menu, strip lighting and loud TV.

La Rotonda   FAST FOOD $$
(11a Calle; mains Q60-100; ⊘ 8am-10pm) Opposite Rutas Orientales bus station, this is a round building with chairs arranged around a circular open-air counter under a big awning. It's a welcoming place – clean and fresh. There are plenty of selections to choose from, including pizza, pasta and burgers.

City Grill   STEAK $$
(cnr 2a Av & 10a Calle, Zona 1; mains Q50-140; ⊘ 8am-10pm) The best steakhouse in town (featuring some of the best steaks for miles around) also serves up some decent seafood and pasta dishes. The pizza is worth a look-in, too.

Restaurant El Angel   CHINESE $$
(☑ 7943-1372; cnr 11a Calle & 2a Av, Zona 1; mains Q50-70; ⊘ 11am-10:30pm) This main-street Chinese eatery does all the standard dishes, plus steaks and a good range of *licuados* (milkshakes). Home delivery is available.

ⓘ Information

Banco Internacional (3a Av 8-87, Zona 1; ⊘ 8am-4pm Mon-Fri, 9am-1pm Sat) Changes cash and traveler's checks, gives cash advances on Visa and MasterCard, is the town's American Express agent and has a Visa ATM.

Post Office (6a Av 2-15) About 10 blocks north of the center.

Telgua (cnr 5a & 9a Calle, Zona 1) Plenty of card phones.

ⓘ Getting There & Away

Buses to Guatemala City (Q60, four hours) arrive and depart hourly from 1:30am to 4:30pm from the **Rutas Orientales bus station** (☑ 7943-1366; cnr 11a Calle & 1a Av, Zona 1), near the entrance to town.

Minibuses to Agua Caliente (Honduran border; Q25, 30 minutes) arrive and depart across the street, leaving every half hour from 5am to 5pm; taxis also wait here, charging the same as minibuses, once they have five passengers.

Minibuses to Chiquimula (Q20, 45 minutes, every 15 minutes) depart from the east end of 11a Calle.

Transportes Guerra (cnr 5a Av & 10a Calle, Zona 1) goes to Anguiatú (El Salvador border; Q20, one hour, every 30 minutes).

CENTRAL & EASTERN GUATEMALA ESQUIPULAS

There are three buses daily for Flores/Santa Elena (Q130, eight hours) from the **Transportes María Elena** (⌨ 7943-0957; 11 Calle 0-54, Zona 1) office. It passes Quiriguá (Q50, two hours), Río Dulce (Q75, four hours) and Poptún (Q100, six hours).

Quiriguá

POP 4800

Quiriguá archaeological site is only 50km from Copán as the crow flies, but the lay of the land, the international border and the condition of the roads make it a journey of 175km. Quiriguá is famed for its intricately carved stelae – the gigantic brown sandstone monoliths that rise as high as 10.5m, like ancient sentinels, in a quiet well-kept tropical park.

From Río Hondo junction it's 67km along Hwy 9 to the village of Los Amates, where there are a couple of hotels, a restaurant, food stalls, a bank and a small bus station. Quiriguá village is 1.5km east of Los Amates,

and the turnoff to the ruins is another 1.5km to the east. The 3.4km access road leads south through banana groves.

History

Quiriguá's history parallels that of Copán, of which it was a dependency during much of the Classic period. Of the three sites in this area, only the present archaeological park is of interest.

Quiriguá's location lent itself to the carving of giant stelae. Beds of brown sandstone in the nearby Río Motagua had cleavage planes suitable for cutting large pieces. Though soft when first cut, the sandstone dried hard in the air. With Copán's expert artisans nearby for guidance, Quiriguá's stone carvers were ready for greatness. All they needed was a great leader to inspire them – and to pay for the carving of the huge stelae.

That leader was K'ak' Tiliw Chan Yo'at (Cauac Sky; r 725–84), who decided that Quiriguá should no longer be under the control of Copán. In a war with his former suzerain, Cauac Sky took Uaxaclahun Ubak K'awil (King 18 Rabbit) of Copán prisoner in 737 and later had him beheaded. Independent at last, Cauac Sky commissioned his stonecutters to go to work, and for the next 38 years they turned out giant stelae and zoomorphs dedicated to his glory.

Cauac Sky's son Sky Xul (r 784–800) lost his throne to a usurper, Jade Sky. This last great king of Quiriguá continued the building boom initiated by Cauac Sky, reconstructing Quiriguá's Acrópolis on a grander scale.

Quiriguá remained unknown to Europeans until the explorer and diplomat John L Stephens arrived in 1840. Impressed by its great monuments, Stephens lamented the world's lack of interest in them in his book *Incidents of Travel in Central America, Chiapas and Yucatan* (1841).

Stephens tried to buy the ruined city in order to have its stelae shipped to New York, but the owner, Señor Payes, assumed that Stephens (being a diplomat), was negotiating on behalf of the US government and that the government would pay. Payes quoted an extravagant price, and the deal was never made.

Between 1881 and 1894, excavations were carried out by Alfred P Maudslay. In the early 1900s all the land around Quiriguá was sold to the US-based United Fruit Company and turned into banana groves. The company is gone, but the bananas and Quiriguá remain. Restoration of the site was carried out by the

Quiriguá Ⓝ
0 —— 200 m
0 —— 0.1 miles

Banana Grove

Carretera al Atlántico
(Hwy 9; 3.4km)

Ticket Office & Snack Stand

Museum & Toilets

P

Stela A
Zoomorph B   Stela C   Stela D
Stela E   Stela F
Zoomorph G
Stela H   Gran
Plaza
Altar L   Stela
I   Stela
Altar M   K
Stela J
Zoomorph
N   Grupo
Oriental
Juego de
Pelota
Acrópolis
Zoomorph P
Zoomorph O

Grupo
Sur

University of Pennsylvania in the 1930s. In 1981 Unesco declared the ruins a World Heritage Site, one of only three in Guatemala (the others are Tikal and Antigua).

◉ Sights

The beautiful parklike archaeological site has a *tienda* (small shop) near the entrance selling cold drinks and snacks, but you'll be better off bringing your own picnic. A small museum just past the entrance has a few information displays and a model of how the site (much of it unexcavated) would have looked in its heyday.

Quiriguá
Archaeological Site   ARCHAEOLOGICAL SITE
(Q80; ⊙ 8am-4:30pm) Despite the sticky heat and (sometimes) bothersome mosquitoes, Quiriguá is a wonderful place. The giant stelae on the Gran Plaza (Great Plaza) are all much more worn than those at Copán. To impede further deterioration, each has been covered by a thatched roof. The roofs cast shadows that make it difficult to examine the carving closely and almost impossible to get a good photograph, but somehow this does little to inhibit one's sense of awe.

Seven of the stelae, designated A, C, D, E, F, H and J, were built during the reign of Cauac Sky and carved with his image. Stela E is the largest Maya stela known, standing some 8m above ground, with another 3m or so buried in the earth. It weighs almost 60,000kg. Note the exuberant, elaborate headdresses; the beards on some of the figures (an oddity in Maya art and life); the staffs of office held in the kings' hands; and the glyphs on the sides of the stela.

At the far end of the plaza is the Acrópolis, far less impressive than the one at Copán. At its base are several zoomorphs, blocks of stone carved to resemble real and mythic creatures. Frogs, tortoises, jaguars and serpents were favorite subjects. The low zoomorphs can't compete with the towering stelae in impressiveness, but as works of art, imagination and mythic significance, the zoomorphs are superb.

⊨ Sleeping & Eating

Hotel y Restaurante Royal   HOTEL $
(☎ 7947-3639; s/d Q140/200; ℗) Of the budget options in town, this is by far the better choice, with spacious clean rooms and a restaurant serving simple, filling meals (Q40-60). Room prices are heavily negotiable.

❶ Getting There & Around

Buses running Guatemala City–Puerto Barrios, Guatemala City–Flores, Esquipulas–Flores or Chiquimula–Flores will drop you off or pick you up here. If you're heading for the hotel, make sure you get dropped at the *pasarela de Quiriguá* (the pedestrian overpass). They'll also drop you at the turnoff to the archaeological site if you ask.

From the highway it's 3.4km to the archaeological site – Q10 by *tuk-tuk* (three-wheeled motor taxi), but if one doesn't come, don't fret: it's a pleasant walk (without luggage) through banana plantations to get there.

If you're staying in Quiriguá village or Los Amates and walking to the archaeological site, you can take a shortcut along the railroad that goes from the village through the banana fields, crossing the access road very near the entrance to the archaeological site. A *tuk-tuk* from Quiriguá village to the site should cost around Q20.

Out on the main highway buses pass frequently for Río Dulce (Q35, two hours), Chiquimula (Q30, two hours) and Puerto Barrios.

COPÁN (HONDURAS)

Copán Site

One of the most important of all Maya civilizations lived, prospered, then mysteriously crumbled around the Copán archaeological site, a Unesco World Heritage Site. During the Classic period (AD 250–900), the city at Copán Ruinas culturally dominated the region. The architecture is not as grand as that across the border in Tikal, but the city produced remarkable sculptures and hieroglyphics, and these days you'll often be virtually alone at the site, which makes it all the more haunting.

The ruins are a pleasant 1km stroll outside of Copán. A visitors center, an excellent sculpture museum and a cafe and gift shop are close to the main entrance. The guides at the Asociación de Guías Copán (☎ 2651-4018; guiascopan@yahoo.com) really know their stuff and hiring one is a worthwhile investment.

The booklet *History Carved in Stone: A Guide to the Archaeological Park of the Ruins of Copán*, by William L Fash and Ricardo Agurcia Fasquelle, is usually available at the site. For further reading see *Scribes, Warriors and Kings* by William Fash (2001), a comprehensible overview of Copán.

History

Pre-Columbian

People have been living in the Copán Valley since at least 1200 BC; ceramic evidence has been found from around that date. Copán must have had significant commercial activity since early times, as graves showing marked Olmec influence have been dated to around 900 to 600 BC.

In the 5th century AD one royal family came to rule Copán, led by a mysterious king named Mah K'ina Yax K'uk' Mo' (Great Sun Lord Quetzal Macaw), who ruled from AD 426 to 435. Archaeological evidence indicates that he was a great shaman, and later kings revered him as the semidivine founder of the city. The dynasty ruled throughout Copán's florescence during the Classic period (AD 250 to 900).

We know little about the subsequent kings who ruled before AD 628. Only some of their names have been deciphered: Mat Head, the second king (no relation to Bed Head); Cu Ix, the fourth king; Waterlily Jaguar, the seventh; Moon Jaguar, the 10th; and Butz' Chan, the 11th.

Among the greatest of Copán's kings was Smoke Imix (Smoke Jaguar; r 628–95), the 12th king. Smoke Imix built Copán into a major military and commercial power in the region. He may have taken over the nearby princedom of Quiriguá, as one of the famous stelae at that site bears his name and image. By the time he died in 695, Copán's population had grown substantially.

Smoke Imix was succeeded by Uaxaclahun Ubak K'awil (18 Rabbit; r 695–738), the 13th king, who willingly took the reins of power and pursued further military conquest.

In a war with King Cauac Sky, his neighbor from Quiriguá, 18 Rabbit was captured and beheaded. He was succeeded by K'ak' Joplaj Chan K'awiil (Smoke Monkey; r 738–49), the 14th king, whose short reign left little mark on Copán. Smoke Monkey's son, K'ak' Yipyaj Chan K'awiil (Smoke Shell; r 749–63), was, however, one of Copán's greatest builders. He commissioned the city's most famous and important monument, the great Escalinata de los Jeroglíficos (Hieroglyphic Stairway), which immortalizes the achievements of the dynasty from its establishment until 755, when the stairway was dedicated. It is the longest inscription ever discovered in the Maya lands.

Yax Pasaj Chan Yopaat (Sunrise or First Dawn; r 763–820; also known as Yax Pac, Yax Pasaj Chan Yoaat and Yax Pasah), Smoke Shell's successor and the 16th king, continued the beautification of Copán. The final occupant of the throne, U Cit Tok', became ruler in 822, but it's not known when he died.

Until recently, the collapse of the civilization at Copán had been a mystery. Now, archaeologists have begun to surmise that near the end of Copán's heyday the population grew at an unprecedented rate, straining agricultural resources. In the end, Copán was no longer agriculturally self-sufficient and had to import food from other areas. The urban core expanded into the fertile lowlands in the center of the valley, forcing both agricultural and residential areas to spread onto the steep slopes surrounding the valley. Wide areas were deforested, resulting in massive erosion that further decimated food production and brought flooding during rainy

Copán Area

0   400 m
0   0.2 miles

seasons. Interestingly, this environmental damage of old is not too different from what is happening today – a disturbing trend, but one that meshes with the Maya belief that life is cyclical and history repeats itself. Skeletal remains of people who died during Copán's final years show marked evidence of malnutrition and infectious diseases, as well as decreased life spans.

The Copán Valley was not abandoned overnight – agriculturists probably continued to live in the ecologically devastated valley for maybe another one or two hundred years. But by the year 1200 or thereabouts even the farmers had departed, and the royal city of Copán was reclaimed by the jungle.

European Discovery

The first known European to see the ruins was a representative of Spanish King Felipe II, Diego García de Palacios, who lived in Guatemala and traveled through the region. On March 8, 1576, he wrote to the king about the ruins he found here. Only about five families were living here at the time, and they knew nothing of the history of the ruins. The discovery was not pursued, and almost three centuries went by before another Spaniard, Colonel Juan Galindo, visited the ruins and made the first map of them.

It was Galindo's report that stimulated John L Stephens and Frederick Catherwood to come to Copán on their Central American journey in 1839. When Stephens published the book *Incidents of Travel in Central America, Chiapas and Yucatán* in 1841, illustrated by Catherwood, the ruins first became known to the world at large.

Copán Today

The history of Copán continues to unfold today. The remains of 3450 structures have been found in the 27 sq km surrounding the Grupo Principal (Principal Group), most of them within about half a kilometer of it. In a wider zone, 4509 structures have been detected in 1420 sites within 135 sq km of the ruins. These discoveries indicate that at the peak of civilization here, around the end of the 8th century AD, the valley of Copán had more than 27,500 inhabitants – a population figure not reached again until the 1980s.

In addition to examining the area surrounding the Grupo Principal, archaeologists continue to make new discoveries in the Grupo Principal itself. Five separate phases of building on this site have been identified; the final phase, dating from AD 650 to 820, is what we see today. But buried underneath the visible ruins are layers of other ruins, which archaeologists are exploring by means of underground tunnels. This is how they found the Templo Rosalila (Rosalila Temple), a replica of which is now in the Museo de Escultura. Below Rosalila is yet another, earlier temple, Margarita, and below that, Hunal, which contains the tomb of the founder of the dynasty, Yax K'uk' Mo' (Great Sun Lord Quetzal Macaw). Two of the excavation tunnels, including Rosalila, are open to the public, though you'll need to pay a second entry fee to access them.

⊙ Sights

Grupo Principal

The Principal Group of ruins is about 400m beyond the visitors center across well-kept lawns, through a gate in a fence and down shady avenues of trees. A group of resident macaws loiter along here. The ruins themselves have been numbered for easy identification and a well-worn path circumscribes the site.

The **visitors center** at the entrance to the ruins houses the ticket office and a small exhibition about the site and its excavation. Nearby are a **cafeteria**, and **souvenir and handicrafts shops**. There's a picnic area along the path to the Principal Group of ruins.

It's a good idea to visit the site with a guide, who can help to explain the ruins and bring them to life. Guides work for the cooperative Asociación de Guías Copán (p201) and charge L660 for groups of up to five. You can find them at the entrance to the parking lot. These prices are just for the main site – guides for the tunnels, Las Sepulturas or Museo de Escultura charge an additional L200 to L300 per site.

Stelae of the Gran Plaza

The path leads to the **Gran Plaza** (Great Plaza; Plaza de las Estelas) and the huge, intricately carved stelae portraying the rulers of Copán. Most of Copán's best stelae date from AD 613 to 738. All seem to have originally been painted; a few traces of red paint survive on Stela C. Many stelae had vaults beneath or beside them in which sacrifices and offerings could be placed.

Many of the stelae on the Gran Plaza portray King 18 Rabbit, including stelae A, B, C, D, F, H and 4. Perhaps the most beautiful stela in the Gran Plaza is **Stela A** (AD 731);

the original has been moved inside the Museo de Escultura, and the one outdoors, like many here, is a reproduction. Nearby and almost equal in beauty are Stela 4 (AD 731); Stela B (AD 731), depicting 18 Rabbit upon his accession to the throne; and Stela C (AD 782), with a turtle-shaped altar in front. This last stela has figures on both sides. Stela E (AD 614), erected on top of Estructura 1 (Structure 1) on the west side of the Gran Plaza, is among the oldest.

At the northern end of the Gran Plaza at the base of Estructura 2, Stela D (AD 736) also portrays King 18 Rabbit. On its back are two columns of hieroglyphs; at its base is an altar with fearsome representations of Chac, the rain god. In front of the altar is the burial place of Dr John Owen, an archaeologist with an expedition from Harvard's Peabody Museum who died during excavation work in 1893.

On the east side of the plaza is Stela F (AD 721), which has a more lyrical design than other stelae here, with the robes of the main figure flowing around to the other side of the stone, where there are glyphs. Altar G (AD 800), showing twin serpent heads, is among the last monuments carved at Copán. Stela H (AD 730) may depict a queen or princess rather than a king. Stela I (AD 692), on the structure that runs along the east side of the plaza, is of a person wearing a mask. Stela J (AD 702), further off to the east, resembles the stelae of Quiriguá in that it is covered in glyphs, not human figures.

Juego de Pelota

South of the Gran Plaza, across what is known as the Plaza Central, is the Juego de Pelota (Ball Court; AD 731), the second largest in Central America. The one you see is the third one on this site; the two smaller courts were buried by this construction. Note the macaw heads carved atop the sloping walls. The central marker in the court is the work of King 18 Rabbit.

Escalinata de los Jeroglíficos

South of the Juego de Pelota is Copán's most famous monument, the Escalinata de los Jeroglíficos (Hieroglyphic Stairway; AD 743), the work of King Smoke Shell. Today it's protected from the elements by a canvas roof. The flight of 63 steps bears a history (in several thousand glyphs) of the royal house of Copán; the steps are bordered by ramps inscribed with more reliefs and glyphs. The story told on the inscribed steps is still not completely understood because the stairway was partially ruined and the stones jumbled, but archaeologists are using 3D-scanning technology to make a digital version of the original, with the hope of one day reading it in its entirety.

At the base of the Hieroglyphic Stairway is Stela M (AD 756), bearing a figure (probably King Smoke Shell) dressed in a feathered cloak; glyphs tell of the solar eclipse in that year. The altar in front shows a plumed serpent with a human head emerging from its jaws.

Beside the stairway, a tunnel leads to the tomb of a nobleman, a royal scribe who may have been the son of King Smoke Imix. The tomb, discovered in June 1989, held a treasure trove of painted pottery and beautiful carved-jade objects that are now in Honduran museums.

Acrópolis

The lofty flight of steps to the south of the Hieroglyphic Stairway mounts the Templo de las Inscripciones (Temple of the Inscriptions). On top of the stairway, the walls are carved with groups of hieroglyphs. On the south side of the Temple of the Inscriptions is the Patio Occidental (West Court), with the Patio Oriental (East Court), also called the Patio de los Jaguares (Court of the Jaguars) to its east. In the West Court, check out Altar Q (AD 776), among the most famous sculptures here; the original is inside the Museo de Escultura. Around its sides, carved in superb relief, are the 16 great kings of Copán, ending with its creator, Yax Pasaj Chan Yopaat. Behind the altar is a sacrificial vault in which archaeologists discovered the bones of 15 jaguars and several macaws that were probably sacrificed to the glory of Yax Pasaj Chan Yopaat and his ancestors.

This group of temples, known as the Acrópolis, was the spiritual and political core of the site – reserved for royalty and nobles, a place where ceremonies were enacted and kings buried.

The East Court also contains evidence of Yax Pasaj Chan Yopaat – his tomb, beneath Estructura 18. Unfortunately, the tomb was discovered and looted long before archaeologists arrived. Both the East and West Courts hold a variety of fascinating stelae and sculptured heads of humans and animals. To see the most elaborate relief carving, climb Estructura 22 on the northern side of the East Court. This was the Templo

Copán

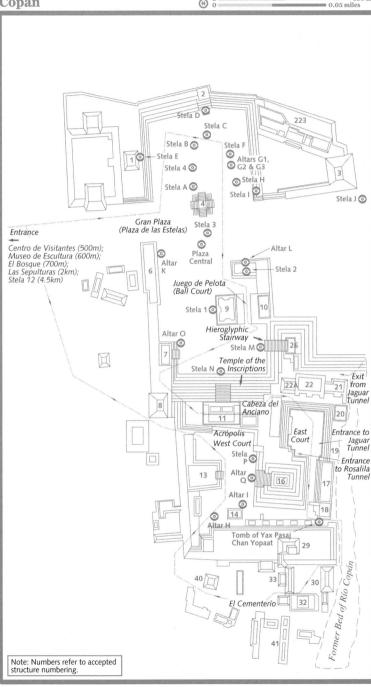

0 ────────── 100 m
0 ────────── 0.05 miles

Entrance
← Centro de Visitantes (500m);
Museo de Escultura (600m);
El Bosque (700m);
Las Sepulturas (2km);
Stela 12 (4.5km)

Stela D
Stela C
Stela B
Stela E
Stela 4
Stela A
Stela F
Altars G1, G2 & G3
Stela H
Stela I
Stela J

1

2

223

3

4

Gran Plaza
(Plaza de las Estelas)

Stela 3

Plaza Central

6

Altar K

Altar L

Stela 2

10

Juego de Pelota
(Ball Court)

Stela 1

9

Hieroglyphic Stairway

Stela M

26

Altar O

7

Temple of the Inscriptions

Stela N

22A 22 21

Exit from Jaguar Tunnel

8

Cabeza del Anciano

11

20

Acrópolis
West Court

East Court

Entrance to Jaguar Tunnel

19

Entrance to Rosalila Tunnel

Stela P

Altar Q

16

17

13

Altar I

14

18

Altar H

Tomb of Yax Pasaj
Chan Yopaat

29

40

33

30

El Cementerio

32

41

Former Bed of Río Copán

Note: Numbers refer to accepted structure numbering.

de Meditación (Temple of Meditation) and has been heavily restored over recent years.

Túnel Rosalila & Túnel de los Jaguares

In 1999 archaeologists opened up the Túnel Rosalila and Túnel de los Jaguares (L330), which allow visitors to get a glimpse of pre-existing structures below the visible surface structures. The first tunnel, Rosalila, is very short and takes only a few visitors at a time. The famous Temple Rosalila is only barely exposed, and is behind thick glass. The other tunnel, Los Jaguares, running along the foundations of Temple 22, was originally 700m in length, but a large section has been closed, reducing it to about 80m. This tunnel exits on the outside of the main site, so you must walk around the base and rear of the main site to get back in again. While fascinating, it's hard to justify the additional entry fee.

Museo de Escultura

While Tikal is celebrated for its tall temple pyramids and Palenque is renowned for its limestone relief panels, Copán is unique in the Maya world for its sculpture. Some of the finest examples are on display at this impressive museum (Museum of Sculpture; L154), which is fully signed in English. Entering the museum is an experience in itself: you go through the mouth of a serpent and wind through the entrails of the beast before suddenly emerging into a fantastic world of sculpture and light.

The highlight of the museum is a full-scale replica of the Rosalila Temple, which was discovered in nearly perfect condition by archaeologists in 1989 by means of a tunnel dug into Structure 16, the central building of the Acrópolis. Rosalila, dedicated in AD 571 by Copán's 10th ruler, Moon Jaguar, was apparently so sacred that when Structure 16 was built over it, Rosalila was not destroyed but was left completely intact. The original Rosalila Temple is inside the core of Structure 16.

El Bosque & Las Sepulturas

Excavations at El Bosque and Las Sepulturas have shed light on the daily life of the Maya in Copán during its golden age. Las Sepulturas, once connected to the Gran Plaza by a causeway, may have been the residential area where rich and powerful nobles lived. One huge, luxurious residential compound seems to have housed some 250 people in 40 or 50 buildings arranged around 11 court-

yards. The principal structure, called the Palacio de los Bacabs (Palace of the Officials), had outer walls carved with the full-sized figures of 10 men in fancy feathered headdresses; inside was a huge hieroglyphic bench. To get to Las Sepulturas you have to go back to the main road, turn right, then right again at the sign (2km from the Gran Plaza).

The walk to get to El Bosque is the real reason for visiting it, as it's removed from the main ruins. It's a 5km (1 hour) walk on a well-maintained path through foliage dense with birds, though there isn't much of note at the site itself save for a small ball court. Still, it's a powerful experience to have an hour-long walk on the thoroughfares of an ancient Maya city all to yourself. To get to El Bosque, go right at the hut where your ticket is stamped. Be sure to slather on the insect repellent before you set off.

Copán Ruinas

POP 10,000

The town of Copán Ruinas, often simply called Copán, is a beautiful place, paved with cobblestones and lined with white adobe buildings with red-tiled roofs. It's also one of the most charming and traveler-oriented places in Honduras, with a friendly local population, widely spoken English and some great hotels and restaurants. Many people come here just to see the famous nearby Maya ruins, but with plenty of other attractions in the town and nearby, there's reason enough to linger.

◎ Sights

Macaw Mountain Bird Park ZOO
(🖉 2651-4245; www.macawmountain.org; L220; ⊙ 9am-5pm) 🐾 Around 2.5km outside Copán Ruinas is an extensive private reserve aimed at saving Central American macaws. There are plenty of them here, along with toucans, motmots, parrots, kingfishers and orioles, all flying around in spacious, humanely constructed cages. In the 'Encounter Center' uncaged birds fly onto your shoulders or hands and you can pose for photos with them.

If caged birds upset you, bear in mind that nearly all of these birds have been donated to the park by owners who didn't want them anymore, or were confiscated from bird smugglers. It's a lovely place to wander around, with plenty of walking trails weaving through the lush forest and over boardwalks to lookout points and swimming holes; there's also a cafe-restaurant on the property. The entrance ticket – which includes a guided tour in English – is valid for three days. To get here, catch a *mototaxi* (three-wheeled motor taxi) for L20 per person.

Memorias Frágiles GALLERY
(☑ 2651-3900; Palacio Municipal, Parque Central; ⊘ 8am-5pm Mon-Fri) FREE This fascinating photo exhibition was a gift from Boston's Peabody Museum; it features a collection of rare photos detailing the first archaeological expeditions to Copán at the turn of the 20th century. Many of these proved essential in later restoration work, as the photos showed the site decades beforehand and offered clues to how the various stone hieroglyphs had lain.

It's located inside the **Palacio Municipal** (City Hall), behind the second door on the left as you enter (you may have to ask for the key).

Museo Digital de Copán MUSEUM
(Parque Central; L66; ⊘ 8am-4pm) This brand-new museum opened in late 2015 as a gift to the people of Copán from Japan and contains some interesting old photographs of Copán. The main reason to visit, though, is to watch the excellent virtual visit to the Copán archaeological site, which can be enjoyed in either Spanish or English at 10am and 3pm each day.

Museo de Arqueología Maya MUSEUM
(☑ 2651-4437; Parque Central; L66; ⊘ 9am-9pm) The Museo de Arqueología Maya is a little dated but still worth a visit. The exhibits include excavated ceramics, fragments from the altars and the supports of the Maya ruins, an insight into the Maya's sophisticated use of calendars and a re-creation of a female shaman's tomb. Some descriptions have English translations.

Courses

Ixbalanque Spanish School LANGUAGE COURSE
(☑ 2651-4432; www.ixbalanque.com; Av los Jaguares) Offers 20 hours of one-on-one instruction in Spanish for L5720 per week, including a homestay with a local family that provides three meals a day.

Guacamaya Spanish Academy LANGUAGE COURSE
(☑ 2651-4360; www.guacamaya.com; Calle de las Gradas, off Av Copán) Offers a package of 20 hours of one-on-one tuition for L3520. For L2200 more you can have full board and lodging with a local family.

Tours

A huge number of tours can be organized from Copán Ruinas; local companies promote these widely. You can go caving, tube a river, visit a Maya village and make tortillas or manufacture ceramics, plunge into hot springs, visit a coffee plantation or head off into the wilds of Honduras.

Birdwatching tours are very popular in the area around Copán – it's said that there are more quetzals in the surrounding cloud forest than there are in the whole of Guatemala (where it's the national bird). One recommended English-speaking birdwatching guide is **Alexander Alvarado** (☑ 9751-1680; alexander.alvarado469@gmail.com).

Horseback riding can be arranged by any of the town's tour companies and most hotels. You can ride to the ruins or make other, lengthier excursions. Three- to five-hour rides out of Café ViaVia (p208) visit the hot springs, Hacienda San Lucas, Los Sapos and the small Ch'orti' village of La Pintada.

Basecamp Tours ADVENTURE TOUR
(☑ 2651-4695; www.basecamphonduras.com; Calle de la Plaza) Located inside Café ViaVia (p208), this outfit offers a range of original and adventurous tours around the local area on foot (L220 to L440) and horseback (L330, three hours). Its highly recommended two-hour 'Alternative Copán' walking tour (L220) delves beneath the glossy surface of the town and investigates the reality of life for many Hondurans.

Yaragua Tours ADVENTURE TOUR
(☑ 2651-4147; www.yaragua.com; cnr Calle de la Plaza & Av Copán) Leads hikes, horseback-riding trips, excursions to Lago de Yojoa and even some outings to nearby caves. Offers guided tours of the Copán archaeological site (per person L770) and a full-day coffee plantation and archaeology tour that includes lunch (per person L1650). Ask for Samuel, a well-respected and trusted local guide.

🛏 Sleeping

Hostel Iguana Azul HOSTEL **$**
(☑ 2651-4620; www.iguanaazulcopan.com; Calle Rosalila; dm/s/d L175/350/400; 🖥) This colonial-style home has eight comfy bunk beds in two rooms and a shared bathroom with hot water; three private rooms sleep two. There's also a pretty back garden. The communal

Copán Ruinas

area has books and lots of travel information, and there's a fridge but no kitchen. This is backpacking elegance at its finest: even a room-cleaning service is included.

★ Hotel Mary
HOTEL **$**

(☑2651-4673; www.comedormary.com; Av Sesesmiles; s/d L600/700) One of the best deals in town, this beautifully presented place has very sweet rooms that are brightly painted and well maintained. There's hot water, ceiling fans, attractive traditional bed covers and a pretty garden to boot.

Hotel & Hostal Berakah
HOSTEL **$**

(☑9951-4288, 2651-4771; www.hotelberakahcopan.hostel.com; Av Copán; dm/d/tw incl breakfast L180/400/440) One of the few true hostels in Copán Ruinas, Berakah is very well set up for backpackers, with a range of different rooms and clean, modern bathrooms. Dorms are rather cramped but a great deal, while the next-door house that functions as a second

site for the hostel has a well-equipped kitchen, a pool table and more dorms.

Café ViaVia
HOTEL **$**

(☑2651-4652; www.viaviacafe.com/en/copan/hotel; Calle de la Plaza; s/d/q from L220/330/440; ☎) This small, Belgian-run, European-style hotel has five spotless rooms with hot-water bathrooms, tiled floors, desks and great beds. There are hammocks, a small garden and enough space to chill out. It's a great place to come for tourist information, and also has an art gallery and lively bar attached, which – be aware – can get noisy.

Casa Doña Elena
GUESTHOUSE **$$**

(☑2651-4029; www.casadonaelena.com; Av Centroamérico; s/d/tr L484/792/1100; ❀☎) This family-run hilltop place enjoys some great views of the town and surrounding valley and has a beautifully tended garden shared by its seven individually named rooms. The rooms themselves are simple, but spacious

Copán Ruinas

and clean, with fans (air-con costs L220 extra per day) and TV. It's a 10-minute sturdy uphill walk from the center of town.

Hotel La Posada
HOTEL **$$**

(☑ 2651-4059; www.laposadacopan.com; Av Centroaméricano; s/d incl breakfast L575/800; ☎) Good value, tranquil and comfortable, La Posada is only half a block from the plaza. Its 19 rooms are set around two leafy patios, are comfortable and clean and have hot-water bathroom, fan and TV.

★ La Casa de Café
B&B **$$$**

(☑ 2651-4620; www.casadecafecopan.com; Calle Rosalila; s/d incl breakfast L1250/1520; ✳☎) This impeccably decorated B&B has rooms adorned with carved wooden doors and Guatemalan masks. The setting is stunning – the view from the lawn over the copious and delicious breakfast service is of morning mists rising around the Guatemalan mountains in the distance. North American owner Howard is a mine of local information and the feeling is very much one of being his personal guest.

La Casa de Café operates an excellent restaurant, open all day. There's also an upscale house and town-house available across the street (L2000 to L2600 a night, rates negotiable for longer stays).

Hotel Yat B'alam
BOUTIQUE HOTEL **$$$**

(☑ 2651-4338; www.yatbalam.com; Calle Independencia; s/d/tr from L1700/1950/2200; ⓟ✳☎) Each of the four beautiful rooms here is spacious and comes with all the usual comforts, as well as minibar and DVD player (the hotel has a selection of movies you can borrow). The whole place is pleasantly decorated with a mix of colonial and indigenous furnishings.

Terramaya
BOUTIQUE HOTEL **$$$**

(☑ 2651-4623; www.terramayacopan.com; Av Centroaméricano; s/d incl breakfast from L2090/2350; ✳☎) This comfortable, stylish newcomer hovers somewhere between a B&B and boutique hotel, offering six smartly appointed rooms, a lovely backyard garden and a candlelit terrace with misty-eyed mountain views. Two upstairs rooms offer spectacular balconies with vistas out to the ruins and the mountains beyond.

✕ Eating

Café ViaVia
INTERNATIONAL **$$**

(www.viaviacafe.com/en/copan; Calle de la Plaza; breakfast L60-80, mains L80-180; ☉7am-10pm; ☎✐) This terrific restaurant serves breakfast, lunch and dinner in a convivial atmosphere, with tables overlooking the street and a replica of Altar Q from the Acrópolis at the Copán Site behind the bar. The organically grown coffee it prepares is excellent, the bread is homemade and there's always a good selection of vegetarian and meat-based dishes on offer.

Asados Copán
STEAK **$$**

(cnr Calle Acrópolis & Av Copán; mains L100-200; ☉8am-10pm) With one of the best settings in town, this large, open-air steakhouse is popular with tourists and locals alike. The menu's simple but effective – a variety of beef and chicken dishes, flame-grilled to perfection.

Casa Ixchel
CAFE **$$**

(Av Sesesmiles; mains L100-200; ☉8am-6pm; ☎) There's a friendly welcome at this serious coffee lover's place, where locally grown Casa Ixchel Arabica coffee is the fuel of choice and the espresso machine is rarely out of use. There's a great little back patio for eating and drinking in the sunshine, and a brunchy menu for tasty breakfasts and light lunches.

Comedor Mary COMEDOR $$
(Hotel Mary, Av Sesesmiles; mains L115-250; ⊙7am-9pm; 🖤) This charming space comprises a garden for alfresco dining and a dining room full of dark wood furniture where excellent *pupusas* are served up. *Comida típica* is also redefined here (try the *lomito de res a la plancha*, a grilled beef tenderloin); service is uncharacteristically friendly and the atmosphere is upscale.

★**Café San Rafael** CAFE, DELI $$$
(Av Centroaméricano; meals L150-335; ⊙11am-11pm Tue-Sat, 8am-6pm Sun & Mon; 🖤) This smart cafe serves organic coffee grown at the *finca* (ranch) of the same name, though it's most famous locally for the various cheeses produced here (platters L120 to L500). Breakfasts (L180) are a filling splurge, while the toasted sandwiches (try the excellent steak and provolone) are a great lunch option. The whole place is gorgeous, overlooking a beautifully maintained lawn, and service is friendly.

El Rincón Colombiano COLOMBIAN $$$
(Calle Acrópolis; mains L150-300; ⊙10:30am-10pm Tue-Sun; 🖤) The 'Colombian Corner' has a great rooftop terrace that's perfect for a light lunch (L140) or an atmospheric dinner, complete with fairy lights. Dishes include *ajiaco* (a chicken soup from Bogotá) and *albóndigas en salsa napolitana de cerveza* (meatballs in a Neopolitan beer sauce), although top billing goes to Solomito de Res – beef medallions in a Dutch cheese sauce with sautéed vegetables.

🍷 Drinking & Nightlife

Given the large traveler presence there's a fair bit of nightlife in town, particularly at weekends – though little goes on beyond 11pm (this is still rural Honduras).

★**Sol de Copán** BAR, BREWERY
(Av Mirador; mains L130-180; ⊙2-10pm Tue-Sat; 🖤) A terrific, German-owned microbrewery in a large basement. The owner, Thomas, is friendly and highly attentive, making sure everyone's regularly topped up with pilsner or lager. Delicious German sausages are served, and there's live music some nights, too. If you're lucky Thomas might show you

some of his fermenting vats out the back. *Baleadas* (L65 to L90) are also available.

❶ Orientation

The town only introduced street names recently, but few people use them; most people know what street their own house or business is on, but everything else works by landmarks. There are no street numbers.

❶ Information

MONEY

US dollars can be changed at most banks, though Guatemalan quetzals can at present only be changed on the black market. The following banks have ATMs that accept foreign cards.

BAC (Parque Central; ⊙9am-5pm Mon-Fri, to noon Sat) Exchanges US dollars and has a 24-hour ATM.

BAC/Bamer (Parque Central; ⊙8am-5pm Mon-Fri, 8:30am-1pm Sat) Has an ATM that accepts Visa and MasterCard.

Banco Atlántida (cnr Calle Independencia & Av Copán) Changes US dollars and has an ATM.

Banco Credomatic (Calle de la Plaza) On the plaza.

Banco de Occidente (cnr Calle 18 Conejo & Av Copán) On the plaza; changes US dollars and gives cash advances on Visa and MasterCard.

POST

Post Office (Calle de la Plaza; ⊙8am-noon & 1-5pm Mon-Sat) A few doors from the plaza.

❶ Getting There & Away

An airport opened here in 2015, but at the time of writing was served only by the occasional charter flight.

Casasola (📞2651-4078; Av Sesesmiles) buses arrive and depart from an open-air **bus depot** (📞2651-4078) at the entrance to town, where destinations include San Pedro Sula (L140, three hours, five daily) and Santa Rosa de Copán (L100, three hours, hourly), from where you can connect easily to Tegucigalpa.

Minibuses to/from the **Guatemalan border** (L20, 20 minutes, every 20 minutes) run between 6am and 5pm from near the town's cemetery at the end of Calle 18 Conejo. On the Guatemala side, buses to Esquipulas and Chiquimula leave the border regularly until about 5pm.

Basecamp Tours (p207) and Hotel Berakah (p208) both run popular shuttle buses between Copán Ruinas and Antigua (L550, six hours) via Guatemala City (L550, five hours). Shuttles also run to El Salvador, stopping at Santa Ana (L640, 4½ hours) and San Salvador (L880, five hours); there's one shuttle to Managua in Nicaragua (L2200, 12 hours) and also one to La Ceiba

(L880, six hours). You can book via Basecamp or other travel agencies.

Hedman Alas (☑ 2651-4037; Km 62 Carretera a San Lucas) has a modern terminal just south of town, where you can get 1st-class buses to San Pedro Sula (L395, three hours) at 11am each day (and also at 2pm on Saturday, Sunday and Monday).

Around Copán Ruinas

The forested hills around Copán Ruinas include a few interesting sights that are well worth visiting while you're staying in the town. Access from Copán Ruinas is easy and cheap using the town's *mototaxis*.

🏃 Activities

Finca El Cisne　　　　　　HORSEBACK RIDING
(☑ 2651-4695; www.fincaelcisne.com; horseback riding tour incl accommodations, 3 meals & thermal baths from L1800) Visiting this working farm 24km from Copán Ruinas is more like an agri-eco experience than a tour. Founded in the 1920s and still operating, the *finca* mainly raises cattle and grows coffee and cardamom. Full-day and overnight packages include guided horseback riding through the forests, and tours of the coffee and cardamom fields and processing plants.

If you come between February and October you can help with the harvest. Lodging is offered in five simple, rustic rooms in the old workers quarters, with meals and a visit to nearby hot springs included. You can book tours in their office inside the Café ViaVia (p208).

Luna Jaguar Spa Resort　　　　　　SPA
(www.lunajaguarsparesort.com; L250; ⊘8am-5pm) Directly across the river from the hot springs is this high-concept Maya day spa – perhaps what the Maya kings would have done to relax if they had the chance. Thirteen 'treatment stations' (offering hot tubs, herbal steam baths and so on) are scattered around the hillside, connected by a series of stone pathways.

The jungle here has been left as undisturbed as possible, and reproduction Maya sculptures dot the landscape. The water used in the hot tub and steam baths comes directly from the volcanic spring. It's an amazing and beautiful spot, worth checking out even if you're not a spa junkie.

Aguas Termales　　　　　　HOT SPRING
(L250; ⊘10am-10pm) This set of hot springs is 24km north of Copán Ruinas, an hour's drive through fertile mountains and coffee plantations. There are a couple of artificial pools, or else you can sit in the river, where the boiling-hot spring water mixes with the cool river water. Bring warm clothes if you come in the evening.

Café ViaVia (p208) can arrange transport here, as does the hot springs' own office in Copán Ruinas, inside Hotel Patty (on Calle Acrópolis).

🛏 Sleeping

★**Hacienda San Lucas**　　　HISTORIC HOTEL **$$$**
(☑ 2651-4495; www.haciendasanlucas.com; s/d/ tr incl breakfast L2860/3300/3960; 🛜) 🍽 This magical place some 3km south of town enjoys sweeping views from its wonderfully maintained gardens. It's a rustic experience – so despite the price tag, don't come expecting luxury. The rooms have stone floors, terracotta roofs, wooden furniture and are stuffed with locally made handicrafts, while the on-site restaurant is superb. The **Los Sapos archaeological site** is on the property.

CARIBBEAN COAST

This is a very different Guatemala – a lush and sultry landscape dotted with palm trees and inhabited by international sailors (around the yachtie haven of Río Dulce and the working port of Puerto Barrios) and one of the country's lesser-known ethnic groups, the Garifuna (around Lívingston).

A boat ride down the Río Dulce is pretty much mandatory for any visit to this region, and many visitors find a few days in Lívingston to be a worthwhile detour. Nature buffs will want to check out the huge wetlands reserves at Bocas del Polochic and Punta de Manabique.

Lago de Izabal

Guatemala's largest lake, to the north of Hwy 9, is starting to earn its place on the travelers' map. Most visitors checking out the lake stay at Río Dulce town, by the long, tall bridge where Hwy 13, heading north to Flores and Tikal, crosses the Río Dulce emptying out of the east end of the lake. Downstream, the beautiful river broadens into a lake called El Golfete before meeting the Caribbean at Lívingston. River trips are a highlight of a visit to eastern Guatemala. If you're looking for lakeside ambiance minus the Río Dulce congestion and pace, head to Chapin Abajo, north of Mariscos or El Estor near the west end of the lake, both of which give access to the rich wildlife of the Bocas del Polochic river delta. There are many undiscovered spots in this area waiting to be explored, so don't limit yourself.

Río Dulce

POP 5200

At the east end of the Lago de Izabal, this town still gets referred to as Fronteras – a hangover from the days when the only way across the river was by ferry, and this was the last piece of civilization before embarking on the long, difficult journey into El Petén.

Times have changed. A huge bridge now spans the water and the Petén region's roads are some of the best in the country. The town sees most tourist traffic from yachties – the US Coast Guard says this is the safest place on the western Caribbean for boats during hurricane season. The rest of the foreigners here are either coming or going on the spectacular river trip between here and Lívingston.

☞ Tours

Ask around at any of the marinas for the latest on which sailboats are offering charter tours.

Aventuras Vacacionales SAILING
(☑7873-9221; www.sailing-diving-guatemala.com) This outfit runs fun seven-day sailing trips from Río Dulce to the Belize reefs and islands (from Q3200) and four-day trips to Lago Izabal (from Q1250). The office is in Antigua but you can also hook up with them in Río Dulce. It makes the Belize and lake trips in alternate weeks.

⛁ Sleeping

Many places in Río Dulce communicate by radio, but all are reachable by telephone. The bar at Bruno's will radio your choice of place to stay if necessary.

On the Water
There are several places to stay just out of town on the water, which is the best place to be. You can call or radio them and they'll come and pick you up. Among these, **Mansión del Río** (☑7930-5020; www.mansion delrio.com.gt; r Q1000) provides all-inclusive resort-style accommodations for those seeking some pampering downtime.

Hotel Kangaroo HOTEL $
(☑5363-6716, in English 4513-9602; www.hotel kangaroo.com; dm Q60, r Q160-200, cabins Q250; @ 🛜) On the Río La Colocha, just across the water from El Castillo de San Felipe, this beautiful, simple Australian/Mexican-run place is built on stilts in the mangroves. Its restaurant's beguiling menu (mains Q50-100) features some Aussie classics and probably the best Mexican food you're likely to find outside of Mexico.

The whole place is constructed from wood, with thatched roofs, and windows are mosquito-netted – there's not a pane of glass in sight.

Wildlife is particularly abundant around here, with blue warblers, pelicans, a seven-foot iguana and turtles making the surrounds their home. There's also a bar-restaurant. Drinks on the deck overlooking the river are a great way to start, finish or while away the day. Call from Río Dulce or San Felipe and they'll come and pick you up for free, even if you're just dropping in for lunch.

Hacienda Tijax HOTEL $$
(☑7930-5505; www.tijax.com; s/d from Q334/372, s/d without bathroom Q160/220; P ❄ 🛜 ≋) This 118-acre hacienda, a two-minute boat ride across the cove from Bruno's, is a special place to stay. Activities include horseback riding, hiking, birdwatching, and walking and canopy tours around the rubber plantation and private nature reserve. Accommodations in lovely little cabins are connected by boardwalks. The pricier ones have kitchens and are well set-up for families.

Most cabins face the water and there's a very relaxing pool/bar area. Access is by boat or by a road that turns off the highway about 1km north of the village. The folks here speak Spanish, English and French, and they'll pick you up from across the river.

El Tortugal BUNGALOW $$
(☑7742-8847; www.tortugal.com; r without bathroom Q300, bungalows from Q400; 🛜) The best-looking bungalows on the river are located here, a five-minute *lancha* (small motorboat) ride east from town. There are plenty of hammocks, the showers are seriously hot and kayaks are free for guest use.

Casa Perico HOSTEL $$
(☑7930-5666; www.casa-perico.com; dm Q60, s/d without bathroom from Q95/140, cabins Q220; @ 🛜) One of the more low-key options in the area, this place is set on a little inlet

about 200m from the main river. Cabins are well built and connected by boardwalks. It offers tours all up and down the river and puts on an excellent buffet dinner (Q90), or you can choose from the menu (Q50 to Q80).

If you want the one cabin with bathroom make sure you book ahead.

Hotel Backpackers HOSTEL $$
(☑ 7930-5480; www.hotelbackpackers.com; dm Q60, r with/without bathroom from Q250/160; @ 🛜) Across the bridge from Río Dulce town, this is a business run by Casa Guatemala and the orphans it serves. It's an old (with the emphasis on old) backpacker favorite, set in a rickety building with very basic rooms. The bar kicks on here at night.

If you're coming by *lancha* (small motorboat) or bus, ask the driver to let you off here to spare yourself the walk across the bridge.

In Town

Hotel Vista al Río HOTEL $
(☑ 7930-5665; dm Q40, r with/without bathroom Q180/120 ; ✳️🛜) Under the bridge just south of Bruno's, this little hotel/marina offers spacious, spotless rooms, the more expensive ones with river views. There's a good restaurant here (mains Q60 to Q100), serving juicy steaks, Southern cooking and big breakfasts.

Bruno's HOTEL $$
(☑ 7930-5721; www.brunoshotel.com; camping per person Q35, dm Q60, s Q110-250, d Q140-350; P ✳️ 🛜 ≋) A path leads down from the northeast end of the bridge to this riverside hangout for yachties needing to get some land under their feet. The dorms are clean and spacious and the new building offers some of the most comfortable rooms in town, with air-con and balconies overlooking the river. It's well set up for families and sleeps up to six.

🍴 Eating

Most of the hotels in town have restaurants. Bruno's serves good breakfasts and gringo comfort food and has a full bar. Hacienda Tijax is a popular lunch spot – give them a call and they'll come pick you up.

⭐ **Sundog Café** INTERNATIONAL $
(sandwiches Q30, meals from Q50; 🕐 noon-9pm) Down a laneway opposite the Litegua bus office (200m up the main street past the end of the bridge), this open-air riverfront bar-restaurant makes great sandwiches on homemade bread and offers a good selection of vegetarian dishes, tasty brick-oven pizzas

and fresh juices. It's also the place to come for unbiased information about the area.

ⓘ Orientation

Unless you're staying at Hotel Backpackers, get off the bus on the north side of the bridge. Otherwise you'll find yourself trudging over what is believed to be the longest bridge in Central America – it's a very hot 3.5km walk.

The main dock is now under the bridge on the opposite side of the main road from Bruno's – you'll see a side road leading down to it.

ⓘ Information

The local online newspaper **Chisme Vindicator** (www.riodulcechisme.com) has loads of information about Río Dulce.

If you need to change cash or traveler's checks, visit one of the banks in town, all on the main road. **Banco Industrial** (🕐 9am-5pm) has a Visa ATM. There's also a trustworthy Visa/MasterCard ATM inside the Despensa Familiar supermarket, also on the main street.

ⓘ Getting There & Away

BOAT

Shared *lanchas* (small motorboats; per person one-way/round-trip Q150/250) go down the Río Dulce (from the new dock) to Lívingston, usually requiring eight to 10 people. The trip is a beautiful one, making a 'tour' of it, with several stops along the way. Boats usually leave from 9am to about 2pm. There are regular, scheduled departures at 9:30am and 1:30pm. Pretty much everyone in town can organize a *lancha* service to Lívingston and most other places you'd care to go, but they charge more.

BUS

The Fuente del Norte and Litegua bus offices are both located on the north side of the bridge, opposite each other.

Beginning at 9:30am, seven Fuente del Norte buses a day head north along a paved road to Poptún (Q40, two hours) and Flores (Q75, four hours). With good connections you can get to Tikal in a snappy six hours. There are also services to San Salvador (El Salvador; Q140) and San Pedro Sula (Honduras; Q150), both leaving at 10am.

At least 11 buses daily go to Guatemala City (Q70, six hours) with Fuente del Norte and Litegua. Línea Dorada has 1st-class buses departing at 1pm for Guatemala City (Q140) and 3pm for Flores (Q140). This shaves up to an hour off the journey times.

Minibuses leave for Puerto Barrios (Q30, two hours) when full, from near the Fuente del Norte office on the main street.

There's a daily shuttle to Lanquín (Q180, five hours), leaving from in front of the Sundog Café (p213) at 1:30pm.

Minibuses leave for El Estor (Q20, 1½ hours, 7am to 6pm hourly) from the San Felipe and El Estor turnoff in the middle of town.

El Castillo de San Felipe

The fortress and castle of San Felipe de Lara, El Castillo de San Felipe (Q25; ⊙8am-5pm), about 3km west of Río Dulce town, was built in 1652 to keep pirates from looting the villages and commercial caravans of Izabal. Though the fortress somewhat deterred the buccaneers, a pirate force captured and burned it in 1686. By the end of the next century, pirates had disappeared from the Caribbean, and the fort's sturdy walls served as a prison. Eventually, though, the fortress was abandoned and became a ruin. The present fort was reconstructed in 1956.

Today the castle is protected as a park and is one of the Lago de Izabal's principal tourist attractions. In addition to the fort itself, there are grassy grounds, BBQ and picnic areas, and the opportunity to swim in the lake. The place rocks during the Feria de San Felipe (April 30 to May 4).

🛏 Sleeping & Eating

There's a surprisingly good range of hotels in the little township around the castle. A few places to eat are located on the street leading down to the entrance to the castle. All the hotels in town have restaurants, too.

Hotel Don Humberto   HOTEL $
(✆7930-5051; s/d Q60/100; P) Near El Castillo, offering basic rooms with big beds and good mosquito netting. It's nothing fancy, but more than adequate for a cheap sleep.

Viñas del Lago   HOTEL $$
(✆7930-5053; s/d Q200/300; P✲@🛜🏊) Near the Hotel Don Humberto, but much fancier, with 18 spacious rooms. The ones out the back have good views. The grounds are large and there's a restaurant (mains Q50 to Q100) with views of Lago de Izabal.

Hotel Monte Verde   HOTEL $$
(✆4953-0840; hotelrestaurantemv@gmail.com; s/d with fan Q120/180, s/d with air-con Q230/300; P✲🏊) One of the best deals for miles around – generously sized rooms, a huge pool set in a lush garden and an on-site bar-restaurant.

❶ Getting There & Away

San Felipe is on the lakeshore, 3km west of Río Dulce. It's a beautiful 45-minute walk between the two towns, or take a minivan (Q15, every 30 minutes). In Río Dulce it stops on the corner of the highway and road to El Estor; in San Felipe it stops in front of the Hotel Don Humberto, at the entrance to El Castillo.

Boats coming from Lívingston will drop you in San Felipe if you ask. The Río Dulce river tours usually come to El Castillo, allowing you to get out and visit the castle if you like, or you can come over from Río Dulce by private *lancha* (small motorboat).

Finca El Paraíso

On the north side of the lake, between Río Dulce and El Estor, Finca El Paraíso (✆7949-7122; admission Q10) makes a great day trip from either place. This working ranch's territory has an incredibly beautiful spot in the jungle where a wide, hot waterfall drops about 12m into a clear, deep pool. You can bathe in the hot water, swim in the cool pool or duck under an overhanging promontory and enjoy a jungle-style sauna.

If you're coming for the waterfall, head north (away from the lake) where the bus drops you off – you pay the admission fee there, from where it's about a 2km walk to the falls. To get to the hotels, head south (towards the lake) for about 3km.

🛏 Sleeping & Eating

There are two accommodations options here, both side by side on the lakefront. One is on the grounds of the Finca El Paraíso (✆7949-7122; with fan/air-con Q220/300) and the other is next door, in the humble little cabins at the Brisas del Lago (✆7958-0309; cabin per person Q120).

Both Brisas del Lago and Finca El Paraíso have restaurants. There is no food available at the waterfall, although a *comedor* sometimes operates at the entrance next to the highway.

❶ Getting There & Away

The *finca* (ranch) is on the Río Dulce–El Estor bus route, about one hour (Q12) from Río Dulce and 30 minutes (Q10) from El Estor. The last bus in either direction passes at around 4:30pm to 5pm.

El Estor

POP 21,100

The major settlement on the northern shore of Lago de Izabal is El Estor, a friendly, somnolent little town with a lovely setting, which provides an easy jumping-off point for Bocas del Polochic, a highly biodiverse wildlife reserve at the west end of the lake. The town is also a staging post on a possible route between Río Dulce and Lanquín.

🛏 Sleeping & Eating

There are no upscale hotels here, but there's a good enough range for the short time you're likely to be here.

Restaurante Típico Chaabil apart, the best place to look for food is around Parque Central.

Restaurante Típico Chaabil   HOTEL $
(☑ 7949-7272; 3a Calle; s/d Q150/250; 🅿) Although they go a bit heavy on the log-cabin feel, the rooms at this place, at the west end of the street, are the best deal in town. Get one upstairs for plenty of light and good views. The restaurant here, on a lovely lakeside terrace, cooks up delicious food, such as *tapado* (Garifuna casserole).

The water here is crystal clear and you can swim right off the hotel's dock.

Hotel Villela   HOTEL $
(☑ 7949-7214; 6a Av 2-06; s/d Q80/120) The rooms are less attractive than the neat lawn and trees they're set around, but some are airier and brighter than others. All have fan and bathroom.

Hotel Vista al Lago   HOTEL $$
(☑ 7949-7205; 6a Av 1-13; s/d Q180/250) Set in a classic historic building down on the waterfront, this place has plenty of style, although the rooms themselves are fairly ordinary. Views from the upstairs balcony are superb.

Restaurante del Lago   INTERNATIONAL $$
(mains Q50-100; ⊗8am-8pm) Catches some good breezes and a bit of a lake view – it has the widest menu in town.

Café Portal   CAFE $$
(5a Av 2-65; mains Q40-60; ⊗7am-9pm) Serves a broad range of fare with some vegetarian options.

ℹ Information

Banrural (cnr 3a Calle & 6a Av; ⊗8:30am-5pm Mon-Fri, 9am-1pm Sat) Changes US dollars and Amex traveler's checks and has an ATM.

Café Portal Provides information, tours and transportation.

Fundación Defensores de la Naturaleza (☑ 7949-7130; www.defensores.org.gt; cnr 5a Av & 2a Calle) Administers the Refugio de Vida Silvestre Bocas del Polochic and the Reserva de Biosfera Sierra de las Minas, among other projects.

ℹ Getting There & Away

El Estor is easily reached from Río Dulce. The road west from El Estor via Panzós and Tucurú to Tactic, south of Cobán, once had a bad reputation for highway holdups and robberies, especially around Tucurú – ask around for current conditions. It's also prone to flooding during the wet season – another reason to inquire. You can get to Lanquín by taking the truck that leaves El Estor's Parque Central at 10:30am for Cahabón (Q50, four to five hours), and then a bus or pick-up straight on from Cahabón to Lanquín the same day. Coming the other way currently involves ungodly departure times and staying the night in Cahabón.

Refugio Bocas del Polochic & Reserva de Biosfera Sierra de las Minas

The Refugio de Vida Silvestre Bocas del Polochic (Bocas del Polochic Wildlife Reserve) covers the delta of the Río Polochic, which provides most of Lago de Izabal's water. A visit here provides great birdwatching and howler-monkey observation. The reserve supports more than 300 species of birds – the migration seasons, September to October and April to May, are reportedly fantastic – and many varieties of butterflies and fish. You may well see alligators and, if you're very lucky, glimpse a manatee. Ask at Café Portal in El Estor for boat guides. The reserve is managed by the Fundación Defensores de la Naturaleza, whose research station, the **Estación Científica Selempim** (camping/dm per person Q20/60), just to the south in Reserva de Biosfera Sierra de las Minas, is open for ecotourism visits. Contact Defensores' El Estor office for bookings and further information.

To explore the reserves you can use canoes free of charge, take boat trips (Q250 to Q400) or walk any of the three well-established trails.

If you want to stay out here, the options are a rustic wood-and-thatch cabin or campground. There's no restaurant, but you can bring food and use the Estación Científica's kitchen.

ℹ Getting There & Away

You can get to the station on a local *lancha* (small motorboat) service leaving El Estor at noon on Monday, Wednesday and Saturday (Q60 round trip, 1¼ hours each way) or by special hire (Q600 for a boatload of up to 12 people).

Puerto Barrios

POP 86,400

The country becomes ever more lush, tropical and humid heading east from La Ruidosa junction toward Puerto Barrios. Port towns have always had a reputation for being slightly dodgy, and those acting as international borders doubly so. Puerto Barrios has an edgy, somewhat sleazy feel; for foreign visitors, it's mainly a jumping-off point for boats to Punta Gorda (Belize) or Lívingston, and you probably won't be hanging around.

◎ Sights

El Muñecón   LANDMARK
(intersection 8a Av, 14a Calle & Calz Justo Rufino Barrios) A statue of a dockworker; this is a favorite landmark and monument in the town.

Cathedral   CATHEDRAL
(8a Av) Puerto Barrios' cathedral is probably one of the least-visited in the country.

🛏 Sleeping

Mostly used as a one-night stopover, Puerto Barrios has a range of decent but unexciting hotels.

Hotel Ensenada   HOTEL $
(🖉 7948-0861; hotelensenadapuertobarrios@hotmail.com; 4a Av btwn Calles 10 & 11; s/d Q150/200; P ❄) Offers tidy little rooms with good bathrooms and OK beds. Get one upstairs to catch a breeze.

Hotel Europa   HOTEL $
(🖉 7948-1292; 3a Av btwn Calles 11a & 12a; s/d with fan Q80/130, s/d with air-con Q130/170; P ❄ 🖥) The best of the budget options in the port area, this hotel, just 1½ blocks from the Muelle Municipal (Municipal Boat Dock), is run by a friendly family and has clean rooms with TV, arranged around a parking courtyard.

Hotel Lee   HOTEL $
(🖉 7948-0685; 5a Av btwn Calles 9a & 10a; s/d with fan Q80/120, d with air-con Q180 ; ❄) This is a friendly, family-owned place, close to the bus terminals. Typical of Puerto Barrios' budget hotels, it offers straightforward, vaguely clean rooms. The little balcony out front catches the odd breeze.

Puerto Bello   HOTEL $$
(🖉 7948-0525; www.hotelpuertobello.com; 8a Av btwn Calles 18 & 19; s/d Q230/350; P ❄ 🖥 ⌨) By far the best-looking hotel in town, marred only by its slightly out of the way location. The rooms are spacious and modern and the lovely garden and pool area is a blessing year-round.

Hotel del Norte   HOTEL $$
(🖉 7948-2116; 7a Calle; s/d with fan Q100/180, s/d with air-con Q180/300; P ❄ @ 🖥 ⌨) A large, classically tropical wooden building with mosquito-screened corridors, the century-old Hotel del Norte is in a class by itself. Its

---

MANATEES

In the days of New World exploration, reports of mermaid sightings were commonplace. Columbus' ship's log from January 1493 recorded: 'On the previous day when the Admiral went to the Río del Oro he saw three mermaids which rose well out of the sea...' It's pretty much accepted now that what sailors were seeing were in fact manatees – who, along with the dugong, belong to the biological order Sirenia, a name taken from the Greek word for mermaid.

Distantly related to elephants, these huge (the largest recorded manatee weighed 1775kg, while newborns weigh around 30kg) vegetarian mammals seem destined to become an endangered species. They were hunted as far back as Maya times – their bones were used for jewelry and their meat (called *bucan*) was prized for its restorative properties. It's believed that the buccaneers (the original pirates of the Caribbean) were so named because they lived almost exclusively on *bucan*.

Some scientists claim that manatees were once sociable creatures who swam in packs and readily approached humans, but have now adapted in response to human hunters, to become the shy, furtive creatures they are today. You have to be extremely fortunate to see one in the wild – they scare easily, can swim in short bursts at up to 30km per hour and can stay underwater for 20 minutes. In Guatemala, your best chance of seeing one is in the Bocas del Polochic (p215) or the Punta de Manabique (p218). Good luck!

weathered and warped frame is redolent of history and the floorboards go off at crazy angles. Pick a room carefully – some are little more than a wooden box, others have great ocean views and catch good breezes.

Rooms with air-conditioning are in the newer, less atmospheric building, but are still an excellent deal. There's a swimming pool beside the sea.

Hotel El Reformador HOTEL **$$**
(☎7948-0533; reformador@intelnet.net.gt; cnr 7a Av & 16a Calle; s/d with fan Q130/200, s/d with air-con Q200/280; P ❄ 📶) Like a little haven away from the hot busy streets outside, El Reformador offers big, cool rooms set around leafy patios. Air-con rooms lead onto wide interior balconies. There is a restaurant (meals Q60 to Q90) here.

Eating

The eating scene in Puerto Barrios is surprisingly varied, and most restaurants are within easy walking distance of where you're likely to be staying.

Kaffa CAFE **$**
(8a Av btwn Calles 7 & 8; sandwiches & breakfast Q40-60; ⏲8:30am-10pm) A hip coffee shop in Puerto Barrios? Well, why not? Let's see how long it lasts. The food's so-so, but the coffee and the breezy deck overlooking the park are both excellent.

Restaurante Morano Calabro MEDITERRANEAN **$$**
(11 Calle btwn 7 & 8 Av; mains Q80-160; ⏲11am-10pm Mon-Sat) Surprisingly good Italian food (the pizzas are the real winners here, but the pasta rates a mention, too) alongside an interesting selection of tapas items. The great wine list, featuring bottles from Spain and South America, rounds out the picture.

★ **Restaurante Safari** SEAFOOD **$$**
(☎7948-0563; cnr 1a Calle & 5a Av; seafood Q70-150; ⏲10am-9pm) The town's most enjoyable restaurant is on a thatch-roofed, open-air platform right over the water about 1km north of the town center. Locals and visitors alike love to eat and catch the sea breezes here. Excellent seafood of all kinds including the specialty *tapado* – that great Garifuna casserole.

Chicken and meat dishes are less expensive than seafood. There's live music most nights. If the Safari is full, the Cangrejo Azul next door offers pretty much the same deal, in a more relaxed environment.

GETTING TO HONDURAS

Minibuses leave for the Honduran frontier (Q30, 1¼ hours) every 20 minutes from 5am to 5pm, from 6a Av outside the market in Puerto Barrios. They stop en route to the border at Guatemalan immigration, where you may be required to pay Q10 for an exit stamp. Honduran entry formalities will leave you around L60 lighter.

La Habana Vieja CUBAN **$$**
(13 Calle btwn Avs 6a & 7a; mains Q50-100; ⏲11am-1pm) A good, wide selection of Cuban classics (including *ropa vieja* – a shredded beef stew) and some straightforward sandwiches. Also has a good bar if you're looking for a quiet drink.

Orientation

Because of its spacious layout, you must walk or ride further in Puerto Barrios to get from place to place. For instance, it's 800m from the bus terminals by the market in the town center to the Muelle Municipal at the end of 12a Calle, from which passenger boats depart. Very few businesses use street numbers – most just label which street it's on, and the cross streets it's in between.

Information

Banco Industrial (7a Av; ⏲9am-5pm Mon-Fri, 9am-1pm Sat) Changes US dollars and traveler's checks, and has an ATM.

Immigration Office (cnr 12a Calle & 3a Av; ⏲24hr) A block from the Muelle Municipal. Come here for your entry or exit stamp if you're arriving from or leaving for Belize. If you're leaving by sea, there is a Q80 departure tax to pay. If you are heading to Honduras, you can get your exit stamp at another immigration office on the road to the border.

Police Station (☎7948-2639; 9a Calle) Police station.

Post Office (cnr 6a Calle & 6a Av; ⏲9am-4pm Mon-Fri, to 1pm Sat) Post office.

Getting There & Away

BOAT

Boats depart from the Muelle Municipal at the end of 12a Calle.

Regular *lanchas* (small motorboats) depart for Lívingston (Q45, 30 minutes, five daily) between 6:30am and 5pm. Buy your ticket as early as you can on the day (you can't book before your day of departure) – spaces are limited and sometimes sell out.

Outside of these regular times, *lanchas* depart whenever they have six people ready to go and cost Q50 per person.

Most of the movement from Lívingston to Puerto Barrios is in the morning, returning in the afternoon. From Lívingston, your last chance of the day may be the 5pm *lancha*, especially during the low season when fewer travelers are shuttling back and forth.

Lanchas also depart from the Muelle Municipal three times daily for Punta Gorda, Belize (Q220, one hour). The 10am departure arrives in time for the noon bus from Punta Gorda to Belize City. Tickets are sold at the dock. Before boarding you also need to get your exit stamp at the nearby immigration office (p217) and pay Q80 departure tax.

If you want to leave a car in Puerto Barrios while you visit Lívingston for a day or two, there are plenty of *parqueos* (parking lots) around the dock area that charge around Q30 per 24 hours. Many of the hotels offer this service, too.

BUS & MINIBUS

Minibuses for Chiquimula (Q50, 4½ hours), also via Quiriguá, leave every half hour from 3am to 3pm, from the corner of 6a Av and 9a Calle. Minibuses to Río Dulce (Q25, two hours) leave from the same location.

Transportes Litegua (⏲7948-1172; cnr 6a Av & 9a Calle) leaves for Guatemala City (Q65 to Q100, five to six hours), via Quiriguá and Río Hondo frequently. *Directo* services avoid a half-hour detour into Morales.

Punta de Manabique

The Punta de Manabique promontory, which separates the Bahía de Manabique from the open sea, along with the coast and hinterland all the way southeast to the Honduran frontier, comprises a large, ecologically fascinating, sparsely populated wetland area. Access to the area, which is under environmental protection as the Área de Protección Especial Punta de Manabique, is not cheap, but the attractions for those who make it there include pristine Caribbean beaches, boat trips through the mangrove forests, lagoons and waterways, birdwatching, fishing with locals, and crocodile and possible manatee sightings.

🛏 Sleeping & Eating

Ecoalbergue GUESTHOUSE $
(⏲5303-9822; www.turismocomunitarioguatema la.com/estero_lagarto.html; Estero Lagarto; per person tents/r Q25/50) The community-run guesthouse in the tiny village of Estero Lagarto offers simple but comfortable rustic beachside accommodations and delicious meals (Q30 to 60), mostly seafood-based.

ℹ Getting There & Away

To visit, get in touch – a week in advance, if possible – with **Estero Lagarto Community Tourism** (⏲5303-9822; www.turismocomuni tarioguatemala.com/estero_lagarto.html).

Lívingston

POP 26,300

Quite unlike anywhere else in Guatemala, this largely Garifuna town is fascinating in itself, but also has the attraction of a couple of good beaches and its location at the end of the river journey from Río Dulce.

Unconnected (for the moment) by road from the rest of the country (the town is called 'Buga' – mouth – in Garifuna, for its position at the river mouth), boat transportation is logically quite good here, and you can get to Belize, the Cayes and Puerto Barrios with a minimum of fuss.

The Garifuna people of Caribbean Guatemala, Honduras, Nicaragua and southern Belize trace their roots to the Caribbean island of St Vincent, where shipwrecked African slaves mixed with the indigenous Carib in the 17th century. It took the British a long time, and a lot of fighting, to establish colonial control over St Vincent, and when they finally succeeded in 1796, they decided to deport its surviving Garifuna inhabitants. Most of the survivors wound up, after many had starved on Roatán island off Honduras, in the Honduran coastal town of Trujillo. From there, they have spread along the Caribbean coast. Their main concentration in Guatemala is in Lívingston but there are also a few thousand in Puerto Barrios and elsewhere. The Garifuna language is a unique mélange of Caribbean and African languages with a bit of French. Other people in Lívingston include the indigenous Q'eqchi' Maya (who have their own community a kilometer or so upriver from the main dock), *ladinos* (people of mixed indigenous and European heritage) and a smattering of international travelers.

◎ Sights

Beaches in Lívingston itself are disappointing, as buildings or vegetation come right down to the water's edge in most places. Those beaches that do exist are often contaminated; however, there are better beaches within a few kilometers to the northwest. You can reach Playa Quehueche near the mouth of the Río Quehueche by taxi (Q30) in about 10 minutes. The best beach in the area is Playa Blanca (Q15), around 12km from Lívingston. This is privately owned and you need a boat to get there.

Los Siete Altares
WATERFALL

(The Seven Altars; Q25) About 5km (1½ hour walk) northwest of Lívingston along the shore of Bahía de Amatique, Los Siete Altares is a series of freshwater falls and pools. It's a pleasant goal for a beach walk and is a good place for a picnic and swim.

Follow the shore northward to the river mouth and walk along the beach until it meets the path into the woods (about 30 minutes). Follow this path all the way to the falls. Boat trips go to Los Siete Altares, but if you're a walker it's better to go by foot to experience the natural beauty and the Garifuna people along the way. About halfway along, just past the rope bridge is Hotel Salvador Gaviota (p221), serving decent food and ice-cold beers and soft drinks. You can stay out here, too.

Rasta Mesa
CULTURAL CENTER

(✉4459-6106; Barrio Nevago; ◷10am-2pm & 7-10pm) This is a friendly, informal little cultural center where you can drop in for classes in Garifuna cooking (per person Q60) and drumming (per person Q100) or just get a massage (from Q150). It also offers volunteering opportunities.

👉 Tours

A few outfits in Lívingston offer tours that let you get out and experience the natural wonders of the area. Exotic Travel (✉7947-0133; www.bluecaribbeanbay.com; Calle Principal, Restaurante Bahía Azul) and Happy Fish Travel (✉7947-0661; www.happyfishtravel.com; Calle Principal, Restaurante Happy Fish) are both well-organized operations. Happy Fish gets extra points for supporting community tourism initiatives in the area and for their willingness to share information on how you can visit many of the local attractions without a guide.

The popular ecological tour/jungle trip (Q70) takes you for a walk through town, out west up to a lookout spot and on to the Río Quehueche, where you take a half-hour canoe trip down the river to Playa Quehueche. Then you walk through the jungle to Los Siete Altares, hang out there for a while, then walk back down the beach to Lívingston. This is a great way to see the area, and the friendly local guides can also give you a good introduction to the Garifuna people who live here.

The Playa Blanca tour goes by boat first to Los Siete Altares and then on to Playa Blanca, the best beach in the area, for two or three hours. This trip goes with a minimum of two people and costs Q100 per person.

Happy Fish offers a return boat trip (Q220) just along the canyon section of Río Dulce (the most interesting and picturesque part), which gives you more time to enjoy the trails, birdwatching and so on than the 'tour' given on the public *lanchas* (small motorboats). It also runs tours to Cueva del Tigre, a community-run tourism project 8km from Lívingston (Q180 for a tour, or they'll tell you how to get there on your own), and offers transport to Lagunita Creek (p224), another community-operated tourism initiative.

Also popular are day/overnight trips to the Cayos Sapodillas (or Zapotillas), well off the coast of southern Belize, where there is great snorkeling (Q500/1200 for one/two days). A minimum of eight people is required and exit taxes and national park fees (Q160 in total) are separate.

Río Dulce Tours

Tour agencies in town offer day trips up the Río Dulce to Río Dulce town (departing at 9:30am and 2:30pm), as do most local sailors at the Lívingston dock. Many travelers use these tours as one-way transportation to Río Dulce, paying Q150/250 one way/round trip. It's a beautiful ride through tropical jungle scenery, with several places to stop on the way.

While a boat ride on the Río Dulce is not to be missed, if you're coming from Guatemala City or Puerto Barrios it makes much more sense to catch a boat from Puerto Barrios to Lívingston and do the tour on your way out.

Shortly after you leave Lívingston, you pass the tributary Río Tatin on the right, then will probably stop at an indigenous arts museum set up by Asociación Ak' Tenamit (p222), an NGO working to improve conditions for the Q'eqchi' Maya population of the area. The river enters a gorge called La Cueva de la Vaca, its walls hung with great tangles of jungle foliage and the humid air noisy with

Lívingston

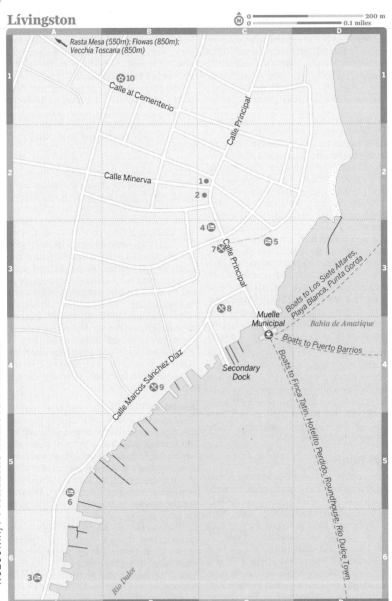

Rasta Mesa (550m); Flowas (850m); Vecchia Toscana (850m)

Calle al Cementerio

Calle Principal

Calle Minerva

Calle Principal

Muelle Municipal

Bahía de Amatique

Boats to Los Siete Altares, Playa Blanca, Punta Gorda

Boats to Puerto Barrios

Boats to Finca Tatín, Hotelito Perdido, Roundhouse, Río Dulce Town

Calle Marcos Sánchez Díaz

Secondary Dock

Río Dulce

the cries of tropical birds. Just beyond that is **La Pintada**, a rock escarpment covered with graffiti. Further on, a **thermal spring** forces sulfurous water out of the base of the cliff, providing a chance for a warm swim. The river widens into **El Golfete**, a lakelike body of water that presages the even more vast expanse of Lago de Izabal further upstream.

On the northern shore of El Golfete is the **Biotopo Chocón Machacas**, a 72-sq-km reserve established within the Parque Nacional Río Dulce to protect the beautiful river land-

Livingston

scape, the valuable forests and mangrove swamps and their wildlife, which includes such rare creatures as the tapir and above all the manatee. A network of 'water trails' (boat routes around several jungle lagoons) provide ways to see other bird, animal and plant life of the reserve. You can stay here, at the community-run lodge Q'ana Itz'am (p224) in Lagunita Salvador but you will have to arrange transportation separately.

Boats will probably visit Islas de Pájaros, a pair of islands where thousands of water-birds live, in the middle of El Golfete. From El Golfete you continue upriver, passing increasing numbers of expensive villas and boathouses, to the town of Río Dulce, where the soaring Hwy 13 road bridge crosses the river, and on to El Castillo de San Felipe on Lago de Izabal.

You can also do this trip starting from Río Dulce.

🎉 Festivals & Events

During Semana Santa (⊙Easter week) Lívingston is packed with merrymakers. Garifuna National Day (⊙Nov 26) is celebrated with a variety of cultural events.

🛏 Sleeping

Prices in Lívingston hit their peak from July to December – outside of these months many midrange and top-end places halve their rates.

Casa de la Iguana   HOSTEL $
(☑7947-0064; www.casadelaiguana.com; Calle Marcos Sánchez Díaz; hammocks/dm Q25/50,

cabins with/without bathroom Q160/120; ☎) A five-minute walk from the main dock, this party hostel offers good-value cabins. They're clean wooden affairs, with simple but elegant decoration. Happy hour here rocks on and you can camp or crash in a hammock.

Flowas   BUNGALOW $
(☑7947-0376; infoflowas@gmail.com; r per person Q120) An extremely laid-back little backpacker enclave, this place offers rustic wood and bamboo cabins set up on the 2nd floor (catching the odd breeze) right on the beachfront. The atmosphere is relaxed and there's good, cheap food available. A taxi (Q15 from the dock) will drop you within 150m of the front gate.

Hotel Salvador Gaviota   BUNGALOW $
(☑7947-0874; www.hotelsalvadorgaviota.com; Playa Quehueche; r per person with/without bathroom Q160/80; @) Beautiful simple wood and bamboo rooms set back a couple of hundred meters from a reasonably clean beach. Day-trippers going to and from Los Siete Altares (p219) drop in for meals (Q50 to Q100) and drinks here – otherwise you may have the place to yourself.

It's 500m from the swing bridge where the road ends – a taxi will charge about Q25 to get you there.

Vecchia Toscana   HOTEL $$
(☑7947-0884; www.vecchiatoscana-livingston.com; Barrio Paris; s/d from Q341/488; ❄@☎🏊) This beautiful Italian-run place down on the beach has some of the best rooms in town. There's a variety of rooms on offer, going up to apartments that sleep eight comfortably. The grounds and common areas are immaculate and there's a good Italian restaurant with sea views out the front. A taxi here from the dock will cost around Q20.

Hotel Ríos Tropicales   HOTEL $$
(☑5755-7571; Calle Principal; s/d Q180/230, s/d without bathroom from Q70/150; ☎) The Ríos Tropicales has a variety of big, well-screened rooms facing a central patio with plenty of hammocks and chill-out space. Rooms without bathroom are more spacious, but others are better decorated.

Posada El Delfín   HOTEL $$$
(☑7947-0976; www.posadaeldelfin.com; Calle Marcos Sánchez Díaz; s/d from Q580/740; ❄☎🏊) Down by the waterfront, this is a big modern construction with reasonably sized,

CENTRAL & EASTERN GUATEMALA LÍVINGSTON

spotless rooms and a great swimming pool overlooking the river. Don't expect views from your room – the recommended 2nd-floor restaurant steals them all.

Hotel Villa Caribe
HOTEL $$$

(☎ 7947-0072; www.hotelvillacaribeguatemala.com; Calle Principal; s/d/bungalows Q790/930/1400; ❄@🎧🅿) The 45-room Villa Caribe is a luxurious anomaly among Lívingston's laid-back, low-priced Caribbean lodgings. Modern but still Caribbean in style, it has many conveniences and comforts, including extensive tropical gardens, a big swimming pool and a large poolside bar.

Rooms are fan-cooled with modern bathrooms; little balconies overlook the gardens and river mouth. The bungalows are air-conditioned.

🍴 Eating

Food in Lívingston is relatively expensive because most of it (except fish and coconuts) must be brought in by boat. There's fine seafood here and some unusual flavors for Guatemala, including coconut and curry. *Tapado,* a rich stew made from fish, shrimp, shellfish and coconut milk, spiced with coriander, is the delicious local specialty. A potent potable is made by slicing off the top of a green coconut and mixing in a healthy dose of rum – these *coco locos* hit the spot.

Calle Principal is dotted with many open-air eateries.

Restaurante Gaby
GUATEMALAN $

(Calle Marcos Sánchez Díaz; mains Q40-80; ⊙8am-9pm) For a good honest feed in humble surrounds, you can't go past Gaby's. She serves up the good stuff: lobster, *tapado* (fish stew), rice and beans, and good breakfasts at good prices. The *telenovelas* (soap operas) come free.

Antojitos Yoli's
BAKERY $

(Calle Principal; baked goods Q15-30; ⊙8am-5pm) This is the place to come for baked goods. Especially recommended are the coconut bread and pineapple pie.

★Restaurante Buga Mama
SEAFOOD $$

(Calle Marcos Sánchez Díaz; mains Q70-120; ⊙noon-10pm; 🎧) This place enjoys the best location of any restaurant in town, and profits go to the Asociación Ak' Tenamit (☎5908-3392; www.aktenamit.org), an NGO with several projects in the area. There's a wide range of seafood, homemade pasta, curries and other dishes on the menu, including a very good *tapado* (fish stew; Q120).

Most of the waiters here are trainees in a community sustainable tourism development scheme, so service can be sketchy, but forgivable.

Happy Fish
SEAFOOD $$

(Calle Principal; mains Q50-120; ⊙7am-10pm; 🎧) This bustling and breezy main street eatery is always busy with locals and tourists, keeping the food fresh and the service snappy. The requisite *tapado* (fish stew) is here, plus a good range of other options.

🍷 Drinking & Nightlife

Adventurous drinkers should try *guifiti,* a local concoction made from coconut rum, often infused with herbs. It's said to have medicinal properties.

A handful of bars down on the beach to the left of the end of Calle Principal pull in travelers and locals at night (after about 10pm or 11pm). It's very dark down here, so take care. The bars are within five minutes' walk of each other, so you should go for a wander and see what's happening. Music ranges from *punta* (a traditional Garifuna dance) to salsa, merengue and electronica. Things warm up on Friday but Saturday is the party night – often going until 5am or 6am.

Happy hour is pretty much an institution along the main street, with every restaurant getting in on the act. One of the best is at Casa de la Iguana (p221).

☆ Entertainment

Quite often a roaming band will play a few songs for diners along the Calle Principal around dinnertime. If you like the music, make sure to sling them a few bucks. Several places around town have live Garifuna music, although schedules are unpredictable.

Diners in the Hotel Villa Caribe restaurant can enjoy a Garifuna show each evening at 7pm.

Café-Bar Ubafu
LIVE MUSIC

(Calle al Cementerio; ⊙6pm-late) Probably the most dependable nightlife option in town. Supposedly has music and dancing nightly, but liveliest on weekends.

❶ Orientation

After being here half an hour, you'll know where everything is. Though there are street names, in reality no one uses them.

ℹ Information

Lívingston has its edgy aspects and a few hustlers operate here – exercise normal precautions. Use mosquito repellent and other sensible precautions, especially if you go out into the jungle; mosquitoes here carry both malaria and dengue fever.

For more on Lívingston, check out its community website (www.livingston.com.gt).

Banrural (Calle Principal; ☉9am-5pm Mon-Fri, 9am-1pm Sat) Changes US dollars and traveler's checks, and has an ATM.

Immigration Office (Calle Principal; ☉6am-7pm) Issues entry and exit stamps for travelers arriving direct from or going direct to Belize or Honduras, charging Q80 for exit stamps. Outside business hours, you can knock for attention at any time.

ℹ Getting There & Away

Frequent boats come downriver from Río Dulce and across the bay from Puerto Barrios. There are also international boats from Honduras and Belize.

Happy Fish (p219) and Exotic Travel (p219) operate combined boat and bus shuttles to La Ceiba (the cheapest gateway to Honduras' Bay Islands) for around Q550 per person, with a minimum of four people. Leaving Lívingston at 6am or earlier will get you to La Ceiba in time for the boat to the islands, making it a one-day trip, which is nearly impossible to do independently.

There's also a boat that goes direct to Punta Gorda (Belize) daily at 7am (Q250, 1½ hours), leaving from the public dock. In Punta Gorda, the boat connects with a bus to Placencia and Belize City. The boat waits for this bus to arrive in Placencia before it sets off back for Lívingston from Punta Gorda at about 10:30am.

If you are taking one of these early international departures, get your exit stamp from immigration in Lívingston the day before.

Around Lívingston

Lanchas traveling between Río Dulce and Lívingston (or vice versa) will drop you at the Hotelito Perdido, Finca Tatin or Roundhouse. These places can also pick you up, charging around Q40 per person from Lívingston, more from Puerto Barrios or Río Dulce.

🛏 Sleeping

★ **Finca Tatin** BUNGALOW $
(☑ 4148-3332; www.fincatatin.com; dm/s/d Q60/180/200, s/d without bathroom Q80/130; 🛜) 🚲
This wonderful, rustic B&B at the confluence of Ríos Dulce and Tatin, about 10km from Lívingston, is a great place to experience the forest. Four-hour guided walks and kayak trips, some visiting local Q'eqchi' villages, are offered. Accommodations are in funky wood-and-thatched cabins scattered through the jungle and some rather spiffy

CATCH THE RHYTHM OF THE GARIFUNA

Lívingston is the heartland of Guatemala's Garifuna community, and it won't take too long before you hear some of their distinctive music. A Garifuna band generally consists of three drums (the *primera* takes the bass part, the other two play more melodic functions), a shaker or maraca, a turtle shell (hit like a cowbell) and a conch shell (blown like a flute).

The lyrics are often call and response – most often sung in Garifuna (a language with influences from Arawak, French and West African languages) but sometimes composed in Spanish. Most songs deal with themes from village life – planting time, harvests, things that happen in the village, honoring the dead and folktales of bad sons made good. Sometimes they simply sing about the beauty of the village.

Traditional Garifuna music has given birth to an almost bewildering array of musical styles, among them Punta Rock, *jugujugu, calachumba, jajankanu, chumba, saranda, sambé* and *parranda*.

Punta Rock is by far the most widely known adaptation of traditional Garifuna rhythms, and you can hear 'Punta' in most discos throughout Central America. The dance that accompanies it (also called *punta*) is a frenzied sort of affair, following the nature of the percussion. The left foot swivels back and forth while the right foot taps out the rhythm. Perhaps coincidentally, this movement causes the hips to shake wildly, leading some observers to comment on the sexual nature of the dance.

If you're interested in learning more about Garifuna culture or want drumming lessons, drop in to Rasta Mesa (p219).

new riverfront cabins with balconies overlooking the water.

There are trails, waterfalls and endless river tributaries that you can explore with one of the *cayucos* (indigenous fishing dugout) available for guest use (per day Q80). Guided night walks through the jungle offer views of elusive nightlife, and cave tours are good for swimming and soaking in a natural sauna. You can walk to Lívingston from here in about four hours, or take a kayak and staff from Finca Tatin will come pick you up.

Roundhouse HOSTEL $

(☑ 4294-9730; www.roundhouseguatemala.com; dm/d without bathroom Q50/110; @ 🖳) 🖉 Unfortunately closed at the time of writing, this medium-sized hostel, 20 minutes by boat from Lívingston, was one of the best on the river. The 1st floor is a riverfront bar/restaurant/hammock area. On the 2nd floor there's a spacious dorm and some good, simple private rooms.

Snorkeling and sailing tours are usually on offer, and the 8.5m pontoon boat is used for booze cruises on the river.

Hotelito Perdido HOTEL $$

(☑ 5725-1576; www.hotelitoperdido.com; dm Q60, s/d bungalows Q200/250, s/d without bathroom Q150/200) 🖉 This beautiful, secluded hideout is a five-minute boat ride from Finca Tatin. The ambiance is superb – relaxed and friendly. The whole place is solar powered and constructed in such a way as to cause minimal impact on the environment.

The two-story bungalows are gorgeous – simple yet well decorated, with a sleeping area upstairs and a small sitting area downstairs. It's a small, intimate place, so it's a good idea to book ahead. You can organize many of the activities available at Finca Tatin from here as well.

Q'ana Itz'am CABIN $$

(☑ 5992-1853; www.lagunitasalvador.com; r with/without bathroom Q200/70, bungalows Q400) 🖉 Midway between Lívingston and Río Dulce, in the small Q'eqchi' community of Lagunita Salvador, this charming community tourism project offers simple accommodations in wooden bungalows connected by boardwalks in the mangroves. There's plenty to do here – birdwatching, jungle walks, kayaking and sampling delicious Q'eqchi' traditional cooking.

The villagers organize traditional dances on request and tours of the friendly village are offered to help give you a better understanding of the way of life in this curious little pocket of the world. Reservations are a must and free transport may be available from Lívingston/Río Dulce.

Lagunita Creek LODGE $$

(☑ 4113-0103; dm/r Q100/400) Heading northwest from Lívingston brings you to the Río Sarstun, which forms the border between Belize and Guatemala. Ten kilometers upstream is the small community of Lagunita Creek, where a community tourism project offers lodging in a simple ecolodge. Simple meals (Q50 to Q70) are available here, or you can bring your own food to cook.

Included in the price is use of kayaks to explore the beautiful, turquoise waters of the river and guided nature walks/birdwatching tours. Transport isn't complicated but it can be expensive – the only way to get here is by boat. *Lanchas* (small motorboats) from Lívingston charge Q1400 per boatload (up to eight people), with a small discount for smaller groups. Happy Fish Travel (p219) in Lívingston offers day/overnight tours here for Q320/560 but require a minimum of six people.

El Petén

Best Places to Eat

➡ Las Orquídeas (p247)

➡ Terrazzo (p239)

➡ Posada & Restaurante Campamento El Chiclero (p257)

➡ Las Mesitas (p238)

➡ Finca Ixobel (p232)

Best Places to Sleep

➡ Finca Ixobel (p232)

➡ Ni'tun Ecolodge (p244)

➡ Chiminos Island Lodge (p232)

➡ Estación Biológica Las Guacamayas (p260)

➡ Alice Guesthouse (p246)

Why Go?

Vast, sparsely populated and jungle-covered, Guatemala's largest and northernmost department is ripe for exploration. Whether it's the mysteries of the Classic Maya, the bounty of the jungle or the chance to lounge lakeside that inspires you, it's all here in abundance. How deeply you choose to delve into the Maya legacy will depend on your willingness to get your feet muddy. The towering temples of Tikal can be reached by tour from just about anywhere, while more remote sites such as El Mirador and Piedras Negras require days of planning and further days of jungle trekking. The Reserva De Biosfera Maya (Maya Biosphere Reserve) covers virtually the entire northern third of El Petén, and together with its counterparts in Mexico and Belize forms a multi-national wildlife haven that spans more than 30,000 sq km.

When to Go

If you're planning to do much jungle trekking to remote archaeological sites, late February to May are best: it's drier, less boggy and you won't have to wade through so much mud, though it can get rather hot and steamy toward late May. The rains begin in June and with them come the mosquitoes – bring rain gear, repellent and, if you plan on slinging a hammock, a mosquito net. September and October are peak hurricane and thunderstorm season, with the rains continuing into November, and are best avoided. December to February, with cool nights and mornings, can be quite a pleasant time to visit El Petén.

El Petén Highlights

1 Gazing over the jungle canopy from towering Temple IV at **Tikal** (p247).

2 Trekking through the jungle to the vast, though still scarcely excavated, Maya city of **El Mirador** (p261).

3 Awakening to the sound of howler monkeys at **Laguna Petexbatún** (p231).

4 Night cruising for crocodiles and spotting macaws at the **Estación Biológica Las Guacamayas** (p260).

5 Lounging lakeside over evening cocktails on the picturesque island/town of **Flores** (p234).

6 Admiring the sunset over Lago de Petén Itzá from your private pier in laid-back **El Remate** (p244).

7 Breaking bread with fellow travelers at the rural retreat of **Finca Ixobel** (p232).

8 Rolling down the **Río de la Pasión** to **Ceibal** (p230), a remote riverside ruin with intricately carved stelae of past Maya rulers.

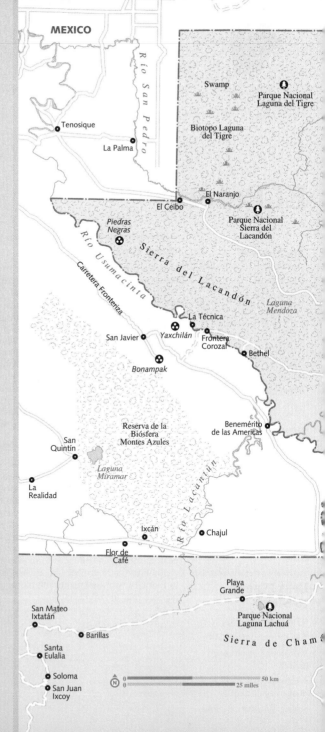

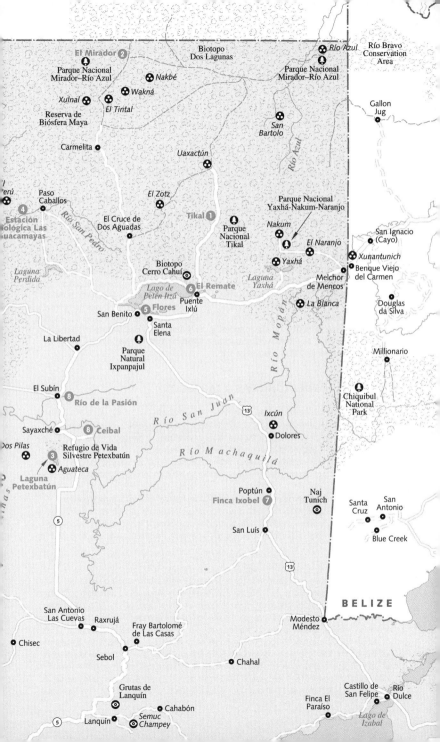

History

Often referred to as the cradle of Maya civilization, El Petén has historically been isolated from the rest of present-day Guatemala, a situation that continued until quite recently. The major Maya population centers – Tikal and El Mirador – had more contact with neighboring settlements in Belize and Mexico than with those down south.

The arrival of the Spanish changed little in this regard. The Itzá, who lived on the island now known as Flores, earned a reputation for cruelty and ferocity which, along with El Petén's impenetrable jungles and fierce wildlife, kept the Spanish at a distance until 1697, about 150 years after the rest of the country had been conquered.

Even after conquest, the Spanish had no great love for El Petén. The island of Flores was a penal colony before a small city was founded, mostly to facilitate the trade in chicle, hardwood, sugarcane and rubber that had been planted in the region.

The big change came in 1970, when the Guatemalan government saw the opportunity to market Tikal as a tourist destination and work began on a decent road network.

El Petén's population boom – largely a result of government incentives for farmers to relocate – has seen the population increase from 15,000 to a staggering 660,000 in the last 50 years.

Some of the new neighbors are not entirely welcome, however – large tracts of land, particularly in the northwest corner and in the Parque Nacional Laguna del Tigre, have been taken over by drug traffickers and people smugglers, capitalizing on the unpatrolled border with Mexico.

❶ Getting There & Around

El Petén's main tourism node is at the twin towns of Flores and Santa Elena, about 60km southwest of Tikal. The main roads to Flores (from Río Dulce to the southeast, from Cobán and Chisec to the southwest, from the Belize border to the east, and from the Mexican border to the northwest) are now all paved and in good condition, except for a few short stretches. Frequent buses and minibuses carry travelers along these routes. Santa Elena also has the only functioning civil airport in the country aside from Guatemala City.

MEXICAN BORDER (CHIAPAS & TABASCO)

Via Bethel & La Técnica and Frontera Corozal

Regular transportation service reaches the Mexican border at Bethel or La Técnica, on the eastern bank of the Río Usumacinta, from where there is a regular ferry service to Frontera Corozal on the Mexican bank. Guatemalan immigration is in Bethel, but the crossing is quicker and much cheaper from La Técnica (Q10 per person). Microbus drivers will normally stop and wait for you to do the formalities in Bethel before proceeding to La Técnica.

Autotransporte Chamoán vans run hourly from Frontera Corozal *embarcadero* (wharf) to Palenque (M$100, 2½ to three hours), with the last departure at 3pm.

To visit the Maya ruins at Yaxchilán on the Mexican side of the river, Escudo Jaguar runs boats from M$950 to M$1300 (five to 10 people), round trip, with a two-hour wait at the ruins.

Via El Ceibo & La Palma

Travelers may enter the Mexican state of Tabasco via the border post by El Ceibo, a village on the Río San Pedro. AMCRU (☎3127-6684) runs regular microbuses from Santa Elena to El Ceibo, more frequently to El Naranjo, which lets you off at 'El Cruce' to catch a shuttle the additional 15 minutes to the border. (In the reverse direction, the last micro from El Ceibo to Santa Elena departs at 5pm.)

A tiny immigration post operates 24 hours on the Guatemalan side, while a huge new facility on the Mexican side is open from 9am to 6pm. From the Mexican side, *tuk-tuks* shuttle travelers around 600m to a little terminal for vans to Tenosique, Tabasco (M$40, one hour, hourly till 6pm). Arriving in Tenosique, get off by the bus terminal to catch an ADO bus to Villahermosa (3½ hours); or get a *tuk-tuk* to where vans leave for Palenque (M$50, 1½ hours) until 7pm.

Sayaxché

POP 114,781

Sayaxché, on the south bank of the Río de la Pasión, 61km southwest of Flores, is the closest town to around 10 scattered Maya archaeological sites, including Ceibal, Aguateca, Dos Pilas, Tamarindito and Altar de Sacrificios. Besides its strategic position between Flores and the Cobán area, it has a riverside appeal all its own, with rickety motorboats and funky barges floating trucks across the broad waterway, the former till sundown, the latter round the clock (pedestrian Q2, car Q15).

Banrural (☺9am-6pm Mon-Fri, 8am-noon Sat, 9am-noon Sun), just below the church toward the river, changes dollars and euros; a nearby branch has a 5B ATM. Get online at Zona X (per hr Q6; ☺8am-6pm), three streets up from the dock on the left.

Bold travelers might venture into the seedy bars alongside the auto ferry, otherwise nightlife here is limited to strolling the dusty streets.

🛏 Sleeping

Though the lodges around nearby Laguna Petexbatún make a far more appealing option, Sayaxché has a few laid-back guesthouses by the riverside.

Hotel Del Río HOTEL $
(☎7928-6138; hoteldelriosayaxche@hotmail.com; s/d Q125/175, with air-con Q150/225; P❈☎) A few steps to the right of the wharf (with your back to the river), this modern hotel is the cushy choice, with huge, sparkling rooms alongside and above an airy lobby.

El Majestuoso Petén HOTEL $
(☎7928-6166; majestuosopeten@gmail.com; s/d Q80/160, without bathroom Q50/100; P❈☎) This establishment has a peaceful setting overlooking a lazy stretch of the Río Petexbatún. Of the simply furnished rooms (with optional air-con), the 'Tikal' and 'San José' have the best river views. From the dock, go up to the first intersection, then three blocks to the right to find the greenish building.

Hospedaje Yaxkín BUNGALOW $
(☎4913-4879; dm Q30, bungalow per person with/without bathroom Q70/35) East of the center are these 15 rustic cabins scattered around a wooded tract. A big open-air restaurant serves pastas, tacos and river fish (Q50). It's two blocks south and three blocks east of the church. Gregarious host don Rosendo will pick you up at the dock if you phone ahead.

🍴 Eating

Decent options are limited to the Café Maya (p229) and the cook shack at Hospedaje Yaxkín (p229). River fish may not be available due to unacceptable pollution levels.

Café Maya GUATEMALAN $
(Calle del Ferry; mains Q40-50; ☺7am-9pm) About the best bet for grub in town is this casual, open-air hall, a popular gathering place both morning and evening. Aside from the usual eggs-and-beans, they do *pinchos* (brochettes), served with abundant portions of salad, beans and rice, and fries, and the papaya smoothies are heavenly.

ℹ Getting There & Away

Southbound from Sayaxché, four microbuses head for Cobán (Q60, four hours) between 5am and 3pm. Every 25 minutes or so, Raxrujá-bound microbuses go to the San Antonio junction (Q30, 1½ hours), from where there are frequent departures for Cobán. Vehicles depart from a lot just up from the ferry dock. From the north side of the Río de la Pasión, microbuses leave for Santa Elena every 15 minutes from 5:45am to 6:30pm (Q23, 1½ hours).

For river transportation, contact **Viajes Don Pedro** (☎4580-9389; servlanchasdonpedro@hotmail.com).

Around Sayaxché

Of the archaeological sites reached from Sayaxché, Ceibal and Aguateca are the most interesting to the amateur visitor. Both are impressively restored and can be reached by boat trips along jungle-fringed waterways followed by forest walks. Most people arrive in the context of a tour but it is possible to make arrangements independently.

Getting to any of the archaeological sites around Sayaxché involves making arrangements with boat operators in Sayaxché, or taking a tour. Viajes Don Pedro (p229) offers a straightforward half-day return trip from Sayaxché to Aguateca, charging Q600 for up to five people. You could, for example, arrange to be dropped at one of the lodges afterwards and be picked up the next afternoon after making a trip to Dos Pilas. **Martsam Travel** (☎7832-2742, US 1-866-832-2776; www.martsam.com; Calle 30 de Junio, Flores) and other outfits in Flores offer one-day tours to Aguateca, including lunch and guide.

Aguateca ARCHAEOLOGICAL SITE

(⊙8am-4:30pm) FREE The ruins of Aguateca stand on a hilltop at the far south end of Laguna Petexbatún. Defended by cliffs and split by a ravine, the city enjoyed military successes (including one over nearby Ceibal) up until about AD 735, according to data gleaned from carved stelae. The site is both the easiest reached and most immediately impressive within reach of Sayaxché.

It's fairly certain that rulers from Dos Pilas abandoned that city for the better-fortified Aguateca around AD 761, and that the city was finally overrun by unknown attackers around 790 – a wealth of arrow-heads and skeletons have been found dating back to that time. It was abandoned shortly afterwards.

The visitor center is a five-minute walk from the dock. Rangers can guide you round the site in about 1½ hours (a small tip is in order). Two main groups feature well-restored structures: the **Grupo del Palacio** where the ruler lived, and the **Plaza Mayor** (Main Plaza) to its south, where fiberglass copies of stelae showing finely attired rulers stand beside the fallen originals. The two groups are connected by a causeway over the ravine.

From the visitor center, you can skirt the cliff wall north to reach a **mirador** (lookout) with views over the rivers and swampland toward the east. The trail then turns left and descends into the ravine, continuing 100m between two sheer limestone walls, then climbs back up to emerge onto the Grupo del Palacio. Proceed through the palatial complex back toward the entrance. At the lower end, turn right to take the causeway over the ravine (70m deep here) to reach the Main Plaza.

Aguateca is a 1¼-hour *lancha* (small motorboat) trip direct from Sayaxché, via the mangrove-fringed Río Petexbatún.

Ceibal

With its strategic position along the west bank of the Río de la Pasión, the independent kingdom of **Ceibal** (Q60; ⊙8am-4pm) amassed considerable power controlling commerce along this key stretch of the waterway. Though architecturally less amazing than some other sites, the river journey to Ceibal is among the most memorable, as is hiking below the jungle canopy with monkeys howling overhead.

There's a large scale model of the site by the entrance. The ceremonial core of the city covers three hills, connected over steep ravines by the original causeways. Smallish temples, many of them covered with jungle, surround two principal groups, A and D. In front of some temples, and standing seemingly alone on paths, are magnificent stelae, their intricate carvings still in excellent condition.

It takes about two hours to explore the site. Bring mosquito repellent.

There's nowhere to eat or sleep at Ceibal. Most visitors arrive in the context of a tour (which usually includes lunch) and stay in Sayaxché or Flores. Your other eating option is to pack a picnic in Sayaxché.

History

Unimportant during most of the Classic period, Ceibal (sometimes spelled Seibal) grew rapidly in the 9th century AD. It attained a population of around 10,000 by AD 900, then was abandoned shortly afterwards. Its low, ruined temples were quickly covered by a thick carpet of jungle. Excavation of the site is ongoing under the supervision of University of Arizona archaeologist Takeshi Inomata.

⊙ Sights

Most of the stelae appear at **Grupo A**, made up of three plazas at the site's highest point. At the best excavated of these, Plaza Sur, stands **Structure A-3**, a pyramidal platform with a stela on each side and one at the top. Some of the characters depicted here have distinctly non-Maya features and dress, which has led to speculation that foreigners once inhabited the area. According to one hotly debated theory, the city was invaded by Putun Maya, a race of merchant-warriors from the Tabasco area of Mexico, around the mid-9th century. This might account for the 'foreign' look of the moustachioed warrior on **stele 11**, for example, who stands on the east side of the platform.

Calzada I leads east to **Grupo D**, a more compact series of temples that backs up on a precipitous gorge. About midway is a turnoff south for Calzada II, just beyond which is the fantastically preserved stela 14, which may depict a tax collector. Proceeding down Calzada II to the south, you reach the intriguing **Structure 79**. Three stone steps surround the unusual ring-shaped structure, which stands alone in a clearing with

Ceibal

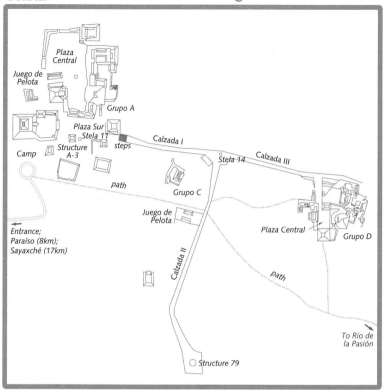

N ↑   0 ▬▬▬▬▬▬▬ 50 m

Plaza Central

Juego de Pelota

Grupo A

Plaza Sur

Stela 11

Calzada I

Camp

Structure A-3

steps

Stela 14

Calzada III

Entrance;
Paraíso (8km);
Sayaxché (17km)

path

Grupo C

Juego de Pelota

Plaza Central

Grupo D

Calzada II

path

To Río de
la Pasión

Structure 79

a small altar in the shape of a jaguar's head. It is believed to have served as an astronomical observatory, from which the inhabitants studied planetary movements.

ⓘ Getting There & Away

Viajes Don Pedro (p229) in Sayaxché, on the north side of the river, runs *lanchas* here (Q600 for up to five passengers). The fee should include a guide, who may actually be the boat operator. In high season, ask the *lancheros* about joining a tour group.

The one-hour boat ride up the Río de la Pasión brings you to a primitive dock. After landing, you clamber up a narrow, rocky path beneath gigantic ceiba trees and jumbles of jungle vines to reach the archaeological zone, perched about 100m above the river.

Alternatively, Ceibal can be reached over land: get any bus, minibus or pick-up heading south from Sayaxché on Hwy 5 (toward Raxrujá and Chisec) and get off after 9km at Paraíso, from where it's an 8km walk east down a dirt track to

Ceibal. About 2km in, where the road bends left by a small farmhouse, continue straight uphill to enter the park – there's no sign. In the rainy season check first that this stretch is passable.

Laguna Petexbatún

Laguna Petexbatún is a 6km-long lake southwest of Sayaxché, approached by an hour's *lancha* ride up the Río Petexbatún, a tributary of the Río de la Pasión. The lake, river and surrounding forests harbor many birds, including kingfishers, egrets, vultures, eagles, cormorants and herons. Within reach of the waterways are five archaeological sites and a pair of jungle-hideaway accommodations.

What we know of the history of these archaeological sites has mostly been unraveled by archaeologists since the late 1980s. Dos Pilas was founded about AD 640 by a prince who left Tikal and later defeated it in two wars, capturing its ruler Nuun Ujol Chaak (Shield Skull) in 679, according to inscriptions at the site. Dos Pilas' second and third rulers carried out monumental building programs, waged wars of conquest and came to dominate most of the territory between the Pasión and Chixoy rivers, but in AD 761 their vassal Tamarindito rebelled and killed the fourth ruler, causing the Dos Pilas nobility to relocate to the naturally fortified site of Aguateca, which was already functioning as a twin capital. Aguateca in turn was abandoned in the early 9th century, around the same time as three defensive moats were cut across the neck of the Chiminos peninsula on the edge of Laguna Petexbatún. Archaeologists surmise that Punta de Chiminos was the last refuge of the Petexbatún dynasty founded at Dos Pilas.

🛏 Sleeping & Eating

Two lodges, one on the Laguna Petexbatún (www.chiminosisland.com; r adult/child under 13yr incl 3 meals Q1030/575) and another (☏5304-1745; www.posadacaribe.com; bungalow Q380) on the river down to it, provide ecologically sound jungle experiences.

Both of the ecolodges at Laguna Petexbatún prepare meals; otherwise there's nowhere to eat around the principal archaeological sites.

❶ Getting There & Away

Laguna Petexbatún is most conveniently reached by motorboat. Most visitors are brought here by one of the lodges in the vicinity or by tour operators in Flores. To arrive independently, try any of the boat operators in Sayaxché, who charge around Q600 for a half-day tour of the lake including a visit to Aguateca (p230).

Dos Pilas

This fascinating site is a mere 16km from Sayaxché, but getting here is a serious undertaking. If you have the time, it's well worth considering for the fine carvings on display, particularly the hieroglyphic staircase, with five 6m-wide steps, each with two rows of superbly preserved glyphs, climbing to the base of the royal palace near the main plaza. (But find out if it's currently visible as archaeologists may cover it up.) In addition, a number of stelae standing here are in excellent shape with clear inscriptions.

Dos Pilas began life as a breakaway from the Tikal group when that city was taken by Calakmul. It appears to have been governed by a set of aggressive rulers – it clashed with Tikal, Ceibal, Yaxchilán and Motul all with-

in 150 years, often ignoring the traditional 'war season', which finished in time for the harvest.

The best way to reach Dos Pilas is by tour from Sayaxché or by staying at the Posada Caribe (p232) and organizing a tour there. Either way, you'll be driven over a rough road to Aldea El Nacimiento (one hour or more depending on the degree of muddiness), then you'll hike for about half an hour to the site. Camping is an option.

Finca Ixobel

This resort (☏5410-4307; www.fincaixobel. com; campsite Q35, dm Q50, s/d Q180/315, without bathroom Q85/135, treehouse from Q90/140; 🅿@🛜) 🦯 is an ecological resort/bohemian hideaway set amid pine forest and patches of jungle between Flores and Río Dulce set in southeast Petén. With a friendly, relaxed atmosphere, a wide range of activities, accommodation options and lip-smacking homemade meals, it's a great place to meet fellow travelers.

Everything at Finca Ixobel works on the honor system: guests keep an account of what they eat and drink and the services they use.

If this place suits your style and you want to help/hang out for six weeks minimum, ask about volunteering.

The grounds contain a natural pool for swimming. Additionally, horseback riding treks (from two hours to four days), cave trips and inner-tubing on the Río Machaquilá (in the rainy season) are all organized on a daily basis. One of the most popular excursions is to the caves of Naj Tunich (p234) with their galleries of Maya painting; the cost of Q310 per person (with a group of four) includes admission, guide and lunch. Another trip combines a visit to ruins at Ixcún, with swimming at the waterfalls on the Río Mopán.

Among the numerous options for bedding down at the Finca are palapas (thatched palm-leaf shelters) for hanging hammocks, bungalows and 'treehouses' – most of which are actually cabins on stilts. The large, grassy camping area has good bathrooms and plenty of shade. Assorted other accommodations include a couple of dormitories and rooms with shared and private bathroom, all with fan, mosquito nets and screened windows.

Meals are excellent, including an eat-all-you-like buffet dinner. Finca Ixobel has its own bakery, grows its own salad ingredients and produces its own eggs. You can cook in the campground if you bring your own supplies.

 Getting There & Away

Finca Ixobel is 5km south of the regional commercial center of Poptún, from where you can take a taxi (Q30) or *tuk-tuk* (Q20). Otherwise, any bus or minibus along Hwy 13 can drop you at the turnoff, from where it's a 15-minute walk to the lodge. Departing, most buses will stop on the highway to pick you up, but not after dark.

The best way to get to Poptún from Flores/ Santa Elena is to take a minibus from the main terminal (Q30, every 10 minutes, 5am to 7pm); tell the driver where you're heading and he'll drop you at the lodge. Coming from Guatemala City or Río Dulce, all Santa Elena–bound buses make a stop in Poptún.

Around Finca Ixobel

◉ Sights

Museo Regional del Sureste de Petén   MUSEUM
(☑ 7926-6033; Q30; ⊗ 8:30am-4:30pm Tue-Sun) Displaying some of the most significant finds from southern Petén sites, this museum is the main draw of Dolores, a town 25km north of Poptún along the CA13. The collection features pottery, arrowheads and stelae dating from throughout the history of Classic Maya civilization.

EL PETÉN FINCA IXOBEL

EXPLORE MORE OF EL PETÉN

The Petén region is literally brimming with archaeological sites in various stages of excavation. Some are harder than others to get to; tour operators in Flores and El Remate can help you reach them. Here are a few of the more intriguing ones that you might want to check out:

San Bartolo Discovered in 2003, this site features one of the best-preserved Maya murals with a depiction of the creation myth from the Popul Vuh. It's approximately 40km northeast of Uaxactún, near the Río Azul.

Piedras Negras On the banks of the Río Usumacinta amid black cliffs, these remote ruins boast impressive carvings and a sizable acropolis complex. It was here that part-time archaeologist Tatiana Proskouriakoff deciphered the Maya hieroglyphic system.

La Blanca Located along the Río Mopan near the Belize border, this palatial complex may have flourished as a trading center in the late Classic period. The acropolis is notable for its remarkably preserved stone walls and an abundance of graffiti. Currently under excavation by a Spanish team. The **Mayan Adventure** (☑ 5830-2060; www.the-mayan-adventure.com; Calle 15 de Septiembre, Flores), based in Flores, leads tours here.

El Zotz This sprawling site occupies its own biotope abutting Tikal National Park. Of the three barely excavated temples, one, the Pirámide del Diablo, can be scaled for views all the way to Tikal. Stick around till dusk to see how the place gets its name – 'The Bat' in Maya. Researchers from the University of Southern California are currently uncovering 23 masks within the tombs of the largest pyramid. INGUAT-authorized guides from the community of Cruce Dos Aguadas (42km north of Flores) lead **tours to El Zotz** (☑ 4646-8019), a 24km hike east through the jungle.

Río Azul Located up near the corner where the Belize, Guatemala and Mexico borders meet, this medium-sized site fell under the domain of Tikal in the early Classic period and became a key trading post for cacao from the Caribbean. Most notable are the tombs with vibrant painted glyphs inside. Campamento El Chiclero (p257) in Uaxactún leads a recommended excursion.

Naranjo Major excavations and restorations are currently going on at this immense site 12km from the Belize border. In the process archaeologists have ascertained that the city was more densely populated than Tikal and possibly larger. Ruled by Princess Six Sky, daughter to a Dos Pilas governor, Naranjo conquered neighboring kingdoms and produced some of the most refined art in the Maya world. Contact Río Mopan Lodge (p240) about visiting the site.

Naj Tunich   CAVE

(☎5034-7317; www.rutanajtunich.com; ⊙8am-6pm) FREE When they were discovered in 1979, these caves created a stir in the archaeological world. Measuring 3km long, they're packed with hieroglyphic texts and Maya murals depicting religious ceremonies, art education, ball games and even sex scenes – though whether they're of a gay nature is still being disputed by anthropologists.

In all, there are 94 images, completed during the Maya Classic period. Scribes and artists traveled from as far away as Calakmul in Mexico to contribute to the murals.

The caves were closed in 1984 due to vandalism, reopened briefly, then closed permanently a decade later for conservation purposes. Fortunately, a superb replica has been created in a nearby cave. Reproductions of the murals were painted by local artists under the supervision of archaeological and cultural authorities.

Finca Ixobel (p232) runs tours to Naj Tunich, traveling by Land Rover to the nearby community of La Compuerta, then continuing on foot to the cave. Proceeds from the tour go to development projects in local communities.

Ixcún   ARCHAEOLOGICAL SITE

(☎7926-6052; www.rutanajtunich.com; Q30; ⊙8am-5pm) The second-largest stela in the Maya world can be viewed amid a protected jungle zone at the remains of a late-Classic Maya kingdom, an hour's walk (7km) north of Dolores. Depicting a ruler wearing a headdress of quetzal feathers, it stands at one end of a large ceremonial center of three plazas, an unrestored temple and an acropolis.

Archaeologists speculate that the complex of structures on the Plaza Principal may have been used as an astronomical observatory. Ixcún's sister city, Ixtontón, a major trading center until the 11th century AD, is another 6km along the Río Mopán.

Flores & Santa Elena

POP 85,000

With its cubist houses cascading down from a central plaza to the emerald waters of Lago de Petén Itzá, the island town of Flores evokes a Mediterranean ambience. A 500m causeway connects Flores to its humbler sister town of Santa Elena on the lake shore, which then merges into the even homelier community of San Benito to the west. The three towns actually form one large settlement, often referred to simply as Flores.

Flores proper is by far the more attractive base. Small hotels and restaurants line the streets, many featuring rooftop terraces with lake views. Residents take great pride in their island-town's gorgeousness, and a promenade runs around its perimeter. Flores does have a twee, built-up edge to it, though, and some Tikal-bound budget travelers opt for the tranquility of El Remate, just down the road.

Santa Elena is where you'll find banks, buses and a major shopping mall.

History

Flores was founded on a *petén* (island) by the Itzáes, who came here after being expelled from Chichén Itzá on Mexico's Yucatán Peninsula, probably in the mid-15th century. They called it Tah Itzá (place of the Itzá), which the Spanish later corrupted to Tayasal. Hernán Cortés dropped in on King Canek of Tayasal in 1525 on his way to Honduras, but the meeting was, amazingly, peaceable. Cortés left behind a lame horse, which the Itzáes fed on flowers and turkey stew. When it died, the Itzáes made a statue of it, which, by the time a couple of Spanish friars visited in 1618, was being worshiped as a manifestation of the rain god Chac. It was not until 1697 that the Spaniards brought the Itzáes of Tayasal – by some distance the last surviving independent Maya kingdom – forcibly under their control. The Spanish soldiers destroyed its many pyramids, temples and statues, and today you won't see a trace of them, although the modern town is doubtless built on the ruins and foundations of Maya Tayasal.

◉ Sights

Flores is great for strolling, especially now that the lakefront promenade that rings the islet is complete – though rising lake levels have submerged much of the northern section. In the center, atop a rise, is the Parque Central, with its double-domed cathedral, **Nuestra Señora de los Remedios**.

Museo Santa Bárbara   MUSEUM

(☎7926-2813; www.radiopeten.com.gt; Isle of Santa Bárbara; Q20; ⊙8am-noon & 2-5pm) On an islet to the west of Flores, this little museum holds a grab bag of Maya artifacts from nearby archaeological sites, plus some old broadcasting equipment from Radio Petén

(88.5 FM), which still broadcasts from an adjacent building. Phone ahead and they'll pick you up (Q20 per person) at the dock behind Hotel Santana (☑7926-5123; www.santanapeten.com.gt; Calle 30 de Junio, Flores; s/d/tr Q385/500/600; ❋@🌐🐕).

After browsing the museum, take a wander round the islet, watch birds poking round the twigs off the banks, then enjoy chilled coconuts at the cafe by the dock.

🏃 Activities

The Guatemalan NGO Arcas (Asociación de Rescate y Conservación de Vida Silvestre; ☑7830-1374; www.arcasguatemala.com/volunteering) has a rescue and rehabilitation center for wildlife on the mainland northeast of Flores, where volunteers 'adopt' and feed animals, such as macaws, parrots, jaguars and coatis, that have been rescued from smugglers and the illegal pet trade. The fee of Q1335 a week covers food and accommodation.

Language schools in nearby San Andrés and San José provide the chance to get involved in community and environmental projects.

👉 Tours

Various travel agencies in Flores offer day tours to archaeological sites such as Tikal, Uaxactún, Yaxhá and Ceibal. Prices, with a guide and lunch, range from Q100 for a basic Tikal tour (by Hostel Los Amigos) to Q1200 for a Ceibal excursion.

More demanding hiking-and-camping experiences to remote archaeological sites such as Nakum, El Perú, El Zotz, El Mirador, Nakbé and Wakná/El Perú are also offered by local tour operators.

Maya Expeditions (p52), based in Guatemala City, offers mild (ie good for families or inexperienced rafters) one- to three-day rafting expeditions on the Río Chiquibul, with options to visit lesser-known sites such as Yaxhá, Nakum and Topoxte for Q650 to Q3490 per person.

Comisión de Turismo
Cooperativa Carmelita Agency   TREKKING
(☑7867-5629; www.turismocooperativacarmelita.com; Calle Centro América, Flores) Flores agency for this Carmelita-based cooperative of trekking guides.

👉 Lake Tours

Boats can be hired for lake tours at the *embarcaderos* opposite Hotel Petenchel and beside the Hotel Santana in Flores, and in the middle of the Flores–Santa Elena causeway. Prices are negotiable. An hourlong jaunt runs around Q150. A three-hour tour, which might include the Petencito Zoo, the isle of Santa Bárbara and its museum and the ruins of Tayazal should cost Q350, with stops and waiting time included.

🛏 Sleeping

Except for a few upscale properties along Santa Elena's waterfront, Flores is by far the more desirable place to stay, unless you have a thing for traffic and dust.

Hostal Frida   HOSTEL $
(☑7926-5427; fridahostel@gmail.com; Callejón El Rosario, Flores; dm Q45) Run by the hospitable Magdalena and family, who also have an alternative beauty salon/cafe nearer the lake, this low-key hostel is in a typical old house with garden at the rear. The dorms are pretty basic with bathrooms behind a partition but it's kept clean. Guest kitchen available.

Hostel Los Amigos   HOSTEL $
(☑7867-5075; www.amigoshostel.com; Calle Central, Flores; dm Q70-90, r with/without bathroom Q320/180; @) Far and away the most popular backpackers haven in El Petén, this hostel has grown organically in its 13 years of existence and now includes various sleeping options, from six- and 10-bed dorms to a treehouse. All the global traveler's perks are here in abundance: herbal steam bath,

EL PETÉN FLORES & SANTA ELENA

TOURS TO LOCAL ARCHAEOLOGICAL SITES

The sample prices are per person for two/three/four-plus people, normally including food, water, sleeping gear and Spanish-speaking guide.

LOCATION	DURATION	COST
El Zotz & Tikal	3 days	Q3300/2455/2110
El Perú & Est Biológica Las Guacamayas	3 days	Q3685/3070/2765
El Mirador-Nakbé-Wakná	7 days	Q5830/4335/3840
Yaxhá & Nakum	2 days	Q2455/2075/1920

Flores

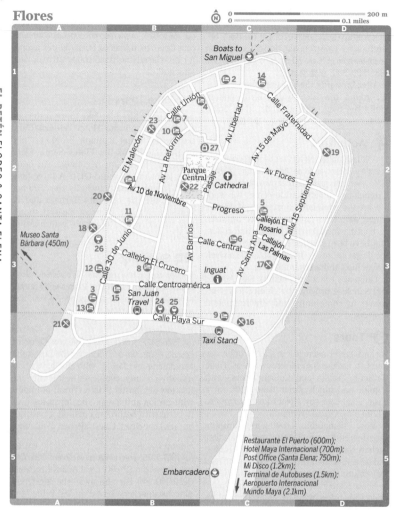

0 ——————— 200 m
0 ——————— 0.1 miles

Boats to San Miguel

Calle Unión
Calle Fraternidad
El Malecón
Av La Reforma
Av Libertad
Av 15 de Mayo
Av 10 de Noviembre
Parque Central
Pasaje
Cathedral
Av Flores
Av 15 de Septiembre
Progreso
Callejón El Rosario
Callejón Las Palmas
Av Barrios
Calle Central
Av Santa Ana
Calle 30 de Junio
Callejón El Crucero
Inguat
Calle Centroamérica
San Juan Travel
Calle Playa Sur
Taxi Stand
Calle Playa Sur
Museo Santa Bárbara (450m)
Embarcadero

Restaurante El Puerto (600m);
Hotel Maya Internacional (700m);
Post Office (Santa Elena; 750m);
Mi Disco (1.2km);
Terminal de Autobuses (1.5km);
Aeropuerto Internacional
Mundo Maya (2.1km)

pool table, hammocks, heaping helpings of organic food, yoga and cut-rate jungle tours.

Despite the good-time atmosphere, it's lights out after 10, but the fun goes on in an ingeniously soundproofed night lounge upstairs. A new annex around the corner is quieter, with seven originally designed rooms.

Hospedaje Doña Goya   HOSTEL $

(✆7867-5513;   hospedajedonagoya@yahoo.com; Calle Unión, Flores; dm Q40, s/d Q120/160, without bathroom Q90/120; 🐾) This family-run guesthouse makes a fine budget choice. Though ultra-basic, the sheets are clean, the fans

work, the water's hot and the paint's fresh. Dorms, too, are spacious and spotless. Best of all is the roof terrace with a palm-thatched shelter and hammocks.

Hotel El Peregrino   HOTEL $

(✆7867-5701;   peregrino@itelgua.com;   Av La Reforma, Flores; s/d Q120/160, without bathroom Q70/120; ❄) El Peregrino is an older, family-run place with home cooking in the front comedor (basic, cheap eatery). Large rooms with tile floors and powerful overhead fans line up along plant-festooned corridors – no views here.

Flores

Posada de la Jungla   HOTEL $

(☑ 7867-5185; lajungla@martsam.com; Calle Centroamérica 30, Flores; s/d Q120/180, with air-con Q190/280; ✳⊜) Worth considering is this slender, three-story building with front balconies. Though a bit cramped, rooms are comfortably arranged, with quality beds.

Hotel Aurora   HOTEL $

(☑ 7867-5516; aldeamaya@gmail.com; Calle Unión, Flores; dm/s/d Q40/Q75/150; ✳@⊜) This backpacker haven's got a jungle theme, with banisters made to look like climbing vines. Rooms are plain, airy and well scrubbed, with screened windows, and most have some kind of view. A super roof terrace features an open-air shelter slung with hammocks. Guest kitchen available.

Hotel Flores de Petén   HOTEL $

(☑ 4718-2635; Calle Sur, Flores; s/d/tr Q125/170/200; ⊜) The first hotel you reach coming off the causeway has bright and spacious rooms with cut-rate furniture and a terrace for lake-gazing. The steady flow of traffic from Santa Elena means you'll probably be up early.

Green World Hotel   HOTEL $

(☑ 7867-5662; greenworldhotel@gmail.com; Calle 30 de Junio, Flores; s/d Q125/175, with air-con Q205/275; ✳@⊜) This low-key shoreline property features an interior patio and an upper sundeck overlooking the lake. Compact, low-lit rooms have safes, enormous ceiling fans and good hot showers – number 8, with its rear balcony, is by far the nicest.

Hotel Santa Bárbara   HOTEL $$

(☑ 7926-2813; radiopeten.com.gt; s/d/tr Q200/400/500; ✳⊜) Part of a trio that includes a museum (p234) and cafe, this is a perfect retreat from the hubbub of Flores on an islet just five minutes west by *lancha* (included in price). Three comfy cabins with big beds and tile floors overlook the lake past a garden brimming with coconut palms and a ceiba tree. Highly recommended.

La Posada de Don José   HOTEL $$

(☑ 7867-5298; cnr Calle del Malecón & Calle Fraternidad, Flores; dm Q60, s/d Q175/250, without bathroom Q125/175; ✳⊜) Near the northern tip of the island, this is an old-fashioned establishment (check the lobby for a portrait of the founder) with rocking chairs scattered around a plant-laden patio and a friendly family that knows your name. The lake level has reclaimed the *malecón* (jetty) here, making the rear terrace infinitely more peaceful than further down.

Besides the neat little rooms, there's a spacious fan-cooled dorm in back.

Hospedaje Yaxha   HOSTEL $$

(☑ 5830-2060; www.cafeyaxha.com; Calle 15 de Septiembre, Flores; dm/s/d Q60/150/200) A haven for archaeologists, historians and fans of pre-Hispanic cuisine, Café Yaxha (p239) now offers a clean and simple place to lay your head. There's a four-bed dorm, private rooms with bathroom, and an apartment – all with quality mattresses and ceiling fans.

Mayaland Plaza Hotel
HOTEL **$$**

(☑ 7926-4976; mayalandplaza@yahoo.com; 6a Av & 4a Calle, Santa Elena; s/d/tr Q225/285/375; **P ✳ @ ☎**) The spacious comfortable rooms are set colonial-style around a peaceful courtyard. All services are on hand, including a recommended restaurant and travel agent.

Hotel La Casona de la Isla
HOTEL **$$**

(☑ 7867-5203; www.hotelesdepeten.com; Calle 30 de Junio, Flores; s/d/tr Q390/450/550; **✳ @ ☎**) Popular with package travelers, this place has a Caribbean flavor. Smallish rooms line a long veranda facing a pool with a rock garden and adjacent lake-view deck for sunset dining. The most appealing units, 31, 303 and 304, have windows facing the lake.

Hotel Petén
HOTEL **$$**

(☑ 7867-5203; www.hotelesdepeten.com; Calle 30 de Junio, Flores; s/d/tr incl breakfast Q380/480/600; **✳ @ ☎ ☎**) Rooms are cheerily decorated here with a dash of chintz. Definitely choose the lake balcony units as they cost no more than interior ones. A good-sized swimming pool straddles the courtyard and rear deck, and the restaurant/bar opens on a lakeside terrace.

Casa Amelia
BOUTIQUE HOTEL **$$**

(☑ 7867-5430; www.hotelcasamelia.com; Calle Unión, Flores; s/d Q350/450; **✳ @ ☎**) Standing tall along Flores' western shore, the Amelia offers bright, stylish chambers with excellent lake views; rooms 301 and 302 are best, opening on the superb balustraded roof terrace.

Casazul
BOUTIQUE HOTEL **$$**

(☑ 7867-5451; www.hotelesdepeten.com; Calle Unión, Flores; d/tr Q440/496; **✳ ☎**) As the name suggests, it's blue all over, from the plantation-style balconies to the nine individually decorated, spacious and comfortable rooms. A couple have their own balconies and everyone can enjoy the beautiful top-floor terrace.

Hotel Isla de Flores
HOTEL **$$$**

(☑ 2476-8775; www.hotelisladeflores.com; Av La Reforma, Flores; s/d Q544/616; **✳ ☎ ☎**) This newish option sports an understated tropical style that's highly appealing. Hardwood beams frame bone-white walls with floral motifs that are echoed on cool stone floors, and large firm beds back up on painted headboards. Though it doesn't stand on the lake shore, the plank-deck roof terrace, with

a small pool, commands fantastic views over the whole island.

Enjoy mojitos and fusion cuisine in the equally stylish street-level cafe.

Hotel del Patio
HOTEL **$$$**

(☑ 7926-0104; http://hoteldelpatio.com.gt; cnr 8a Av & 2a Calle, Santa Elena; r Q780; **P ✳ @ ☎ ☎**) Shady corridors lined with terracotta floors wind around a stunning courtyard, centered on a gurgling fountain. Rooms are tasteful and comfortable, though not quite as luxurious as the courtyard.

Hotel Maya Internacional
HOTEL **$$$**

(☑ 7926-2083; www.villasdeguatemala.com; Calle Litoral del Lago, Santa Elena; s/d/tr incl breakfast Q465/550/670; **P ✳ @ ☎ ☎**) One of the best reasons to stay in Santa Elena is this tropical-chic resort spreading over a landscaped marsh by the waterfront. The big-top dining room is the center of activity; an adjacent wooden deck with a small infinity pool is great for sunset daiquiris. A boardwalk snakes through tropical gardens to reach the 26 thatch-and-teak rooms.

Rooms 49 to 54 have the best lake views.

✖ Eating

As might be expected, Flores is rife with tourist-oriented joints pitching a bland melange of 'international' fare to the package crowd. Nevertheless, a few local gems rise above the pack.

Las Mesitas
GUATEMALAN **$**

(El Malecón, Flores; snacks Q5-10; ⏱ 3-10pm) Every evening, but especially Sundays, there's a street party on the waterfront promenade, as local families fix enchiladas (actually *tostadas* topped with guacamole, chicken salad and so on), tacos and tamales, and dispense fruity drinks from giant jugs. All kinds of cakes and puddings are served, too. Everyone sits on plastic chairs or low barrier walls.

Cool Beans
CAFE **$**

(☑ 5571-9240; Calle 15 de Septiembre, Flores; breakfast Q25-35; ⏱ 7am-10pm Mon-Sat; ☎) Also known as Café Chilero, this laid-back place is more clubhouse with snacks than proper restaurant, featuring salons for chatting, watching videos or laptop browsing. The lush garden with glimpses of the lake makes a *tranquilo* spot for breakfast or veggie burgers. Be warned – the kitchen closes at 9:01pm sharp.

Restaurante El Mirador
GUATEMALAN $

(☑ 7867-5246; Parque Central, Flores; set menu Q25; ☉ 7am-10pm Mon-Sat) Refreshingly not aimed at foreign travelers, this traditional eatery does toothsome home cookin'. You'll find such hearty options as *caldo de res* (beef stew), served with all the trimmings, and *fresco* (fruit drink) in the bright lunch hall that looks over the treetops. It's next to the basketball court on the Parque Central.

Café/Bar Doña Goya
CAFE $

(El Malecón, Flores; breakfast Q35-50; ☉ 6:30am-10pm; 🛜) Doña Goya's is good for an early breakfast or sunset snack, with a pretty terrace facing the lake. Toward the weekend, it blends into the nightlife scene along this stretch of the promenade, with occasional live music.

Restaurante Mijaro
RESTAURANT $

(☑ 7926-1615; www.restaurantemijaro.com; 6a Av, Santa Elena; meals Q25-40; ☉ 7am-10pm) You'll find good home cooking at this locally popular *comedor* a few blocks south of the causeway, with an airy thatch-roofed garden area. Besides the grub, they do good long *limonadas* (lime-juice drinks).

⭐Terrazzo
ITALIAN $$

(Calle Unión, Flores; pasta Q70-80; ☉ 8am-10pm Mon-Sat) Inspired by a chef from Bologna, this Italian gourmet restaurant covers a romantic rooftop terrace. The fettuccine, tortellini and gnocchi are all produced in house, the pizzas (made of seasoned dough) are grilled rather than baked, and the fresh mint lemonade is incredible. All this, and the service is the most attentive in town.

Antojitos Mexicanos
STEAK $$

(Calle Playa Sur, Flores; grilled meats Q50-60; ☉ 7-10pm) Every evening at the foot of the causeway these characters fire up the grill and char steak, chicken and pork ribs of exceptional quality. Their specialty is *puyazo* (sirloin) swathed with garlic sauce. Sit outside facing the twinkly lights on the lake or, if it's raining, inside under a tin roof. Staff behave with all the formality of an elegant restaurant. Also known as 'Don Fredy.'

Raíces
STEAK $$

(☑ 7867-5743; Calle Sur, Flores; mains Q90-175; ☉ noon-10pm) A broad deck and a flaming grill are the main ingredients at this stylish lakefront restaurant/bar, possibly the prettiest setting in Flores for dinner. Chargrilled meats and seafood are the specialty; they also do wood-oven pizzas.

Restaurante El Peregrino
GUATEMALAN $$

(☑ 7867-5115; Av La Reforma, Flores; mains Q40-60; ☉ 7am-10pm) Part of the hotel of the same name, this humble *comedor* serves heaping helpings of home-cooked fare such as pork-belly stew and breaded tongue. Ask for the daily lunch specials (Q25).

Café Arqueológico Yaxha
CAFE $$

(☑ 4934-6353; www.cafeyaxha.com; Calle 15 de Septiembre, Flores; mains Q45-70; ☉ 6:30am-10pm) Apart from the usual egg-and-bean breakfasts, what's special here are the pre-Hispanic and Itzá items – pancakes with *ramón* seeds, yucca scrambled with *mora* herbs, chicken in *chaya* sauce.

Restaurante El Puerto
SEAFOOD $$

(1a Calle 2-15, Santa Elena; mains Q90-100; ☉ 11am-11pm) Seafood is the star attraction at this breezy, open-air hall by the lakefront in Santa Elena, with a well-stocked bar at the front. It's an ideal setting to enjoy shellfish stews, *ceviches* or the famous *pescado blanco* – whitefish from the lake.

🍷 Drinking & Nightlife

Flores' little Zona Viva is traditionally the strip of bars along Calle Sur, but there's plenty of action around the bend, along the lakefront promenade north of Hotel Santana.

Qué Pachanga
CLUB

(El Malecón, Flores) One of a pair of lively nightspots round the west side of the island, this room gets heavy most evenings, when young Guatemalans decked out in their tightest possible jeans gyrate to a continuous barrage of throbbing reggaetón and *cumbia* (Colombian dance tunes).

El Trópico
BAR

(Calle Sur, Flores; ☉ 4:30pm-1am Mon-Sat) Longest running of the bars along the southern bank, El Trópico supplies tacos and *cerveza* (beer) to a mostly older Guatemalan clientele. The candlelit terrace is a nice spot to start the night, as the lights of Santa Elena reflect pleasingly off the lake. Many gallos (tortilla sandwiches) later, the pulse picks up and DJs work the crowd.

Jamming
BAR

(Calle Sur, Flores) One of several nightlife venues along the southern bank, Jamming sports a reggae theme though there's more beer guzzling than ganja smoking. It attracts a younger set of middle-class Guatemalans.

Shopping

Castillo de Arizmendi HANDICRAFTS
(Parque Central, Flores; ⊙9am-6pm) A monument to Martín de Ursúa Arizmendi y Aguirre, who snatched the island from the Maya in 1697, the castle on the main plaza's north side houses a series of shops with local handicrafts, particularly tropical hardwood carvings by artists from El Remate working in mahogany, cedar and *chicozapote*.

Information

EMERGENCY
Hospital Privado Santa Elena (☑7926-1140; 3a Av 4-29, Zona 2, Santa Elena)
Police Station (☑7926-1365; Calle Límite 12-28, San Benito)
Tourist Police (Proatur; ☑5414-3594; proatur. peten1@gmail.com; Calle Centro América)

MONEY
Banrural (Av Flores, Flores) bank, just off the Parque Central, changes US dollar and euros, cash or traveler's checks. Many travel agencies and places to stay will change cash US dollars and sometimes traveler's checks, though at poorer rates.

The only **ATM** (Calle 30 de Junio, Flores) in Flores is at the Fotomart convenience store, opposite Capitán Tortuga. There are plenty of other banks with ATMs along 4a Calle in Santa Elena.

POST
Post Office (4a Calle & 4a Av; ⊙8am-5pm Mon-Sat) Inside Centro Comercial Karossi, Santa Elena.

TOURIST INFORMATION
INGUAT (☑2421-2800, ext 6303; info-ciudad flores@inguat.gob.gt; Calle Centro América, Flores; ⊙8am-4pm Mon-Sat) The official INGUAT office provides basic information. There's another **branch** (☑7926-0533; info-mundomaya@inguat.gob.mx; Aeropuerto Internacional Mundo Maya; ⊙7am-noon & 3-5pm) at the airport.

ⓘ Getting There & Away

AIR
Aeropuerto Internacional Mundo Maya is on the eastern outskirts of Santa Elena, 2km from the causeway connecting Santa Elena and Flores. **Avianca** (www.avianca.com) has two flights daily between here and Guatemala City. The Belizean airline **Tropic Air** (☑7926-0348; www. tropicair.com) flies once a day to/from Belize City, charging around Q1500 each way for the one-hour trip.

BUS
Long-distance buses use the Terminal Nuevo de Autobuses in Santa Elena, located 1.5km south of the causeway along 6a Av. It is also used by a slew of *aka expresos* (microbuses), with frequent services to numerous destinations. Second-class buses and some micros make an additional stop at 5a Calle, in the market area (the 'old' terminal) before heading out. You can reduce your trip time by 15 minutes by going straight to the market, though the vehicle may be full by then.

As always, schedules are highly changeable and should be confirmed before heading out.

In addition to the destinations shown in the table, the following can be reached with some changes:

Cobán Take a bus or minibus to Sayaxché, from where connecting microbuses leave for Cobán.

Puerto Barrios (Q115, six hours) Take a Guatemala City–bound Fuente del Norte bus and change at La Ruidosa junction, south of Río Dulce.

Río Dulce (Q100, four hours) Take a Guatemala City–bound bus with Fuente del Norte or Línea Dorada.

CROSSING THE BELIZEAN BORDER

It's 100km from Flores to Melchor de Mencos, the Guatemalan town on the border with Belize. From the Tikal junction at Puente Ixlú, 27km from Flores, the good paved road continues to the border with a brief stretch of rough rutted surface.

Most travelers pass through Melchor, though there is an actual town across the Río Mopán, with hotels, banks and businesses. There's little reason to linger but if you're done traveling for the day, Melchor has one fine place to stay, the **Río Mopan Lodge** (☑7926-5196; avinsa@yahoo.com; r with/without air-con Q244/122; 🅿❄🛜). Set back from the road in lush, jungle grounds, it's so tranquil that you'll find it hard to comprehend you're just 50m from the immigration booth. The rooms are big and cool with Maya decor and nice balconies overlooking the river. It's between the bridge and Guatemalan immigration.

BUSES FROM SANTA ELENA

DESTINATION	COST	DURATION	FREQUENCY	CONNECTIONS
Belize City	Q160	5hs	Línea Dorada (☎ 7924-8535) leaves at 7am, returning from Belize City at 1pm.	This bus connects with boats to Caye Caulker and Ambergris Caye.
Bethel/ La Técnica (Mexican border)	Q45	4-4½hr	AMCRU runs 12 microbuses to Bethel between 4:15am and 4:30pm, eight of which continue on to La Técnica.	
Carmelita	Q40	4½hr	Two Pinitas buses depart at 5am and 1pm from the market.	
El Ceibo/ La Palma (Mexican border)	Q40	4hr	El Naranjo–bound microbuses depart every 20 minutes, from 4:20am to 6:30pm, stopping at the El Ceibo junction, from where there are shuttles to the border (Q10, 15 minutes). Five of these go all the way to El Ceibo (Q45).	At La Palma, on the Mexican side, you can find transport to Tenosique, Tabasco (one hour), and onward to Palenque or Villahermosa.
El Remate	Q20	45min	ATIM microbuses leave every half hour from 6:30am to 7pm.	Buses and minibuses to and from Melchor de Mencos will drop you at Puente Ixlú junction, 2km south of El Remate.
Guatemala City	Q130-225	8-9hr	Línea Dorada (☎ 7924-8535) runs four first-class buses between 6:30am and 10pm (Q225). Autobuses del Norte (☎ 7924-8131) has buses at 9pm and 10pm (Q180). Fuente del Norte runs at least 11 buses between 4am and 10:30pm (Q130), including five deluxe buses (Q180),	
Melchor de Mencos (Belizean border)	Q50	2hr	Microbuses go about every hour 5am to 6pm. Línea Dorada Pullmans en route to Belize City depart at 7am (Q40).	
Poptún	Q30	2hr	Microbuses, via Dolores, every 10 minutes 5am to 7pm.	
San Andrés/ San José	Q8	35-40min	Microbuses depart around every 15 minutes, from 5am to 6:40pm, from the left side of the terminal entrance.	
Sayaxché	Q23	1½hr	Microbuses depart about every 15 minutes from 5:35am to 5pm.	
Tikal	Q30	1¼hr	Six microbuses by ATIM between 6:30am and 3pm, the last returning at 5pm. You could also take the Uaxactún-bound bus (Q40) at 2pm, which goes a bit slower.	

CAR

Several car-rental companies have desks at the airport.

Hertz (☎ 3724-4424; www.guatemalarent car.com)

Tabarini (☎ 7926-0253; www.tabarini.com)

SHUTTLE MINIBUS

Maayach Expeditions offers a shuttle service at 8am (Q150), picking up passengers from their hotels; purchase tickets at **San Juan Travel** (☎ 4068-7616; Calle Playa Sur, Flores). San Juan Travel operates shuttle minibuses to Tikal (one way/return Q50/80). There are five departures between 4:30am and 1pm. Most hotels and travel agencies can book these shuttles and they will pick you up from where you're staying. Returns leave Tikal at 12:30pm, 3pm and 5pm. If you know which round-trip you plan to be on, ask your driver to hold a seat for you or arrange one in another minibus. If you stay overnight in Tikal and want to return to Flores by minibus, it's a good idea to reserve a seat with a driver when they arrive in the morning.

ℹ Getting Around

A taxi from the airport to Santa Elena or Flores costs Q30. *Tuk-tuks* will take you anywhere between or within Flores and Santa Elena for Q5 to Q10; the *tuk-tuk* service stops after 7pm.

Around Flores

Petencito Zoo ZOO
(Q40; ☉8am-5pm) A couple of dozen native critters, including pumas, ocelots, spider monkeys, crocodiles and macaws, dwell around and within a lagoon at this secluded zoo east of Flores on the opposite bank. Laced with interpretive trails, the reserve is connected by floating bridge to an islet, the domain of turtles and crocodiles. Camping is permitted (Q25 with tent). Boat operators from Flores charge Q200, including an hour's wait while you tour the zoo.

Cuevas de Ak'tun Kan CAVE
(Q25; ☉7am-6pm) Try spelunking at the impressive limestone caverns of Ak'tun Kan, which translates from Q'eqchi' Maya as 'Cave of the Serpent'. The cave-keeper provides the authorized interpretation of the weirdly shaped stalagmite and stalactite formations, including the Frozen Falls, the Whale's Tail, and the Gate of Heaven, the last within a great hall where bats flutter in the crevices. If you haven't got a flashlight, you can rent one. Explorations take 30 to 45 minutes. It's 2km south of Flores; take a *tuk-tuk* there (Q10).

Parque Natural Ixpanpajul WILDLIFE RESERVE
(☑2336-0576; www.ixpanpajul.com; zip-line tour adult/child Q170/100; ☉7am-6pm) At Parque Natural Ixpanpajul you can ride horses, mountain bikes or tractors, or zip-line your way through the jungle canopy. The big attraction is the Skyway, a 3km circuit of stone paths and six linked suspension bridges through the upper levels of the forest. Camping and cabins are available for overnight stays. It's 8km east of Flores.

The park offers shuttle service from Flores at 8am and 2pm daily; phone to reserve and they'll pick you up at your hotel.

Hotel Villa Maya RESORT $$$
(☑7931-8350; www.villasdeguatemala.com; s/d Q800/940; ⓟ@☞☒) At Laguna Petenchel, a small lake east of Santa Elena, this hotel is among the finest in the area. Ensconced within its own wildlife refuge, the blissfully quiet accommodations include 10 two- to three-level bungalows and 10 cabins. It's 4km north of the crossroads where the Guatemala City road diverges from the Tikal road.

San Miguel & Tayazal

Covering the western end of the San Miguel peninsula, reached by frequent ferries from Flores, are the remains of **Tayazal** (Q5; ☉8am-5pm), among the last of the Maya capitals. It was settled by the Itzáes, refugees from the destroyed city of Chichén Itzá in Yucatán, who held out against the Spanish until 1697. Scholars concur that Tayazal was actually centered on the island of Flores, but remnants of the Itzáes' reign are scattered around the peninsula. The chiefly Classic-era mounds are overgrown by vegetation, and a few pockmarked stelae have been recovered. The real draw, though, is the chance to wander the forested spine of the peninsula, taking in panoramic views of the lake.

To reach the ruins, walk 250m to the left along the shore from where the boat drops you, then turn up the paved street to the right. After 300m, turn left at the 'Playa' sign, passing a football field on your right. About another 600m on, a trail on the right leads to **Playa El Chechenal**, a swimming beach with a dock extending over turquoise waters and a few picnic tables (admission Q5). Continue west another 300m to reach the main entrance to the site. From here it's a precipitous climb up the hillside – actually one of the pyramids of ancient Tayazal – to reach **El Mirador del Rey Canek**, an observation point with 360-degree views around Lago de Petén Itzá. The archaeological site can be visited by circling round the base of the tower and skirting the lake back toward the village. Around 800m further, go left up a hill (past a building foundation), then follow a dirt road left to reach the Gran Plaza, where you'll find some weathered stelae dating from the late Classic period.

Lago de Peten Itzá

San Miguel itself is a quiet, slow-moving place. A short boat ride from busy cosmopolitan Flores, it has a far more idyllic vibe, especially along the waterfront promenade. Steps from the dock stands a stone horse, dedicated in 2014 to the 'wisdom and bravery of the indomitable Itzá people.'

🛏 Sleeping & Eating

Easily accessible as it is from Flores, staying in San Miguel is an excellent option and the one shoreline hotel here is a gem.

Posada San Miguel   HOTEL $
(📞7867-5312; laposadasanmiguel.com; s/d Q70/100) This amiably managed little lakefront hotel is on the incredibly idyllic Peninsula San Miguel, just a five-minute passage over from Flores by *lancha* (Q5, running all night). There's a section of newly minted rooms with orthopedic beds along a fabulous terrace with painted-wood lounge chairs. From the dock, head left and go round the bend. A café prepares *pescado blanco* (whitefish) from the lake and other local specialties.

ⓘ Getting There & Away

Lanchas (Q5 per person) make the five-minute crossing to San Miguel village from the north side of Flores whenever they have a boatload.

San José & San Andrés

POP 9340

San Andrés and San José, a pair of similarly sized, small towns at the northwest corner of Lago de Petén Itzá, are just a few kilometers apart but are distinct in character.

In San Andrés, a jumble of mismatched houses covers a precipitous hillside interwoven with lushly overgrown paths, all imbued with the calming presence of the lake.

San José is peopled by Itzá Maya, descendants of the area's pre-Hispanic inhabitants. The extraordinarily neat and orderly village descends steeply from its little blue church to the lakefront, site of a waterslide park and a couple of seafood shacks.

🏃 Activities

Each town has a language school, and their relative isolation makes it easier to learn Spanish as there are more chances to interact with locals.

Escuela Bio-Itzá   LANGUAGE COURSE
(www.bioitza.com; San José) The community-owned Escuela Bio-Itzá is part of an association working to keep Itzá traditions and language alive. The group also manages a 36-sq-km nature reserve bordering the southern section of the Biotopo El Zotz, which is being outfitted for ecotourism. Students participate in community projects such as producing cosmetics from the medicinal plant garden, or helping the reserve rangers monitor wildlife.

Cost for the usual 20 hours of one-on-one Spanish classes is Q1230 per week to live with a local family, or Q1540 to stay on the reserve. Bio-Itzá also offers single day and overnight tours of the reserve to non-students with a focus on bird-watching, archaeology, medicinal plants and the work of the *chiceros* who harvested the sap of the chicozapote tree for the production of chewing gum.

NIGHT OF THE SKULLS

San José is a special place to be on the night of October 31, when perfectly preserved human skulls, normally housed in the church, are paraded around town on a velvet pillow followed by devotees in traditional dress, carrying candles. Throughout the night, the skulls make visits to predetermined houses, where blessings are sought, offerings made and a feast eaten.

Eco-Escuela de Español   LANGUAGE COURSE
(☑ 3099-4846;   ernestoalonso75@hotmail.com; San Andrés) This community-owned school in San Andrés emphasizes ecological and cultural issues and organizes environmental trips and volunteer opportunities, such as installing trails in the woods or classifying medicinal plants. Room and board with a local family is provided for Q1150 a week.

🛏 Sleeping & Eating

Most visitors to the area stay at one of two lakefront lodges, though it is also possible to find accommodations within either community through their respective language institutes.

Besides a lakefront grill by the waterslide park at the west end of San José, both of the resort-style lakefront lodges prepare meals for guests.

Hotel Bahía Taitzá   HOTEL $$
(☑ 7928-8125; www.taitza.com; d/tr Q300/400) West of the village, this is an elaborate spread where you can truly unwind. Eight well-designed rooms with tropical hardwood furnishings and lovely porches are in two buildings facing the lake across a lawn dotted with ficus and almond trees. The new units in a row on a rise are less exotic but more spacious.

Wood-fired pizzas, vegetarian curries and such are served under a beachfront *palapa*.

Ni'tun Ecolodge   RESORT $$$
(☑ 5201-0759; www.nitun.com; s/d incl breakfast from Q1100/1770; P@) West of San Andrés and down a gravel road, Ni'tun is set on a 35-acre patch of protected secondary forest where six species of hummingbird nest year-round. Four spacious huts built from indigenous materials feature handcrafted furniture and wraparound screened windows. Superb meals are prepared in the open-air clubhouse with a lounge on the upper deck.

Bernie and Lorena, Guatemalan conservationists, built and operate the lodge and coordinate adventure excursions through their affiliated company, Monkey Eco Tours (☑ 5201-0759; www.nitun.com; San Andrés).

ⓘ Getting There & Away

Microbuses depart around every 15 minutes from 5am to 6:40pm from the left side of the main terminal in Santa Elena, stopping in San Andrés (Q8, 35 minutes) and continuing another five minutes along the shore to San José.

El Remate

This idyllic spot at the eastern end of Lago de Petén Itzá makes a good alternative base for Tikal-bound travelers – it's more relaxed than Flores and closer to the site. Just two roads, really, El Remate has a ramshackle vibe all of its own.

El Remate begins 1km north of Puente Ixlú, where the road to the Belize border diverges from the Tikal road. The village strings along the Tikal road for 1km to another junction, where a branch heads west along the north shore of the lake.

El Remate is known for its wood carving. Some fine examples of the craft are sold from stalls along the main road.

You can change US dollars and euros or check your email at Horizontes Mayas (☑ 5825-8296; www.horizontesmayas.com; Ruta a Tikal), adjacent to Hotel Las Gardenias.

✦ Activities

Most El Remate accommodations can book two-hour boat trips for bird-watching or nocturnal crocodile spotting (each Q100 per person). Try Hotel Mon Ami (p246), which also offers sunset lake tours with detours up the Ixlu and Ixpop rivers (Q150 per person).

Asunción, found by the second speed bump from the north shore junction, rents kayaks (Q35 per hour) and bicycles (per hour/day Q10/70). He also guides horseback rides to Laguna Sacpetén and a small archaeological site there (Q150 per person, 2½ hours).

Biotopo Cerro Cahuí NATURE RESERVE

(Q40; ⊙7am-4pm) Comprising a 7.3-sq-km swath of subtropical forest rising up from the lake over limestone terrain, this nature reserve offers mildly strenuous hiking and excellent wildlife watching, with paths to some brilliant lookout points. As a bonus, there's an adjacent lakeside park with diving docks for a refreshing conclusion to the tour.

More than 20 mammal species roam the reserve, including spider and howler monkeys, white-tailed deer and the elusive Mesoamerican tapir. Bird life is rich and varied, with the opportunity to spot toucans, woodpeckers and the famous ocellated turkey, a big bird resembling a peacock. Trees include mahogany, cedar, *ramón*, and cohune palm, along with many types of bromeliads, ferns and orchids.

A network of loop trails ascend the hill to three lookout points, affording views of the whole lake and of Laguna Sacpetén to the east. The trail called Los Escobos (4km long, about 2¼ hours), through secondary growth forest, is good for spotting monkeys.

The admission fee includes the right to camp or sling your hammock under small thatch shelters inside the entrance. There are toilets and showers. The reserve is 1.75km west along the north-shore road from El Remate.

Project Ix-Canaan VOLUNTEERING

(www.ixcanaan.com) This group supports the improvement of health, education and opportunities for rainforest inhabitants. Operating here since 1996, they run a community clinic, women's center, library and research center. Volunteers work in the clinic, build and maintain infrastructure, and assist in various other ways.

🧭 Tours

La Casa de Don David (p246) offers tours to Yaxhá (Q460 per person, minimum two people), and Tikal (Q479). Prices include an English-speaking guide and lunch but not admission to the site. Horizontes Mayas has slightly cheaper tours and runs collective excursions to Yaxhá at 7am and 1:30pm (Q100 per person, minimum three people).

🛏 Sleeping

Most hotels are set up for swimming in – and watching the sun set over – the lake.

📋 Along the Main Road

Hotel Las Gardenias HOTEL $

(☑5936-6984; www.hotelasgardenias.com; Ruta a Tikal; s/d from Q90/150, with air-con Q150/200; ❄@🛜) Right at the junction with the north shore road, this cordial hotel/restaurant/shuttle operator has two sections: the wood-paneled rooms at the front are bigger, those in the rear are appealingly removed from the road. All feature comfortable beds with woven spreads, attractively tiled showers and porches with hammocks.

Posada Ixchel HOTEL $

(☑3044-5379; hotelixchel@yahoo.com; s/d Q90/120) This family-owned place near the village's main junction is a superior deal, with spotless, wood-fragrant rooms featuring fans and handcrafted mosquito nets. The cobbled courtyard has inviting little nooks with tree-log seats.

Hotel Sun Breeze HOTEL $

(☑5898-2665; sunbreezehotel@gmail.com; Main Rd; s/d Q80/120; ℗) The nearest place to the junction, this excellent-value homey guesthouse has neatly kept and well-ventilated rooms with screened windows and porches. Rear units are best, at the back of a pleasant patio. It's a short stroll to the public beach.

Hostal Hermano Pedro HOSTEL $$

(☑5164-6485; www.hhpedro.com; Calle Camino Biblico 8055; dm/s/d incl breakfast Q96/152/208; 🛜) About 150m from the north shore junction, this two-level wooden structure has a relaxed environment, with plenty of hammocks in the patio and along the verandas. Recycled elements are cleverly incorporated into the decor of the spacious rooms, which feature big fans and lacy curtains. Guests can use the kitchen.

Hotel Palomino Ranch HOTEL $$

(☑3075-4189; hotelpalominorancho@gmail.com; Km 30 Carretera a Tikal; s/d Q300/448; ℗❄🛜🏊) An incongruous slice of the old west in El Remate, Hotel Palomino Ranchhas air-conditioned rooms with a cowpoke motif. There's a swimming pool and stable: guests are allowed to ride around the grounds for free from 7am to 4pm, and trail rides can be arranged as well. Food and beverages are served all day long in the vintage saloon.

Along the North Shore Road

Casa de Doña Tonita
HOSTEL $

(☑5767-4065; dm/s/d Q30/40/80) This friendly family-run place has four basic, adequately ventilated rooms, each with two single beds and screened windows, in a two-story clapboard *rancho* (small house), plus a dorm situated over a restaurant that serves tasty, reasonably priced meals. There's just one shower. Across the road is a pier's end hut for sunset gazing.

★ Alice Guesthouse
BUNGALOW $$

(☑3087-0654; alice.gwate@gmail.com; dm Q60, bungalow Q200) As in Wonderland, that is. Fruit of the budding imaginations of a Franco-Belgian pair, this slightly remote spread looks not at the lake but at a swath of jungle. Free-form, friendly and fun, it has dorms in fanciful huts with conical thatch roofs, a pair of neat colorful cabins and a tropical shower in a roundhouse, all connected by pebbly paths.

An open-air kitchen is the domain of a chef imported from Nantes. To reach Alice, go down the Jobompiche road about 1.5km; a signed track on the right angles uphill.

★ Posada del Cerro
BUNGALOW $$

(☑5376-8722; www.posadadelcerro.com; dm/s/d/tr Q100/220/330/450; P⑦) ✎ This ecologically sound option blends brilliantly into its jungle setting, close enough to the Cerro Cahui biosphere reserve to hear the monkeys howl the evening in. Ten thoughtfully furnished rooms occupy stone-and-hardwood houses and solitary huts scattered over the hillside; one is open to the woods with its own lake-view deck. There's also an eight-bed hut for groups.

Herbs from the forest are stirred into local recipes in the neat, thatched-roof restaurant.

Gringo Perdido Ecological Inn
RESORT $$

(☑5804-8639; www.hotelgringoperdido.com; Jobompiche Rd; campsite Q40, s/d with breakfast & dinner Q380/760; P) ✎ Ensconced in a paradisaical lakefront setting within the Cerro Cahui biosphere reserve, this jungle-style lodge offers a bank of rooms with full-wall roll-up blinds to give you the sensation of sleeping in the open air. A few lakeside bungalows offer a bit more seclusion. There's also a grassy campground with thatched-roof shelters for slinging hammocks, and a Maya sauna.

The Gringo Perdido is 3km along the north shore from the main Tikal road.

La Casa de Don David
HOTEL $$

(☑5306-2190; www.lacasadedondavid.com; Jobompiche Rd; s/d incl breakfast or dinner from Q273/436; ⊗restaurant 6:30am-9pm; ❋@⑦) Just west of the junction, this full-service outfit has spotless, modern rooms decorated with Maya textiles. All feature verandas and hammocks facing the broad garden that's been cultivated into an incredible aviary. Whether or not you're staying here, don't miss the ceiba tree and Maya calendar arrangement in the rear garden designed by owner David Kuhn (the original Gringo Perdido).

Hotel Mon Ami
HOTEL $$

(☑3010-0284; www.hotelmonami.com; Jobompiche Rd; dm/s/d Q75/150/200, s/d without bathroom Q100/150; ⑦) A 15-minute walk from the Tikal road, Santiago's place maintains a good balance between jungle wildness and Euro sophistication. Quirkily furnished cabins and dorms with hammocks are reached along candlelit paths through gardens bursting with local plant life. And the pier opposite is a delight. Fans of French cuisine will appreciate the open-air restaurant.

Pirámide Paraiso
HOTEL $$$

(http://hotelgringoperdido.com/hotel-piramide-paraiso; Jobompiche Rd; r from Q1550; P⑦) Built in time for the dawn of the new *bak-tún* (a *baktún* equals about four centuries) of the Maya calendar (in 2012) is this glitzy addition to the Gringo Perdido Ecological Inn, a smooth white structure that rises surreally from the forest like a Maya temple. Each of the eight huge, luxuriously decorated suites features its own exterior Jacuzzi.

✖ Eating

Most hotels have their own restaurants and there are simple *comedores* (cheap eateries) scattered along the main road.

La Piazza
CAFE $

(☑5951-7338; mains Q30-40; ⊗5am-9pm) Step into this breezy open-air pavilion any time for espresso and tasty snacks. Run by sweet-tempered staff who make brilliant papaya milkshakes and mighty fine pineapple cake. It's right at the junction.

★ **Las Orquídeas** ITALIAN **$$**
([☑]5819-7232; Jobompiche Rd; pastas Q55-80;
[☺]noon-9pm Tue-Sun) Almost hidden in the
forest, a 10-minute walk down the north
shore from the Tikal junction, is this marve-
lous open-air dining hall. The genial Italian
owner-chef blends *chaya*, a local herb, into
his own tagliatelle and *panzarotti* (smaller
version of calzones). There are tempting des-
serts, too.

Mon Ami FRENCH **$$**
(mains Q35-55; [☺]6am-9pm) Down the north
shore road, here's the French jungle bistro
you've dreamed of, a peaceful palm-thatched
affair. Try the lake whitefish or the big *ensalada francesa* (French salad).

❶ Getting There & Away

El Remate is linked to Santa Elena by frequent
minibus service (Q20) till around 7pm.

For Tikal, a collective shuttle departs at
5:30am, starting back at 2pm (one-way/round
trip Q30/50). Any El Remate accommodations
can make reservations. Or catch one of the ATIM
(p254) or San Juan Travel (p241; Q20) shuttles
passing through from Santa Elena to Tikal from
5am to 3:30pm.

For taxis, ask at Hotel Sun Breeze (p245). A
one-way ride to Flores costs about Q300; round
trip to Tikal costs Q350.

For Melchor de Mencos on the Belizean border,
get a minibus or bus from Puente Ixlú, 2km south
of El Remate (Q20, 1¼ hours). Additionally, Horizontes Mayas (p244) offers daily departures to
Belize City (Q150) via Melchor at 5:30am and 8am.

Tikal

The most striking feature of Tikal ([☑]2367-
2837; www.parque-tikal.com; Q150; [☺]6am-6pm)
is its towering, steep-sided temples, rising
to heights of more than 44m, but what dis-
tinguishes it is its jungle setting. Its many
plazas have been cleared of trees and vines,
its temples uncovered and partially restored,
but as you walk from one building to another you pass beneath the dense canopy of
rainforest amid the rich, loamy aromas of
earth and vegetation. Much of the delight
of touring the site comes from strolling
the broad causeways, originally built from
packed limestone to accommodate traffic
between temple complexes. By stepping
softly you're more likely to spot monkeys,
agoutis, foxes and ocellated turkeys.

Tikal is a popular day trip from Flores or
El Remate, so is much quieter in the late afternoon and early morning, which makes an
overnight stay an attractive option.

History

Tikal is set on a low hill, which becomes
evident as you ascend to the Gran Plaza
from the entry road. Affording relief from
the surrounding swampy ground, this high
terrain may explain why the Maya settled
here around 700 BC. Another reason was
the abundance of flint, used by the ancients
to make clubs, spear points, arrowheads and
knives. The wealth of this valuable stone
meant good tools could be made, and flint
could be traded for other goods. Within 200
years the Maya of Tikal had begun to build
stone ceremonial structures, and by 200 BC
there was a complex of buildings on the site
of the Acrópolis del Norte.

Classic Period

The Gran Plaza was beginning to assume
its present shape and extent by the time
of Christ. By the dawn of the early Classic
period, around AD 250, Tikal had become
an important religious, cultural and commercial city with a large population. King
Yax Ehb' Xooc, in power about AD 230, is
looked upon as the founder of the dynasty
that ruled Tikal thereafter.

Under Chak Tok Ich'aak I (King Great
Jaguar Paw), who ruled in the mid-4th
century, Tikal adopted a brutal method of
warfare, used by the rulers of Teotihuacán
in central Mexico. Rather than meeting
their adversaries on the battlfield in hand-
to-hand combat, the army of Tikal used aux-
iliary units to encircle the enemy and throw
spears to kill them from a distance. This
first use of 'air power' among the Maya of
Petén enabled Siyah K'ak' (Smoking Frog),
the Tikal general, to conquer the army of
Uaxactún; thus Tikal became the dominant
kingdom in El Petén.

By the middle of the Classic period, in the
mid-6th century, Tikal's military prowess
and its association with Teotihuacán allowed
it to grow until it sprawled over 30 sq km and
had a population of perhaps 100,000. But in
553, Yajaw Te' K'inich II (Lord Water) came
to the throne of Caracol (in southwestern
Belize), and within a decade had conquered
Tikal and sacrificed its king. Tikal and other Petén kingdoms suffered under Caracol's
rule until the late 7th century when, under
new leadership, it apparently cast off its op-
pressor and rose again.

Tikal

SURVEYING THE CLASSIC MAYA KINGDOM

Constructed in successive waves over a period of at least 800 years, Tikal is a vast, complicated site with hundreds of temples, pyramids and stelae. There's no way you'll get to it all in a day, but by following this itinerary you'll see many of the highlights. Before setting out be sure to stop by the visitor center and examine the scale model of the site. The small **Museo Sylvanus G Morley 1** usually houses a wealth of kings, although the majority of its contents (other than Stela 31) are currently located in the CCIT research center while the museum is indefinitely under restoration. Present your ticket at the nearby control booth and when you reach the posted map, take a left. It's a 20-minute walk to the solitary **Templo VI 2** . From here it's a blissful stroll up the broad Méndez causeway to the **Gran Plaza 3** Tikal's ceremonial core, where you may examine the ancient precinct of the **North Acropolis 4** . Exit the plaza west, and take the first left, along a winding path, to **Templo V 5** . Round the rear to the right, a trail encircles the largely unexcavated South Acropolis to the **Plaza de los Siete Templos 6** .

Immediately west stands the great pyramid of the **Mundo Perdido 7** . From here it's a quick stroll and a rather strenuous climb to the summit of **Temple IV 8** , Tikal's tallest structure.

Templo IV
Arrive in the late afternoon to get magically tinted photos of Temples I, II and III poking through the jungle canopy. If you're lucky you might also get a glimpse of an orange-crested falcon swooping around the treetops.

Mundo Perdido
The smaller temple to the west of the great pyramid may look familiar to those who've visited Teotihuacán near Mexico City, with its elegant stepped *talud-tablero* design, a vivid reminder of that distant kingdom's influence.

TOP TIPS

» Bring food and water.
» If you enter after 3pm, your ticket is good for the next day.
» Stay at one of the onsite hotels to catch the sunset/sunrise.
» To watch the sunset/sunrise from Temple IV, you'll need to purchase an additional ticket (Q100).
» Bring mosquito repellent.

Gran Plaza

Though the surreally tall Templo I, a mausoleum to the Late Classic ruler Ah Cacao, is off-limits to climbers, you're welcome to ascend the almost-as-tall Templo II across the plaza.

North Acropolis

Amid the stack of smaller and much older temples that rise up the hillside north of the plaza, take a peek beneath the two thatched shelters on a ledge to find a pair of fearsome masks.

Museo Sylvanus G Morley

Volumes have been written about the remarkably preserved Stela 31, a portrait of the ruler Stormy Sky crowning himself, flanked by spear-toting warriors in the attire of (ally or overlord?) Teotihuacán.

DEAGOSTINI /GETTY IMAGES ©

4

Ticket Booth **1**

Posted Map

Visitor Centre

CCIT

2

Templo VI

The secluded temple has a lengthy set of glyphs inscribed on the back of its lofty roof comb, recording the lineage of successive kingdoms. Be patient: the contents of the weathered slab may take some effort to discern.

Plaza de los Siete Templos

Seven miniature temples line up along the east side of this grassy courtyard. Climb the larger 'palace' at the south end to get a sightline along the septet.

Templo V

As steep as it is massive, Tikal's second tallest temple (52m) has unusual rounded corners. Tempting as it may seem to climb, the broad front staircase is off-limits.

TONY WHEELER/GETTY IMAGES ©

Tikal's Renaissance

A powerful king named Ha Sawa Chaan K'awil (682–734, also called Ah Cacao or Moon Double Comb), 26th successor of Yax Ehb' Xooc, restored not only Tikal's military strength but also its primacy in the Maya world. He conquered the greatest rival Maya state, Calakmul in Mexico, in 695, and his successors were responsible for building most of the great temples around the Gran Plaza that survive today. King Ah Cacao was buried beneath the staggering height of Templo I.

Tikal's greatness waned around 900, but it was not alone in its downfall, which was part of the mysterious general collapse of lowland Maya civilization.

Rediscovery

No doubt the Itzáes, who occupied Tayazal (now Flores), knew of Tikal in the late Post-classic Period. Perhaps they even came here to worship at the shrines of old gods. Spanish missionary friars who moved through El Petén after the conquest left brief references to these jungle-bound structures, but their writings moldered in libraries for centuries.

It wasn't until 1848 that the Guatemalan government sent out an expedition, under the leadership of Modesto Méndez and Ambrosio Tut, to visit the site. This may have been inspired by John L Stephens' bestselling accounts of fabulous Maya ruins, published in 1841 and 1843 (though Stephens never visited Tikal). Like Stephens, Méndez and Tut took an artist, Eusebio Lara, to record their archaeological discoveries. An account of their findings was published by the Berlin Academy of Science.

In 1877 the Swiss Dr Gustav Bernoulli visited Tikal. His explorations resulted in the removal of carved wooden lintels from Templos I and IV and their shipment to Basel, where they are still on view in the Museum für Völkerkunde.

Scientific exploration of Tikal began with the arrival of English archaeologist Alfred P Maudslay in 1881. Others continued his work, Teobert Maler, Alfred M Tozzer and RE Merwin among them. Tozzer worked at Tikal on and off from the beginning of the 20th century until his death in 1954. The inscriptions at Tikal were studied and deciphered by Sylvanus G Morley.

Archaeological research and restoration was carried on by the University of Pennsylvania and the Guatemalan Instituto de Antropología e Historia until 1969. Since 1991, a joint Guatemalan–Spanish project has worked on conserving and restoring Templos I and V. The Parque Nacional Tikal (Tikal National Park) was declared a Unesco World Heritage Site in 1979.

◉ Sights

◉ Gran Plaza

The path comes into the Gran Plaza around the **Templo I**, the Templo del Gran Jaguar (Temple of the Grand Jaguar). This was built to honor – and bury – Ah Cacao. The king may have worked out the plans for the building himself, but it was actually erected above his tomb by his son, who succeeded him to the throne in AD 734. The king's rich burial goods included stingray spines, which were used for ritual bloodletting, 180 jade objects, pearls and 90 pieces of bone carved with hieroglyphs. At the top of the 44m-high temple is a small enclosure of three rooms covered by a corbeled arch. The sapodilla-wood lintels over the doors were richly carved; one of them was removed and is now in the Basel Museum für Völkerkunde. The lofty roofcomb that crowned the temple was originally adorned with reliefs and bright paint. When it's illuminated by the afternoon sun, it is still possible to make out the figure of a seated dignitary.

Although climbing to the top of Templo I is prohibited, the views from **Templo II** just across the way are nearly as awe-inspiring. Templo II, also known as the Temple of the Masks, was at one time almost as high as Templo I, but it now measures only 38m without its roofcomb.

Nearby, the **Acrópolis del Norte** (North Acropolis) significantly predates the two great temples. Archaeologists have uncovered about 100 different structures, the oldest of which dates from before the time of Christ, with evidence of occupation as far back as 600 BC. The Maya built and rebuilt on top of older structures, and the many layers, combined with the elaborate burials of Tikal's early rulers, added sanctity and power to their temples. The final version of the acropolis, as it stood around AD 800, had more than 12 temples atop a vast platform, many of them the work of King Ah Cacao. Look especially for the two huge, powerful wall masks, uncovered from an earlier structure and now protected by roofs. On the plaza side of the North Acropolis are two rows of stelae. These served to record the great deeds of the kings, to sanctify their memory and to add power to the temples and plazas that surrounded them.

◉ Acrópolis Central

South and east of the Gran Plaza, this maze of courtyards, little rooms and small temples is thought by many to have been a palace where Tikal's nobles lived. Others think the tiny rooms may have been used for sacred rites and ceremonies, as graffiti found within them suggest. Over the centuries the configuration of the rooms was repeatedly changed, suggesting that perhaps this 'palace' was in fact a noble or royal family's residence and alterations were made to accommodate groups of relatives. A hundred years ago, one part of the acropolis provided lodgings for archaeologist Teobert Maler when he worked at Tikal.

◉ Templo III

West of the Gran Plaza, across the Calzada Tozzer (Tozzer Causeway) stands Templo III, still undergoing restoration. Only its upper reaches have been cleared. A scene carved into the lintel at its summit, 55m high, depicts a figure in an elaborate jaguar suit, believed to be the ruler Dark Sun. In front of it stands stela 24, which marks the date of its construction, AD 810. From this point, you can continue west to Templo IV along the Calzada Tozzer, one of several sacred byways between the temple complexes of Tikal.

◉ Templo V & Acrópolis del Sur

Due south of the Gran Plaza, Templo V is a remarkably steep structure (57m high) that was built sometime between the 7th and 8th centuries AD. It consists of seven stepped platforms and, unlike the other great temples, has slightly rounded corners. A recent excavation of the temple revealed a group of embedded structures, some with Maya calendars on their walls. Tempting as it may seem, you are not allowed to scale the broad central staircase.

Excavation has hardly even begun on the mass of masonry just west of the temple, known collectively as the Acrópolis del Sur (South Acropolis). The palaces on top are from the late Classic Period (the time of King Moon Double Comb), but earlier constructions probably go back 1000 years.

◉ Plaza de los Siete Templos

To the west of the Acrópolis del Sur is this broad grassy plaza, reached via a path to its southern edge. Built in the late Classic Period, the seven temples with their stout roofcombs line up along the east side of the plaza. On the south end stand three larger 'palaces'; on the opposite end is an unusual triple ballcourt.

◉ El Mundo Perdido

About 400m southwest of the Gran Plaza is El Mundo Perdido (Lost World), a complex of 38 structures with a huge pyramid in its midst, thought to be essentially Preclassic (with some later repairs and renovations). The pyramid, 32m high and 80m along the base, is surrounded by four much-eroded stairways, with huge masks flanking each one. The stairway facing eastward is thought to have functioned as a platform for viewing the sun's trajectory against a trio of structures on a raised platform to the east, a similar arrangement to the astronomical observatory at Uaxactún. Tunnels dug into the pyramid by archaeologists reveal four similar pyramids beneath the outer face; the earliest (Structure 5C-54 Sub 2B) dates from 700 BC, making this pyramid the oldest Maya structure at Tikal.

A smaller temple to the west, dating from the early Classic Period, demonstrates Teotihuacán's influence, with its *talud-tablero* (stepped building) style of architecture.

◉ Templo IV & Complejo N

Templo IV, at 65m, is the highest building at Tikal and the second-highest pre-Columbian building known in the western hemisphere, after La Danta at El Mirador. It was completed about AD 741, probably by order of Ah Cacao's son, Yax Kin, who was depicted on the carved lintel over the middle doorway (now in a museum in Basel, Switzerland), as the western boundary of the ceremonial precinct. A steep wooden staircase leads to the top. The view east is almost as good as from a helicopter – a panorama across the jungle canopy, with (from left to right) the temples of the Gran Plaza, Temple III, Temple V (just the top bit) and the great pyramid of the Mundo Perdido poking through.

Between Templo IV and Templo III is Complejo N, an example of the 'twin-temple' complexes erected during the late

Classic Period. This one was built in AD 711 by Ah Cacao to mark the 14th *katun*, or 20-year cycle, of *baktún* 9. The king himself is portrayed on the remarkably preserved stela 16 in an enclosure just across the path. Beside the stelae is altar 5, a circular stone depicting the same king accompanied by a priestly figure in the process of exhuming the skeleton of a female ruler.

Templo de las Inscripciones (Templo VI)

Templo VI is one of the few temples at Tikal to bear written records. On the rear of its 12m-high roofcomb is a long inscription – though it will take some effort to discern it in the bright sunlight – giving us the date AD 766. The sides and cornice of the roofcomb bear glyphs as well. Its secluded position, about a 25-minute walk southeast of the Gran Plaza along the Calzada Méndez, makes it a good spot for observing wildlife. From here, it's a 20-minute hike back to the main entrance.

Northern Complexes

About 1km north of the Gran Plaza is **Complejo P**. Like Complejo N, it's a late-Classic twin-temple complex that probably commemorated the end of a *katun*. **Complejo M**, next to it, was partially torn down by the late-Classic Maya to provide building materials for a causeway, now named after Alfred P Maudslay, which runs southwest to Templo IV. **Grupo H**, northeast of Complexes P and M, with one tall, cleared temple, had some interesting graffiti within its temples.

Complejo Q and **Complejo R**, about 300m north of the Gran Plaza, are very late-Classic twin-pyramid complexes with stelae and altars standing before the temples. Complex Q is perhaps the best example of the twin-temple type, as it has been partly restored. Stelae 22 and altar 10 are excellent examples of late-Classic Tikal relief carving, dated to AD 771.

Museums

Museo Sylvanus G Morley MUSEUM

(Museo Cerámico; Museum of Ceramics; Q30, also valid for Museo Lítico; ⌚8am-4pm) This museum exhibits a number of superb ceramic pieces from excavations, including incense burners and vases, with descriptions of their uses and significance (in Spanish). The usual museum building is under restoration indefinitely, during which time the ceramics are displayed at the CCIT.

Two of the most highly prized items, the elaborately carved Stela 31 dedicated to the ruler Stormy Sky-Double Comb, and the simulated tomb of King Moon Double Comb with the precious items unearthed from his burial site beneath Temple I, remain inside the museum, and the guard can show them to you on request.

CCIT MUSEUM

(Centro de Conservación e Investigación de Tikal; ⌚8am-noon & 1-4pm) FREE This Japanese-funded research center is devoted to the identification and restoration of pieces unearthed at the site. The 1300-sq-meter facility has a huge cache of items to sort through, and you can watch the restorers at work. Though not strictly a museum per se, it features an excellent gallery on the different materials used by Maya craftspeople.

The center is home to the Museo Sylvanus G Morley for an indefinite period while that museum is under restoration.

Museo Lítico MUSEUM

(Stone Museum; Q30, also valid for Museo Sylvanus G Morley; ⌚8am-4:30pm Mon-Fri, 8am-4pm Sat & Sun) The larger of Tikal's two museums is in the visitor center. It houses a number of carved stones from the ruins. The photographs taken by pioneer archaeologists Alfred P Maudslay and Teobert Maler of the jungle-covered temples in various stages of discovery are particularly striking. Outside is a model showing how Tikal would have looked around AD 800.

Activities

Canopy Tours Tikal ADVENTURE TOUR

(☎5615-4988; www.tikalcanopy.com; tours Q230; ⌚7am-5pm) By the national park entrance, this outfit offers a one-hour tour through the forest canopy, with the chance to ride a harness along a series of cables linking trees up to 300m apart and to cross several hanging bridges. The fee includes transport from Tikal or El Remate.

Tours

Archaeologist **Roxy Ortiz** (☎5197-5173; http://www.tikalroxy.blogspot.com) has 32 years' experience trekking throughout the Maya world and does early-morning tours around Tikal from her base at the Tikal Inn. She also does personalized treks to Uaxactún, Yaxhá and other less-visited sites with her 15-seat military vehicle.

Multilingual guides are available at the information kiosk. These authorized guides display their accreditation carnet, listing the languages they speak. Before 7am, the charge for a half-day tour is Q80 per person with a minimum of five persons. After that you pay Q475 for a group tour.

🛏 Sleeping

Staying overnight enables you to relax and savor the dawn and dusk, when most of the jungle birds and animals can be seen and heard (especially the howler monkeys). Other than camping, there are only three places to stay, and tour groups often have many of the rooms reserved. Almost any travel agency in Guatemala offers Tikal tours, including lodging, a meal or two, a guided tour and transportation.

There's no need to make reservations if you want to stay at Tikal's campground (campsite per person Q50, hammock with mosquito net Q85), behind the research center. This is a large, grassy area with a clean bathroom block and *palapa* for hanging hammocks.

Tikal Inn   HOTEL $$
(☑ 7861-2444; www.tikalinn.com; s/d Q500/730; Ⓟ @ 🛜 ☀) Built in the late '60s, this resort-style lodging offers rooms in the main building and thatched bungalows alongside the pool and rear lawn, with little porches out

front. All are simple, spacious and quite comfortable. The most secluded accommodations are the least expensive, in a handful of cabins at the end of a sawdust trail through the forest.

Jungle Lodge   HOTEL $$$
(☑ 7861-0446; www.junglelodgetikal.com; s/d Q695/810, without bathroom Q370/385; Ⓟ @ ☀) Nearest of the hotels to the site entrance, this was originally built to house archaeologists working at Tikal. Self-contained bungalows, plus a bank of cheaper units, are well spaced throughout rambling, jungle grounds. Some newer suites feature jungle-chic decor and outdoor rain-showers. The restaurant-bar (mains Q80 to Q100) serves veggie pastas, crepes and other international dishes in a tropical ambience.

Jaguar Inn   HOTEL $$$
(☑ 7926-2411; www.jaguartikal.com; campsite per person Q50, with tent Q115, s/d/tr Q580/695/925; Ⓟ ❄ @ 🛜) The inn of choice for youthful, independent travelers has duplex and quad bungalows with thatched roofs and hammocks on the porches, plus a smart little restaurant with a popular terrace out front. For those on a tight budget there are tents for rent on a platform.

🍴 Eating

Along the right-hand side of the access road stand a series of little *comedores*, offering bland versions of standards such as grilled

---

BIRD-WATCHING AT TIKAL

As well as howler and spider monkeys romping through the trees of Tikal, the plethora of birds flitting through the canopy and across the green expanses of the plazas is impressive. The ruined temple complexes present ideal viewing platforms for this activity, often providing the ability to look down upon the treetops to observe examples of the 300 or so bird species (migratory and resident) that have been recorded here. Bring binoculars and a copy of *The Birds of Tikal: An Annotated Checklist*, by Randell A Beavers, available at the visitor-center shop. Tread quietly and be patient, and you'll probably see some of the following birds in the areas specified:

Templo de las Inscripciones Tody motmots, four trogon species and royal flycatchers

El Mundo Perdido Two oriole species, keel-billed toucans and collared aracaris

Complejo P Great curassows, three species of woodpecker, crested guans, plain chachalacas and three tanager species

Aguada Tikal (Tikal Reservoir) Three kingfisher species, jacanas, blue herons, two species of sandpiper, and great kiskadees

Entrance path Tiger herons sometimes nest in the huge ceiba tree located here

Complejo Q Red-capped and white-collared manakins

Complejo R emerald toucanets

chicken and grilled steak (Q40 to Q50). All are open from 5am to 9pm daily.

Picnic tables beneath shelters are located just off Tikal's Gran Plaza, with soft-drink and water vendors standing by, but no food is sold. If you want to spend all day at the ruins without having to make the 20- to 30-minute walk back to the *comedores*, carry food and water with you.

Comedor Tikal   RESTAURANT $$

(Visitor Center; mains Q60-70; ⊙6:30am-8:30pm) This is one of a series of little open-air *comedores* along the right-hand side of the access road to Tikal. Pasta and hamburgers are among the offerings.

❶ Orientation

The archaeological site is at the center of the 550-sq-km Parque Nacional Tikal. The road from Flores enters the park 19km south of the ruins. From the parking lot at the site, it's a short walk back to the junction where there's an information kiosk. Immediately south of this junction, a visitor center sells books, maps, souvenirs, hats, insect repellent, sun block and other necessities; it also houses a restaurant and museum (p252). Near the visitor center are Tikal's three hotels, a campground, a few small *comedores* and a modern research center containing a second museum (p252).

It's a five-minute walk from the ticket control booth to the entry gate. Just beyond, there's a large map posted. From here, it's a 1.5km walk (20 minutes) southwest to the Gran Plaza. From the Gran Plaza west to Templo IV it's more than 600m.

❶ Information

Everyone must purchase a ticket at the entry gate on the road in; tickets purchased after 3pm are valid for the whole next day. Those staying more than one day can purchase additional tickets at the ticket control booth along the path to the site entrance. Seeing the sunrise from Templo IV at the west end of the main site is possible from about October to March, but to enter the park before or after visiting hours you must purchase an additional ticket for Q100, presumably to pay the guide who must accompany you.

The core of the ancient city takes up about 16 sq km, with more than 4000 structures. To visit all the major building complexes, you must walk at least 10km, so wear comfortable shoes with good rubber treads that grip well. The ruins here can be slick from rain and organic material, especially during the wet season. Bring plenty of water, as you'll be walking around all day in the heat.

Please don't feed the coatis (pisotes) that wander about the site.

MONEY

The Jaguar Inn (p253) will exchange US dollars cash and traveler's checks (at a poor rate).

RESOURCES

For more complete information on the monuments at Tikal, pick up a copy of *Tikal – A Handbook of the Ancient Maya Ruins*, by William R Coe, which is available in Flores and at Tikal. A book you're best off finding before you come is *The Lords of Tikal*, by Peter D Harrison, a vivid, cogent summary of the city's history. Guards at the ticket booth sell you a useful site map (Q20).

❶ Getting There & Away

Six microbuses by **ATIM** (ATIM; ☑5905-0089) depart Flores between 6:30am and 3pm (Q30, 1½ hours), the last returning at 5pm. They return from Tikal at noon, 1:30pm, 3pm and 6pm. You could also take the Uaxactún-bound bus from the market of Santa Elena at 3:30pm, which goes a bit slower. San Juan Travel (p241) runs five shuttles daily from Flores (one way/round trip Q50/80, including guide Q150) between 4:30am and 1pm, the last returning at 6pm.

From El Remate, a collective shuttle departs at 5:30am for Tikal, starting back at 2pm (one way/ round trip Q30/50). Any El Remate accommodations can make reservations.

If traveling from Belize, get a Santa Elena–bound microbus to Puente Ixlú, sometimes called El Cruce, and switch there to a north-bound microbus for the remaining 36km to Tikal. Heading from Tikal to Belize, start early and get off at Puente Ixlú to catch a bus or microbus eastward. Be wary of shuttles to Belize advertised at Tikal: these have been known to detour to Flores to pick up passengers!

Uaxactún

POP 700

Uaxactún (wah-shahk-*toon*), 23km north of Tikal along an unpaved road through the jungle, was Tikal's political and military rival in late Preclassic times. It was conquered by Tikal's Chak Tok Ich'aak I (King Great Jaguar Paw) in the 4th century, and was subservient to its great sister to the south for centuries thereafter, though it experienced an apparent resurgence during the Terminal Classic, after Tikal went into decline.

Villagers make an income from collecting chicle, *pimienta* (allspice) and *xate* (low-growing palm, exported to Holland for floral arrangements) in the surrounding forest. In the *xate* warehouse at the west end

Uaxactún

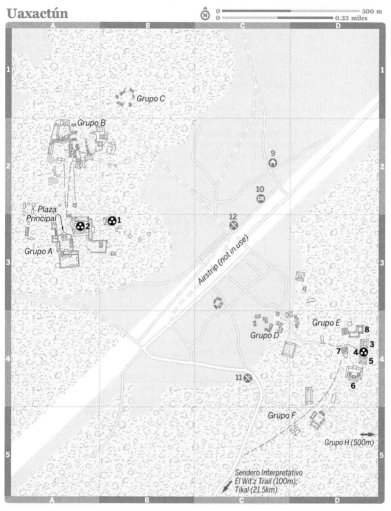

Uaxactún

of town, women put together bunches of the plants for export.

Much of the attraction here is the absolute stillness and isolation. Few visitors make it up this way.

At the time of writing there was no cellphone coverage and just one public phone, in an office (⊙to 6pm) on the south side of the airstrip.

An interpretive nature trail, the Sendero Interpretativo El Wit'z, runs 1.7km through the jungle, initiating from a point 200m beyond the Comedor Imperial Okan Arin and ending up at Grupo H of the Uaxactún archaeological site. Moving from cultivated to preserved sections of the forest, it is meant to demonstrate the effectiveness of conservation in preserving the environment. Chicozapote, *ramón* and other native trees grow in the protected part.

◉ Sights

Research performed by the Carnegie Institute in the 1920s and '30s laid the groundwork for much of the archaeological study that followed in the region, including the excavations at Tikal.

The fee of Q50 to enter Uaxactún is collected at the gate to Tikal National Park, though there is no ticket control at the site itself.

Colección Dr Juan Antonio Valdés MUSEUM
(Campamento El Chiclero) FREE The collection on display here, on the north side of the airstrip, holds a remarkable wealth of Maya pottery from the Uaxactún, Yaxhá and as far away as Oaxaca, Mexico. There are vases, cups, plates, bowls, incense burners and tall vessels for drinking chocolate. Caretaker Neria can tell you the history, origin, meaning and use of each one.

A case contains some of the most precious finds: stone earrings, arrowheads and three plates showing the dance of the corn god.

Although there's no admission fee, donations are appreciated.

◎ Grupo E

The buildings here are grouped on five low hills. From the airstrip find the sign pointing to Grupo E between the Catholic and Evangelical churches on the right side, from where it's a 10- to 15-minute walk. The most significant temple here is Templo E-VII-Sub, among the earliest intact temples excavated, with foundations going back perhaps

to 2000 BC. The pyramid is part of a group with astronomical significance: seen from it, the sun rises behind Templo E-I on the longest day of the year and behind Templo E-III on the shortest day. The four jaguar and serpent masks affixed to the main temple's staircase were painstakingly restored in 2014 by a group of Slovak archaeologists, but then covered up again for conservation.

Templo E-X ARCHAEOLOGICAL SITE
This is the tallest and possibly the oldest of a set of temples at Grupo E. Archaeologists date the structure to around 400 BC. Standing north of the central plaza, it can be recognized by its prominent central staircase.

Templo E-II ARCHAEOLOGICAL SITE
This is the middle of three temples that together form an astronomical observatory at Grupo E. Viewed from Templo E-VII-Sub, the sun sets behind Templo E-II at the start of spring and autumn.

◎ Grupos B & A

About a 20-minute walk to the northwest of the airstrip are Grupo B and Grupo A, the latter featuring the more formidable structures around the city's main square. Palacio V, on the east side of the square, is considered a model for Tikal's North Acropolis. In 1916 the American archaeologist Sylvanus Morley uncovered a stelae dating from the 8th *baktún* at Grupo A. Thus the site was called Uaxactún, meaning 'eight stone.' Behind Palacio V, along a path back toward the village, is the imposing Palacio A-XVIII, affording the most panoramic view of the site from its summit.

Stela 5, at Grupo B, displays Tikal's signature glyph, from which archaeologists deduced that Uaxactún was under that city's sway by the date inscribed, 358.

☞ Tours

Tours to Uaxactún can be arranged in Flores or at the hotels in El Remate and Tikal.

In Uaxactún, Hector Aldana Nuñez from Aldana's Lodge is an English-speaking guide specializing in nature-oriented tours of the region. He leads three-day treks to El Zotz and Tikal for around Q1300 per person. He also offers survival training (Q350 per day), in which participants learn to find sustenance and shelter in the jungle; machetes are provided.

Campamento El Chiclero can organize trips to more remote sites such as El Mirador, Río Azul (three days), Xultún, Nakbé and San Bartolo.

🛏 Sleeping & Eating

If you arrive here by public bus, you'll need to spend the night, since the only return trip is early in the morning. There are two places to stay, one basic, the other rustic.

A few basic cookshacks provide food, including Comedor Uaxactún (mains Q20; ⊙ 8am-8pm) and Comedor Imperial Okan Arin (mains Q20; ⊙ 7am-7pm), and the village's main lodging prepares all meals.

Posada & Restaurante Campamento El Chiclero HOTEL $

(☎ 5780-4855; campamentochiclero@gmail.com; campsite/r per person Q30/Q75) On the north side of the airstrip, this place has 10 spartan, institutional green rooms underneath a thatched roof, with decent mattresses and mosquito-netted ceilings and windows. Clean showers and toilets are in an adjacent outbuilding; lights out at 9pm. Perky owner Neria does the best food in town (Q50 for soup and a main course with rice).

Aldana's Lodge HUT $

(☎ 7783-3931; campsite/r per person Q20/Q25) To the right off the street leading to Grupos B and A, the Aldana family offers half a dozen clapboard cabins, with thin mattresses on pallets. Father and son Alfido and Hector Aldaña lead tours to jungle sites, and Amparo prepares good meals.

ℹ Orientation

Uaxactún village lies either side of a disused airstrip, a remnant of the age when planes were the only way to reach this inaccessible spot. The strip now serves as pasture and a football field. About halfway along the airstrip, roads go both left and right to the ruins. Village boys will want to guide you: you don't need a guide to find the ruins, but you might want to let one or two of them earn a small tip.

ℹ Getting There & Away

A Pinita bus leaves the main terminal of Santa Elena for Uaxactún (Q40) at 2:15pm, then migrates to the market terminal, finally leaving town at 3:30pm. This bus passes through El Remate around 4:30pm and Tikal by 5pm. The following day it starts back for Santa Elena from Uaxactún at 7am. This means you'll need to spend two nights in Uaxactún to see the ruins.

Otherwise, tours from El Remate to Uaxactún and back by Casa de Don David (p246) cost Q615 for up to five persons.

If you're driving, the last chance to fill your fuel tank as you come from the south is at Puente Ixlú, just south of El Remate. During the rainy season (from May to October, sometimes extending into November), the road from Tikal to Uaxactún can become pretty muddy. From Uaxactún, unpaved roads lead to other ruins at El Zotz (about 30km southwest), Xultún (35km northeast) and Río Azul (100km northeast).

Yaxhá

The Classic Maya sites of Yaxhá, Nakum and El Naranjo form a triangle that is the basis for a national park covering more than 370 sq km and bordering the Parque Nacional Tikal to the west. Yaxhá, the most visited of the trio, stands on a hill between two sizable lakes, Lago Yaxhá and Lago Sacnab. The setting, the sheer size of the site, the number of excellently restored buildings and the abundant jungle flora and fauna all make it particularly worth visiting. The site is 11km north of the Puente Ixlú–Melchor de Mencos road, accessed via unpaved road from a turnoff 32km from Puente Ixlú and 33km from Melchor de Mencos.

⊙ Sights

Occupied as early as 600 BC, Yaxhá (translated as 'blue-green water') achieved its cultural apex in the 8th century AD, when it counted some 20,000 inhabitants and 500 buildings, including temples, palaces and residential complexes.

It takes about two hours to wander round the main groups of ruins, which have been extensively excavated and reconstructed. Pick up an excellent map/information guide (Q20), in English, at the ticket booth. One approach is to cover the site in a clockwise fashion, traversing the original road network. The first group of buildings you come to, Plaza C, is one of a pair of astronomical observatories. Take the Calzada de las Canteras to the South Acropolis, a complex of palatial structures from which Yaxhá's aristocracy could watch the games going on in the ball court below. To the northwest stands one of Yaxhá's most ancient constructions, the Greater Astronomical Complex (Plaza F). The arrangement is similar to the one at Uaxactún's Grupo E, with an observation tower (unexcavated)

Yaxhá

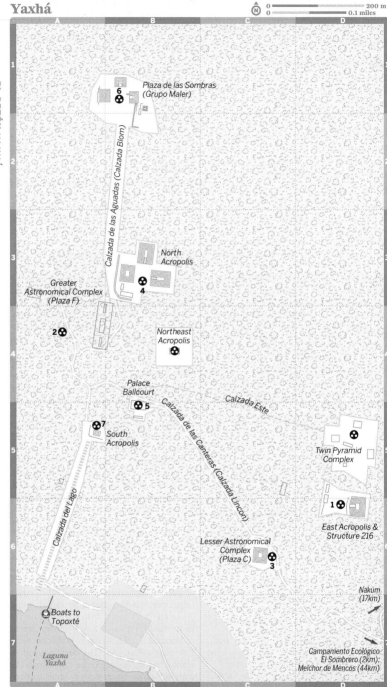

Plaza de las Sombras
(Grupo Maler)

6

Calzada de las Aguadas (Calzada Blom)

North
Acropolis

4

Greater
Astronomical Complex
(Plaza F)

2

Northeast
Acropolis

Palace
Ballcourt

5

Calzada Este

Calzada de las Canteras (Calzada Lincon)

7
South
Acropolis

Calzada del Lago

Twin Pyramid
Complex

1

East Acropolis &
Structure 216

Lesser Astronomical
Complex
(Plaza C)

3

Boats to
Topoxté

Laguna
Yaxhá

Nakúm
(17km)

Campamento Ecológico
El Sombrero (2km);
Melchor de Mencos (44km)

0   200 m
0   0.1 miles

Yaxhá

facing a three-part platform for tracking the sun's trajectory through the year. You can ascend the pyramidal tower (there's a wooden staircase alongside) for jaw-dropping views of the **North Acropolis** to the northeast, with a formidable temple rising above the jungle foliage. From here, take the Calzada de las Aguadas north to reach the **Plaza de las Sombras** (aka Grupo Maler), where archaeologists believe throngs of citizens once gathered for religious ceremonies. Return toward the entrance along the Calzada Este to reach the high point of the tour (literally), **Structure 216** in the East Acropolis. Also called the Temple of the Red Hands, because red handprints were discovered there, it towers over 30m high, affording views in every direction.

On an island near the far (south) shore of Laguna Yaxhá is a late Postclassic archaeological site, **Topoxté**, where the dense covering of ruined temples and dwellings harbor some 100 structures. Evidence shows two distinct periods of occupation here, the latter, as late as AD 1450, by a migrant group from the Yucatán Peninsula. At the bottom of the Calzada del Lago is the **boat landing**, from where a boat operator might be willing to take you to Topoxté for around Q250.

A trail from the boat landing leads along the lake shore to a new **Interpretive Center**, which displays ceramic pieces, musical instruments and jewelry unearthed from the site, along with descriptions of its discovery and excavation.

🛏 Sleeping & Eating

El Sombrero Eco-Lodge (☑4215-8777; elsombreroecolodge.com; s/d/tr Q544/880/1216, s/d/tr without bathroom Q144/288/416; 🅿) 🍽 offers comfortable lodging 2km from the archaeological site. On the lake shore below the Yaxhá ruins is **Campamento Yaxhá** `FREE`, where you can camp for free on raised platforms with thatched roofs. Outbuildings have showers and toilets. Drinking water can be purchased at a store, but you must bring food. There's no need to purchase another admission ticket if you'd like to stay another day or two.

The nearest place to eat is El Sombrero Eco-Lodge, with quality Italian food; otherwise you'll find home-cooked meals at the turnoff from the Puente Ixlú–Melchor road.

ⓘ Getting There & Away

Agencies in Flores and El Remate offer organized trips to Yaxhá, some combined with Nakum and/or Tikal. Horizontes Mayas (p244) in El Remate runs tours (Q125 per person, minimum three people), including guide and entrance fee, at 7am and 1pm, returning at 1pm and 6:30pm. Otherwise, take a Melchor de Mencos–bound microbus and get off at Restaurante El Portal de Yaxhá, opposite the Yaxhá turnoff, and they can arrange transport to the site by pickup truck or motorcycle (Q65 return).

Nakum

A contemporary of Tikal, Nakum was a significant port on the Holmul river, a waterway that linked Tikal with the Caribbean coast, though it reached its cultural peak in the Late Classic period, well past Tikal's prime. It's 17km north of Yaxhá, a 1½ hour drive over a rough road that's impassable from August to January (though it was improved by the crew of Survivor Guatemala, which was shot here).

Remote as this spot is, it's particularly exciting to find such a formidable group of structures here. The excavated section is not huge but it packs a lot in. Major excavations of the site have recently been completed. Archaeological research focused on the predominance of *talud-tablero* (stepped building style, with alternating vertical and sloping sections) type structures in the south section, suggesting a connection with Teotihuacán in Mexico. The question remains why Nakum flourished during the Terminal Classic at a time when its contemporaries were collapsing all around it.

The site features two major architectural groups, the North and South Sectors, connected by a causeway; most of the excavated structures are in the latter. The most interesting of these, in the part dubbed the Plaza Central, features an unusually well-preserved roofcomb with a clearly visible mask. In tandem with the pyramidal structure opposite, it presumably served as some kind of astronomical observatory.

Moving south from the Plaza Central, you enter the South Acropolis, a walled compound on a raised platform comprising 12 courtyards surrounded by 33 buildings that housed palatial residences. This arrangement was in place around AD 900, though there is evidence that the site had been occupied for the previous 14 centuries. What's unique about some of the courtyards here, like Patio 1, is that they were completely enclosed by buildings, a layout not found elsewhere in the Maya world. Outside the South Acropolis to the east are stelae bearing dates from the 9th century, among the latest recorded dates in the Maya lowlands.

Campamento Ecológico El Sombrero (p259) in Yaxhá can arrange horseback rides with a night spent sleeping in hammocks. To get here independently, you'll need a 4WD and a permit from the park's administration at Yaxhá. Should you wish to spend the night, Nakum has a handful of tent platforms, free of charge, but bring food and water.

Parque Nacional Laguna del Tigre

A vast expanse of seasonally flooded forest cut through by slow-moving rivers, this 3340-sq-km park in the northwest corner of El Petén forms the largest protected wetlands area in Mesoamerica. Though its northwestern reaches are threatened by petroleum extraction operations and drug-running activities, it remains a haven for endemic wildlife.

El Perú (Waká)

Trips to El Perú are termed La Ruta Guacamaya (the Scarlet Macaw Trail) because the chances of seeing these magnificent birds are high, chiefly during their nesting season (February to June). Several important Classic-period structures and stelae at the jungle site have led archaeologists to believe it may have allied with Calakmul, Tikal's great rival to the north.

El Perú is 62km northwest of Flores in the Parque Nacional Laguna del Tigre. From the riverbank, it's a half-hour walk to the site entrance, then an hour's climb through primary-growth forest to the ruins.

Though there are no excavated buildings here, a number of stelae, in various states of deterioration, occupy four plazas. Stela number 16 in plaza 3 (the original lies under a thatched roof next to a fiberglass replica) portrays Siyaj K'ak', aka Smoking Frog, a warrior from Teotihuacán who arrived here in 378 and apparently allied with El Perú in a campaign to overthrow Tikal.

Most visitors stay at Estación Biológica Las Guacamayas, 20 minutes by motorboat up the Río San Pedro, but there are tent platforms at the ranger station for those who like to camp out.

There is no restaurant or snack bar at the site; pack a lunch or make arrangements with your tour guide.

The most practical way to get to El Perú is by tour through the Estación Biológica Las Guacamayas, usually as part of a two- or three-day package. They can convey you to the site by *lancha* or through the jungle by buggy; tours are conducted by guides from the nearby community of Paso Caballos.

Estación Biológica Las Guacamayas

A scientific research center within the Parque Nacional Laguna del Tigre, the **Estación Biológica Las Guacamayas** (Scarlet Macaw Biological Station; ✆ 5699-3735; www.lasguacamayas.org) offers wildlife watching and archaeology tours, and the chance to tag along with researchers as they monitor macaws and butterflies. Overlooking the broad lazy river, it's a splendidly isolated spot and there is comfortable, ecofriendly accommodations in several thatched-roof houses.

One-day birding tours are devoted to spotting and photographing not just macaws but more than 300 other avian species found in and around the reserve, including the red-capped manakin, red-legged honeycreeper and long-tailed hermit. Two- to three-day tours consist of some combination of a visit to the archaeological site of El Perú, 20 minutes west down the Río San Pedro, and nighttime observation of the endemic Morelet's crocodile, along with the chance to fish for the renowned *pescado blanco* (whitefish).

Volunteering is possible, with the chance to contribute to infrastructure, maintain trails, cultivate the butterfly garden or support environmental education projects among the Q'eqchi' community in Paso Caballos. There's a minimum two-week commitment, and volunteers pay Q620 per week for accommodation, food and transport to the site.

The 15 newly installed rooms are semi-luxurious jungle affairs featuring bamboo-frame beds, mahogany furniture, screened picture windows and porches overlooking the river. The rate per person on a two-day stay (for two people) is around Q2000, including accommodations, meals and transport; for a three-day stay it's Q3000.

There's a *comedor* on site, where healthy meals are prepared.

The reserve (p260) provides transport from Flores as part of its packages. The journey involves a 2½-hour drive to Paso Caballos, followed by a 20-minute motorboat trip to the station.

El Mirador

Buried within the furthest reaches of the Petén jungle, just 7km south of the Mexican border, the late-Preclassic metropolis at El Mirador (Lookout; www.miradorbasin.com; ⏲24hr) FREE contains the largest cluster of buildings of any single Maya site, among them the biggest pyramid ever built in the Maya world. Ongoing excavations have only scratched the surface, so many are still hidden beneath the jungle.

El Mirador was so-named by local *chicleros* (chicle harvesters) for the excellent views provided by some of the pyramids. La Danta (the Tapir) looms 70m above the forest floor. El Tigre is 55m high with a base covering 18,000 sq meters. At its height, the city spread over 16 sq km and supported tens of thousands of citizens. It was certainly the greatest Maya city of the Preclassic era, far exceeding in size anything built subsequently in the Maya world.

The temples erected here display the unusual 'triadic' style, in which three pyramids crown a large platform, with the one in the middle dominating the other two, which face each other at a lower level. The facades of these buildings were once embellished with carved masks.

Scholars are still figuring out why and how El Mirador thrived (there are few natural resources and no water sources save for the reservoirs built by ingenious, ancient engineers) and what led to its abandonment in 150 AD. Some five centuries after that date, El Mirador appears to have been resettled, as suggested by the existence of Classic architecture among the older structures. Pottery unearthed from this era displays highly refined codex-style of decoration, in which calligraphic lines are painted on a cream-colored surface, with designs believed to resemble Maya codices.

Richard Hansen, a professor from Idaho State University, is leading the effort to map the Mirador basin, a vast swath of northern El Petén comprising dozens of interconnected cities, with funding from an assortment of international and Guatemalan foundations and private sources. In March 2009, Dr Hansen and his crew made a significant

EL PETÉN EL MIRADOR

THE MIRADOR BASIN

The 2169 sq km of tropical forest surrounding El Mirador harbors dozens of substantial cities that flourished during the middle- and late-Preclassic eras. At least six major causeways connected El Mirador to these satellites, an engineering feat that enabled it to become what was possibly the New World's first political state. The four largest cities in the vicinity are all within a day's walk of El Mirador.

El Tintal (23km southwest of El Mirador) One of the largest and most important Preclassic cities, with a moat surrounding the civic center both to defend the city and ensure a year-round water supply.

Wakná (15km south) Built around what is possibly the largest astronomical observatory in the Maya world, with Preclassic murals and a series of internal causeways.

Nakbé (13km southeast) Established around 1200 BC, it grew to be one of the most important Preclassic sites. El Mirador was probably modeled upon this predecessor. All the characteristic features of Maya civilization – monumental architecture, palaces, causeways and ball courts – had appeared here by 600 BC.

Xulnal (7km west of El Tintal) Discovered in 2001. Pottery found here is evidence of some of the earliest occupation in the Mirador Basin.

discovery when they excavated a 4m frieze at the base of La Danta, dating from 300 BC, which they surmise decorated a royal pool. The carved images upon it depict the twin heroes Hunahpú and Ixbalnqué swimming through the underworld domain of Xibalbá, a tale that is related in the Popol Vuh (the Maya 'Bible'). The finding underlines the importance of El Mirador in establishing the belief system of Classic era civilizations.

🛏 Sleeping & Eating

If arriving at the site by tour, your guides will set up camp with mosquito netting at Tintal, El Mirador and Nakbe. In Carmelita (launching point for the trek), local families offer beds.

Trekking guides prepare snacks along the trail and meals at campsites, though it's a good idea to pack a few of your preferences. Neria from Posada del Campamento Chiclero (p257) is famed for her culinary skills.

ℹ Getting There & Away

A visit to El Mirador involves an arduous jungle trek of at least five days and four nights (it's about 60km each way), with no facilities or amenities aside from what you carry in and what can be rustled from the forest. During the rainy season, especially September to December, the mud can make it extremely difficult; February to June is the best period to attempt a trek.

The trip usually departs from a cluster of houses called Carmelita, 82km up the road from Flores. The Comisión de Turismo Cooperativa Carmelita (p235), a group of 16 INGUAT-authorized guides, can make all arrangements for a trek to El Mirador, with optional visits to the Preclassic sites of Nakbé, El Tintal, Wakná and Xulnal. Travelers who participate in these treks should be in good physical shape, able to withstand high temperatures (average of nearly 38°C) and humidity (average 85%) and be prepared to hike or ride long distances (up to 30km per day).

On the first day of a typical six-day itinerary, you'll hike six hours through mostly agricultural country to El Tintal, where you'd camp for the night. On the second day, after a look around El Tintal, you proceed through denser forests to El Mirador and set up camp there. The next day is reserved for exploring El Mirador. On day four, you hike four hours southeast to arrive at Nakbé and camp there. The next day the expedition begins the return south via an eastern trail, stopping for the night at the site of La Florida. On day six, you head back to Carmelita.

For a five-/six-/seven-day trip, the cooperative charges Q1915/2300/2700 per person in a group of at least three people. The fee includes tents, hammocks and mosquito netting; all meals and drinking water; Spanish-speaking guide; mules and muleskinners; and first-aid supplies.

Two buses daily travel from Flores to Carmelita, at 5am and 1pm (Q40). Generally you'd take the morning bus and start hiking straight away.

It's also possible to get here from Uaxactún, a longer but gentler approach since there are fewer bajos (seasonal swamps) and it's less affected by agricultural clearing, so you're underneath the jungle canopy from the outset. Posada Campamento del Chiclero (p257) offers a six-day tour at Q1900 per person per day. On the first leg of the journey you're driven in a monster truck to a campground at the former chiclero camp of Yucatán, a five-hour journey. The next morning the group is outfitted with mules and proceeds to another camp, La Leontina, a four-hour tramp through the jungle. The following day it's a three-hour walk to Nakbé. After visiting that site, the expedition continues to El Mirador. The journey back follows the same route in reverse.

If expense is not a concern, you can go the easy way: by helicopter. During selected periods throughout the year, **TAG Airlines** (☎ 2380-9400; www.tag.com.gt) offers chopper packages from Flores to El Mirador, including guided commentary by longtime site archaeologist Richard Hansen, plus meals and accommodation for about Q10,340 per person. Contact the airline to find out about the current schedule.

Understand Guatemala

Guatemala Today

Guatemalans are struggling. Over half the population lives below the poverty line and gang membership is rising as an overwhelmed and under-resourced police force struggles to maintain order. Against this increasingly bleak backdrop, scores of grass-roots organizations have sprung up, tirelessly combating Guatemala's many problems. While successive governments continue to make promises, it is Guatemalans themselves who are delivering solutions.

Best on Film

Aquí me Quedo (Rodolfo Espinoza; 2010) Subtle political commentary, black comedy and satire abound in this story of a kidnapping, shot in and around Quetzaltenango.

When the Mountains Tremble (Pamela Yates & Newton Thomas Sigel; 1983) Documentary about the civil war, featuring Susan Sarandon and Rigoberta Menchú.

Capsulas (Verónica Riedel; 2011) A look at greed, corruption and the drug trade from one of Guatemala's few female directors.

Ixcanúl (Jayro Bustamante; 2015) Multi-award-winning film about a young Kaqchikel girl's coming of age.

Best in Print

The President (Miguel Ángel Asturias; 1946) Nobel Prize–winning Guatemalan author takes some not-too-subtle jabs at the country's long line of dictators.

A Mayan Life (Gaspar Pedro Gonzáles; 1995) The first published novel by a Maya author is an excellent study of rural Guatemalan life.

The Art of Political Murder (Francisco Goldman; 2008) Meticulously researched account of the assassination of Bishop Gerardi.

Neither Corrupt nor a Thief

The elections that followed ex-president Otto Pérez Molina's impeachment were won by Jimmy Morales, a popular television comic whose popularity partly stemmed from the fact that he came from outside the country's political elite. Morales ran with the slogan *'Ni corrupto, ni ladrón'* (neither corrupt nor a thief), which obviously touched some chords in a country that now had its previous president and vice-president in jail. Morales took office in January 2016. Hopes were high that change was finally in the air, but the new president's ties to the military establishment (themselves seen as the core of the country's real political elite) gave way to concerns that the country was in for more of the same, again.

A Question of Security

Guatemala still struggles with violence. The National Gun Registry campaign started off well, but continues to falter. There are 11 guns for every 100 people in Guatemala, of which only three are registered.

The police force, understaffed and under-resourced, has struggled to keep up with the rise in drug-related crime, particularly in urban areas and most notably in Guatemala City. A measure of their failure to do so is the fact that there are an estimated 150,000 private security guards employed nationwide, as compared to just 30,000 police officers. It won't take you too long on your travels before you start spotting heavily armed young (sometimes scarily young) men in official-looking uniforms, guarding everything from private residences to pharmacies and fast-food restaurants.

Global Policy

Global policy continues to affect Guatemala. A possibly unforeseen consequence of the move toward renewable fuels worldwide has seen corn-tortilla prices skyrocket in Guatemala, as the United States uses up to 40% of its corn crop to make biofuel. Corn is a staple in Guatemala – pretty much the one ingredient you are guaranteed to see at every meal – and despite widespread plantations the country pays over US$200 million per year to import corn.

One very touchy subject in rural Guatemala has to do with large (often foreign-administered) projects such as hydroelectric dams and mineral mines. Amnesty International reports state that international companies regularly flaunt Human Rights conventions when displacing local communities, and that the worst-affected are impoverished rural indigenous communities.

The Slow Road to Recovery

Guatemala is on the slow road to recovery from its Civil War wounds. While this is in part due to the passing of generations who lived through the war, official recognition of some atrocities has been an important step in the recovery process. Though President Morales has stated he does not believe the genocide in the Ixil triangle ever took place, a campaign is underway to exhume clandestine cemeteries used by the military to bury 'disappeared' dissidents and the legal processes have at last begun, with some war criminals being brought to justice. So far the heftiest penalty to be handed down was to ex-Military Commissioner Lucas Tecún, who was sentenced to 7710 years in prison.

In March 2012, in a move that shocked many hardened cynics, a Guatemalan judge removed the final obstacle barring former dictator Efraín Ríos Montt from facing trial on charges of genocide. At first he was convicted to 80 years prison, but a later court ruling overturned the conviction, then called for a retrial, citing Ríos Montt's alleged senility.

Grass Roots Movement

In the face of official indifference and/or inability to deal with the country's myriad problems, many community-based organizations and NGOs are moving in to fill the void. Large segments of the Guatemalan population are becoming active in volunteer work, focusing on everything from neighborhood-watch-type programs in areas unpatrolled by police to larger efforts focusing on food security and housing for the poor. This community spirit is also evident after natural disasters hit the country, as citizens band together to deliver aid to affected families.

The mass protests against the Pérez Molina government, mainly non-politically aligned and organized chiefly through social media, seem to have sparked a new interest in politics among young Guatemalans, with alliances being formed from previously disparate groups.

POPULATION: **14,919,000**

AREA: **108,889 SQ KM**

GDP: **US$63.22 BILLION**

INFLATION: **2.2%**

POPULATION BELOW
POVERTY LINE: **54%**

if Guatemala were 100 people

59 would be Mestizo (person of mixed ancestry)
40 would be Maya
 1 would be other

Guatemalan diaspora
(% of migrating population)

84 — USA
10 — Mexico
2 — Canada
4 — Other

population per sq km

Guatemala   Mexico   USA

👤 ≈ 35 people

History

Tumultuous barely begins to describe the series of events that this small piece of land has seen over the past few millennia. Great empires have risen and fallen, conquerors have come and gone, and the population has repeatedly found itself trapped in the crossfire of war.

The Ancient Maya, by Robert J Sharer, is a 1990s update of Sylvanus G Morley's classic 1940s tome of the same name, and is admirably clear and uncomplicated.

Preclassic Period (2000 BC–AD 250)

The Preclassic Period is generally thought to have coincided with the emergence of stable social structures and early forms of agriculture, pottery and tool-making in what is now Mexico and Guatemala. The improvement in the food supply led to an increase in population, a higher standard of living and developments in agricultural and artistic techniques. Decorative pots and healthier, fatter corn strains were produced. Even at the beginning of the Preclassic period, people in Guatemala spoke an early form of the Maya language.

By the middle Preclassic period (800–300 BC) there were rich villages in the Copán Valley, and villages had been founded at what would become the majestic city of Tikal, amid the jungles of El Petén. Trade routes developed, with coastal peoples exchanging salt and seashells for highland tribes' tool-grade obsidian.

As the Maya honed their agricultural techniques, including the use of fertilizer and elevated fields, a noble class emerged, constructing temples that consisted of raised platforms of earth topped by thatch-roofed shelters. The local potentate was buried beneath the shelter, increasing the site's sacred power. Such temples have been found at Uaxactún, Tikal and El Mirador. Kaminaljuyú, in Guatemala City, reached its peak from about 400 BC to AD 100, with thousands of inhabitants and scores of temples built on earth mounds.

In El Petén, where limestone was abundant, the Maya began to build platform temples from stone. As each succeeding local potentate demanded a bigger temple, larger and larger platforms were built over existing platforms, eventually forming huge pyramids. The potentate was buried deep within the stack of platforms. El Tigre pyramid at El Mira-

TIMELINE	3114 BC	1100 BC	c 250 BC
	The Maya creation story says that the world was created on August 13 of this year, which corresponds to the first date on the Maya Long Count Calendar.	Proto-Maya settlements begin to appear in the Copán Valley. By 1000 BC settlements on the Guatemalan Pacific coast show early signs of developing a hierarchical society.	Early Maya cities El Mirador and Kaminaljuyú flourish between 250 BC and 100 AD due to tactical and commercial advantages. Agricultural techniques are refined as the trade in obsidian and jade booms.

dor, 18 stories high, is believed to be the largest ever built by the Maya. More and more pyramids were built around large plazas. The stage was set for the flowering of Classic Maya civilization.

Classic Period (AD 250–900)

The Classic Maya were organized into numerous city-states. While Tikal began to assume a primary role around AD 250, El Mirador had been mysteriously abandoned about a century earlier. Some scholars believe a severe drought hastened this great city's demise.

Each city-state had its noble house, headed by a priestly king who placated the gods by shedding his blood by piercing his tongue, penis or ears with sharp objects. As sacred head of his community, the king also had to lead his soldiers into battle against rival cities, capturing prisoners for use in human sacrifices.

A typical Maya city functioned as the religious, political and market hub for the surrounding farming hamlets. Its ceremonial center focused on plazas surrounded by tall temple pyramids and lower buildings with warrens of small rooms. Stelae and altars were carved with dates, histories and elaborate human and divine figures.

In the first part of the Classic period, most of the city-states were probably grouped into two loose military alliances centered on Calakmul, in Mexico's Campeche state, and Tikal.

In the late 8th century, trade between Maya states waned and conflict grew. By the early 10th century the cities of Tikal, Yaxchilán, Copán, Quiriguá and Piedras Negras had reverted to minor towns or even villages, and much of El Petén was abandoned. Many explanations, including population pressure, drought and ecological damage, have been offered for the collapse of the Classic Maya period.

Postclassic Period (900–1524)

Some of the Maya who abandoned El Petén must have moved southwest into the highlands of Guatemala. In the 13th and 14th centuries they were joined by Maya-Toltecs from the Tabasco or Yucatán areas of Mexico. Groups of these newcomers set up a series of rival states in the Guatemalan highlands: the most prominent were the K'iche' (or Quiché; capital, K'um'arkaj, near modern Santa Cruz del Quiché), the Kaqchiquels (capital, Iximché, near Tecpán), the Mam (capital, Zaculeu, near Huehuetenango), the Tz'utujil (capital, Chuitinamit, near Santiago Atitlán) and the Poqomam (capital, Mixco Viejo, north of Guatemala City). Another group from the Yucatán, the Itzáes, wound up at Lago de Petén Itzá in El Petén, settling in part on the island that is today called Flores.

The Maya, by Michael D Coe, is probably the best single-volume telling of the ancient Maya story. Coe's *Breaking the Maya Code* recounts the modern decipherment of ancient Maya writing, and his *Reading the Maya Glyphs* will help you read ancient inscriptions.

Archaeologists estimate that only 10% of Tikal – one of the country's biggest and most famous Maya sites – has been uncovered.

HISTORY CLASSIC PERIOD (AD 250–900)

AD 230	682	900	c 13th century
El Mirador begins to decline in importance. King Yax Ehb' Xooc of Tikal establishes the dynasty that will make Tikal the dominant city of the southern Maya world.	King Moon Double Comb, or Lord Chocolate, ascends Tikal's throne and begins remodeling and reconstructing Tikal's grand plazas and temples that had been destroyed by Caracol and Calakmul.	The collapse of Classic Maya civilization begins, and the Postclassic era starts. A century-long exodus from Tikal commences, after which the city will never be inhabited again.	Ruthlessly organized Toltec-Maya migrants from southeast Mexico establish kingdoms in Guatemala. Highlands Maya organize into competing kingdoms, establishing language and cultural groupings that survive today.

Spanish Conquest

The Blood of Kings: Dynasty & Ritual in Maya Art, by Linda Schele and Mary Ellen Miller, is a heavily and fascinatingly illustrated guide to the art and culture of the ancient Maya.

Spaniards under Hernán Cortés defeated the Aztec Empire based at Tenochtitlán (modern Mexico City) in 1521. It only took a couple of years for the conquistadors to turn to Guatemala in their search for wealth. Pedro de Alvarado, one of Cortés' most brutal lieutenants, entered Guatemala in 1524, forging temporary alliances with local Maya groups while murdering and subjugating their rivals. And then laying waste to them.

And so it went throughout Guatemala as Alvarado sought fortune and renown. The one notable exception was the Rabinal of present-day Baja Verapaz, who survived with their preconquest identity intact and remain one of Guatemala's most traditional groups to this day.

Alvarado moved his base to Santiago de los Caballeros (now called Ciudad Vieja) in 1527, but, shortly after his death in 1541, Ciudad Vieja was destroyed by a flood. The Spanish capital was relocated under the same name to a new site nearby, known today as Antigua.

Colonial Period (1524–1821)

The Spanish effectively enslaved Guatemala's indigenous people to work what had been their own land for the benefit of the Spanish, just as they did throughout the hemisphere. Refusal to work meant death. The colonists believed themselves omnipotent and behaved accordingly.

Enter the Catholic Church and Dominican friar Bartolomé de Las Casas. Las Casas had been in the Caribbean and Latin America since 1502 and had witnessed firsthand the near complete genocide of the indigenous populations of Cuba and Hispaniola. Horrified by what he had seen, Las Casas managed to convince Carlos V of Spain to enact the New Laws of 1542, which technically ended the system of forced labor. In reality, forced labor continued, but wanton waste of Maya lives ceased. Las Casas and other friars went about converting the Maya to Christianity.

Returning from the Americas, Christopher Columbus introduced Europeans to a whole range of foods they'd never seen before – including tomatoes, sweet potatoes, squash, potatoes, avocados, corn and cocoa.

A large portion of the church's conversion success can be attributed to its peaceful approach, the relative respect extended to traditional beliefs, and the education provided in indigenous languages.

Independence

By the time thoughts of independence from Spain began stirring among Guatemalans, society was already rigidly stratified. Only the European-born Spaniards had any real power, but the *criollos* (Guatemalan-born Spaniards) lorded it over the *ladinos* (of mixed Spanish and Maya blood), who in turn exploited the indigenous population who still remained on the bottom rung of the socioeconomic ladder.

Angered at being repeatedly passed over for advancement, Guatemalan *criollos* successfully rose in revolt in 1821. Independence changed

1523	1542	1609–1821	1773
Spaniard Pedro de Alvarado begins the conquest of Guatemala. Alvarado quickly conquers much of the country, although parts of the highlands hold out for years and El Petén is not subdued for another 170 years.	Spain enacts the New Laws, officially banning forced labor in its colonies. Catholic influence becomes more institutionalized and traditional Maya social structures are transformed.	The Captaincy General of Guatemala comprises what are now Costa Rica, Nicaragua, Honduras, El Salvador, Guatemala and the Mexican state of Chiapas, with its capital at Antigua, then at Guatemala City.	Antigua, a jewel in the colonial crown, complete with a university, a printing press, schools, hospitals and churches, is destroyed by an earthquake. The new capital is founded at present-day Guatemala City.

little for Guatemala's indigenous communities, who remained under the control of the church and the landowning elite.

Mexico, which had recently become independent, quickly annexed Guatemala, but in 1823 Guatemala reasserted its independence and led the formation of the United Provinces of Central America (July 1, 1823), along with El Salvador, Nicaragua, Honduras and Costa Rica. Their union lasted only until 1840 before breaking up into its constituent states. This era brought prosperity to the *criollos*, but worsened the lot of the Guatemalan Maya. The end of Spanish rule meant that the crown's few liberal safeguards, which had afforded the Maya a minimal protection, were abandoned. The Maya, though technically and legally free, were enslaved by debt peonage to the big landowners.

Mesoweb (www.mesoweb.com) is a great resource on the Maya, past and present.

The Liberals & Carrera

The ruling classes split into two camps: the elite conservatives, including the Catholic Church and the large landowners, and the liberals, who had been the first to advocate independence and who opposed the vested interests of the conservatives.

A short succession of liberal leaders ended when unpopular economic policies and a cholera epidemic led to an indigenous uprising that brought a conservative *ladino* pig farmer, Rafael Carrera, to power. Carrera held power from 1844 to 1865, undoing many liberal reforms and ceding control of Belize to Britain in exchange for construction of a road between Guatemala City and Belize City, a road that was never built.

Liberal Reforms of Barrios

The liberals returned to power in the 1870s, first under Miguel García Granados, next under Justo Rufino Barrios, a rich, young, coffee-plantation owner who held the title of president, but ruled as a dictator (1873–79). Barrios modernized Guatemala's roads, railways, schools and banking system and favored the burgeoning coffee industry disproportionately. Under Barrios' successors a small group of landowning and commercial families came to control the economy, while foreign companies were given generous concessions, and political opponents were censored, imprisoned or exiled.

Estrada Cabrera

Manuel Estrada Cabrera ruled from 1898 to 1920, bringing progress in technical matters, but placing a heavy burden on all but the ruling oligarchy. He fancied himself a bringer of light and culture to a backward land, styling himself the 'Teacher and Protector of Guatemalan Youth.'

In reaction to Cabrera's doublespeak, the *Huelga de Dolores* (Strike of Sorrows) began around this time. Students from Guatemala City's

1823–40	1838	1840	1870s
Guatemala, El Salvador, Honduras, Nicaragua and Costa Rica form the United Provinces of Central America. Liberal reforms are enacted, and vehemently opposed by conservative groups and the Catholic Church.	Much of southwestern Guatemala declares independence, becoming the sixth member of the United Provinces. The new state, called Los Altos, has its capital at Quetzaltenango. It will secede, briefly, in 1844, 1848 and 1849.	Rafael Carrera seizes power and declares Guatemala fully independent and reincorporates Los Altos into Guatemala. He sets about dismantling many of the liberal reforms of the United Provinces.	Liberal governments modernize Guatemala, but turn indigenous lands over to coffee plantations. European newcomers are given preferential treatment, further disenfranchising the Maya.

San Carlos University took to the streets during Lent – wearing hoods to avoid reprisals – to protest against injustice and corruption. The tradition caught on in university towns across the country, culminating with a parade through the main streets on the Friday before Good Friday, a tradition that continues to this day.

Jorge Ubico

Estrada Cabrera was overthrown in 1920 and Guatemala entered a period of instability, ending in 1931 with the election of General Jorge Ubico as president. Ubico insisted on honesty in government, and modernized the country's health and social welfare infrastructure. His reign ended when he was forced into exile in 1944.

Arévalo & Arbenz

Guatemala finally recognized Belizean independence in 1992, but the exact border remains in dispute. An agreement to take the matter to the International Court of Justice was signed in 2008.

Just when it appeared that Guatemala was doomed to a succession of harsh dictators, the elections of 1945 brought a philosopher – Juan José Arévalo – to the presidency. Arévalo, in power from 1945 to 1951, established the nation's social security system, a bureau of indigenous affairs, a modern public health system and liberal labor laws. He also survived 25 coup attempts by conservative military forces.

Arévalo was succeeded by Colonel Jacobo Arbenz, who continued Arévalo's policies, instituting agrarian reforms designed to break up the large estates and foster productivity on small, individually owned farms. He also expropriated vast, unused lands conceded to the United Fruit Company during the Estrada Cabrera and Ubico years. Compensation was paid at the value declared for tax purposes (far below its real value), and Arbenz announced that the lands were to be redistributed to peasants and put into cultivation for food. The announcement set off alarms in Washington, and in 1954 the US, in one of the first documented covert operations by the CIA, orchestrated an invasion from Honduras. Arbenz stepped down, and the land reform never took place.

Arbenz was succeeded by a series of military presidents. More covert (but well documented) support came from the US government, in the form of money and counterinsurgency training. Violence became a staple of political life, land reforms were reversed, voting was made dependent on literacy (disenfranchising around 75% of the population), the secret police force was revived and military repression was common.

In 1960, left-wing guerrilla groups began to form.

The Civil War Begins

Guatemalan industry developed fast, but the social fabric became increasingly stressed as most profits flowed upwards. Labor unions organized, and migration to the cities, especially the capital, produced urban

1901	1940s	1945–54	1954
President Manuel Estrada Cabrera courts the US-owned United Fruit Company to set up shop in Guatemala. United Fruit soon takes on a dominant role in national politics.	Bowing to pressure from the US (buyers of 90% of Guatemala's exports at the time), President Jorge Ubico expels German landowners from the country. Their lands are redistributed to political and military allies.	Juan José Arévalo, elected with 85% of the popular vote, comes to power, ushering in an era of enlightened, progressive government that is continued by his successor Jacobo Arbenz.	Effecting the country's first serious attempt at land reform, Arbenz appropriates Guatemalan lands of the US-owned United Fruit Company. He is soon deposed in a US-orchestrated coup.

sprawl and slums. A cycle of violent repression and protest took hold and by 1979 Amnesty International estimated that 50,000 to 60,000 people had been killed during the political violence of the 1970s alone.

A severe earthquake in 1976 killed some 22,000 people and left around one million homeless. Most of the aid sent for those in need never reached them.

1980s

In the early 1980s four disparate guerrilla groups united to form the URNG (the Guatemalan National Revolutionary Unity) and military suppression of antigovernment elements in the countryside peaked, especially under the presidency of General Efraín Ríos Montt, an Evangelical Christian who came to power by coup in March 1982. Huge numbers of people – mainly indigenous men – from more than 400 villages were murdered in the name of anti-insurgency, stabilization and anticommunism.

It was later estimated that 15,000 civilian deaths occurred as a result of counterinsurgency operations during Ríos Montt's term of office alone, not to mention the estimated 100,000 refugees (again, mostly Maya) who fled to Mexico. The government forced villagers to form Patrullas de Autodefensa Civil (PACs; Civil Defense Patrols), who were later accused of some of the worst human rights atrocities committed during Ríos Montt's rule.

As the civil war dragged on and both sides committed atrocities, more and more rural people came to feel caught in the crossfire.

In August 1983 Ríos Montt was deposed by General Oscar Humberto Mejía Victores, but the abuses continued. Survivors were herded into remote 'model villages' surrounded by army encampments. The ongoing reports of human rights violations and civilian massacres led the US to cut off military assistance to Guatemala, which in turn resulted in the 1986 election of a civilian president, Marco Vinicio Cerezo Arévalo of the Christian Democratic Party.

There was hope that Cerezo Arévalo's administration would temper the excesses of the powerful elite and the military, and establish a basis for true democracy. But armed conflict festered in remote areas and when Cerezo Arévalo's term ended in 1990, many people wondered whether any real progress had been made.

Early 1990s

President Jorge Serrano (1990–93) from the conservative Movimiento de Acción Solidaria (Solidarity Action Movement) reopened a dialogue with the URNG, hoping to bring the decades-long civil war to an end. When the talks collapsed, the mediator from the Catholic Church blamed both sides for intransigence.

In *Silence on the Mountain,* Daniel Wilkinson uncovers in microcosm the social background to the civil war as he delves into the reasons for the burning of a coffee estate by guerrillas.

HISTORY 1980S

La Hija del Puma (The Daughter of the Puma), directed by Ulf Hultberg, is a powerful 1994 film, based on a true story, about a K'iche' Maya girl who survives the army massacre of her fellow villagers and sees her brother captured. She escapes to Mexico, but then returns to Guatemala in search of her sibling.

1950s–1960s	1967	1976	1982
Military dictators rule the country, reversing liberal reforms of previous governments. Crackdowns lead to the formation of left-wing guerrilla groups. The civil war begins.	Guatemalan writer and diplomat Miguel Ángel Asturias, credited as a pioneer of modernist Latin American literature, is awarded the Nobel Prize for Literature for his political novel *El Señor Presidente*.	Earthquake kills 22,000 in Guatemala. Reconstruction efforts help to consolidate leftist opposition groups, who are met with fierce military reprisals. The Carter administration bans military aid to Guatemala.	Four powerful guerrilla organizations unite to form the URNG (Guatemalan National Revolutionary Unity). An estimated half a million people actively support the guerrilla movement.

Human-rights abuses continued during this period despite the country's return to democratic rule. In one dramatic case in 1990, Guatemalan anthropologist Myrna Mack, who had documented army violence against the rural Maya, was fatally wounded after being stabbed dozens of times. Former head of the Presidential Guard, Colonel Juan Valencia Osorio, was found guilty of masterminding the assassination and sentenced to 30 years' imprisonment, but went into hiding before he could be arrested.

RIGOBERTA MENCHÚ TUM

Of all the unlikely candidates for the Nobel Prize throughout history, a rural indigenous Guatemalan woman would have to be near the top of the list.

Rigoberta Menchú was born in 1959 near Uspantán in the highlands of Quiché department and lived the life of a typical young Maya woman until the late 1970s, when the country's civil war affected her tragically and drove her into the left-wing guerrilla camp. Her father, mother and brother were killed in the Guatemalan military's campaign to eradicate communism in the countryside.

Menchú fled to exile in Mexico, where her story *I, Rigoberta Menchú: An Indian Woman in Guatemala* was published and translated throughout the world, bringing the plight of Guatemala's indigenous population to international attention. In 1992 Rigoberta Menchú was awarded the Nobel Prize for Peace, which provided her and her cause with international stature and support. The Rigoberta Menchú Tum Foundation (www.frmt.org), which she founded with the US$1.2 million Nobel Prize money, works for conflict resolution, plurality, and human, indigenous and women's rights in Guatemala and internationally.

Guatemalans, especially the Maya, were proud that one of their own had been recognized by the Nobel committee. In the circles of power, however, Menchú's renown was unwelcome, as she was seen as a troublemaker.

Anthropologist David Stoll's book *Rigoberta Menchú and the Story of All Poor Guatemalans* (1999) contested the truth of many aspects of Menchú's book, including some central facts. The *New York Times* claimed that Menchú had received a Nobel Prize for lying, and of course her detractors had a field day.

Menchú took the controversy in her stride, not addressing the specific allegations, and the Nobel Institute made it clear that the prize was given for Menchú's work on behalf of the indigenous, not the content of her book. More than anything, the scandal solidified support for Menchú and her cause, while calling Stoll's motives into question.

In 1994 Menchú returned to Guatemala from exile. Since then her work with the Foundation has continued, alongside efforts to promote greater access to low-cost, generic pharmaceuticals and a stint as a UN goodwill ambassador for the Peace Accords. In 2007 she decided to run for president. The problematic, often fragmented nature of indigenous politics was highlighted when the World Indigenous Summit of that year chose not to support her. Menchú's party won a little over 3% of the popular vote in the presidential elections.

1982–83	1990	1992	1996
State terror against rural indigenous communities peaks during the rule of General Efraín Ríos Montt. Peasants, particularly in the highlands, begin an exodus to Mexico to escape violence from both sides.	The army massacres 13 Tz'utujil Maya (including three children) in Santiago Atitlán. Outraged, the people of Santiago fight back, becoming the first town to succeed in expelling the army by popular demand.	Indigenous rights and peace activist Rigoberta Menchú is awarded the Nobel Prize for peace. Menchú receives the award while living in exile in Mexico, returning to Guatemala two years later.	After nearly a decade of talks, the Peace Accords are signed, bringing to an end the 36-year civil war in which an estimated 200,000 Guatemalans died.

Serrano's presidency came to depend more on the army for support. In 1993 he tried to seize absolute power, but after a tense few days was forced to flee into exile. Congress elected Ramiro de León Carpio, an outspoken critic of the army's strong-arm tactics, as president, to complete Serrano's term.

Peace Accords

President de León's elected successor, Álvaro Arzú of the center-right Partido de Avanzada Nacional (PAN; National Advancement Party), took office in 1996. Arzú continued negotiations with the URNG and, finally, on December 29, 1996, 'A Firm and Lasting Peace Agreement' was signed. During the 36 years of civil war, an estimated 200,000 Guatemalans had been killed, a million made homeless, and untold thousands had disappeared.

Guatemala Since the Peace Accords

Any hopes for a truly just and democratic society have looked increasingly frayed in the years since 1996. International organizations regularly criticize the state of human rights in the country and Guatemalan human rights campaigners are threatened or simply disappear on a regular basis. The major problems – poverty, illiteracy, lack of education and poor medical facilities (all much more common in rural areas, where the Maya population is concentrated) – remain a long way from being resolved.

The 1999 presidential elections were won by Alfonso Portillo of the conservative Frente Republicano Guatemalteco (FRG). Portillo was seen as a front man for FRG leader, ex-president General Efraín Ríos Montt. At the end of his presidency Portillo fled the country in the face of allegations that he had diverted US$500 million from the treasury to personal and family bank accounts. Having evaded prosecution for years, Portillo was finally charged by the United States for laundering money using US banks, and looks set to be extradited and put on trial there.

Ríos Montt was granted permission by Guatemala's constitutional court to stand in the 2003 elections, despite the fact that the constitution banned presidents who had taken power by coup in the past, as Ríos Montt had in 1982.

Berger and the 'New' Guatemala

In the end Guatemala's voters dealt Ríos Montt a resounding defeat, electing Oscar Berger of the moderately conservative Gran Alianza Nacional (GANA) as president. Berger managed to stay relatively untouched by political scandal, critics saying this was because he didn't really do anything, let alone anything bad.

The Central America Free Trade Agreement (CAFTA; TLC or Tratado de Libre Comercio, in Spanish) was ratified by Guatemala in 2006.

Searching for Everardo, by US attorney Jennifer K Harbury, tells of how she fell in love with and married a URNG guerrilla leader who then disappeared in combat, and of her dedicated struggles with the US and Guatemalan governments – including a hunger strike outside the White House – to discover his fate.

Guatemala: Nunca Mas (1998), published by ODHAG (Human Rights Office of the Archbishopric of Guatemala) and REMHI (Recovery of Historical Memory), details many of the human-rights abuses committed during Guatemala's civil war, and includes moving testimonials.

1998	2000–4	2006	2011
The true nature of peace is questioned as Bishop Gerardi, author of a paper blaming the army for the overwhelming amount of civil-war deaths, is found bludgeoned to death in his home.	Presidency of Alfonso Portillo of the FRG party, led by Efraín Ríos Montt. Portillo begins by prosecuting those responsible for the death of Bishop Gerardi, but is soon mired in corruption allegations.	Guatemala ratifies CAFTA, a free-trade agreement between the US and Central America. Massive street protests and seemingly endless media discussion have little effect on the final document.	First Lady Sandra Torres announces she will divorce the president in order to run for upcoming elections, or in her words, 'marry the people.' The move is slammed as electoral fraud by the opposition.

Supporters claim it frees the country up for greater participation in foreign markets, while detractors state that the agreement is a bad deal for the already disenfranchised rural poor.

Another round of elections was held in late 2007, bringing to power Álvaro Colom of the center-leftist Unidad Nacional de la Esperanza (UNE). Colom followed Berger's example of steady, minimalist governance and spearheaded some much-needed improvements to the country's infrastructure. Unfortunately, his entire presidency was dogged by corruption claims, from straight-out vote buying to back-room deals granting contracts to companies who had contributed to his campaign fund.

But probably the most bizarre twist of the Colom presidency happened as he was leaving office. The Guatemalan constitution prohibits members of the president's family from running for the subsequent presidency (supposedly an anti-dictatorship measure), so Colom and his wife filed for divorce in the lead-up to the 2011 elections in an attempt to make her a valid candidate. The Constitutional Court banned her candidature anyway, leaving the door open for hard-line, ex–civil war general Otto Pérez Molina to take office in early 2012.

Pérez Molina's election was always going to be controversial – he was a general in Ríos Montt's army in the period when the worst atrocities occurred, in the regions where they occurred. Guatemalans had grown tired of the growing lawlessness in their country, though, and turned a blind eye to history in the hope that Molina would deliver on his two campaign promises – jobs and security.

For the latest on human rights in Guatemala, visit the Guatemala Human Rights Commission/USA website (www. ghrc-usa.org) or click on 'Human Rights' on the website of the US embassy in Guatemala City (http://guate mala.usembassy. gov).

Despite some heavy-handed reactions to protesters (the army killed seven and wounded 40 in one incident at an anti-dam and anti-mining protest), Pérez Molina did little to combat real crime, and his early presidency was plagued by vague rumors of corruption in the administration. In April 2015, the UN anti-corruption agency CICIG issued a report and things got a whole lot less vague.

The report claimed several senior members of the Pérez Molina administration were involved in taking bribes from importers in return for reduced customs fees. Within days, mass protests were organized over social media and tens of thousands turned out in downtown Guatemala City. Vice president Roxana Baldetti was the first to go – she resigned in early May, unable to explain how she paid for her US$13 million helicopter, among other things.

In the following months more than 20 officials resigned and many were arrested as the scandal snaked its way to the top. Mass protests continued as more findings were released. Baldetti was arrested in August amid calls for Pérez Molina's impeachment. The president hung on for a few weeks more, then resigned in the face of impending impeachment. He was arrested in early September.

Jan 2012	Dec 21, 2012	2015	2016
Ex-civil war general Otto Perez Molina takes office as president, having won the election promising a reign of 'mano dura' (iron fist) as a solution to Guatemala's burgeoning crime problems.	Despite end-of-the-world predictions from non-Mayans, Baktun 13 ends without major incidents and a new Great Cycle of the Mayan Long Count calendar begins.	UN anti-corruption agency CICIG publishes report claiming widespread government corruption. Vice president Baldetti and President Pérez Molina resign in August and September respectively following mass protests.	Sandra Morán, the first openly LGBT member of Guatemalan congress is sworn in on the same day as new president and ex-comedian Jimmy Morales, an evangelical Christian who has publicly opposed same-sex marriage.

Guatemalan Way of Life

The usual socioeconomic dividers aside, the *way* you live in Guatemala depends largely on *where* you live – the differences between the coast and the highlands, big cities and small villages are so marked that sometimes it feels like that one-hour bus ride has taken you into another country. Some things are common to all Guatemalans, though – a set of national characteristics that when taken together largely define the essence of *ser Chapín* (being Guatemalan).

Bright Lights, Big City

Around half of all Guatemalans live in what are classified as 'urban environments,' but it's important to remember that by international standards, Guatemala City is the country's only really big city: while the capital has more than 4 million inhabitants, Quetzaltenango (the second-largest city) is yet to hit 200,000.

Life in the capital (and even in the larger cities) resembles life in any big city in many ways. There are slums, middle-class neighborhoods and exclusive gated communities. Overcrowding and an ever-growing car culture make for traffic jams that wouldn't be out of place in London or New York. Guatemala City, in particular, has a bad reputation for street crime and it's rare to see people out walking at night. The capital is also where you'll see the most fortified homes, with razor wire, barred windows and closed-circuit camera surveillance – people tend to take as many measures as they can afford to guard against burglars and home invasion.

The standard of living in Guatemala City is slowly improving, thanks largely to the efforts of ex-President and five-time mayor Álvaro Arzú, whose initiatives to open up public spaces and create pedestrian-only streets have earned him the nickname 'El Jardinero' (the gardener) from critics.

Life on the Mountain

Guatemala's mountainous regions also happen to be the most indigenous. As a result, Maya culture and tradition is much stronger in the mountains than on the coastal plain and in the capital. Even in larger cities you'll see many more women (and even some men) dressed in traditional Maya clothing, and no doubt you'll hear locals speaking in their dialect. Many people from these regions, particularly from older generations, speak Spanish as a second language, and some don't speak it at all.

The cold is a factor in the mountains – towns like Quetzaltenango and Todos Santos regularly register below-freezing temperatures in December. Another sight you're likely to see is men chopping and hauling firewood, which is used for both heating and cooking in many traditional homes.

The highlands' rich volcanic soil also makes for some of the best farmland in the country. Vegetables grown in the Western Highlands are exported as far away as Belize, while the Cobán region has become a leading exporter of cardamom – much of it going as far away as India and the Middle East. Many mountain-dwellers work in agriculture, either tending small subsistence plots or working on larger commercial farms.

Down on the Coast

The pace of life on the coast – where midday temperatures regularly hit 40°C (104°F) – slows right down. There's very little industry in these parts, and economic opportunities are few. The big employers on the coast are the sugar cane, chicle and African palm farms, which provide seasonal work. It's hardly cushy employment (imagine cutting cane with a machete in 40°C heat) and many coastal-dwellers migrate to the cities in search of better opportunities.

Fishing is another income source. There are a few large industrial operations, but the bulk of fishermen (Guatemalan fisherwomen are extremely rare) either work independently, selling the day's catch at market, or in small cooperatives.

Housing on the coast is radically different to the rest of the country. Due to the extreme heat, cinderblock is not the popular construction material it is elsewhere, nor is corrugated iron for roofing. The classic coastal house will be open plan, often with wooden walls and a thatched roof. Doors will always be open and windows often lack glass, instead just having wooden shutters to keep out the monsoonal downpours of the rainy season.

Village Life

Guatemala's rural areas, while undoubtedly the country's most picturesque, are the epicenter for many of the country's persistent problems. Life in many villages has barely changed over the last hundred years, as subsistence farmers eke out a daily existence on tiny plots of land. The precariousness of this life is emphasized with every flood, drought, plague or crop failure – the smallest of any of these being enough to place entire families in danger of starvation.

While many rural houses now have running water, the village *pila* (communal laundry trough) remains a place to get together and exchange gossip.

Guatemalan governments have ignored villages, and infrastructure levels can be dire. Many children have to travel for hours to attend the local school and what they call a school may not be something that you recognize as such. Access to health care is equally limited – at best a village will have a small medical clinic, capable of dealing with minor complaints. Patients requiring hospitalization may need to be transported several hours away. Many smaller villages don't even have a doctor, and medical care is provided by *curanderas* (healing women), *comadres* (midwives) and maybe a pharmacist.

Despite all of these drawbacks, Guatemalan villages are often stunningly beautiful – surrounded by lush countryside, with dirt roads winding between adobe huts, an old colonial church on the plaza and chickens and horses roaming about, as barefoot children play in the streets in a carefree way unseen in the rest of the country.

Being Guatemalan

Despite these huge regional differences, there is such a thing as *ser Chapín*. With a few unfortunate exceptions, you'll be amazed when you first reach Guatemala by just how helpful, polite and unhurried Guatemalans are. Everyone has time to stop and chat and explain what you want to know. This is apparent even if you've just crossed the border from Mexico, where things aren't exactly rushed either. Most Guatemalans like to get to know other people without haste, feeling for common ground and things to agree on, rather than making blunt assertions and engaging in adversarial dialectic.

What goes on behind this outward politeness is harder to encapsulate. Few Guatemalans exhibit the stress, worry and hurry of the 'developed' nations, but this obviously isn't because they don't have to worry about money or employment. They're a long-suffering people who don't expect wealth or good government, but make the best of what comes their way – friendship, family, a good meal, a bit of good company.

The tales of violence – domestic violence, civil-war violence, criminal violence – that one inevitably hears in Guatemala sit strangely with the mild-mannered approach you will encounter from nearly everybody. Whatever the explanation, it helps to show why a little caution is in order when strangers meet.

Religion

Guatemalans are a religious bunch – atheists and agnostics are very thin on the ground. People will often ask what religion you are quite early in a conversation. Unless you really want to get into it, saying 'Christian' generally satisfies.

Orthodox Catholicism is gradually giving way to Evangelical Protestantism among the *ladinos* (people of mixed indigenous and European parentage), with the animist-Catholic syncretism of the traditional Maya always present. The number of new Evangelical churches, especially in indigenous Maya villages, is astonishing. Since the 1980s, Evangelical Protestant sects, around 58% of them Pentecostal, have surged in popularity and it is estimated that 30% to 40% of Guatemalans are now Evangelicals.

Catholicism's fall can be attributed in part to the civil war. On occasion, Catholic priests were (and still are) outspoken defenders of human rights, attracting persecution (and worse) from dictators at the time, especially from the Evangelical Ríos Montt.

Catholicism is fighting back with messages about economic and racial justice, papal visits and new saints – Guatemala's most venerated local Christian figure, the 17th-century Antigua-hospital-founder Hermano Pedro de San José de Bethancourt, was canonized in 2002 when Pope John Paul II visited Guatemala.

Catholicism in the Maya areas has never been exactly orthodox. The missionaries who brought Catholicism to the Maya in the 16th century

GETTING ALONG WITH GUATEMALANS

While Guatemalans tend to give foreigners a fair amount of leeway, at least trying to adapt to local ways is bound to make your travels run more smoothly.

➡ Even in such routine situations as entering a store or taking a bus seat, a simple greeting is often exchanged: *buenos días* or *buenas tardes* and a smile is all that's needed.

➡ When leaving a restaurant, it is common to wish other diners *buen provecho (bon appétit)*.

➡ In general, the Maya are a fairly private people and some communities are still recovering from the nightmare of the civil war. People may be willing to share their war stories, but don't dig for information – let your hosts offer it.

➡ Referring to a Maya person as *indio* (Indian) is considered racist. The preferred term is *indígena*.

➡ When dealing with officialdom (police, border officials, immigration officers), try to appear as conservative and respectable as possible.

➡ Dress modestly when entering churches or attending family gatherings.

wisely permitted aspects of the existing animistic, shamanistic Maya religion to continue alongside Christian rites and beliefs. Syncretism was aided by the identification of certain Maya deities with certain Christian saints, and survives to this day. A notable example is the deity known as Maximón in Santiago Atitlán, San Simón in Zunil and Rilaj Maam in San Andrés Itzapa near Antigua, who seems to be a volatile combination of Maya gods, the Spanish conquistador Pedro de Alvarado and Judas Iscariot.

To get a handle on Maximón and shamanism around Lago de Atitlán, check out *Scandals in the House of Birds: Shamans and Priests on Lake Atitlán*, by anthropologist and poet Nathaniel Tarn.

Family Life

Despite modernizing influences – education, cable TV, contact with foreign travelers, international popular music, time spent as migrant workers in the USA – traditional family ties remain strong at all levels of society. Large extended-family groups gather for weekend meals and holidays. Old-fashioned gender roles are strong too: many women have jobs to increase the family income, but relatively few have positions of much responsibility.

Cynics say that much of this closeness has more to do with economics than sentiment – that it's hard to be distant when there are three generations living under the same roof. But this doesn't really play out. You see the strong bonds of family among middle- and upper-class Guatemalans, and one of the questions you're bound to get asked at least once (and possibly many more times) while on your travels is if you miss your mother.

Despite this closeness, it's rare to meet a family who doesn't have at least one member who has emigrated to the United States to work – the couple of hundred dollars that these emigrants send back per month is the sole income for some families, and, when tallied up, equals around half of what Guatemala earns from exports.

Women in Guatemala

One of the goals of the 1996 Peace Accords was to improve women's rights in Guatemala. By 2003 the Inter-American Commission on Human Rights had to report that laws discriminating against women had yet to be repealed. Women got the vote and the right to stand for election in 1946, but in 2015 only 13% of congressional deputies were women.

THE BIGGEST PARTY IN TOWN

It's Friday night in any small town in Guatemala. The music's pumping, there's singing and hands are clapping. Have you just stumbled onto a local jam session? Sorry to disappoint, but what you're most likely listening to is an Evangelical church service.

The Evangelicals are the fastest-growing religion in Latin America – one estimate puts the number of new Latino converts at a staggering 8000 per day.

The Catholic Church is worried – this is their heartland, after all, and the reasons that they're losing their grip aren't all that easy to identify.

Some say it's the Evangelicals' use of radio and TV that brings them wider audiences; for some it's their rejection of rituals and gestures and customs in favor of real human contact. Others say it's the way the newcomers go to the roughest barrios and accept anybody – including 'the drunks and the hookers,' as one priest put it.

For some, they're just more fun – they fall into trances and speak in tongues, heal and prophesize. And then there's the singing – not stale old hymns, but often racy pop numbers with the lyrics changed to more spiritual themes.

One thing's for sure – an Evangelical makes a better husband: drinking, smoking, gambling and domestic violence are all severely frowned upon. Maybe, once again in Guatemala, it's the wives who are really calling the shots.

Women's leaders repeatedly criticize Guatemala's *machista* culture, which believes a woman's place is in the home. The situation is, if anything, worse for indigenous women in rural areas, who also have to live with most of the country's direst poverty.

The international organization Human Rights Watch reported in 2002 that women working in private households were persistently discriminated against. Domestic workers, many of whom are from Maya communities, lack certain basic rights, including the rights to be paid the minimum wage and to work an eight-hour day and a 48-hour week. Many domestic workers begin working as young adolescents, but Guatemalan labor laws do not provide adequate protection for domestic workers under the age of 18.

Probably of greatest concern are the reports of escalating violence against women, accompanied by a steadily rising murder rate. These victims were once brushed off as being 'just' gang members or prostitutes, but it is now clear that murder, rape and kidnapping of women is a serious issue. The international community has begun to put pressure on Guatemala to act, but the realities of *machista* society mean that even with the passing of legislation specifically aimed at protecting women, crimes against women are seldom investigated and rarely solved.

For information on Guatemalan women's organizations (and much, much more) visit www. entremundos.org.

Education in Guatemala

Education is free and, in theory, compulsory between the ages of seven and 14. Primary education lasts for six years, but the average school-leaving age is 11 years, according to UN statistics. Secondary school begins at age 13 and comprises two cycles of three years each, called *básico* and *magisterio*. Not all secondary education is free – a major deterrent for many. Some people continue studying for their *magisterio* well into adulthood. Completing *magisterio* qualifies you to become a school teacher yourself. It's estimated that only about 34% of children of the 13-to-18 age group are in secondary school. Guatemala has five universities.

Overall, adult literacy is around 81% in Guatemala, but it's lower among women (76%) and rural people. Maya children who do seasonal migrant work with their families are least likely to get an education, as the time the families go away to work falls during the school year. It is estimated that 21% of Guatemalans between the ages of five and 14 work instead of attending school.

A limited amount of school teaching is done in Maya languages – chiefly the big four, K'iche', Mam, Kaqchiquel and Q'eqchi' – but this rarely goes beyond the first couple of years of primary school. Spanish remains the necessary tongue for anyone who wants to get ahead in life.

Sport (aka Futból)

If there's one thing that unites almost all Guatemalans, it is their passion and enthusiasm for *fútbol* (soccer). If you'd like a universal talking point, you could do worse than brush up on your soccer teams. Many Guatemalans keep a keen eye on their local team, the Guatemalan national team and at least one European team (Barcelona being by far the most popular Spanish side). Although Guatemalan teams always flop in international competition, the 10-club Liga Mayor (Major League) national competition is keenly followed by reasonably large crowds. Two seasons are played each year: the Torneo de Apertura (Opening Tournament), from July to November, and the Torneo de Clausura (Closing Tournament), from January to May. The two big clubs are Municipal and Comunicaciones, both from Guatemala City. The 'Classico Gringo' is when teams from Quetzaltenango and Antigua (the two big tourist towns) play.

For up-to-the-minute news on the football scene in Guatemala, log on to www. guatefutbol.com.

Maya Heritage

The ancient Maya constructed a civilization that was vastly impressive, complex and fruitful. While some legacies, such as the archaeological sites, are obvious, scholars are still working to put together the various pieces of how Maya society worked. Here we present a summary of some of the things that are known about the Maya, from traditions long lost to rituals still carried out in modern times.

Ancient Maya Beliefs

Mayan Folktales, edited by James D Sexton, brings together the myths and legends of the Lago de Atitlán area, translated into English.

The date of creation that appears in inscriptions throughout the Maya world is 13.0.0.0.0, 4 Ahaw, 8 Kumk'u, or August 13, 3114 BC on our calendar.

On that day the creator gods set three stones in the dark waters that covered the primordial world. These formed a cosmic hearth at the center of the universe. They then struck divine fire by means of lightning, charging the world with life.

The gods made three attempts at creating people before getting it right. First they made deer and other animals, but not being able to speak properly to honor the gods, the animals were condemned to be eaten.

Next was a person made from mud. At first, the mud person spoke, 'but without knowledge and understanding,' and he soon dissolved back into the mire.

The gods' third attempt was people carved from wood. These too were imperfect and also destroyed. The *Popol Vuh,* a book compiled by members of the Maya nobility soon after the Spanish conquest, says that the survivors of these wooden people are the monkeys that inhabit the forests.

The gods finally got it right when they discovered maize, and made mankind from the yellow ears and white ears of this indispensable grain.

The Maya Cosmovision

For the ancient Maya, the world, the heavens and the mysterious underworld called Xibalbá were one great, unified structure that operated according to the laws of astrology, cyclical time and ancestor worship.

The towering, sacred ceiba tree symbolized the world-tree, which united the heavens (represented by the tree's branches and foliage), the earth (the trunk) and the nine levels of Xibalbá (the roots). The world-tree had a sort of cruciform shape, so when the Franciscan friars came bearing a

---

MAYA BEAUTY

The ancient Maya considered flat foreheads and crossed eyes beautiful. To achieve these effects, children would have boards bound tight to their heads and wax beads tied to dangle before their eyes. Both men and women made cuts in their skin to gain much-desired scar markings, and women sharpened their teeth to points, another mark of beauty – which may also have helped them to keep their men in line!

MAYA WRITING

During the Classic period, the Maya lowlands were divided into two major linguistic groups. In the Yucatán Peninsula and Belize people spoke Yucatec, and in the eastern highlands and Motagua Valley of Guatemala they spoke a language related to Chol. People in El Petén likely spoke both languages. Scholars have suggested that the written language throughout the Maya world was a form of Chol.

Long before the Spanish conquest, the Maya developed a sophisticated hieroglyphic script that is partly phonetic (glyphs representing sounds) and partly logographic (glyphs representing words).

cross and required the Maya to venerate it, the symbolism meshed easily with established Maya beliefs.

Each point of the compass had a color and a special religious significance. Everything in the Maya world was seen in relation to these cardinal points, with the world-tree at the center.

Blood-letting ceremonies were the most important religious ceremonies for the Maya – a way for humans to link themselves to the underworld – and the blood of kings was seen as the most acceptable for these rituals. Maya kings often initiated blood-letting rites to heighten the responsiveness of the gods.

Maya ceremonies were performed in natural sacred places as well as their human-made equivalents. Mountains, caves, lakes, cenotes (natural limestone cavern pools), rivers and fields were – and still are – sacred. Pyramids and temples were thought of as stylized mountains. A cave was the mouth of the creature that represented Xibalbá, and to enter it was to enter the spirit of the secret world. This is why some Maya temples have doorways surrounded by huge masks: as you enter the door of this 'cave' you are entering the mouth of Xibalbá.

Ancestor worship was very important to the ancient Maya, and when they buried a king beneath a pyramid or a commoner beneath the floor or courtyard of a *na* (thatched Maya hut), the sacredness of the location was increased.

The Ball Game

The recreation most favored by the Maya was *juego de pelota* (a ball game), courts for which can still be seen at many archaeological sites. It's thought that the players had to try to keep a hard rubber ball airborne using any part of their body other than their hands, head or feet. In some regions, a team was victorious if one of its players hit the ball through stone rings with holes little larger than the ball itself.

The Maya Counting System

The Maya counting system's most important use – and the one you will encounter during your travels – was in writing dates. It's an elegantly simple system: dots are used to count from one to four; a horizontal bar signifies five; a bar with one dot above it is six, a bar with two dots is seven, and so forth. Two bars signifies 10, three bars 15. Nineteen, the highest common number, is three bars stacked up and topped by four dots.

To signify larger numbers the Maya stack numbers from zero to 19 on top of each other. Thus the lowest number in the stack shows values from one to 19, the next position up signifies 20 times its face value, the third position up signifies 20 times 20 times its face value. The three positions together can signify numbers up to 7999. By adding more positions one can count as high as needed. Zero is represented by a stylized picture of a shell or some other object.

The Foundation for the Advancement of Mesoamerica Studies website (www.famsi. org) is incredibly detailed, with information ranging from current and past research to studies on writing, educational resources, linguistic maps and more.

The Maya Calendar

The ancient Maya's astronomical observations and calculations were un-cannily accurate and time was, in fact, the basis of the Maya religion. Per-haps the best analogy to the Maya calendar is the gears of a mechanical watch, where small wheels mesh with larger wheels, which in turn mesh with other sets of wheels to record the passage of time.

Tzolkin or Cholq'ij or Tonalamatl

To translate a date using the Maya calendar, visit the Maya Date Calculator at www.mayan-cal endar.com/calc. html.

The two smallest 'wheels' were two cycles: one of 13 days and another of 20 days. As these two wheels meshed, the passing days received unique names. The two small wheels thus created a larger wheel of 260 days, called a *tzolkin, cholq'ij* or *tonalamatl*.

Vague Year (Haab)

Another set of wheels in the Maya calendar comprised 18 'months' of 20 days each, which formed the basis of the solar year or *haab* (or *ab'*). Eighteen months, each of 20 days, equals 360 days, a period known as a *tun;* the Maya added a special omen-filled five-day period called the *uayeb* at the end of this cycle in order to produce a solar calendar of 365 days.

Calendar Round

The huge wheels of the *tzolkin* and the *haab* also meshed and repeated every 52 solar years, a period called the Calendar Round. The Calendar Round was the dating system used not only by the Maya, but also by the Olmecs, Aztecs and Zapotecs of ancient Mexico.

Long Count

The Calendar Round has one serious limitation: it only lasts 52 years. Hence the Long Count, which the Maya developed around the start of the Classic period.

The Long Count uses the *tun*, but ignores the *uayeb*. Twenty *tuns* make a *katun* and 20 *katuns* make a *baktun*. Curiously for us today, 13 *baktuns* (1,872,000 days, or 5125 Gregorian solar years) form some-

---

THE MAYA BURY THEIR DEAD

It is the night before the funeral, and the shaman is in the house of the deceased, wash-ing candles in holy water. If he misses one, a family member could go blind or deaf. He has counted off the days, and divined that tomorrow will be propitious for the burial.

He prays to the ancestral spirits, asking for the health of the family and the absence of disaster. The list is long and detailed. Personal objects are placed in the coffin; if they're not, the man's spirit might return home looking for them.

Members of the *cofradía* (fraternity) bear the coffin to the cemetery, a trail of mourn-ers following. Four stops are made on leaving the house: at the doorway, in the yard, on entering the street, and at the first street corner. At each stop, mourners place coins on the coffin – in reality to buy candles, symbolically so that the spirit can buy its way out of purgatory and into heaven.

As the coffin is lowered into the ground, mourners kiss handfuls of dirt before throwing them on top. Once the coffin is buried, women sprinkle water on top, packing down the soil and protecting the corpse from werewolves and other dark spirits.

Every All Soul's Day (November 2) the family will come to the cemetery to honor their dead. Sometimes this will stretch over three days (beginning on the first). They will come to clean and decorate the grave, and set out food such as roasted corn, sweet potatoes, vegetable pears (*chayote* or chokos), and other fresh-picked fruit of the field. The church bells will ring at midday to summon the spirits, who feast on the smells of the food.

thing called a Great Cycle, and the first Great Cycle began on August 11, 3114 BC, which means it ended on December 23 (or 25), AD 2012. The end of a Great Cycle was a time charged with great significance – you may have noticed a little (non-Maya) end-of-the-world panic around Christmas 2012.

Maya Architecture

Ancient Maya architecture is a mixed bag of incredible accomplishments achieved despite severe limitations. The Maya's great buildings are both awesome and beautiful, with their aesthetic attention to intricately patterned facades, delicate 'combs' on temple roofs, and sinuous carvings. These magnificent structures, such as the ones found in the sophisticated urban centers of Tikal, El Mirador and Copán, were created without beasts of burden (except for humans) or the luxury of the wheel. Once structures were completed, experts hypothesize, they were covered with stucco and painted red with a mixture of hematite and most probably water.

Although formal studies and excavations of Maya sites in Guatemala have been ongoing for more than a century, much of their architectural how and why remains a mystery. For example, the purpose of *chultunes,* underground chambers carved from bedrock and filled with offerings, continues to baffle scholars. And while we know that the Maya habitually built one temple on top of another to bury successive leaders, we have little idea how they actually erected these symbols of power. All the limestone used to erect the great Maya cities had to be moved and set in place by hand – an engineering feat that must have demanded astronomical amounts of human labor.

Mary Ellen Miller's well-illustrated *Maya Art and Architecture* paints the full picture from gigantic temples to intricately painted ceramics.

Modern Maya Rituals

Many sites of ancient Maya ruins – among them Tikal, Kaminaljuyú and K'um'arkaj – still have altars where prayers, offerings and ceremonies continue to take place today. Fertility rites, healing ceremonies and sacred observances to ring in the various Maya new years are still practiced with gusto. These types of ceremony are directed or overseen by a Maya priest known as a *tzahorín* and usually involve burning candles and copal (a natural incense from the bark of various tropical trees), making offerings to the gods and praying for whatever the desired outcome may be – a good harvest, a healthy child or a prosperous new year, for example. Some ceremonies involve chicken sacrifices as well. Each place has its own set of gods – or at least different names for similar gods.

Visitors may also be able to observe traditional Maya ceremonies in places such as the Pascual Abaj shrine at Chichicastenango, the altars on the shore of Laguna Chicabal outside Quetzaltenango, or El Baúl near Santa Lucía Cotzumalguapa, but a lot of traditional rites are off-limits to foreigners.

Arts & Architecture

For such a poor and troubled country, Guatemala has produced more than its share of important artists and groundbreaking artistic achievements. The enduring legacy of Maya architecture and weaving cannot be denied, and the country has produced writers and musicians who have attained international fame. Many traditional crafts survive as well, with handicrafts manufactured both as everyday items and for sale as souvenirs.

Literature

Guatemala's first great literary figure was poet and Jesuit priest Rafael Landívar, whose collection of poetry *Rusticatio Mexicana,* containing 5348 verses in Latin, was published in 1781.

A great source of national pride is the Nobel Prize for Literature that was bestowed on Guatemalan Miguel Ángel Asturias (1899–1974) in 1967. Best known for *Men of Maize,* his magical-realist epic on the theme of European conquest and the Maya, and for his thinly veiled vilification of Latin American dictators in *The President,* Asturias also wrote poetry. He served in various diplomatic capacities for the Guatemalan government.

Other celebrated Guatemalan authors include short-story master Augusto Monterroso (1921–2003), who is credited as having written the shortest story in published literature, *El Dinosaurio*. Look also for his published work *The Black Sheep and Other Fables*. Luis Cardoza y Aragón (1901–92) is principally known for his poetry and for fighting in the revolutionary movement that deposed dictator Jorge Ubico in 1944. Gaspar Pedro Gonzáles' *A Mayan Life* is claimed to be the first novel written by a Maya author.

Guatemalan-born Arturo Arias is an author and professor of Spanish-American literature at the University of Texas. His most famous works include *Itzam Na* (1981), *Jaguar en llamas* (1990) and *The Rigoberta Menchú Controversy* (2001), in which he examines the heated debate that ensued after Menchú won the Nobel Prize.

Born in the US to a Guatemalan mother, Francisco Goldman is probably the most famous author writing about Guatemala in modern times. Primarily a novelist, Goldman has also written a non-fiction account of the assassination of Bishop Gerardi, *The Art of Political Murder,* that won him international and critical acclaim and a good selection of enemies from within Guatemala's power structure.

One of Central America's largest literary competitions, the Juegos Florales Hispanoamericanos, is held in Quetzaltenango in September to coincide with Independence Day celebrations.

Painting

Precolonial

No discussion of painting in Guatemala would be complete without a mention of the fabulous mural work that the Maya created long before the Spanish arrived. Most have been severely worn by time and vandals, but a few archaeological sites such as San Bartolo and Río Azul have paintings that remain surprisingly vivid.

Early Postcolonial

One of the earliest postcolonial painters of note was Tomás de Merlo, widely credited as the father of the 'Antigua Baroque' movement. You can see many of his works in the National Museum of Colonial Art, in Antigua, and hanging on church walls in Antigua, too.

Modern Maya Painting

One truly Guatemalan genre of painting, dubbed 'Maya naïve art' was spearheaded by Andrés Curruchich, a native of San Juan Comalapa near Lago de Atitlán. Curruchich's works depicted the simple rural scenes of the Guatemalan countryside you can still see today. There is a permanent exhibition of Curruchich's work in the Ixchel museum in Guatemala City. While the artist died in 1969, his legacy continues – there are an estimated 500 artists working in San Juan Comalapa today, many of them trained by Curruchich himself. Juan Sisay was another Maya primitivist painter from the Atitlán region to gain international fame.

Contemporary Artists

Of all modern Guatemalan artists, the architect, muralist, painter and sculptor Efraín Recinos is probably the most famous. His murals grace Guatemala City's National Music Conservatory and he is also responsible for the facade of the National Library and the design of the Centro Cultural Miguel Ángel Asturias, both also in Guatemala City. Recinos was awarded Guatemala's highest honor, the Order of the Quetzal, in 1999, and the country went into mourning when he died in 2011.

Music

Folk Music

Guatemalan festivals provide great opportunities to hear traditional music featuring instruments such as cane flutes, square drums and the *chirimía,* a reed instrument of Moorish roots related to the oboe.

The other popular form of 'folk' music is made by the Garifuna people who live around the country's Caribbean coast. Completely different from traditional Maya music, the Garifuna's most popular style is Punta Rock, variants of which you can hear in dance clubs around the country.

Modern Music

Guatemalan tastes in pop music are greatly influenced by the products of other Latin American countries. Reggaetón is huge – current favorites include Pitbull, Nicky Jam and J Balvin.

THE MARIMBA

The marimba is considered the national instrument, although scholars cannot agree whether this xylophone-type instrument already existed in Africa long before and was brought to Guatemala early on by slaves. Marimbas can be heard throughout the country, often in restaurants or in plazas in the cool of an evening.

The earliest marimbas used a succession of increasingly large gourds as the resonator pipes; modern marimbas are more commonly fitted with wooden pipes, though you may see the former type in more traditional settings. The instrument is usually played by three people and there is a carnival-like quality to its sound and compositions.

Jazz buffs should be familiar with the sound of the marimba – the instrument became hip in the 1940s when jazz greats such as Glenn Miller started to include it in their compositions.

The only record label seriously promoting new Guatemalan artists (mostly in the urban/hip-hop vein) is Guatemala City–based Outstanding Productions.

Guatemalan rock went through its golden age in the '80s and early '90s. Bands from this era such as Razones de Cambio, Bohemia Suburbana and Viernes Verde still have their die-hard fans. The most famous Guatemalan-born musician is Ricardo Arjona.

To find out about up-and-coming Guatemalan rock bands, check out www.rockrepublik.net.

Architecture

Modern Guatemalan architecture, apart from a few flashy bank and office buildings along Av La Reforma in Guatemala City and the work of Efraín Recinos, is chiefly characterized by expanses of drab concrete. Some humbler rural dwellings still use a traditional wall construction known as *bajareque,* where a core of stones is held in place by poles of bamboo or other wood, which is faced with stucco or mud. Village houses are increasingly roofed with sheets of tin instead of tiles or thatch – less aesthetically pleasing, but also less expensive.

Colonial Architecture

During the colonial period (the early 16th to early 19th centuries), churches, convents, mansions and palaces were all built in the Spanish styles of the day, chiefly Renaissance, baroque and neoclassical. But while the architectural concepts were European-inspired, the labor used to realize them was strictly indigenous. Thus, Maya embellishments – such as the lily blossoms and vegetable motifs that adorn Antigua's La Merced – can be found on many colonial buildings, serving as testament to the countless laborers forced to make the architectural dreams of Guatemala's newcomers a reality. Churches were built high and strong to protect the elite from lower classes in revolt.

Guatemala does not have the great colonial architectural heritage of neighboring Mexico, partly because earthquakes destroyed many of its finest buildings. But the architecture of Antigua is particularly striking, as new styles and engineering techniques developed following each successive earthquake. Columns became lower and thicker to provide more stability. Some Antigua buildings, including the Palacio de los Capitanes and Palacio del Ayuntamiento on the central plaza, were given a double-arch construction to strengthen them. With so many colonial buildings in different states of grandeur and decay, Antigua was designated a World Heritage Site by Unesco in 1979.

After the 1773 earthquake, which prompted the relocation of the capital from Antigua to Guatemala City, the neoclassical architecture of the day came to emphasize durability. Decorative flourishes were saved for the interiors of buildings, with elaborate altars and furniture adorning churches and homes. By this time Guatemalan architects were hell-bent on seeing their buildings stay upright, no matter how powerful the next earthquake. Even though several serious quakes have hit Guatemala City since then, many colonial buildings (such as the city's cathedral) have survived. The same cannot be said for the humble abodes of the city's residents, who suffered terribly from the devastating quake of 1976.

For an extensive, searchable database of photographs of pre-Columbian ceramics, have a look at www.mayavase.com.

Handicrafts

Guatemalans make many traditional handicrafts, both for everyday use and to sell to tourists and collectors. Crafts include basketry, ceramics and wood carving, but the most prominent are weaving, embroidery and other textile arts practiced by Maya women. The beautiful, handmade *traje* (traditional clothing) worn by local women is one of the most awe-inspiring expressions of Maya culture.

Weaving

The most arresting feature of Maya traditional clothing is the highly colorful weaving and embroidery, which makes many garments true works of art. It's the women's *huipil*, a long, sleeveless tunic, that receives the most painstaking, loving care in its creation. Often entire *huipiles* are covered in a multicolored web of stylized animal, human, plant and mythological shapes, which can take months to complete. Each garment identifies the village from which its wearer hails (the Spanish colonists allotted each village a different design in order to distinguish the inhabitants from each other) and within the village style there can be variations according to social status, as well as the creative individual touches that make each garment unique.

Maya men now generally wear Western clothing, except in places such as Sololá and Todos Santos Cuchumatán, where they still sport colorful *trajes*. Materials and techniques are changing, but the pre-Hispanic backstrap loom is still widely used. The warp (long) threads are stretched between two horizontal bars, one of which is fixed to a post or tree, while the other is attached to a strap that goes round the weaver's lower back. The weft (cross) threads are then woven in. Throughout the highlands you can see women weaving in this manner outside the entrance to their homes. Nowadays, some *huipiles* and other garments are machine made, as this method is faster and easier than weaving by hand.

Yarn is still hand-spun in many villages. For the well-to-do, silk threads are used to embroider bridal *huipiles* and other important garments. Vegetable dyes are not yet totally out of use, and red dye from cochineal insects and natural indigo are employed in several areas. Modern luminescent dyes go down very well with the Maya, who are happily addicted to bright colors, as you will see.

The colorful traditional dress is still generally most in evidence in the highlands, which are heavily populated by Maya, though you will see it in all parts of the country. The variety of techniques, materials, styles and designs is bewildering to the newcomer, but you'll see some of the most colorful, intricate, eye-catching and widely worn designs in Sololá and Santiago Atitlán, near Lago de Atitlán; Nebaj, in the Ixil Triangle; Zunil, near Quetzaltenango; and Todos Santos and San Mateo Ixtatán in the Cuchumatanes mountains.

You can learn the art of backstrap weaving at weaving schools in Quetzaltenango, San Pedro La Laguna and other towns. To see large collections of fine weaving, don't miss the Museo Ixchel in Guatemala City or the shop Nim Po't in Antigua.

Well-illustrated books on Maya textiles will help you to start identifying the wearers' villages. Two fine works are *The Maya of Guatemala – Life and Dress,* by Carmen L Pettersen, and *The Maya Textile Tradition,* edited by Margot Blum Schevill.

Other Handicrafts

The Maya, particularly in the highlands, have a long tradition of skilled artistry, products of which you can see in nearly every market in the country. The small town of Totonicapán has dozens of tiny workshops that are open to visitors where you can see tinsmiths, potters, wood carvers and instrument makers at work.

Jade was a sacred stone to the Maya and remains a popular material for jewelers. To see the finest pieces you can tour the workshops and showrooms in Antigua.

Some of the most popular Guatemalan souvenirs are the wooden masks used for village festivals. Many display a curious mixture of pre- and post-Columbian influences, such as the very devilish-looking masks used to depict the Spanish colonizers. Again, masks are in markets everywhere, but to see the best selection, go to Chichicastenango, and for the best prices, head to Panajachel or Antigua.

Landscapes & Wildlife

Even 'city people' will have to admit that some of the best parts of Guatemala are in the countryside. The ever-changing terrain takes in the balmy coast, the harsh highlands, cool cloud forest, lush jungle and desert-like savannah. Many animals have, quite frankly, been eaten, but there are still enough exotic critters and creatures around to keep most wildlife-spotters happy.

The Land

Tajumulco (4220m), northwest of Quetzaltenango, is the highest peak in Central America. La Torre (3837m), north of Huehuetenango, is the highest nonvolcanic peak in Central America.

Guatemala covers an area of 108,889 sq km – a little less than the US state of Louisiana, a little more than England. Geologically, most of the country lies atop the North American tectonic plate, but this abuts the Cocos plate along Guatemala's Pacific coast and the Caribbean plate in the far south of the country. When any of these plates gets frisky, earthquakes and volcanic eruptions ensue. Hence the major quakes of 1917, 1918 and 1976 and the spectacular chain of 30 volcanoes – some of them active – running parallel to the Pacific coast from the Mexican border to the Salvadoran border. North of the volcanic chain rises the Cuchumatanes range.

North of Guatemala City, the highlands of Alta Verapaz gradually decline to the lowland of El Petén, occupying northern Guatemala. El Petén is hot and humid or hot and dry, depending on the season. Central America's largest tracts of virgin rainforest straddle El Petén's borders with Mexico and Belize, although this may cease to be true if conservation efforts are not successful.

Northeast of Guatemala City, the valley of the Río Motagua (dry in some areas, moist in others) runs down to Guatemala's short, very hot Caribbean coast. Bananas and sugarcane thrive in the Motagua valley.

Between the volcanic chain and the Pacific Ocean is the Pacific Slope, with rich coffee, cotton, rubber, fruit and sugar plantations, cattle ranches, beaches of black volcanic sand and a sweltering climate.

Guatemala's unique geology also includes tremendous systems of caves. Water coursing for eons over a limestone base created aquifers and conduits that eventually gave way to subterranean caves, rivers and sinkholes when the surface water drained into underground caverns and streams. This type of terrain (known as karst) is found throughout the Verapaces region and makes Guatemala a killer spelunking destination.

Wildlife

Guatemala's natural beauty, from volcanoes and lakes to jungles and wetlands, is one of its great attractions. With an astonishing range of different ecosystems, the variety of fauna and flora is great – and if you know where to go, opportunities for seeing exciting species are plentiful.

To see rare scarlet macaws in the wild, the place to head is La Ruta Guacamaya (the Scarlet Macaw Trail) of El Perú ruins in El Petén.

Animals

Estimates point to 250 species of mammals, 600 species of birds, 200 species of reptiles and amphibians, and many of butterflies and other insects.

The national bird, the resplendent quetzal (for which the national currency is named), is small but exceptionally beautiful. The male sports a bright-red breast, brilliant blue-green neck, head, back and wings, and a blue-green tail several times as long as the body, which stands only around 15cm tall. The female has far duller plumage. The quetzal's main habitat is the cloud forests of Alta Verapaz.

Exotic birds of the lowland jungles include toucans, macaws and parrots. If you visit Tikal, you can't miss the ocellated turkey (also called the Petén turkey), a large, multicolored bird reminiscent of a peacock. Tikal is an all-round wildlife hot spot: you stand a good chance of spotting howler and spider monkeys, coatis (locally called *pisotes*) and other mammals, plus toucans, parrots and many other birds. Some 300 endemic and migratory bird species have been recorded at Tikal, among them nine hummingbirds and four trogons. Good areas for sighting waterfowl – including the jabiru stork, the biggest flying bird in the western hemisphere – are Laguna Petexbatún and the lakes near Yaxhá ruins, both in El Petén, and the Río Dulce between Lago de Izabal and Lívingston.

Guatemala's forests still host many mammal and reptile species. Petén residents include jaguars, ocelots, pumas, two species of peccary, opossums, tapirs, kinkajous, agoutis (*tepescuintles*; rodents 60cm to 70cm long), white-tailed and red brocket deer, and armadillos. Guatemala is home to at least five species of sea turtle (the loggerhead, hawksbill and green ridley on the Caribbean coast, and the leatherback and olive ridley on the Pacific) and at least two species of crocodile (one found in El Petén, the other in the Río Dulce). Manatees exist in the Río Dulce, though they're notoriously hard to spot.

Les D Beletsky's *Belize & Northern Guatemala: The Ecotravellers' Wildlife Guide* is a comprehensive, all-in-one guide to flora and fauna in the region. The book features hundreds of illustrations and photos and some welcome splashes of humor.

Endangered Species

Guatemala's wildlife faces two major threats. The first is the loss of habitat, as more land is turned over to farming. The second threat is hunting, which is mostly done for food, but also takes place for the collection of skins and other products, as is the case for deer, turtles and some reptiles. Endangered mammals include jaguars, howler monkeys, manatees, several species of mice and bats, and the Guatemalan vole.

DON'T LET YOUR MOM READ THIS

We don't want to worry you, but Guatemala, along with being the Land of the Eternal Spring, the Land of Smiles and the Land of the Trees also seems to be the Land of the Natural Disaster. Don't panic – there are really only three biggies you have to worry about:

Earthquakes Sitting on top of three tectonic plates hasn't really worked out that well for Guatemala. The present-day capital was founded after Antigua got flattened, but Guatemala City still got pummeled in 1917, 1918 and 1976. This last one left 23,000 people dead.

Hurricanes Nobody likes a hurricane. They're windy and noisy and get mud and water everywhere. Guatemala has two coastlines so theoretically the hit could come from either angle, although it's statistically more likely to come from the Pacific side. Hurricane Stan in 2005 was the worst the country's seen, killing more than 1500 and affecting nearly half a million people. Hurricane season runs June to November – for the latest news, you can check with the National Hurricane Center & Tropical Prediction Center (www.nhc.noaa.gov).

Volcanoes Great to look at, fun to climb, scary when they erupt. Guatemala has four active volcanoes: Pacaya, Volcán de Fuego, Santiaguito and Tacaná. The nastiest event to date was back in 1902 when Santa María erupted taking 6000 lives. In recent years Pacaya and Fuego (both outside of Antigua) have been acting up, with increased lava flow and ash. Fuego's recent eruptions have led to over 5000 people being evacuated from nearby communities. If you feel you need to keep an eye on it, log on to the Smithsonian's volcano page (www.volcano.si.edu).

More than 25 bird species native to the region are listed as endangered, including the Atitlán grebe (found only in Guatemala) and the national bird, the resplendent quetzal. Many reptiles, including the Morelet's crocodile are likewise disappearing.

Plants

Guatemala has more than 8000 species of plants in 19 different ecosystems ranging from mangrove forests and wetlands on both coasts to the tropical rainforest of El Petén, and the pine forests, open grasslands and cloud forests of the mountains. The cloud forests, with their epiphytes, bromeliads and dangling old-man's-beard, are most abundant in Alta Verapaz. Trees of El Petén include the sapodilla, wild rubber trees, mahogany, several useful palms and Guatemala's national tree for its manifold symbolism to the Maya, the ceiba (also called the kapok or silk-cotton tree in English). Cities such as Antigua become glorious with the lilac blooms of jacaranda trees in the early months of the year.

The national flower, the *monja blanca* (white nun orchid), is said to have been picked so much that it's now rarely seen in the wild; nevertheless, with 550 species of orchid (one third of them endemic to Guatemala), you shouldn't have any trouble spotting some. If you're interested in orchids, be sure to visit the Vivero Verapaz orchid nursery at Cobán and try to land in town for their annual orchid festival, held every December.

Domesticated plants, of course, contribute at least as much to the landscape as wild ones. The *milpa* (maize field) is the backbone of agricultural subsistence everywhere. *Milpas* are, however, usually cleared by the slash-and-burn method, which is a major factor in the diminution of Guatemala's forests.

Parks & Protected Areas

Guatemala has more than 90 protected areas, including *reservas de biosfera* (biosphere reserves), *parques nacionales* (national parks), *biotopos protegidos* (protected biotopes), *refugios de vida silvestre* (wildlife refuges) and *reservas naturales privadas* (private nature reserves). Even though some areas are contained within other, larger ones, they amount to 28% of the national territory. Tikal National Park is the only such area on the Unesco World Heritage list in Guatemala, and owes half its listing to the archaeological site found within.

Many of the protected areas are remote and hard to access for the independent traveler.

Environmental Issues

Environmental consciousness is not enormously developed in Guatemala, as the vast amounts of garbage strewn across the country and the choking clouds of diesel gas pumped out by its buses and trucks will quickly tell you. Despite the impressive list of parks and protected areas, genuine protection for those areas is harder to achieve, partly because of official collusion to ignore the regulations and partly because of pressure from poor Guatemalans in need of land.

Guatemala's popularity as a tourist destination leads to a few environmental problems – the question of sewerage and trash disposal around

Bird-lovers must get hold of either *The Birds of Tikal: An Annotated Checklist*, by Randell A Beavers, or *The Birds of Tikal*, by Frank B Smithe. If you can't find them elsewhere, at least one should be on sale at Tikal itself, and both are useful much further afield.

Jonathon Maslow's *Bird of Life, Bird of Death* begins as a story about a naturalist's search for the quetzal, but quickly develops into a terrifying portrait of Guatemala during the civil war.

SNAKE IN THE GRASS

The Central American or common lancehead, also called the fer-de-lance (locally known as *barba amarilla*, or 'yellow beard') is a highly poisonous viper with a diamond-patterned back and an arrow-shaped head. The *cascabel* (tropical rattlesnake) is the most poisonous of all rattlers. Both inhabit jungles and savannah.

PARKS & PROTECTED AREAS

PROTECTED AREA	FEATURES	ACTIVITIES	BEST TIME TO VISIT
Área de Protección Especial Punta de Manabique	large Caribbean wetland reserve; beaches, mangroves, lagoons, birds, crocodiles, possible manatee sightings	boat trips, wildlife observation, fishing, beach	any
Biotopo Cerro Cahuí	forest reserve beside Lago de Petén Itzá; Petén wildlife including monkeys	walking trails	any
Biotopo del Quetzal (Biotopo Mario Dary Rivera)	easy-access cloud-forest reserve; howler monkeys, birds	nature trails, birdwatching, possible quetzal sightings	any
Biotopo San Miguel La Palotada	within Reserva de Biosfera Maya, adjoins Parque Nacional Tikal; dense Petén forest with millions of bats	jungle walks, visits to El Zotz archaeological site and bat caves	any, drier Nov-May
Parque Nacional Grutas de Lanquín	large cave system 61km from Cobán	bat-watching; observation of the nearby Semuc Champey lagoons and waterfalls	any
Parque Nacional Laguna del Tigre	remote, large park within Reserva de Biosfera Maya; freshwater wetlands, Petén flora and fauna	wildlife-spotting, including scarlet macaws, monkeys, crocodiles; visiting El Perú archaeological site; volunteer opportunities at Las Guacamayas biological station	any, drier Nov-May
Parque Nacional Laguna Lachuá	circular, jungle-surrounded, turquoise lake, 220m deep; many fish, occasional jaguars and tapir	camping, swimming	any
Parque Nacional Mirador–Río Azul	national park within Reserva de Biosfera Maya; Petén flora and fauna	jungle treks to El Mirador archaeological site	any, drier Nov-May
Parque Nacional Río Dulce	beautiful jungle-lined lower Río Dulce between Lago de Izabal and the Caribbean; manatee refuge	boat trips	any
Parque Nacional Tikal	diverse jungle wildlife among Guatemala's most magnificent Maya ruins	wildlife-spotting, seeing spectacular Maya city	any, drier Nov-May
Refugio de Bocas del Polochic	delta of Río Polochic at western end of Lago de Izabal; Guatemala's second-largest freshwater wetlands	birdwatching (more than 300 species), howler monkey observation	any
Refugio de Vida Silvestre Petexbatún	lake near Sayaxché; water birds	boat trips, fishing, visiting several archaeological sites	any
Reserva de Biosfera Maya	vast 21,000-sq-km area stretching across northern Petén; includes four national parks	jungle treks, wildlife-spotting	any, drier Nov-May
Reserva de Biosfera Sierra de las Minas	cloud forest reserve of great biodiversity; key quetzal habitat	hiking, wildlife-spotting	any
Reserva Natural Monterrico-Hawaii	Pacific beaches and wetlands; birdlife, turtles	boat tours, birdwatching and turtle-watching	Jun-Nov (turtle nesting)

Lago de Atitlán being a major one, and some inappropriate development in the rainforests of El Petén being another. Infrastructure development in Guatemala is moving at such a pace, though, that these problems seem minor compared to some of the other challenges that environmentalists face.

Deforestation is a problem in many areas, especially El Petén, where jungle is being felled not just for timber but also to make way for cattle ranches, oil pipelines, clandestine airstrips, new settlements and new maize fields cleared using the slash-and-burn method.

Oil exploration is a concern all over the country – Guatemalans are scrambling to start drilling in El Petén, as the Mexicans have been doing for years, tapping into a vast subterranean reserve that runs across the border. In his short stint in office, then-president Alfonso Portillo proposed drilling for oil in the middle of Lago de Izabal. The plan was shelved after massive outcry from international and local environmental agencies and some not too subtle pressure from Guatemala's trading partners. It's a project that's gone, but not forgotten.

Large-scale infrastructure projects are being announced with regularity, often in environmentally sensitive areas. The most controversial of these is the almost complete Northern Transversal, a strip of highway consolidating existing roads that will stretch from the Mexican border at Gracias a Dios, pass Playa Grande and eventually connect up to Modesto Méndez, where a new border crossing for Belize is planned. Concerns with the project are many, as the road passes through sites of archaeological, environmental and cultural significance. Local environmental groups fear its construction will facilitate oil exploration in the Ixcán. One component of the plan is the construction of the Xalalá dam, a hydroelectric project. Despite claims that the dam will produce 886GWh of hydroelectric energy per year, thus reducing the country's energy deficit and reliance on fossil fuels, the project has run into stiff opposition as detractors claim that construction will displace local communities, affect water quality downstream and alter the ecology of the area through habitat loss.

Transnational mining companies are moving in, most notably in San Marcos in the Western Highlands and the Sierra de las Minas in the southeast. Without the proper community consultation called for by law, the government has granted these companies license to operate open-cut mines in search of silver and gold. Chemical runoff, deforestation, eviction of local communities and water pollution are the main issues here. Police have been used to forcibly evict residents and quash community groups' peaceful protests.

Environmental Organizations

Despite such a dire-sounding list of obstacles, a number of Guatemalan organizations are doing valiant work to protect their country's environment and biodiversity. The following are good sources of information for finding out more about Guatemala's natural and protected areas:

Arcas (www.arcasguatemala.com) NGO working with volunteers in sea turtle conservation and rehabilitation of Petén wildlife.

Asociación Ak' Tenamit (www.aktenamit.org) Maya-run NGO working to reduce poverty and promote conservation and ecotourism in the rainforests of eastern Guatemala.

Cecon (www.cecon.usac.edu.gt) Manages six public *biotopos* and one *reserva natural*.

Fundación Defensores de la Naturaleza (www.defensores.org.gt) NGO that owns and administers several protected areas.

ProPetén (www.propeten.org) NGO that works in conservation and natural resources management in Parque Nacional Laguna del Tigre.

For information about the spectacular Chelemhá cloud forest, check out www.chelemha.org.

Timber, Tourists, and Temples, edited by Richard Primack and others, brings together experts on the forests of Guatemala, Mexico and Belize for an in-depth look at the problems of balancing conservation with local people's aspirations.

Ecotravels in Guatemala (www.planeta.com/guatemala.html) has arresting articles, good reference material and numerous links.

Survival Guide

Directory A–Z

Accommodations

Guesthouses, Hostels & Hotels

Guatemalan accommodations range from luxury hotels to budget hotels to ultrabudget guesthouses called *hospedajes, casas de huéspedes* or *pensiones.*

Places at the lower end of the budget range are generally small, dark and not particularly clean. Security may not be the best. At the upper end of the budget range you should expect a clean, sizable room, with bathroom, TV and, in hot parts of the country, a fan (and possibly air-con).

Hostels are becoming more prevalent, particularly in tourist hotspots such as Antigua, Flores and Lanquín. While sleeping arrangements in these places can be barebones (a bunch of bunk beds crammed in a room), facilities often include bars and restaurants, tour services, swimming pools and other amenities. They're great places to meet other travelers.

Midrange rooms are almost always comfortable: private hot-water bathroom, TV, decent beds, fan and/or air-con are standard. Good midrange hotels often have attractive public areas such as dining rooms, bars and swimming pools.

Top-end accommodation mainly consists of Guatemala City's international-class, business-oriented hotels, Antigua's finest hostelries, and a few resort hotels elsewhere. These places offer all the comforts (and many more) that you expect for the price.

Room rates often go up in places popular with tourists during Semana Santa (the week leading up to Easter Sunday), over Christmas and New Year, and in July and August. Semana Santa is the major Guatemalan holiday period, and prices can rise by anything from 30% to 100% in Antigua, on the coast and in the countryside – anywhere Guatemalans go to relax. At this time advance reservations are a very good idea.

Regardless of your budget, if you're planning on staying for longer than a few days, it's worth asking for a discount.

Room rates are subject to two large taxes – 12% IVA (value-added tax) and 10% to pay for the activities of the Guatemalan Tourism Institute

SLEEPING PRICES

The following price ranges refer to a double room with bathroom in high (but not absolute peak) season. Unless otherwise stated, taxes of 22% are included in the price.

$ less than Q200

$$ Q200–Q550

$$$ more than Q550

(Inguat). All prices listed include both taxes. Some of the more expensive hotels forget to include them when they quote their prices.

Camping

Camping in Guatemala can be a hit-or-miss affair as there are few designated campgrounds and safety is rarely guaranteed. Where campsites are available, expect to pay from Q20 to Q50 per person per night.

Homestays

Travelers attending Spanish school have the option of living with a Guatemalan family. This is usually a pretty good bargain – expect to pay between Q300 and Q600 a week on top of your tuition for your own room, a shared bathroom, and three meals a day except Sunday. Find a homestay that gels with your goals – some families host several students at a time, creating more of an international hostel atmosphere than a family environment.

Children

Young children are highly regarded in Guatemala and can often break down barriers and open doors to local hospitality. However, Guatemala is so culturally dense, with such an emphasis on history and archaeology, that children can easily get bored. To keep kids entertained, try to make a point of breaking up the trip with visits to places such as Guatemala City's **Museo de los Niños** (Children's Museum; Map p50; ☑2475-5076; www.museodelosninos.com.gt; 5a Calle 10-00, Zona 13; Q40; ☺8am-noon & 1-4:30pm Tue-Fri, 9:30am-1:30pm & 2:30-6pm Sat

& Sun) and **La Aurora Zoo** (Map p50; ☑2472-0507; www.aurorazoo.org.gt; 5a Calle, Zona 13; adult/child Q30/15; ☺9am-5pm Tue-Sun), **Autosafari Chapín** (☑2222-5858; www.autosafarichapin.com; Carretera a Taxisco, Km 87.5; adult/child Q60/50; ☺9:30am-5pm Tue-Sun), and Retalhuleu's **Xocomil** (☑7772-9400; www.irtra.org.gt; Carretera CITO, Km 180.5; adult/child Q100/50; ☺9am-5pm Thu-Sun) water park and **Xetulul** (☑7772-9450; www.irtra.org.gt; Carretera CITO, Km 180.5; adult/child Q100/50; ☺10am-5pm Fri-Sun) theme park. Most Spanish schools are open to kids, too, and many older children will enjoy activities such as zip lining, kayaking and riding.

For general information on traveling with children, have a look at Lonely Planet's *Travel with Children*.

Customs Regulations

Normally customs officers won't look seriously in your luggage and may not look at all. Guatemala restricts import/export of pretty much the same things as everybody else (weapons, drugs, large amounts of cash, etc).

Electricity

120V/60Hz

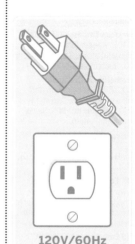

120V/60Hz

Climate

Guatemala City

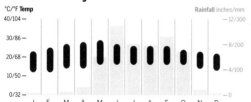

Huehuetenango

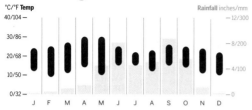

Río Dulce

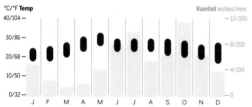

Embassies & Consulates

Citizens from countries that do not have embassies generally end up having to go to Mexico City (unless the consulate can be of help).

Australian Honorary Consulate (☎2328-0300; sdr@australian consulate.com.gt; 2a Calle 23-80, Edificio Avante, Oficina 701, Zona 15)

Belizean Embassy (☎2367-3883; www.embajadadebelize. org; 5a Av 5-55, Europlaza 2, Office 1502, Zona 14, Guatemala City)

Canadian Embassy (☎2363-4348; www.guatemala.gc.ca; 13a Calle 8-44, 8th fl, Edificio Edyma Plaza, Zona 10, Guatemala City)

French Embassy (☎2421-7370; www.ambafrance-gt.org; 5a Av 8-59, Zona 14, Guatemala City)

German Embassy (☎2364-6700; www.guatemala.diplo. de; Avenida La Reforma 9-55, Edificio Reforma 10, 10th fl, Zona 10, Guatemala City)

Honduran Consulate (☎2332-6281; embhond@intelnet.net. gt; Av La Reforma 6-64, Zona 9, Guatemala City)

Irish Honorary Consulate (☎5353-5349; irelandgua@ gmail.com; 19a Av, Zona 15, Guatemala City)

Mexican Embassy (☎2420-3400; www.embamex.sre.gob. mx/guatemala; 2a Av 7-57, Zona 10, Guatemala City)

Netherlands Consulate (☎2296-1490; guatemala@ nlconsulate.com; Carretera a El Salvador Km 14.5, Santa Catarina Pinula)

Salvadoran Embassy (☎2245-7272; www.embajadaguate mala.rree.gob.sv; 15a Av 12-01, Zona 13, Guatemala City)

UK Embassy (☎2380-7300; www.ukinguatemala.fco.gov. uk; 16a Calle 0-55, 11th fl, Torre Internacional, Zona 10, Guatemala City)

US Embassy (☎2326-4000; http://guatemala.usembassy. gov; Av La Reforma 7-01, Zona 10, Guatemala City)

Food

What you eat in Guatemala will be a mixt of Guatemalan food, which is nutritious and filling without sending your taste buds into ecstasy, and international traveler/ tourist food, which is available wherever travelers and tourists hang out. Your most satisfying meals in both cases will probably be in smaller eateries where the boss is in the kitchen themselves.

GLBTI Travelers

Few places in Latin America are outwardly gay-friendly and Guatemala is no different. Technically, homosexuality is legal for persons over 18 years, but the reality can be another story, with harassment and violence against gays too often poisoning the plot. Don't even consider testing the tolerance for homosexual public displays of affection here.

Though Antigua has a palatable – if subdued – scene, affection and action are still kept behind closed doors; the chief exception is the gay-friendly club **La Casbah** (Map p66; ☎3141-5311; www.lasvibrasantigua. com; 5a Av Norte 30; ⊙5pm-1am Wed-Sat). In Guatemala City, **Genetic** (Map p46; Ruta 3 3-08, Zona 4; from Q30; ⊙9pm-1am Fri & Sat) and the **Black & White Lounge** (Map p46; www.blackandwhite bar.com; 11a Calle 2-54, Zona 1; ⊙7pm-1am Wed-Sat) are the current faves. Mostly, though, gay travelers in Guatemala will find themselves keeping it low-key and pushing twin beds together.

Gay.com has a personals section for Guatemala, and the Gully (www.thegully. com) usually has some articles and information relevant to Guatemala. The best site, Gay Guatemala (www.gayguatemala.com), is in Spanish.

Health

Staying healthy in Guatemala involves some common-sense precautions and a few destination-specific ones.

Before You Go
HEALTH INSURANCE

Despite relatively low costs for health care, it is generally recommended that travelers take out travel insurance, which almost always covers medical costs. Check your policy carefully to see what is and is not covered before buying.

VACCINATIONS

Discuss your requirements with your doctor, but the vaccines that are usually recommended for travel to Central America are hepatitis A and B and typhoid. If you are planning to spend time handling animals or exploring caves, consider getting vaccinated for rabies.

In Guatemala
AVAILABILITY & COST OF HEALTH CARE

Larger towns have both public (cheap, with long waiting times) and private (expensive, but faster) hospitals, often with doctors who speak at least a little English. In smaller towns there will be a health clinic, and in villages there is usually a doctor. Guatemala City naturally has the best range of health services in the country. Health care is relatively cheap in Guatemala (around Q25 for a standard doctor's consultation).

While 'medical tourism' is taking off in Guatemala (dentistry, for example, is a serious bargain compared to what you will pay elsewhere), if you have a serious complaint that does not require immediate attention, consider returning to your home country for treatment.

HEALTHY EATING

By far the most common health issue that travelers to Guatemala experience is stomach-related. This can range from serious diseases such as cholera to simple cases of diarrhea. Watch what you eat, drink and generally put in your mouth. Here are a few simple guidelines to keep you out of the bathroom and on the road:

➡ Wash your hands thoroughly before eating or touching your face.

➡ Eat only in places that appear to be clean (conditions in the dining room are sometimes a good indicator of what's going on in the kitchen).

➡ To ensure the food you eat is fresh and freshly cooked, eat only in busy places around mealtimes.

➡ Peel, cook or disinfect fruits and vegetables.

➡ Be very selective when it comes to street food.

➡ Avoid tap water unless it has been boiled thoroughly or disinfected. Ice in more expensive restaurants is made from purified water, but order drinks without it if you want to be really cautious.

➡ If you do get sick and it lasts longer than a few days, take a stool sample to the laboratory (even the smallest towns have them) for analysis. You'll get a possibly alarming readout of exactly what kinds of bugs you have. Any pharmacist will be able to use the readout to prescribe the appropriate medicine.

MOSQUITOES

Mosquitoes can transmit two serious diseases: malaria and dengue fever. Malaria tablets are available and recommended if you are planning to travel in rural areas at altitudes lower than 1500m, especially in the rainy season (June to November). It's worth noting that there is no malaria risk in Antigua or around Lake Atitlán. The best prevention against mosquito-borne diseases is to avoid getting bitten. In high-risk areas this means a DEET–based insect repellent (bring one from home), long sleeves and pant legs, avoiding being outside around sunrise and sunset, and checking window screens and mosquito nets in hotel rooms for holes.

ZIKA VIRUS

In late 2015 it was reported that the Zika virus had reached Guatemala, and by early 2016 there were over 100 confirmed cases. Also spread by mosquitoes, Zika's symptoms include fever, rash, joint pain and red eyes, and sufferers tend to recover after a week or so. Complications for pregnant women and infants are more serious – see the Center for Disease Control website (www.cdc.gov) for details. As with other mosquito-borne diseases, the best prevention is not getting bitten.

TAP WATER

While many Guatemalans drink the tap water (often through necessity rather than choice), it is not recommended that foreigners do so. Purified water is cheap and readily available in tourist areas and many back-country regions as well, and picking up a stomach bug is no fun.

Insurance

Getting travel insurance to cover theft, loss and medical problems is recommended. Some policies specifically exclude dangerous activities, which can include scuba diving, motorcycling and even trekking.

You may prefer a policy that pays doctors or hospitals directly, rather than you having to pay on the spot and claim later. If you have to claim later, ensure you keep all documentation.

Check that the policy covers ambulances or emergency flight home.

Worldwide travel insurance is available at www.lonelyplanet.com/travel-insurance. You can buy, extend and claim online anytime – even if you're already on the road.

Internet Access

Most travelers make constant use of internet cafes and free web-based email. Most towns have cybercafes with fairly reliable connections. Internet cafes typically charge between Q5 and Q10 an hour.

Wi-fi is becoming readily available across the country, but can only really be counted on in large and/or tourist towns. Most (but not all) hostels offer wi-fi, as do many hotels in the midrange and up category. The best reliable source of wi-fi around the country is at Pollo Campero restaurants – they're in pretty much every town of any size and all offer free, unsecured access.

Language Courses

Guatemala is celebrated for its many language schools. A spot of study here is a great way not only to learn Spanish, but also to meet locals and get an inside angle on the culture. Many travelers heading south through Central America to South America make Guatemala an early stop so they can pick up the Spanish skills they need for their trip.

Guatemalan language schools are some of the

cheapest in the world, but few people go away disappointed. There are so many schools to choose from that it's essential to check out a few before deciding.

You can start any day at most schools, and study for as long as you like. If you're coming in peak season and hoping to get into one of the more popular schools, it's a good idea to book ahead, although many schools charge around Q380 for phone or internet reservations. All decent schools offer a variety of elective activities, from salsa classes to movies to volcano hikes. Many schools offer classes in Maya languages as well as Spanish.

Where to Study

Antigua is the most popular place to study. Quetzaltenango is second, perhaps attracting a more serious type of student; Antigua has a livelier students' and travelers' social scene. Outside of these areas, there are Spanish schools scattered across the country. Schools charge from Q1500 to Q2400 for four hours of one-on-one classes five days a week and accommodation with a local family.

Studying in a small town has its pros and cons. On the upside, you may be the only foreigner around, so you won't be speaking any English. On the downside, Spanish may be the second language of the inhabitants of the village (including your teacher), meaning that you could pick up all sorts of bad habits.

Choosing a School

Choosing between the mass of Spanish schools in Guatemala can be tough. Many schools don't have in-house teacher training programs, so there aren't so many 'good schools' as there are 'good teachers.' It's best to pay for as little time as possible (a week, usually) so you can change if you're really unhappy. You should be completely up-front about what your goals are (conversation,

grammar, vocabulary etc) are when starting, as well as any specialized interests that you have (politics, medical, legal etc) so the school can design a curriculum and assign you a teacher to best suit your needs. If you end up liking the school, but not the teacher, ask for a new teacher as soon as possible – personality conflicts occur, and four or five hours of one-on-one with someone you don't like can soon turn into hard work.

For (completely unverified) reviews of some of Guatemala's Spanish schools by ex-students, check out www.guatemala365.com.

Legal Matters

You may find that police officers in Guatemala are, at times, somewhat unhelpful. Generally speaking, the less you have to do with the law, the better.

Whatever you do, don't get involved in any way with illegal drugs – even if the locals seem to do so freely. As a foreigner you are at a distinct disadvantage and you may be set up by others. Drug laws in Guatemala are strict, and though enforcement may be uneven, penalties are severe. If you do get caught doing something you shouldn't, your best line of defense is to apologize, stay calm and proceed from there.

While many commentators claim that corruption is rife in Guatemala, don't take this to mean you can buy your way out of any situation. If it does seem that you can 'make everything go away' by handing over some cash, proceed cautiously and tactfully.

Money

Guatemala's currency, the quetzal (ket-sahl, abbreviated to Q), has been fairly stable at around Q7.5 = US$1 for years, with fluctuations owing more to the unstable

dollar than to movements in the quetzal. The quetzal is divided into 100 centavos.

ATMs

You'll find ATMs (cash machines, *cajeros automáticos*) for Visa/Plus System cards in all but the smallest towns, and there are MasterCard/Cirrus ATMs in many places, too, so one of these cards is the best basis for your supply of cash in Guatemala. The 5B network is widespread and particularly useful, as it works with both Visa and MasterCard cards.

Be aware that card skimming is a problem in Guatemala. Avoid ATMs that are left unguarded at night (ie those in the small room out front of the bank) and look for one that is in a secure environment (such as those inside supermarkets or shopping malls). Failing that, keep your hand covered when entering your PIN and check your balance online.

Cash

Cash is king in Guatemala, although carrying too much of it makes getting robbed a bigger pain than it would otherwise be. Some towns suffer from change shortages: always try to carry a stash of small bills. Keep a small supply of low-denomination US dollars (which are accepted pretty much anywhere, at various rates of exchange) as an emergency fund.

While everybody accepts dollars, you will almost always get a better deal by paying in quetzals.

Currencies other than the US dollar are virtually useless, although a small handful of places now change cash euros.

Credit Cards

Many banks give cash advances on Visa cards, and some on MasterCard. You can pay for many purchases with these cards or with American Express (Amex) cards – particularly in higher-end hotels and restaurants. Paying with credit card can attract a service charge of up to 5% – be sure to ask if there is a *recargo* (transaction fee).

Tipping

A 10% tip is expected in restaurants (often automatically added to your bill in tourist towns such as Antigua). In small *comedores* (basic, cheap eateries) tipping is optional, but follow local practice and leave some spare change.

Travelers Checks

If you're not packing plastic, a combination of Amex US-dollar traveler's checks and some cash US dollars is the way to go. Take some of these as a backup even if you do have a card. Many banks change US-dollar traveler's checks, and tend to give the best rates. Amex is easily the most recognized traveler's check brand. Few businesses will accept traveler's checks as payment or change them for cash.

Opening Hours

Hours provided are general guidelines, but there are many variations. Restaurant times, in particular, can vary by up to two hours either way.

The Ley Seca (dry law) stipulates that bars and *discotecas* must close by 1am, except on nights before public holidays; it is rigidly followed in large cities and universally mocked in smaller towns.

Banks 9am–5pm Monday to Friday, 9am–1pm Saturday

Bars 11am–midnight

Cafes & Restaurants 7am–9pm

Government offices 8am–4pm Monday to Friday

Shops 8am–noon and 2pm–6pm Monday to Saturday

Photography

Photography is a sensitive subject in Guatemala. Always ask permission before taking portraits, especially of Maya women and children. Don't be surprised if your request is denied. Children often request payment (usually Q1) in return for posing. In certain places, such as the church of Santo Tomás in Chichicastenango, photography is forbidden. Maya ceremonies (should you be so lucky to witness one) are off-limits for photography unless you are given explicit permission to take pictures. If local people make any sign of being offended, put your camera away and apologize immediately, both out of decency and for your own safety. Never take photos of army installations, men with guns or other sensitive military subjects.

Post

The Guatemalan postal service was privatized in 1999. Generally, letters and parcels take eight to 10 days to travel to the US and Canada and 10 to 12 days to reach Europe. Almost all cities and towns (but not villages) have a post office where you can buy stamps and send mail. If you want to get a package couriered to you, make sure the courier company has an office in the town where you are staying; otherwise you will be charged some hefty 'handling fees.'

Public Holidays

Guatemalan public holidays include the following:

New Year's Day (Año Nuevo) January 1

Easter (Semana Santa; Holy Thursday to Easter Sunday inclusive) March/April

Labor Day (Día del Trabajo) May 1

Army Day (Día del Ejército) June 30

Assumption Day (Día de la Asunción) August 15

Independence Day (Día de la Independencia) September 15

Revolution Day (Día de la Revolución) October 20

All Saints' Day (Día de Todos los Santos) November 1

Christmas Eve afternoon (Víspera Navidad) December 24

Christmas Day (Navidad) December 25

New Year's Eve afternoon (Víspera de Año Nuevo) December 31

Safe Travel

While crime definitely happens in Guatemala, and definitely happens to tourists, these days the most frequently reported type of nasty incident involves robbery on walking trails.

The days of robbers targeting tourist buses out on the open highway seem to be thankfully in the past,

GOVERNMENT TRAVEL ADVICE

The following government websites offer travel advisories and information on current hot spots. Please bear in mind that these sites are updated occasionally and are obliged to err on the safe side – many, many travelers visit Guatemala and don't experience any of the reported problems.

Australian Department of Foreign Affairs (www.smartraveller.gov.au)

British Foreign Office (www.fco.gov.uk)

Canadian Department of Foreign Affairs (www.dfait-maeci.gc.ca)

US State Department (http://travel.state.gov)

although some tourists in rental cars have been targeted. This information is incredibly fluid – check with **Proatur** (☑in English 1500) for the latest.

The crime you're most likely to become a victim of involves pickpocketing, bag-snatching, bag-slitting and the like in crowded streets, markets, bus stations and on buses, but also in empty, dark city streets.

Tips

➡ It's best to travel and arrive in daylight hours. If that's not possible, travel at night using 1st-class buses and catch a taxi to your hotel once you arrive.

➡ Only carry the money, cards, checks and valuables that you need. Leave the rest in a sealed, signed envelope in your hotel's safe, and obtain a receipt for the envelope.

➡ Don't flaunt jewelry, cameras or valuable-looking watches. Keep your wallet or purse out of view.

➡ On buses keep your important valuables with you, and keep a tight hold on them.

➡ Use normal precautions when using ATMs (and be aware that card skimming is a reality here).

➡ Hiking in large groups and/or with a police escort reduces the risk of robbery.

➡ Resisting or trying to flee from robbers usually makes the situation worse.

➡ Hiking on active volcanoes obviously has an element of risk. Get the latest story before you head out. In the wet season, hike in the morning before rain and possible thunderstorms set in.

➡ Be careful, especially in rural areas, when talking to small children, always ask permission to take photographs, and generally try not to put yourself in any situation that might be misinterpreted.

Scams

➡ One common scenario is for someone to spray ketchup or some other sticky liquid on your clothes. An accomplice then appears to help you clean up the mess and robs you in the process. Other methods of distraction, such as dropping

a purse or coins, or someone appearing to faint, are also used by pickpockets and bag snatchers.

➡ Regrettably, ATM card cloners have moved into Guatemala, targeting Guatemalans and foreigners alike. They operate by attaching a card reading device to the ATM (often inside the slot where you insert your card) and once they have your data, proceed to drain your account. There have been reports of card cloning in all the major tourist destinations. The only way to avoid it is to use ATMs that cannot be tampered with easily (inside supermarkets or shopping malls). The ATMs most prone to tampering are the ones in the little unlocked room at the front of a bank. Note that you should *never* have to enter your PIN number to gain access to an ATM room.

Telephone

Guatemala has no area or city codes. Calling from other countries, you just dial the international access code (☑00 in most countries), then the Guatemala country code (☑502), then the eight-digit local number. Calling within Guatemala, just dial the eight-digit local number. The international access code from Guatemala is ☑00.

Many towns and cities frequented by tourists have privately run call offices where you can make international calls for reasonable rates.

Don't use the black phones placed strategically in tourist towns that say 'Press 2 to call the United States free!' This is a bait-and-switch scam; you put the call on your credit card and return home to find you have paid between US$8 and US$20 per minute.

Many travelers use an account such as Skype. If an internet cafe does not have Skype installed, it can usually be downloaded in a matter

---

REPORTING A CRIME

Reporting a crime is always a toss-up in Guatemala. If you're the victim of something really serious, of course you should take it to the police – the phrase you're looking for here is '*Yo quisiera denunciar un crimen*' (I'd like to report a crime). If you've been robbed, get a statement filed so you can show your insurance company.

If it's a minor thing, on the other hand, you might want to decide whether or not it's really worth your while reporting it to the police.

Specially trained tourist police (often English speaking) operate in some major tourist areas – you can call them in **Antigua** (☑5578-9835; operacionesproatur@inguat.gob.gt; 6a Calle Poniente Final; ☺24hr) and **Guatemala City** (Tourist Police; ☑2232-0202; 11 Calle 12-06, Zona 1; ☺24hr).

Outside of those areas (and normal office hours) your best bet is to call **Proatur** (☑in English 1500), which operates a 24-hour nationwide toll-free hotline in English and Spanish. It can give you information and assistance, help deal with the police and even arrange a lawyer if need be.

of minutes. If you're planning on using internet cafe computers to make calls, buy earbuds with a microphone attached before you leave – you can plug them into the front of most computers.

Cell Phones

There are three cell companies in the country – Movistar (www.movistar.com.gt) tends to have the cheapest rates, with coverage limited to not much further than major cities, while Tigo (www.tigo.com.gt) and Claro (www.claro.com.gt) have the best coverage.

It's possible to bring your cell phone from home, have it 'unlocked' for use in Guatemala (this costs between Q50 and Q100 in Guatemala, depending on the make of the phone), then substitute your SIM card for a local one. This works on some phones and not others and there doesn't appear to be a logic behind it.

Guatemalan phone companies work on either 850, 900 or 1900 MHz frequencies – if you have a tri- or quad-band phone you should be OK. Compatibility issues, and the possibility of theft (cell phones are a pickpocket's delight) makes buying a cheap prepaid phone on arrival the most popular option.

Prepaid phones are available pretty much everywhere and cost around Q100 to Q150, often coming with Q100 or so in free calls. Cards to restock the credit on your phone are sold in nearly every corner store. Calls cost Q1.50 per minute anywhere in the country, the same for calls to the US (depending on the company you're with), and up to five times that for the rest of the world.

Phonecards

The most common street phones (although becoming increasingly rare as everybody goes cellular) are those of Telgua, for which you need to buy a Telgua phone card (*tarjeta telefónica de Telgua*) from shops, kiosks and the like. Card sales points may advertise the fact with red signs saying '*Ladatel de Venta Aqui.*' The cards come in denominations of Q20, Q30 and Q50: you slot them into a Telgua phone, dial your number, and the display will tell you how much time you have left. Telgua street phones bear instructions to dial ☑147110 for domestic collect calls and ☑147120 for international collect calls.

Time

Guatemala runs on North American Central Standard Time (GMT/UTC minus six hours). The 24-hour clock is often used, so 1pm may be written as 13 or 1300. When it is noon in Guatemala, it is 1pm in New York, 6pm in London, 10am in San Francisco and 4am the next day in Sydney. For more time conversions, see www.timeanddate.com/worldclock.

Toilets

➡ You cannot throw *anything* into Guatemalan toilets, including toilet paper. Bathrooms are equipped with some sort of receptacle (usually a small wastebasket) for soiled paper.

➡ Toilet paper is not always provided, so always carry some. If you don't have any and need some, asking a restaurant worker for *un rollo de papel* (a roll of paper), accompanied by a panicked facial expression, usually produces fast results.

➡ Public toilets are rare. Use the ones at cafes, restaurants, your hotel and archaeological sites. Buses rarely have toilets on board and if they do, don't count on them working.

Tourist Information

Guatemala's national tourism institute, Inguat (www.visitguatemala.com), has information offices in major tourist areas. A few towns have departmental, municipal or private-enterprise tourist information offices. **Proatur** (☑in English 1500), a joint private-government initiative, operates a 24-hour toll-free advice and assistance hotline.

Travelers with Disabilities

Guatemala is not the easiest country to negotiate for travelers with a disability. Although many sidewalks in Antigua have ramps and cute little inlaid tiles depicting a wheelchair, the streets are cobblestone, so the ramps are anything but smooth and the streets worse!

Many hotels in Guatemala are old converted houses with rooms around a courtyard; such rooms are wheelchair accessible, but the bathrooms may not be. The most expensive hotels have facilities such as ramps, elevators and accessible toilets. Transportation is the biggest hurdle for travelers with limited mobility: travelers in a wheelchair may consider renting a car and driver as the buses will prove especially challenging due to lack of space.

Mobility International USA (www.miusa.org) advises travelers on mobility issues, runs exchange programs (including in Guatemala) and publishes some useful books. Also worth consulting are Access-Able Travel Source (www.access-able.com) and Accessible Journeys (www.disabilitytravel.com).

Antigua-based Transitions (www.transitionsfoundation.org) is an organization aiming to increase awareness and access for people with disabilities in Guatemala.

Download Lonely Planet's free Accessible Travel guide from http://lptravel.to/AccessibleTravel.

Visas

Citizens of the US, Canada, EU countries, Norway, Switzerland, Australia, New Zealand, Israel and Japan are among those who do not need a visa for tourist visits to Guatemala. On entry into Guatemala you will normally be given a 90-day stay. (The number '90' will be written in the stamp in your passport.)

Citizens of some Eastern European countries are among those who do need visas to visit Guatemala. Inquire at a Guatemalan embassy well in advance of travel.

In August of 2006 Guatemala joined the Centro America 4 (CA-4) trading agreement with Nicaragua, Honduras and El Salvador. Designed to facilitate the movement of people and goods around the region, it has one major effect on foreign visitors – upon entry to the CA-4 region, travelers are given a 90-day stay for the entire region. You can get this extended once, for an additional 90 days, for around Q120. The exact requirements change with each government, but here's how it was working in Guatemala at the time of writing: you needed to go to the **Departamento de Extranjería** (Foreigners Office; Map p46; ☎2411-2411; www.migracion.gob.gt; 6a Av 3-11, Zona 4, Guatemala City; ⊙8am-2:30pm Mon-Fri), with all of the following:

Two black-and-white cédula-sized photos on matte paper; a valid passport; two copies of the photo page of your passport and one copy of the page with the entry stamp on it; credit (not debit) card with a photocopy of both of its sides (or US$400 worth of travelers' checks or a ticket out of the country or proof of flight reservation on travel agency letterhead, signed and sealed by a travel agent).

Extensions can take up to a week to process, but this period is also very flexible – it's worth asking about before you start the process.

If you have been in the CA-4 for your original 90 days and a 90-day extension, you must leave the region for 72 hours (Belize and Mexico are the most obvious, easiest options), after which you can return to the region to start all over again. Some foreigners have been repeating this cycle for years.

Visa regulations are subject to change – it's always worth checking with a Guatemalan embassy before you go.

Volunteering

If you want to get to the heart of Guatemalan matters, consider volunteer work. Opportunities abound, from caring for abandoned animals to writing grant applications to tending fields. Travelers with specific skills such as nurses, doctors, teachers and website designers are particularly encouraged to investigate volunteering in Guatemala.

Most volunteer posts require basic or better Spanish skills and a minimum time commitment. Depending on the organization, you may have to pay for room and board. Before making a commitment, you may want to talk to past volunteers and read the fine print associated with the position.

An excellent information source on volunteer opportunities is Quetzaltenango-based **EntreMundos** (Map p138; ☎7761-2179; www.entre mundos.org; 6a Calle 7-31, Zona 1; ⊙2-4pm Mon-Thu). The website has a huge range of volunteer opportunities. Many language schools have close links to volunteer projects and can introduce you to the world of volunteering – often the best option if you are only looking to commit for a few weeks. A worldwide site for volunteer positions (with many Guatemala listings) is www.idealist.org.

Women Travelers

Women should encounter no special problems traveling in Guatemala. The primary thing you can do to make it easy for yourself while traveling here is to dress modestly. Modesty in dress is highly regarded, and if you practice it, you will usually be treated with respect.

Specifically, shorts should be worn only at the beach, not in town, and especially not in the highlands. Skirts should be at or below the knee. Going braless is considered provocative. Many local women swim with T-shirts over their swimsuits.

Women traveling alone can expect plenty of attention from talkative men. Often they're just curious and not out for a foreign conquest. It is, of course, up to you how to respond, but there's no need to be intimidated. Consider the situation and circumstances, and stay confident. Try to sit next to women or children on the bus. Local women rarely initiate conversations, but usually have lots of interesting things to say once the ball is rolling.

While there's no need to be paranoid, the possibility of rape and assault does exist. Use your normal traveler's caution – avoid walking alone in isolated places or through city streets late at night, and skip hitchhiking.

Work

Some travelers find work in bars, restaurants and places to stay in Antigua, Panajachel or Quetzaltenango, but the wages are just survival pay. If you're looking to crew a yacht, there's always work being offered around the Río Dulce area, sometimes for short trips, sometimes to the States and further afield. Check noticeboards and online forums for details.

Transportation

GETTING THERE & AWAY

With land borders on three sides, river and sea port entries and two international airports, it's not hard to get into or out of Guatemala. Flights, cars and tours can be booked online at lonelyplanet.com/bookings.

Air

Guatemala City's Aeropuerto La Aurora (GUA) is the country's major international airport. The only other airport with international flights (from Belize City) is Flores (FRS). The Guatemalan national airline, Avianca, is a subsidiary of the Colombian company of the same name.

There are direct flights from the USA with airlines including Avianca (www.avianca.com). Aero-Mexico (www.aeromexico.com) and Interjet (www.interjet.com.mx), flying direct from Mexico City. Avianca and Alternative Airlines (http://taca.alternativeairlines.com) have flights from most Central American capitals. If you are coming from elsewhere, you will almost certainly be changing planes in the US, Mexico or elsewhere in Central America.

Land

It's advisable to get through all borders as early in the day as possible. Onward transportation winds down in the afternoon and border areas are not always the safest places. There is no departure tax when you leave Guatemala by land, although many border officials will ask for Q10. If you're willing to argue and wait around, this may be dropped, but most travelers take the path of least resistance and simply pay up.

Border Crossings

Guatemala has official border crossings with all neighboring countries. Check visa requirements (p16) before arrival.

BELIZE

➡ Melchor de Mencos (GUA) – Benque Viejo del Carmen (BZE)

EL SALVADOR

➡ Ciudad Pedro de Alvarado (GUA) – La Hachadura (ES)

➡ Valle Nuevo (GUA) – Las Chinamas (ES)

➡ San Cristóbal Frontera (GUA) – San Cristóbal (ES)

➡ Anguiatú (GUA) – Anguiatú (ES)

HONDURAS

➡ Agua Caliente (GUA) – Agua Caliente (HND)

➡ El Florido (GUA) – Copán Ruinas (HND)

➡ Corinto (GUA) – Corinto (HND)

MEXICO

➡ Ciudad Tecún Umán (GUA) – Ciudad Hidalgo (MEX)

➡ El Carmen (GUA) – Talisman (MEX)

➡ La Mesilla (GUA) – Ciudad Cuauhtémoc (MEX)

CLIMATE CHANGE & TRAVEL

Every form of transport that relies on carbon-based fuel generates CO_2, the main cause of human-induced climate change. Modern travel is dependent on airplanes, which might use less fuel per kilometer per person than most cars but travel much greater distances. The altitude at which aircraft emit gases (including CO_2) and particles also contributes to their climate change impact. Many websites offer 'carbon calculators' that allow people to estimate the carbon emissions generated by their journey and, for those who wish to do so, to offset the impact of the greenhouse gases emitted with contributions to portfolios of climate-friendly initiatives throughout the world. Lonely Planet offsets the carbon footprint of all staff and author travel.

TRANSPORTATION RIVER

DEPARTURE TAX

Guatemala levies a departure tax of US$30 on outbound air passengers, which is nearly always included in your ticket price. If it's not, it has to be paid in cash US dollars or quetzals at the airline check-in desk.

Bus

Bus is the most common way to enter Guatemala by land. Most first-class international buses run nonstop from Guatemala City. First-class buses for Belize also depart from Flores/Santa Elena. On first-class buses (particularly to Honduras and El Salvador) the driver may take your passport and complete border formalities for you. Going to Belize or Mexico, you will have to do them yourself. Border fees (official or otherwise) will not be included in the ticket price.

Second-class buses tend not to cross the border.

Car & Motorcycle

The mountain of paperwork and liability involved with driving into Guatemala deters most travelers. You will need the following documents, all clear and consistent, to enter Guatemala with a car:

➡ current and valid registration

➡ proof of ownership (if you don't own the car, you'll need a notarized letter of authorization from the owner that you are allowed to take it)

➡ your current and valid driver's license or an International Driving Permit (IDP), issued by the automobile association in your home country

➡ temporary import permit (available free at the border, good for maximum 90 days).

Insurance from foreign countries is not recognized by Guatemala, forcing you to purchase a policy locally. Most border posts and nearby towns have offices selling liability policies. To deter foreigners from selling cars in Guatemala, the authorities make you exit the country with the vehicle you used to enter it. Don't be the designated driver when crossing borders if you don't own the car, because you and it will not be allowed to leave Guatemala without each other.

Gasoline is readily available in all but the tiniest of villages. If you see a kid waving a funnel at you, it means he's selling cheap contraband Mexican gas – some swear by it, others claim its high sediment content ruins engines.

Mechanics are everywhere. Authorized agencies can only be found in larger cities. Generic parts are easy to come by, but if you're looking for originals, Toyota is by far the most popular make in the country, followed (distantly) by Mazda and Ford.

River

There are two crossings from Mexico's Chiapas State to El Petén – the most commonly used crosses at the Mexican town of Frontera Corozal to either La Técnica or Bethel in Guatemala. Frontera Corozal has good transport connections to Palenque in Mexico and there are regular buses from La Técnica and Bethel to Flores/Santa Elena. The other river route from Mexico into Guatemala's Petén department is up the Río de la Pasión from Benemérito de las Américas, south of Frontera Corozal, to Sayaxché, but there are no immigration facilities or reliable passenger services along this route.

Sea

Public boats connect Punta Gorda in Belize with Lívingston and Puerto Barrios in Guatemala. Punta Gorda services connect with bus services to/from Belize City There is a Q80 departure tax when leaving Guatemala by sea.

GETTING AROUND

Air

At the time of writing the only scheduled internal flights were between Guatemala City and Flores, a route operated daily by Avianca (www.avianca.com) and TAG (www.tag.com.gt).

Bicycle

Guatemala's mountainous terrain and occasionally terrifying road conditions make intercity pedaling hard going. But if you have your wits about you, cycling is a great way to get around smaller towns – Antigua, Quetzaltenango and San Pedro La Laguna are among the towns where you can rent reasonable mountain bikes (you don't want skinny wheels here). There are bike shops in almost every town where you can buy a new bike starting from around Q800.

Boat

The Caribbean town of Lívingston is only reachable by boat, across the Bahía de Amatique from Puerto Barrios or down the Río Dulce from the town of Río Dulce – both great trips. In Lago de Atitlán fast fiberglass launches zip across the waters between villages – by far the best way to get around.

Bus & Minibus

Buses go almost everywhere in Guatemala. Most are ancient school buses from the US and Canada. It is not unusual for a local family of five to squeeze into seats that were originally designed for two child-sized bottoms. They're known as chicken buses, after the live cargo accompanying many passengers. They are frequent, crowded and cheap. Expect to pay Q10 (or less!) for an hour of travel.

Chicken buses will stop anywhere, for anyone. Helpers will yell '*hay lugares!*' (eye loo-gar-ays), which literally means 'there are places.' The same helpers will also yell the bus's destination. Tall travelers will be especially challenged on these buses. To catch a chicken bus, simply stand beside the road with your arm out parallel to the ground.

Some routes, especially between big cities, are served by more comfortable buses with the luxury of one seat per person. The best buses are labeled 'Pullman,' '*especial*' or '*primera clase.*' Occasionally these may have bathrooms (don't count on them working), televisions and even food service. Pullman routes always originate or end in Guatemala City.

In general, more buses leave in the morning (some as early as 2am) than the afternoon. Bus traffic drops off after about 4pm; night buses are rare and not recommended. An exception are the overnight buses from Guatemala City to Flores, which have been relatively drama-free for some years now.

Distances in Guatemala are not huge and, apart from the Guate–Flores run, you won't often ride for more than four hours at a time. On a typical four-hour bus trip you'll cover 175km to 200km for Q60 to Q100.

For a few of the better services you can buy tickets in advance; this is generally worth doing as it ensures that you get a place.

On some shorter routes, minibuses, usually called 'microbuses,' are replacing chicken buses. Operated with the same cram-'em-all-in principle, they can be even more uncomfortable because they have less leg room. Where neither buses nor minibuses

roam, *picop* (pick-up) trucks serve as buses; you hail them and pay for them as if they were the genuine article.

At least a couple of times a month, a chicken bus plunges over a cliff or rounds a blind bend into a head-on collision. Newspapers are full of gory details and diagrams of the latest wreck.

Shuttle Buses

Shuttle minibuses run by travel agencies provide comfortable and quick transport along the main routes plied by tourists. You'll find these heavily advertised wherever they are offered. With a few notable exceptions, they're much more expensive than buses (anywhere between five and 15 times as expensive), but more convenient – they usually offer a door-to-door service, with scheduled meal and bathroom breaks. The most popular shuttle routes include Guatemala City airport–Antigua, Antigua–Panajachel, Panajachel–Chichicastenango and Lanquín–Antigua.

Car & Motorcycle

You can drive in Guatemala with your home-country driver's license or with an International Driving Permit (IDP). Driving etiquette will probably be very different from what you're used to at home: passing on blind curves, ceding the right of way to vehicles coming uphill on narrow passes and deafening honking for no

apparent reason are just the start. Expect few road signs and no indication from other drivers of what they are about to do. Do not pay any attention to turn signals – they are rarely used. Hazard lights generally mean that the driver is about to do something foolish and/or illegal.

A vehicle coming uphill always has the right of way. *Túmulos* are speed bumps that are generously (sometimes oddly) placed throughout the country, usually on the main drag through a town. Use of seat belts is obligatory, but generally not practiced.

In Guatemala driving at night is a bad idea for many reasons, not the least of which are armed bandits, drunk drivers and decreased visibility.

Every driver involved in an accident that results in injury or death is taken into custody until a judge determines responsibility.

If someone's car breaks down on the highway (particularly on mountain roads), they'll warn other drivers by putting shrubs or branches on the road for a few hundred meters beforehand. If you're driving and you see these, it's best to be cautious and slow down.

Rental

While car hire is possible, if you're sticking to the main sights, logistically it is rarely a good idea – Antigua is best seen on foot, the villages around Lake Atitlán are best visited by boat, and the distance from either of those to

A CHICKEN BUS IS HATCHED

If you rode the bus to school 10 years ago or more in the US, you might just end up meeting an old friend in Guatemala, resurrected and given new life as a 'chicken bus.' Love 'em or hate 'em, chicken buses (*camionetas* or *parrillas* to Guatemalans) are a fact of life in traveling around Guatemala. A lot of times there is no alternative.

In the US, once school buses reach the ripe old age of 10 years or do 150,000 miles, they're auctioned off. They then get towed through the States and Mexico, taken to a workshop where they are refitted (bigger engine, six-speed gearbox, roof rack, destination board, luggage rack, longer seats) and fancied up with a paint job, CD player and chrome detailing. Drivers then add their individual touches – anything from religious paraphernalia to stuffed toys and Christmas lights dangling around the dashboard area.

If you've got a choice of buses to go with, looks *are* important – chances are if the paint is fresh and the chrome gleaming, the owner also has the cash to spend on new brakes and regular maintenance. And, with a conservative estimate of an average of one chicken-bus accident per week in Guatemala, this is something you may want to keep in mind.

Tikal makes it a much better idea to catch a bus or fly. That said, for freedom and comfort, nothing beats having your own wheels.

There are car-hire places in the major tourist cities. To rent a car you need to show your passport, driver's license and major credit card. Usually, the person renting the vehicle must be 25 or older. Insurance policies accompanying rental cars may not protect you from loss or theft, in which case you could be liable for hundreds or even thousands of dollars in damages. Be careful where you park, especially in Guatemala City and at night. If your hotel does not have parking, they will know of a secure garage nearby.

Motorcycles are available for rent in Antigua and around Lake Atitlán. Bringing safety gear is highly recommended.

Hitchhiking

Hitchhiking in the strict sense of the word is generally not practiced in Guatemala because it is not safe. However, where bus service is sporadic or nonexistent, pick-up trucks and other vehicles may serve as public transport. If you stand beside the road with your arm out, someone will stop. You are expected to pay the driver as if you were traveling on a bus and the fare will be similar.

This is a safe, reliable system used by locals and travelers, and the only inconvenience you're likely to encounter is full-to-overflowing vehicles.

Any other form of hitching is never entirely safe, and we don't recommend it. Travelers who hitch should understand that they are taking a small but potentially serious risk.

Local Transportation
Bus & Minibus

Public transportation outside Guatemala City is chiefly provided by newish, crowded minibuses. They're useful to travelers mainly in more spread-out cities such as Quetzaltenango and Huehuetenango. Guatemala City has the old red buses (that are not recommended for safety reasons) and newer fleets of TransMetro and TransUrbano buses.

Shuttle minibuses run by travel agencies provide comfortable, quick transport along main routes plied by tourists. You'll find these heavily advertised wherever they are offered. With a few exceptions, they're much more expensive than buses (anywhere between five and 15 times more), but more convenient – they usually offer a door-to-door service, with scheduled meal

and bathroom breaks. Popular shuttle routes include Guatemala City airport–Antigua, Antigua–Panajachel, Panajachel–Chichicastenango and Lanquín–Antigua.

Taxi

Taxis are fairly plentiful in most significant towns. A 10-minute ride can cost about Q60, which is relatively expensive – expect to hear woeful tales from taxi drivers about the price of gasoline. Except for some taxis in Guatemala City, they don't use meters: you must agree upon the fare before you set off – best before you get in, in fact.

If you feel reluctant to take on Guatemalan roads, an alternative to car hire can be to hire a taxi driver for an extended time. This is often only slightly more expensive than renting and gives you all the freedom and comfort without the stress of having to drive.

Tuk-tuk

If you've spent any time in Asia, you'll be very familiar with the *tuk-tuk,* a three-wheeled minitaxi nominally seating three passengers and a driver, but obviously capable of carrying twice that amount. Named for the noise their little lawnmower engines make, *tuk-tuks* are best for short hops around town – expect to pay somewhere around Q5 per person. Hail them the way you would a normal taxi.

Language

There are around 20 Maya indigenous languages used in Guatemala, but Spanish is the most commonly spoken language.

SPANISH

Latin American Spanish pronunciation is easy, as most sounds have equivalents in English. Note that kh is a throaty sound (like the 'ch' in the Scottish *loch*), v and b are like a soft English 'v' (between a 'v' and a 'b'), and r is strongly rolled. There are some variations in spoken Spanish across Latin America, the most notable being the pronunciation of the letters *ll* and *y*. In our pronunciation guides they are represented with y because they are pronounced as the 'y' in 'yes' in most of Latin America. Note, however, that in some parts of the continent they sound like the 'lli' in 'million'. If you read our colored pronunciation guides as if they were English, you'll be understood. The stressed syllables are indicated with italics in our pronunciation guides.

The polite form is used in this chapter; where both polite and informal options are given, they are indicated by the abbreviations 'pol' and 'inf'. Where necessary, both masculine and feminine forms of words are included, separated by a slash and with the masculine form first, eg *perdido/a* (m/f).

Basics

Hello.	*Hola.*	o·la
Goodbye.	*Adiós.*	a·dyos

WANT MORE?

For in-depth language information and handy phrases, check out Lonely Planet's *Latin American Spanish Phrasebook*. You'll find it at **shop.lonelyplanet.com**, or you can buy Lonely Planet's iPhone phrasebooks at the Apple App Store.

How are you?	*¿Qué tal?*	ke tal
Fine, thanks.	*Bien, gracias.*	byen gra·syas
Excuse me.	*Perdón.*	per·don
Sorry.	*Lo siento.*	lo syen·to
Please.	*Por favor.*	por fa·vor
Thank you.	*Gracias.*	gra·syas
You are welcome.	*De nada.*	de na·da
Yes./No.	*Sí./No.*	see/no

My name is ...
Me llamo ...   me ya·mo ...

What's your name?
¿Cómo se llama Usted?   ko·mo se ya·ma oo·ste (pol)
¿Cómo te llamas?   ko·mo te ya·mas (inf)

Do you speak English?
¿Habla inglés?   a·bla een·gles (pol)
¿Hablas inglés?   a·blas een·gles (inf)

I don't understand.
Yo no entiendo.   yo no en·tyen·do

Accommodations

I'd like a single/double room.
Quisiera una   kee·sye·ra oo·na
habitación   a·bee·ta·syon
individual/doble.   een·dee·vee·dwal/do·ble

How much is it per night/person?
¿Cuánto cuesta por   kwan·to kwes·ta por
noche/persona?   no·che/per·so·na

Does it include breakfast?
¿Incluye el desayuno?   een·kloo·ye el de·sa·yoo·no

campsite	*terreno de*	te·re·no de
	cámping	kam·peeng
guesthouse	*pensión*	pen·syon
hotel	*hotel*	o·tel
youth hostel	*albergue*	al·ber·ge
	juvenil	khoo·ve·neel

air-con	aire acondicionado	ai·re a·kon·dee·syo·na·do
bathroom	baño	ba·nyo
bed	cama	ka·ma
window	ventana	ven·ta·na

Directions

Where's ...?
¿Dónde está ...?   don·de es·ta ...

What's the address?
¿Cuál es la dirección?   kwal es la dee·rek·syon

Could you please write it down?
¿Puede escribirlo, por favor?   pwe·de es·kree·beer·lo por fa·vor

Can you show me (on the map)?
¿Me lo puede indicar (en el mapa)?   me lo pwe·de een·dee·kar (en el ma·pa)

at the corner	en la esquina	en la es·kee·na
at the traffic lights	en el semáforo	en el se·ma·fo·ro
behind ...	detrás de ...	de·tras de ...
in front of ...	enfrente de ...	en·fren·te de ...
left	izquierda	ees·kyer·da
next to ...	al lado de ...	al la·do de ...
opposite ...	frente a ...	fren·te a ...
right	derecha	de·re·cha
straight ahead	todo recto	to·do rek·to

Eating & Drinking

Can I see the menu, please?
¿Puedo ver el menú, por favor?   pwe·do ver el me·noo por fa·vor

What would you recommend?
¿Qué recomienda?   ke re·ko·myen·da

Do you have vegetarian food?
¿Tienen comida vegetariana?   tye·nen ko·mee·da ve·khe·ta·rya·na

I don't eat (red meat).
No como (carne roja).   no ko·mo (kar·ne ro·kha)

Question Words

How?	¿Cómo?	ko·mo
What?	¿Qué?	ke
When?	¿Cuándo?	kwan·do
Where?	¿Dónde?	don·de
Who?	¿Quién?	kyen
Why?	¿Por qué?	por ke

That was delicious!
¡Estaba buenísimo!   es·ta·ba bwe·nee·see·mo

Cheers!
¡Salud!   sa·loo

The bill, please.
La cuenta, por favor.   la kwen·ta por fa·vor

I'd like a table for ...	Quisiera una mesa para ...	kee·sye·ra oo·na me·sa pa·ra ...
(eight) o'clock	las (ocho)	las (o·cho)
(two) people	(dos) personas	(dos) per·so·nas

Key Words

bottle	botella	bo·te·ya
breakfast	desayuno	de·sa·yoo·no
(too) cold	(muy) frío	(mooy) free·o
dinner	cena	se·na
fork	tenedor	te·ne·dor
glass	vaso	va·so
hot (warm)	caliente	kal·yen·te
knife	cuchillo	koo·chee·yo
lunch	comida	ko·mee·da
plate	plato	pla·to
spoon	cuchara	koo·cha·ra

Meat & Fish

beef	carne de vaca	kar·ne de va·ka
chicken	pollo	po·yo
duck	pato	pa·to
lamb	cordero	kor·de·ro
pork	cerdo	ser·do
prawn	langostino	lan·gos·tee·no
salmon	salmón	sal·mon
tuna	atún	a·toon
turkey	pavo	pa·vo
veal	ternera	ter·ne·ra

Fruit & Vegetables

apple	manzana	man·sa·na
banana	plátano	pla·ta·no
beans	judías	khoo·dee·as
cabbage	col	kol
capsicum	pimiento	pee·myen·to
carrot	zanahoria	sa·na·o·rya
cherry	cereza	se·re·sa
corn	maíz	ma·ees
cucumber	pepino	pe·pee·no
grape	uvas	oo·vas
lemon	limón	lee·mon
lettuce	lechuga	le·choo·ga

Signs

Abierto	Open
Cerrado	Closed
Entrada	Entrance
Hombres/Varones	Men
Mujeres/Damas	Women
Prohibido	Prohibited
Salida	Exit
Servicios/Baños	Toilets

mushroom	*champiñón*	cham·pee·*nyon*
nuts	*nueces*	*nwe*·ses
onion	*cebolla*	se·*bo*·ya
orange	*naranja*	na·*ran*·kha
peach	*melocotón*	me·lo·ko·*ton*
peas	*guisantes*	gee·*san*·tes
pineapple	*piña*	*pee*·nya
plum	*ciruela*	seer·*we*·la
potato	*patata*	pa·*ta*·ta
spinach	*espinacas*	es·pee·*na*·kas
strawberry	*fresa*	*fre*·sa
tomato	*tomate*	to·*ma*·te
watermelon	*sandía*	san·*dee*·a

Other

bread	*pan*	pan
butter	*mantequilla*	man·te·*kee*·ya
cheese	*queso*	*ke*·so
egg	*huevo*	*we*·vo
honey	*miel*	myel
jam	*mermelada*	mer·me·*la*·da
pepper	*pimienta*	pee·*myen*·ta
rice	*arroz*	a·*ros*
salt	*sal*	sal
sugar	*azúcar*	a·*soo*·kar

Drinks

beer	*cerveza*	ser·*ve*·sa
coffee	*café*	ka·*fe*
(orange) juice	*zumo (de naranja)*	*soo*·mo (de na·*ran*·kha)
milk	*leche*	*le*·che
red wine	*vino tinto*	vee·no *teen*·to
tea	*té*	te
(mineral) water	*agua (mineral)*	*a*·gwa (mee·ne·*ral*)
white wine	*vino blanco*	vee·no *blan*·ko

Emergencies

Help!	*¡Socorro!*	so·*ko*·ro
Go away!	*¡Vete!*	ve·te

Call ...!	*¡Llame a ...!*	*ya*·me a ...
a doctor	*un médico*	oon *me*·dee·ko
the police	*la policía*	la po·lee·*see*·a

I'm lost.
Estoy perdido/a. es·*toy* per·*dee*·do/a (m/f)

I'm ill.
Estoy enfermo/a. es·*toy* en·*fer*·mo/a (m/f)

I'm allergic to (antibiotics).
Soy alérgico/a a (los antibióticos). soy a·*ler*·khee·ko/a a (los an·tee·*byo*·tee·kos) (m/f)

Where are the toilets?
¿Dónde están los baños? *don*·de es·*tan* los *ba*·nyos

Shopping & Services

I'd like to buy ...
Quisiera comprar ... kee·*sye*·ra kom·*prar* ...

I'm just looking.
Sólo estoy mirando. *so*·lo es·*toy* mee·*ran*·do

Can I look at it?
¿Puedo verlo? *pwe*·do *ver*·lo

I don't like it.
No me gusta. no me *goos*·ta

How much is it?
¿Cuánto cuesta? *kwan*·to *kwes*·ta

That's too expensive.
Es muy caro. es mooy *ka*·ro

There's a mistake in the bill.
Hay un error en la cuenta. ai oon e·*ror* en la *kwen*·ta

ATM	*cajero automático*	ka·*khe*·ro ow·to·*ma*·tee·ko
internet cafe	*cibercafé*	see·ber·ka·*fe*
market	*mercado*	mer·*ka*·do
post office	*correos*	ko·*re*·os
tourist office	*oficina de turismo*	o·fee·*see*·na de too·*rees*·mo

Time, Dates & Numbers

What time is it?	*¿Qué hora es?*	ke o·ra es
It's (10) o'clock.	*Son (las diez).*	son (las dyes)
It's half past (one).	*Es (la una) y media.*	es (la oo·na) ee *me*·dya

morning	mañana	ma·nya·na
afternoon	tarde	tar·de
evening	noche	no·che
yesterday	ayer	a·yer
today	hoy	oy
tomorrow	mañana	ma·nya·na

Monday	lunes	loo·nes
Tuesday	martes	mar·tes
Wednesday	miércoles	myer·ko·les
Thursday	jueves	khwe·ves
Friday	viernes	vyer·nes
Saturday	sábado	sa·ba·do
Sunday	domingo	do·meen·go

1	uno	oo·no
2	dos	dos
3	tres	tres
4	cuatro	kwa·tro
5	cinco	seen·ko
6	seis	seys
7	siete	sye·te
8	ocho	o·cho
9	nueve	nwe·ve
10	diez	dyes
20	veinte	veyn·te
30	treinta	treyn·ta
40	cuarenta	kwa·ren·ta
50	cincuenta	seen·kwen·ta
60	sesenta	se·sen·ta
70	setenta	se·ten·ta
80	ochenta	o·chen·ta
90	noventa	no·ven·ta
100	cien	syen
1000	mil	meel

Transportation

boat	barco	bar·ko
bus	autobús	ow·to·boos
plane	avión	a·vyon
train	tren	tren

A ... ticket, please.	Un billete de ..., por favor.	oon bee·ye·te de ... por fa·vor
1st-class	primera clase	pree·me·ra kla·se
2nd-class	segunda clase	se·goon·da kla·se
one-way	ida	ee·da
return	ida y vuelta	ee·da ee vwel·ta

first	primero	pree·me·ro
last	último	ool·tee·mo
next	próximo	prok·see·mo

bus stop	parada de autobuses	pa·ra·da de ow·to·boo·ses
cancelled	cancelado	kan·se·la·do
delayed	retrasado	re·tra·sa·do
ticket office	taquilla	ta·kee·ya
timetable	horario	o·ra·ryo
train station	estación de trenes	es·ta·syon de tre·nes

I want to go to ...
Quisiera ir a ... — kee·sye·ra eer a ...

Does it stop at ...?
¿Para en ...? — pa·ra en ...

What stop is this?
¿Cuál es esta parada? — kwal es es·ta pa·ra·da

What time does it arrive/leave?
¿A qué hora llega/sale? — a ke o·ra ye·ga/sa·le

Please tell me when we get to ...
¿Puede avisarme — pwe·de a·vee·sar·me
cuando lleguemos a ...? — kwan·do ye·ge·mos a ...

I want to get off here.
Quiero bajarme aquí. — kye·ro ba·khar·me a·kee

I'd like to hire a ...	Quisiera alquilar ...	kee·sye·ra al·kee·lar ...
bicycle	una bicicleta	oo·na bee·see·kle·ta
car	un coche	oon ko·che
motorcycle	una moto	oo·na mo·to

helmet	casco	kas·ko
mechanic	mecánico	me·ka·nee·ko
petrol/gas	gasolina	ga·so·lee·na
service station	gasolinera	ga·so·lee·ne·ra

Is this the road to ...?
¿Se va a ... por — se va a ... por
esta carretera? — es·ta ka·re·te·ra

(How long) Can I park here?
¿(Cuánto tiempo) — (kwan·to tyem·po)
Puedo aparcar aquí? — pwe·do a·par·kar a·kee

The car has broken down (at ...).
El coche se ha averiado — el ko·che se a a·ve·rya·do
(en ...). — (en ...)

I have a flat tyre.
Tengo un pinchazo.   *ten·go oon peen·cha·so*

I've run out of petrol.
Me he quedado sin   *me e ke·da·do seen*
gasolina.   *ga·so·lee·na*

MODERN MAYA

Since the pre-Columbian period, the two ancient Maya languages, Yucatec and Cholan, have subdivided into more than 20 separate Maya languages (such as Yucatec, Chol, Ch'or-ti, Tzeltal, Tzotzil, Lacandón, Mam, K'iche' and Kakchiquel). Indigenous languages are seldom written, but when they are, the Roman alphabet is used. Most Maya speakers will only read and write Spanish – they may not be literate in Maya.

Maya pronunciation is pretty straightforward. There are just a few rules to keep in mind: **c** is always a hard 'k' sound, as in 'cat'; **j** is similar to the 'h' in 'half'; **u** is pronounced as in 'prune', but at the beginning or end of a word, it's like English 'w'; and **x** is pronounced like the 'sh' in 'shoes'. The consonants followed by an apostrophe (**b'**, **ch'**, **k'**, **p'**, **t'**) are pronounced more forcefully and explosively. Vowels followed by an apostrophe (') indicate a glottal stop (like the sound between the two syllables in 'uh-oh'.) Stress usually falls on the last syllable.

K'iche'

K'iche' is spoken throughout the Guatemalan highlands, from around Santa Cruz del Quiché to the area around Lago de Atitlán and Quetzaltenango. There are around two million K'iche' Maya in Guatemala.

Good morning.	*Saqarik.*
Good afternoon.	*Xb'eqij.*
Good evening/night.	*Xokaq'ab'.*
Goodbye.	*Chab'ej.*
See you soon.	*Kimpetik ri.*
Excuse me.	*Kyunala.*
Thank you.	*Uts awech.*
What's your name?	*Su ra'b'i?*
My name is ...	*Nu b'i ...*
Where are you from?	*Ja kat pewi?*
I'm from ...	*Ch'qap ja'kin pewi ...*

Where is a/the ...?	*Ja k'uichi' ri ...?*
bathroom	*b'anb'al chulu*
bus stop	*tek'lib'al*
doctor	*ajkun*
hotel	*jun worib'al*

Do you have ...?	*K'olik ...?*
boiled water	*saq'li*
coffee	*kab'e*
rooms	*k'plib'al*

bad	*itzel*
blanket	*k'ul*
closed	*tzapilik*
cold	*joron*
good	*utz*
hard	*ko*
hot	*miq'in*
open	*teb'am*
sick	*yiwab'*
soft	*ch'uch'uj*
vegetables	*ichaj*

north (white)	*saq*
south (yellow)	*k'an*
east (red)	*kaq*
west (black)	*k'eq*

1	*jun*
2	*keb'*
3	*oxib'*
4	*kijeb'*
5	*job'*
6	*waq'ib'*
7	*wuqub'*
8	*wajxakib'*
9	*b'elejeb'*
10	*lajuj*

Mam

Mam is spoken in the department of Huehuetenango. This is the language you'll hear in Todos Santos Cuchumatán. Note that many Mam words have been in disuse for so long that the Spanish equivalent is used almost exclusively. The numbers from one to 10 are the same as in K'iche', and for numbers higher than 10, Spanish words are used.

Good morning/ afternoon/evening.	*Chin q'olb'el teya.* (sg inf) *Chin q'olb'el kyeyea.* (pl inf)
Goodbye.	*Chi nej.*
See you soon.	*Ak qli qib'.*
Excuse me.	*Naq samy.*
Thank you.	*Chonte teya.*
How are you?	*Tzen ta'ya?*
What's your name?	*Tit biya?*

My name is ...	Luan bi ...
Where are you from?	Jaa'tzajnia?
I'm from ...	Ac tzajni ...
Where is a/the ...?	Ja at ...?
bathroom	bano
doctor	medico/doctor
hotel	hospedaje
Is there somewhere we can sleep?	Ja tun kqta'n?
Where is the bus stop?	Ja nue camioneta?
How much are the fruit and vegetables?	Je te ti lobj?
Do you have ...?	At ...?
boiled water	kqa'
coffee	café

rooms	cuartos
I'm cold.	At xb'a'j/choj.
I'm sick.	At yab'.
bad	k'ab'ex/nia g'lan
closed	jpu'n
good	banex/g'lan
hard	kuj
hot	kyaq
open	jqo'n
soft	xb'une
north (white)	okan
south (yellow)	eln
east (red)	jawl
west (black)	kub'el

GLOSSARY

Apartado Postal – post-office box; abbreviated Apdo Postal

Ayuntamiento – often seen as H Ayuntamiento (Honorable Ayuntamiento) on the front of town hall buildings; translates as 'Municipal Government'

barrio – district, neighborhood

billete – bank note

boleto – ticket (bus, train, museum etc)

bolo – colloquial term for drunk (noun)

cabañas – cabins

cacique – Maya chief; also used to describe provincial warlord or strongman

caféteria – literally 'coffee-shop,' but refers to any informal restaurant with waiter service; not usually a cafeteria in the North American sense of a self-service restaurant

cajero automático – automated teller machine(ATM)

callejón – alley or narrow or very short street

camión – truck or bus

camioneta – bus or pickup truck

cardamomo – cardamom; a spice grown extensively in the Verapaces and used as a flavor enhancer for coffee and tea

casa de cambio – currency exchange office; offers exchange rates comparable to those of banks and is much faster to use, though uncommon in Guatemala

cenote – large, natural limestone cave used for water storage (or ceremonial purposes)

cerveza – beer

Chac – Maya god of rain

chac-mool – Maya sacrificial stone sculpture

chapín – slang term for citizen of Guatemala

charro – cowboy

chicle – sap of the sapodilla tree; used to manufacture chewing gum

chicleros – men who collect chicle

Chinka' – small, non-Maya indigenous group living on the Pacific Slope

chuchkajau – Maya prayer leader

chuj – traditional Maya sauna; also known as tuj

chultún – artificial Maya cistern

cigarro – cigarette

cocina – kitchen; also used for a small, basic one-woman place to eat, often located in or near a municipal market, and in the phrases cocina económica (economical kitchen) or a cocina familiar (family kitchen)

cofradía – religious brotherhood, most often found in the highlands

colectivo – jitney taxi or minibus that picks up and drops off passengers along its route

comal – hot griddle or surface used to cook tortillas

comedor – basic and cheap eatery, usually with a limited menu

completo – full; a sign you may see on hotel desks in crowded cities

conquistador – explorer-conqueror of Latin America from Spain

copal – tree resin used as incense in Maya ceremonies

correos – post office

corte – Maya wraparound skirt

costumbre – traditional Maya rites

criollos – people born in Guatemala of Spanish blood

cruce – crossroads, usually where you make bus connections; also known as entronque

cuadra – a city block

curandero – traditional indigenous healer

damas – ladies; the usual sign on toilet doors

dzul, dzules – Maya for foreigners or 'townsfolk'

faja – Maya waist sash or belt

ferrocarril – railroad

finca – plantation, farm

galón, galones – US gallons; fluid measure of 3.79L

glyph – symbolic character or figure; usually engraved or carved in relief

gringo/a – a mildly pejorative term applied to a male/female North American visitor; sometimes applied to any visitor of European heritage

gruta – cave

guayabera – man's thin fabric shirt with pockets and appliquéd designs on the front, over the shoulders and down the back; often worn in place of a jacket and tie on formal occasions

hacienda – estate; also 'treasury,' as in Departamento de Hacienda, Treasury Department

hay – pronounced like 'eye,' meaning 'there is' or 'there are'; you're equally likely to hear no hay, meaning 'there isn't' or 'there aren't'

hombre/s – man/men

huipil – Maya woman's woven tunic; often very colorful and elaborately embroidered

IVA – *impuesto al valor agregado* or value-added tax; on hotel rooms it is 12%

juego de pelota – ball game

kaperraj – Maya woman's all-purpose cloth; used as a head covering, baby sling, produce sack, shawl and more

Kukulcán – Maya name for the Aztec-Toltec plumed serpent Quetzalcóatl

ladino – person of mixed indigenous and European race; a more common term in Guatemala than *mestizo*

lancha – motorboat used to transport passengers; driven by a *lanchero*

larga distancia – long-distance telephone

lavandería – laundry; a *lavandería automática* is a coin-operated laundry

leng – in the highlands, a colloquial Maya term for coins

libra – pound; weight measurement of 0.45kg

lleno – full (fuel tank)

machismo – maleness, masculine virility

malecón – waterfront boulevard

manglar – mangrove

manzana – apple

mariachi – small group of street musicians featuring stringed instruments, trumpets and often an accordion; sometimes plays in restaurants

marimba – Guatemala's xylophone-like national instrument

mestizo – person of mixed indigenous and European blood; the word *ladino* is more common in Guatemala

metate – flattish stone on which corn is ground with a cylindrical stone roller

milla – mile; distance of 1.6km

milpa – maize field

mirador – lookout, vista point

mochilero – backpacker

mordida – 'bite'; small bribe paid to keep the wheels of bureaucracy turning

mudéjar – Moorish architectural style

mujer/es – woman/women

na – thatched Maya hut

onza – ounce; weight of 28g

palacio de gobierno – building housing the executive offices of a state or regional government

palacio municipal – city hall; seat of the corporation or municipal government

palapa – thatched shelter with a palm-leaf roof and open sides

panza verde – literally 'green belly,' a nickname given to Antigua residents who are said to eat lots of avocados

parada – bus stop; usually for city buses

picop – pickup truck

pie – foot; measure of 0.30m

pisto – colloquial Maya term for money, quetzals

posada – guesthouse

propino, propina – a tip, different from a *mordida*, which is really a bribe

punta – sexually suggestive dance enjoyed by the Garífuna of the Caribbean coast

puro – cigar

Quetzalcóatl – plumed serpent god of the Aztecs and Toltecs; see also Kukulcán

rebozo – long woolen or linen scarf covering the head or shoulders

refago – Maya wraparound skirt

retablo – ornate, often gilded altarpiece

retorno – 'return'; used on traffic signs to signify a U-turn or turnaround

sacbé, sacbeob – ceremonial limestone avenue or path between great Maya cities

sacerdote – priest

sanatorio – hospital, particularly a small private one

sanitario – literally 'sanitary'; usually means toilet

secadora – clothes dryer

stela, stelae – standing stone monument(s); usually carved

supermercado – supermarket; anything from a corner store to a large, US-style supermarket

taller – shop or workshop

taller mecánico – mechanic's shop, usually for cars

teléfono comunitario – community telephone; found in the smallest towns

tepezcuintle – edible jungle rodent the size of a rabbit

tienda – small store that may sell anything from candles and chickens to aspirin and bread

típico – typical or characteristic of a region; particularly used to describe food

tocoyal – Maya head covering

traje – traditional clothing worn by the Maya

tzut – Maya man's equivalent of a *kaperraj*

viajero – traveler

vulcanizadora – automobile tire repair shop

zonas – zones

zotz – bat (the mammal) in many Maya languages

FOOD GLOSSARY

a la parrilla – grilled, perhaps over charcoal
a la plancha – grilled on a hotplate
aguacate – avocado
ajo – garlic
almuerzo – lunch
antojitos – snacks (literally 'little whims')
arroz – rice
atole – a hot gruel made with maize, milk, cinnamon and sugar
aves – poultry
azúcar – sugar

bebida – drink
bistec or bistec de res – beef steak

café (negro/con leche) – coffee (black/with milk)
calabaza – squash, marrow or pumpkin
caldo – broth, often meat-based
camarones – shrimps
camarones gigantes – jumbo shrimp
carne – meat
carne asada – grilled beef
cebolla – onion
cerveza – beer
ceviche – raw seafood marinated in lime juice and mixed with onions, chilies, garlic, tomatoes and cilantro (coriander leaf)
coco – coconut
chicharrón – pork crackling
chile relleno – bell pepper stuffed with cheese, meat, rice or other foods, dipped in egg whites, fried and baked in sauce
chuchito – small tamal
chuletas (de puerco) – (pork) chops
churrasco – slab of thin grilled meat

ensalada – salad

filete de pescado – fish fillet
flan – custard, crème caramel
fresas – strawberries

frijoles – black beans
frutas – fruits

guacamole – avocados mashed with onion, chili sauce, lemon and tomato
güisquil – type of squash

hamburguesa – hamburger
helado – ice cream
huevos fritos/revueltos – fried/ scrambled eggs

jamón – ham
jícama – a popular root vegetable resembling a potato crossed with an apple
jocón – green stew of chicken or pork with green vegetables and herbs

leche – milk
lechuga – lettuce
legumbres – root vegetables
licuado – milkshake made with fresh fruit, sugar, and milk or water
limón – lemon
limonada – drink made from lemon juice

mantequilla – butter
margarina – margarine
mariscos – seafood
mesa – table
melocotón – peach
miel – honey
milanesa – crumbed, breaded
mojarra – perch
mosh – oatmeal/porridge

naranja – orange
naranjada – like a *limonada* but made with oranges

pacaya – a squash-like staple
papa – potato
papaya – pawpaw
pastel – cake
pato – duck
pavo – turkey

pepián – chicken and vegetables in a piquant sesame and pumpkin seed sauce
pescado – fish (fried in butter and garlic)
piña – pineapple
pimienta – pepper (black)
plátano – plantain (green banana), edible when cooked (usually fried)
plato típico – set meal
pollo (asado/frito) – (grilled/ fried) chicken
postre – dessert
propina – tip
puerco – pork
puyaso – a choice cut of steak

queso – cheese

refacciones – snacks; see *antojitos*

sal – salt
salchicha – sausage
salsa – sauce made with chilies, onion, tomato, lemon or lime juice, and spices
sopa – soup

taco – a soft or crisp corn tortilla wrapped or folded around meat and salsa
tamal – corn dough stuffed with meat, beans, chilies or nothing at all, wrapped in banana leaf or corn husks and steamed
tapado – a seafood, coconut milk and plantain casserole
tarta – cake
tenedor – fork
tocino – bacon
tomate – tomato
tostada – flat, crisp tortilla topped with meat or cheese, tomatoes, beans and lettuce

vaso – glass
verduras – green vegetables

zanahoria – carrot

Behind the Scenes

SEND US YOUR FEEDBACK

We love to hear from travelers – your comments keep us on our toes and help make our books better. Our well-traveled team reads every word on what you loved or loathed about this book. Although we cannot reply individually to your submissions, we always guarantee that your feedback goes straight to the appropriate authors, in time for the next edition. Each person who sends us information is thanked in the next edition – the most useful submissions are rewarded with a selection of digital PDF chapters.

Visit **lonelyplanet.com/contact** to submit your updates and suggestions or to ask for help. Our award-winning website also features inspirational travel stories, news and discussions.

Note: We may edit, reproduce and incorporate your comments in Lonely Planet products such as guidebooks, websites and digital products, so let us know if you don't want your comments reproduced or your name acknowledged. For a copy of our privacy policy visit lonelyplanet.com/privacy.

OUR READERS

Many thanks to the travelers who used the last edition and wrote to us with helpful hints, useful advice and interesting anecdotes:

Kurt Annen, Karen Bidmead, Amanda Bresnan, Sofia Gazon, Pete Harvey, Rita Jaros, Pauline Kennedy, Lora Liegel, Lorette Medwell, Mark Nakano, Zack Rath, Hank Raymond, Nina Stelzig, Xabier Urrutia

AUTHOR THANKS

Lucas Vidgen

Thanks once again to the Guatemalans for making such a great country in which to work, live and travel. Specifically, thanks to Johann in Guate for all the inside juice *and* a great night out, Denis in Río Dulce and Charlie in Monterrico. To all the readers who wrote in with tips and info – *gracias*! And thanks as always to my partner, América, for giving me all I ever wanted, including Sofía and Teresa.

Daniel C Schechter

A number of *chapines* and *semi-chapines* generously pitched in their knowledge and expertise to this edition. To name but a few: Azucena Soto and Ángel Quiñones in Antigua;
Christian Behrenz, Stefanie Zecha, Matt Purvis, and Steve and Kat Kmack at Lago de Atitlán; William Paxtor, Martha 'la nicaraguense' Munguia, Marieke Smulders, Jacco Windt and Marcos Cifuentes in Quetzaltenango; Pauline Décamps and Mario Rolando Gutiérrez in Huehuetenango; Jeovani Tut Rodríguez and Marco Gross in El Petén; and Juan Pablo Viegas who described his experience crossing the border at La Mesilla. *¡Gracias a todos!*

ACKNOWLEDGEMENTS

Climate map data adapted from Peel MC, Finlayson BL & McMahon TA (2007) 'Updated World Map of the Köppen-Geiger Climate Classification', *Hydrology and Earth System Sciences*, 11, 163344.

Illustration pp248–9 by Michael Weldon.

Cover photograph: Iglesia y Convento de Nuestra Señora de la Merced, Antigua; Aurora Photos/AWL ©.

THIS BOOK

This 6th edition of Lonely Planet's *Guatemala* guidebook was researched and written by Lucas Vidgen and Daniel C Schechter, who also wrote the last two editions. This guidebook was produced by the following:

Destination Editor Bailey Johnson

Associate Product Director Angela Tinson

Product Editors Carolyn Boicos, Kate Chapman, Jenna Myers

Senior Cartographers Mark Griffiths, Anthony Phelan

Book Designer Virginia Moreno

Assisting Editors Judith Bamber, Charlie Claxton, Melanie Dankel, Bruce Evans, Samantha Forge, Kate James, Katie O'Connell, Saralinda Turner, Maja Vatrić

Cover Researcher Naomi Parker

Thanks to Victoria Harrison, Andi Jones, Kirsten Rawlings, Tony Wheeler

Index

Map Legend

Sights

- Beach
- Bird Sanctuary
- Buddhist
- Castle/Palace
- Christian
- Confucian
- Hindu
- Islamic
- Jain
- Jewish
- Monument
- Museum/Gallery/Historic Building
- Ruin
- Shinto
- Sikh
- Taoist
- Winery/Vineyard
- Zoo/Wildlife Sanctuary
- Other Sight

Activities, Courses & Tours

- Bodysurfing
- Diving
- Canoeing/Kayaking
- Course/Tour
- Sento Hot Baths/Onsen
- Skiing
- Snorkeling
- Surfing
- Swimming/Pool
- Walking
- Windsurfing
- Other Activity

Sleeping

- Sleeping
- Camping

Eating

- Eating

Drinking & Nightlife

- Drinking & Nightlife
- Cafe

Entertainment

- Entertainment

Shopping

- Shopping

Information

- Bank
- Embassy/Consulate
- Hospital/Medical
- Internet
- Police
- Post Office
- Telephone
- Toilet
- Tourist Information
- Other Information

Geographic

- Beach
- Gate
- Hut/Shelter
- Lighthouse
- Lookout
- Mountain/Volcano
- Oasis
- Park
- Pass
- Picnic Area
- Waterfall

Population

- Capital (National)
- Capital (State/Province)
- City/Large Town
- Town/Village

Transport

- Airport
- Border crossing
- Bus
- Cable car/Funicular
- Cycling
- Ferry
- Metro station
- Monorail
- Parking
- Petrol station
- Subway/Subte station
- Taxi
- Train station/Railway
- Tram
- Underground station
- Other Transport

Routes

- Tollway
- Freeway
- Primary
- Secondary
- Tertiary
- Lane
- Unsealed road
- Road under construction
- Plaza/Mall
- Steps
- Tunnel
- Pedestrian overpass
- Walking Tour
- Walking Tour detour
- Path/Walking Trail

Boundaries

- International
- State/Province
- Disputed
- Regional/Suburb
- Marine Park
- Cliff
- Wall

Hydrography

- River, Creek
- Intermittent River
- Canal
- Water
- Dry/Salt/Intermittent Lake
- Reef

Areas

- Airport/Runway
- Beach/Desert
- Cemetery (Christian)
- Cemetery (Other)
- Glacier
- Mudflat
- Park/Forest
- Sight (Building)
- Sportsground
- Swamp/Mangrove

Note: Not all symbols displayed above appear on the maps in this book

`DA   11/16`

OUR STORY

A beat-up old car, a few dollars in the pocket and a sense of adventure. In 1972 that's all Tony and Maureen Wheeler needed for the trip of a lifetime – across Europe and Asia overland to Australia. It took several months, and at the end – broke but inspired – they sat at their kitchen table writing and stapling together their first travel guide, *Across Asia on the Cheap*. Within a week they'd sold 1500 copies. Lonely Planet was born.

Today, Lonely Planet has offices in Dublin, Franklin, London, Melbourne, Oakland, Beijing and Delhi, with more than 600 staff and writers. We share Tony's belief that 'a great guidebook should do three things: inform, educate and amuse'.

OUR WRITERS

Lucas Vidgen

Guatemala City, The Pacific Slope, Central & Eastern Guatemala Born and raised in Melbourne, Australia, Lucas has been traveling and working in Latin America for nearly 20 years. He ended up living in Quetzaltenango for over a decade, having gone there for a few weeks to study Spanish. He currently divides his time between Melbourne and Quetzaltenango where he publishes – and very occasionally contributes to – the city's leading nightlife and culture magazine, *XelaWho*. Lucas has contributed to a range of Lonely Planet titles over the years, mostly on Central and South America. His Spanish is OK but he still can't decide if a *pupusa* is better than a potato cake. Lucas also wrote the Plan Your Trip, Understand Guatemala and Survival Guide sections.

Daniel C Schechter

Antigua, The Highlands, El Petén A native New Yorker, Daniel has been poking around Latin America for so long it sometimes makes more sense to him than his place of birth. After living in Colombia and Puerto Rico, he called Mexico home for over a decade. During that time he spanned the Mundo Maya on various forays, discovering and writing about such places as Campeche, Calakmul and Tikal, and cultivating an enduring interest in Classic Maya history. Daniel currently lives in the Netherlands, where he blogs on cycling (http://netherlandsbikeways.blogspot.nl).

Published by Lonely Planet Global Limited
CRN 554153
6th edition – October 2016
ISBN 978 1 78657 114 4
© Lonely Planet 2016   Photographs © as indicated 2016
10 9 8 7 6 5 4 3 2 1
Printed in China